WILLIAM FAULKNER'S
YOKNAPATAWPHA

WILLIAM FAULKNER'S YOKNAPATAWPHA

"A Kind of Keystone in the Universe"

Elizabeth M. Kerr

New York
FORDHAM UNIVERSITY PRESS
1985

Printed in the United States of America

Contents

ABBREVIATIONS

AA	*Absalom, Absalom!*
AILD	*As I Lay Dying*
CS	*Collected Stories of William Faulkner*
FD	*Flags in the Dust*
GDM	*Go Down, Moses*
ID	*Intruder in the Dust*
KG	*Knight's Gambit*
LA	*Light in August*
R	*The Reivers*
RN	*Requiem for a Nun*
San.	*Sanctuary*
Sar.	*Sartoris*
Snopes: A Trilogy	
H	*The Hamlet*
T	*The Town*
M	*The Mansion*
SF	*The Sound and the Fury*
U	*The Unvanquished*
ESPL	*William Faulkner: Essays, Speeches, and Public Letters*
FN	*Faulkner at Nagano*
FU	*Faulkner in the University*
FWP	*Faulkner at West Point*
LG	*Lion in the Garden: Interviews with William Faulkner, 1926–1962*

1

Themes and Thematic Symbols

I • CONSCIOUS AND UNCONSCIOUS SYMBOLISM

REPETITION OF CONCRETE DETAILS and recurrence of characters and places in the Yoknapatawpha chronicles contribute to a flexible unity of the whole body of fiction and to the three-dimensional effect of the land and the people. These devices, however, usually serve an even more vital purpose: when repeated within a work and reappearing in others, they develop symbolic values related to the themes of the separate narratives and to the encompassing mythology. Characters, episodes, and dramatic tableaux combine symbolic details in impressive configurations pregnant with meaning. But before the total mythology and meaning can be discerned, the function and effect of symbolism in individual works or narrative sequences must be recognized.

In reading most of the Yoknapatawpha fiction, one receives the impression that Faulkner is using symbolic images in profusion but without consistency, and even without complete awareness of suggested meanings. This impression is confirmed by Faulkner's answers to questions about symbolism. Although his own words cannot be taken as conclusive evidence, on this point he did not seem to have his tongue in his cheek, as he occasionally did, or to be as disparaging of critical analysis, as he sometimes was.

In response to a question on the Freudian implications which critics have found in his writings, Faulkner stated his general attitude toward such interpretation of literature:

> I'm convinced . . . that that sort of criticism whether it's nonsensical or not is valid because it is a symptom of change, of motion, which is life, and also it's a proof that literature—art—is a living quantity in our social condition. If it were not, then there'd be no reason for people to delve and find all sorts of symbolisms and psychological strains and currents in it [*FU* 65].

In his own writing Faulkner was not always conscious of symbolic meanings, but he did not deny the existence of unpremeditated symbols or the validity of the search for such symbols:

> . . . some people get a certain amount of pleasure in hunting around in an author's work for reasons, for symbols, for similarities, and of course they are very likely all there, but the writer himself is too busy simply writing about people in conflict with themselves and their background to wonder or even care whether he repeats himself or whether he uses symbols or not. He would use a symbol at the drop of a hat if that was the simplest way to throw the light on the particular incident he's telling about, and it's perfectly valid, I think, for anyone to seek for those symbols [*FU* 121].

In reply to a question on Freudian symbolism, Faulkner expressed the same idea concerning the role of the critic and the primary concern of the writer, and explained the source of much symbolism:

> I think that in the same culture the background of the critic and of the writer are so similar that a part of each one's history is the seed which can be translated into the symbols which are standardized within that culture. That is, the writer don't have to know Freud to have written things which anyone who does know Freud can divine and reduce into symbols. And so when the critic finds those symbols, they are of course there. But they were there as inevitably as the critic should stumble on his own knowledge of Freud to discern symbol [sic] [*FU* 147].

Faulkner's brief period of association with other writers occurred at the period when Freud was being discussed, and he was exposed to such influences as are discussed by Frederick Hoffman in *Freudianism and the Literary Mind*. Of the four groups of writers of the post–World War I period listed by Hoffman according to their knowledge and use of Freud, Faulkner seems to belong to the fourth: (1) those who read Freud in the original and had an accurate understanding of him; (2) those who read Freud in translation; (3) those who read summaries of Freud and heard lectures on Freud; (4) those who gained their knowledge of Freud through discussion of Freud on social occasions. In his introduction to *William Faulkner: New Orleans Sketches*, Carvel Collins referred to "the people who ran" *The Double Dealer* in New Orleans and with whom Faulkner associated in 1925 and 1926 as being "extremely aware of the intellectual and aesthetic currents which were making the twenties so important in American literary history."

Where Faulkner's symbolism is not obviously derived from the current culture and where it seems to be or is acknowledged to be unconscious, it is possible that Faulkner's creative imagination instinctively seized upon details and images from what Jung calls the "collective unconscious." Without mentioning Jung, Faulkner gives a completely Jungian explanation for much of his symbolism:

> They found symbolism that I had no background in symbolism to put in the books. But what symbolism is in the books is evidently instinct in man, not in man's knowledge but in his inheritance of his old dreams, in his blood, perhaps his bones, rather than in the storehouse of his memory, his intellect [*FN* 68].

It is immaterial whether Faulkner was familiar with Jung's theories or was conscious of the resources from which he drew. What David Daiches said about Shakespeare's psychological insights may well apply not only to Freudian and Bergsonian elements in Faulkner but also to his symbolism: "remarkable insight into human nature" may be confirmed by psychological knowledge without any implication of the author's familiarity with psychological theory. Ruel Foster stated that, although Faulkner dealt with the primacy of the unconscious in human behavior, he was not significantly influenced by systematic psychology. Although Jungian psychology may have been a less prevalent part of the culture and literary climate than Freudian or Bergsonian psychology, Joseph Warren Beach recognized Jungian aspects in poetic "obsessive images" current not only in the 1930s and 1940s but also in the nineteenth century; some of these images appear in Faulkner, and his essentially poetic approach to fiction and his interest in poetry would render him sensitive to this aspect of the climate of literary ideas.

The cultural and literary climate, in conjunction with the literary tradition of realistic novels, favorable to the use of objective details which may have symbolic meaning, is partial explanation of the kinds of symbols to be found in Faulkner's fiction and the ways in which he used them.

In considering unconscious symbolism in the works of Melville, Gide, D. H. Lawrence, and Faulkner, William Tindall quotes Faulkner as saying: "Maybe all sorts of symbols and images get in. I don't know. When a good carpenter builds something, he puts the nails where they belong. Maybe they make a fancy pattern when he's through, but that's not why he put them in that way." Jung would say that he got the pattern from the collective unconscious.

A sentence Tindall quotes from André Gide's Preface to *Paludes* might be true also of Faulkner: "And my interest is what I have put into the work without knowing it,—that unconscious part that I like to call God's." Tindall remarks also that the author "if he is an artist like Faulkner" may use symbols "as elements in a design." Although Faulkner is only occasionally a symbolist, depending on "image, pattern, or rhythm" rather than "narrative or discourse" in his novels, the statement with which Tindall ended his definition of the symbolist novel applies to all the Yoknapatawpha novels: "details of actuality, no longer there for their own sake or to serve a sociological point, carry meaning outside the limits to which they seem confined." Claude-Edmonde Magny, herself a critic of Faulkner, also quoted Gide's remark, in a context relevant to the role of imagery and symbolism:

> There are two parts in every book, as in every work of art. . . . on the one hand, the author's conscious and expressly intended message the effect for which he purposely fitted out his machine . . .; on the other, the truth which he reveals without realizing it, the aspect of the world which he has discovered almost in spite of himself, in the course of the actual experience of composition; which is doubtless more or less what Gide, in the Preface to *Paludes*, refers to as "God's share."

Magny's further remark that "to the extent that an author is over-successful in communicating his conscious message, the jealous gods refuse him their collaboration" may explain why *A Fable* is inferior to the works in which Faulkner's symbolism is less conscious. In the following chapters, the second, the symbolic, part of Faulkner's "works of art" will be of primary concern. A statement by A. C. Bradley, quoted by Maud Bodkin, may well be true also of Faulkner. Shakespeare discovered or created "a mass of truth about life, which was brought to birth by the process of composition, but never preceded it in the shape of ideas, and probably never, even after it, took that shape in the poet's mind." One may observe and interpret what is in the "mass of truth" without committing either the intentional or the unintentional fallacy: the validity and effectiveness of symbols do not depend on whether they are conscious or unconscious.

Before consideration of the themes and symbols by means of which Faulkner discovered or created his "mass of truth about life," examination of basic concepts and definition of key terms in Jung's *Psyche and Symbol* may be useful. Remarkably close to Faulkner's statement about himself is Jung's theory of the collective unconscious, upon which the theory of archetypes and archetypal patterns is based. The theory of the collective unconscious is based on "the hypothesis of an omnipresent, but differentiated psychic structure which is inherited and which necessarily gives a certain form and direction to all experience." Like the organs of the body, "the archetypes, as organs of the psyche, are dynamic, instinctual complexes which determine psychic life to an extraordinary degree. . . . The layer of unconscious psyche which is made up of these universal dynamic forms I have termed the *collective unconscious.*" The archetypes which "are the imperishable elements of the unconscious" are continually changing and are interwoven in meanings, but "do form units that are accessible to intuition." The total reservoir, as it were, of the collective unconscious is "the microcosm which contains 'the image of all creation.'" The other hypothesis which would explain some of the phenomena Jung ascribes to the collective unconscious is that of transmigration of souls, with an individual surviving many incarnations. Faulkner's fondness for the term *avatar*, a noticeable feature of his style, may signify the nature of his creative imagination: he may have projected into his characters a kind of alternative explanation of the psychic experience he ascribed to himself as author.

II • SYMBOLS, IMAGES, AND ARCHETYPES

The proliferation of works on symbolism within recent years, however, is by no means a wholly Jungian phenomenon, nor are all symbols in Faulkner archetypal. Tindall succinctly defined his subject, *the literary symbol*, and its purpose: "The literary symbol, an analogy for something unstated, consists of an articulation of verbal elements that, going beyond reference and the limits of discourse, embodies and offers a complex of feeling and thought." Universal symbols need not be buried in the unconscious and be dredged up by instinct: images of things common to all men have universal and unlimited evocative power. Such symbols, food and drink for example, may be used consciously by the author on the material, realistic level and be interpreted by readers on both that level and the symbolic level of spiritual communion. Repetition of symbols or clustering of symbols introduces a structural, unifying function; the interweaving of disparate elements organizes experience for aesthetic purposes. As Charles Feidelson explains, by constituting "a key term, the center of many overlapping circles of metaphorical meaning," a symbol may stand "as a kind of synecdoche for the metaphors into which it has entered," the part retaining "its organic character as part of a whole." In his excellent introduction to *A Dictionary of Symbols*, J. E. Cirlot quoted the succinct definition of *symbolism* by Ananda Coomaraswamy: "The art of thinking in images." Cirlot's own designation of the field open to the use of symbols is almost equally terse: "The influence of the symbol must be allowed to pervade all levels of reality; only then can it be seen in all its spiritual grandeur and fecundity."

Symbols not only enrich meaning and unify structure but achieve connotative power. Alfred North Whitehead found in the extension of meaning through symbols the basis of literature: "In every effective symbolism there are certain aesthetic features shared in common. The meaning acquires emotion and feeling directly excited by the symbol. This is the whole basis of the art of literature, namely that the emotions and feeling directly excited by the words should fitly intensify our emotions and feelings arising from the contemplation of the meaning."

In explaining the origin of symbols, Erich Kahler suggests the distinction between archetypal symbols and conscious symbols: "The symbol originates in the split of existence, the confrontation and communication of an inner with an outer reality, whereby a meaning detaches itself from sheer existence." Although he limits the use of symbols, he recognizes the difficulty in strictly applying his limitation: "Only consciously formed images are real symbols. To be sure, borderlines between unconscious operation, between sheer expression and intentional representation, are fluid, and, as Jung has amply demonstrated, archetypal patterns, which operate in the unconscious, pass over into the conscious work of artists, poets, thinkers, who create cultic images."

This relationship between the symbol from the common past and that from an author's culture is confirmed by Jung's translator and editor, in *Psyche and Symbol*:

> The living symbol expresses an essential unconscious factor. The more widely this factor operates, the more generally valid is the symbol, for in every soul it evokes a resonance. . . . it must proceed from the most complex and subtle strata of the contemporary psychological atmosphere. Conversely, the effective, living symbol must also contain something which is shared by considerable numbers of men: it embraces that which is common to a larger group. Consequently it must include those

primitive elements, emotional and otherwise, whose omnipresence stands beyond all doubt.

To reinforce his statement in *Man and His Symbols* that "symbols . . . are natural and spontaneous products," Jung suggested an impossible image: "No genius has ever sat down with a pen or brush in his hand and said: 'Now I am going to invent a symbol.'"

The primitive elements which are collective rather than personal are archetypal symbols. "The universal dispositions of the mind" Jung compares with "Plato's forms (*eidola*), in accordance with which the mind organizes its contents." These forms, however, are "categories of imagination" and hence "are always in essence visual," with the character of "*typical* images," for which Jung borrows the term *archetypes* from St. Augustine. Jung finds "rich mines of archetypes" in comparative religion and mythology and in psychoses and the psychology of dreams.

> The astonishing parallelism between these images and the ideas they serve to express has frequently given rise to the wildest migration theories, although it would have been far more natural to think of the remarkable similarity of the human psyche at all times and in all places. Archetypal fantasy-forms are, in fact, reproduced spontaneously anytime and anywhere, without there being any conceivable trace of direct transmission. . . . The archetypes are, so to speak, organs of the prerational psyche. They are eternally inherited forms and ideas which have at first no specific content. Their specific content only appears in the course of the individual's life, when personal experience is taken up in precisely those forms.

In "Dream-Work in the Quentin Section of *The Sound and the Fury*," James Cowan showed that "psychoanalytic concepts and the techniques of dream-work are particularly useful in rendering" Quentin's consciousness.

Faulkner's responsiveness to the collective unconscious, if that is the explanation of his use of archetypal themes, no doubt reflected his particular temperament and creative imagination and his long residence in a region in which his family had lived since the youth of his great-grandfather. Thus Faulkner's personal experience and that of his family compressed into a few generations the span between savage wilderness and a decadent civilization. To the inherent richness of this environment in archetypal images and patterns Faulkner was attuned, the degree of his conscious awareness being less significant than the manifestations of his predisposition.

The responsiveness of the reader to archetypal patterns accounts in part for the great interest in Faulkner's works despite their difficulty. Regardless of the conscious intent of the author, the archetypal symbol evokes response at all times, everywhere. But archetypes are what Northrop Frye calls "complex variables," "associative clusters," and modern writers, Frye says, prefer to keep their archetypes "as versatile as possible, not pinned down exclusively to one interpretation." Whether Faulkner was thus motivated or was as unconscious of possible interpretations as he claimed to be, the wide range of interpretations of his major works is due very largely to the complex symbolism, much of which is archetypal. Frye points out the necessity of some center, to create a real structure: "The study of archetypes is the study of literary symbols as parts of a whole." We shall be concerned here with two wholes and sometimes three: the individual work and the Yoknapatawpha chronicles and related sequences within the chronicles such as the trilogy, *Snopes*. Throughout the Yoknapatawpha fiction the interlacing of symbols and of themes which the symbols designate builds "a real structure" for which one must seek a center.

A distinctive aspect of that structure is due to the fact that Faulkner's imagination operated like that of the narrative poets of ancient times as described by Erich Kahler, clustering "around a core of reality pre-established by old-age events or by long-grown incarnations of true emotions and drives in the human being." His approach to his material is also analogous to that of the ancients in that he works from the legends provided by his society and contributes his own interpretations to familiar patterns, the ideas often growing out of the images.

The frequent use of *images* in the remarks on symbols necessitates some clarification of the relation between images and symbols. Perhaps the simplest distinction is that, using the term *symbols* in the Jungian sense of visual images, symbols are images but not all images are symbols, that is, not all images represent more than the concrete reality. Tindall's definition is based on examples: "The image, like the symbol of which it is a principal kind, appears to be a verbal embodiment of thought and feeling. . . . the image presents what it carries. The word image may refer to the symbolic whole or to an element depending for part of its burden upon context." Tindall notes that images are most important when the structure to which they are central limits and enhances them. Although Faulkner's images are generally realistic, he sometimes presents an image that, though composed of realistic elements, suggests the poetic objective correlative: "a verbal formula outside poet and reader for presenting something inside them but to neither alike." Such an image, central to the structure and meaning of *Sanctuary*, is that of Temple leaving the courtroom surrounded by her father and brothers.

Faulkner's admiration for Thomas Mann may explain his use of the leitmotif as a subsidiary device. Thomas Mann, influenced by Wagner, gave his own definition: like a motif in music, "The leitmotif is the technique employed to preserve the inward unity and the abiding presentness of the whole at each moment." The leitmotif elaborates a theme, is repeated, and does not depend on time sequence; it is especially suited to link the parts of the Yoknapatawpha chronicles and to suggest Faulkner's concept of time in its timelessness. In "Coordinate Structures in Four Faulkner Novels," William Ramsey identifies structural patterns by "the non-contiguous, thematic arrangement of coordinate motifs"; leitmotifs have the subordinate function of drawing attention to the coordinations between larger motifs. A leitmotif with thematic but not structural function is the name of the jailer's daughter scratched on the window in *The Unvanquished* (p. 17), *Intruder in the Dust* (pp. 50, 51), and *Requiem for a Nun* (p. 229), where it is developed into a major symbolic motif. The leitmotifs of Flem Snopes's little bow ties and his constant chewing make him seem impervious to time.

In a paradox worthy of his own fictional world, Faulkner succeeded in creating, out of the "well of the past," a highly original body of fiction in which the symbol, archetypal or personal, achieved its maximum effect as defined by Kahler:

> . . . inasmuch as artistic representation is not just mimesis, the rendering of an already patent reality, but rather an evocation of a latent, heretofore unseen reality, it carries out in its artistic performance a supra-artistic, a human deed of the greatest consequence: *the creation of a new form of reality*. Such coincidence, indeed identity, of the artistic and the human act, is the supreme reach of the symbol.

In the Yoknapatawpha chronicles Faulkner's individual creative process accounts for the fact that most of his symbols can be taken at face value and serve to provide realistic elements in character or setting; the symbolic significance is an added dimension that enhances the meaning but is not essential on the narrative level. Faulkner's account of the genesis of *The Sound and the Fury* seems typical of his creative imagination at work: "It began with a mental picture. I didn't realize at the time it was symbolical. The picture was of the muddy seat of a little girl's drawers in a pear tree, where she could see through a window where her grandmother's funeral was taking place . . ." (*LG* 245). Faulkner belongs among those whose concrete approach to symbols, as de-

scribed by Northrop Frye, "begins with images of actual things and
works outward to ideas and propositions."

If objects have symbolic value in themselves or through association
with a character, the author need only suggest, sometimes merely by
means of repetition, the symbolism inherent in the object. Thus, fiction
may be realistic and still be highly charged with symbolic meanings.
This is particularly true, as Philip Wheelwright notes, in fiction which
is close to nature: "Each thing in nature that stirs us deeply seems at
once valuable in itself and a kind of gateway or threshold to an unex-
plored Something More." Yoknapatawpha County is virtually unique
in containing a people close to the soil, whose lives are attuned to the
rhythm of the seasons, but among whom there are sensitive and even
highly sophisticated characters whose intellectual activity coexists
with sympathetic observation of nature.

A brief classification of the chief types of symbols found in the
Yoknapatawpha chronicles may be a helpful preliminary to discussion
of individual works and of the functions of symbols in them. The natural, universal symbols, suitable to the rural and small-town settings,
include the cosmos, the four elements, the weather, and other aspects
of nature and geographical features of Yoknapatawpha County. Such
symbols may be used as universal collective symbols, like the long
summer in *The Hamlet*, or as recurrent personal symbols, like honeysuckle in Quentin's memories in *The Sound and the Fury*, or as specific
symbols, like the snake Ike McCaslin sees in "The Bear."

Artifacts may be collective symbols, like the jail and the courthouse,
or family or group symbols, like Sutpen's Hundred or the Compson
house, or objects associated with persons, like the stained glass Aunt
Jenny Du Pre brought to Sartoris from Carolina.

Titles and names of characters are often symbolic. Faulkner said that
his characters named themselves: "I never have to hunt for their
names. Suddenly they tell me who they are. In the conception quite
often, but never very long after I have conceived that character, does
he name himself. When he doesn't name himself, I never do" (*FN* 78).
The names they tell him, however, are for the most part local names;
when he says that he never uses the name of a real person (*FU* 206), he
means the complete name, which would identify an individual; the
Oxford *Eagle* and the Oxford telephone directory are full of family
names found in Faulkner's works, names which, A. F. Beringause
observes, "help Faulkner achieve an organic relationship of form and
meaning and intensify the emotional impact of the very plots whose
construction they bolster." Faulkner's choice of names is in harmony

with his mythic approach; in the mythical consciousness, according to Ernst Cassirer, the awe of proper names is due to the belief that a name "expresses what is innermost and essential in the man." A dissertation by Frances Pate, "Names of Characters in William Faulkner's Mississippi," and Joseph Blotner's *Faulkner: A Biography* reveal that most of the names in the fiction are selected, rather than invented. Although "Snopes" is invented, it has possible sources: a character in Augustus Longstreet's *Georgia Scenes* is Ransy Sniffle, and Faulkner's friend John Cullen in *Old Times in the Faulkner Country* refers to the son of Senator Snipes "(not Snopes)" as the seducer of a girl at "Miss Reba's." Beringause comments on the usefulness of onomatology to Faulkner critics and on the function of names in building up Faulkner's illusion "of a world within a world": "he defines his mythical county with almost literal accuracy, perhaps to remind readers that Yoknapatawpha is not entirely a realm of imagination."

Not only objects, natural or man-made, or characters, but whole scenes, like tableaux or dramatic images, may be charged with complex symbolism derived from clusters of symbolic details of any or all of the types listed above.

Symbols, images, and archetypal patterns may have varied functions. Faulkner's prevailing irony and paradox may be symbolically indicated with thematic imagery serving to create dramatic tensions, or to confirm, amplify, or contradict the plot. Walter Slatoff's study of polarity in Faulkner and Victor Strandberg's study of "the technique of inversion" are relevant to aspects of symbolism as well as to structure and style. Anse Bundren's false teeth and Dewey Dell's quest for an abortion are symbols which deny the unselfish heroism suggested by the journey of the Bundrens; much of the difficulty critics have had with *As I Lay Dying* was due to failure to recognize the symbols as clues to the predominant pattern, an ironic inversion of the quest romance. Most frequently and significantly, symbols point to the themes and aid in their development: "the overtones of meaning which are thrown off by the main images and image-patterns" are as vital in Faulkner's major works as Wheelwright, in "Thematic Patterns in the *Oresteia*," shows them to be in Aeschylus.

In this chapter collective symbols which are not associated with or limited to single works or characters will be dealt with as symbols drawn from the natural world or from the world of artifacts. Symbols related to a traditional mythic pattern, such as the quest-hero or the hero of an initiation, will be dealt with in Chapter 2. Part V of this chapter will include other personal and family symbols.

III • THE NATURAL WORLD AS SYMBOL

In the last paragraph of the interview with Jean Stein, Faulkner used three metaphors in referring to his mythical county, Yoknapatawpha: he discovered that his "own little postage stamp of native soil" was worth writing about, so, he said, "I created a cosmos of my own." The last metaphor is a kind of macrocosm version of the microcosm in the first one: "I like to think of the world I created as being a kind of keystone in the universe; that, small as that keystone is, if it were ever taken away, the universe itself would collapse." My first book on Faulkner bears the title *Yoknapatawpha: Faulkner's "Little Postage Stamp of Native Soil."* The title of this volume was chosen to signify that I am following Faulkner's progress from the provincial to the universal, as he so helpfully suggested. In between my two subtitles lurks a third, which a study of the natural world of Yoknapatawpha and its symbolic significance should recognize. The cosmic dimensions of Yoknapatawpha have been perceived by several critics. In a dissertation, "Religious Themes and Symbols in the Novels of William Faulkner," Stanley Elkin regretted the tendency of critics to "regionalize Faulkner" and thus to miss "the real microcosmic implications of his mythical county." Lawrence Dembo observed a fusion of naturalism and morally sensitive symbolism in the works of T. S. Eliot, James Joyce, Robert Penn Warren, and William Faulkner. In his study of "The Symbolic Action of Sin and Redemption" in five Yoknapatawpha novels, Dembo commented that the "strata of symbolic reference" of literal action were adaptable to psychology, sociology, and cosmology. Dembo, Elkin, and I were all exploring Yoknapatawpha County for our diverse purposes before American astronauts landed on the moon, but Michael P. Routh, with a 1973 dissertation, no doubt belongs to the space age and accepted the challenge in "The Story of All Things: Faulkner's Yoknapatawpha Cosmology by Way of 'Light in August.'" The cosmological perspective now having been established, I shall limit myself to the universal.

The natural world is the environment of Faulkner's fiction, the town of Jefferson being too small and too dependent on the countryside to separate its inhabitants from nature. The concept of the frontier presented by Henry Nash Smith in *Virgin Land: The American West as Symbol and Myth* applied especially to northern Mississippi, the last area in the state to be settled. Having noted these historical facts in "Primitivism in the Fiction of William Faulkner," George W. Sutton described Faulkner and his area as "at the core of America itself." The inevitable involvement of both natives and transients with nature provided one aspect of the good/evil polarity in the Yoknapatawpha fiction: harmony with nature is common to all the characters who are admirable and lack of such harmony is evident in the weak or vicious. The confrontation of Horace Benbow and Popeye at the spring in *Sanctuary*, the most striking single scene illustrating this polarity, was strategically placed at the beginning in Faulkner's revision of the unpublished galleys of *Sanctuary*, as Gerald Langford's collation of the galleys with the published book makes clear. The world of nature may be used impersonally or in relation to personal awareness and reactions or as a causal factor in situations. In this survey of basic general symbols, characters and situations will merely be suggested if the work is to be dealt with later in detail.

Of the four elements, Faulkner deals most frequently with earth, partly because of the major theme of the exploitation of the land, partly because water, the other most useful element for symbolic purposes, is present in Yoknapatawpha County only in limited degree. The all-embracing historical view in *Requiem for a Nun* covers Yoknapatawphan earth from the Creation to about 1950. The right relationship to the land and its use is represented in the Indians before the white man came, when they owned the land communally, and in the Negroes. *Go Down, Moses* best represents this relationship. In his analysis of the short stories about Indians, such as "Red Leaves," "A Justice," and "A Courtship," Sutton shows that corruption of the Indians had been effected in the three generations from the coming of the white man to the forced migration of the Indians to Oklahoma. In *Go Down, Moses* Sam Fathers is the only surviving Indian who maintains the old relationship of mutual respect with the white hunters. Sam dies in "The Bear." *The Hamlet* most fully develops the theme of the exploitation of the land and the corruption of the white owners.

In *Sartoris*, the one novel in which the air is used as a dominant symbol, there seems to be a clear contrast between the earth as a symbol of reality, growth, acceptance, and life and the air as a symbol of rejection of life. Young Bayard almost achieved reconciliation to life during the late summer and fall after his marriage, when he was interested in the seasonal activities on the plantation and in hunting. His suicidal last flight, as a test pilot, was a deliberate rejection of earth and of life.

Water in Yoknapatawpha County takes the form of small streams or rivers. It is used realistically, as a force of nature which man must cope with, in *As I Lay Dying* and "The Bear." The plantations in the bottomlands, owing their existence to the streams, symbolize man's use of water. Parchman, the actual name of the state prison farm, provides a symbolically suitable contrast outside the county. Water is used symbolically as representing innocence or redemption, as in "The Bear" where Ike's immersion in the river may be a kind of baptism, or in *The Unvanquished*, "Raid," where the Negroes swarm into the river as into the river Jordan. But conversely, water may be associated with corruption: the branch and Caddy's muddied drawers in *The Sound and the Fury* introduce the water motif, "the dominant symbolic motif," and the motif of ritual cleansing, repeated in both I and II, as William Grant indicates in "Benjy's Branch: Symbolic Method in Part I of *The Sound and the Fury*." Caddy having failed to restore her purity by ritual cleansing, Quentin drowned himself in the Charles River, the symbol of death, as the branch was the symbol of sin.

Fire Quentin thought of as a purgatorial purifying "clean flame," an image and significance recalling Dante's wall of fire in the *Purgatorio*, where love is purified. Quentin's flame, however, is that of everlasting hell. To Benjy, fire is a friendly element, perhaps a symbol of Caddy's love; the fire that finally destroys Benjy and the Compson house suggests the destruction that Caddy bought upon her brothers through their inability to love her unselfishly (*M* 322). As it is for Benjy, fire in "The Fire and the Hearth" and "Pantaloon in Black" is a symbol also of love and security, here specifically of married love. Other uses of fire are destructive: the fire of hate and revenge in the burning of Joanna Burden's house in *Light in August*, and in Ab Snopes's "Barn Burning" and the threat of it in *The Hamlet*; the fire of the destructiveness of war, in *The Unvanquished* and *Requiem for a Nun*; the fire of mob hatred in *Sanctuary* and the threat of it in "The Fire and the Hearth" and *Intruder in the Dust*. The burning coffin in *As I Lay Dying* combines symbolisms: a cleansing fire to end corruption, from Darl's point of view (*FU* 110), and a test of love and fulfillment of prophecy for Jewel, who saved Addie "from the water and from the fire" (*AILD* 160). Enrico Garzilli noted that the "water, fire and fish all have mythical and religious overtones."

Universal symbols like the elements, the seasons, and weather figure prominently in relation to tone, mood, and action in many stories, but only *Sartoris* is based on the cycle of the whole year; it covers slightly more than a year and the time pattern is a chief structural device. There is no consistent relation of the season to events: the death of old Bayard occurred in winter, followed by a kind of spiritual death of young Bayard, who could not face the consequences of his act, but his own death occurred in summer.

Spring is significant, in harmony or more often in ironic discord, in *The Hamlet, The Sound and the Fury, Sanctuary*, and *Intruder in the*

Dust. Summer is the most common seasonal setting and symbolism, with emphasis on heat, dryness, and despair as well as on fruition. The two extremes are combined in *Light in August*, in the Joe–Lena polarity. In the green wilderness of early summer Ike first sees Old Ben ("The Bear"). "The Long Summer" in *The Hamlet* is a pastoral idyll chiefly for Ike Snopes and the cow. In *The Unvanquished*, summer is the time of military activity; in *Sanctuary*, it is the time for the trial and lynching of Lee Goodwin. For Quentin in *The Sound and the Fury*, the roses of summer are associated with Caddy's wedding and thus are a symbol of despair which drives him to suicide in June. In *As I Lay Dying*, the stench of corruption hangs over the summer pilgrimage of the Bundrens.

Autumn is used most symbolically in some of the short stories: in "Red Leaves," the title symbolizes "that the red leaves had nothing against him when they suffocated him and destroyed him"—the slave is the victim of "normal deciduation" (*FU* 39). In "Dry September," as the title suggests, the weather exacerbates the nerves of the people until the rumor started by Miss Minnie Cooper goes through the "bloody September twilight, aftermath of sixty-two rainless days . . . like a fire in dry grass" (*CS* 169). Dust is used as a motif. "An Odor of Verbena" is the only story in *The Unvanquished* with an autumnal setting, perhaps to represent both the death of Colonel Sartoris in his prime and the growth of Bayard to moral maturity when he succeeds his father as "the Sartoris." In *Absalom, Absalom!* the heat and dryness and dust of September hang over Quentin as he listens to Miss Rosa and his father and accompanies Miss Rosa to Sutpen's Hundred. In "The Old People" and "The Bear," the buck and Old Ben are killed at the end of autumn.

Most symbolic is the season in "Delta Autumn"; the passing of the wilderness, the old age of Uncle Ike McCaslin, the memory of hunting days of the past, and the dying out of the old code of not killing does are all relevant to the title and the season. Jung, in *Man and His Symbols*, cites the ancient symbolism of the deer hunt as "one of the countless symbolic or allegorical images of the sexual act." When Ike in his youth hunted in Yoknapatawpha, not the Delta, the only does in his consciousness had four legs. The only festive family occasion directly presented in Yoknapatawpha is the Sartoris Thanksgiving dinner, with Horace and Doctor Peabody and his son as guests. Before Christmas old Bayard was dead and young Bayard was a fugitive.

Throughout the chronicles, winter is used often and always with grimness or dreariness. In *The Unvanquished*, Granny's murder by Grumby and Bayard's and Ringo's pursuit of Grumby and their savage vengeance took place in winter, in snow and iron frost and rain (p. 186). Ike found Fonsiba and her husband in December, in destitute misery (*GDM* 277). The end of the story of Labove's obsessing love for Eula Varner is the only winter episode in *The Hamlet*: "a gray day, of the color and texture of iron, one of those windless days of a plastic rigidity too dead to make or to release snow" (p. 124). The "strange iron New England snow" on Shreve's overcoat sleeve, as Quentin, in their room at Harvard, tells the story of the Sutpens, is a symbol of the contrast between the North and the South, and Quentin is "panting in the cold air, the iron New England dark" when he affirms that he does not hate the South (*AA* 378).

There are few natural symbols which, like the northern winter, go beyond Yoknapatawpha County. The dominant features of the landscape, other than the rivers dealt with as water symbols, are the wilderness during the early period and the rural landscape traversed by roads in the twentieth century. The wilderness represents a way of life and values which cannot survive the access provided by roads and modern transportion for the agents of materialism. Faulkner said: "The wilderness to me was the past, which could be the old evils, the old forces, which were by their own standards right and correct, ruthless, but they lived and died by their own code—they asked nothing" (*FN* 50). *Requiem for a Nun* in the prologues traces the whole process of the vanishing of the wilderness; some of the short stories and *Go Down, Moses* develop the theme in detail. Faulkner was more consciously using symbolism in "The Bear" than, apparently, in any other one work. The wilderness is the background for a cluster of nature symbols which will be discussed later. Other than the Tallahatchie River, the wilderness northwest of Jefferson had no distinctive features except the Indian mounds referred to in "A Bear Hunt," where they symbolize "inference of secret and violent blood, of savage and sudden destruction" (*CS* 64).

The excellent and extremely perceptive study, "The Landscape," in François Pitavy's *Faulkner's "Light in August,"* deals with subtle and unique qualities; a synthesis of his comments on specific aspects will suffice to suggest how felicitous Pitavy's observations are in this context of the world created by William Faulkner. The descriptions

are glimpses of a landscape seen through a character's perceptions or related to his acts, so that Faulkner's scenery always appears to be somehow inhabited. . . . It is thus not surprising that the landscape should bear a strange resemblance to the characters inhabiting it, and have the same quality of unreality and haunting actuality. . . . The landscape is in fact largely defined in terms of light and shade, and of stillness and movement [p. 85]. On this August afternoon, the landscape and all that Lena sees seem to be, like her, suspended outside time, as though, with the absence of movement, time or timelessness were merged with space and took on all its attributes. . . . The landscape in *Light in August* is never immutable or dead; it retains potential movement as do the momentarily stilled characters. In fact, as in a dream or nightmare, the landscape is slowly altered, and the shadows quiver and swell monstrously; or it can appear to glide past the characters, while they remain apparently stationary [p. 86]. Light, or its absence, is the color of sunrise . . . before the harsh, implacable glare has obliterated every nuance of color [p. 87]. The landscape is less remarkable for its colors than for the striking use of black and white, light and shadow [p. 88].

Pitavy's broader generalizations anticipate his concluding chapter and the suggested "Interpretations":

This landscape is unreal and impossible, but as actual and as inevitable as the closed world of dreams, where, isolated from outside comparison with reality, the landscape becomes perfectly coherent and real [p. 89]. Faulkner's landscape is as physically "depthless" as his characters. In the blaze of noon, the landscape dissolves in too much light, yet remains actual and visible; in the evening, the several planes reappear, but separately, not forming a solid world. As much as his characters, Faulkner's landscapes remain in suspension [pp. 90–91].

The interpretations François Pitavy suggests for *Light in August* are valid for most of the Yoknapatawpha fiction: the first, Gothic, is the basis of my book *William Faulkner's Gothic Domain*; the other two, Mythological and Existentialist and Humanist, are covered in this volume, which was in process in the 1960s. It is pleasant to realize that we were following parallel trails.

Of the characters through whose perceptive eyes Yoknapatawpha is most extensively and intensively viewed, the chief ones, Gavin Stevens and Charles Mallison, his nephew, present two complementary and comprehensive views. Gavin as narrator addresses the reader; Charles, as central intelligence, is presented in the third person, past tense. Gavin viewed Jefferson and the county at night, from Seminary Ridge:

First is Jefferson, the center, radiating weakly its puny glow into space; beyond it, enclosing it, spreads the County, tied by the diverging roads to that center as is the rim to the hub by its spokes, yourself detached as God Himself for this moment above the cradle of your nativity . . . then and last on to where Frenchman's Bend lay beyond the southeastern horizon, cradle of Varners and ant-heap for the northwest crawl of Snopes [*T* 315–16, 317].

On a bright morning in May, during an interlude in the traumatic experience of his initiation into the responsibilities of a Southern man, Charles was being driven by Gavin into the hill country, "up and onto the last crest":

> now he seemed to see his whole native land, his home . . . unfolding beneath him like a map in one slow soundless explosion: to the east ridge on green ridge tumbling away toward Alabama and to the west and south the checkered fields and the woods flowing on into the blue and gauzed horizon beyond which lay at last like a cloud the long wall of the levee and the great River itself . . . the umbilicus of America . . . [*ID* 151].

The full effect of cosmic dimensions cannot be gained from such curtailed quotations, but the images of the enclosing hills strengthen the significance of Yoknapatawpha County as a microcosm peripheral to the navel of America.

The vegetation of this microcosm is used realistically as well as symbolically. As the basis of the economy, cotton pervades the fiction with its seasonal phases. But it also becomes a symbol of the exploitation of the land and of man. The quick returns of this one crop which exhausted the soil had made slavery profitable. Faulkner's Muse must have selected his birthplace with great care: he was born in northern Mississippi approximately one hundred years after the invention of the cotton gin in 1793. This invention determined the future of the South in general and of Yoknapatawpha in particular; Faulkner in the first sentence of *Requiem for a Nun* said that the town "began somewhere under the turn of the century." At that time the growth of the materialistic spirit and a vast westward migration brought new settlers into Mississippi with dreams of owning cotton plantations and with slaves as a labor force. The most unfortunate effect of the cotton gin, according to Clement Eaton, was "the revitalization of the moribund institution of slavery." By 1860, Eaton said, Mississippi was the leading cotton-growing state. Lafayette–Yoknapatawpha County, however, was poor cotton-growing land except in flat river bottoms such as those of the Tallahatchie and Yocona (Yoknapatawpha) rivers. But cotton-growing even on a small scale contributes its own patterns to the landscape, with the seasonal variations in the appearance of the crop, the activities of the workers, and the autumn traffic of cotton-laden trucks to cotton gins.

For glimpses of cotton country Faulkner not only used the perceptions of a character, as Pitavy observed, but chose a character who had not seen his own kind of cotton country for thirty-eight years. On his pedestrian journey from Memphis to Jefferson, Mink Snopes, preoc-

cupied with worries about his pistol, realized he had turned into "a dirt
crossroad" and noticed "the wisps of cotton lint snared into the road-
side weeds and brambles from the passing gin-bound wagons": "a
Negro road, a road marked with many wheels and traced with cotton
wisps, yet dirt, not even gravel" because the people who lived on it
lacked both voting power and money to get a better road. Then he
found "what he had expected": "a weathered paintless dog-trot cabin
enclosed and backed by a ramshackle of also paintless weathered
fences and outhouses—barns, cribs, sheds—on a rise of ground above
a creek-bottom cotton patch . . ." (*M* 398–99). To the Negro who hired
him to pick cotton, Mink boasted that he was on his way to his daughter's home in the Delta, and the man replied, "I made a Delta cotton
crop one year myself." Mink's rediscovery of the seasons when he left
Parchman evoked the memory of an autumn in the hills when he had
the rare experience of enjoying the beauty of nature. He had stolen a
gun to shoot some squirrels for his ailing foster mother and saw the
land "gold and crimson with hickory and gum and oak and maple,
and the old fields warm with sage and splattered with scarlet
sumac . . ." (*M* 104).

Trees and flowers are likely to be referred to as personal symbols:
Benjy Compson's deadly jimson weed, Quentin's sexy honeysuckle,
Drusilla's verbena that smelled of courage. Before Charles Mallison
reached the crest and had his vision of his native land, "he could see
the white bursts of dogwood in the hedgerows . . . or standing like
nuns in the cloistral patches and bands of greening woods and the pink
and white of peach and pear and the pinkwhite of the first apple trees in
the orchards . . ." (*ID* 146). In Jefferson all the townspeople were
familiar with the heaven-tree (Pawlonia) beside the jail, where the
friends of the Negro murderer in the jail gathered and sang spirituals
and the murderer himself sang, "de bes ba'ytone singer in nawth
Mississippi!" (*San.* 110–11). The heaven-tree had shed its trumpet-
shaped purple blooms when the murderer sang for the last time before he
was "hanged without pomp and buried without circumstance"
(p. 127). Both the tree and the jail in Oxford are gone but the older
generation remember them.

Faulkner used animals also with both general and specific symbolic
meaning. The wild animals always have a special significance as well as
sharing the symbolism of the vanishing wilderness, but they are never
used without relation to characters. Domestic animals, especially the
horse and the mule, have a kind of communal meaning as well as
symbolizing qualities in a character, as Jewel's horse, in *As I Lay
Dying*, is a substitute also for wife and mother. Horses are the most

common domestic animals in Yoknapatawpha; they are both a natural part of the environment and a reflection of Faulkner's "family heritage" of love for horses from which he learned "to have sympathy for creatures not as wise, as smart, as man, to have pity for things that are physically weak" (*FN* 91, 92). This particular interest survived to the very end of Faulkner's writing and appears there in its most directly autobiographical reference: in *The Reivers*, the father of Lucius had a livery stable. The horse in general symbolizes male prestige, virility, and aspiration. It was the supreme status symbol before the automobile.

In contrast with the horse is the mule, a symbol of the cotton-growing economy, compared with and sometimes symbolizing the Negro in humble endurance (*GDM* 295). The well-known panegyric to the mule (*Sar.* 278–79), echoed in *The Reivers* (pp. 121–24), makes clear this general symbolism, and individual mules are seldom given other significance. The Negro and the mule together constitute "the land's living symbol—a formal group of ritual almost mystic significance" (*ID* 147). Both horses and mules as essential means of transportation are associated with road symbolism.

Identifying "the major issue involved in the Sutpen tale" as "inhuman abstraction" which reduces human dignity, Donald Foran devotes a chapter to images equating people with livestock: "Of Cattle, Chattel, and Pallets." Slaves and women were like other property. The pallet, a most insignificant man-made object, was "one measure of the existing stratification": it was the kind of cot Thomas Sutpen slept on as a child and to which those of "pariah status" were later assigned in the Sutpen family.

IV • THE MAN-MADE WORLD AS SYMBOL

Concentration upon Yoknapatawpha County as the setting of his fiction enabled Faulkner to make extensive use of man-made objects as recurrent symbols. In *Requiem for a Nun*, using the courthouse and the jail as nuclei for clusters of symbolic objects, Faulkner reviewed the whole history of the town and county and thereafter continued to repeat artifacts as symbols until *The Reivers* ended the chronicles. Since these symbols reflect the stages in the development and history of white society, chronological arrangement, by time of action, will be helpful. The symbols of a group tradition can serve the individual in Yoknapatawpha County as Maud Bodkin said they served Clarissa Dalloway, "amid the flux of an individual sensibility": "The function fulfilled by such symbols in the life of an individual today is the same that was performed by the images and dogma of institutional religion, more widely in the past. . . ." In a community in which the past is a religion, the symbols are doubly effective.

One of the most striking deliberate uses of symbolic images in *Requiem for a Nun* is the passage in which history is traced in terms of footgear (pp. 217–20). Specific symbolic value is given to these symbols of the human occupation—moccasins, fitted shoes, brogans—by the image of Mohataha, with a slave carrying her slippers, riding westward, followed by her young men in broadcloth trousers and boiled shirts, carrying New England-made shoes: the true owners of the land were first corrupted by the white man and then dispossessed (pp. 216–17, 220). The symbol of the white man's shoes which the Indian cannot wear had been used earlier of Moketubbe in "Red Leaves." Because the act of setting foot on new soil is in itself symbolic, footgear automatically takes on symbolic meaning from the familiar act. Furthermore, since one of Faulkner's main themes is the exploitation of the land, the article of apparel which is in contact with the land is significant. (In *Heart of Darkness*, the bloody shoes which Marlow, "out of sheer nervousness," threw overboard are invested with such symbolic meaning.) The fact that Moketubbe and Mohataha cannot walk and cannot wear slippers thus symbolizes both the Indians' loss of land and their greed and corruption.

The roads, which in time criss-crossed the county, unify the region with an imperfect wheel-like pattern, with Jefferson the hub and the roads the spokes, as Gavin noted in the view from Seminary Ridge. (There are no straight roads in Lafayette County.) In Faulkner the wheel is a symbol of change, related to the theme of change and flux. Ernst Cassirer's contrast between the Heraclitean wheel as a symbol of change and the Buddhist wheel as a symbol of escape from change is relevant to Faulkner's themes and symbols. The journey pattern of some novels and recurrent shorter journeys in others lend a general theme of quest or pilgrimage to the chronicles and a contrasting one of flight. William Ramsey included journeying as one of the coordinating motifs in *The Sound and the Fury*. Jefferson is the mecca of the quest in "An Odor of Verbena," in *As I Lay Dying*, in Flem Snopes's rise in *The Hamlet*, and in Mink Snopes's revenge in *The Mansion*. In *The Unvanquished*, "The Bear," *Intruder in the Dust*, and *The Reivers*, Jefferson is the point of departure and return for young men who must leave the security of home to achieve self-knowledge. The contrasting pattern, centrifugal from Jefferson, is used in the flight of Granny Millard and the boys from Sartoris in *The Unvanquished* and in the flight of Joe Christmas after he fled from the Burden house.

Because Yoknapatawpha County, like Lafayette County, is not industrialized, the modern age in Faulkner is not the machine age in
general but the automotive age. The development of transportation
began with the roads, which all led to Jefferson, and hence vehicles of
various kinds have a general symbolic significance in the history of the
county and of Jefferson, its hub. The pony express of Pettigrew and its
successor, the stagecoach from Memphis, belong to the time when the
trails became roads and wheeled vehicles became symbols of both
business and professional activity and of courtship. In *The Hamlet*,
Ratliff's wagon and Varner's buggy represent commercial activity,
and the buggies of Eula's suitors are the modern equivalent of the
chariots of the wooers of Helen of Troy (pp. 127–33). Doc Habersham
in *Requiem for a Nun* (p. 216) and Doc Peabody in *As I Lay Dying*
covered the county in their buggies. Wagons, strictly utilitarian, both
ushered out the old, Mohataha and her retinue (*Requiem for a Nun*,
pp. 216–17), and ushered in the new. Wagons served life in *The Unvanquished* and death in *As I Lay Dying*. They marked a stage in the
progress of an individual, for both Ratliff and Flem in *The Hamlet*
(pp. 13, 361). Carriages and fine horses were a symbol of antebellum
aristocracy, especially to the older Sartorises before they yielded to the
insinuating delights of speed in 1920, and to the Compsons who had to
make do with the relics of their former splendor, Queenie and the
surrey, in 1928 (*SF* 398–401).

After the Civil War in Jefferson the railroad succeeded the steamboat as the symbol of progress but, unlike the steamboat, was identified in the Yoknapatawpha chronicles with an individual, Colonel John
Sartoris. In "An Odor of Verbena" it was his dream for the community
and for his own prestige and power (pp. 169–72), but it became his
doom when his former partner shot him. The story is retold in *Requiem
for a Nun* (pp. 238–39). In "The Bear," the logging railroad symbolizes
the commercial interests which doom the wilderness to extinction;
unlike the railroad through Jefferson, this line serves only a temporary
function and goes out of existence like the wilderness. When the automobile and the airplane became common, the railroad, except for
freight, went the way of the steamboat as an obsolete form of transportation.

In 1919 Horace Benbow arrived home by train and was met at the
depot by Narcissa; train and platform porters were available to cope
with his "astonishing impedimenta" and to retrieve the hand luggage
he left on the platform (*Sar.* 161, 196). In 1937 Chick Mallison and
Gavin Stevens met Linda Kohl at the Memphis airport, eighty miles
from Jefferson, and Chick drove the car back to Jefferson with Linda
and Gavin in the back seat (*M* 179, 199).

The most dramatic evidence of the fading of Colonel John Sartoris' dream and of his role as a public benefactor is the experience of Mink Snopes in 1946, after thirty-eight years at Parchman. He followed the railroad tracks into Jefferson to avoid being seen. Reminded of the night he spent watching the passenger trains go through Jefferson on the railroad that ran from Chicago to the Gulf of Mexico, he discovered that it "was now a fading weed-grown branch line knowing no wheels any more save two local freight trains more or less every day" (*M* 406).

After 1905, the automobile is the ubiquitous symbol of progress, speed, excitement, and love. A thumbnail sketch of the automobile in the life of Jefferson, from old Bayard Sartoris' law prohibiting the operation of a mechanically propelled vehicle in Jefferson streets to the period after World War II, is given in *Requiem for a Nun*, "The Jail," but it scarcely suggests the prominent role the automobile played in action and in the lives and deaths of the characters. It largely but not entirely succeeds the horse as a masculine symbol. In fact, in Faulkner's last novel, *The Reivers*, the auto plays its first major role, chronologically, in the chronicles and shares the honors with the sardine-addict horse through whose victory in the race the automobile belonging to Boss Priest would be recovered. The irresistible delight of a trip to Memphis in a Winston Flyer was the occasion of young Lucius' first venture into Non-virtue. Here also we learn the whole story of the occasion for the law against mechanically propelled vehicles, "that arrogant decree of Colonel Sartoris's" which Boss Priest "could not allow to stand" (pp. 25–30). In *My Brother Bill*, John Faulkner gave the facts of the edict, passed by his grandfather, in local history; it is "still on the books, for the simple reason that it has never been rescinded" (p. 104).

Sartoris covers only a little more than a year in time, but, as Walter Brylowsky indicated, it focuses on three societies, symbolized by the horse, the automobile, and the plane. Bayard used his new car to fight against the old society, terrifying Negroes and mules, almost killing himself, and killing his grandfather. Presumably he could have mastered the stallion—Brylowski notes the centaur image—but was thrown when he saved a child. He flew a plane in World War I but was killed in a test flight in a plane no other test pilot would fly. The automobile is the symbol of Bayard's psychic wound. In proving his courage and his wish to die, he brought into symbolic union the three stages of man's progress in self-propelled transportation. To Jason Compson in *The Sound and the Fury* and to Flem Snopes in *The Town*, both in the 1920s, an automobile was a status symbol, not a source of enjoyment or a means of displaying skill and courage.

The Town picks up the story of the automobile at its beginning in

Jefferson, with Manfred de Spain's racer a symbol of his love affair with Eula as the suitors' buggies had been in *The Hamlet*. In *Intruder in the Dust*, about 1940, cars and trucks are the indispensable means of performing actions and the symbol of the mob and its shamed flight. Except for *Sartoris*, planes play a part only in offstage action. By using the automobile as a symbol of aspirations and status, of materialistic ambition and the lack of it, of personal rivalries and triumphs, Faulkner converts a means of transportation into a symbol of the century. Although this is scarcely an archetypal symbol, it is the modern avatar of the ancient wheel and the descendant of the chariot of Phaëthon.

In the Square around which the cars merrily whiz, buildings are collective symbols, recurring throughout the chronicles. Only in *Requiem for a Nun* is the story told of the chest and the lock and the ledger, the germ out of which the town and the country grew (pp. 3–31). The jail, however, figures prominently throughout the chronicles and is a center of action in *Intruder in the Dust*; in addition to Lucas Beauchamp, it housed at various times Mink Snopes, Lee Goodwin, Joe Christmas, and Nancy Mannigoe. The story of the jailer's daughter who inscribed her name on the window pane is stated in *The Unvanquished*; in *Intruder in the Dust* and *Requiem for a Nun*, the motif of the window pane, this frail fragment of perishable stuff, is raised to a symbol not only of private life and love but also of the ironic survival of the symbol long after the people are dust. This maiden and youth, memorialized in a pane of glass, are Faulkner's symbol of life and time, comparable to his favorite "Grecian Urn" which makes time stand still. The real-life original was Jane T. Cook, who did scratch her name on a piece of glass preserved in the Mary Buie Museum in Oxford. According to E. O. Hawkins, she so aroused the admiration of General Forrest's son, a captain in a troup which she "cursed . . . Out" for retreating, that he returned after the war and married her.

Though the jail survived the burning of the Square (and stood until 1962), the courthouse was burned in 1863 but survived (*RN* 46), to rise again like a phoenix after a restoration period of twenty-five years. Except in *Requiem for a Nun*, neither edifice was invested with symbolic significance in the chronicles before the Civil War. As the center of the Square, the courthouse is literally the point around which the life of the community revolves. Like the primitive "ceremonial house" which Mircea Eliade explains, in *The Sacred and the Profane*, as a part of "the cosmic symbolism of the village," the courthouse was four-square, with four pillars each on the identical north and south porticos. Like the sacred lodge of the Sioux, "the roof symbolizes the dome of the sky, the floor represents earth, the four walls the four directions of cosmic space." (In Oxford, the two wings which destroy the symbolic squareness were added in the 1950s.) Having cited ancient European countries as well as American Indians, Eliade concludes: "We constantly find the same cosmological schema and the same ritual scenario: *settling in a territory is equivalent to founding a world.*" It appears that Faulkner had created his cosmos before he realized the implications: his Genesis, in *Requiem for a Nun*, very properly comes a long time after the Creation.

The Confederate monument in front of the south portico of the courthouse is a literal symbol, but it is also one of the cluster of points on the Square which comprise a whole constellation. Other points are the Holston House, the hardware store, with Gavin Stevens' office above it, the federal courthouse, and the barbershop. These are all collective symbols, common to people in both town and county and scenes where action takes place.

Outside of Jefferson, only one community has buildings invested with somewhat comparable collective significance. In Frenchman's Bend, Varner's store is to the Bend what the area surrounding the courthouse is to Jefferson, the place where men sit and talk, but it is much more the scene of discussion of local affairs by Ratliff and the natives than the courthouse is for Jefferson. Varner's store and gin and the Old Frenchman place also are symbols of Flem's rise to power. The barrel chair at the Old Frenchman's is the throne on which Will Varner is succeeded by Flem Snopes. The use of these same old ruins in *Sanctuary* invests the scene with a different symbolic meaning: in the chronology of events, from the barrel chair to the corncrib is a progress from greed and lust to greed and impotence and then to lust and impotence.

From the single perspective of Charles Mallison in *Intruder in the Dust* the reader learns an amazing amount about the world of Yoknapatawpha and its history. His description of the jail is to be treasured now that it can no longer be seen: "It still looked like a residence with its balustraded wooden gallery stretching across the front of the lower floor. But above that the brick wall was windowless except for the single tall crossbarred rectangle" (p. 51). There were, of course, only one courthouse and one jail, but many churches. After digging up a corpse at night at Caledonia Chapel, Charles really looked at the chapel for the first time the next morning: " . . . a plank steepleless box . . . paintless too yet . . . not shabby and not even in neglect or disrepair . . . standing among the trunks of the high strong constant shaggy pines . . . and he remembered the tall slender spires which said Peace and the squatter utilitarian belfries which said Repent and he remembered one which even said Beware but this one said simply: Burn . . ." (*ID* 157). In *The Town* Charles speaks of the two oldest churches in Yoknapatawpha: "a small Episcopal church in Jefferson, the oldest extant building in town" and "a Presbyterian congregation too, the two oldest congregations in the county . . ." (pp. 306–307). William and Estelle Faulkner were married in the Presbyterian church, at College Hill; in Oxford they attended the Episcopal church, St. Peter's, and their daughter Jill was married there. Charles referred to the Baptists and Methodists as "incorrigible nonconformists" who "usurped and dispossessed" the other two congregations (p. 307).

Jessie Coffee's "Empty Steeples: Theme, Symbol, and Irony" takes its title from the meditations of Hightower, in *Light in August*, in which he experienced a kind of tragic enlightenment after he was wounded by Joe Christmas. He realized that what was destroying the church was "the professionals who control it and who have removed the bells from its steeples. He seems to see them, endless, without order, empty, symbolical, bleak, skypointed not with ecstacy or passion but in adjuration, threat, and doom" (p. 461). Symbolism in Faulkner not infrequently is used ironically, to represent an absence or inversion of what the symbol traditionally signifies.

Beginning in *Sartoris*, the cemetery is a recurrent scene. In Oxford it is St. Peter's Cemetery but is used by the whole community. The chief difference between the real and the fictitious cemeteries is that the statue of Colonel John Sartoris is not in St. Peter's, which is east, not west, of the central north–south street. Otherwise the reader will find "symbolical urns and doves . . . surrounded by clipped, tended sward green against the blanched marble and the black cedars . . ." (*Sar.* 373). Even two tombstones bear familiar inscriptions: "I bare him on eagles' wings and brought him unto me" is on the grave of Dean Faulkner, not John Sartoris, and the monument with a marble head carved on it, in the same lot, is that of Faulkner's grandmother, not of Eula Varner, though "Her Children Rise and Call Her Blessed" is on both monuments. Anyone familiar with the Yoknapatawpha fiction will see many familiar names on tombstones; the lot next to the older Falkner lot is that of the Buffalo family; in fiction, *The Reivers*, and in fact, *My Brother Bill*, Mr. Buffalo built the first automobile in Jefferson–Oxford. In a newer part of the cemetery, the graves of William and Estelle Faulkner, side by side, are utterly lacking in "the pagan symbols of . . . vainglory and the carven gestures of it in enduring stone" which so roused Aunt Jenny's scorn: Sartoris men, she thought "can't even lie dead in the ground without strutting and swaggering" (*Sar.* 376, 374).

As Panthea Broughton stated, "Statuary and machinery and stone may be impregnable to human anguish, but they are also impervious to human bliss." In characters described in terms of "rocklike stability," "fixity of these shapes seems to imply imperviousness, yet it establishes lifelessness." The most devastating examples of such vainglory are the headstones in the Sutpen family graveyard, "bombastic and inert carven rock" brought from Italy during the war and referred to as "Colonel" and "Mrs. Colonel" by the troops who bore that dead weight, and Judith's headstone bearing Rosa's admonition "*Pause, Mortal; Remember Vanity and Folly and Beware*" (*AA* 211). No Sutpen still lived to beware.

Broughton is not the only one to note that machinery is among the symbolic objects with unfavorable or evil significance. Mary Culley consigned to Hell the image of useless, discarded machinery and compared it with Conrad's use of such images. George Sutton viewed machinery and gadgets with disapproval and even begrudged Mrs. Snopes the separator which she had to use for reruns. Ab was not "curdled then" and said: "It looks like she is fixing to get a heap of pleasure and satisfaction outen it" (*H* 47). The absolutely perfect example of machinery dumps is the automobile dumps common at the edge of towns and cities especially in the South, including Oxford, Mississippi.

Mechanical objects include the pistols and shotguns without which some men fear their manhood itself will be in question. The farcical conflict between Boon and Ludus at the beginning of *The Reivers* hinges on John Powell's having his pistol in the livery stable against the rules because "the pistol was the living symbol of his manhood" and he could not leave the pistol at home (p. 7). Precisely the same code explained why Lucas Beauchamp had his pistol the day Crawford Gowrie tricked Lucas into firing at a target and then accused Lucas of the murder Crawford himself committed: Lucas wore the pistol on Saturday when he dressed up, just as old Carothers had done (*ID* 226). The Sartoris dueling pistols Bayard rejected in "An Odor of Verbena," but they were still among the Sartoris treasures when he was an old man (*Sar.* 91).

Sportsmanship and game consciousness are closely allied and so significant in Yoknapatawpha chronicles that two dissertations have been written on them: Stewart Rodnon dealt with "Sports, Sporting Codes, and Sportsmanship" in the work of Ring Lardner, Farrell, Hemingway, and Faulkner. Nicholas M. Rinaldi's subject is less extensive and more intensive: "Game-consciousness and Game-metaphor in the Work of William Faulkner." Relevant ethical and moral principles will be considered in a broader context, but literal games with visible symbols link Yoknapatawpha with the Western world and its cultures. Episodes in which games influence events, sometimes matters of life and death, are significant enough in the Yoknapatawpha chronicles to be worth special consideration. Of the games which require familiar equipment with symbolic implications and metaphors, chess and card playing preserve terms from the Middle Ages in Europe and traditions of much more ancient origin. According to Cirlot, "The entire pack of playing-cards is symbolic in origin." (Unfortunately, the Tarot pack, with its appropriate symbolism, was not used in Yoknapatawpha: "the Tarot cards comprise an image . . . of the path of initiation.") Dice have been found in ancient Egyptian tombs and were used in Greece and Rome. Checkers were used in Europe in the sixteenth century and were derived from an ancient game.

Two allusions to games in Faulkner's early Yoknapatawpha novels express a fatalistic view that should not be identified with Faulkner without qualifications. At the end of *Sartoris* is the famous passage: "But the Player, and the game He plays . . . He must have a name for His pawns, though. But perhaps Sartoris is the game itself—a game outmoded and played with pawns shaped too late and to an old dead pattern, and of which the Player himself is a little wearied." The only Sartoris in the context is Aunt Jenny, whose comment on those sentiments would be "Fiddlesticks!" Applied to Faulkner as the creator of *Sartoris* it makes good sense, but not as applied to the creator of Yoknapatawpha. The nihilistic philosophy of Mr. Compson is expressed in two game metaphors in rapid succession: "man . . . is conceived by accident and . . . every breath is a fresh cast with dice already loaded against him . . . he risks everything on a single blind turn of a card . . . even the despair or remorse or bereavement is not particularly important to the dark diceman . . ." (*SF* 220–21). Acceptance of that statement as truth impelled Quentin to commit suicide.

The game episodes are varied in situations, characters involved, and effects. The checker game between Mink and Lump Snopes in *The Hamlet* creates an extraordinary feeling of tension: Mink was playing a stalling action to keep Lump from going with him to get the supposed fifty dollars from the pockets of the dead Houston. The board is a piece of plank, "marked off with charcoal," the checkers, a can containing "a handful of small china- and glass-fragments in two colors, apparently from a broken plate and a blue glass bottle." Lump set the score: "We'll play a nickel a game against that fifty dollars." Mink played with "a cold and deadly deliberation and economy of moves, the other with a sort of clumsy speed and dash . . . with an incredible optimism, an incorrigible dishonesty long since become pure reflex . . ." (p. 250).

When Lump realized that when he "had won all of his [Mink's] share he won't need to risk going where it's at," "he reversed himself. Whereupon it was as if even dishonesty had foresworn him" (p. 246). When Lump would not leave, Mink set out with Lump following and in the dark managed to knock Lump out by a blow on the head and tied him up and proceeded in search of the body. The contrast between the two kinsmen, the little murderer with his integrity and the completely greedy and unprincipled Lump, would-be accessory after the fact, sustains the suspense.

The two successive poker games in "Was" involve serious issues to be determined by the outcome. Hubert Beauchamp was trying to get his sister Sibbey married off to Uncle Buck McCaslin. The marriage of the two slaves, Tennie and Tomey's Turl, will cost one man $300 to buy one slave from the other so that husband and wife will be together. Uncle Buck lost, and had to be saved by his twin Uncle Buddy, from the fate, worse than death, of having to marry Sibbey. McCaslin Edmonds, the young nephew of the twins, went back to the McCaslin plantation and got Uncle Buddy to go back to Warwick and rescue Buck. No one but a dedicated poker player could follow the games. But at the end, when Hubert had to call or pass, he asked Uncle Buddy who dealt the cards. In *this* game, if Uncle Buddy won, if Hubert called Buddy, Hubert would have to buy Tomey's Turl. Hubert tilted the light so that it fell on the arms of Tomey's Turl, which "were not quite white," and said, "I pass" (p. 29). *Go Down, Moses* is the story of the McCaslin–Beauchamp family, descended from Carothers McCaslin: Uncle Buck eventually did marry Sibbey and their son was Ike McCaslin. The Beauchamps were descended from Carothers also: Tomey's Turl, both the son and the grandson of old Carothers, and Tennie were the ancestors of the black Beauchamps. The poker games, exercises in one-upmanship, show clearly how the entire future of slaves was subject to the whims of their owners, even as the initial pursuit of Tomey's Turl by Uncle Buck was a parody of a fox hunt.

There is nothing complicated or amusing about the dice game in "Pantaloon in Black." Rider's grief over the death of his wife had driven him to such despair that when he joined members of his timber gang and the white night watchman in a dice game, he exposed the second pair of dice held by the white man and cut the man's throat before the man could seize his pistol. The deputy who tells the story of the lynching of Rider remarked to his wife that "Birdsong had been running crooked dice on them mill niggers for fifteen years" (p. 156). Rider's inconsolable grief is beyond the comprehension of the deputy.

Although the chess game in "Knight's Gambit" reflects a very serious situation, the dialogue between Gavin Stevens and his nephew has a tone of humorous geniality that modifies the threat of violence involving men and horses. Both the action in the past and the action in the narrative present are too complicated to summarize. The pattern of the chess game was introduced when Chick and Gavin were playing and Chick "checked his uncle's queen and her castle both with the horse" and found he had made an error: "Maybe I should have taken the queen twenty minutes ago when I could, and let the castle go." Gavin replied, "You couldn't have taken them without two moves. And a knight can move two squares at once and even in two directions at once. But he can't move twice" (p. 176). The queen was Mrs. Harriss, her castle, her mansion; the knight was a captain from Argentina who checked queen and castle at one move. But it was the princess, not the queen, whom the knight desired. Gavin prevented murder of the knight by the girl's brother, and made a trade with him to enlist, in part by using a "playing the game" analogy, based on the "unspoken obligation" one assumes to his partners to finish the game (*KG* 225). Gavin finally got both the queen and the castle.

The chess pattern as such is less significant, however, than the fact that Gavin's courtly lover role in *The Town* and *The Mansion* turns out to be oddly an extension and a contradiction of "Knight's Gambit": he refused to marry Linda Snopes because the queen and the castle would reappear in due time, and he would cease to play the courtly lover role and become the husband, with a grown stepson and stepdaughter and a stepson-in-law who had ceased to be the knight as centaur or unicorn (*KG* 165) when he joined "a 1942 United States Army cavalry which had abolished horses" (p. 243).

But what about the most cherished symbol of all, the stately mansion with its Greek revival pillars? Has it gone with the wind? In fact, no, as spring pilgrimages in the South, including Oxford, Mississippi, prove. Faulkner's Rowan Oak is a modest example, on a small scale. But in Yoknapatawpha, with both the Sutpen mansion and the decayed Compson house burned down after the war and the Sartoris house burned during the war, with a post-bellum substitute, there are two restorations of plantation houses. Gavin and his wife are living in one in *The Mansion*, as it had been fearfully and wonderfully transformed by Melisandre's first husband, a wealthy bootlegger:

> . . . the new house was going to occupy the same ground as the old one would have occupied if there had been four of them just alike nailed together. It had been just a house, of one storey, with the gallery across the front where the old master would sit in his home-made chair with his toddy and his Catullus; when Harriss got through with it it looked like the

formal violence," held out to him the pistols with which to execute vengeance (*U* 267–73). She put verbena in his lapel and kissed his hand, "communicating to it that battery charge dark, passionate and damned forever of all peace" (p. 274). Bayard confronted Redmond unarmed and escaped unscathed; there was no dead Redmond to match the dead Grumby. But there was a sprig of verbena, on Bayard's pillow, Drusilla's parting accolade to a courage unlike her own of "an endless feud of an eye for an eye." (*FU* 42).

The minor themes anticipate major ones and may even anticipate individual symbols: Ab Snopes, greedy, opportunistic, like Flem later, used people for his purposes and even, like Flem, chewed on something all the time. The comparison of Ab Snopes with a thawed-out water moccasin prepares for the recurrent comparison of Snopeses to animals in *Snopes* (*U* 198).

The images of the railroad, symbolically interpreted by Bayard, are clearly related to minor themes: to the Negroes it represents the passing of the old plantation order, "a delusion, a dream, a bright shape" to follow; the story of the two locomotives is a latter-day equivalent of medieval single combat, "like a meeting between two iron knights of the old time," a symbol of the gallant but futile gesture, "proving nothing save the finality of death and the vanity of all endeavor" (*U* 80). Colonel John Sartoris' dream of the railroad is a dream of the new order, of doing something for everyone, black and white, an "operation bootstrap" (p. 169).

The Sartoris story really began in Faulkner's first Yoknapatawpha novel, *Flags in the Dust*, which was completed in September 1927. After the manuscript had been rejected by twelve publishers, Faulkner finally yielded to the offer of Alfred Harcourt to publish it if it were reduced to a specified length. Absorbed in writing *The Sound and the Fury*, Faulkner allowed his friend Ben Wasson to make the necessary revision. The shortened version was published as *Sartoris* in January 1929. The original version with the original title was published by Random House, in 1973, edited and with an introduction by Douglas Day from which the above information was taken. Unless the omission in *Sartoris* of a portion of the original manuscript is of specific significance, *Flags in the Dust* will not be dealt with.

When Colonel John Sartoris is first heard of, he is already a legend, more magnified and glorified by old man Falls than by young Bayard in *The Unvanquished*. In *Sartoris*, Bayard, an old man, listened to old Falls retelling the old tales, and his father's old pipe evoked the Colonel's "bearded, hawklike face" (p. 1). In the first three parts of *Sartoris* he is a living legend, and in Four and Five he is presented in effigy, his monument in the cemetery. Dead, Colonel John was a more vital presence than his living son.

The house John Sartoris built after the Yankees burned the first one is described only in *Sartoris*; it symbolizes his sense of dignity and importance, with the drawing room in his day "a pageantry of color and scent and music against which he moved with his bluff and jovial arrogance" (p. 59). The colored glass is still a symbol of Aunt Jenny. The shrouded drawing room of 1920 and the cemetery, with the statue of Colonel John Sartoris looking over the railroad he built and the graves of the rest of the Sartoris men, "their dust moldering quietly beneath the pagan symbols of their vain glory and the carven gestures of it in enduring stone" (p. 376), symbolize the dead end of a sterile tradition and a closed pattern of life.

Another device is used twice in *Sartoris* to symbolize the past, first in direct relation to the time of *The Unvanquished*. In the chest in the attic old Bayard, who was young Bayard in *The Unvanquished*, found symbolic family heirlooms: brocade; a fine rapier, "just such an imple-ment as a Sartoris would consider the proper equipment for raising tobacco in a virgin wilderness"; the cavalry sabre which had hung at his father's side; the two dueling pistols which Drusilla had handed to him, "slender and invincible and fatal as the physical shape of love" ("An Odor of Verbena," p. 273); a stubby derringer; the long-necked silver oil-can engraved with the picture of the first locomotive on the railroad; the brass-bound Bible in which Bayard recorded the deaths of his grandson John, and of Young Bayard's first wife and son (*Sar.* 90–92). In this collection of Sartoris heirlooms the phallic symbolism of rapier, sabre, pistols, and derringer is more obvious than it was in the scattered appearance of most of them in *The Unvanquished*. Young Bayard burned the relics in his treasure chest: the paw of the first bear his twin brother had killed; a New Testament; a canvas hunting coat (pp. 214–15). These two parallel scenes are empty rituals in a dead tradition: the brass-bound Bible records death; the unopened Testa-ment cannot release the living from guilty and grief-stricken devotion to the dead.

To the themes of Sartoris foolhardiness and valor continued from *The Unvanquished* and symbolized in the legends of both Johns and of the Carolina Bayard in *Sartoris* is added, in contrast with the theme of Bayard in *The Unvanquished*, the theme of young Bayard's boredom, despair, and guilt. The symbols of this theme are physically apparent: he has the hawk-like face and abrupt actions of Colonel John (*Sar.* 43–44), but his eyes are bleak, and his "false and stubborn pride" and his violence find their outlet in fighting animals and machines. The

archetypal symbol of the man on the horse recurs when Bayard rides
the stallion and almost kills others and himself (pp. 132–34). The automobile, cause of injury and death, is a symbol, not of transportation,
for Bayard had no real destination, but of self-destruction which
he finally achieved in an airplane. His flight on horseback to the
MacCallums after his grandfather's death and by mule and wagon from
the Negro cabin to the railroad completed in sober calm the transportation gamut, with an intervening interlude in which cold and death
imagery predominate. Although Richard Carpenter sees the parallel to
the Ninth Circle of Dante's Hell—"the December chill is the objective
correlative of his psychic state," his inability to love anyone except his
brother John and his self-isolating spiritual agony—there is a parallel
also with Dante's Suicidal Wood and the profligates, destroyers of
property, who spend eternity in mad flight. In *Sartoris* the pattern of
flight, in widening gyres, is associated with means of flight.

Aunt Jenny still looks like the Sartorises and still cherishes beauty,
supervising flower-growing to show the harmony with nature symbol-
ized in her name, Du Pre, "of the meadow." The new main characters
are Narcissa and Horace Benbow. With *Benbow* then suggesting only
Treasure Island, not, as it does now in Oxford, the Admiral Benbow
Motor Lodge, name symbolism rested in *Horace* and *Narcissa*.
Horace suggests the scholarly, rather ineffectual kind of person
Horace is, associated with books, glass-blowing, gardens, and women.
Narcissa is almost allegorically symbolic; the white purity her name
suggests is emphasized by her white garments and Horace's epithets of
"Serene" and "Thou still unravished bride of quietness" (*Sar.* 82).
The fragile glass vase he made is an obvious female symbol of Narcissa, who is further associated with flowers, which she passively
accepts but does not grow, and piano playing. The classical allusion
in *Narcissa* is the clue to her worship of her self-image, patterned
on the Southern stereotype of the "lady." The stereotype and Narcissa
as a spurious imitation of it are dealt with in my article, "William
Faulkner and the Southern Concept of Women." The hilarious fact
disclosed in Joseph Blotner's *Faulkner: A Biography* is that in the
summer of 1933 Mammy McEwen joined the Faulkner household as
nurse for baby Jill. Mammy of course was black, and was slightly over
five feet tall and weighed more than two hundred pounds. And her first
name was Narcissus! Previously she had worked for "Miss Lida,"
Faulkner's mother-in-law, so it seems likely that in 1926, when he
created Narcissa Benbow, he knew Narcissus but changed the ending
to the feminine *a*. This example is further evidence that the names in
Yoknapatawpha are basically realistic, even the most improbable ones.

The image of purity which Narcissa created by her dress and manner she showed to be false when she kept the vulgar mash notes of Byron Snopes. These notes are a recurrent symbol or motif, like the orders on Union army letterheads which symbolized Granny's tragic flaw in *The Unvanquished*. The exposure of Narcissa's nature and motives in "There Was a Queen" adds the image of Narcissa and her son Benbow sitting with their clothes on in the branch to wash away Narcissa's sin of having slept with the FBI agent in order to get back from him the letters through which Byron, the bank robber, was being traced. The title of the story is anticipated in *Sartoris*: "Others spoke to her [Aunt Jenny] as to a martial queen" (p. 93). *Byron Snopes* was a perfect name: *Byron* for his romantic longings and missives of which Narcissa was the object and *Snopes* for his ignorance, vulgarity, and greed.

The tableaux in *Sartoris* combine in memory the distant and the recent past: The Carolina Bayard jumping his horse over the breakfast table (p. 17); Colonel John taken by surprise, when sitting with his sock feet on the railing opposite the salvia bed (p. 21); Colonel John shooting the Burdens (p. 22); Aunt Jenny dancing with Jeb Stuart in Baltimore in '58 (p. 19); the last flight of John Sartoris in World War I (pp. 252, 321). The images of collision or confrontation, dealt with by Allen Guttmann as symbolic of the collision of the old and new orders, are frequent in the accounts of the twins, but the peacetime dangers they faced involved no agent of conflict or force except physical laws: John swinging off the water tank and parachuting from a balloon (pp. 71–72); Bayard on the stallion (pp. 132–34); the non-combat airplane images; and all the automobile incidents. Bayard's perils are symbolic rather of his personal psychosis; the new order exists for him chiefly as it provides more numerous and exciting hazards. Olga Vickery rightly interprets the car and plane incidents as "propitiatory" rituals to Colonel John and young John, demonstrations, in the terms of modern experience, of the courage the legend demands. The quest for danger to heighten the sense of life had become a quest for death, a degeneration, Faulkner said, into moral weakness (*FU* 119).

Absalom, Absalom! is the perfect example of the symbolic title which conveys more meaning than Faulkner consciously intended. The idea of the man who wanted sons and the title came simultaneously, Faulkner said (*FU* 76). Although Faulkner was taking his title from 2 Samuel 18:33 and 19:4, David's lament for Absalom, the story of Amnon, Tamar, and Absalom, in 2 Samuel 13, suggests parallels to the incest theme involving Henry and Judith Sutpen and Charles Bon, with a resultant serendipitous accretion of symbolism: "the Biblical references provide," in John Hardy's terms, "a further dimension of symbolic significance that is ultimately ahistorical."

Names of the characters are largely symbolical. J. R. Cofield, Faulkner's Oxford photographer, thought that his name might have suggested *Coldfield*. If so, the change created the symbolism: the bleak sterility of the aliens from the North. *Rosa* adds an ironic touch, suitable to one who was nipped in the blighted bud. *Sutpen* is rare, perhaps invented, with no apparent meaning. *Thomas* and *Henry*, like the Sartoris *John*, are neutral. But Judith's childhood taste for violence and bloodshed and her womanly fortitude call to mind the Biblical Judith, although of the latter's fervent faith and intelligent, courageous, and ruthless action, Judith Sutpen showed less evidence than did Granny Millard, another *Rosa*, in *The Unvanquished*. The name of Charles Bon, Charles the Good, probably named by Sutpen himself (*AA* 265), was corrupted in local speech to Bond, the slave: proper names thus become metaphors of the spiritual effect of caste on both races. Sutpen named Clytie, Mr. Compson guessed, in confusion between Clytemnestra and Cassandra; either name serves the purpose of recalling the story of Agamemnon's return and the doom of the House of Atreus.

But Thomas Sutpen is the Atreus–Agamemnon who both brings and suffers the family doom. The themes center in the grand design: the innocence which conceived it and the ruthless determination which carried it out; the subordination of human values to megalomaniac ambition which resulted in the rejected son's search for a father, the web of incest and miscegenation which entangled the three children and caused Henry to murder Charles, and the final extinction of the family after Sutpen had again rejected his own offspring. William Tindall recognized the house as "the central image": "designed to shelter a great family, constructed in fury, almost attaining magnificence, the great house falls into decay at last and final destruction."

To the factual details in the legend, the narrators add imaginative touches: the "short reddish beard . . . *resembled a disguise*," "his pale eyes had *a quality at once visionary and alert*," the flesh of his face was like "*pottery . . . colored by that oven's fever either of soul or environment . . . a dead impervious surface as of glazed clay*" (*AA* 32, 33); italics indicate non-objective details added by the narrator. His big roan horse and his pistols are symbols of his masculinity. The Spanish gold coins, exchanged for a hundred square miles of rich bottomland, symbolize the unsavory mystery surrounding him. On his second appearance, the town observed other symbolic details: the covered wagon with its Negro cargo and the French architect, in his Paris hat, symbolize Sutpen's subordination of people to his design; the two females in the "black tunnel filled with still eyeballs and smelling like a wolfden" symbolize the particular ruthlessness with which he would beget and discard what was not "conjunctive to" his design, would sow the dragon's teeth (p. 62). The building of Sutpen's Hundred elaborates on these first details: living an animal existence, naked master and naked slaves cut the timber and made the bricks and built the house. The supreme symbol of Sutpen's vainglory is the Italian marble tombstone which he had brought through the blockade and transported to Jefferson by his troops who called them "colonel" and "Mrs. Colonel" (pp. 189, 270). At this time he wore the symbols of his military achievement: in shabby uniform, "worn gauntlets and faded sash . . . the plume in his hat broken and frayed and soiled" (p. 271), and mounted "on the gaunt black stallion" he returned to war (p. 275). Instead of occasional terms such as *hawklike* in *Sartoris*, epic and Wagnerian epithets and leitmotifs are paralleled in the multitude of *demons* and *Faustuses* and *Beelzebubs*, with qualifying details. Ellen Coldfield, Stupen's wife, is reduced to one such leitmotif: the "swamp-hatched butterfly" which lives for a brief and frivolous summer (pp. 69, 74, 85).

Of the three children of Sutpen, Judith is the most vivid, associated with such concrete symbolic objects as the pictures of herself, of Charles Bon, and of Charles Bon's wife and child, with the letter which Quentin saw, and with the wedding dress (*AA* 142, 130, 132, 172). Clytie, a "tiny gnome-like creature in headrag and voluminous skirts," with the "worn coffee-colored face," is symbolized to Rosa in the brown hand, the "bitted bridle-curb to check and guide the furious and unbending will" (p. 139), the hand which Rosa struck away the second time and knocked Clytie down, in a heap of rags, like "a handful of sticks concealed in a rag bundle"—a recurrent image for old and frail people. In a last gesture of protection, the hand of Clytie set fire to the ruined mansion.

The tableaux of scenes of action in *Absalom, Absalom!* are particularly numerous: the boy at the door, the germinal scene which causes Sutpen to conceive and execute his grand design (pp. 229, 233); his arrival and his return (pp. 8, 31–32) with all the means for exploitation of land and people; the hunting of the architect in the light of pine torches, with the dogs and the naked Negroes (p. 245); the wedding procession between two lines of hostile faces lighted by torches (pp. 56–57); the race to church "in a thunder and a fury of wildeyed horses and of galloping and of dust" (p. 23); the fight in the stable with one of his own slaves, while his daughters, white and black, looked on (p. 29); his return from war, projecting himself "ahead like a mirage" in his impatience (p. 159). The fine figure of a man on the black stallion was cut down with a rusty scythe by Wash Jones as time cut down

Sutpen's design when he used human beings as means to his end and discarded them.

The galloping image, the apotheosis Mr. Compson conjectured, may have been in Wash's mind in the moment when Sutpen entered the cabin—"the proud galloping image" in "the fine climax where it galloped forever and forever immortal beneath the brandished sabre and the shot-torn flags rushing down a sky in color like thunder"—when Wash heard Sutpen speak one sentence to Milly (pp. 287–88). De Spain saw the living image which had annihilated the man on the horse: Wash was "running into the lanterns" so that "they could see his face, his eyes too, as he ran with the scythe above his head, straight into the lanterns and the gun barrels, making no sound, no outcry . . ." (p. 292). The moment of death of both Sutpen and Wash is omitted in "Wash" and *Absalom, Absalom!* in Faulkner's frequent technique of "freezing motion" before its bloody end.

Quentin Compson is the link between *Absalom, Absalom!* and *The Sound and the Fury*. The structural scenes in which he hears and tells the story of the Sutpens belong among the tableaux: in the "dim hot airless room" smelling of wistaria, Miss Rosa upright in the straight chair with feet dangling in "impotent and static rage" and "wan haggard face," as she conjured up the "man-horse-demon" and his "band of wild niggers" (pp. 7–9); at twilight on the front gallery, the smell of wistaria and of his father's cigar mingled (p. 31); in the dust and the dark with Miss Rosa on the way to Sutpen's Hundred while she told him of that other summer of wistaria when she saw the photograph of Charles Bon and of the closed door which, years later, kept her from seeing Charles, dead (pp. 143–45, 147, 150, 175); in the cold room at Harvard, in January with snow on Shreve's coat sleeve and the memory of the "dead summer twilight—the wistaria, the cigar-smell, the fireflies—attenuated . . . into this strange room" (p. 173).

Robert Musil commented on the greater complexity of the structuring of the tableau in the scene of Quentin and Shreve in which the mental pictures are present and charged with meaning. Musil did not stress the climax in which Quentin and Shreve simultaneously share the experience and thoughts of Henry Bon, signaled by the omniscient author's introducing the shift to italics: "They were both in Carolina and the time was forty-six years ago, and it was not even four now but compounded still further, since now both of them were Henry Sutpen and both of them were Bon, compounded each of both yet either neither, smelling the very smoke which had blown and faded away forty-six years ago . . ." (*AA* 351). At the end of Chapter VIII the return to Shreve as interpreter, with Quentin saying only "Yes"

(p. 359), leads into Quentin's reliving in memory the night trip with Miss Rosa to Sutpen's, followed by return to Shreve's commentary and his apocalyptic glimpse of the future and Quentin's denial that he hates the South.

In *Doubling and Incest/Repetition and Revenge: A Speculative Reading of Faulkner*, John Irwin analyzes the two Quentin stories as *"elements in a holistic structure."* There are only two parts in Irwin's book, the introduction and the text, because doublings by nature are inseparable. His insistence that analysis of these two novels depends on the interplay between them applies to a lesser degree to the body of fiction that makes up the cosmos called Yoknapatawpha. Irwin does not comment, however, on why, in these two novels, Faulkner illogically departed from his usual method of providing, within the narratives, the interconnections that his creation of Yoknapatawpha necessitates. In *Absalom, Absalom!* Caddy and the events of the summer of 1909 are obliterated from Quentin's thoughts and his memory and from the narration by Mr. Compson. In particular the relevance of the Henry–Judith relationship to that of Quentin and Caddy and the implication of a homosexual relationship between Henry–Charles and Quentin–Shreve and, potentially, between Quentin and Dalton Ames is so carefully concealed that readers of *Absalom, Absalom!* who encounter Quentin for the first time would never know that he had a sister. Irwin's procedure certainly is valid and his conclusions are generally convincing. The "perspectival elements of the structure" with which he is concerned include: "spatial and temporal doubling, spatial and temporal incest, narcissism, the Oedipus complex, the castration complex, repetition, sameness and difference, recollection, repression, revenge, substitution, reversal, sacrifice and mediation" (p. 6). The inclusion of elements including themes, ordering of content, mental processes, and serious psychological problems shows comprehensive treatment. But the puzzle remains of why the reader of *Absalom, Absalom!* cannot imagine Mr. Compson, the narrator, as the nihilist in *The Sound and the Fury* in the father–son struggle from which Quentin could escape only in death.

The title of *The Sound and the Fury* is the most significant in the Yoknapatawpha chronicles as a clue to themes and characters, but it cannot be assumed that it expresses Faulkner's view of life. He said: "The title, of course, came from the first section, which was Benjy . . . though the more I had to work on the book, the more elastic the title became, until it covered the whole family" (*FU* 87). The whole passage suggests a pattern involving the Compson family seen in "the petty pace" of their futility. "All our yesterdays have lighted fools /

The way to dusty death" approximates the cynical and cheerless nihilism of Mr. Compson and suggests the recurrent death, funeral, and
graveyard motifs which eventually make death dusty. "Life's but a
walking shadow" no doubt is the source of the shadow image char-
acterizing Quentin, who is "heard no more" after II. (The reappearance of Quentin was a late development in the writing of the Sutpen
story.) Jason "struts and frets," and Mrs. Compson "frets," both
being addicted to role-playing. And of course Benjy's tale is the "tale
told by an idiot, full of sound and fury, signifying nothing," Luster's
first remarks to Benjy include "Hush up that moaning" (p. 2); but
before he finally hushes, when order has been restored in his world,
Benjy bellows in "horror; shock; agony eyeless, tongueless; just sound"
(p. 400). But it is invested with universal significance: "It might have
been all time and injustice and sorrow become vocal for an instant by a
conjunction of planets" (p. 359). It is remarkable that the cosmic
symbolism is suggested so early in the creation of Yoknapatawpha.

In addition to these themes suggested by the title there are the
themes related to Caddy: virginity and incest, sin and expiation, love
and hate. There are the themes of time and eternity. There are the
themes of the decadence and chaos of the family, rooted in the selfishness and irresponsibility of the parents, and of the order provided by
Dilsey's compassion and selfless love and devoted care. Implied is the
comprehensive theme of a family lacking parental love and spiritual
vitality to provide values for life and motives for living.

Quentin's name suggests Scott's Quentin Durward and romantic
chivalry and its gyneolatry, but in a society where "get thee to a
nunnery" was not an acceptable way of preserving purity. Benjy's
second name was chosen, after his mental deficiency was recognized,
to signify that he was the son of Mrs. Compson's old age (*SF* 109), and,
of course, to remove from the Bascomb family the stigma of having
produced an idiot. Considering what Uncle Maury was like, it might
have been a prudent move had not all Jefferson already known the
previous name. If *Jason* had been used only once, for Jason IV, it
would have an appropriate mythical connotation, for Jason IV's gold-
seeking obsession impelled him to fleece his mother. For Jason III, the
name has no significance. The chief reason for *Candace* seems to be
that when the pasture became a golf course, Benjy was reminded of his
sister every time he heard the players call "caddie."

Like the Sutpen mansion, the Compsons' house is in a state of decay
by the time of the main action: both "the square, paintless house with
its rotting portico" (p. 372) and the description of Benjy (p. 342) startle
the reader, having been obliged for so long to depend on his own

imagination. Luster getting Benjy seated "looked like a tug nudging at a clumsy tanker in a narrow dock" (p. 356). The environs have symbolic meanings and associations: the golf course occupies the land sold to send Quentin to Harvard, the pasture Benjy had loved. The memories of both Benjy and Quentin center in the small area in which Benjy is confined. The cabin of Dilsey was a refuge to the children in crises. The tree Caddy climbed to look into the window, after she had been playing in the branch, the initial image from which the book evolved, reappears near the end: "A pear tree grew there, close to the house. It was in bloom and the branches scraped and rasped against the house and the myriad air, driving in the window, brought into the room the forlorn scent of the blossoms" (p. 352). Symbolic details drawn from their surroundings, too numerous to cover fully, characterize Benjy and Quentin and represent interrelated themes.

The tree image exemplifies the richness of symbolism which may be contained in a familiar object in the natural world. M.-L. von Franz explained that in Jungian psychology a tree in dreams symbolizes involuntary and natural psychic growth, precisely what Benjy in his idiocy and Quentin in his obsession would deny Caddy. Using a Calvinistic approach, Mary Fletcher interpreted Benjy's small natural world as an Edenic state of innocence and the tree up which Versh pushed Caddy as the Forbidden Tree (pp. 46–47). The tree and Caddy's muddy drawers symbolize her fall from innocence, a stain which ritual cleansing, such as Dilsey's scrubbing, could not remove. In his idiotic innocence, Benjy insisted on Caddy's cleansing herself of the smell of perfume each time she did not smell of trees. In Quentin's memory of the scene in Caddy's room he remembered "*the odor of the apple tree*" (p. 130), making explicit the Forbidden Tree symbolism.

Of the man-made symbols, the mirror which reflects the fire and, in Quentin's memory, Caddy as a bride may also, Lawrance Thompson suggested, symbolize Caddy, who is a mirror of Benjy's instinctive values, and Benjy, who reflects the whole family. Faulkner explained Caddy as being all the world to Benjy, with his perceptions "flashes that were reflected on her as in a mirror" (*FU* 64).

The emphasis on weddings and funerals, especially in Benjy's section, is related to the theme of "self-centeredness of innocence" (*FN* 103) which would hold Caddy captive and to the theme of a loveless mother who forced Caddy into a loveless marriage to preserve outward respectability. One may recall, as a kind of ironic echo, Yeats's "How but in custom and ceremony / Are innocence and beauty born" ("A Prayer for my Daughter"). *Ceremony* and *innocence* occur in conjunction in other poetry of the period quoted by J. W. Beach in *Obsessive Images*.

Another "custom and ceremony" of innocence, provided by Dilsey and scorned by Mrs. Compson, is the birthday cake for Benjy, with its thirty-three makeshift candles (*SF* 69). The Christ symbolism is too obvious to ignore and too tenuous to emphasize. In *Man in the Modern Novel* John Hardy referred to the tradition "of the idiot as the favorite of God," and comments that "Faulkner's Christ figures are all of sub- or extra-intellectual intelligence." Hardy's ingenious identification of Miss Quentin as the Christ figure, "undergoing a 'passion' in these three days," resurrected on Sunday and leaving behind not an empty tomb but an empty room, shows the extravagant lengths to which a critic can go by failing to realize that such parallels in Faulkner are more likely to be ironic inversions than what would be a sacrilegious Christ figure. (Benjy is a Christ figure ironically, too, but he may exemplify the Biblical verse: "Except ye be converted and become as little children, ye shall not enter the kingdom of heaven.") Hardy's interpretation of *The Sound and the Fury* as "a fairly simple kind of satire on the neo-Pagan character of this 'Christian' community" would make irony entirely suitable as a satiric device. Although I have never been in Oxford when there was a carnival on Good Friday, I have observed that the three-hour church services and closing of many commercial establishments customary in all the northern cities I have lived in are not noticeable in Oxford. Hardy's general statement about symbolic significance in Faulkner is excellent: Faulkner's mind was so "steeped in the traditions of Protestant Christianity" that "beyond the legend . . . of the immediate regional history . . . —the Biblical references provide a further dimension of symbolic significance that is ultimately ahistorical."

All the death symbols in I prepare for the death theme in Quentin's section: Nancy's bones, the smell of death, the buzzards. Benjy's favorite flower, the jimson weed, is a poisonous plant of the deadly nightshade family which is popularly called "angel's trumpet" because of its white, trumpet-shaped blossoms. The flower is particularly suitable for Benjy's graveyard, but one wonders at the ignorance and indifference of the elder Compsons; the poisonous effects of jimson weed are fairly well known. "Angel strumpet" is a natural mispronunciation and may be intended as a punning reference to Caddy, an angel to Benjy and a strumpet to Jason and Quentin. Benjy's other favorite flower, the narcissus, obviously symbolizes the idiot's self-centered, self-enclosed world.

The most frequent images in II are those of time: the broken watch, the clocks, the sound of clocks striking, finally, just before Quentin goes out to escape time in the river. Quentin's last purity rituals— cleansing of his garments, brushing his teeth, brushing his hat, getting a clean handkerchief—suggest by ironic reversal a passage in Conrad Aiken's *Preludes for Memnon*: "Stand, take off the garments time has lent you, / The watch, the coins, the handkerchief, the shoes." Although Faulkner expressed a high regard for Aiken's poetry in a review of *Turns and Movies* (*William Faulkner: Early Prose and Poetry*, pp. 74–76), *Preludes for Memnon* (1931) was too late to influence Faulkner in *The Sound and the Fury*. Looking into the river, Quentin had been reminded of Benjy's mirror, and in that last scene he literally looked into a mirror. Water, a symbol of death *"peaceful and swift not goodbye"* (*SF* 214) and a symbol of both purity and stain, is recurrently combined with Quentin's shadow, the most frequent symbolic image which is inseparable from Quentin. The life–death symbolism of the river is confirmed by the trout passage, in which the flames of hell, in Quentin's thoughts, alternate with the trout he sees in the river (pp. 144–45).

"The *shadow*, the *anima*, and the *animus*," Jung explained in *Psyche and Symbol*, are archetypes that were present from the beginning in the collective unconscious. The shadow, "the negative side of the personality," represents "the personal unconscious, and its content can therefore be made conscious without too much difficulty." But, as Jung explained, the "contrasexual figure," the anima for Quentin, is so far from consciousness that it is "seldom if ever realized." In a purely fictional character presented by a technique which presents the incredible, the thoughts of a character the day he committed suicide, the psychological possibilities appeal to the imagination, not to scientific belief. In "Quentin and the Walking Shadow," Louise Dauner discussed the various meanings of the shadow symbolism, including that of the anima, and regarded the shadow as the most meaningful symbol in Quentin's section, in the narrative present as well as in memory, and as evidence of his psychic immaturity in denying his instinctual nature and in refusing to acknowledge the dark side of his nature. Mary Fletcher explained Quentin's denial of the forces of darkness in terms of his Calvinist background and his final ritual as an enactment of the Puritan principle that "cleanliness is next to godliness."

Symbols of Caddy in Quentin's mind, like the smell of trees in Benjy's, are the smell of honeysuckles, a symbol of Caddy's lost virginity, and of roses, a symbol of her wedding, a ceremony of guilt which made Caddy's sin respectable by concealing it. Puritan respectability in Yoknapatawpha seemed to function on the principle "Save the surface and you save all." In one memory image, roses are combined with the mirror, Caddy in her wedding dress, and moonlight (*SF* 100). Honeysuckles, cedars, and the swing combine symbols of sex and of fertility with a symbol of death. Quentin imagined Death and his dead grandfather as "waiting on a high place beyond cedar trees" for Colonel Sartoris to come down from a higher place (p. 218). The smell of water "after the honeysuckle got all mixed up in it" came "to symbolize night and unrest" (p. 211). The corridor image which follows, an "objective correlative" of a sense of shadowy unreality, Ruel Foster suggested may be a version of tunnel images which symbolize the sex act; this interpretation fits the context. The reference to *door* in the preceding sentence and the conjunction of *door* and *corridor* later strengthen this interpretation (p. 215).

References to Quentin's lack of virility involve contrasts with the men in Caddy's life. Quentin broke his leg riding a horse, but Dalton Ames was a horseman. The automobile Herbert Head gave Caddy was a symbol of his male superiority and of Caddy's shame, the price of respectability. The male symbols of knife and pistols were used to show Quentin's ineffectualness, again in contrast with Dalton's skill (pp. 188–89). The flatirons are the first obvious symbol of Quentin's intention to drown himself (p. 98). The clean flame of hell is an isolating image and is comparable to the desert island image in *Absalom, Absalom!*, but the flame more obviously symbolizes incestuous love. The images from *Othello* and Frazer reflect Quentin's obsession with the animalistic physical aspects of sex. Richard Adams identified the reference to "the swine of Euboeleus running" (*SF* 184) as an allusion to the abduction of Persephone by Pluto as related by Frazer in *The Golden Bough*. The symbolic details associated with Quentin center on his obsession with Caddy and with his own inadequacy, his rejection of temporal experience, and his consequent isolation.

The limitations in Jason's nature are apparent in the poverty of symbols. He is symbolized by his eyes "like marbles" (*SF* 348), his habit of keeping his hands in his pockets—"Jason going to be rich man. . . . He holding his money all the time" (p. 43)—and his preoccupation with letters, checks, and telegrams which are not, like Quentin's suicide notes, communication of feeling but symbols of Jason's greed and deception. He never kept "a scrap of paper bearing a woman's name" and forbade Lorraine to write to him (pp. 240–41). His auto symbolized his deception of his mother for status, not pleasure; his inability to enjoy driving it may indicate more than an allergy to the smell of gasoline. Faulkner apparently substituted the auto for the horse as a symbol of virility. Jason was a reluctant driver. Horace Benbow was too inept to drive. Flem Snopes in *The Mansion* did not drive. He was known to be impotent. The only evidence of Jason's virility is what Lorraine told other men about him: "he may not drink but if you don't believe he's a man I can tell you how to find out" (pp. 290–301). As the mechanical man, Popeye in *Sanctuary* was impotent but could drive and shoot. To Quentin, the smell of gasoline symbolized Jason. Both Jason and his mother were addicted to camphor. The sight of water made Jason sick. The red tie, "the latch string to hell" (p. 301), is repeated from I, distinguishing Miss Quentin's lover from her mother's. Jason is too imperceptive to dwell on natural details: references to money, to stock market reports, to the passes to the show which he burns before Luster's covetous eyes, constitute the chief symbolic pattern. The supreme symbols are the phony checks (which his mother burned every month, happily unaware that Jason cashed the good ones and kept the money), the key to his room, and the money box. His references to Caddy are in terms of money, and "once a bitch always a bitch," the term which is the key to his whole cynical view of life.

The tableaux, many of them recurrent, are particularly important in *The Sound and the Fury* because Quentin's section, in repeating incidents and scenes which occur in Benjy's, makes clear what happened and what the significance is, and because in I and II memory images bear more symbolic weight than present action. (Present action follows an initiation pattern which will be dealt with in Chapter 2.) It is simplest to deal with these symbolic "stills" or tableaux, which are not limited to visual details, in relation to the central figure.

Similar images in Benjy's past differ in significant details: fire, the cushion, the mirror, and Caddy represent contentment for Benjy, running through the memories of the rainy night when his name was changed to Benjy (pp. 74–83); later there is a dark place on the wall, like a door, where the mirror had been and Benjy has Caddy's slipper, with the fire and cushion, to quiet him (pp. 79–80); the absence of the mirror and of Caddy may be equated: the loss of the sister is the loss of the mirror which reflects the characters of the whole family. In Benjy's fragmentary impressions, as the unreflecting "camera eye," Caddy is frequently the central figure; Caddy getting wet in the branch, up in the tree looking in the window, and being unsuccessfully scrubbed behind with her wet, muddy drawers by Dilsey form a sequence of stills symbolizing the whole story of Caddy; her headstrong daring and her consequent defilement (pp. 19, 47, 91). The scenes of Caddy in the door, then standing with her back to the wall looking at Benjy as he cried and pulled at her dress, then upstairs in the bathroom door, are repeated by Quentin, with Benjy completely in the picture (pp. 84, 154, 185); Quentin's succeeding image of Caddy "lying in the water her head on the sand spit" and the conversation which follows confirm the symbolism of the door as sexual and the ablutions as ritual cleansing. The scenes of Benjy at the gate are symbolic parallels of those of Caddy in the door, but it is doubtful that Benjy's pushing Caddy into the bathroom is to be interpreted as manifesting his sexual impulses. Lawrence Bowling stressed Benjy's desire to communicate, his "trying to say," as his motive when he got through the gate. Bowling suggested that Jason deliberately left the gate open so that there would be a good reason to send Benjy to Jackson. It does seem in character: "Just like Jason!"

The day Benjy pulled Caddy into the bathroom (p. 185) Quentin associated with the day Caddy lay down in the branch, when he reminded Caddy of the muddy drawers incident, and then held "the point of the knife at her throat" (pp. 188–89), apparently to kill her and then kill himself. Water and the smell of honeysuckles are the symbolic sense impressions (pp. 190, 191). Caddy as a bride, with shining veil and flowers in her hair, is a fleeting image in Benjy's memory (p. 47); in Quentin's, the separate components of the bride picture—roses, the nuptial song, "The Voice That Breathed o'er Eden," the mirror—are scattered through many passages but are all gathered together more or less coherently as she runs "out of the mirror," veil swirling behind her, into the moonlight to still Benjy's bellowing (p. 100). Quentin adds the scene in Caddy's room the night before, with the fragrant apple tree in bloom outside and the more fragrant bridal clothes on the bed (pp. 130, 139). Caddy as a mother is seen only through the eyes of Jason; in the glimpse of Caddy running after the hack when Jason let her see the baby for even less than the stipulated minute (p. 255), Jason's cold heartlessness and Caddy's love for her child are imaged.

In addition to the images of Caddy, Quentin's section is full of tableaux of himself, past, present, and after death. The death motif of bones in I reappears in II as Quentin's bones, "murmuring bones and the deep water like wind, like a roof of wind," until at the Last Judgment, "the Day when He says rise," only the flatirons "would come floating up" (pp. 98, 139). An ultimate note of hope appears in the other visualization of death. "And maybe when He says Rise the eyes will come floating up too, out of the deep quiet and the sleep, to look on glory" before the flatirons float (p. 144). One image combines several symbolic details related to death: "Trampling my shadow's bones into the concrete with hard heels and then I was hearing the watch, and I touched the letters through my coat" (p. 118). Dalton Ames, the symbol of virility to Quentin, as well as the seducer of Caddy, "looked like he was made out of bronze in his khaki shirt" (p. 197). Dalton holding Quentin's wrists with one hand, taking out his pistol, loosing Quentin, then showing his marksmanship and handing Quentin the gun which

Quentin rejects in favor of fists is, on both the realistic and the symbolic level, a demonstration of virility contrasted with girlish weakness. The fact that Dalton, after his offer of his horse to the beaten Quentin, rides off adds the horse symbol to the pistol.

The recurrent image of a gull hovering as if fixed on wires is explained by Mr. Compson's remark that "time is your misfortune": "A gull on an invisible wire attached through space dragged. You carry the symbol of your frustration into eternity" (p. 129). It appears most significantly in a tableau of stasis and action, of time rushing away and time conquered, as Gerald rows beneath a "terrifically motionless" gull (p. 149).

In addition to the image of himself and Caddy in hell, one other purely symbolic image, the objective correlative of the failure of the parents which brought disaster to the children, presents what Kathryn Gibbons interpreted as a Jungian anima–animus dream mandala: Quentin recalled a picture of "a dark place into which a single weak ray of light came slanting upon two faces lifted out of the shadow," which he identified with his mother and father, "upward into weak light holding hands and us lost somewhere below even them without even a ray of light" (p. 215). Caddy's reaction was to break the place open and whip the prisoners.

The tableaux in which Mrs. Compson appears condemn her as a woman and mother: in black dress and veil, weeping, mourning over Caddy's lost virginity (p. 286); in mourning weeds again at her husband's funeral, with Uncle Maury patting her hand and chewing on cloves (pp. 244–45). As a spectacle of "correct" grief she is less appalling than when flirting with Herbert Head, whom she had ensnared to give her unborn grandchild a name (pp. 116–17). The image of Mrs. Compson lying on her bed, camphor-soaked cloth on her head, and asking Dilsey to hand her her Bible epitomized her whole selfish, self-indulgent, hypocritical life (pp. 374–75). Every month she observed a ritual of rejecting the wages of sin: "She struck the match and lit the check and put it in the shovel, and then the envelope, and watched them burn" (p. 273). (Jason, of course, cashed the real checks and hoarded the money.) Miss Quentin, pathetically painted and dressed like a woman from Gayoso or Beale Street in Memphis, is symbolized by her eyes, those of a cornered animal, and by her anonymous room with its "evidences of crude and hopeless attempts to feminize it" but only "giving it that dead and stereotyped transience of rooms in assignation houses" (p. 352). The blooming pear tree outside should have symbolized the delicate purity of girlhood but instead was the means of her escape to ruin less terrible than Jason's authority. Jason, grabbing from his mother "a huge bunch of rusty keeys on an iron ring like a mediaeval jailer's" to get into Miss Quentin's room and then looking at his treasure box, minus its valuable contents, is a Balzacian image of ruthless greed reduced to desperation (p. 351).

The Easter tableaux are in sharp contrast to Jason's frantic pursuit of Miss Quentin and his money: the weathered church "lifted its crazy steeple" and the whole scene was as "flat and without perspective as a painted cardboard set upon the ultimate edge of the flat earth, against the windy sunlight of space and April and a mid-morning filled with bells" (p. 364); the minister, "his monkey face lifted and his whole attitude that of a serene, tortured crucifix that transcended its shabbiness and insignificance" (p. 368); Dilsey with Benjy, her hand on his knee: "Two tears slid down her fallen cheeks, in and out of the myriad coruscations of immolation and abnegation and time" (p. 368). Victor Strandberg found in the sermon an example of Faulkner's inversion analogous to the Biblical "the last shall be first" inversion, with allusions which fit the Compsons, as "Wuz a rich man . . . . Whar he now?" fits Jason. The tableaux of Benjy moaning beside his "graveyard," with the "withered stalk of jimsonweed," of Benjy bellowing when Luster violates the order of the universe, and of Benjy finally serene with his broken narcissus when each familiar object is "in its ordered place" epitomize the Compson family: the chaos and disorder of their lives and the frailty of their hope without a sustaining faith are embodied in the idiot who in his dumb and selfish way loved Caddy and beauty and order (pp. 393, 399–401). Dilsey is the only one who brings beauty and order into their lives.

Even an incomplete survey of symbolism in *The Sound and the Fury* demonstrates the textural and sensuous richness that accompanies the structural and stylistic virtuosity.

In contrast to the prevailing subjective symbolism in *The Sound and the Fury*, the symbolism of *Sanctuary* is conveyed through a multitude of objective details and numerous scenes of "collisions and confrontations" derived in part from the structural polarity of characters and settings. The themes center on the problem of evil and of justice, on attitudes toward sex, and on disparity between appearance and reality. Conventional "respectable" citizens value the preservation of the appearance of innocence more than the carrying out of justice, to free the innocent and punish the guilty.

Faulkner said that the title "meant that everyone must have some safe secure place to which he can hurry, run, from trouble" (*FN* 143). Ironically, although the novel abounds in enclosed places, few of the characters find sanctuary, a "safe secure place." The other meaning of *sanctuary*, in the medieval sense, is a sanctified place where a criminal is safe from the law. In that sense, Temple finds sanctuary in Southern tradition, social conventions, and her own family. The name *Temple* is almost a synonym for *Sanctuary* in this sense of a sanctified place. Southern gyneolatry puts a white woman of high social class on a pedestal; Narcissa Benbow's self-image is based on this tradition. Sexual violation is thus violation of a temple, of something sacred. The irony of the narrative events in the other sense of *sanctuary* is matched by the irony of Temple's unworthiness of her first name and of the tradition in which she finds sanctuary. *Drake* may symbolize lust; the heroine's name expresses the basic polarity. The male term *Drake* suggests androgyny; Temple was a typical flapper at a time when short skirts and short hair and boyish freedom in behavior were combined with girlish enticement, symbolized by her long legs and her compact with mirror and powder.

Names of a few other characters have some significance. Horace has been dealt with in *Sartoris*. Ruby Lamar and Lee Goodwin, faithful but unmarried and therefore social outcasts in Jefferson, have names which are chiasmatically parallel. *Ruby* recalls the verse in Proverbs 31:10: "Who can find a virtuous woman? for her price is far above rubies." Ruby was in essential respects a devoted wife and mother and thus virtuous. *Lamar* is the most glorious name in nineteenth-century Oxford, Mississippi, history: L. Q. C. Lamar had a distinguished career in public and military affairs before, during, and after the Civil War. *Lee* is similarly the most glorious name in the Southern history of the Civil War. It is scarcely possible that the use of two such names is accidental. And if *Ruby* suggests a virtuous woman, *Goodwin* could be "good friend" or, more likely, "God's friend." Though both names are obviously ironic, Faulkner treats Ruby and Lee with sympathy throughout, without glossing over their sins and weaknesses. Popeye's name suggests his grotesque and inhuman characteristics. Intended to be "another lost human being" (*FU* 72), he seems to be a symbol of evil in modern society, especially because of his complete alienation from nature. According to Joseph Blotner, the name *Popeye* Faulkner probably took from Popeye Pumphrey, one of the notorious criminals in Memphis when it was "Murder Capital of the U.S.A." in 1929, the time of action in *Sanctuary*. Faulkner began writing *Sanctuary* in January 1929. The other possible source of the name, the comic-strip Popeye, appeared that month in Elzie Segar's "Thimble Theatre," too late to take precedence over Popeye Pumphrey. Thomas McHaney, using 1929 as the date for the action, discovered mythic correspondence in the dates of action and noted the appearance of Popeye. I have dealt with these facts in "The Creative Evolution of *Sanctuary*," in *Faulkner Studies I*.

Places show the same polarity as is seen in Horace and Popeye, Temple and Ruby: the Old Frenchman place, a sinister ruin, frequented by lawbreakers; the Sartoris and Benbow houses, old and respectable residences of the gentry. Horace finds little sanctuary with Narcissa at Sartoris and little in his own house. Miss Reba's in Memphis is Temple's "sanctuary," which she accepts without much protest, although it is, to anyone but Virgil and Fonzo, a brothel; the old woman's, where Ruby is driven by the respectable women of Jefferson, like the Old Frenchman place is the weed-surrounded haunt of the disreputable (*San.* 41, 193). Even the jail offers little sanctuary to Lee Goodwin: trusting the law in his innocence of the crime with which he was charged, he fears being shot by Popeye through the window of his cell (pp. 127–28). Outside the jail the heaven tree sheds its trumpet-shaped blooms (p. 122). The courtroom which should symbolize justice is the scene of Temple's perjury and of her rescue by the five Drake "knights." The beginning, in May, is in the season of growth and fertility rites; the trial is in the summer of fruition; only the ending, "in the season of rain and death," is directly, not ironically, symbolic. The lynching of Lee Goodwin, one of the few terrible scenes directly presented by Faulkner, was added in Faulkner's revision of the unpublished galleys, collated with the published book by Gerald Langford. Having lost "the safe and glittering regions beyond the moon" (*Sar.* 180), the sanctuary of his idealism, and having witnessed the fiery death of Lee Goodwin, Horace returned to Belle and shrimp toting. Previously having found sanctuary from justice in the terror he inspired and in the ulterior motives of "good" people, Popeye was executed, without protest before the trial and without appeal after the death sentence, for a crime he did not commit, having been too busy at that time killing someone elsewhere. The scenes of Popeye in the jail and his execution are parallel to the jail and lynching scenes in Jefferson.

Each character in appearance and in possessions and attitudes symbolizes his thematic function. Horace is indifferent to dress but carries a book on his flight from his wife. Popeye dresses in black, and carries a gun and a platinum penknife, both ironic phallic symbols; his eyes are like "two knobs of soft black rubber," and he has "that vicious depthless quality of stamped tin" (p. 4). This recurrent image in Faulkner Richard Adams traced to a passage in *The Nigger of the Narcissus* and concluded that both Conrad and Faulkner used it to suggest a "mechanistic alienation from nature." The brilliantine on his hair contrasts with Horace's "thinning and ill-kempt hair" (p. 16). Popeye's last words before execution were "Fix my hair, Jack" (p. 308). Popeye's fear of nature is the preliminary evidence that he is an artificial and probably unfeeling person, in contrast to Horace who loves nature. Although Popeye may himself be a phallic symbol, as his possessions also suggest, he is ironically so, being impotent. There is, however, no evidence of Horace's virility. Neither one is the source of new life.

Temple is what Ruby calls "a cheap sport," enticing men without being capable of real love; her constant use of her compact, her "grimace of taut, toothed coquetry" (p. 47) at Popeye are the visible signs of the "actual pride, a sort of naïve and impersonal vanity" which makes her try to attract or propitiate every man she sees and even causes her to take satisfaction in telling Horace her story (p. 209). Her name in the station lavatory was seen twice, by Gowan and Horace (pp. 34, 168), lest the reader might miss a single instance of such a telling detail. At Miss Reba's, Temple was surrounded by objects and possessions which symbolize her nature, the wages of her sin: the clock, with its four china nymphs, represents Miss Reba's taste but symbolizes Temple's nymphomania. Temple selected her fine clothes, her cosmetics and perfumes, and her platinum bag, paid for by Popeye (p. 218). Lacking moral sensitivity, she carried into the courtroom the bag which was the badge of the shame she concealed by perjury. As he denied the shame, her father repudiated the price; when Temple dropped the bag in the courtroom, "with the toe of his small gleaming shoe the old man flipped the bag into the corner where the jury box joined the Bench, where a spittoon sat . . ." (p. 282). With "her mouth painted into a savage and perfect bow, . . . like something both symbolical and cryptic cut carefully from purple paper and pasted there" (p. 277), Temple is blatantly deliberate and artificial in her allurement.

The minor characters also are contrasted, with clearly symbolic details. Gowan's plump conceit and Narcissa's impervious stupidity and the desire of both to be taken as representing an ideal—Gowan the Virginian gentleman who can hold his liquor, Narcissa the virtuous and pure lady—make them comparable; both betray the ideal, Gowan by folly and cowardice and Narcissa by selling out justice and humanity for conventional respectability. In contrast with Temple's finery and Ruby's own previous "three fur coats," Ruby's faded pink undergarment, her old and worn but neat gray dress and hat (pp. 42, 112), show the price she has paid for her fidelity to Lee and the status of wife and mother. Miss Reba's two dogs, named for herself and Mr. Binford, are the symbol of her grief and, probably, of her particular female nature. "We was happy as two doves," she wailed, choking, her rings smoldering in hot glints within her billowing breast'' (p. 153). Love and devotion are pathetically symbolized in Ruby and grotesquely in Miss Reba, in contrast with Temple's lack of anything but physical feeling for Red and her willingness to be a kept woman and unwillingness to admit it. Judge Drake, with his silver hair and mustache, his pouched eyes and "small paunch . . . buttoned snugly into his immaculate linen suit" (p. 281), sits with his "hands crossed on the head of his stick" (p. 309), like the old blind man at Lee Goodwin's (p. 41); the identical attitude may symbolize Judge Drake's moral "blindness." Little Belle, in her white dress, is revealed by her reflection in the mirror to be, not Nature, symbolized by the grape arbor, but Progress, symbolized by the mirror (pp. 14–15), and is revealed by her photograph, again envisioned in terms of "sympathy with the blossoming grape," to be "suddenly older in sin than he would ever be" (pp. 162–63). A parallel image of innocence transmuted to depravity occurs in *Crime and Punishment*, in Svidrigailov's dream of the five-year-old girl who revealed the "shameless face of a French harlot" (Part Six, Chapter Six). Temple's mental image of herself and Horace's image of Belle, which identifies her with Temple, are objective correlatives of sex fantasies (pp. 215–16), Temple's of rape, castration, and death, according to Lawrence Kubie. Horace's images of Narcissa and Little Belle in white symbolize his attempt to hide incestuous desire beneath a mask of purity.

The wealth of single symbolic scenes or tableaux is due to the basic polarity and the thematic confrontation of good with evil. The first scene, with Horace and Popeye at the spring, immediately establishes the central polarity: Horace, the man of intellect and goodwill, in harmony with nature, confronting and held immobile by the man of evil and ill-will, who has power only because he has a gun, who fears the birds and the trees, and who defiles nature by spitting into the spring. This scene, Langford's collation shows, was placed at the beginning in Faulkner's revision of the galleys. Later when Ruby, beside the spring, confronted Popeye: "Somewhere in the swamp a bird sang" (p. 94). When Horace is in bed, again immobilized, he is confronted by Narcissa, with her demand that he sacrifice the living to honor the dead, and cease to help Ruby and Lee (p. 179). He is confronted by Clarence Snopes, again as by Popeye in natural surroundings: the "black-and-silver tunnel of cedars" in the moonlight, with fireflies "in fatuous pinpricks" and whippoorwills calling and the fragrance of honeysuckle (p. 196). In this moonlit scene Clarence as informer and his information are equally incongruous: he tells Horace that Temple is in a Memphis whorehouse. The confrontations between Horace and Ruby take place in Horace's house, in the hotel in Jefferson, and in the jail, those with Lee in the jail; upon these depend all the others. The confrontation of Horace and Temple occurs at Miss Reba's, in a setting as alien to Horace as the spring was to Popeye. Temple receives him in bed (as Ruby did not), but with rouge on her cheeks and "her mouth painted into a savage cupid's bow," suggesting that she is not in an alien setting (p. 207). The interview between Horace and Temple physically and symbolically is the reverse of the scene between Horace and Narcissa. The absence of directed confrontation in the courtroom, where Temple is called as a witness by Horace but never looks at him and is questioned only by the District Attorney, symbolizes Horace's failure to prevail over the forces ranged against him to suppress the truth (pp. 277–81). The clue to Temple's failure to tell the truth is the confrontation between Narcissa and the District Attorney, between Respectability and Political Ambition. The confrontation of Popeye and Clarence, of Sadist and Snoop, at Miss Reba's, the ironic parallel to that of Horace and Temple, presents Clarence at the keyhole of Temple's room, like Lovelace at Clárissa's, and Popeye holding a match to Clarence's neck (p. 203).

Temple as the central figure is presented most frequently in symbolic scenes: the first, as she watches the train disappear at Taylor, signifies her deliberate choice of what she knows must be evil because it is forbidden (*RN* 136). Gowan, her companion, spends his brief time at the Old Frenchman place in collisions: with the tree in the road and with Van. The absence of the confrontation with Temple to which he was morally obligated symbolizes his responsibility for what follows: "The prospect of facing Temple again was more than he could bear" (p. 83). Temple on the bed, wearing the raincoat, first fluffing her hair and powdering her face and then lying "like an effigy on an ancient tomb," suggests both a sacrifice and a harlot, fear and enticement (p. 69). The scenes in the corncrib in May (pp. 90–91, 96–99) have both obvious and hidden symbolism: *crib* has a triple meaning; *corn* suggests fertility rites, one feature of which in some societies was rape. Frazer's *The New Golden Bough* cites a fertility festival in Central America in which men and boys ran naked across a field and violated any woman they overtook. In that society Temple's frantic flights would have been interpreted as provocative rather than evasive. The desolation of the Goodwin place, uncultivated and overgrown with weeds, adds to the ironic inversion of symbols. That Carvel Collins gives, as the possible source of Temple's story, the experience of a girl from Cobbtown does not invalidate symbolic interpretations; it merely shows what Faulkner's imagination could do with a suggestion. In the corncrib, Temple was first confronted by a rat, with eyes "like two tiny electric bulbs," which leaped at her but then backed into the corner, and, "its forepaws curled against its chest," squeaked "in tiny plaintive gasps" (pp. 90–91). In its offensive and defensive attitudes the rat symbolizes both Popeye and Temple. Tommy as a guard, a "natural" man, responsive to Temple's helplessness but too innocent of evil to fear Popeye, increased the antithesis between nature and the unnatural evil symbolized by Popeye. Temple's impassivity, when Popeye came down the ladder, and the sound of the shot, "a short, minor sound," understate the violence.

On the road from the spring, Temple, the cause of the murder, and Popeye, the murderer, confronted the wife of the man who was to die for their deeds: Popeye made no sign; Temple "looked the woman full in the face without any sign of recognition whatever" (p. 100). Ironically, when Temple and Popeye rode through the countryside it was a May Sunday of a lavender spring (p. 133). In Memphis, however, the dingy street which led to Miss Reba's was suitably sordid.

There, with Temple the victim–enticer, the pattern of confrontation is repeated, recalling Temple's first coquettish grimace and the scene in the raincoat: "She writhed slowly in a cringing movement, cringing upon herself in as complete an isolation as though she were bound to a church steeple. She grinned at him, her mouth warped over the rigid, placative porcelain of her grimace" (p. 154). At the Grotto, surrounded by Popeye and his gunmen, Temple is the enticer, who brings Red to his death, and who tries to disarm Popeye. With Red, her sexuality is unrestrained. With a last confrontation of Red as he "made her a short, cheery salute," Temple is hustled off by Popeye's gunnmen. Her final confrontation with Popeye symbolically prefigures Red's murder; Popeye flips the dying match as casually as he shoots Red: "The match flipped outward like a dying star in miniature, sucked with the profile into darkness by the rush of their passing" (p. 234).

The tableau at the end of the court scene, when Temple leaves with her father, symbolizes Southern Womanhood protected by Southern Chivalry; it also symbolizes, perhaps, the stifling, by forces of convention, of the impulse to tell the truth and save a life:

Again the girl stopped. She began to cringe back, her body arching slowly, her arm tautening in the old man's grasp. He bent toward her, speaking; she moved again, in that shrinking and rapt abasement. Four younger men stood like soldiers, staring straight ahead until the old man and the girl reached them. Then they moved and surrounded the other two, and in a close body, the girl hidden among them, they moved toward the door. Here they stopped again; the girl could be seen shrunk against the

wall just inside the door, her body arched again. She appeared to be
clinging there, then the five bodies hid her again, and again in a close
body the group passed through the door and disappeared [p. 282].

Ruby's father had shot Ruby's suitor (p. 56); Temple's father has in
effect set the match to Ruby's "husband."

The scenes of death and violence for which *Sanctuary* was notorious
are actually few: the killing of Tommy is merely suggested by a sound
"no louder than the striking of a match" (p. 98); the rape is indicated
by the corncob and by Temple's plaints on the trip to Memphis; the
killing of Red is done offstage. Instead of seeing Tommy dying we see
Tommy dead at the undertaker's, with the younger men of Jefferson
coming to look at him: "He lay on a wooden table, barefoot, in overalls, the sun-bleached curls on the back of his head matted with dried
blood and singed with powder . . ." (p. 108). This is innocence, after
meeting and not recognizing evil.

Red was not innocent. His last appearance, the famous scene in the
Grotto, is sophisticated, as befits sexuality destroyed by perverted
trafficking with evil: black and silver coffin on a crap table draped in
black; the Negro waiters in black shirts and white jackets like photograph negatives; the bowl of punch on a black-draped table; the or-
chestra playing "Nearer My God to Thee" lest anything more suited to
Red should start the mourners dancing. When the regular customers
invaded the dice-room, the corpse was tumbled out of the coffin and
the hole in the forehead exposed. Although the macabre humor of the
funeral and the session at Miss Reba's seems irrelevant to the main
story except as disreputable persons show more feelings than "good"
people, William Stein found the Grotto scene richly and ironically
symbolic, a profane Mass for the Dead which ends in a travesty of the
Crucifixion.

The death of Lee Goodwin, like Red guilty of trafficking with evil
but, unlike Red, doing so with the support of respectable citizens, is
the most horrible, the most infernal scene: the black figures seen
against the flames, the screams of the man whose oil-can exploded, but
no sound from "the central mass of fire": "It was now undistinguish-
able, the flames whirling in long and thunderous plumes from a white-
hot mass out of which there defined themselves faintly the ends of a
few posts and planks" (pp. 288–89). Horace, who confronts the horror,
is rendered almost senseless by it. (In the first galleys of *Sanctuary*,
Lee was not lynched.) Lee burns as a sacrificial victim, a scapegoat, to
the god of respectability and of innocence, which need not exist in
reality if the mask of innocence can be preserved. The only characters

who show depth of feeling and have real vitality are Lee and Ruby; by comparison with the rest, except Horace who is a victim also of his society, Lee Goodwin and Ruby Lamar are less ironically named than Temple.

In both date of publication and time of action, *Light in August* follows *Sanctuary*. There is some similarity also in themes and in the sharply defined contrasts. The double story, however, of Lena and Byron Bunch and of Joe Christmas accentuates the polarity of symbols and images and increases the complexity of the thematic structure. The themes may be grouped in three classes: those dealing with society, chiefly religion, the race problem, and the glorification of the past; those dealing with the problems of individuals, derived from social attitudes but manifest in the individual isolated from society; and third, archetypal patterns. Because *Light in August* is so complex and significant, it is necessary to review each major theme and the characters and situations it involves before dealing with the thematic symbols. The religion represented by McEachern, Doc Hines, and Joanna Burden is strongly Calvinistic, characterized by repression and by a sense of being an instrument of the divine purpose, an attitude also reflected in Percy Grimm. Joanna says, "I don't ask it. It's not I who ask it. Kneel with me" (*LA* 267). Doc Hines's refrain is "The Lord told old Doc Hines what to do and old Doc Hines done it" (p. 361). In "The Calvinistic Burden in *Light in August*," Ilse Lind noted that the themes of religion and repression link the stories of Hightower and Joe and Lena, each story having its own mood and tempo: tragedy for Joe, problem novel for Hightower, comedy for Lena and Byron. The problem of race centers in the Southern concept of the Negro, a concept closely linked with religion: Doc Hines and Joanna show the opposite extremes, unreasoning hatred of and unreasoning love for Negroes. Only with McEachern, of the Calvinistic figures, is race not an issue, and that only because he is unaware of Joe's possible Negro blood. Joe is central to all these themes. The problems of individuals are closely related to these themes of society: repression causes sexual aberrations in Joanna and Joe which are further complicated by the racial attitudes. The recurrent themes of isolation as they are developed in Joe and Joanna Burden directly involve the racial problem: Joanna is an outcast because of her work for Negroes, and Joe rejects both white and Negro society because of his suspicion that he has Negro blood. In Joe, tragedy of isolation also involves the theme of the search for identity and the action patterns of flight and pursuit. Less sympathetic characters like Doc Hines and McEachern and Joanna are isolated by rigid codes which prevent participation in the community, but Hightower is isolated by obsession and by rejection of conventional codes. Absence of family ties contributes to the isolation of Joe, Joanna, Hightower, Lena, and Byron. Lena and Byron seek and secure response from others in the community: their isolation diminishes as Byron's growing sense of commitment and responsibility brings him closer to Lena's wholesome, natural acceptance of life.

The other aspect of society, the glorification of the past, is responsible for the strength of traditional attitudes toward Negroes, but Hightower, the individual who is most devoted to the past, is isolated by his idealization of his grandfather, not by religion or race concepts. Joanna Burden is isolated by all three. The tradition of the past which was transmitted to her by her family included northern Calvinistic religion and dedication to the mission of raising the shadow of the black man (LA 239–40). This tradition, by isolating her from the community, led to her psychological problems. The vision of the black shadow as a cross from which white babies were struggling to escape (p. 239) is part of the archetypal pattern of crucifixion, repeated in the death of Joe and joined with the archetype of nativity in the birth of Lena's baby, mistaken for Joe by Mrs. Hines. This death–birth pattern, which is also one of negation and affirmation, is even more general and universal an archetype than that of the dying god or of the crucifixion. Thus the themes range from archetypal to specific aspects of a society and the psychological and spiritual problems of individuals.

The story of Lena, the most positive and vital figure, is not an appendage to the story of Joe Christmas but is the origin of the entire novel and is the basis of the symbolism in the title:

> . . . in August in Mississippi there's a few days somewhere about the middle of the month when suddenly there's a foretaste of fall, there's a lambence, a luminous quality to the light, as though it came not from just today but from back in the old classic times. It might have fauns and satyrs and the gods . . . —from Greece, from Olympus in it somewhere. It lasts just for a day or two . . . but every year in August that occurs in my country, and that's all that title meant, it was just to me a pleasant evocative title because it reminded me of that time, of a luminosity older than our Christian civilization. Maybe the connection was with Lena Grove, who had something of that pagan quality of being able to assume everything, . . . she was never ashamed of that child whether it had any father or not, she was simply going to follow the conventional laws of the time in which she was and find its father. But as far as she was concerned, she didn't especially need any father for it, any more than the women . . . on whom Jupiter begot children were anxious for a home and a father. It was enough to have had the child. And that was all that was meant, just that luminous lambent quality of an older light than ours [FU 199].

The expression "the lambent suspension of August" (*LA* 465) is used, however, in connection with Hightower. Faulkner said in another session that the story began with "the idea of the young girl with nothing, pregnant, determined to find her sweetheart" and that it grew out of his admiration "for the courage and the endurance of women" (*FU* 74). So although the title has little to do with the story, it has much to do with the character of Lena.

Faulkner's remarks concerning the pagan quality of Lena lend plausibility to Beach Langston's theory that Lena Grove's name has symbolic significance, identifying her with Diana of Nemi, Diana of the Woods whose sacred grove stood on the lake of Nemi. The fact that the festival of Diana of Nemi gave place to the festival of the Assumption of the Virgin on August 15 offers an obvious basis for the combination in Lena of pagan qualities and of attributes associated with the Virgin Mary. Furthermore in *The Golden Bough* Sir James G. Frazer noted that Diana of Nemi was the goddess of childbirth and that "fire seems to have played a foremost part in her ritual." The Festival of Diana occurred on August 13. The smoke from the burning Burden house was the first evidence that the wagon in which Lena was riding was approaching Jefferson (p. 26). The birth of Lena's child and the death of Joe Christmas could have occurred on Monday, August 13, 1928, the festival of Diana, or on Monday, August 15, 1932, the festival of the Assumption of the Virgin Mary. The Madonna details and the fact that the book was published in 1932 make the latter date seem preferable. Certainly Robert Slabey, in "Myth and Ritual in *Light in August*," was correct in describing Lena as "a primordial image," not limited by Western and Christian convention, "a concrete personification of tranquility, the eternal renewal of life, and the triumph of the 'pure in heart.'"

A symbolic name parallel to Lena's, according to Langston, was *Lucas Burch*, the equivalent of the Latin for a grove sacred to deity. He thus might be the ironic counterpart of the priest of the wood of Diana, described by Frazer, who must be slain in single combat by whoever would be his successor. Lucas won in single combat with Byron Bunch but ran away and Byron won by default. The name *Bunch*, common in Lafayette County, suggests "one of the bunch," the common man. *Byron* is purely ironic, as with Byron Snopes; neither man, despite, one assumes, his mother's romantic yearnings, had any Byronic fascination for women. One of the Lafayette County Bunch tribe was named Homer.

The name of Joe Christmas, however, is purely symbolic; found on Christmas, by the "divine intervention" of Doc Hines (p. 362), the child was given a name that set him apart, so that, as a man's name "can be somehow an augur of what he will do," Joe "carried with him his own unmistakable warning, like a flower its scent or a rattlesnake its rattle" (p. 29). The name and his initials J C presage his crucifixion. Joanna Burden has a name equally symbolic. The corruption of the original *Burrington* to *Burden* (p. 228) befits the family who assume the burden of slavery and the curse of the white race represented by the black man (pp. 239–40). *Calvin* symbolizes the Calvinistic temper of the Unitarian Burdens, who seem to have been unusual among Unitarians in that respect. Calvin Burden is quoted as saying to his children, "I'll beat the loving God into the four of you as long as I can raise my arm" (p. 230).

Undue significance has been given to the detail that Joanna almost had her head cut off, ascribing to Faulkner symbolic intention that he probably did not have. (Decapitation has been interpreted as an allusion to John the Baptist or to the false Prophets in Dante's *Inferno*, Canto XX, who had their heads turned backward.) An unforgettable event occurred in Oxford in September 1908, shortly before Faulkner's eleventh birthday. Faulkner's friend John Cullen described it in *Old Times in the Faulkner Country*. Mrs. McMullen was murdered by Nelse Patton, a Negro, and Cullen quoted a newspaper account as saying that Patton drew a razor and "cut Mrs. McMullen's throat from ear to ear, almost severing the head from the body." Quoting the passage in *Sanctuary* about the murderer in jail awaiting execution, Cullen said that it was "almost exactly" a description of the same murder. Cullen not only saw the body at the scene of the crime but was the fourteen-year-old who shot Patton twice during the pursuit and was present at the lynching. Living in Oxford and keeping up with the local news and reading the Old Testament provided Faulkner with many of the boards from his "lumber room" (*FU* 103).

Similarly, too much significance has been read into Gail Hightower's name. *Hightower* is the name of a prominent Oxford, Mississippi, family, of which one member was named Gaines. Hightower's name nicely suits him, especially his remoteness from the life of the town and his habit of sitting in his window, but Faulkner did not coin the name. Phyllis Hirshleifer's interpretation that *Gail* means that the grandfather sowed the wind and Gail reaped the whirlwind is acceptable if one does not exaggerate the significance. Faulkner had Hightower himself explain the symbolism of Gail: he had thought that being a minister would provide a place "where the spirit could be born anew sheltered from the harsh gale of living . . ." (p. 453). The most significant statement Faulkner made, in referring to Hightower, used "tower" symbolically:

"I think that the worse perversion of all is to retire to the ivory tower. Get down in the market place and stay there" (*FWP* 55).

The Burden and the Hightower property, the focal points of the major August events, in their lack of activity and of relationship with the white community symbolize the bondage to the past and the isolation and withdrawal of the inmates. Joe understood what went on at the Burden house during the day: "Negro women . . . came to the house from both directions up and down the road, following paths which had been years in the wearing and which radiated from the house like wheelspokes" (p. 243). Byron viewed the place after the house burned; once a plantation, it was overgrown with scattered Negro cabins and a clump of oaks marking the site of the house (p. 402). Hightower's small bungalow was so hidden by bushes that the street was visible only from his study window, a "dead and empty small house" on a "dead and empty little street" (p. 293).

Integration of themes is achieved by use of these settings, by descriptive details of symbolic significance, and by recurrent images and motifs, and by even more frequent use than in *Sanctuary* of confrontations and encounters which visually dramatize the conflicting attitudes and values.

The descriptions of Lena stress her calm, serene, and peaceful air and her blue dress: by these details and by the slow journey, the image of a rustic madonna is built up before the nativity scene. Her bundle and her palm leaf fan are her sole pssessions. Joe Christmas is repeatedly described in white and black terms, symbolizing his mixed blood. His bearing when he first appears in Jefferson bespeaks his character and circumstances; in pride, isolation, and rejection of the supposed Negro part of his inheritance, he dresses like a city white man:

> His shoes were dusty and his trousers were soiled too. But they were of decent serge, sharply creased, and his shirt was soiled but it was a white shirt, and he wore a tie and a stiffbrim straw hat that was quite new, cocked at an angle arrogant and baleful above his still face. He did not look like a professional hobo in his professional rags, but there was something definitely rootless about him, as though no town nor city was his, no street, no walls, no square of earth his home. And that he carried his knowledge with him always as though it were a banner, with a quality ruthless, lonely, and almost proud [p. 27].

After work, Joe always changed from his overalls before going to town (p. 226). Concern with his dress began early; at McEacherns', he sold his cow to buy a new suit and a watch (p. 160), when he was wooing Bobbie. Dress is related to sexual prowess, and Mr. McEachern regarded the suit as a sign of lechery (p. 188). Various references to shoes are retrospectively given significance when Joe, donning the Negro brogans to escape from the posse and the dogs, accepted them as a symbol of his Negro blood (pp. 313, 321). His appearance and conduct in Mottstown before he was arrested are symbolic: freshly shaven, in clean new clothes except for the Negro brogans, "he walked the streets in broad daylight, like he owned the town" (p. 331). What amazed and angered the townspeople was this unconventional behavior, symbolized in his respectable appearance, when he should have been skulking, muddy and dirty, in the woods.

Being shaved was characteristic: the razor, before being put to its grim use, was one of the objects associated with Joe. It was the only thing he owned when he arrived at Joanna Burden's (p. 223). During the night he used his knife to cut off the buttons which are a symbol of the services of women (pp. 99, 100). The next morning he carefully shaved and put on a tie before emerging from the woods to go to a country store (p. 103). The revolver, "like the arched head of a snake," was not his weapon; after it misfired he took it. At the end he had a nickle-plated pistol (p. 437). These objects may be phallic symbols. Pistols and guns figure also in the stories of Doc Hines and Percy Grimm. The snake-like rope with which Joe got out at night at McEachern's was "the implement of his sin" (p. 179). Money is used as a sex symbol, from the time that the dietician gave Joe a dollar to conceal her affair with the doctor (p. 117); Richard Chase sees the dollar as a symbol of the circle Joe cannot break through. He took money from Mrs. McEachern's secret hoard for Bobbie, finally taking all of it so that he could marry Bobbie (p. 195). The blonde woman gave him money after Bobbie and her companions had taken Joe's money and left (p. 208). Food also is a sex symbol, especially of Joe's need of and rejection of women. The notes from Joanna, hidden in the hollow stump or left on his bed, serve as sex symbols (pp. 245, 257, 263).

Other characters are less frequently described in symbolic terms. Byron is neat and self-effacing; we seldom "see" him. His silver watch is his symbol: he is his own timekeeper until Lena enters his life and he ceases to avoid temptation by working on Saturday (p. 45). David Frazier noted that Lucas Burch, Byron Bunch, and Joe Christmas form a thematic triad. Christmas opposes religion, is repelled often by sexuality, never experiencing wholesome sex relations; he lives in isolation and rejects responsibility; Byron is religious, comes to accept responsibility and with it Lena's natural, vital sexuality, and participates in human affairs; Burch is without awareness of religion, is sexually casual and irresponsible, and seeks only easy and selfish gain.

Burch sells Joe; Byron tries to save him. Burch is lazy and undependable, and Byron works beyond what would seem to be his strength (pp. 35–36, 42–43). Hightower is related to this triad in that, in his avoidance of involvement in human affairs and his attempt to preserve in Byron his own non-participation, he would hand Lena over to Burch, putting the biological fact of paternity above the welfare of Lena and the child. Hightower is always described in terms of self-neglect—dirty, unshaven, slovenly in "respectable" clothes (p. 291)—in contrast to the other three men: Byron neat and clean, Christmas "soberly austere," Burch flashy (p. 36). Hightower's appearance symbolizes tradition decayed, all vestiges of gentility in his dress being contradicted by his filthy and flabby self-neglect.

Another isolated character who shows remnants of gentility, in this instance pathetic, is Mrs. Hines, with her purple silk dress and hat with a plume and her umbrella (p. 333). Her husband, "a dirty little old man," has divested himself of whatever signs of respectability may have given rise to theories about his former status as minister or public official and appears "collarless, in dirty blue jean clothes and with a heavy piece of handpeeled hickory worn about the grip dark as walnut and smooth as glass" (p. 324). Doc Hines's stick, his shotgun, and his pistol are the symbols of his violence, directed equally against "bitchery and abomination" and the Negro race. Negroes fed him as the women whom his grandson Joe despised fed Joe.

Joanna is first seen by candlelight, "quiet, grave, utterly unalarmed" (p. 218), looking much younger than her actual age. She dressed like a country woman in "clean calico house dresses" and sometimes a sunbonnet (p. 220). When she was in the throes of nymphomania, her clothing was torn to ribbons and her hair hung in "octopus tentacles," Medusa-like (p. 245). The contrast symbolizes the repression of her previous life and the violence of her release from it. In the last phase she reverts to cold stillness, and her graying hair, severe garments, and steel-rimmed spectacles symbolize her return to sexless fanaticism (p. 260).

Light in August is particularly rich in recurrent images and motifs which are not associated with a single character but may cluster chiefly around one or a pair and may be created by the author or the character or both. Richard Chase identifies "a texture of mechanics and dynamics," involving images of stasis and motion, circle and sphere or line, light and dark. He stresses images of "linear discreteness" associated with Joe—street car windows, picket fence, streets—with images of curve associated with Lena, the cycles of nature contrasted with the symbols of modernism. Joe's street becomes an imprisoning circle;

Lena's curve is the curve of earth's surface upon which she advances
with delight and wonder.

According to Aniela Jaffé, in "Symbolism in the Visual Arts:
The Symbol of the Circle," the circle "as the symbol of the Self
. . . expresses the totality of the psyche in all its aspects, including the
relationship between man and the whole of nature . . . it always points
to the single most vital aspect of life—its ultimate wholeness." But
when Joe Christmas realized that he had "never got outside" the
paved street that made a circle he had been inside for thirty years, that
he had "never broken out of the ring" of what he had already done and
could not undo (p. 321), he decided to give himself up and took a
"direction as straight as a surveyor's line . . . like a man who knows
where he is and where he wants to go and how much time . . . he has
to get there in" (p. 320). Joe had no roots in the cycle of nature, and
when he becomes aware of what he must do, "he desires to see his
native earth for the first or the last time" (p. 320). Joe chose the
straight road back into the modern world to face the consequences of
what he had done. Lena's progress follows the curves of the earth and
the cycles of nature no matter what road she takes into an indeter-
minate future.

The many corridor and street images are both sex symbols and symbols of flight and pursuit. Images of roundness and containment represent to Joe female symbols contrasted with male trees, posts, roads;
the urns of his adolescent vision are the objective correlative of the
female "periodical filth" (pp. 173, 177); he destroys the whisky tins
before going the last time to Joanna's house (p. 105). The pit or abyss is
an image which serves as the objective correlative of Joe's engulfment
in Negro femaleness, analogous to the urns and following the incident
of the whisky tins: he stood in the hollow in Freedman Town as at "the
bottom of a thick black pit," with "the bodiless fecundmellow voices
of Negro women" on all sides, "as though he and all other manshaped
life about him had been returned to the lightless hot wet primogenitive
Female" (pp. 106–107). He fled back to the street and the rows of white
houses. During Joanna's nymphomania "he began to see himself as
from a distance, like a man being sucked down into a bottomless
morass," seeing by contrast "the street, lonely, savage, and cool" (p.
246). He also saw Joanna as a dual nature: "like two moongleamed
shapes struggling drowning in alternate throes upon the surface of a
black thick pool beneath the last moon," the second one trying "to
drown in the black abyss of its own creating that physical purity which
had been preserved too long now even to be lost."

Many of the window images are sex symbols, from the first time

Lena climbed out the window until Lucas Burch escaped from her by
climbing out another window (pp. 3, 409). This group of images suggests
the custom among German peasants of "window visits," an example of
prenuptial license as a basis for choice of a bride. Malinowski's emphasis
on the fact that the modern flapper was acting like the girl in a primitive or
European peasant society throws some light on Lena as a child of nature
in the 1930s. Instinctively and without shame she was acting as sophisti-
cates of the same period were doing in defiance of tradition. Joanna's
three phases are pictured as they seemed to Joe: the first "had been as
though he were outside a house where snow was on the ground, trying to
get into the house"; in the second "he was at the bottom of a pit in the hot
wild darkness"; in the third "he was in the middle of a plain where there
was no house, not even snow, not even wind" (pp. 254–55). Previously
Joe climbed out the window to go to Bobbie (p. 159); he climbed in the
window the first time he entered Joanna's house (p. 216). The next time,
when he found the door unlocked, "it was like an insult" (p. 224). The
window in which Hightower sits may well symbolize his sexless life, since
he looks out on a little patch of street and is visited only by Byron and the
Hineses; it is through Hightower's door that Joe finally enters to seek
refuge and is instead castrated and killed.

Minor motifs which become significant with repetition are the mask
images noted by Slabey, as symbolic of concealment of true nature, a
concomitant of isolation and withdrawal; and the use of light and dark,
of flight and repose, of motion and stasis. Many of these are brief and
seemingly casual. The wheel image, however, is related to both motion
and stasis and is developed finally at length in Hightower's last meditation; Lena's travels by wheeled vehicles are summed up in a female
image of stasis: "like something moving forever and without progress
across an urn" (p. 5). Faulkner's fondness for Keats's "Ode to a
Grecian Urn" is reflected here as elsewhere in an image of stasis. Lena
moves across the countryside: "The wagon goes on, slow, timeless.
The red and unhurried miles unroll beneath the steady feet of the
mules, beneath the creaking and clanking wheels" (p. 25). At the end
of the book, she is "looking out and watching the telephone poles and
the fences passing like it was a circus parade." Contrasted with Lena's
serene passage across the countryside while she is fulfilling her nature
by seeking the rightful father before giving birth to her child is Joe's
frantic flight in which "the thousand streets ran as one street." At
intervals, trying to escape himself, he rode "on trains and trucks, and
on country wagons" (p. 210). "But the street ran on in its moods and
phases, always empty: he might have seen himself as in numberless
avatars, in silence, doomed with motion, driven by the courage of

flagged and spurred despair; by the despair of courage whose opportunities had to be flagged and spurred'' (p. 213).

Juxtaposition of Lena and Joe Christmas is a reminder of the significant fact that never in the novel do they meet. The pillar of smoke is a
kind of symbol of the way in which the lives of diverse people meet in a
focal point: Lena and the wagon driver see the smoke (p. 26); Byron
sees it, "the yellow smoke standing straight as a monument on the
horizon" (p. 44), not long before Lena appears, expecting to see Lucas
Burch. "It seemed to him that fate, circumstance, had set a warning in
the sky all day long in that pillar of yellow smoke, and he too stupid to
read it" (p. 77). The smoke brings the people to the fire: it is the signal
which sets the forces of justice in motion.

The confrontations and encounters provide so many scenes in which
a thematic idea is impressively symbolized that relatively few can be
cited. Lena's confrontations with chance-met country people secure
response because of her cheerful serenity and her confident expectation that she will be treated kindly. One scene at Armstids' seems to
have a definitely Biblical significance. Lena sitting in her blue dress,
"her hands motionless in her lap," while Martha Armstid bustles and
clashes the stove savagely recalls the story of Mary and Martha,
with an overtone of the Virgin Mary in the color of Lena's dress and
her "inwardlighted quality of tranquil and calm unreason and detachment," "her soft and musing face" (pp. 15, 17). Lena's confrontation
with Byron symbolizes acceptance and participation, Byron's instinctive and unaccustomed response to her need, seeing his time-clock
time contrasted with her natural time: "A few minutes wouldn't make
no difference, would it?" (p. 47). Her confrontation with Burch is the
precise opposite: he climbs out the window to escape his actual responsibility (p. 409). Byron's confrontation with Burch is a fight which
he loses physically but wins when Burch passes on the train he has
"jumped," leaving the field to Byron: "They see one another at the
same moment: the two faces, the mild, nondescript, bloody one and
the lean, harried, desperate one contorted now in a soundless shouting
above the noise of the train, passing one another as though on opposite
orbits and with an effect as of phantoms or apparitions" (p. 417). This
image symbolizes not only the relationship between the two men but
also the isolation that, in this novel, is the prevailing human condition.

The scenes between Byron and Hightower are a kind of duel of wills:
Byron, having accepted the present and responsibility, moves from
uncertainty, symbolized by his stumbling on the step, to commitment,
symbolized by his ceasing to stumble (pp. 70, 294). And Hightower
hates it worse, as Byron says, when Byron does not stumble. The first
time they face each other across the desk, Byron tells about Lena and

"Brown" and the murder, while Hightower sits motionless (pp. 80, 82, 85–86). At the end Hightower has his eyes closed and sweat runs down his face like tears as he says, referring to Joe's supposed Negro blood and what will happen when he is caught, "Poor man. Poor mankind" (p. 93).

In these scenes, their opposition is visible: they sit on opposite sides of the desk and Byron, with his "still, stubborn ascetic face," "does not look up" (p. 286). Hightower's confrontation with the storekeeper, with the counter between them, reveals his motives: he wants peace, thinking that he has bought immunity, that he can withdraw from involvement in human affairs (pp. 291–94). To Byron, Hightower's nose is a symbol, holding "invincibly to something yet of pride and courage above the sluttishness of vanquishment like a forgotten flag above a ruined fortress" (p. 343). When Byron confronts Hightower with the news that Christmas has been arrested, Hightower weeps in impotence, faced with his duty as a man of God and with the penalty he must pay for goodness. He foresees the crucifixion of Joe as inherent in the nature of the people and their religion. Again confronted by Byron and Doc and Mrs. Hines, he is forced to hear the terrible story of how Joe's father and mother died. He sits beyond the desk "like an awkward beast tricked and befooled of the need for flight, brought now to bay by those who tricked and fooled it" (p. 365). To Byron's plea that he give Joe an alibi, as his way of paying for being good, Hightower responds by ordering them out of his house and falling forward on the desk which has been his barrier against commitment to life. At the last confrontation between Byron and Hightower, Hightower yields and goes to Lena when her baby is born and is rewarded by "a glow, a wave, a surge of something almost hot, almost triumphant" (p. 382), and when he returns and she looks at him with "an expression serene and warm," he responds "with an expression on his face gentle, beaming, and triumphant" (pp. 385–86). He has re-entered the world and sees "the good earth" being peopled with "good stock" (p. 384). The final physical confrontation of Hightower is with the fugitive Joe Christmas and his pursuers, when, struck down by Joe's manacled hands, Hightower, "his big pale face streaked with blood," still tries to give Joe the false alibi he had refused earlier (p. 349). Moral struggle is presented in physical images of confrontation.

Finally Hightower confronts the truth: in his meditation in the window he sees his past life and its phantoms, his flight to Jefferson to live in a trance of the past, and sees that he accepted religion as a barricade against truth and served it for his own desire (p. 461). The wheel of thinking carries him to the truth that his grandfather was a swaggering and chastened bravo and his own life "a single instant of darkness in which a horse galloped and a gun crashed'' (pp. 462, 465). With the last "of honor and pride and life'' he again has the vision, the moment of courage and action. The implication seems to be that his enlightenment was not redemptive. The horse symbol is common in Faulkner as a symbol of masculinity. (To Joe also horses are a male symbol: "Even a mare horse is a kind of a man'' [p. 101].) Hightower's recurrent vision is interpreted by Campbell and Foster as showing "the glorious futility of Civil War heroes and the ghostly tragedy of present-day Southern retrospective nostalgia.''

The story of Joe is a complex sequence of confrontations in which the issues are more complex and varied than those between Byron and Hightower. The first confrontations are with adult authority: the dietician motivated by guilt; Doc Hines, by racial hatred; McEachern, by religious fanaticism. The search for identity and the obsession with women and food begin, the toothpaste and the dietician linking the two, and in addition introducing the money-sex symbol in the dollar she gives him. Prayer and punishment are combined in the conflict with McEachern over learning the catechism and over the new suit (pp. 137–43, 154), with Joe's calm, peaceful look and contemplative musing, "remote with ecstasy and self-crucifixion'' (pp. 143, 150), anticipating the image of his death. In his search for identity, Joe rejected the name *McEachern* and retained *Christmas*. Confrontation with sex first sickened Joe (pp. 146–48), then aroused his innocent idealism toward Bobbie. The stallion image (p. 167) and the escape from the dance hall on the horse on which McEachern had pursued him symbolize masculinity and escape from honor and law (p. 194), with a Faustian sense of power. The horse is also a symbol of the Oedipal displacing of the father, when Joe knocked out McEachern in the dance hall and took the horse. In encounters with women, Joe was confronted with weak, ingratiating, and basically undependable women like the dietician or Mrs. McEachern, whom he rejected in preferring the hard but predictable masculinity of McEachern, perhaps as an expression of latent homosexuality. The scene when Joe was brought to McEachern's and Mrs. McEachern washed his feet contributes to the Christ symbolism (p. 156); his rejection of food is an inversion of communion—Joe carried the tray "as if were a monstrance''—and is a repeated symbol of rejection of women (pp. 145, 224–25). His other encounters with women are with cynical, experienced women like Mame and Bobbie, his innocence and poverty and idealism being faced by sex for hire. In his defeat and rejection by Bobbie and her group, sex rather than religion is the cause of physical brutality at the hands of adults.

With Joanna, patterns are repeated: Joe is confronted by an older woman secretly offering him food. When Joanna confronts him in his cabin, it is the first time he has seen her head bare; the Burden history is presented to him, with its combination of the Calvinism of his foster father and the Burden sense of mission to Negroes (pp. 228–41). In her third phase Joanna confronts Joe, not as a woman and a mistress but as an authoritative elder, insisting on repentance and expiation and trying to force upon him the identity of a Negro; as they had earlier, they stood to talk (p. 264). The final confrontation, to which he went with a sense of destiny, repeats the pattern of their confrontations—the dark bedroom, the only room except the kitchen in which he had ever seen her—but adds the pattern of the confrontations with McEachern, the command to kneel (p. 267). This also repeats Faulkner's understated handling of violence by omission of images: there is a lapse from the moment when the gun fails to fire until Joe stops a car, confronting the boy and girl, gun in hand, and terrifying them. The murder is the climax of the series of symbolic confrontations in which Joe's search for identity brings him into conflict with those who are older than he and who try to force him into social, religious, and sexual patterns which will determine his whole life, in contrast with Hightower's confrontations which involve a moral choice between life and a living death for a relatively few remaining years.

In "Who Killed Joanna Burden?" Stephen Meats raised a significant but usually ignored question that requires a careful review of the information we are given. After Joe entered Joanna's room he "laid the razor on the table" and lighted the lamp (p. 266). There is no evidence that he picked up the razor. When Joanna aimed her old "cap-and-ball" revolver at Joe, he watched "the shadow of the pistol on the wall; he was watching when the cocked shadow of the hammer flicked away" (pp. 266, 267).

A hiatus follows in the text, apparently representing Joe's lapse of consciousness. When the narrative continues, Joe was "standing in the middle of the road." He flagged a car with his right hand. When he leaped out of the car, something fell and "struck him on the flank." Only then did he realize why the couple in the car were so agitated: what had struck him was "the ancient heavy pistol" in his right hand. "He did not know that he had it" or remember picking it up. He examined it and found that the hammer had fallen on one chamber which had not exploded, and that the other chamber was still loaded: "'For her and for me,' he said." There is no evidence that he had a bloody razor, but the young people had seen him and he knew that he must flee, even though he had not shot Joanna. He was in danger without further evidence: he realized that the customary manhunt would be under way, by men "with pistols already in their pockets," seeking "someone to crucify" (p. 272).

The implication as to who murdered Joanna is in the facts that come out. Brown was in the Burden house when the fire was discovered (p. 274). Joe's razor was still on the table. Joe had proved his superiority to Brown twice (pp. 259–60). As soon as a reward was offered, Brown revealed that Christmas had Negro blood, confirming the assumption when a Negro was questioned by the sheriff and the deputy (pp. 275–79).

The implications of these facts in the interpretation of Joe as a Christ figure are significant. Burch's role as a disciple had been indicated: he imitated Joe "as if the very attitude of the master's dead life motivated, unawares to him, the willing muscles of the disciple who had learned too quick and too well" (p. 40). His betrayal of Joe immediately followed the news that Joanna's nephew "offered a thousand dollars' reward for the capture of her murderer" (p. 278). At nine o'clock that evening "Brown" reappeared, seeking the sheriff, and claimed the reward as soon as he confronted the sheriff (p. 279). Although the above "case" was presented without reference to the article by Meats in order to make it as short and simple as possible, his conclusion admirably expresses my own concluding thought: "On the basis of this insufficient knowledge all of us—the sheriff, Gavin Stevens, Percy Grimm, the community, the reader—are more than ready to pass judgment."

It is well to have in mind the known facts before considering the last days of Joe's life. In his flight Joe confronts the Negro congregation like a white devil and rejects them and curses God (pp. 304–308). His successive confrontations of country people symbolize his complete alienation from human life until he steps into the Negro shoes and later finds himself at a table with food being set before him and thinks, "and they were afraid. Of their brother afraid" (p. 317). His re-entry thereafter into the human community is symbolized by his asking the time and washing and shaving and going into Mottstown, meeting and being recognized by people along the way and desiring "to see his native earth in all its phases for the first or the last time" (p. 320). In Mottstown the street that ran for thirty years becomes a circle, a ring which he cannot break out of, and the Negro shoes on his feet are a black tide moving up his legs like death (p. 321).

When Joe is no longer subjectively presented, the scenes of confrontation shift to Doc and Mrs. Hines, Doc confronting Joe in Mottstown, and demanding his death, symbolizing the fanaticism of religion when combined with racial hatred (pp. 326–27). Mrs. Hines confronts Doc with her demand, after thirty years, that he tell her what he did with Milly's baby (p. 330). The parallel between Joe's foster parents and his grandparents is part of the pattern of brutality and fanaticism of husbands and subjection of wives that is seen in all families except Hightower's. Impelled by love for her grandson, Mrs. Hines successively confronts her husband, the deputy, the station agent, and Hightower; impelled by hate, Doc tells his story of being the instrument of God which has doomed the bastard, Joe, of whom God says to him, "He's a pollution and a abomination on My earth" (p. 365).

Percy Grimm is the instrument of God in the last scene in Joe's life, the end of the flight and pursuit: when Joe re-enters the human community and allows himself to be taken, he attains, as Kazin says, "in this first moment of selfhood, the martyrdom that ends it." Joe's motives in this last flight are not given; the pursuit ends at Hightower's where Joe confronts Hightower and then Percy Grimm, exalted like "a young priest." At the moment of death, Joe's spirit confronts the three men with Grimm and soars into their memories forever (p. 439). This last episode combines the themes of fanatic religion, of race, of isolation involving flight and pursuit, of commitment, of death and of crucifixion not only in connection with Joe and Hightower, as noted previously, but also in Joanna's vision of the black crosses (p. 221), which Lind interprets as prefiguring "her own crucifixion on the black cross of her elected mission" (p. 89). John Hardy comments on the episode where Joe is taken for the devil: "a mistake . . . that was made concerning Christ himself": "this kind of Christ, this monstrous mockery of Him . . . is the only kind that properly can appear in a society that has already completely rejected Christ."

The meditations of Hightower return to the theme of the past. The birth of Lena's baby, the same day that Joe was killed, and the end of Lena's and Byron's story constitute a return to the themes of life and affirmation and introduce the beginning of the life of Byron and Lena and the baby as a family, a kind of flight into Egypt.

The intricate interweaving of themes and symbols invests with significance almost every realistic detail, but no one pattern, especially the pattern of Christ symbolism, should be subjected to the test of strict consistency and made to bear the burden of the meaning. The novel is a configuration of themes and symbols; it means as much as the total configuration suggests, which is more than the sum of the various strands of symbolism. It is extraordinarily rich in scenes in which, figuratively speaking, the images may be frozen and the separate details and attitudes of characters be found on every re-examination to reveal new overtones and nuances of thematic meaning.

Radically different in content, themes, and narrative method from
Light in August, *Snopes* nevertheless provides numerous symbols,
many of them repeated in the three volumes in the trilogy, and dramatizes themes in symbolic tableaux. Discussion here will be limited to
the main themes and characters and related symbols, excluding the
host of minor Snopeses and episodes in which they figure. Neither the
success story of Flem nor the love theme centered in Eula and Linda
involves traditional symbols or displays dramatic structure, being
interspersed with action and reminiscence related to the whole Jefferson story. The revenge tragedy of Mink is similarly alternated with
stories of individuals and the community.

Mink and Flem share chiefly the name of *Snopes*. *Flem* suggests
both Flem's phlegmatic impassivity and his habitual spitting. *Mink*
reflects the recurrent use of animal terms to describe the Snopeses.
Mink is referred to as a half-starved little wildcat, and Flem has "a tiny
predatory nose like the beak of a small hawk" (*H* 51). The only time
when Mink's clothes symbolize anything but destitution they display
the newness of the clothes provided to the discharged convict (*M* 104).
In contrast, Flem's clothes symbolize his ascent from destitution to
affluence, Jefferson-style. From the white shirts, streaked from sun-
marks on the bolt of cloth, the tennis shoes, the little black tie, and the
cap which were his "uniform" in Frenchman's Bend, Flem's clothes
are his chosen status symbols. The significance of Flem's clothes is
underlined in his last appearance, as Mink saw him through the window: "the black planter's hat he had heard about in Parchman but the
little bow tie might have been the same one he had been wearing forty
years ago behind the counter in Varner's store, the shirt a white city
shirt and the pants the dark pants too and the shoes polished city shoes
instead of farmer's brogans" (*M* 412–13).

The swivel chair in which Flem is seated is the successor to the
barrel chair which was the symbol of his success in Frenchman's Bend.
Except for the water tower, Flem's "monument" (*T* 29), Flem is symbolized by his possessions: the house he rented, then bought, the mansion he bought and restored to columnar grandeur, the black cars
which took him nowhere for pleasure. He bought Eula's tombstone,
perhaps as partial repayment for what he was paid to marry her. Mink,
however, owned nothing, not even the hovel which housed him, except
the antiquated gun which sufficed to kill Flem.

Gavin Stevens and V. K. Ratliff are as distinctive in appearance as
Flem, but with more individual taste apparent. Ratliff's tieless blue
shirts and bland, brown, inscrutable face are as distinctive as Gavin's
mop of whitening hair, his corncob pipe, and his Phi Beta Kappa key.

V. K.'s exotic name, Vladimir Kyrilytch, was inherited from his Russian ancestor who fought in the British army during the Revolutionary War; the name seems to have no symbolic meaning except that Eula's knowing his name indicates that she and V. K. were better acquainted than Gavin had realized (*T* 323). As Ratliff has his successive vehicles of business, his wagon and converted automobile and pickup truck, bearing the "house" which contained his demonstrator sewing machine and the radio and television supplies, so Gavin has his unchanging office, overlooking the Square. Gavin's name, however, suggests *Gawain* and has definite chivalric connotations and possible mythic parallels. Ratliff's own house, with its Allanovna necktie under glass, figures late in *Snopes* but symbolizes his immaculate competence and intuitive good taste. Gavin's house and his Cadillac convertible symbolize only his wife's wealth and her gangster first husband's taste and Gavin's indifference to the male status symbols of his society, his lack of interest in both horses and automobiles. Gavin's failure as a romantic lover is symbolized by Manfred de Spain's E.M.F. sportscar and Matt Levitt's homemade racer, with open cutout or double-barrel brass horn, respectively, driven defiantly and triumphantly past the Stevens–Mallison residence (*T* 186). The new Jaguar in which Linda left Jefferson after Mink murdered Flem is the final symbol of Gavin's failure in romantic love and of his unrewarded—by his own choice—devotion to his goddesses: it reveals to him that he has been an accessory before the fact in the murder of Flem. He could not even blame the automotive age: he would also have been a failure as a knight on a horse.

One nature image in *The Hamlet* is used in an unusual way as a unifying thematic symbol: the moon represents love and fertility and in combination with the flowering pear tree symbolizes both romance and profit. The moon is waning when Ike Snopes renders devoted service to the cow (*H* 180). Houston's house is completed "in time to catch the moon's full of April through the window where the bed was placed" in the belief "that the full moon of April guaranteed the fertilizing act" (*H* 215, 216). Houston remembers his blasted hopes just before he is shot by Mink (*H* 217). The flowering pear tree outside Mrs. Littlejohn's appears first (*H* 276) and last in the moonlight, but on its last appearance Varner's comment reduces it to a symbol of profit rather than a serene symbol of romance and fruitfulness: "Then the pear tree came in sight. It rose in mazed and silver immobility like exploding snow; the mocking bird still sang in it. 'Look at that tree,' Varner said, 'It ought to make this year, sho' " (p. 307).

On the preceding page is Ratliff's unuttered vision of Eula standing

in the moonlight like Brunhilde or a Rhinemaiden or Helen of Troy, the
tableau which most directly and impressively presents Eula in her
mythic role. In the other tableaux in *The Hamlet* in which she figures
as representing the theme of love and fertility, she is not alone. Having
repelled Labove, "old headless horseman Ichabod Crane," "she stood
over him, breathing deep but not panting and not even dishevelled" (*H*
122). With Hoake McCarron, she was reported as beating back their
assailants with the buggy whip and later was imagined as supporting
Hoake by her braced arm on his injured side (p. 139). Finally Ratliff
saw "the calm beautiful mask" through the window of a moving train,
leaving on her honeymoon with "the froglike creature which barely
reached her shoulder" (p. 147).

In *The Town* and *The Mansion* the theme of love centers on Gavin,
and is represented in tableaux with his rivals and with the ladies whom
he serves: fighting with Manfred de Spain over Eula, "getting up from
the alley again with his face all bloody" (*T* 76); and taking Matt Levitt's
blows as champion of Linda (p. 190); eye to eye with Eula when he
proves more gentleman than man and "buys Flem" (pp. 94, 95); facing
Eula across the desk when she wants him to marry Linda (pp. 320–22);
with Linda in the drugstore, "forming her mind" (p. 180); with Linda
watching the sunset through the "tall and ragged palms and pines" on
the Gulf coast when she wants him to get married (*M* 248); standing
side by side with Linda at the mantel when she gives him the money for
Mink, the reward for the murder in which she involved Gavin as an
accessory before and after the fact (p. 426). Because of the limits of the
narrative method, there are no tableaux representing Eula and
Manfred, just a brief motion picture of them dancing with no moments
"frozen" (*T* 74, 75).

In part because of the narrative method but in part because the
theme of money and profit is less concentrated in *The Town* and *The
Mansion*, tableaux representing that theme are more frequent in *The
Hamlet*. The episode of the spotted horses most fully presents the male
motives of desire for a bargain and desire for possession of horses,
symbols of male prestige and virility. The succession of static and
violent images is noteworthy: the men ranged along the fence (p. 286),
Mrs. Armstid in the battered wagon (pp. 289–90), Flem among the men
at the fence after the auction is over (p. 293)—these "stills" are in
sharp contrast with the horses breaking through the barn door (p. 283)
and crashing through the lot gate (p. 302), and the one horse racing
through Mrs. Littlejohn's boardinghouse (pp. 302–303). The recurrent
images of Mrs. Littlejohn pursuing her peaceful and sensible domestic
chores, such as washing clothes in an iron wash pot in the back yard,

provide contrapuntal tableaux which underscore the folly of male activity, as does the image of Ratliff in his underclothes looking out the window—until the horse comes in the door and Ratliff jumps out the window (p. 303).

These community tableaux represent the horse-trading competition to which the success of Flem can be ascribed. That success has its own images: Flem giving Mrs. Armstid a nickel bag of candy for the "chaps," while refusing to refund the five dollars paid by the deluded Henry marks the climax of the spotted horses drama as an episode in the career of Flem (*H* 317); his career as Varner's clerk was climaxed when Flem sat at the scales at the cotton gin, steadily chewing (pp. 59–60). The final gesture in *The Hamlet*, when Flem, on his way to Jefferson with his family, spits over the wagon wheel beside the trench where the insane Henry Armstid is digging (p. 366), is matched by his farewell to Linda beside the grave and tombstone of her mother: "He leant a little and spit out of the window and then set back in the seat. 'Now you can go,' he says" (*T* 355).

The other tableaux in which Flem figures in *The Town* symbolize his desire for respectability: dropping the key to Montgomery Ward Snopes's studio on Gavin's desk after planting evidence to get M. W. sent to Parchman and counting out the price of ridding Jefferson of I. O. Snopes (pp. 176, 253). The limitation of view in *The Town* is clearly apparent when, in *The Mansion*, Montgomery Ward Snopes supplies a necessary scene of confrontation between himself and Flem and reveals Flem's real motive in getting him sent to Parchman (pp. 66–67). A vital confrontation is missing from *The Mansion*: the scene between Jason Compson and Flem Snopes when Flem bought the Compson place (p. 325). The most memorable Snopesian tableaux of greed and corruption in *The Mansion* do not involve Flem: Clarence with the dogs lined up behind him and in the car circled by dogs on three legs (pp. 317–18); Res holding the frying pan with the cold fried egg as Gavin sells him the mutilated rifle for a deed to Essie Meadowfill of the strip of land wanted by the oil company (p. 347).

The last tableau in which Flem appears is the climax, not to the theme of profit but to that of revenge. Mink as the active agent in this theme is represented in a series of tableaux in *The Mansion*, some of which are repeated from *The Hamlet*: almost ridden down by Houston, the man on the horse, angered by Houston's arrogance (*M* 8); in jail at the window watching for Flem (p. 40); at his trial, watching the door at the rear instead of the judge (p. 41); finally, thirty-eight years later, confronting Flem, motionless in the swivel chair, and twice pulling the trigger of the "toad-shaped iron-rust-colored weapon" for the single shot which killed Flem. Flem's offenses against human dignity and family loyalty and Mink's outraged sense of manhood are symbolized; Mink's motives for revenge are similar to Linda's when she confronts him, returns to him the pistol he threw at her, and shows him the way out (pp. 415–16). After the scene in which Mink, kneeling in the old cistern, confronts Ratliff and Gavin and takes the money sent by Linda, Mink risks the power of the earth as he lies down, facing the exact east, "equal to any, good as any, brave as any, being inextricable from, anonymous with all of them" (pp. 432, 435).

Unlike *Snopes*, structure and symbols in "The Bear," perhaps the Yoknapatawpha narrative richest in symbolism, chiefly follow a traditional pattern, that of initiation, which will be dealt with in Chapter 2. Other aspects of "The Bear" and of the volume in which it and the other Ike McCaslin stories are published, *Go Down, Moses*, are relevant here. The title, *Go Down, Moses*, refers explicitly to the Negro descendants of Carothers McCaslin: in the Negro spiritual, the Lord is telling Moses to go down to Egypt and deliver the Hebrew children from bondage. The Negro race still needs to be delivered at the end of the story of Ike. The title of the first of the trio of hunting tales, "The Old People," refers not only to the Indians, the "old people" who disappear with the wilderness, but to the other dispossessed people, the Negroes, and to the theme of injustice visited upon those who happen to be "red in color or black in color" (*FN* 86–87). "The Bear" is a self-explanatory title. "Delta Autumn" has a double symbolism: "Delta" signifies the passing of the old wilderness in Yoknapatawpha County and the moving of the hunt more than two hundred miles into the Delta country (p. 340); "autumn" is not only the season of the hunt but also the season of Ike's life and that of the wilderness: "He seemed to see the two of them—himself and the wilderness—as coevals, . . . the two spans running out together, not toward oblivion, nothingness, but into a dimension free of both time and space . . ." (*GDM* 354). It is the twilight season, the *Götterdämmerung* of the old gods and heroes.

In these stories the setting is completely thematic: the few scenes which do not take place in the wilderness or in De Spain's hunting camp symbolize the application of wilderness values, the passing of the wilderness, or the loss of wilderness values: in Memphis, Boon is merely grotesque (*GDM* 231); Ike looks at the plantation commissary and its ledgers with the insight gained in the wilderness (*GDM* 255–56); Hoke's logging camp marks the passing of the wilderness (p. 318); the Delta camp marks the extinction of both the old wilderness and its values, the new breed of hunters being killers of does, lesser men by their own admission than their predecessors (pp. 345–47).

Faulkner's own statement about the wilderness and its significance relates the two major themes represented in the story of the hunt and the story of Ike McCaslin's repudiation of his inheritance:

> The wilderness to me was the past, which could be the old evils, the old forces, which were by their own standards right and correct, ruthless, but they lived and died by their own code—they asked nothing. . . . To me, the wilderness was man's past, that man had emerged. The bear was a symbol of the old forces which in man's youth were not evil, but that they were in man's blood, his inheritance, his . . . impulses came from that old or ruthless malevolence, which was nature. . . . this story was to me a universal story of the man who, still progressing, being better than his father, hoping that his son shall be a little better than he, had to learn to cope with and still cope with it in the terms of justice and pity and compassion and strength [*FN* 50–51].

Nature as revealed in the wilderness and its creatures is the basic theme. It is both the source of spiritual truth and the victim of white rapacity. Man has to learn the rules of the wilderness and prove himself worthy before he will be accepted, before he will have his vision, but having had his vision he will lose the wilderness. That is the theme of Ike's hunting experiences in "The Old People" and "The Bear." There is another theme with two aspects: the wilderness is an Eden of innocence, from which, as Olga Vickery said, Ike as Adam must depart "to discover his humanity"; and it is the second chance for redemption offered to man by God: "a new world where a nation of people could be founded in humility and pity and sufferance and pride of one to another"; "a refuge and sanctuary of liberty and freedom from . . . the old world's worthless evening" (*GDM* 258, 283). To Ike, the wilderness is a peaceful retreat, a way of life in a lost Golden Age, rather than a vacation interlude in a life lived in the world of the present. The men of that golden age were "the Old People," of whom Sam Fathers told Ike, "those dead and vanished men of another race" and of old times which became "a part of the boy's present" (*GDM* 171).

Sam Fathers is so called because he had two fathers, the Indian chief who swapped him and his Negro mother to Carothers McCaslin for a gelding (*GDM* 263) and his mother's Negro husband. The name *Fathers* symbolizes Sam's role as spiritual father to Ike and may even suggest the primordial Mothers in Goethe's *Faust*. Isaac McCaslin recognizes the symbolic meaning of his own name: "an Isaac born into a later life than Abraham's and repudiating immolation; fatherless and therefore safe declining the altar because maybe this time the exasperated Hand might not supply the kid" (*GDM* 283). Stanley Sultan sees in the outcast Sam a symbol of Ishmael, the son of a slave woman and dweller in the wilderness, denied his inheritance. Ike's father and uncle, twins, were named *Theophilus* and *Amodeus*, both names meaning "dear to God." God chose them in their time to do the will of God, as He chose Ike in Ike's time (*GDM* 299). Even these symbolic and unlikely names Faulkner found in Oxford: the great-uncles of Phil Stone were Theophilus and Amodeus Potts, called Buck and Buddy.

As Old Ben, the bear, symbolizes the forces of nature, Lion, whose name is symbolic of courage, may perhaps symbolize also the destruction of the old forces of nature by man-created forces: his color is that of "a gun or pistol barrel" or "like a blued gun-barrel"; he has "cold and almost impersonal malignance like some natural force"; he combines courage with "the will and desire to endure beyond all imaginable limits of flesh in order to overtake and slay" (*GDM* 216, 218, 237).

In addition to objects which symbolize Ike's initiation, such as his gun and his hunting horn, other objects associated with him symbolize his family inheritance: the family ledgers are the record of the past injustices which Ike repudiated, the symbol of the plantation system founded upon human bondage; the Bible, however, from which Ike learned the truths of the heart is not concretely represented (*GDM* 255, 257). The silver cup filled with gold coins which was to be his inheritance from his maternal uncle is transmuted into the tin coffee-pot, filled with IOU's and coppers, one of his few personal possessions which included his iron cot and mattress and his carpenter's tools (*GDM* 300).

Because the story of Ike McCaslin is told through his memories, some experiences are not presented as clearly visualized, dramatic scenes. In addition to the tableaux which represent initiation, to be dealt with later, are those which represent the passing of the wilderness: the logging train, like "a small dingy harmless snake vanishing into weeds" which flung "its bitten laboring miniature puffing into the immemorial woodsface with frantic and bootless vainglory" and frightened a bear cub (*GDM* 318, 320); the graves of Lion and Sam, and the tree with the axle-grease tin with its offerings to Sam of the few comforts of civilization which he had enjoyed—tobacco, peppermint candy, a new bandanna (p. 328). Ike hailed the snake as Sam greeted the phantom buck: "Chief, . . . Grandfather" (p. 330): the snake is both the spirit of the wilderness and the serpent of Eden, but guiltless of its destruction; the real destroyer of Eden is the real grandfather, old Carothers, who brought slavery into the wilderness. Ike's final sight of the wilderness, Boon under the gum tree hammering the breach of his dismembered gun with the barrel and shouting that all the squirrels are his, has symbolic but cryptic meaning. If Boon, a notoriously poor shot, means that he expects to shoot all the squirrels, he has been corrupted by the white man's possessive attitude toward nature. If he is destroying his gun and wishes to protect the squirrels, he is the last defender of the wilderness. Ruel Foster interpreted this scene as the objective correlative of Ike's mental state at the loss of his own glory with the passing of the wilderness. In Webb and Green's *William Faulkner of Oxford*, Bramlett Roberts tells a story he heard from Faulkner about a man whose gun went to pieces when he shot it at squirrels in a large tree in a clearing: "Bill went up and was going to kill some of the squirrels . . . . And Wes said, 'Oh no, don't bother 'em! They're mine!'" Faulkner's explanation of Boon in "The Bear" agrees with the actual character and circumstances: "he didn't want anybody else to shoot the squirrels until he could get his gun fixed" (*FU* 8).

The tableaux and confrontations in the fourth part of "The Bear" center on the themes of exploitation of the land and the people and of moral regeneration. One group deals with the Negro descendants of Carothers McCaslin: the confrontation of McCaslin Edmonds by the suitor of Fonsiba who comes as a man, not as a Negro, to "the chief of her family" because "no man of honor could do less" (*GDM* 275); Ike's confrontation of Fonsiba and her husband, reading with lenseless gold-framed spectacles, who answers Ike's protests at his destitute idleness with "measured and sonorous imbecility of the boundless folly and the baseless hope" (p. 279), physical needs being of no concern to one who is free. Lucas confronts Ike to collect what Carothers McCaslin had willed him (p. 282). The story of the Beauchamps and Ike's legacy from Uncle Hubert is presented in another sequence of scenes, dominated by the burlap-wrapped parcel and the anticlimactic opening of it on Ike's twenty-first birthday (p. 306). The last confrontation in 4 is that in which Ike's wife offers herself to him, naked, to induce him to take back his inheritance: for a moment he weakens and says yes and she gives him his one chance to have a son (p. 315).

It must be the memory of this time, which "was like nothing he had ever dreamed" (p. 315), that Ike recalls when he says, in "Delta Autumn," that "at that instant the two of them together were God" (p. 348). The first of two major confrontations in "Delta Autumn" is that in which Ike faces Roth and affirms his faith in man and in the code of the hunt which does not permit the killing of does (pp. 345–49) and expresses the judgment which God will visit on man: "The woods and the fields he ravages and the game he devastates will be the consequence and signature of his crime and guilt, and his punishment" (p. 349). In Ike's confrontation with the girl, mother of Roth's son, Ike shows how limited his moral regeneration has been and how disastrous his relinquishment of responsibility: he offers the girl the money Roth left for her, thus repeating the gesture of old Carothers, who found it cheaper to will money to his Negro offspring than to say "My son to a nigger." Roth had not learned from Ike, who shirked his responsibility, the code which Ike learned from his foster fathers. The touch of the hands of Ike and the girl symbolizes the slightness of Ike's grasp of human affairs and family duty: "the gnarled, bloodless, bone-light bone-dry old man's fingers touching for a second the smooth young flesh where the strong old blood ran after its long lost journey back to home" (p. 362).

The stories in *Go Down, Moses* which do not deal with Ike McCaslin repeat the themes of the exploitation of people and of racial injustice. Lucas Beauchamp and his family are the central characters through whom these themes are developed. "The Fire and the Hearth" takes its title from the fire on Lucas' hearth which is the deliberate symbol of marital fidelity and family unity, imitated by Rider in "Pantaloon in Black." Lucas, grandson of old Lucius Quintus Carothers McCaslin, shortened his first name to Lucas and dropped the other names, symbolizing his independence even of the grandfather of whose blood he was proud. *Beauchamp*, "beautiful field," ironically symbolizes the plantation country which is a major setting in *Go Down, Moses*. Because Lucas reappears, in *Intruder in the Dust*, from the point of view of Charles Mallison, details of his appearance and his house are more clearly presented in the later work. His dress is inherited from old Carothers and proudly, arrogantly worn, "as if he refused, declined to accept even that little of the pattern not only of Negro but of country Negro behavior": the black broadcloth suit, "the raked fine hat and the boiled white shirt . . . and the tieless collar and the heavy watch-chain and the gold toothpick" (*ID* 24). His house, on ten acres held in perpetuity by his heirs, is distinguished from other Negro houses by the portrait of Lucas in his white man's clothes and Molly in a hat, symbolizing Lucas' refusal to have a "field nigger" picture in the house (pp. 14, 15).

Lucas' rejection of the traditional role of the Negro is symbolized in tableaux in both *Go Down, Moses* and *Intruder in the Dust*. Guilty in his treasure-hunting mania of the same misuse of the land represented in Henry Armstid's actual insanity in *The Hamlet*, Lucas is represented in tableaux of digging and using the gold-hunting machine, a white man's method substituted for the dowsing scenes in *The Hamlet* (*GDM* 38, 86, 93). The tableaux in which Lucas gives Molly a bag of candy, in token of reconciliation, and takes the gold-hunting machine to Roth Edmonds signify his abjuration of his misuse of the land and his acceptance of the truth stated by Molly: "God say, 'What's rendered to My earth, belong to Me unto I resurrect it. And let him or her touch it, and beware'" (p. 102). Tableaux of confrontation more obviously and more frequently symbolize Lucas' rejection of his racial role. Most detailed and dramatic is the scene recalled in "The Fire and the Hearth" when he faced Zack across the bed and gripped hands with him, the pistol between them, the jealous husband challenging his rival, regardless of color (p. 56). Although *Intruder in the Dust* as the story of Charles Mallison's initiation will be dealt with later, Charles's own confrontations with Lucas and scenes he observed or heard about provide a whole series of tableaux of the "uppity nigger": turning his hand and dropping on the floor the coins with which Charles had paid for his dinner (*ID* 15–16); walking erect and unseeing, in grief, down the street in his white man's clothes (p. 25); imperturbably eating gingersnaps in the country store in front of a homicidal white man (p. 19); brushing his fine hat when it was knocked off as he was being taken into the jail (p. 44); looking at Charles and saying, "Tell your uncle I wants to see him" (p. 45); in jail, facing first Gavin and Charles and then Charles alone through the barred door, wanting to hire a lawyer or pay a boy to prove his innocence (pp. 59–61, 73); and finally paying what Gavin asks for expenses and waiting for his receipt (pp. 246–47).

Examination of the separate works in the Yoknapatawpha chronicles reveals the consistent care with which Faulkner used both explicit and implicit symbolism to point to themes, from titles of works and names of characters to details of dress, from the world which man created to the natural world of Yoknapatawpha. The multiplicity of details which are realistically authentic but which sustain thematic meaning is impressive, especially in the cumulative effect secured by recurrence of details in different works. Variations in the use of symbols and of symbolic tableaux are due in part to the different narrative methods. The wealth of symbols and of symbolic scenes in *Sanctuary* and *Light in August* is related to the combination in them of symbols provided by the author and the objective views of characters and their observations and memories of events. Strictly speaking, all the symbols and tableaux in *The Sound and the Fury*, Parts I, II, and III, and in *Absalom, Absalom!* are created by the characters, in their selection of details from experience or legend; the richness of I and II, *The Sound and the Fury*, in symbolic details and the poverty of III strikingly demonstrate the dependence of symbolism on the consciousness of characters in subjective methods of narration. *Absalom, Absalom!* differs from the narrator device as used in *The Town* and *The Mansion* in the more deliberate and extensive creation of complete scenes by the narrators, stimulated by listeners and by their own attempt to re-create or to remember in order to understand or to justify. But regardless of the narrative method of a particular work, the characters are placed in the same natural world and society from which the author or the characters make their choices, with both selection and omission of images and symbols carrying implications in relation to the whole world of Yoknapatawpha. The impressive total, even in a far from exhaustive representation, of tableaux of confrontation between races or between individuals engaged in moral choices confirms the thematic significance of such scenes in any one work. Themes and symbols of separate works contribute to the interpretation of the Yoknapatawpha chronicles as a whole.

2

The Mythology
of Yoknapatawpha

FROM SYMBOLS TO MYTH is an easy step on either the religious or the secular path of literary criticism. In "Baptism in the Forest," a title referring to Ike McCaslin in "The Bear," Thomas Merton defined symbols as "signs which release the power of imaginative communion" which are "basic archetypal forms anterior to any operation of the mind, forms which have risen spontaneously with awareness in all religions and which have everywhere provided patterns for the myths in which man has striven to express his search for ultimate meaning and for union with God." "Myth" Merton defined as "a tale with an archetypal pattern capable of suggesting and implying that man's life in the cosmos has a hidden meaning which can be sought and found by one who somehow religiously identifies his own life with that of the hero in the story." In *Go Down, Moses* Merton perceived "a conscious and deliberate construction of myth in order to convey a sense of initiatory awakening into the deeper meaning of life in terms of a tradition of natural wisdom." John Macquarrie, a Protestant professor of theology, defined myth as bearing metaphysical truth and mythology as expressing "in a symbolic manner truths about man's own life and thought." In *Love in the Western World*, Denis de Rougemont interprets myth directly in relation to secular literature and society. "A myth," he said, is "a symbolical fable as simple as it is striking—which sums up an infinite number of more or less analogous situations: a myth makes it possible to become aware at a glance of certain types of *constant relations* and to disengage these from the welter of everyday appearances." In terms most directly relevant to the mythology of Yoknapatawpha. Rougement said that "a myth expresses the *rules of conduct* of a given social or religious group. It issues accordingly from whatever *sacred* principle has presided over the formation of this group."

The Yoknapatawpha chronicles present a whole society and its history; cumulatively they build up a mythology by which that society and its culture may be interpreted, a mythology covering the history of the county and of the chief families and the lives of individual heroes and heroines. Since a mythology is not dependent upon literary forms and structures, individual works will here be of less consequence than the stories of individuals, families, and the community as they may be put together from all the works in the chronicles. The meaning of the Yoknapatawpha chronicles lies essentially in the mythology and in the universal patterns which evolve from the realistic material pertaining to a particular time and place. Fidelity to a social reality is compatible with fidelity to universal truths; to discount either the regional or the universal elements in Faulkner is to misinterpret and undervalue his literary achievement. The themes of separate works and the symbols which point to the themes are part of the mythology but take on a deeper meaning when viewed in relation to the larger themes and patterns of the complete Yoknapatawpha chronicles. From constellations of symbols we turn to the whole solar system.

Most of the Yoknapatawpha fiction was written or at least planned before the approach to literature as myth was well established in modern criticism; Faulkner contributed more to that approach than he was influenced by it. Therefore, both literary and non-literary views of myth are relevant to the Yoknapatawpha fiction, a body of literature which grew out of a society with its own well-developed mythology. Anthropology, philosophy, and psychology afford insights useful in interpreting both the social and literary mythologies. The broad and loose use of *myth* having deprived it of "cognitive utility," as Henry Murray observed in his Introduction to *Myth and Mythmaking*, the "complete and concise view of current usage of the term" in Mark Schorer's *William Blake* provides a definition as useful in this context as in Murray's: "A myth is a large, controlling image that gives philosophical meaning to the facts of ordinary life; that is, which has organizing value for experience. A mythology is a more or less articulated body of such images, a pantheon. . . . All real convictions involve a mythology," either broad or private, literary, social, and religious or fantastic, private, and fanatical. The imagery of myth activates ideologies and influences behavior, and "rational belief is the intellectual formalization of that imagery." Thus "myth is fundamental, the dramatic representation of our deepest intellectual life" and even in modern life is "still the essential substructure of all human activity." Schorer's distinction between "myth" and "mythology" will generally be observed, "mythology" being used to refer to Yoknapatawpha fiction as a whole and "myth" to refer to single novels or to stories of individuals or families.

Myths modern or ancient serve familiar functions. The function of myth in modern times, as stated by William York Tindall, suggests why man's need for myth has been recognized and served by modern writers:

> With ritual it may serve to support belief, but even for those without it, myth retains something of its old potency. Serving the individual as it once served the group, myth may unite him with tradition or society, and, in literature, while uniting the conscious mind with the primitive or unconscious, myth may express the inner by the outer, the present by the past.

Individual and *group* suggest the distinction between ancient and modern myths: modern myths are created by an identified individual, to be read and responded to by an individual.

Ancient myths were anonymous and traditional, shared by groups when literature was still of necessity a source of collective entertainment and instruction. Except for this difference in origin, the ancient myths, like modern ones, were, in the words of René Wellek and Austin Warren, stories "telling of origins and destinies, the explanations a society offers its young of why the world is and why we do as we do, its pedagogic images of the nature and destiny of man." In specific characteristics, ancient myths resemble modern myth-making fiction and poetry, a resemblance unusually strong and consistent in the Yoknapatawpha fiction. Myth, Philip Wheelwright says, has a "radically cognitive function": "Myth . . . is not in the first instance a fiction imposed on one's already given world, but is a way of apprehending that world. Genuine myth is a matter of perspective first, invention second." What knowledge is available concerning the creation of the Yoknapatawpha myth confirms this order of the intellectual processes and the accuracy of applying *myth* rather than *new myth* to

Faulkner's work, with the distinction made by Paul Tillich: "All the talk about the 'new myth' is an indication of how remote the new myth is in actuality. A myth that is sought for as myth is for that very reason repelled. Only when one's thinking has objective reference can a truly mythical element pulsate through it." The first of Herbert Weisinger's four approaches to myth is used here: the poetic approach to myth as primitive, communal, and religious, based on an indispensable principle of unity in the lives of individuals and society. It is derived from Jungian archetypes and from the works of Ernst Cassirer and Bronislaw Malinowski.

In culture, as Malinowski explains, myth plays "a leading part in moral conduct and social organization," constituting "the charter of social organization and the precedent of religious ritual": "Myth, ritual and ethics are definitely but three facets of the same essential fact: a deep conviction about the existence of a spiritual reality which man attempts to control, and by which in turn man is controlled." Paul Tillich similarly accords to myth a primary place in culture, along with language, art, and philosophy also "manifested in symbols": "Cultural reality is in its essence symbolic reality; not because in itself it reflects a reality but rather because, being free from anything-in-itself beyond the empirical, it creates a world of cultural objects." In the breakdown of myth into the religious, the scientific, and "the truly mythical," "the mythical stands forth in its purity and in its true character, as a necessary element in the construction of a meaningful reality."

But myth apprehends the world and reality by including more than the objective aspects of life. According to Otto Rank, in *The Myth of the Birth of the Hero*, myth owes its unanimity to its foundation in "general traits of the human psyche," including particularly and essentially the imaginative faculty and the irrational, man's unconscious and the dreams to which it gives birth. The world of myth, like the world of dreams, reflects human desires: "In terms of narrative," Northrop Frye says, "myth is the imitation of actions near or at the conceivable limits of desire." Like dreams also, myth creates images, annihilates time in an eternal present, and lends itself to varied interpretations.

Because myth has as its function, as Suzanne Langer observes, not escape into the world of fairy tales but "moral orientation," it "does not exhaust its whole function in the telling, and . . . separate myths cannot be left entirely unrelated to any others" but "tend to become systematized." Especially is this true of the Yoknapatawpha chronicles, in which the characters, however sharply differentiated, reflect the characteristic of myth in terms of their society: in Ernst Cassirer's words, "myth binds particulars together in the unity of an image, a mythical figure," such as the stereotypes of the class-caste system. Cassirer described qualities of myth which are particularly relevant to the myth of the South: myth involves an active attitude, a "life feeling" aroused from within and manifest in "love and hate, fear and hope, joy and grief," engendering "mythical fantasy" which "creates a world of specific representatiớns." A perfect exemplification of these qualities, including a proliferation of symbols and rituals, is provided by a "home" football game at "Ole Miss," the University of Mississippi.

The creator of myth, however, has distinctive qualities not found in the society which provides his myth. As a modern creator of myths, Thomas Mann's concept of myth, in "Freud and the Future," may resemble Faulkner's:

> For the myth is the foundation of life; it is the timeless schema, the pious formula into which life flows when it reproduces its traits out of the unconscious. Certainly when a writer has acquired the habit of regarding life as mythical and typical there comes a curious heightening of his artistic temper, a new refreshment to his perceiving and shaping powers, which otherwise occurs much later in life; for while in the life of the human race the mythical is an early and primitive stage, in the life of the individual it is a late and mature one.

Such a "mythically oriented artist," Mann says, looks upon life with "an ironic and superior gaze, . . . for the mythical knowledge resides in the gazer and not in that at which he gazes," and the origin of mythical values "lies in the unconscious." Hans Meyerhoff's two reasons why myths are chosen as literary symbols supplement Mann's statement: "to suggest, within a secular setting, a timeless perspective of looking upon the human situation; and to convey a sense of continuity and identification with mankind in general."

The specific application of modern myth to the novel, the form of literature in which it now finds its greatest scope, is made by Dorothy Van Ghent, referring to *Clarissa Harlowe* in terms equally appropriate to Faulkner's fiction:

> Myth is a dramatic vision of life, and we never cease making myths, accepting myths, believing in myths; even in our own positivistic age, we see life dramatically through the myths offered us by Hollywood, by the commercial advertisements, by the detective story, by local politics, by international diplomacy, or by the physicists. Myth appears in a novel when the action and the particular set of manners represented in the book are organized in a total symbolic construct of such a kind that it not only reflects the aspirations and ideals, the attitudes and customs of a large social group, but also seems to give to these attitudes and customs the sanction of some "higher authority," perhaps the authority of ancient

tradition, perhaps supernatural authority, perhaps the authority of some vaguely defined power-and-knowledge concept such as "law" or "government" or "science" or even "society" itself. Finally, this total symbolic construct is, in myth, projected dramatically. . . . Myth does not offer an intellectual system. What it offers is the dramatization of powers that are assumed to have universal authority over the actions of men. The dominion of allegory (as a total system) is the intellect; the dominion of myth is the irrational.

The irony specified by Mann should be kept in mind in relation to the above remarks on authority which refer to the un-ironic Samuel Richardson.

The dominion of myth being the irrational, the modern creator of myths belongs to the Jungian type of artist, instinctively tapping the resources of the collective unconscious rather than consciously constructing an intellectual allegory. But there is a dual process at work, both unconscious and conscious. The artist's "predisposing factors" enable him, Maud Bodkin said, to assimilate forms from his environment and to objectify what has been "in the fantasy of the community": "Thus he attains for himself vision and possession of the experience engendered between his own soul and the life around him, and communicates that experience, at once individual and collective, to others, so far as they can respond adequately to the words and images he uses." But the artist is also sensitive to the current trends in his culture and creates his myth by conscious transformation of his material into art which expresses his times as well as his unique vision.

Realism being the prevailing trend in the American novel, the combination of myth with realism is natural. Northrop Frye explains the relation of myth to realism: "In myth we see the structural principles of literature isolated; in realism we see the *same* structural principles (not similar ones) fitting into a context of plausibility" by devices called displacement used for making mythical structure plausible in realistic fiction. He finds three organizations of myths and archetypal symbols: undisplaced myth, romance, and realism. "Ironic literature begins with realism and tends toward myth, its mythical patterns being as a rule more suggestive of the demonic than of the apocalyptic. . . ." Precisely this relation between realism and irony is the subject of my article "*As I Lay Dying* as Ironic Quest," and is an aspect of other Yoknapatawpha fiction. The realistic basis of Faulkner's mythical county is the subject of my first book on Yoknapatawpha: *Yoknapatawpha: Faulkner's "Little Postage Stamp of Native Soil."*

The technical virtuosity with which Faulkner handled his realistic material is further evidence, as Hyatt Waggoner noted, of his being attuned to the literary trends of his time: "the fiction of William Faulkner springs not only from the soil of Yoknapatawpha, the sociology of which it reports with such amazing and wonderful verisimilitude; it springs equally . . . from the soil prepared by Eliot and Joyce and the others who were initiating the 'mythological method.' . . ."

Because the mythology of Yoknapatawpha developed gradually, as did the fiction about it, critics for a time failed to recognize the mythic element or, if they did recognize it, misinterpreted the partial version. The attempts of George Marion O'Donnell and Malcolm Cowley to provide coherence for the fiction of Faulkner were unsuccessful because their view was partial. Granted that Wright Morris was correct, that "the final act of coherence is an imaginative act—not a sympathetic disposal of parts—and the man who created the parts must create the whole into which they fit," the parts are now all completed and the man who created them went as far as time permitted him in creating the whole. The act of coherence must be performed by readers.

Malcolm Cowley's modification, in the revised edition of *The Portable Faulkner*, of O'Donnell's "Faulkner's Mythology" corrected only in part O'Donnell's unsound interpretation of early works and fallacious extrapolation from the meaning he discerned. O'Donnell tried to read into Faulkner's mythology the popular myth of the South. He also made the mistake of identifying Faulkner with his neurotic heroes, despite the obvious fact that Faulkner, unlike any of his characters, was a serious, disciplined, impersonal artist. O'Donnell deserves mention here because he had a seminal idea that was right, however wrong he was in his assumptions about what the myth was and in interpretation of particular details. Since O'Donnell and Cowley and Robert Penn Warren pointed out the way, the basic concept of Yoknapatawpha as a mythical world has become common, but it is viewed in different lights, with different emphases, from Greek to Gothic, from geographical to mystical. In *William Faulkner's Gothic Domain* I deal with Gothicism in seven of the Yoknapatawpha novels plus *Snopes*; these novels cover the whole spectrum of Gothicism, which is much broader than most readers realize. The most remarkable feature of Faulkner's use of Gothicism is that he never repeated narrative structure and techniques. After "Faulkner and the Myth of the South" (1961), Richard P. Adams devoted *Faulkner: Myth and Motion* (1968) to Faulkner's use of myth and legend and his own myth of Yoknapatawpha, based on his philosophy of life as motion and change.

What has largely escaped critics who have dealt with Faulkner's mythology is the pervading irony of Faulkner's view and of his art, and the relation between the melodramatic elements which so distressed early critics and the irony those critics missed. In *Anatomy of Criticism* Northrop Frye's Theory of Myth (pp. 147–56) provides the clue to the demonic imagery in Faulkner: it is appropriate to the ironic mode, a late phase in the return to Myth. "Demonic modulation" reverses the usual moral associations of archetypal patterns or images. This demonic imagery may have parody as its theme as in the idyll of Ike Snopes and the cow in *The Hamlet*.

Demonic imagery Frye arranges in a kind of chain of being. The demonic divine world is one of "inscrutable fate or external necessity," giving "the sense of human remoteness and futility in relation to the divine order," a concept akin to Mink Snopes's of Old Moster who will neither help nor hinder (*M* 403). The demonic human world is held together by loyalty to the group "which diminishes the individual" or "contrasts his pleasure with his duty or honor." In Faulkner, individuals are sacrificed to both concepts, to the point of being required to participate in individual revenge or mass lynching. At opposite poles Frye notes the tyrant-leader—rare in Faulkner—and the sacrificed victim; both are illustrated in *Light in August* by Percy Grimm and Joe Christmas. The demonic imagery which parodies the Eucharist symbolism is imagery of torture and mutilation, again illustrated by Percy and Joe. "The demonic erotic relation," symbolized by a harlot who "can never be possessed," is doubly illustrated by Temple Drake and the impotent Popeye, who cannot possess. "The demonic parody of marriage" is incest or homosexuality, which will be specifically dealt with later. Demonic society is the mob, looking for a victim, one of Faulkner's most terrifying repeated images. The animal world is represented by beasts of prey, such as Faulkner's Old Ben and Lion; the serpent, also impressive in "The Bear," is common. The demonic vegetable world may be a waste land—like the Old Frenchman place in *Sanctuary*—or the sinister parody of the tree, the gallows, converted to modern life in Faulkner by the use of burning instead of hanging, as one burns oil instead of wood. The inorganic world may be desert or ruins—ruined mansions in Faulkner—or dead or evil machines, like Bayard's auto and airplane and Lucas' gold-hunting machine. Sinister geometric images are the cross, the circle, the spiral, and the labyrinth, all with their non-sinister counterparts. In *Light in August*, Joe's streets and circle and Lena's roads beautifully illustrate the contrast between sinister and benign versions of the same image.

The elements of fire and water in the demonic world are destructive, not purifying, cleansing, or life-sustaining. The fire Benjy loved finally destroyed him and the Compson house (*M* 322). The "clean flame" which Quentin envisioned was his eternal punishment in hell, not the purifying punishment in Dante's *Purgatorio* from which souls would ultimately emerge and ascend to heaven. The branch in which Caddy played and soiled her drawers was the ominous parallel to the river in which Quentin drowned himself as the consequence of Caddy's defilement. The most horrendous example of the ironic inversion of an ancient mythical ritual into a modern realistic event is that of the European spring fertility rites described by Sir James G. Frazer in *The Golden Bough* in which straw men or witches were burned in effigy to ensure the welfare of the community. Such rites originated in pagan times, and Frazer noted that the heathen rites were believed to have involved human sacrifice. The straw man in Jefferson, destroyed first by the respectable citizens and then burned by a mob led by drummers from out of town, was Lee Goodwin, found guilty of one crime and lynched for another, but innocent of both. The ritual began with anointing the sacrificial victim with coal oil before setting fire to him; the coal oil can exploded and the man carrying it met the same death that Lee did. The fact that there was no such demonic ending in the unrevised galleys of *Sanctuary* is evidence that Faulkner was not trying to reduce the horror in making his revisions. The demonic images which color the Yoknapatawpha chronicles must be recognized as ironic inversions if Faulkner's intent is to be understood.

The definition of irony given by Edwin Honig applies as well to Faulkner's encompassing mythology as it does to allegory, Honig's main concern: "Irony is the traditional mode of the satirist hunting down the disparities which are understood to exist between man's moral and physical nature, between all sanguine expressions of hope in social ideals and in benevolent intentions and the unregenerate condition of human actuality." Irony also provides an "apparently endless continuum of integrative allusions" and symbols "for the unfolding of the basic thematic ambiguity" for Honig's allegorical action or for Faulkner's mythological action. Honig's example is taken from Hawthorne's "Rappaccini's Daughter." Hawthorne and Melville are members of the party of Irony added by R. W. B. Lewis to Emerson's party of Hope and party of Memory: the party of Irony is characterized by its "curious, ambivalent, off-beat kind of traditionalism," expressed in narrative which "revealed its design through an original use of discredited traditional materials." Faulkner's resemblance to both Hawthorne and Melville, particularly in his mythical quality, has often been noted. Irony as a common element in all three is less frequently identified.

Approaching the Yoknapatawpha chronicles as myth, frequently ironic, enriches our responses and lends valuable perspective by serving some of the same functions which Honig attributes to typology: "Typology is . . . an invaluable critical resource because it helps one discern common literary structures in many works, which would otherwise elude one's scrutiny of the individual work. . . . Typology provides a generalized framework for appraising characteristic relationships among different works, not legislative acts to which the works must be made to conform." The combination of typology and mythology, for example, reveals in *As I Lay Dying* the quest romance structure, "an original use of discredited traditional materials," and the mythical significance of the hero's adventures, all instinct with irony.

These perspectives reveal not only literary form but also the function of myth: to aid the individual and society to understand themselves and the rituals of their culture by discovering in myth the basic human patterns. Modern culture and the individual author respond to the same need, as stated by C. G. Jung (*Psyche and Symbol*), to find an antidote for "lifeless rationalism": to "frame a view of the world which adequately explains the meaning of human existence in the cosmos" and which "springs from out psychic wholeness." In *Memories, Dreams, and Reflections*, Jung explained myth as "the revelation of a divine life in man. It is not we who invent myth, rather it speaks to us as a word of God." Culture and an author follow analogous processes in learning "to accept and integrate the irrationality of one's own life and life in general"; tapping the collective unconscious, the author creates the myth in which his readers recognize the elemental human patterns.

The reawakened interest in myth was explained by Joseph Warren Beach as a reaction to "a culture that has deprived us of our primitive mythologies without having weakened the savagery of our passions." Myth provides cultural incentives that serve as what Malinowski calls "integrative imperatives" in times of calamity and thus prevent individual and group disorganization.

Such "integrative imperatives" as determinants of behavior are closely allied to tradition and ritual. Ritual as socially sanctioned action gives man a sense of communal participation and of harmony with nature: the fusion of the two values is particularly evident in "The Bear." The significance of ritual as a way of establishing relationship with the past is manifest in both the action and title of the preceding story, "The Old People." Thus myth unites the public world of ritual and the private world of dream. In myth the individual may find vital links with his personal and cultural past dramatized in literature, a kind of objectification of his experience through imaginative art. His conscious and his unconscious selves are united, as he is united with his society.

In his lifework of creating the mythology of Yoknapatawpha, Faulkner began with the human condition and used the tools at hand, his own county and town (*FU* 168). This material was not only American but definitely Southern. Faulkner could retain the close, accurate observation which is one of the delights and values in his work and still make Yoknapatawpha universal by using archetypal patterns and building them into a total mythology.

II • THE TRADITIONAL MYTH OF THE SOUTH

The mythic approach to his material was made easier and more natural for Faulkner, as a Southern writer, by the fact that the South has preserved, through oral and literary tradition, its own myth, upon which its children are nurtured. Probably in no other part of the United States is there an equally strong sense of tradition or an equally cherished legend. The Southern myth was self-engendered and self-nurtured. It was a dream, W. J. Cash said, dreamed by a region in which "criticism, analysis, detachment" all "took on the aspect of high and aggravated treason," in which "conformity made a nearly universal law," and in which the individual identified himself with the South to such an extent that any "question or doubting of the South in any respect" was taken as a personal challenge. The myth of the South illustrates general principles observed by Ernst Cassirer which help to explain its potency: upon a foundation of a cult (white supremacy) it builds a world and reality to which "all reality seems subject," and believes in this world so intensely that "what seemed to free the spirit from the fetters of things becomes a new fetter which is all the stronger since it is not a mere physical force but a spiritual one."

To suggest how and by what people the myth of the South after the Civil War was created and propagated, two events in 1936 will serve as examples. Margaret Mitchell's *Gone with the Wind* was published and would have been a tremendous success in both the North and the South even if it had not been filmed; William Faulkner's *Absalom, Absalom!* was published and would not have been a popular success even if it had been filmed. The novels of Sir Walter Scott had been a staple of the literary diet before the Civil War, especially in the South, and had contributed to the feudal and chivalric aspects of social ideals which were already anachronistic when the South was first settled. Margaret Mitchell belonged to the tradition of plantation novelists like Thomas Nelson Page, whose novels after the Civil War had a nostalgic appeal. But the gospel of the Southern myth was both conceived and disseminated by writers such as Thomas Dixon whose basic propagandist purpose, according to Gavin Davenport, was "the preservation of Anglo-Saxon supremacy." In *The Myth of Southern History*, Davenport gives a lengthy account of Dixon's novels, of which *The Clansman* was the most influential in the North in the motion-picture version, D. W. Griffith's *The Birth of a Nation*. In 1915 Dixon persuaded President Wilson to approve the showing of the film against the protests of the NAACP and white liberals. Davenport commented that the South "needed a myth to replace the one shattered by the Civil War and Reconstruction." But the one fostered by Dixon catered to desires and illusions, not to the needs of active life.

Cultural and moral awakening in the South, therefore, demands as a preliminary step the correction of the myth by another which can furnish valid imperatives and provide an applicable code, retaining the best of the old in terms of universal human values. The South and with it the nation need to be liberated as a people from a myth which has kept them enslaved, black and white alike, and has stifled development of potentialities. As Joanna Burden's father put it: "You must struggle, rise. But in order to rise, you must raise the shadow with you" (*LA* 222). The individual needs to be liberated from the ghosts created by the collective unconscious. Maud Bodkin might have been speaking of Faulkner's heroes haunted by the past, like Quentin Compson and Gail Hightower: "Every individual in whose fantasy such mighty ghosts arise, with their superhuman claims and relationships, must learn to distinguish such claims from those of the personal self; while yet the personal self may be enriched through the conscious experience of its relation to the great forces which such figures represent." The collective unconscious, she continues, "in its spontaneous movement toward expression generates alike the hero figures of myth and legend"; the "mind of the South" in similar fashion generated, from the recent past, figures of legend that even more potently "appearing in individual fantasy, may overwhelm the personal consciousness." Gail Hightower in *Light in August* was overwhelmed by one image of his grandfather; Quentin was overwhelmed by all the stories he had to listen to too long (*AA* 207). If the need for liberation is more prevalent than the achievement of liberation, that fact may explain why it seemed to many readers, during the evolution of the Yoknapatawpha chronicles, that Faulkner, who was trying to show the need, was pessimistic and that he painted a picture of hopeless gloom, and why, by contrast, in Faulkner's fiction and in the legend, the ante-bellum past looked brighter.

The spell of the legend of the South is so strong, thanks to fiction and moving pictures which are as popular in the North as in the South, that one expects a Southern writer to subscribe to it. The moonlight and

magnolia romance, with a backdrop of gleaming white columns pic-
turesquely enhancing the dalliance of beautiful young ladies and gallant
young gentleman, had little basis in reality in the late-settled and poorly
endowed region of northern Mississippi. In chronology of early settlement, southeastern Wisconsin, for example, is precisely comparable
with northern Mississippi. Faulkner varies little from actual dates in his
account of Jefferson, to which Sutpen came in 1833, when there were
only a tavern and a store where the square was to be; Milwaukee was a
village in 1835. The University of Mississippi opened the same year as
Milwaukee–Downer Seminary, 1848, and a year before the University
of Wisconsin, 1849. Middlewest northerners are apt to be misled by
the legend and to think of their own region as raw and new and of the
South east of the Mississippi as mellow and old. Cash sums up the
"Old South of the legend in its classical form":

> Its social pattern was manorial, its civilization was that of the Cavalier,
> its ruling class an aristocracy coextensive with the planter group—
> . . . in every case descended from the old gentlefolk who for many centu-
> ries had made up the ruling classes of Europe.
>   They dwelt in large and stately mansions, preferably white and with
> columns and Grecian entablature. Their estates were feudal baronies,
> their slaves quite too numerous ever to be counted, and their social life a
> thing of Old World splendor and delicacy . . . a world singularly polished
> and mellow and poised, wholly dominated by ideals of honor and chival-
> ry and *noblesse*—all those sentiments and values and habits of action
> which used to be, especially in Walter Scott, invariably assigned to the
> gentleman born and the Cavalier.

This ruling class, according to the legend, was Anglican (p. 55). Far
below this master class were the poor whites, "a physically inferior
type" whose "ideas and feelings did not enter into the make-up of the
prevailing Southern civilization." In the legend, this Old South was
completely destroyed by the Civil War and the New South is an industrialized and modernized region. Cash concludes with the idea that the
break between the Old and the New South "has been vastly exaggerated" and that "the mind of the section . . . is continuous with the
past," the thesis which he then develops in *The Mind of the South*.
This, Richard King said, "can be read as a gloss on much of Faulkner's
work."

Cash's explanation of how this legend grew up and of how it deviates
from the facts applies particularly to such parts of the South as
Yoknapatawpha County represents. By the Civil War and Reconstruction the master class was halted in its march toward the aristocracy
that had not been achieved in the short period of a generation between

settlement of the country and the Civil War. Trying to cling to their ascendancy, the master class looked back on the past "with an intense regret and nostalgia": "while the actuality of aristocracy was drawing away toward the limbo of aborted and unrealized things, the claim of its possession as an achieved and essentially indefeasible heritage, so far from being abated, was reasserted with a kind of frenzied intensity." The legend of the Old South took form during this period:

> Perpetually suspended in the great haze of memory, it hung, as it were, poised somewhere between earth and sky, colossal, shining, and incomparably lovely—a Cloud-Cuckoo-Land wherein at last everybody who had ever laid claim to the title of planter would be metamorphosed . . . into the breathing image of Marse Chan and Squire Effingham, and wherein life would move always in stately and noble measure through scenery out of Watteau.

The common whites took pride in the legend, which shed some of its glory on them—Wash Jones, the perfect example, identified himself so fully with Sutpen, as Mr. Compson conjectured, that "the actual world was the one where his own lonely apotheosis . . . galloped on the black thoroughbred," and that Wash "would look at Sutpen and think *A fine proud man. If God Himself was to come down and ride the natural earth, that's what He would aim to look like*" (*AA* 282).

This stereotype of the ante-bellum plantation system as an aristocratic timocracy included several other features of the social structure inherent in the basic concept and, like it, derived from the Southern tendency toward unreality, romanticism, and sentimentality. This society was exclusive in the aristocratic class, patriarchal in the family, and paternalistic in the self-contained world of the plantation. The common whites were loyal and subservient because they saw in the planter "their obviously indicated captain in the great common cause" of white supremacy (Cash, p. 69). The plantation owner was lord and master in his own household and the protector of the white women in his family. And he was the Great White Father to the Negroes:

> The South's perpetual need for justifying its career, and the will to shut away more effectually the vision of its mounting hate and brutality toward the black man, entered into the equation also and bore these people yet further into the cult of the Great Southern Heart. The Old South must be made not only the happy country but the happy country especially for the Negro. . . . The only bonds were those of tender understanding, trust, and loyalty.

Writing later than Cash, the year of the centennial celebration of the Civil War in 1961, Frank Vandiver examined "The Confederate myth,

. . . a vital part of life in the South." "Key elements in the Southern mode of living," he said, "were tradition, dedication to the protocols of lineage, land, cotton, sun, and vast hordes of blacks." Using the monuments of the dead heroes as a symbol, Vandiver explained what had happened: "Their stone faces look from countless shafts to the past, and their sons, grandsons, and great-grandsons look with them." But the mythmakers, "falsifiers of history," changed the Confederate "from a human, striving, erring being to something much different. All Confederates automatically became virtuous, all were the defenders of the rights of states and individuals, all were segregationists, all steadfast, all patriotic. . . . Like all lasting myths, this one had enough validity to sound good."

The defense of tradition was the defense of the interests and the continued prestige of the aristocrats; consequently the tradition served to foster idealized and romanticized concepts of gentlemen and ladies whose high estate would be clearly no more than their due. The ideal hero was characterized by his courage, even foolhardiness; by his fondness for living the noble role in which he had cast himself, with its magniloquent speech and splendid gestures; and by his obedience to the code of honor and chivalry within his own class.

The great-grandson looking at the stone face described by Vandiver could be William Faulkner looking at the monument of Colonel William C. Falkner, the model for that of Colonel John Sartoris in the cemetery in Jefferson (*Sar.* 375). The original is still in the cemetery at Ripley, Mississippi. Col. Falkner seems to have taken the ideal hero as a model, although in the booming days before the Civil War he was a self-made man, not an aristocrat. He was rewarded for his ambition by becoming a legend which owed not a little to his ability as his own press agent and to his tendency to recast the events of his life to suit his purpose. John Philip Duclos found the reality quite different from the legend as it has been preserved by Mississippians: "In capturing word-pictures of a glorified, fictionalized, even gallant old Southern gentleman, they have created a new man who bears only the slightest resemblance to the man who really lived."

Colonel Falkner's life was one of those which contributed to the legend of the Old South: from the beginning it was characterized, as Duclos said, by a pattern of "violence, ambition, daring, and even arrogance in which he would be catapulted to local fame and notoriety throughout his life." Old man Falls in *Sartoris* exemplifies the way in which the legend was built and preserved, and illustrates the point made by Irving Howe in "The Southern Myth and William Faulkner": "the Southern emphasis on honor and heroism may often have been a means of salvaging pride from defeat or a token of uncertainty about the moral value of its cause."

The ideal heroine, like the hero, would have been at home in a Scott romance. The cult of courtly love, however, was transformed in the Southern legend to what Cash describes as a cult of gyneolatry, in which the practical consideration of insuring the purity of the legitimate line was masked by the myth of passionless purity of aristocratic white women. The unspeakable atrocity of rape of white women figured much more prominently in the myth than did miscegenation owing to white male aggression; the prominence of the themes seems to have been in a kind of inverse proportion to the incidence of the offenses. Cash estimated that a white woman was less likely to be raped by a Negro than to be struck by lightning.

The myth of the "Southern Lady" to modern readers, especially women, is the least credible part of the myth of the South. Based on what Cash called gyneolatry, the secular version of Mariolatry, it owes much to the tradition of medieval chivalry, kept alive in the South by the novels of Sir Walter Scott. The glorification of women in the Southern myth is firmly rooted in the patriarchal society where women had roles only as wives and mothers. Male homage was one means of "conditioning" women to accept their submissive roles. Anne F. Scott's study *The Southern Lady: From Pedestal to Politics, 1830–1930* is based chiefly on unpublished letters and diaries which confirm what one would suspect, that the mythic image of feminine perfection did have some power to shape the reality and to make piety and virtue and wifely devotion goals to strive for. The universal view in the male-dominated society was that Southern ladies were not erotic. Only one life was possible for a Protestant lady, who could not get her to a nunnery: marriage or else! "If you defy the pattern and behave in unlady-like ways you will be unsexed, rejected, unloved, and you will probably starve." The same dismal fate confronted spinster ladies in Victorian England. In her introduction to *Suffer and Be Still: Women in the Victorian Age*, Martha Vicinus said of spinsters of good social status who had no relative with whom they could live: "few survived at the same social level they had been born to." She concluded: "All social forces combined to leave the spinster emotionally and financially bankrupt."

A dismal picture of the Southern lady when she was off her pedestal is presented in Mary Boykin Chesnut's *A Diary from Dixie*. Her opportunities for observing Southern life were exceptionally broad; being childless, she had more freedom to come and go and she moved in the best society. An exceptional woman herself, her evidence of Southern life from 1861 to 1886 is "a masterpiece of history in the highest and fullest sense," in the words of Ben Ames Williams, the editor of the 1961 edition.

But the Southern lady of the myth of the South was not invented by Southern gentlemen. The essays in *Suffer and Be Still: Women in the Victorian Age* which present the Victorian ideal of the "perfect lady" show that ideal to be basically the same as the myth of the South. But the Victorian men who promoted the ideal were not seeking to preserve the outmoded social system of the plantation and slavery. The introductory description of the Victorian ideal "most fully developed in the upper middle class" fits the ladies of Yoknapatawpha so well that it will aid the modern reader to realize imaginatively why Faulkner's women acted as they did and in particular how few choices were available to them.

> Before marriage a young girl was brought up to be perfectly innocent and sexually ignorant. The predominant ideology of the age insisted that she have little sexual feeling at all, although family affection and the desire for motherhood were considered innate. Morally she was left untested, and kept under the watchful eye of her mother in her father's home. . . . Once married, the perfect lady did not work; she had servants. She was mother only at set times of the day, even of the year; she left the heirs in the hands of nannies and governesses. Her social and intellectual growth was confined to the family and close friends. Her status was totally dependent upon the economic position of her father and then her husband. In her most perfect form, the lady combined total sexual innocence, conspicuous consumption and the worship of the family hearth.

For the Southern lady, read "mammies" for "nannies." Governnesses were rare except in Gothic romances "displaced" to America.

Martha Vicinus, editor of the book and author of the introduction, points out that the ideal was far removed from the "objective situations of countless women" and that "few women could afford to pursue" the ideal, "economically, socially, or psychologically." But these practical considerations were ignored. A girl's education "was to bring out her 'natural' submission to authority and innate maternal instincts. Young ladies were trained to have no opinions lest they seem too formed and too definite for a young man's taste and thereby unmarketable as a commodity." As one would expect, "few women of character fit the ideal lady." But the role was made attractive enough to innocent girls by the "chaste woman" being seen as "exerting an all-pervasive moral influence within the home" to make women "the greatest enforcers of standards of moral behavior (defined in purely sexual terms). . . ."

The essay in *Suffer and Be Still* which is most pertinent to Faulkner's ladies is "Innocent Femina Sensualis in Unconscious Conflict," by Peter T. Cominos. Because Faulkner did not give the reader access to the consciousness of women except the Bundrens, who were not ladies, I had entertained many questions about Faulkner's ladies which Cominos answers. Some of the basic elements in the "unconscious conflict" will be illustrated in girls and women in Yoknapatawpha. The innocence which represses sexual desires renders the conflict unconscious between those desires and the ideals women aspired to. To respectable Victorians "innocence" or "inherent purity" was considered "an exalted state of feminine consciousness," and daughters were preserved in a state of mindlesness in which they were "forbidden knowledge of their own sexuality, instincts, and desires as well as the knowledge of good and evil." "Once innocence was lost, the daughter's chastity became vulnerable." Because "repressive innocence created psychological resistance to the conscious acknowledgment of sexual realities" unacceptable to "the world of respectability," "innocent Femina Sensualis was beset by an unconscious conflict between a repressed conscience and unconscious sexual desires." As a consequence of this conflict, girls would suffer guilt and anxiety which would arouse their doubts as to "the completeness . . . of their innocence."

Men were the same in England or Yoknapatawpha: the "double standard" allowed men to protect the innocence of their wives and daughters and to obey the nature of their own desires without scruples. The motto of gentlemen seems to have been the Rabelaisian "Fay ce que vouldras." In *The Other Victorians* Steven Marcus exposes the secret life of some Victorian gentleman to whom Miss Reba's establishment would have been as respectable, comparatively speaking, as she could have wished.

Having no choice but to submit to parents or husbands, ladies had no responsibility. Gentlemen were supposed to be "masters of themselves and self-controlled," but ladies "were to be controlled or 'protected' by others." Men could sublimate their sexual instincts by their occupation or profession, but the only channel of sublimation available to most women was religion. "In the Evangelical version of ideal love, passion was completely deflected from all other human beings to the love of Christ."

The theory of the "seduction of the innocent" in the 1850s and 1860s put the responsibility on the man, not on the "angelic, non-seductive, non-cooperative, naïve, helpless victim." By the 1890s this theory was revised, and seductive and cooperative women might be guilty

(Jefferson still clung to the old theory, rooted in the myth, in 1929). Unchastity turned a woman into a prostitute or a mistress. A woman was classified by her known sexual behavior: she was either "a respectable member of the family or one who had fallen below the line of respectability into . . . prostitution, the negation of the family."

It is clear that "women were classified into polar extremes," sexless "ministering angels" or "oversexed temptresses" of the devil. These polarities of prostitution and the family in the world of respectability caused women's depravity to be lamented and their "angelic innocence" to be exalted and women "to be placed on a pedestal." And the innocence of women caused the "daughter's first love to be authoritarian," a father figure. But prostitutes and madams, "having acquired the price of their withdrawal . . . chose to make a dash for respectability."

Cominos ends with a paraphrase of the Communist Manifesto: "The Womanly Woman had nothing to lose but her tightly corseted existence, hang-ups, guilt-feelings, crucified flesh, innocent mindlessness, and self-absorbing roles of daughter, wife and mother."

The similarities between the England of Dickens and the Mississippi of Faulkner are greater than the influence of Dickens would explain. But the similarities of the two societies confirm the broader scope of the Yoknapatawpha myth than the myth of the South with its outmoded political, social, and economic goals. The roles of women in that myth are not adequately accounted for by such extravagant homage as the fraternity toast Wilbur Cash quoted from Carl Carmer: acolytes carry "a long cake of ice" and "the leader mounted on a table," lifts a glass of water and proposes this toast: "To Woman, lovely woman of the Southland, as pure and chaste as this sparkling water, as cold as this gleaming ice, we lift this cup, and we pledge our hearts and our lives to the protection of her virtue and chastity" (p. 340). The leader is not pure, chaste, or sober; this is a cult ritual, which could never be addressed to the ideal lady of Victorian England. But the myth of the South and Faulkner's imagination cannot be credited—or discredited—with responsibility for the patriarchal society and the feminine stereotypes to which women were forced to conform.

Not only the ideal of the family but the importance of consanguinity is reflected in the patriarchal society of the myth of the South. The multitude of cousins and of uncles and of aunts in Southern families, the proverbial "kissing kin," rivals the consanguineous entourage of the Rt. Hon. Sir Joseph Porter in *H.M.S. Pinafore*. The myth does not stress the fact, noted by Cash (pp. 28–29), that the aristocracy often had kin far below their own exalted rank. The isolation of plantation life, in myth and fact, strengthened family ties and fostered hospitality to friends and kinfolk for extended visits which enlivened daily routine or holiday celebrations in the mansion. Family ties with any off-white members of the household were rarely honored, in myth or fact. The deviations in Yoknapatawpha from the mythic family patterns will be dealt with later.

In the post-bellum legend, the ante-bellum history of a community, like the history of a plantation family, came to follow a characteristic pattern. Men of wealth came into the new territory, with slaves and money, and bought great tracts of land on which they developed prosperous plantations and lived lives of elegance. The prototypes of these men and their splendid estates were to be found in the Tidewater plantations and in New Orleans: Cash says, "Here, indeed, there was a genuine, if small, aristocracy. Here was all that in aftertime was to give color to the legend of the South."

During the Civil War, men of these families, in Mississippi often the very founders themselves, distinguished themselves as valiant leaders, sacrificing personal advantage to the Cause and often losing all they possessed except the land itself; the lucky ones returned to find the mansion still standing, in disrepair if not in ruins.

During the Reconstruction period, the former army officers retained their leadership over the whites in their communities in the struggle with the carpetbaggers, striving to retain white supremacy and to rehabilitate their plantations: in this conflict, the gentlemen with noble principles were pitted against crass and vulgar opportunists, black or white. The sentimental cult of the Confederate hero, part of the legendary heritage, was vividly described by Cash:

> Every boy growing up in this land now had continually before his eyes the vision, and heard always in his ears the clamorous hoofbeats of a glorious swashbuckler, compounded of Jeb Stuart, the golden-locked Pickett, and the sudden and terrible Forrest (yes, and, in some fashion, of Lord Roland and the douzepers) forever charging the cannon's mouth with the Southern battle flag.

The authenticity of this account of the legend is vouched for, by implication, in the very similar passage in *Intruder in the Dust* (pp. 194–95), reflecting the youthful experiences of Gavin Stevens and Charles Mallison. Having known misfortune and tragedy, the Southern aristocrats, in poetic justice, unconsciously ironic, took satisfaction in regarding themselves as the Chosen People, even as their slaves had done before them. (The longing and suffering which the slaves put into the spiritual "Go Down, Moses" provided Faulkner with a title.) "For is it not written that whom He loves He chastens?'' Thus could the defeat of the South be interpreted as a sign of God's favor (Cash, p. 135). From such concepts, proponents of the myth of the South, notably Thomas Dixon, were inspired with a sense of the mission of the South to redeem the nation through a national mythology which would, as Garvin Davenport said, ''eliminate the Negro from political and social participation in American life.'' As new sources of wealth developed and common men prospered through adapting themselves to the new economy, these men, Cash said, were unfavorably compared with the old pattern of success, with ''its contempt for mere money-grubbing, and its positive pride in a certain looseness of attention to affairs, in scorn for thrifty detail; the careless tolerance of innefficiency and humane aversion for the role of harsh taskmaster.''

And if the succeeding generations of the old aristocratic families found themselves reduced to genteel poverty, living in the decayed mansion and served by devoted black servants, their fine possessions gaining luster by becoming only a memory, those survivors became invested with a melancholy radiance from the past glory of which they dreamed.

Evidence that Faulkner's myth of Yoknapatawpha influenced Southern historians and critics of literature appears in *Myth and Southern History* as a kind of thematic prelude, before the table of contents and the introduction: the passage from *Intruder in the Dust* is quoted which describes the feeling for history of ''every Southern boy fourteen years old'' (pp. 194–95). This collection of essays, edited by Patrick Gerster and Nicholas Cords, reflects the depth and breadth of studies of the myth of the South which followed the publication in 1964 of George B. Tindall's ''Mythology: A New Frontier in Southern History.'' *Myth and Southern History* and the appended ''Suggestions for Further Reading'' are invaluable for readers who are interested in the mythic approach to the study of Faulkner and other Southern writers. The departure of the myth of the South from historical fact is a major topic in a number of the essays by authorities on social, political, and literary history.

But Faulkner's myth of Yoknapatawpha touches so slightly on historical events that it is not the historical truth or falsity of the myth which concerns us but rather its effect on the society represented in Yoknapatawpha. The paralyzing effect of the myth illustrates Malinowski's principle that culture acts as a vast ''conditioning apparatus'' on social organization and conduct. If a life of poverty and idleness is accepted by ''the people who really count'' in a community, and if the energetic people who prosper through their own efforts are scorned as vulgar materialists, indolence may be more attractive than industry. The myth shapes the culture, which "thus produces individuals whose behavior cannot be understood by the study of anatomy and physiology alone, but has to be studied through the analysis of cultural determinism—that is, the process of conditioning and molding."

Faulkner's myth of Yoknapatawpha is not the simple one George Marion O'Donnell took it to be, a losing struggle of Sartorian virtue against Snopesian evil. Having been himself conditioned by the myth, Faulkner soon broke away from the conventional pattern which he said had no place for the creative artist (*FU* 197). His new myth, rooted in a searching examination of the values and motives which impel man to action, is a kind or ironic inversion, at key points, of the traditional myth: not a negation of genuine values of that myth but a repudiation of its falsities. He saw his society, like Hightower in his window, paralyzed by its nostalgic absorption in the dream of the past, and in effect conveyed his message: "life is motion and the only alternative to motion is stasis—death. It's bound to change whether we like it or not" (*FWP* 98).

III • POLARITY OF YOKNAPATAWPHA THEMES

The dynamic quality of the mythology of Yoknapatawpha, as it is built up by the narratives and themes of individual works, reflects Faulkner's concept of life as motion and the tensions created by sharply contrasted themes. From the duality of good and evil and the thematic polarities, the dominant patterns of the mythology gradually emerge in separate works and reveal an evolving design in the whole body of Yoknapatawpha fiction.

But the dualism is much older and more pervasive than that of any one religion or society. It is as old as light and darkness and the powers of light and darkness which pervaded Faulkner's cosmos, as Michael Routh perceives it in "The Story of All Things": the Life Force struggling against "the world's ambiguities." In *The Quest* Mircea Eliade said that "the cosmic polarity, expressed by the symbols *yang* and *yin* . . . furnished quite early the model for a universal classification" in China. *Yang* as representing a masculine nature and *yin* a feminine one, "the ritual opposition of the two sexes . . . expresses simultaneously the complementary antagonism of two modes of being and the alternation of two cosmic principles, *yang* and *yin*." In *Memories*, C. G. Jung described the psyche as a flow of energy between two poles. In *Man and his Symbols*, M.-L. von Franz, one of Jung's coauthors, explains another Jungian theory: "every personfication of the unconscious—the shadow, the anima, the animus, and the Self—has both a light and a dark aspect. . . . The anima and animus have dual aspects: They can bring life-giving development and creativeness to the personality, or they can cause petrification and physical death." In society, the polarities range from sacred and profane time and space to the male–female polarity. And within the female sex, especially in the myth of the South and of Yoknapatawpha, to use Naomi Jackson's title, we have "Faulkner's Woman: Demon–Nun and Angel–Witch." The Victorians had prostitutes and ideal women.

Dualism or polarity being so universal in the cosmos, in living beings, in the human race and society, and in psychology and experience, and in the apocalyptic and demonic worlds of myth, according to Northrop Frye's theory of myth, it seems unnecessary to apply the religious term "Manichean" to Yoknapatawpha, as Heinrich Straumann did, an unlikely context for Faulkner's kind of dualism. It is interesting, however, that Richard King described Wilbur Cash's "Man at the Center" in the South at the beginning of the Civil War as "possessed of a Manichean world-view." Although such "a dualistic view is rejected by Christianity," as John Macquarrie said (*Principles of Christian Theology*), the Calvinistic denominations were still strong in the South, well into the twentieth century. Calvinistic separation of souls into the elect and the damned and the self-righteousness of the elect, like Doc Hines and Percy Grimm, suggests that both Cash and Faulkner recognized this aspect of the myth of the South. In *Light in August* Faulkner linked good–bad, elect–damned polarity with the white–black racial division in society, as Gavin Stevens did in explaining Joe's good white blood as keeping him from shooting someone in his last flight. The myth of the South had as its goal the permanent inequality of the two races, with white society dominant.

Jung's theory about how a symbol is born illuminates Faulkner's polarity of imagination and the creative process by which he produced his myth:

> Only the passionate yearning of a highly developed mind, for which the conventional symbol no longer expresses in one image the ultimate reconciliation of painfully conflicting elements, can create a new symbol. Yet, inasmuch as the symbol not only proceeds from man's most complex mental achievement, but has at least an equal source in the lowest and most primitive motions of his psyche. . . . such a condition necessarily entails a violent disunion with oneself, even to the point where the conflicting elements mutually deny each other, while the ego nevertheless is forced to acknowledge their existence and its own participation in the

conflict. The energy engendered by the tension of the opposites flows
into the creation of the symbol . . . .

This explanation of Jung's theory, from Violet de Laszlo's introduction
to *Psyche and Symbol*, brought to my mind the perfect example provided in the myth of the South: the Ku Klux Klan's fiery cross. By
pure serendipity I later found in *Man and His Symbols* a photograph of
white-robed Klansmen in front of a blazing cross, exemplifying an
example of " 'a collective infection' that can weld people into an irrational mob—and to which the *shadow* (the dark side of the ego-per-
sonality) is vulnerable.'' The statement about the symbol applies also
to the myth, extending the application of the basic idea to the more
complex creative process.

"Tension" and "energy" in the above passage are terms relevant
not only to the polarity of themes but also to Faulkner's prevailing
concept of life as motion, developed at length in Warren Beck's *Man in
Motion* on the trilogy, *Snopes*, and by Richard Adams in *Faulkner:
Myth and Motion*. This concept casts light upon a group of themes
related to time, space, and motion. Life is flux, is change, is motion, to
which the only alternative is death and nothingness. Peace is a condition which man is incapable of achieving in the present, "a condition
in retrospect, when the subconscious has got rid of the gnats and the
tacks and the broken glass in experience and has left only the peaceful
pleasant things . . . . Maybe peace is not is but was" (*FU* 190, 267, 67).

The polarities in the human psyche do not require a choice of one or
the other pole but a synthesis. Stasis is as unnatural to man as peace: a
dynamic–static polarity equates life with motion. In the first chapter of
Quest for Failure, "Motion and Immobility," Walter Slatoff traced the
antithesis through the Yoknapatawpha fiction and some works outside
Faulkner's "cosmos." Slatoff showed antithesis to be "part of the
very form and texture of experience and events," related to "the
protracted physical movements such as journeys, races, pursuits, and
flights." After Slatoff's book was published, *The Reivers* confirmed
Slatoff's comment on the importance of physical movement by devoting a whole novel to journeys and races and, as a kind of valedictory of
Faulkner to his cosmos and his readers, provided what Slatoff had
sought in vain: a triumph of virtue over evil. Slatoff conceived of Faulkner's work as based on a choreography of motion including "even the
earth itself, spinning, slowing, or racing to destruction"; he ascribed
much of Faulkner's power to this "dance" and "its continual stimula-
tion of kinesthetic and motor responses in the reader." The contrasting
images of stasis, of arrested or frozen motion, heighten the effect of

motion. In "Flux and the Frozen Moment" (1956) and "Faulkner's Garden: Woman and the Immemorial Earth" (1956), Karl Zink had dealt with the basic antithesis and with the theme of flux. Gary Lee Stonum in *Faulkner's Career* (1979) identifies the theme of motion and the concept of arrested motion as significant aspects of the "procession" of "transformations" which constituted Faulkner's career.

Recognition of Faulkner's concept of change and motion and its relation to the antithetical themes of tradition and progress would have prevented misinterpretation based on the assumption, especially in the early stages of the creation of Yoknapatawpha, that Faulkner would be pro-tradition. In his later works as well as in public statements Faulkner made it clear that he viewed change and motion and progress as inescapable facts of human life and that "the only alternative to progress is death" (*FU* 5). Faulkner of course recognized the need for acceleration of spiritual progress to keep it apace of mechanical and technological progress, but man has no alternative but to compromise and cope with progress (*FU* 68, 98). Man's responsibility is therefore to control change to keep it from being destructive and to initiate change for worthy motives and ends. The wilderness can be replaced by something better if men choose to plan and act wisely: to provide more food and education for people, more leisure for enjoyment of the good things in life, rather than extend the "agrarian economy of peonage" (*FU* 277).

Faulkner's characters may indulge in nostalgia for the good old days or want to stop the clock of time or regard with pessimistic resignation a degenerating society in which man seems helpless to control his fate and better his condition. The theme of tradition and the past versus progress and the present and future is another basic theme, with a realistic preponderance of characters representing tradition; not only social classes are involved, with the decline of the aristocrats and the rise of the common man, but also all individuals of any class whose lives are materially and spiritually affected by their attitudes toward tradition and the past.

Faulkner's attitude toward the past was psychologically and sociologically sound. He recognized that as people grow old, they look back nostalgically at the past; his own feeling that "the old times were the best times" (*FU* 68) was a psychological feeling, not a philosophical conviction. He would have agreed with Jung on the danger of the rigidity that may accompany age in those who cling to the old views: "They are not defaulters, merely slowly dying trees, or . . . 'witnesses of the past.' But the accompanying symptoms, the rigidity, the narrow-mindedness, the lagging behind of these *laudatores temporis acti* are undesirable manifestations." The solution Jung indicates is also one which Faulkner would have agreed with and which he himself experienced, according to the testimony of his writings: "the retaining of the former values together with a recognition of their opposites. This naturally means conflict and division within oneself." What is true of the individual is also true of society and social institutions: as Malinowski said, institutions are subverted by "blind adherence to outworn truths and obsolete habits" and by the concept, a relic of loyalty to the tribe, that progress is evil or sinful. Ernst Cassirer's statement about Taoism shows the consequences of raising traditionalism to a religious doctrine and ethical principle: "the future has religious justification only insofar as it can legitimize itself as a simple continuation, an exact and faithful copy of the past"; thus "the given order of things . . . is perpetuated and sanctified."

To hold progress in check and to return to the past are equally impossible; the tradition–progress antithesis is parallel to the nature–civilization antithesis, which, however, can use setting as the base of essential symbols. Despite his regret at the passing of the wilderness, his own image of nature, Faulkner was neither an agrarian when that cultural ideal flourished nor a Rousseauistic advocate of a return to nature. When asked specifically whether he agreed with the idea "that we should return to nature to recover our whole and proper humanity," Faulkner replied:

> I don't hold to the idea of a return. That once the advancement stops, then it dies. It's got to go forward and we have got to take along with us all the rubbish of our mistakes and our errors. We must cure them; we mustn't go back to a condition, an idyllic condition, in which the dream [made us think] we were happy, we were free of trouble and sin. We must take the trouble and sin along with us, and we must cure that trouble and sin as we go [FN 77–78].

Although Faulkner used nature as a positive value in human life and used harmony with nature as a characteristic of his admirable characters, he was, as Wilson Clough said, neither a primitivist nor a romanticist dreaming of a lost paradise nor a Hawthorne nor a Conrad using the forest as a symbol of the heart of darkness. The noble savage and the state of nature have their elegy in the death of Sam Fathers, the one "child of nature" who could resist corruption by the white man. Faulkner did not show the Negro as a child of the wilderness. Lucas Beauchamp was at home in cultivated nature and was sophisticated in the ways of men in civilization. Go Down, Moses, especially "The Old People" and "The Bear" and the short stories about Indians, best represents these themes of the wilderness and the encroachment of civilization, symbolized by the logging camp and the railroad. *Absalom, Absalom!* dramatizes the conversion of the wilderness into incongruous magnificence. *Requiem for a Nun* embraces the whole span of time in this little spot of earth and the stages in the progress of civilization as it supplanted the wilderness.

Here Faulkner carried to its limit the eternal–temporal theme and reveals the universal and cosmic dimensions of his vision. The earth, as Karl Zink said, is the setting for the human drama: "Faulkner casts the human condition against fundamental processes, the raw common denominator of life on Earth, and it is quite possible that the male's ambiguous fear and hatred and love of woman must be explained in terms of his fear and hatred and love of the old Earth itself, to which Woman is so disturbingly related." The timelessness of Faulkner's vision, its almost Greek sense of elemental truths, is expressed also by Millar MacLure: "For his vision of humanity draws its power from blood and earth as religious entities, *daimonoi*, demanding initiation, permitting passion and honor and even a little justice, promising dust." What was revealed by the mythic consciousness of William Faulkner in his own cosmos was explained by Jung, in *Man and His Symbols*, in psychological terms:

> Today . . . we talk of "matter." . . . But the word "matter" remains a dry, inhuman, and purely intellectual concept, without any psychic signifi-cance for us. How different was the former image of matter—the Great Mother—that could encompass and express the profound emotional meaning of Mother Earth. In the same way, what was spirit is now identified with intellect and thus ceases to be the Father of All. It has degenerated to the limited ego-thoughts of man; the immense emotional energy expressed in the image of "our Father" vanishes into the sand of an intellectual desert.

The racial polarity in Yoknapatawpha, although it suggests the black–white contrast traditionally associated with evil and good, car-ries no such conventional moral symbolism nor the ironic reversal, equating black with good and white with evil. Although Negroes are credited with distinctive virtues and with capacity to survive, Faulkner's subject is man. The basic theme involving the racial polar-ity is the exploitation of human beings and the concomitant injustice. The particular nature of the exploitation is determined by the setting, whether the workers are black or white. Faulkner said that the problem was not racial nor ethnic but economic (*FN* 77).

In collective aspects, the social and economic themes are inseparable from the moral themes, which are polarized essentially in the dream of innocence and the nightmare fact of guilt. Faulkner fulfilled what Leslie Fiedler, in *An End to Innocence*, saw as the function of the American writer: "the recorder of the encounter of the dream of innocence and the fact of guilt, in the only part of the world where the reality of that conflict can still be recognised." The fundamental theme is the exploitation of the land, linked with the exploitation of the people by whose labors the land was ravished. All misuses of land are covered, from private ownership itself to exhaustion of the soil by owners greedy for quick and excessive profit. Even the violation of the land by digging it up in search of buried treasure is presented twice, in *The Hamlet* and in "The Fire and the Hearth." The land, misused, accomplished its own revenge, even as the wilderness did (*GDM* 364). That revenge is Southern poverty and racial problems, caused by the crushing of human potential of the exploited race and by the corruption of the exploiters by their own power.

The two myths of the land in American folklore are identified by Daniel Hoffman: the Adamic view of man, involving the prelapsarian concept of nature as an Eden, and the Calvinistic view of original sin as the inescapable root of human nature. Both are reflected in the Yoknapatawpha chronicles in concepts held by characters. The views expressed by Ike McCaslin on the communal ownership of land by the Indians, in contrast with private ownership (*GDM* 254–55), are based on a historic fact concerning those Indians but are extended to a romantic view at variance with anthropological facts. Bronislaw Malinowski declared: "Complete communism of land actually under cultivation is never found in any primitive society." He dismissed scornfully the myth of the Golden Age and "the cry of return to nature" as "junk," of no value "to serve as a beacon towards which humanity has to progress." "In every human society there is a fair balance between individual property and the partial surrender for the common treasury, in cooperative work, in contributions, and in taxation."

Evidence that Faulkner did not share Ike McCaslin's view is implicit in his discussion of the Indians' communal ownership of land: he stressed the unjust way in which the Indians were dispossessed and exiled by treaty, rather than condemning private ownership as an evil in itself. In citing a Choctaw chief, Greenwood LeFlore, as "wise enough to get a patented deed to his land and to take up the white man's ways," Faulkner did not imply that LeFlore was ethically wrong in so doing (*FU* 43–44). Although Wilson Clough seems to regard Ike as more nearly ideal than Faulkner did, Clough's remark on Hawthorne is applicable to Ike: "The unpardonable sin . . . is to cut oneself off from the common stream; and the dread punishment is isolation from one's fellowmen." Faulkner himself was more like Emerson's ideal: "the great man is he who in the midst of the crowd keeps with perfect sweetness the independence of solitude." Of course, one cannot guarantee the perfect sweetness.

Since Ike's ideals are shown to be invalid, in that he failed to achieve maximum effectiveness as an individual and as a member of society, his romantic concept should not be taken without reservation. He belongs to a well-defined American tradition, in literature and in individual beliefs, a Thoreau who failed, however, to outgrow the hunter stage, rather than an Emerson, striving for a balance between withdrawal and conformity. The theme of primeval nature and fertility, as contrasted with the plantation system, offers a parallel to the Edenic and the Calvinistic views of man; primeval nature, however, is both Edenic and pagan. In *Occidental Mythology*, Joseph Campbell cites primitive examples of the Garden in which "there is no Fall, no sense of sin or exile . . . . They are affirmative, not critical of life." In *The Hamlet* and in *Light in August*, Eula Varner and Lena Grove are earth goddesses; Lena is invested also with Christian significance.

The curse upon the land is slavery, "an intolerable condition," the most extreme form of the sin against humanity of using people as things and having contempt for them. Charles Bon and Thomas Sutpen in *Absalom, Absalom!* "epitomize a constant general condition in the South" (*FU* 79, 98, 94). The themes of the exploitation of land and of the people are the major themes which recur throughout the Yoknapatawpha chronicles in the stories of individuals, of families, and of communities.

Centered in two communities, Jefferson and Frenchman's Bend, are the themes of love and greed, polarized in *Snopes* in the women who love and are loved, Eula and Linda, and in the man, Flem Snopes, who wants only money and respectability. The contrast between the theme of Eula as the Earth and that of Flem perfectly illustrates a change Joseph Campbell described as taking place with the growth of the "new mythology of the great gods": from "a state of indifference to the modalities of time," "the plane of attention . . . shifted to the foreground figures of duality and combat, power, profit and loss, where the mind of the man of action normally dwells." This theme is focused on individuals and on the conflict between Flem and the community more than on families, but *Snopes* traces the rise of the Snopes family.

The theme of the vitiation of the moral forces of the community, as in *The Hamlet* and *Sanctuary*, is paralleled by that of the decay or disintegration of families. This theme may involve lack of love; love and the lack of love or the search for love are antithetical themes in Yoknapatawpha and occasionally are clearly defined themes within a novel, as in *The Sound and the Fury*. In *Go Down, Moses* lack of love in the white families is contrasted with capacity for love in Negro families descended also from old Carothers McCaslin. Love is rarely a force in Yoknapatawpha, perhaps because love, which Joseph Campbell called "the true pedagogue of the open free society" of Periclean Athens, finds little place in *Mississippi: The Closed Society*, as Faulkner's friend James Silver called it.

Individuals, whether or not involved in family relationships or community activities, show antitheses of life and death, fertility and sterility, innocence and guilt, reason and instinct. The problem may be that of avoiding one-sidedness, the reaching a balance between reason and instinct, for example, or of succumbing to or of conquering a fatal illusion or an untenable principle. Of the various polarities, the guilt–innocence theme is the most characteristic of fiction and poetry of the mid-twentieth century. William Van O'Connor identified two major visions: "the vision of innocence and the vision of horror" or "the dream of innocence and the sense of guilt." In poetry also, as Joseph Warren Beach observed, "the sense of guilt and the longing for innocence are perhaps, along with fear and anxiety, the dominant emotions of the period in which we live." Innocence in Faulkner ranges from Sutpen's "innocence," a lack of moral perception caused by the blindness of hybris and by exaggerated rationality, to the mindless innocence of Benjy Compson, the idiot. These inner conflicts of individuals, however, represent also the conflicts of the society which created the myth of the South to demonstrate its innocence and conceal its guilt and which, by so doing, chose sterility instead of vitality, chose the overly rational or the overly irrational course instead of instinct balanced by reason, chose the way of death instead of the way of life—motion and change. But the mythology of Yoknapatawpha which Faulkner created in contrast to the myth of the South does not express unrelieved pessimism and despair.

IV • FAULKNER'S MYTHOLOGY OF YOKNAPATAWPHA

In the last paragraph of Jean Stein's interview with William Faulkner in 1956, Faulkner revealed his concept of Yoknapatawpha in two contrasting metaphors which I have used as subtitles: "little postage stamp of native soil" and "a kind of keystone in the universe." One other term he used unites the metaphors: "I created a cosmos of my own": the microcosm "of native soil" and the macrocosm of "the universe" are neatly hitched by "cosmos," with the emphasis on completeness and universality, not on size. Despite this clue to critics to approach his Yoknapatawpha fiction as a cosmic myth, even the mythic approach to separate novels was non-existent in 1956, according to the index in Thomas McHaney's *William Faulkner: A Reference Guide*. Until Faulkner's death, shortly after *The Reivers* was published, a study of Yoknapatawpha as a cosmos would have been premature.

The fact that Claude-Edmonde Magny recognized the cosmic concept in *The Age of the American Novel*, published in 1948, is noteworthy. Her comparison of Faulkner with Balzac, in a section entitled "Rivalry with God the Father—Faulkner and Balzac," is predictable, but her observation of "a simultaneity of vision that precedes, in Balzac as in Faulkner, the actual transcription of the work," as explaining gaps between dates of composition and publication, was confirmed repeatedly in Joseph Blotner's *Faulkner: A Biography*. Faulkner's last novel was an excellent example of a fairly frequent dormant period between the idea for a story or novel and the writing of it. Faulkner's idea for "a sort of Huck Finn story" was outlined in a letter to Robert Haas in May 1940; it became *The Reivers*, published shortly before Faulkner's death in July 1962. Mme Magny's assumption that Faulkner had an Old Testament concept of time and that he resembled T. S. Eliot and James Joyce in that respect was incorrect but in 1948 was not unreasonable. At that time Faulkner's views could not be distinguished with real assurance from those of his characters.

In 1968 the merits of a study of mythic elements in Faulkner's novels was established by the publication of *Faulkner: Myth and Motion* by Richard Adams and *Faulkner's Olympian Laugh: Myth in Faulkner's Novels* by Walter Brylowski. Neither book, however, dealt with the Yoknapatawpha fiction as constituting a mythic cosmos. Recognition of the cosmos need not, however, entail a study of the whole creation. In a dissertation, "The Monument and the Plain: The Art of Mythic Consciousness in William Faulkner's *Absalom, Absalom!*," Oliver Billingslea wanted to show, in part, that "what William Faulkner sought to create was a cosmos of spatial and temporal phenomena in which man must face the universal problem of the 'human heart in conflict with itself'" and that "the basis for Faulkner's art is a 'mythic consciousness' inherent in all mankind." Thus "the reader is able to approach the cosmos with some certainty of understanding the greater issues of the human spirit" (vii).

From recognizing Yoknapatawpha as a cosmos to studying it as

cosmology is a logical step which Michael Routh took in his dissertation, "The Story of All Things: Faulkner's Yoknapatawpha County
Cosmology by Way of *Light in August*." Although "Yoknapatawpha is
a physical place," Routh says, "inhabited by 'real' people, . . . it
constitutes a massive symbol for the whole cosmos" and "represents . . . the soul of a cosmic universal creature, a Mesocosmic
Being." In the Yoknapatawpha novels Faulkner used "the history of
the South as it is capsuled into the saga of Yoknapatawpha County as a
metaphor with which to make a cosmological statement on the human
condition." "Cosmological literature . . . is a mythopoeic impulse."

"The Mesocosmic Being," Routh explains, "serves as a joining link
between the little world, man, and the great world, the universe."
Routh continues his explanation in terms of Jungian psychology of the
Self and of Joseph Campbell's *The Hero With a Thousand Faces*. In
coincidental relation to the polarity of themes already dealt with,
Routh cites Cirlot: " 'Universal Man' implies hermaphroditism" and a
statement by the Jungian psychologist M.-L. von Franz that the
hermaphrodite as a symbol "reconciles one of the most important pairs
of psychological opposites—man and woman."

The creation of man and woman in Genesis follows the account of
the creation of the world and of other creatures; this is the Judeo-
Christian cosmogony. The Yoknapatawpha cosmogony took place
later, and it took Faulkner a little longer than it did God to look on his
work and call it good. In this cosmos of polar opposites, in "the
eschatological conception," according to Mircea Eliade, the "two
essential moments" are the creation of the world and the end of the
world. Study of the cosmology of Yoknapatawpha would suggest the
posibility of an eschatological approach, a study of the last things. The
possible is the actual: a dissertation by Mary Margaret Culley,
"Eschatological Thought in Faulkner's Yoknapatawpha Novels." The
usual four Protestant "last things" are included: Death, Judgment,
Heaven, and Hell. Like Dante, modern Catholics would include Purgatory. Closely associated with eschatology is the apocalypse, the Revelation in the New Testament book by St. John. The apocalyptic world
has distinctive imagery, described by Northrop Frye in *Anatomy of
Criticism*, which is the polar opposite of the demonic imagery already
described. By the imagery in the short story "Wash," Jack Stewart
identified this version of Wash's revenge murder of Sutpen as Wash's
one act of courage and conviction, his apotheosis, in the apocalyptic
climax of Time, Death, and Judgment for Sutpen and Wash.

When William Faulkner created his own cosmos of Yoknapatawpha,
it was less than a hundred years since that part of Mississippi was

settled by white men, an event which paralleled the stage of civilization which Eliade described; "settlement in a new, uncultivated country" was regarded as "equivalent to an act of creation" and was symbolically performed in a "ceremonial taking possession of newly discovered land." Eliade cited the Spanish and Portuguese conquistadors setting up a cross and taking possession in the name of Christ and the English navigators taking possession in the name of their king. Sutpen seems to have taken possession of the land after he purchased it from the Indians without any sacred ritual to transform the land from chaos to cosmos.

The symbolism of the center, the *axis mundi*, is based on the belief in the "Sacred Mountain—where heaven and earth meet—situated at the center of the world." Eliade explains that each religion would have its own Sacred Mountain. For Christianity it is Golgotha, where Christ died and where Adam was buried, to be redeemed by the blood of Christ. A temple or a sacred city or a royal residence would be regarded as a Center, an *axis mundi*.

After the discovery of North America, a new world open to its first civilized inhabitants, the concept of the end of the world as described in Revelation was modified. The world would be destroyed by fire, but after the purifying fire had destroyed the wicked, there would be "a new golden age" or "millennium of bliss." By the time settlers were coming to America, Christian thought had, Eliade said, "undertaken to transcend all the other archaic viewpoints by revealing the importance of the religious experience of faith and that of the value of the human personality." In *Virgin Land* Henry Nash Smith explained that the myth of the Garden of the World, with Edenic echoes, was dominated by "the heroic figure of the idealized frontier farmer . . . with . . . his sacred plow," cultivating, Eliade would say, sacred space. But unfortunately the inhabitants made it a "profane space," being already fallen when they arrived in Eden. The chapter on the Southern version of the Garden Smith entitled "The South and the Myth of the Garden." The Southern version of the myth of the garden and its symbols was based on the "powerful and persuasive myth of the Southern plantation," created, as Smith said, "to express the ideal ends of the slave system."

The pertinence to Yoknapatawpha of Eliade's account of sacred and profane space is demonstrated in a dissertation by Edward L. Corridori, "The Quest for Sacred Space: Setting in the Novels of William Faulkner." The sacred and the profane pertain to time as well as to space. Eliade defines sacred time as "*a primoridial mythical time made present*" by rites and festivals. "Just as a church constitutes a

break in plane in the profane space of a modern city, the service celebrated inside it marks a break in profane temporal duration."

The Western world is so accustomed to "time" as referring to linear,
historical time which can be measured without heeding sun time that
the concept of living in sacred, cyclical time measured by natural
phenomena is difficult to imagine. An example of mythic, cyclical time
and linear, historical time being lived within one family group in
Mississippi in the twentieth century may help to clarify the difference.
In Eudora Welty's *Losing Battles*, the Vaughns at a family reunion in
the 1930s are embattled against any threat of change, identified chiefly
in Gloria, the young wife of the future head of the Vaughn tribe. Taught
by Miss Julia Mortimer to think for herself and to plan for the future,
Gloria is determined to get Jack, her husband, and their child in a
house by themselves and not to be swallowed up by Jack's relatives
and their devotion to old ways which required neither thought nor
energy. Michael Kreyling's "Myth and History: The Foes in *Losing
Battles*" gives a good account of the cyclical and the linear time concepts as they affect characters. Characters in Faulkner can be judged
by the same concepts. Both communities reveal the irony of the myth
of the South: the founding fathers and the heroes of the past are being
lauded for the very qualities their descendants lack: courage and
energy to risk their future and establish their families in unknown
territory. The Vaughns are like archaic man as explained by Eliade in
Cosmos and History: his life is "repetition of archetypal acts, . . . the
unceasing rehearsal of the same primordial myths"; he lives in time but
"does not bear the burden of time, does not record time's irreversibil-
ity."

Eliade's contrast between the archaic man and modern man is of
significance to Faulkner's cosmos: modern man can reproach archaic
man "imprisoned within the mythical horizon of archetypes and repetition, with his creative impotence, or . . . his inability to accept the
risks entailed by every creative act. For the modern man can be creative only insofar as he is historical: in other words, all creation is
forbidden him except what has its source in his own freedom; and,
consequently, everything is denied him except the freedom to make
history by making himself." Only this creative freedom, Eliade said,
"is able to defend modern man from the terror of history—a freedom
. . . which has its source and finds its guaranty and support in God."
The title of a dissertation by Vernon Hornback sounds like an echo of
Eliade: "William Faulkner and the Terror of History: Myth, History,
and Moral Freedom in the Yoknapatawpha Cycle."

Reverting to mythical time without regard to historical dates, what

Mircea Eliade said of "Territories, Temples, and Cities" and of "The Symbolism of the Center" and of "Rituals" can be said of Yoknapatawpha: "The cosmogony first of all represents the Creation." Faulkner extended the myth of Yoknapatawpha beyond earth and time, but only after he had been recounting the chronicles for almost twenty-five years. According to Blotner's *Biography*, Faulkner was writing about the Sartorises and the Snopeses in 1926; "A Name for the City" ("The Courthouse" in *Requiem for a Nun*) was published in 1950. Almost as if he had been reading Eliade, he went back to the Creation in the history of the state capitol in Jackson: "The Golden Dome (Beginning Was the Word)." "In the beginning," as in Genesis, stated more concisely, "The earth was without form and void." After eight lines Faulkner's earth was ejaculated from the "moil of litter from the celestial experimental Work Bench." Faulkner's non-stop sentences (he does compromise with a semicolon at the end of each paragraph) cannot be quoted; what seems like verbosity is actually incredible conciseness, retaining colorful details and precise events in the history of Mississippi and arriving at 1903, when the Capitol, "the golden dome . . . the gilded pustule," was completed, in eleven pages (*RN* 99–110). Although the last line in "The Golden Dome," in a kind of guidebook entry about Jackson, is "Diversions: acute: Religion, Politics," it is noteworthy that the prologues to Act One and Act Three, respectively, are "The Courthouse" and "The Jail": only one of the two acute diversions is represented as an act of creation in new territory. The facts that the building of a church as a creation of "sacred space" is absent and that the jail was built before the courthouse and before even the site had been determined show a lack of a sense of sacred space on the part of the town founders where it would be most obviously evoked. But politics did stir the mythic consciousness: "a by-neo-Greek-out-of-Georgian-England" edifice was "set in the center of what in time would be the town Square (as a result of which, the town itself had moved one block south . . .)" (p. 213). The positions of the jail and the courthouse are strictly realistic; when the old jail was torn down in 1961, the new one was built on the same site, now badly overcrowded. The fact that the town was populated from the beginning by Protestant denominations explains why there was no such communal effort to build a church as there was to build a courthouse. Faulkner put into the words of Gavin Stevens the explanation of the order in which public buildings were erected: "if you would peruse in unbroken—ay, overlapping—continuity the history of a community, look not in the church registers and the courthouse records, but beneath the successive layers of calsomine and creosote and white-

wash on the walls of the jail, since only in that forcible carceration does
man find the idleness in which to compose . . . the gross and simple
recapitulations of his gross and simple heart'' (p. 214). Gavin outlined
the stages in the history of Jefferson: "from a halting-place: to a community: to a settlement: to a village: to a town . . ." (p. 214).

The cosmogony of Yoknapatawpha is the foundation of the myth.
All three prologues merit careful consideration; "The Courthouse"
and "The Jail" deal with Yoknapatawpha and introduce the founders
of the leading families at times earlier than the narrative action, except
Sutpen, who not only helped with the building of the courthouse but
provided the aid of his French architect (p. 40). Grenier never appears
again as a character nor does Jason Lycurgus Compson I. The infiltra-
tion of settlers, symbolized by "prints of horses and men" (p. 215), and
the dispossession of Mohataha, the Indian queen, and her subjects are
among the most memorable of the events, presented with such wealth
of symbols that the history of more than a hundred years is covered in
less than fifty pages in "The Jail." But then the history outside of
Yoknapatawpha from the Creation to 1903 is given in eleven pages!
(99–110).

Although we shall have occasion to refer to myth and ritual in relation to specific characters and events, it must be kept in mind that there
were no profane activities in the archaic world. Eliade sums up the acts
which have "a definite meaning" and therefore were sacred: "hunting,
fishing, agriculture; games, conflicts, sexuality." The best example of
ritual conflict which pertained to the South is the duel. One is reminded
of the Sartoris dueling pistols and Drusilla in "An Odor of Verbena."
Eliade's explanation of "the ritual role of hostilities" includes the
"magical and pharmaceutical value of certain herbs," among which he
cites the verbena. According to tradition, it first grew on the Mount of
Calvary, "the 'center' of the Earth." Outmoded ritualized hostilities
survived in the South, thanks to the influence of Sir Walter Scott: in
The Waning of the Old South Civilization, Clement Eaton records "a
romantic tournament of knights and their fair ladies" in Burlington,
North Carolina, in 1872. The Oxford *Eagle*, December 10, 1936, gave
an account of such a tourmanent held in Oxford in 1867.

From the warp and woof of polarized themes, with embroidery of
symbols, Faulkner wove the mythology of Yoknapatawpha County
which, compared to the myth of the South, shows only partial or ironic
parallels. From the version of the myth in *Requiem for a Nun* and the
separate stories and novels one can construct an outline of the mythology according to the main stages in the history of the county.

The coming of the white men was the first chapter: the cheating and dispossession of the Indians is a dominant theme in Yoknapatawpha. The only detailed example of the building of a plantation in the wilderness is Sutpen's Hundred, created out of the chaos of primeval forest and swamp by the fiat of Sutpen, executed by the captive French architect and naked Negroes. Whether it was Sutpen or Sartoris or Compson or McCaslin, the Indians were first cheated, then corrupted, and finally exiled. In "Faulkner's 'Waste Land' Vision in *Absalom, Absalom!*" Robert M. Slabey sees in *Absalom, Absalom!* "a symbolic picture of the Fall and the exile from the Garden," and compares this picture with T. S. Eliot's Waste-Land vision.

The other plantations are not presented directly in narrative or are not described in detail: Grenier's ruined mansion, the Old Frenchman place, in *The Hamlet*, is all we see where was once "an enormous house," stables and slave quarters, gardens and "brick terraces and promenades" (*H* 3). Similarly the Compson domain has been reduced to a "square, paintless house with its rotting portico," "the kitchen-garden and the collapsing stables and one servant's cabin," its former splendor of one square mile, many buildings, and "formal lawns and promenades and pavilions" now only a memory (*SF* 372, 410, 407). The McCaslin plantation house in *Go Down, Moses* in 1859, the time of Buck and Buddy, was an unfinished big house in which Negroes lived, while Buck and Buddy lived in one of the slave cabins. At the same time the Beauchamp estate had front gate posts but no gate, rotted floor boards on the gallery, and broken shutters (*GDM* 6, 9, 10). Sartoris as it was rebuilt after the war (*Sar.* 6–8) seems more elegant than the original plantation house, as one envisions it from Bayard's references to it in the early stories in *The Unvanquished*. In short, Faulkner never presents directly the elegant antebellum mansions and the cultured life of the wealthy aristocracy, comparable with Tidewater society, which the legend of the South features. Sutpen's estate comes closest to the traditional picture, but Sutpen was never a member of aristocratic society and his elegance was a veneer, a sign of the culture he desired, not of what he actually was.

And Sutpen was by origin a poor white, Grenier was a French Huguenot, McCaslin apparently the pioneer type, but of good stock; only John Sartoris definitely came from an old, wealthy South Carolina family, an aristocrat and presumably an Anglican as Granny Millard was. Thus only one of Faulkner's first families fits the traditional pattern of the legend, and the founder of that family in Mississippi regarded his pride in family with ironic realism. "In the nineteenth century . . . genealogy is poppycock. Particularly in America, where only what a man takes and keeps has any significance and where all of us have a

common ancestry and the only house from which we can claim descent
with any assurance is the Old Bailey. Yet the man who professes to
care nothing about his forbears is only a little less vain than the man
who bases all his actions on blood precedent. And I reckon a Sartoris
can have a little vanity and poppycock, if he wants it" (*Sar.* 92).

In a dissertation, "The Fatal Illusions: Self, Sex, Race, and Religion
in William Faulkner's World," Jewell Gresham examined the
Yoknapatawpha novels with feudal chivalry as an analogue; the four
illusions are represented by four novels, after the first chapter,
"Yoknapatawpha and the Chivalric Myth: The South as Invention":
The Cavalier Myth: *Sartoris* (Self); The Cult of Virginity: *The Sound
and the Fury* (Sex); The Black Scapegoat: *Light in August* (Race);
Blood Guilt and Cultural Casualties: *Absalom, Absalom!* (Religion).
Light in August would seem to represent religion best, but a scheme of
one illusion to a novel overrules other considerations.

Faulkner's detailed account in *Requiem for a Nun* of the courthouse
and the jail and his many references to the first banks and his accounts
of John Sartoris' railroad (*Requiem for a Nun, Sartoris, The Reivers,
The Unvanquished*), and of the history of roads and automobiles, show
an interest in the development of social institutions, commerce, and
transportation which is not typical of the legend.

None of the leading men of Yoknapatawpha County had really distinguished military careers. John Sartoris left his regiment when he was
demoted and was a guerrilla leader under Forrest. The most glowing
account of John Sartoris as a military leader comes from Uncle Buck
and deals in glittering generalities (*U* 58–60). Although Thomas Sutpen acquitted himself creditably in the war, acting in accordance
with the code of the class to which he aspired and in defense of the
society he had chosen, he put pride above military duty when he had
tombstones for his wife and himself brought from Italy in blockade
runners and transported from Pennsylvania to Mississippi by his
regiment, "starved gaunt men and gaunt spent horses knee deep in an
icy mud or snow" (*AA* 189). The living could scarcely be more ruthlessly sacrificed to the dead and to a megalomaniac's dream. General
Compson, the highest ranking army officer from Jefferson, is not presented directly, but we are told in the Appendix to *The Sound and the
Fury* that he "failed at Shiloh in '62 and failed again though not so
badly at Resaca in '64" and "spent the next forty years selling frag-
ments" of the Compson Domain "to keep up the mortgage on the
remainder" (p. 408). It is significant that Faulkner omitted from his myth
any army leader, historical or fictitious, who represents the romantic
legend, as based on men like Jeb Stuart; Stuart, as recalled in a minor

incident (*Sar.* 11–19), suggests an implicit comparison between the historical and fictional leaders.

The losses suffered by the Sartorises and the Sutpens are typical of both facts and legend: the Sartoris house was burned and the Sutpen house fell into disrepair and both plantations deteriorated. Sartoris recouped his fortunes and took on new enterprises; Sutpen put having a dynasty before anything else and was killed for treating Wash's granddaughter worse than a mare. McCaslin Edmonds even prospered after the war. The ante-bellum plantation house on the site comparable to that of the Sartoris house was not destroyed during the war. It has been restored to its original elegance and is the home of Faulkner's nephew Jimmy.

Just as Faulkner did not stress the sacrifices and losses of the aristocrats, he touched only lightly the Reconstruction period. Except for a brief reference in "The Bear" (GDM 291), there is no account of terror and suffering under carpetbag rule, such as were prominent in the novels of Thomas Dixon. In "Skirmish at Sartoris," Colonel John Sartoris is the villain, shooting a one-armed old man and a youth, Joanna Burden's grandfather and her brother. In the direct account, in "Skirmish at Sartoris," Bayard was not a witness. Old man Falls told the story to Bayard when they were both old men and denounced Colonel Sartoris for having become a killer (*Sar.* 22–23). Joanna could understand why her grandfather did not shoot first: "a man would have to act as the land where he was born had trained him to act" (*LA* 241).

Bayard Sartoris was the only aristocrat who met a moral crisis with notable choice and a fine sense of personal honor, but it was his one distinctive achievement in a long life. He acted in direct violation of the legendary code of revenge ("An Odor of Verbena"). The two instances of aristocrats who proved competent to cope with changing conditions in a creditable way are not presented directly and dramatically; Bayard remembered Colonel John's railroad after receiving news of his death; Ike McCaslin remembered that McCaslin Edmonds, as a mere youth, faced the "debacle and chaos" after the war and cared for the workers and animals and enlarged the plantation (*U* 259; *GDM* 298). Neither the suffering nor the achievements of this period are stressed to evoke sympathy and admiration for Southern gentry, as legendary accounts of the Reconstruction were designed to do.

The Southern gentry who are most nostalgically committed to the past are unsympathetically portrayed or pay the penalty for their rejection of life in the present. The most notable of those who reject life, Quentin Compson and Gail Hightower, have qualities which evoke some sympathy. Mr. and Mrs. Compson withdrew from life almost as much as Hightower did and in their inertia and self-pity victimized their children, sacrificing them to the legend of gyneolatry and to family pride and defeatism. In sharp contrast to Mrs. Compson are two more genuinely aristocratic ladies: Aunt Jenny Du Pre and Miss Habersham. Aunt Jenny loved to recall the family legend but she saw the legend for what it was, faced the present realistically, and provided the family with its chief energy and affection. Miss Habersham with dignity earned a living for herself and her servants by useful labor traditionally held to be beneath a gentlewoman. Her treatment of her servants showed her responsibility and sympathy; Aunt Jenny's showed her sense of being "quality" and her exasperation with inefficiency, but she was not unkind. Elnora served her with devoted pride. Mrs. Compson, on the other hand, was demanding, inconsiderate, and unappreciative, clear signs that she was not really "quality." Dilsey's devotion was to helplessness, not to "quality."

The departures from the legend observed up to this point and the additions of modern developments implicitly suggest certain criticisms of the legend. The degeneration in the Compsons and the Sartorises, among the leading families, was due to inherent weaknesses, not to the economic and social effects of the war. Faulkner said of the Sartorises: "the Southern men were the ones that couldn't bear . . . having lost the war. The women were the ones that could bear it because they never had surrendered. The men had given up and in a sense were dead and even generations later were seeking death" (*FU* 254). The members of the De Spain family do not appear in Yoknapatawpha in the early period, but they were among the earlier settlers and were superior to the Sartorises and Compsons: the De Spain blood "was stronger, it was less prone to the aberrations, to the degeneracy into semimadness which the Compsons reached. It didn't degenerate into the moral weakness of the Sartorises, it was tougher blood. It may be it wasn't quite as exalted as theirs was at one time, that . . . it kept a certain leaven of a stronger stock by instinctive choice" (*FU* 119). In Manfred de Spain, that strength is manifest in his love for Eula Snopes, without benefit of clergy though it was; his healthy instincts and courage and fidelity were inadequate to save Eula and himself.

The fact that the De Spains were originally not as aristocratic as the Sartorises illustrates another deviation of Faulkner's mythology from the legend of the South: Faulkner draws no class lines between admirable and despicable characters. The two most despicable are Jason Compson, scion of one of the "first families," and Flem Snopes, a poor white. Wallstreet Panic Snopes, of low "Snopes" origin, and

Ratliff, descended from poor whites, are both admirable, and their rise in the social scale is viewed sympathetically because they used legitimate means and did not victimize people to gain economic advantage. Ratliff and Wall together were able to succeed in spite of Flem because they were not guilty of weaknesses which would give Flem a hold over them. (In *The Hamlet*, Ratliff had learned his lesson not to let greed betray him into Flem's hands.) Contrasts between characters on the same high social level show similar lack of class distinctions between weak and admirable characters. Ike McCaslin was chiefly admirable, but his kinsman Roth lacked Ike's moral convictions and unselfish conduct and showed the same weakness as did his ancestor, Carothers McCaslin. Gavin Stevens and Quentin Compson belonged to the same generation, Quentin being, if anything, of higher social class; both went to Harvard; both were devoted to their sisters, and Gavin suffered from unrequited love; both were by nature idealists. Quentin committed suicide, and Gavin lived a useful, public-spirited life. The same contrast is apparent between Gavin and Bayard Sartoris and Horace Benbow: all returned from World War I, Gavin to pursue a career, Bayard to yield to his neurotic lack of purpose and seek a Sartoris death, and Horace to let himself be seduced and casually to carry on his inherited law practice. Neither family status nor the fortunes of war set a pattern for characters; the stereotypes of legend yielded to highly individualized characters.

Nor is the final view of the South one of hopelessness and defeat: the chronicles end almost a hundred years after the Civil War, the latest time of action being 1946, in *The Mansion*, and the latest mental perspective that of Lucius Priest, in *The Reivers*, in 1961. In *The Mansion* the conflict between Snopesism and the best principles of the old tradition seems likely to be won by the proponents of civic virtue and integrity: Ratliff and Gavin Stevens and Charles Mallison have united in active participation in community affairs and politics. The presiding genius of *The Mansion* is Athena, Miller MacLure notes, as Eros was of *The Hamlet* and Hermes, the trickster, of *The Town*: the cycle has moved from love to barter to wisdom. The "good guys" have learned that it is not enough to have high principles: "One has got to belong to the human family and to take a responsible part in the human family . . ." (*FU* 81). By the same token, Flem and Snopesism are self-defeated: "The Snopeses will destroy themselves" (*FU* 282).

Disintegration in the world of Yoknapatawpha is not inevitable because Faulkner's themes are not those of the Old South. The changes in the themes and the legend which we have observed testify to a re-reading of the past in a new light: the loss of belief in the old legend and of faith in the old ruling class is accompanied in Faulkner by a sense of the potentialities not only of the Gavin Stevenses and the Ratliffs and the Charles Mallisons who live and strive in the present but even of the Mink Snopeses, in whom poverty and ignorance have not killed a sturdy integrity and narrow but intense concept of honor.

In the familiar myth of the South, poor whites, such as Mink, and Negroes appear chiefly as recipients of white benevolence, demonstrating the felicity of their lot in a paternalistic society. In Faulkner's mythology the Negroes constitute a possible hope of redemption for the South, if the South can be redeemed by love and kindness and forgiveness. Two of Faulkner's most impressive and convincing characters are Dilsey, who represents the best of the old tradition, and Lucas Beauchamp, who is unique but suggests a possible new direction for the Southern Negro. Dilsey served and endured; she had boundless compassion even for those who were ungrateful to her. Dilsey "knew her place" because she was a Christian and could accept her lot in a Christian spirit. Lucas, as a recognized descendant of Carothers McCaslin, had economic and social security unique among Negroes in the community. He did not accept the demeaning racial etiquette, and he rejected white patronage, dealing with white men as man to man. Furthermore, he had an ideal of family life and marital fidelity that resembles the best in the white tradition: the fire on the hearth symbolizes a rejection of the loose family ties and the matriarchal system which originated during slavery. Lucas' folly which drove Molly to seek a "voce" was white folly and he gave it up to save his marriage.

Faulkner's mythology seems to imply that the hope for the South lies in the poor whites and the Negroes and those of the upper classes who are willing to treat people with human dignity, regardless of race or class: the Gavin Stevenses and Ratliffs and Miss Habershams, for example. And the despair of the South lies in those like Mrs. Compson and Jason and Roth, who are selfish and arrogant and victimize the helpless, as well as in the Flem Snopeses who rise in life by taking advantage of the weaknesses of others.

V • FAMILY MYTHS

Only the prologues in *Requiem for a Nun* cover the whole scope of the mythology; presentation in direct narrative centers on families and individuals whose stories may be compared, as parts of the mythology, with such Greek myths as those of the House of Atreus and the Theban cycles. But added to the archetypal patterns in the Yoknapatawpha family cycles are the patterns of modern novels tracing the rise or decline of families, thus fusing the psychological and the economic-sociological aspects of family histories. The Yoknapatawpha cycle does not, however, trace the history of any family unbroken for several generations nor present typical family groups and individual experience of family life throughout a whole life-span.

The family is a universal subject for fiction in that the purpose of the family, the typical family group, and the experience of individuals within the family have certain universal characteristics, regardless of radical differences in cultures. The purpose of marriage in all societies, according to Malinowski, "is the licensing of parenthood rather than of sexual intercourse." The family exists for the benefit of the children whose place in society is thus provided for. Malinowski states the universal principle: "The most important moral and legal rule concerning the physiological side of kinship is that no child should be brought into the world without a man—and one man at that—assuming the role of sociological father, that is, guardian and protector, the male link between the child and the rest of the community." In essentials, marriage and the family are as universal as any aspect of human life can be:

> through all the changes and vicissitudes, all history, all development, all geographical setting, the family and marriage still remain the same twin institutions; they still emerge as a stable group showing throughout the same fundamental features—a group consisting of a father, of mother and of children, forming a joint household, co-operating economically, united by a contract and surrounded by religious sanctions which make the family into a moral unit.

To the typical family of both parents and several children of both sexes there would usually be added, in the past and in an agricultural economy, other relatives, especially grandparents and often aunts and uncles. The parents are directly responsible for the care and education of the children. The father ensures the social status of the children and exercises the authority in the family. The mother's role is to provide tender care, symbolized by nursing the infant. Lena Grove is the only mother figure so presented in Yoknapatawpha. She was only a transient in Jefferson and was deserted by the father of the child. Had she remained in Yoknapatawpha and belonged to a higher social class, her baby would have had a black mammy, very likely a wet nurse at first. Lillian Smith remembered seeing a mammy nursing a black and a white baby at the same time. She observed that to Southerners who had had two mothers, of two colors and two cultures, the Oedipus complex would seem a comparatively "simple adjustment."

The stages in the life of the individual involve changing relationships within the family; after puberty, often marked by special initiation rites, the young person has increased independence, especially independence of boys from their mother's influence. Courtship and marriage and the setting up of a new household are followed by the individual's experience of parenthood through all the periods of the children's lives. Then the family may be reduced to husband and wife, after the children are grown up and married. As grandparents, in their last years, they may be dependent on grown children. In the South particularly, large families, rural life, and social custom gave the kinship group some of the characteristics of the clan.

In his account of the Southern Renaissance of the 1930s and 1940s, Richard King was particularly concerned with the efforts of Southern writers "to come to grips with the tradition of the Southern family romance," which was "progressively demystified and rejected." The family romance dealt with the "planter elite" which dominated Southern life before the Civil War. It was "a patriarchal hierarchical" society which cultivated leisure and social graces but failed to balance "democratic aspirations" with "aristocratic ethos." After the war the segregation of races had been established under the "Jim Crow laws" by the 1890s, when the blacks were disfranchised in Mississippi. By the early 1900s, "the South was a solidly one-party section, dominated by a white elite," and remained so until the 1950s. In the tradition of the family romance, King said, "culture and civilization are seen as literally and symbolically *of* the father." When the family was disrupted by the loss or the inadequacy of the father, the ordered world collapsed. Measured by "the heroic generation of the grandfathers, the fathers seemed rather unheroic and prosaic to their sons."

If "grandfathers" were changed to "great-grandfathers," King's statement would apply to Faulkner, whose "attitude toward his family tradition reflects the classical pattern of the family romance, but also departs significantly from it." Faulkner was as ambivalent "in his attitude toward his male ancestors" as toward his own vocation. The Sartorises represent "the historical world in which the Southern tradition has grown destructive."

But the "constitutive rules of the Southern family romance" appear in *Absalom, Absalom!*, not in *Sartoris*: in the consciousness of Quentin Compson, "the violations of these rules become emblems of the disorder at the core of the tradition." The family romance is "decomposed into its constitutive opposites," with no mediating influences.

Obvious facts about families and the patterns of their lives have been stated here because, among the major families in Faulkner's mythology, there is no typical family or individual life history. In the twentieth century Faulkner does not present directly any family with more than one child that is ruled by the traditional code of family duty and responsibility of parents toward children or children toward parents except the MacCallums and the Gowries, each family all-male and close knit. Jason Compson in *The Sound and the Fury*, *in loco parentis*, outwardly observed the forms of family life but violated the spirit.

The Sutpen family is traced most completely among Yoknapatawpha families, through five generations, from Thomas Sutpen's parents to his great-grandson, the idiot Jim Bond. But this family is never presented directly, only through various narrators of whom only Rosa actually knew Thomas and his own family. Despite this oblique method and many deviations from what is typical, the life of Thomas Sutpen comes closest, in the Yoknapatawpha chronicles, to a typical life history. It is the styles of the narrators which invest that history with a legendary quality. But beneath the surface Donald Kartiganer perceived the universal myth of fathers and sons, kings and heirs, and the myth of ascendancy and doom.

Sutpen was a poor white, one of several children. His mother died when he was a child. When he was still in his teens, he rejected his family and set forth alone to seek his fortune. Both of his marriages were marriages of convenience, to further his grand design of establishing an estate and a dynasty. Neither marriage involved the free choice of both parties, based on mutual attraction, which Bronislaw Malinowski stated is the normal marriage in all communities.

Sutpen's second marriage took place in Jefferson; the wedding, the only one in Yoknapatawpha which is described in any detail, was a travesty: of the hundred guests who had been invited, only ten, including the wedding party, were present, and a hostile mob gathered outside the church. Even without Malinowski's authority, "the rich and varied symbolism" of the marriage ceremony is familiar. It is remarkable, therefore, that the only other weddings presented, in brief or fragmented fashion, are those forced upon girls by conventional mothers: Drusilla's wedding in *The Unvanquished* and Caddy's wedding in *The Sound and the Fury*.

Sutpen had at least five children: three were legitimate but the oldest, Charles Bon, was denied recognition as Sutpen's son. Bon, presumably, and Clytie had Negro blood. Clytie and the white daughter of Sutpen, Wash's granddaughter, were illegitimate. The family group at Sutpen's Hundred was not a typical group in a general sense. It was not untypical in Faulkner's fiction, nor, unfortunately, in fact. Henry and Judith were brought up with their half-sister Clytie; their recognition of the fact of the relationship was not typical. Both Wilbur Cash and Mary Boykin Chesnut confirm the basic realism of the situation but indicate that white women, at least, were supposed to feign ingorance of such relationships.

Thomas Sutpen fulfilled his role as father better than did his wife, Ellen, her role as mother: the "butterfly" was capable of little but shopping for Judith's trousseau. Ellen's delegation of a mother's responsibility to her sister Rosa was anthropologically typical, according to Malinowski; it was unique in Yoknapatawpha and unusual in any society in Rosa's being so young. Ellen had no sense of qualifications of a person for a family role; Rosa's youth made her even less capable than Ellen had been. Sutpen experienced a paternal relationship with only Henry and Judith, of his five children. Because of her Negro blood Clytie was more a slave than a daughter. When Sutpen refused to accept responsibility for his last white daughter, Wash killed him. In either a primitive or a civilized society, Sutpen's rejection of both mother and child would have been reprehensible.

None of Sutpen's children lived a complete or typical life. Henry shot Charles Bon to keep Charles from marrying Judith, his half-sister: presumably it was the miscegenation, not the incest which Henry could not accept (*AA* 356). Henry disappeared, returned many years later, lived as a recluse and fugitive from the law, and died with only his half-sister Clytie as companion and nurse. Judith never married but took care of Charles Bon's son and grandson. Denied recognition as Sutpen's son, Charles Bon grew up fatherless and himself knew fatherhood only in his son's infancy. That son, denied acceptance in white society despite his gentle upbringing, defied all social conventions by marrying a very black and uncouth woman, the mother of his son, Jim Bond the idiot, Sutpen's last descendant.

Patricia Tobin uses the term "genealogical imperative" for the kind of family novel which equates temporal form with the dynastic line; chronological succession guarantees identity and legitimacy if individuals can trace their lineage to its origin. ". . . ontological priority is conferred upon mere temporal anteriority, the historical consciousness is born and time is understood as a linear manifestation of the genealogical destiny of events." Thus the "genealogical imperative" is the opposite of mythic time and of the mythic search for fusion of discontinuous identities in ritual.

Concerned with space more than with time, Edward Corridori uses the concept of sacred and profane space of Eliade in "The Quest for Sacred Space: Setting in the Novels of William Faulkner." Corridori traces four basic images and their significance: (1) thresholds or doorways, (2) imagery of creation, (3) dwellings, (4) the land or earth. Quentin he considers the protagonist, a "questor figure," searching for meaning in a desacralized world. In "his night journey into his own heritage" and meeting with Henry, Quentin experienced Eliade's "terror of history" and found no cosmology to justify events or redeem himself from Sutpen's "irreversible linearity of time." Such cosmology depends on being rooted in the earth and identifying with cyclical time. The contrast between cycles of earth and seasons and the ripples in water (*AA* 261) and Quentin's choice of drowning to end the ripples confirms his lack of roots. The most significant interpretation in terms of Eliade's concepts is that of Sutpen, whose failure to bring order out of chaos by sacred, ritual acts doomed his design. His creation was no *axis mundi*, a center of activities for others than those he possessed, as slaves or offspring. His design being profane, his life was profane: he used land and people as mere instruments.

Dealing with *Absalom, Absalom!* with direct reference to the myth of the South and "the imagery of neoclassical architecture," Davenport said: "For Dixon, the plantation house with its Grecian columns and white portico represented the order and simplicity of a social order based on white supremacy. For Faulkner, the house and the style represented irresponsible innocence, greed, social irresponsibility, and, in general, the decay of the Old South, mythical or otherwise." Being "about American history and the American burden of innocence," "the story could generally be best expressed within the framework of classical myth and symbol (that is, the title, itself a reference to the Biblical story of David and his sons, and the analogies to Greek families and characters), and specifically could best be illustrated by the South's entanglement with history through the burden of the Negro and the burden of defeat." "The burden of history" Davenport defined in terms relevant to the myth of the South: it "suggests that the defeat, the humiliation, and the social catastrophe give fruitful knowledge of the human condition rather than the impotent, self-destructive idea of self-sufficient innocence; responsibility rather than irresponsibility; motion and action to replace political immobility and moral stagnation."

The title of Maxine Rose's dissertation on the Sutpen story indicates that the scope in space and time cannot be exceeded: "From Genesis to Revelation: The Grand Design of Faulkner's *Absalom, Absalom!*." Her study shows "the unique influence of the Bible on the style, structure, and technique," beginning with the first clue, the ironic title: David's lament for Absalom, of which there is not even an echo in Sutpen's story. We are concerned here with the parallels in the stories of David and Sutpen as heads of families. The Absalom and Amnon and Tamar story has parallels with that of Henry and Charles Bon and Judith, with the addition of miscegenation to incest in the Sutpen story. Rose considers both Henry and Charles Bon to have Absalom–Amnon characteristics. She also interprets Bon as a Christ figure: "the expositor of love and the victim of sacrifice" and, in the combined roles, "a god-man who offers salvation and redemption." Sutpen is "at once a Jehovah figure, a 'demon,' King David, and the dragon of the Apocalypse," plus minor parallels with other Biblical figures from Adam on. The polarity of themes is particularly impressive in this approach: "The two major antagonists of the Bible, God–Jesus and Satan–demon–dragon, offer powerful cosmic parallels for Sutpen and Bon, with possibilities for divine and human qualities, and paradoxical God–Satan combinations."

The extension of this study to cover both the Old Testament and the New Testament enhances the significance of the Sutpen–Bon contrast. Sutpen represents the Old Law, "a rigid and inflexible code," and Bon the New Law "of love and grace" which abolishes social and racial distinctions. Bon is loving and involved with the lives of others, showing "compassion, pity, sacrifice, love." (No mention is made of the lack of objective information about Bon.) "Non-human" and "Satanic" may be too extreme terms for Sutpen, but he certainly was "rigid, inflexible, lacking in love, not involved in the lives of others, and incapable of dealing with his own son compassionately, wisely, and kindly." The title of this study was justified: it does "cover the span of the whole human race" and "extend the scope to heaven and hell and the time to eternity."

In contrast with the Sutpen family story of the rejection of one son and estrangement from the other is the story of the Sartoris family, in which the most satisfactory father–son relationship in Yoknapatawpha is presented in narrative form. But the Sartoris family was never complete or typical. In *The Unvanquished* the family consisted of Colonel John, his mother-in-law, Rosa Millard, and his son Bayard. Bayard's mother never appeared as a character, and the three daughters of Colonel John mentioned in *Sartoris*, the first Yoknapatawpha novel, were never mentioned in *The Unvanquished*. A pleasantly untypical aspect of the Sartoris family, in terms of satiric stereotypes, is the relationship of Colonel John with his mother-in-law: it could not have been better if she had been his own mother.

Bayard is the only Sartoris followed in direct narrative from adolescence to death. An only child in *The Unvanquished*, he was brought up by his father and Granny Millard and, after Granny's death, by his father's sister, Aunt Jenny, apparently the only available mother-substitute. Bayard's training and family life in childhood and youth were excellent. The only complication occurred after his father married Drusilla, whose fiancé was killed during the Civil War. Bayard as a young man found his stepmother taking an unmotherly interest in him, like Phaedra's in Hippolytus in Greek myth ("An Odor of Verbena"). Bayard's maturity, from when he was in his twenties until he was in his seventies, is omitted from the narratives. He is never shown as husband and father, and little is told about this major portion of his life (*Sar.* 91–92). As a grandfather he was benevolent but ineffectual in dealing with his grandson, Bayard, the only one who is a character in direct narrative.

After young Bayard's father died in 1901, Bayard and his twin brother John were brought up by their grandfather and their grandfather's aunt, Jenny Du Pre. Only a year of young Bayard's life is covered in *Sartoris*. His two brief marriages, the first of which ended with the death of his wife before the novel opens, showed no sense on Bayard's part of the purpose of marriage and family life and gave him no experience of fatherhood. His closeness to his twin brother John was reflected in his reminiscence of their boyhood. Judging by Bayard's thoughts when he returned home, the only meaningful family relationship had been that with John. After he had injured himself by his reckless driving and been taken home by a Negro and his son in their wagon, Bayard would not let Simon send for a doctor but took all his keepsakes that had been Johnny's and burned them (*Sar.* 214–15).

To understand Bayard's second marriage, one must know not only what is told about Narcissa Benbow in *Sartoris* but what is later divulged in "There Was a Queen." In *Sartoris*, and even more explicitly in *Flags in the Dust*, her brother Horace's incestuous love for Narcissa and his influence in providing her with a role to play by idealizing her as the pure white Southern lady, always dressed in white, have been made clear. Narcissa was both attracted by the Sartoris twins and repelled by their violence. In *Sartoris* Narcissa had sought the favor of Aunt Jenny so that her presence as a visitor at Sartoris would be established before Bayard returned after the war. While he was immobilized after his accident she stayed with him when Aunt Jenny was not at home. He seemed to be first a captive and then a suitor. After their marriage Bayard seemed contented for a while, taking part in plantation activities and hunting. But when he killed his grandfather by causing old Bayard to have a heart attack during a narrow escape from a car crash, he fled and never returned to Jefferson. His son and Narcissa's was born the day he was killed in a plane no one else was suicidal enough to fly.

In "There Was a Queen" Aunt Jenny's memories fill in some details from before the beginning of *Sartoris*: Narcissa was already engaged to Bayard when she was coming out to visit Aunt Jenny. Aunt Jenny knew about the obscene letters Narcissa was receiving from Byron Snopes but not about the engagement. Aunt Jenny's death was caused by learning that Narcisssa spent a weekend with a federal agent and paid the price he demanded for returning the letters Byron had stolen after Narcissa married Bayard and had lost as he fled after robbing the bank. The ritual cleansing after her sin Narcissa achieved by sitting fully clothed with her son in, as Aunt Jenny said, "Jordan at the back of a country pasture in Missippi [sic]" (*CS* 741).

Narcissa is the perfect example of the phony Southern lady who concealed her basic immorality and self-righteousness by playing the role to such perfection that she fooled even Aunt Jenny. The reader might well be fooled by Narcissa in *Sartoris* if he did not recognize the stereotype. But Elnora, Aunt Jenny's servant and half-sister of old Bayard, knew from the beginning that Narcissa was trash, as she told Isom (*CS* 727, 734). Through Elnora's thoughts, her unreserved conversations with Isom, and her prudent remarks to Aunt Jenny, we learn much about Narcissa that is most significant in understanding the Southern myth and Faulkner's attitude toward it. "Quality," Elnora said, "ain't *is*, it's *does*" (*CS* 711). To Aunt Jenny she said, "Ain't no Sartoris man never missed nobody" (p. 730). That might well apply to many Yoknapatawpha men if "nobody" is changed to "no woman." Young Bayard's twinship made his grief and guilt over Johnny's death less an exception than it seems: Bayard had lost part of himself, and the better half. Elnora also knew why Narcissa did not marry again: "She ain't going to leave this place, now she done got in here" (p. 729). ("There Was a Queen" was published in 1933, before any of the stories in *The Unvanquished*; in "There Was a Queen" the Sartoris house was built when John Sartoris came "from Carolina and built it" (*CS* 727); at the end of "Retreat" the house was burned and in "Skirmish at Sartoris" it was being rebuilt.)

What Narcissa wanted was status, which the Sartoris name and mansion gave her. Benbow Sartoris, brought up by Narcissa, with even Aunt Jenny's alleviating influence ended with her death when Benbow was a child, was still at Sartoris in 1937, when he was seventeen and a good bird shot (*M* 306). There seems little hope of Benbow's reviving the Sartoris family.

In "The Role of Women in Faulkner's Yoknapatawpha," Maureen Waters treats Narcissa with the scorn that she deserved. Narcissa appears again in *Sanctuary*, in which she is even more despicable, as will be apparent. Waters' interpretation of Narcissa in *Sartoris* is uneven; she did not have the advantage of having read Blotner's biog-

raphy or *Flags in the Dust* which are aids in interpreting both Faulkner's attitudes toward women and Narcissa's attitudes toward men.
Waters considered Benbow to be crippled by his possessive mother, a
sound assumption, in light of his Benbow–Sartoris heritage.

Elnora's verdict, "town trash," applies to the contrast between
Aunt Jenny, who loved flowers and devoted much time to cultivating
them, and Narcissa, who used Aunt Jenny's flowers as an excuse for
going to Sartoris. Edward Corridori divided characters into those who
are attuned to nature and regard the earth as sacred space and those
who lead profane lives: the only life-cherishing, vital Sartoris was Aunt
Jenny, at ninety, until the life-destroying Narcissa revealed the truth
about her conduct and lack of integrity which Aunt Jenny could not
live with.

The Sartorises and the Compsons, the families in the first two
Yoknapatawpha novels, seem very different in personalities of the
individual members and in characteristics as families. But they both
illustrate the failure of the aristocrats to maintain their social and moral
leadership in the community.

The Compson family was more prolific than the Sartorises, having
four children of one marriage, but the number of children was no
guarantee of the continuity of the family. Three generations of the
Compsons are presented directly: the parents, Jason III and Caroline;
the children, Quentin, Jason IV, and Benjy (Caddy is seen only
through the memories of her brothers); and Caddy's daughter, Miss
Quentin. Damuddy, the maternal grandmother, is presented only
through the memories of Benjy and Quentin, and the paternal grandfather, General Compson, only through the memories of Quentin in
Absalom, Absalom! and incidentally in some short stories, such as "A
Justice."

Quentin, Caddy, and Benjy knew little of parental care and love
except that of Dilsey, a surrogate mother. Mrs. Compson used up her
maternal feelings on Jason IV, the only real Bascomb in the Compson
family. Quentin and Caddy never knew maternal love or observed
marital love. Victims of the myth of the South which denied that
women had sexual impulses, Caddy yielded to her impulses and
Quentin, believing the myth, condemned her for her loss of chastity.
Forced into a loveless marriage to preserve the family respectability by
giving her unborn child a father and a name, Caddy was cast out by her
husband and was denied access to her child after she gave it up to her
parents. Her disastrous life was predictable from the time Mrs.
Compson put on mourning because Caddy had let a boy kiss her. After
the destruction of his own ideals by Caddy's loss of virtue and his
father's nihilistic cynicism, Quentin committed suicide rather than face

maturity. Benjy, the idiot, responded to Caddy's love with possessive devotion, but merely registered the deficiencies of his parents. Jason, a confirmed bachelor, was the head of the family after Mr. Compson's death. As guardian of his niece, Miss Quentin, Jason was a parody of his uncle Maury's irresponsibility: he kept a watchful eye on Miss Quentin and by his sadistic persecution drove her to repeat the error of her mother and accept whatever means of escape she could find as a substitute for a loveless family life. We are never told what became of Miss Quentin, but in the Appendix to *The Sound and the Fury* Faulkner confirmed the readers' suspicions about the man she eloped with: he "was already under sentence for bigamy" (p. 426). Thus ended the Compson family, even while Benjy and Jason and Mrs. Compson still lived.

Except for the very short period of Bayard's and Narcissa's married life, no Sartoris marriage is presented and no family of parents and children. The chivalric ideal thrived in the successive generations of men. In the Compson family, however, another cultural influence prevailed, that of Calvinism. Mr. Compson was a nihilist, but regarded women with Calvinistic distrust, as irrational creatures with an affinity for evil. In Mrs. Compson, Calvinistic beliefs and attitudes were most apparent and were most damaging to the children. Predestination is a very sustaining belief for those who are convinced that they are among the elect. In "William Faulkner: The Calvinistic Sensibility," Mary Fletcher noted the relation of the Compson pride to their Calvinistic background. Proud of her ignorance of sin, Mrs. Compson disowned Caddy and would not let her name be spoken in the Compson home while Caddy's daughter, Miss Quentin, was growing up there. To Quentin, as to his mother, loss of chastity without the sanctification of marriage was the unpardonable sin of Caddy. But Mrs. Compson found a husband for Caddy and flirted coyly with him before he married Caddy. When he found out how he had been hoodwinked, he divorced Caddy. Mrs. Compson is a parody of the myth of the Southern ideal woman, and in her way is as devastating as Narcissa Benbow Sartoris in imposing her own superficial standards on others: both Caddy and Quentin believed that they were damned, and Mrs. Compson had no sense of responsibility for their fates. Predestination can be a comforting belief. Fletcher pointed out the relation between Jason's ambitions and the Calvinistic support of capitalistic ethics. Jason's unethical behavior, particularly by cashing the checks Caddy sent for her daughter and letting his mother think that she was untainted with Caddy's sin when she burned the phony checks, is all of a piece with her role-playing and self-deception. Caddy's real sin was dooming her child to the same fate as befell her—being brought up in the Compson family, under Mrs. Compson's influence. But a Southern lady of Caddy's social class would know nothing of how to support herself and her child in a socially respectable fashion.

Dilsey is the real mother in the Compson family, but none of the Compson children learned from their parents to appreciate and respect Dilsey. And, as Frank Thomas pointed out, Dilsey had to subordinate the needs of her own children to the demands of the Compsons.

From John Faulkner's *My Brother Bill* and from Joseph Blotner's *Faulkner: A Biography*, it is evident that Faulkner had a very keen sense of responsibility to his family. But nowhere in his fiction did he present the larger family group traditional in the South and a reality in Faulkner's family, as he told Robert Linscott. Only in *The Reivers* did he present a three-generation family of grandparents, parents, and children which closely resembles his own family when he was a child.

The McCaslin genealogical table gives a misleading first impression of a family. The white family of Carothers McCaslin, the only one that counts in Southern society, dies out in the third generation in the male line and in the seventh in the female line, in which it has descended through the slender links of a single child in each generation. The family of Isaac McCaslin, the only one developed in any detail, is untypical and ends with Isaac. He is the only child of a late and strange marriage: his father, Uncle Buck, was ensnared, at the tender age of about sixty-five, by Sophonsiba Beauchamp as the only available male who could provide her with the marital status society required; as Malinowski says, "The attainment of a full tribal status is always a powerful motive for marriage." She is the one McCaslin wife presented with any details, but only in the memory of the boy, Cass Edmonds. As the son of such a marriage, Ike never experienced typical family life: Uncle Buck died when Ike was about six, and Sophonsiba when Ike was ten. Ike was rather fortunate in enjoying a father–son relationship with his cousin's son, McCaslin Edmonds, sixteen years older than Ike, with Sam Fathers, and with the group of men at the hunting camp ("The Bear"). In none of these relationships is there any evidence that Ike observed or shared family life. Ike married a woman who, Faulkner said, thought sex was evil and married him only "to be chatelaine of a plantation" (*FU* 275). She gave Ike one last chance to have a son ("The Bear," p. 315); Ike was father to none but "uncle" to many. Judging by Roth, this avuncular relationship was not as effective as was the relationship between Cass Edmonds and Ike: in "The Fire and the Hearth" and "Delta Autumn" Roth showed no signs of having learned such "truths of the heart" as Ike learned from Cass's tutelage and example.

The collateral line of the Edmondses repeats the motherless–only-child pattern represented in the male line: Zack and Roth are both only children, and, according to "The Fire and the Hearth," Roth was left motherless as a newborn infant. In 1941, when we last see him, Roth has one illegitimate, unacknowledged child and is unmarried, as he seems to be in 1961, when we last hear of him (*The Reivers*, p. 61). His child, last of the McCaslin tribe, at least has a mother whose Negro blood is, judging from the rest of the family, likely to make her a better mother than the white mothers.

The Negro side of the family is, of course, negligible, from the point of view of white society, but it is worth looking at anthropologically. Tomey's Turl, presumably son of Carothers McCaslin and his own daughter, Thomasina, was the father of six children, of whom only three lived to grow up, such being the rigors of infant existence among Negroes in those turbulent times. Of these three children, only two produced families, so far as we know: James was the grandfather of the girl who bore Roth's child; Lucas, who married Molly Worsham, had three children but in 1941 had only one grandchild: Samuel Worsham Beauchamp, who was electrocuted in "Go Down, Moses." Thus in 1941, Roth's child is the only one living of the combined white and Negro lines. There are no white children, and no children of either Henry or Nat Beauchamp, Lucas' son and daughter. The only family *group* in either white or Negro lines is that of which Lucas and Molly are parents, which included Roth Edmonds, as a foster brother of Henry until he assumed his white status and withdrew. From what we are told about Lucas and Molly, we can infer that they were good, responsible parents, the adolescent delinquency of their grandson Samuel being inadequate as evidence to the contrary.

Among the yeomen, rather than the aristocrats, we find the best example of a large, companionable family, with a seemingly ideal father–son relationship. But the MacCallums are a family of men, with Negro servants. In *Sartoris* none of the five sons, ranging from twenty to fifty-two, is married (pp. 309 ff.). Buddy, the youngest, son of old Virginius' second wife, is expected to perpetuate the family. In "The Tall Men" (1941) Faulkner confirmed his account of the MacCallums in 1919, except that the name is now spelled "McCallum"; the family is still united by strong ties and ruled by a code of respect for the father. During World War II, Buddy is, predictably, the only one of the five brothers who has sons, twins. Buddy, a widower, and the twins, of draft age and unmarried, live with Buddy's four brothers until the twins leave to enlist. Marshal Gombault accompanied a federal investigator to the McCallum farm to see why the twins had not registered for the draft and told the investigator the family history, from old Anse who as a young man walked from Mississippi back to Virginia, which he had never seen, to fight in the Confederate army. Any suspicions of the young heirs to the McCallum tradition are effectively dispelled. The twins, Anse and Lucius, are, Gombault says, "the livin', spittin' image of old Anse McCallum" (*CS* 55). Buddy is about to have his leg amputated at home. Informed that the twins are subject to arrest for failing to register for the draft, Buddy sends them to enlist, preferably in "the old Sixth Infantry" where he used to be, in World War I: "The Government done right by me in my day, and it will do right by you." The twins silently "kiss their father on the mouth" and then "turn as one," as they speak as one (p. 54), and set out to war.

This situation scarcely augurs a bright future for the McCallum family. The obvious truth about this unnatural family is immediately apparent if one changes it to a family of a mother with spinster daughters. Albert Devlin was the first to deal with the unideal aspects of the family, in "*Sartoris*: Rereading the MacCallum Episode," an expansion of the MacCallum part of a dissertation, "Parent–Child Relationships in the Works of William Faulkner."

A parallel that reinforces this prediction is Ike McCaslin's waking dream of heavenly bliss, a white man's happy hunting grounds, where he will rejoin his old hunting companions and "the wild strong immortal game" (*GDM* 354). In both the myth of the South and the myth of Yoknapatawpha, men put women on pedestals; in Yoknapatawpha, some men took a wife off her pedestal long enough to bear a child, then put her in a coffin and lived contentedly with the services of a Negro mammy.

One other all-male family in Yoknapatawpha, the Gowries of Beat Four, would not have Negroes in the household. "Nub" Gowrie, a one-armed widower, ruled his family of six sons in a "twenty-year womanless house" (*ID* 219). Clement Eaton's account, in *The Waning of the Old South*, of deeply religious people, generally fundamentalists, who had "a strong puritanical streak" but were given to "outbursts of violence" fits the Gowries. The most notorious example of such a family and community, Sullivan's Hollow, has been recorded by Chester Sullivan and published by the University Press of Mississippi. In Mississippi, as the author said, the name is "a synonym for lawlessness."

The other leading family of yeoman class and the most prosperous was the Varners, of Frenchman's Bend. They too were atypical but in a quite different way. Although we are told that Will Varner fathered sixteen children (*H* 5), the only ones presented directly are Jody, the incorrigible bachelor, and Eula, the frustrated earth-mother, who had one illegitimate daughter, Linda, for whose sake Eula let herself be married to the impotent and detestable Flem Snopes. In 1946, at the end of *The Mansion*, Linda is a childless widow.

United by respect and affection and fairly normal except in having only one child is the Mallison family, in *Knight's Gambit, Intruder in the Dust*, and in *The Town* and *The Mansion*. At first the family group included Grandfather Stevens, his daughter Margaret Mallison and her husband and their son Charles, and Margaret's brother, Gavin Stevens.

Gavin Stevens had been a Yoknapatawpha character since he appeared as a minor character, known to the narrator, in "Hair" (1931). He had had a brief speaking part in *Light in August* (1932), when he explained to a newly arrived guest how Joe Christmas' white blood would not let him shoot the pistol his black blood snatched up, so that he was shot to death "with that loaded and unfired pistol in his hand" (*LA* 425). In "Monk" (1937), narrated by his nephew, Charles Mallison, Gavin first appeared in a family context. In "An Error in Chemistry" (1946), Gavin was clearly living in the same house with Charles; Charles referred to "my own father before he died" (*KG* 127). In "Knight's Gambit," Charles's mother was referred to as a friend of Melisandre Backus. They were classmates at the Academy before Melisandre married when she was seventeen. In December 1941, the marriage of Melisandre, a widow with grown children, to Gavin is imminent, as Charles's "Bless you, my children" intimates (p. 238). When he comes home the next spring, he is met at the depot by Gavin, his new aunt Melisandre, and his mother (p. 240). Although the period covered in *The Town* ends in 1929, Faulkner had decided to resurrect Mr. Mallison but not to annul the marriage of Gavin and Melisandre by letting Gavin marry Linda. To prepare the reader for what will happen in *The Mansion*, after 1941, Charles tells us about his Uncle Gavin's attempt to form a girl's mind before he tried it again with Linda Snopes. His mother and his father tell him about Melisandre, now Mrs. Harris, as she was in "Knight's Gambit." In *The Town*, she is five years younger than Margaret Mallison, and is a wealthy widow with two children. In *The Mansion*, however, Margaret and Gavin are twins, with the bond of twinship a major aspect of their relationship.

It is obvious that, whatever Faulkner's addiction to twins indicates, it does not indicate that he considered twins likely to marry young and have many children.

Despite the closeness of the bonds which unite the Stevens–Mallison family, there are unusual aspects in addition to Charles's being an only child. The maternal uncle, Gavin, usurps the father role and plays a much larger part in the education, in the broad sense, of Charles than does his own father. Here the influence of the uncle is good, not the road to ruin as it was for Miss Quentin Compson with Uncle Jason as surrogate father. But Gavin was so well satisfied with the Mallisons as a substitute for a family of his own, with a tireless listener in Charles for his incorrigible loquacity, so lacking in a realistic and aggressive approach to sex, and so romantic and permanently adolescent that he married late, in 1942, and had no children of his own. It is possible that he was a step-grandfather in 1946, at the end of *The Mansion*. At that time Charles Mallison was still unmarried, but he had served in World War II from 1941 to 1945. Thus the most sane, wholesome, and affectionate members of the upper class who play major roles in Yoknapatawpha seem to be doing nothing to perpetuate the family. Stuart and Rafe, the twins in Buddy's generation, were not identical twins, but all five sons had "dark, saturnine faces all stamped clearly from the same die" (*Sar.* 319). Albert Devlin analyzed the abnormalities which were created and fostered by this atypical patriarchal family. Only in a male chauvinist society could this family be considered admirable and enviable. In "The Tall Men," during World War II, Buddy, now a widower, has twin sons, of draft age and unmarried, living with their father and uncles. This situation scarcely augurs well for the future of the family, especially when the twins enlist in the army.

Unlike such atypical families, the Mallisons are united by respect and affection and fairly normal in make-up. Furthermore, they are leading characters in *Knight's Gambit, Intruder in the Dust, The Town,* and *The Mansion*. The family group includes three generations: Grandfather Stevens, his son Gavin and daughter Margaret Mallison, her husband, and their son Charles. But Charles is an only child, Gavin seems to be an incorrigible bachelor who mysteriously has achieved twinship with his sister and usurps a father's role in the education of his nephew. He enjoyed a comfortable life with little responsibility and cherished its romantic dreams until his belated marriage in 1942. Charles is thirty-two at the end of *The Mansion* and Gavin is still childless. They will not regenerate Yoknapatawpha society, provide a viable new myth for the South.

If Faulkner had lived longer and had wished to continue the Yoknapatawpha chronicles beyond *The Reivers*, there was another leading family through whom the best of the old tradition might have been preserved. The Priests, a branch of the Edmonds family identified for the first time in *The Reivers*, are an admirable family. In retrospect, old Lucius Priest presents a picture of a complete family of four little boys, their parents and paternal grandparents, and Uncle Ike McCaslin and Cousin Zachary Edmonds. Young Lucius, as seen by his elderly self, was a boy who proved capable of gaining wisdom from experience without losing his sensitive conscience. His grandfather proved capable of coping wisely and tenderly with the boy's spiritual crisis. By implication, in view of old Lucius' story told to his grandson, the family has not only survived to the fifth generation from that of Boss Priest, grandfather of the narrator, but has maintained admirable family relationships. This family is much more like Faulkner's own family, with his three brothers and grandchildren, than is the Sartoris family, in which Faulkner's generation was extinct in 1920 and there were no grandchildren in 1961, when *The Reivers* was narrated. The parallels between Colonel John Sartoris and Colonel William C. Falkner are the chief resemblances between fact and fiction in the Sartoris story. It is pleasant to meet the Priest family in 1961, typifying the best in the Southern tradition and in family life in general and closely resembling the Faulkners as they are represented in John Faulkner's *My Brother Bill* and Blotner's *Faulkner: A Biography*. The four Faulkner brothers, of the generation of Lucius Priest, grandfathered twelve grandchildren, including Jill Faulkner's three boys, the only ones not born as Faulkner. (Faulkner also regarded as among his grandchildren the children of his stepson and his stepdaughter.)

As Otto Schlumpf observed, "Only in *The Reivers* is nobility still full-blooded among the aristocrats. . . ." But it is not in the direct line of the male descendants of the founders of Yoknapatawpha, and the preservation of honor is less rooted in the past. In seeking to come to terms with the "Southern family romance," Faulkner presented in one novel what Richard King defined as the structure of "the literal and symbolic family," grandfather, father, and son. Faulkner also illustrated the truth of King's statement that "once the family romance was demythologized" and the white families had to recognize their black children, "the incest and miscegenation taboo had to go as well." Young Lucius was taught by his mother to call Ned McCaslin, "the family skeleton," "Uncle Ned McCaslin," because he was "an actual grandson" of old Lucius Quintus Carothers McCaslin (and thus the counterpart of Lucas Beauchamp in *Go Down, Moses*). And Lucius was taught by his grandfather before Lucius could remember that "no gentleman ever referred to anyone by his race or religion" (p. 143).

The absence in Yoknapatawpha of vigorous families like the Faulkners is a symptom of a decaying society. But, although it is true, as Olga Vickery said, that "each dynasty carries the seeds of its own destruction," the "seeds" vary, and each family must be examined to see why it breaks off when it does. Vickery used a neat and attractive scheme, based on *Mosquitoes*, of dynasties having stages like those of

individuals: elemental being, in the frontiersman period; doing, represented in men of action of the settlement and war periods; thinking
represented in lawyers; and remembering, seen in those who, though
young, "relive the lives of their ancestors." But the reasons behind
those stages vary with families and individuals, and the differences are
as significant as the similarities.

The decline of a family may be caused by a lack of physical vitality
or of healthy sexuality or it may be psychic, lack of the will to live. The
Compson family represent various shades of an inherent opposition to
life, except Caddy and Miss Quentin, who had to escape from the
family in order to live in whatever dubious fashion was available. Mr.
Compson, Jason III, begot four children, the fourth an idiot, and then
retreated to a life of alcoholic indolence that contributed to Quentin's
disillusionment and defeatism and rejection of life and to Jason IV's
selfish cynicism and unwillingness to marry and increase the burdens
which were all he inherited from his father. Mrs. Compson played the
role of a Southern lady: she imposed her creed of chastity on both
Caddy and Quentin and thereby drove Caddy to believe in her own
damnation and Quentin to share that belief and drown himself. But he
courteously finished the year at Harvard which had gratified his
mother's pride. Mrs. Compson's ladylike hypochondria was the feminine equivalent of Mr. Compson's alcoholism and no doubt a cause of
it. The Sartorises had a much better example to follow in Colonel John
than the Compsons had in General Compson: his third avatar, after
"the one as son of a brilliant and gallant statesman, the second as
battleleader of brave and gallant men," was spent at "the hunting and
fishing camp in the Tallahatchie river bottom" as a "pseudo-Daniel
Boone–Robinson Crusoe, who had not returned to juvenility because
actually he had never left it" (*SF* 409). The Sartorises did not fare
much better, though they were more agreeable as people. (Aunt Jenny
was superior to the male Sartorises but was widowed when young and
never remarried.) It is questionable whether the last scion of the
Sartorises, Benbow, is preferable to Caddy's daughter, Miss Quentin,
the victim of both Mrs. Compson and Jason and therefore even more
unfortunate than Caddy.

Three young men of the same generation contribute to the end of
their respective families by a psychic and a psychological impediment
to marriage. Horace Benbow, Quentin Compson, and Gavin Stevens
are all quixotic idealists, lacking in vigorous and healthy sexuality—
Quentin perhaps lacking in heterosexuality—and all three too strongly
attached to a sister to seek other feminine companionship. Horace was
ensnared by a married woman, the opposite of his seemingly chaste

and serene sister, suitably named Narcissa. Quentin was seduced by Little Sister Death, because his sister was *not* chaste and serene. Gavin's sister Margaret was the most normal and admirable of the three sisters. But after Margaret miraculously became Gavin's twin, the strong bond between them and the pleasant home she provided for Gavin and their father, Judge Stevens, apparently made Gavin prefer dreams of courtly love for first Eula and then her daughter, Linda, to the realities of marriage. Neither Gavin nor Horace had any children.

Gavin Stevens of *The Town* had not been conceived of when Faulkner wrote *Sartoris* and *Sanctuary*: to use one of Faulkner's favorite words, Gavin was an avatar of Horace. When Faulkner planned the *Snopes* trilogy, there was no role for such a person as Horace or Gavin in *The Town*, according to a synopsis of the trilogy which Faulkner sent to Robert Haas in 1938 (Blotner, II 1006–1008). Faulkner intended to have Eula Varner Snopes's daughter meet the son of Sarty Snopes, the little boy who ran away in "Barn Burning," and bring about a meeting between him and a remote Snopes cousin. The consequences of this marriage of Sarty's son to another Snopes brings about—or was intended to bring about—more dire consequences than one could imagine. But before Faulkner began to write *The Town*, he met Joan Williams and created Eula's daughter Linda more or less in Joan's image. Gavin Stevens, of Eula's generation, was already created. In *The Town* Gavin devoted the fervor of his courtly love to Eula Snopes. After her suicide, he ended the chivalric-Platonic relationship that had developed between him and Linda as she grew up and sent her to Greenwich Village, in 1929. The letters of Faulkner to Joan Williams which have been published by Blotner, in the *Biography* and the *Selected Letters*, are useful in interpreting *The Town* but have little relevance to the Gavin–Linda story in *The Mansion*.

Somewhat different attitudes toward women may have similar consequences in the history of a family: idealization of woman may prevent marriage, but marriage chiefly for procreation may result in brief marriages if the wife dies after having had one or two children. By the MacCallums and the Gowries and the McCaslins and the white Beauchamps, wives can be dispensed with. The mothers in these families, whether the children were few or many, we are told nothing about. Ike McCaslin might never have been born if Miss Sophonsiba had waited to be wooed by Uncle Buck. "Was" suggests that by the time the Civil War was over, Sophonsiba must have reached a state of desperation that forced her to abandon her Southern lady act and that the male–female roles were reversed in the Grecian Urn scene: "What mad pursuit? What struggle to escape?" There were always plenty of black women to take care of children and domestic chores. Ike McCaslin lost his one chance to have a son, but he also failed to vitalize his ideals by fulfilling his responsibilities as the oldest man in the McCaslin family or by participating in the life and activities of the community.

To both the McCaslins and the MacCallums, the male world of hunting and of life close to nature—without, for Ike, cultivating the soil—seemed more attractive than the world of marriage and family life which is shared with white women. Once Hubert Beauchamp got his sister off his hands by her marriage to Uncle Buck, he lived an irresponsible and irregular life, keeping a Negro mistress until Sophonsiba drove her out (*GDM* 302–303). Hubert used up the inheritance intended for Ike and died destitute, his dying gaze still "innocent and immortal and amazed and urgent" (*GDM* 306). A kind of arrested development kept some men in these three families in Vickery's first stage, that of "elemental being," in which the responsibilities of marriage and parenthood were postponed until too late or evaded altogether.

The fate of the Sutpen family is the only instance in Yoknapatawpha of the dying out of a family primarily because of the errors of its founder. Thomas Sutpen's attempt to live by the traditional code without any conception of the ethical aspects of that code, his patriarchal domination of the family, and his sacrifice of his own children to his megalomaniac grand design were the causes of his failure and of the extinction of the family. The Civil War contributed more directly to the decline of the Sutpens than to that of other families. Time was against Sutpen in his attempt after the war to rehabilitate the plantation and to have a son to continue the dynasty. "Doing" proved as unsuccessful a state of being for Sutpen as the other stages did for other families. Even had Henry not renounced his heritage and become a murderer and a fugitive, it is unlikely that he could have carried on the family: he was very similar, it seems, to Quentin Compson.

So far only the major upper-class families have been discussed. What were the patterns of family life among the Snopeses? Is Yoknapatawpha an example of the decay of the aristocracy and the vitality of the proletariat? Not exactly. Prolific as the tribe of Snopeses seems to be, there is no single family that is large and vigorous, and no individual of Snopesian nature has the ability and initiative to succeed the impotent Flem. Ab, the founder of the family, had two sons, Colonel Sartoris Snopes, and Flem, and two bovine daughters. Sarty disappeared at the end of "Barn Burning." As Flem was impotent, that branch of the Snopes family in Yoknapatawpha is extinct in the male line. Considering what Faulkner had planned in his synopsis, it is just as well that Sarty did not reappear. Flem's household was a travesty of the typical family. Eula was his wife and Linda was his daughter in name only, and all that he could provide was the material means of life and the veneer of respectability. Mink Snopes had two daughters by his ex-prostitute wife. All three women were the victims of Mink's poverty and misfortune, the girls going the way of their mother. Clarence Snopes is the only one of the family whose fortunes we can trace to the end of *The Mansion*, when his political career had been blasted. Byron Snopes's savage brood had been sent back where they came from: at the end of *The Town* they are on the train, headed for El Paso.

The one Snopes family which seems to hold some hope for continuity and satisfactory family life is that of Eck Snopes, who was Snopes only in name. The fine father–son relationship between Eck and young Wall in *The Hamlet* was the only such example in the Snopes annals, after Sarty's disillusionment and flight in "Barn Burning." Eck's honesty, but not Eck's ineptness, was inherited by Wallstreet Panic Snopes. He chose a good wife and was a good husband to her and brother to Admiral Dewey Snopes.

The absence of normal family patterns and the psychological aberrations in some family relationships which have already been indicated affect the survival of the family. These aberrations and others also affect relationships within the family. The mythology of Yoknapatawpha repeats archetypal patterns in family relationships, but the same patterns are also found in Southern life. The strong family ties, the exclusive social life of the aristocrats, who comprise only a small group in a limited geographical area, and the isolation of plantation life are typical aspects of the culture. We are now concerned with these aspects of culture in relation to myth, which from the Greek myths to the present has been concerned with the family and the emotional reactions engendered by family relationships and family life.

Although the parent–child relationship, as Malinowski says, "remains one of the dominant sentiments in human life, manifesting itself in moral rules, in legal obligations, in religious ritual," those relationships can be destructive as well as constructive. Some kinds of Utopian societies, from Plato to Aldous Huxley, do away with the family, not only to subordinate the family to the state but to protect the child against pernicious effects of family life. In the Yoknapatawpha chronicles, although the ideal of family life is not attacked, harmonious and mutually satisfactory relationships between parents and children are rare. Parents fail to give children the love and security the children need or children resent parental authority and rebel against it.

Except for Colonel John Sartoris and Bayard, Eck Snopes and Wall, and "Mister Ernest" and his foster son in "Race at Morning," the father who wins his son's admiration and respect without exerting domination over the son is absent. Father–son relationships may involve the traditional and universal conflict between generations, a conflict that in Faulkner's works usually does not involve Oedipal rivalry. The conflict between Ike McCaslin and his substitute father, Cass Edmonds, was over ideals and principles. But Ike's relinquishment of his inheritance may have been one cause of the decline of the family: if he had made his wife "chatelaine of a plantation," he might have had sons (*FU* 275–76). Ike's conflict with Cass may be Oedipal in the sense in which Rank used the term: a rebellion against the role of son and father and a desire "to grow up a free man in the wilderness." This pattern is stressed by Leslie Fiedler in *Love and Death in the American Novel*, but only Ike McCaslin fits the pattern in Yoknapatawpha. Uncle Buck and Uncle Buddy suggest Fiedler's "pure marriage of males," with a bit of incest added to dilute the purity. Ike's subsequent marriage would seem to weaken the interpretation as an Oedipal conflict to escape responsibility, did not his memory of his marriage and the story of his father's marriage seem to suggest that marriage was the woman's idea.

In *William Faulkner: An Interpretation*, Irving Malin dealt with the father–son myth, based upon the themes of rigidity and the need to rebel against it. These themes do not cover all aspects of the father–son myth in Faulkner's works. Quentin and Jason Compson reacted in very different ways to their father: Quentin rejected his father's philosophy and Jason rejected his father, holding him in scorn and bearing a grudge because he did more for Quentin than he did for Jason. Henry Sutpen renounced his heritage and by so doing destroyed his father's design. This is the clearest example of Rank's type of the son's rebellion against the father's design.

A strong attachment between father and son or between mother and daughter was recognized by Otto Rank as reverse Oedipal. The feeling between Colonel John and Bayard Sartoris seems too moderate and wholesome to be called reverse Oedipal. Irving Malin regarded their relationship as nearly ideal. Beyond planning for Bayard to study law to meet the needs of changing times (*U* 266), Colonel John did not try to impose his will on Bayard. His death left Bayard free before beginning his career.

The most extreme example of the reverse Oedipal relationship, that in the MacCallum family between Virginius and his sons in *Sartoris* and between Buddy and his twin sons in "The Tall Men," has already been dealt with, as preventing normal family and individual patterns of life.

The relationship between Charles Mallison and his uncle, Gavin Stevens, especially in *Intruder in the Dust* and *The Mansion*, resembles a reverse Oedipal complex. An unusual variation is suggested in *The Town* and *The Mansion*, in which Gavin and Charles's mother are twins: Charles's attachment to Gavin may involve an Oedipal element transferred to the male twin.

Rebellion against the father or attachment to the father are opposite relationships. A third possibility occurs when the son has no father, when he has lost his father, or when his father refuses to fulfill his paternal responsibilities. The search for a father is a search for security, for authority, often a search for God as a father-image. Rank said: "the child has to discover or create his parents as he needs them, which is actually realized in the idea of God." Charles Bon is the one son who is most clearly seeking a father, desiring acknowledgment as a son. Bon is presented, however, in Quentin Compson's version of the story of the Sutpens. Quentin's rebellion against his father may be the obverse of his search for a father, for superior wisdom which could so present the world to Quentin that he could accept it. Since much of Quentin's interpretation of the Sutpen story is a projection of his own problems, this may be another instance of such projection. Ike McCaslin is a clear example of the search for a father. Fatherless, with a guardian, Cass Edmonds, not old enough to be his father, Ike turned to Sam Fathers, whose age and wisdom could fill Ike's needs and who sought an heir to the tradition of the Old People.

The father–daughter relationship, like the mother–son relationship, may have sexual implications. Rank explained the father's preference for a daughter as possibly betokening an unwillingness to be a father and therefore as revealing an incestuous element. The clearest suggestion of such an attitude is a father's jealous reaction toward a daughter's suitors. In addition to Miss Emily's father, in "A Rose for Emily," whom we see in the tableau imagined by the townspeople, Miss Emily in the open doorway, her father in front of her with a horsewhip (*CS* 123), Ruby's father, in *Sanctuary*, used a gun, not a whip, and her brother kept Ruby from interfering (*San.* 56). The fact that Ruby told the story to Temple may imply a parallel between Judge Drake and Temple and Ruby and her father, as Ruby suggested. Temple's disobedience and the tableau of Temple leaving the courthouse surrounded by her father and four brothers (p. 282) may symbolize male chivalry protecting feminine virtue or incestuous feelings within the family group, from which Temple seemed to flee.

The relationship between child and parent may be caused by circumstances and tensions in the family rather than by instinctive attraction or repulsion. Condemned and rejected by her mother, Caddy Compson turned to her father for love and sympathy. A child may create a father-image out of the most unlikely person, as Linda did out of Flem in *The Town*, according to Eula's last conversation with Gavin before she committed suicide (pp. 323–34). The relation which this bit of self-deception on Linda's part, in addition to her bitterness over her mother's suicide, may bear to Linda's ultimate assistance in destroying Flem, in *The Mansion*, is left to the reader's imagination.

The non-Oedipal emphasis in Faulkner's mythology is most apparent in the relationships between mothers and sons. Only in the Bundren family was strong attachment between mother and son reciprocal. But Jewel used his horse as a surrogate for his mother, an outlet for violent affection and abuse. Except for his one soliloquy, the only overt evidence of his feeling was his heroic effort to get Addie's body safely to Jefferson. Mrs. Compson's preference for Jason, as a Bascomb, did not evoke equal warmth from Jason. Considering that Benjy was the only male Compson left in Jason's section, her preference was scarcely a flattering choice. Narcissa Benbow Sartoris dominated her fatherless son, Benbow, but not to the exclusion of other men, younger than herself, such as Gowan Stevens (*Sanctuary*).

The one dangerously close approach in Yoknapatawpha to violation of the universal taboo, cited by Malinowski, of sexual interest between unmarried members of a family group is also a parallel to an ancient myth: Drusilla made advances to her stepson Bayard, as Phaedra did to Hippolytus. But unlike Hippolytus, who literally preferred death to Phaedra, Bayard responded to Drusilla. But when he kissed her, he thought "of the woman of thirty, the symbol of the ancient and eternal snake" (*U* 262). Of the numerous examples of serpent or snake symbolism in Cirlot, the "clear connexion between the snake and the feminine principle" is the most pertinent to Bayard's thought. In loyalty to his father, Bayard told of his disloyalty, but "it didn't even matter" to Colonel Sartoris, preoccupied with his need for "moral housecleaning" of his own (*U* 266).

Faulkner obviously forgot this episode and thought that "Drusilla would have made no effort to bring out that ["romantic attraction"] in that boy because her husband . . . was her knight"; Faulkner further explained that the authority of Colonel John and Bayard's concern for his father's honor would have made such an attraction unthinkable (*FU* 256). In view of Faulkner's later ideas, this episode should be neither overstressed nor forgotten. The mythic quality in Faulkner's imagination may have diminished as he grew older and his memory may consequently have become unreliable.

Drusilla's relationship with "Aunt Louise," her mother, is parallel with the rebellion of son against father, except that Drusilla was not rebelling merely against her mother but against the whole traditional concept of woman and her function. In turning to Colonel Sartoris for refuge, she was rejecting marriage and motherhood. But she was forced into marriage against her will to prevent social ostracism. Drusilla is also the only example of a mother-dominated mature woman. Unlike Caddy Compson or Judith Sutpen, she had no father to turn to from her weak and shallow but strong-willed mother.

The infrequency of Freudian implications in parent–child relations may indicate Faulkner's lack of interest in that aspect of psychology or in families which are typical enough to fit the pattern. Few children in Yoknapatawpha have two parents living who are at all comparable in strength of character or influence; this peculiarity of the family pictures may signify that incomplete families are a cause of the doom of families and individuals. Faulkner had no objection to dealing with incestuous relationships, but they were those between brother and sister instead of between child and parents. The strongest family relationships in Yoknapatawpha are those between brother and sister or between twins, of the same or opposite sex.

Two aspects of incestuous attachment between brother and sister are relevant to the myth of the South and to the conditions of Southern society: incest was a royal prerogative, according to Otto Rank, a means of preserving the exclusiveness of the chosen few; it was also a consequence of the isolated life on plantations which often deprived the white children of companionship with other white children of their own social class. None of the upper-class families in Faulkner's mythology has enough relatives to break the isolation by family visits which were customary in the South. Another explanation of incestuous inclinations refers to the psychology of the individual: according to Rank, it is a way of escaping the compulsion of racial immortality through sex, a way of escaping the responsibility of marriage and parenthood, similar to the preference of a father for a daughter.

The taboo on incest is most familiar and universal; therefore violations of it spring from deep and powerful impulses, strongly stated by Malinowski: "The taboo on incest is a universal rule throughout humanity, endures through life, and is usually the strongest, most deeply felt moral prohibition"; it is "mainly directed towards the separation of brother and sister." Faulkner's characters illustrate that last point and the reason for it: Freud explains the taboo against incest as evidence of strong instinct in favor of incestuous relationships which requires a strong taboo as a check. In Yoknapatawpha the brother–sister relationships range from strong affection through suggested incestuous feelings to fully recognized incestuous desire.

Horace and Narcissa Benbow were orphans at the beginning of *Sartoris*. Horace had been devoted to Narcissa since her birth when he was seven. He idealized her and cared for her after the death of their parents: his emphasis on her purity and serenity, upon which she based her own self-image, may have been a means of ensuring that he would not violate those qualities. Horace was responsive to other women, not so chaste and serene: his feelings toward his female relations, by blood or by marriage, have an ambiguity in both *Sartoris* and *Sanctuary* that is lacking in *Flags in the Dust* and the unpublished galleys of *Sanctuary*. *Flags in the Dust* made explicit Horace's feelings toward all the females in his life: his mother, Narcissa, Belle Mitchell, her eight-year-old daughter, Little Belle, and even Belle's sister Joan, "a lady tiger in a tea-gown" (*FD* 292), whom Ben Wasson removed completely when he shortened the role of Horace in cutting down *Flags in the Dust* to an acceptable length. When Faulkner revised the unpublished galleys of *Sanctuary*, he followed Wasson's principle of omitting numerous passages presenting the inner consciousness of Horace Benbow. One's assumption in *Sanctuary* that Horace was naïvely unaware of the true nature of his feeling for Little Belle and of unhealthy elements in his devotion to Narcissa is disproved in the deleted portions of *Flags in the Dust* and of the galleys.

The strongest bonds of brother–sister love are combined in Gavin Stevens and his sister, Margaret Mallison, who resemble Horace and Narcissa in some ways but are much more admirable. The devotion between Gavin and Margaret is strongest in *The Town* and in *The Mansion* where she is his twin, not a younger sister. In *The Town* Margaret was willing to overstep the bounds of convention to gratify Gavin in his devotion to Eula, but her feeling for Gavin had not kept her from marrying and being a good wife, whose husband seems not to have objected to having Gavin a member of the household. Gavin's devotion to Eula and later to Linda suggests that his feeling for Margaret was not unacceptably intense. His "courtly love" tendency to carry on protracted love affairs on a high spiritual level and at a safe distance, his late marriage, and his failure to have children, Charles being almost like a son to him, may indicate that his attachment to Margaret lessened his ability or desire fully to love other women. Jean-Marie Magnan includes Gavin and Margaret as examples of incest in "Incest et mélange des sangs dans l'œuvre de William Faulkner."

Analogy as a means of discovering hidden truths is fundamental to the story of Quentin in *Absalom, Absalom!*. Faulkner's omission of any reference to the happenings in *The Sound and the Fury* is an inexplicable deviation from his usual practice of linking stories in the Yoknapatawpha chronicles which have recurrent characters. Readers of *The Sound and the Fury* who know when and why Quentin committed suicide assume that Quentin's feeling for Caddy inspired his and Shreve's interpretation of Henry Sutpen's feeling for Judith, for which there was no possible evidence. Mr. Compson's theory about Henry, Bon, and Judith is purely conjectural, but the story of Quentin in *The Sound and the Fury* makes his acceptance of his father's interpretation credible and convincing. Idelle Sullens distinguished four themes related to the incest themes in *Absalom*: male and female virginity; self-identification of brothers (Quentin and Henry) with sisters (Caddy and Judith) and unconscious response to the sisters' lovers; miscegenation; man's concept of woman as a receptacle for man's regeneration. The last theme is not germane to this discussion. Concentrating on Quentin's attitudes, since much about Henry is based only on Quentin's conjectures and therefore reflects his projection of his own feelings into his explanation of Henry, the most salient fact is that Quentin could accept and justify either bigamy, Charles Bon's marriage to the octoroon, not legally binding in the South, or incest, which preserves the aristocratic inheritance, but not miscegenation, which corrupts the inheritance and in the South was the ultimate sin. Quentin and Shreve, identifying with Henry and Charles Bon, imagined what preceded Henry's shooting of Charles Bon (*AA* 351): after Henry's meeting with Colonel Sutpen, Bon, they imagined, said: "*So it's the miscegenation, not the incest, which you can't bear*" (*AA* 356); then, still in the tent in Carolina, facing Henry, Bon offered his pistol to Henry and said: "*I'm the nigger that's going to sleep with your sister, Unless you stop me, Henry*" (*AA* 358). The italicized passage that began on p. 351 ends with the same description of Henry and Bon and "*—You will have to stop me, Henry.*" Then Shreve's narration continues, with his account of the shooting of Bon by Henry at the gate of Sutpen's Hundred and the events learned from Rosa. The mystery concerning how Quentin knew Henry's motive for the murder remains. Between the possibility, not probability, that Quentin learned the truth from Henry when he saw him at Sutpen's Hundred, an episode presented entirely in Quentin's memory, including the dialogue with Henry, and Quentin's intuition concerning the only possible reason why Henry would shoot Bon, intuition is sufficient as providing an answer to "What is worse than bigamy or incest?"

The degree to which Henry's feeling for Charles Bon, as represented by Quentin, after Mr. Compson's conjectures, reflects Quentin's feeling for Dalton Ames, the only possible parallel to Charles Bon among Caddy's lovers, is hypothetical. Faulkner's own explanation of Quentin in the appendix to *The Sound and the Fury*, written after *Absalom, Absalom!*, and the story of Henry and Judith as given by the narrators would suggest that in both families the incestuous feeling went no further than the brother's identification with the sister and the direction of his desire toward the sister to the exclusion of other girls. Mr. Compson first presented the homosexual-incest theory (*AA* 95–99).

In *Doubling and Incest/Repetition and Revenge*, John T. Irwin examined the whole story of Quentin in *Absalom, Absalom!* and *The Sound and the Fury*, including relationships between brother and brother (Henry Sutpen and Charles Bon, doubled in Quentin and Shreve) and homosexuality (doubled in Henry–Bon and Quentin–Shreve, Quentin–Dalton Ames), as well as between Henry–Judith and Quentin–Caddy. The doubling includes also father–son, Sutpens and Compsons, author and characters, the significance of "doubling and incest as images of the self-enclosed" and also "as symbols of the state of the South after the Civil War, symbols of a region turned in upon itself." "The circle of the self-inclosed," Irwin explains, "repeats itself through time as a cycle," in the individual and in the family in "successive generations" (p. 59). Irwin assumes the interrelationship of *Absalom, Absalom!* and *The Sound and the Fury* as basic to an understanding of Quentin but does not deal with Faulkner's deviation from his usual practice in his complete omission of allusions to *The Sound and the Fury* in *Absalom, Absalom!*, particularly the absence of Caddy from narrative dialogue and Quentin's thoughts.

An additional interpretation of Quentin's incestuous attraction to Caddy as his sister is quite credible. Caddy may be a mother-substitute for both Quentin and Benjy. Quentin's scrap of inner monologue, "*if I'd just had a mother so I could say Mother Mother*" (p. 190), plus the painfully clear and unsympathetic picture of Mrs. Compson in his memories, lends credence to this theory of Quentin's desire and need for a mother. An impressive collection of images have Freudian meanings: the tree Caddy climbs may be the tree of life; water is a maternal symbol, associated with birth as well as death, the explicit association; the grandmother's death and Caddy's wedding both signify loss to Quentin and Benjy. Jung's account of the shadow, "the dark aspects of the personality" or the personal unconscious, is suggested by the extensive use of the shadow image in Quentin's section. Jung's explanation of the anima as an archetype, the contrasexual figure which is the source of projections in a man, includes a statement which describes Quentin: "a man living regressively, seeking his childhood and his mother, fleeing from a cold cruel world which denies him understanding." His own mother being unsympathetic, Quentin substitutes one of the other images in "the realm of his psyche," the sister, the beloved. The significance of this part of the mythology of Yoknapatawpha is the indication that the Compson family die out because of the psychic problems derived from both inheritance and conditions of family life related to the tradition of the South. The Waste Land sterility of Yoknapatawpha, like that of ancient Thebes, may be related to incest.

For Quentin, family affection is centered solely on Caddy, quite understandably when one considers the rest of the family. But among the families of Yoknapatawpha, brotherly love is rare: there is absence of feeling, as in Benjy and Quentin, or hostility, or too great attachment between brothers. Jason showed hostility toward Quentin in childhood and jealousy after Quentin's death because Quentin wasted the opportunities which were denied Jason; he showed sadistic scorn toward Benjy. In the Bundren family, not a leading family but noteworthy here as having four brothers, brotherly relationships vary. Cash and little Vardaman show some kindly feeling toward Jewel and Darl. Between Darl and Jewel there is hostility, Darl the son rejected by Addie, the mother, and Jewel the favored son. The combined hostility of Jewel, Anse, the father, and Dewey Dell, the sister, results in Darl's being sent to the insane asylum, despite Cash's regret.

Twin brothers show great devotion toward each other, to the exclusion of other affection. Buck and Buddy McCaslin lived as bachelors until they were over sixty, when Sophonsiba outwitted them and subsequently got Buck as her husband, by what other scheming we are not told. Young Bayard Sartoris' grief and guilt over his twin brother John's death were stronger than his love for his wife, Narcissa. The MacCallum family included two sets of twins, in two generations, but fraternal relationships among the brothers were so strong that twinship was not distinctive. Fraternal affection in the McCaslin, Sartoris, and MacCallum families in these instances apparently inhibited heterosexual love and led to late marriage, unsatisfactory marriage, or failure to marry.

These family situations suggest homosexuality but do not offer proof of it. When homosexuality occurs within the family, it is, like incest, a violation of the taboo against sexuality within the family, outside of the marital relation. Otherwise it is a violation of the general taboo against rejection of heterosexuality: such rejection places the self above the

melodrama. Carothers McCaslin's story is the simple one of a lonely man who, like all his class, had power over slave women but who had somewhat more conscience than most of his caste: although he would not say "my son" to a nigger, he would acknowledge his offspring in his will. But he knowingly exercised his *droit de seigneur* with his own daughter. Roth's repetition, through ignorance but also through inherited character, of the original moral offense, with the granddaughter of James Beauchamp, represents the never-ending chain of injustice. The relationship was too remote to be incestuous, but Roth knew it was miscegenation. The girl's love gave Roth the power that status gave his ancestor. Even Ike sinned against humanity by denying the ties of kinship because of miscegenation, for which his white kinsmen were responsible ("Delta Autumn"). This is the guilt of the South: making the victims of injustice bear the consequences, and denying both the Christian brotherhood of man and the blood brotherhood. This guilt is epitomized in the Sutpen family, whose fate symbolizes that of the South: the grand design failed and the family was ruined because those with Negro blood were denied a place in the family. The universal problem of man's inhumanity to man is presented in terms of the violation of the most sacred rights of human beings and the degradation and corruption of both the aggressors and the victims. The myth of the South presents as its supreme horror the rape of white women by Negroes; the mythology of Yoknapatawpha County presents as its supreme horror the absence of the very concept of rape of Negro women by white men.

In all this sprawling McCaslin and Edmonds and Beauchamp tribe, the family of Lucas and Molly best represents a normal family. What is omitted from the leading white families is as significant as what is included. The Sartorises and the Mallisons are the only families united by a healthy love and congeniality and including a grandparent and an aunt or uncle in the family group. The Mallisons are the only family which in 1946, at the end of *The Mansion*, have a male heir who is likely to marry and have a family.

The contrast between fiction and fact narrows a bit at this time. In "Knight's Gambit" Charles Mallison was eighteen just before Pearl Harbor and enlisted in the Air Force immediately. Jimmy Faulkner, Faulkner's nephew, was born in 1923 and joined the Air Force, and Faulkner took great satisfaction in Jimmy's war record. The fact that in 1946 Charles was not yet married is of no significance. Jimmy was not married until 1950, and fathered two sons and a daughter. Faulkner was particularly pleased when his grandniece was born, after Jimmy and his brother Chooky had five sons, all living in Oxford. The convergence of the Mallison and Faulkner families in this "fiction meets fact" fashion serves to emphasize the divergence thereafter: the Faulkners have thrived but no family in Yoknapatawpha equalled them.

No other family had enough physical vitality and natural sexual feeling to ensure its continuity. There is no family of children, except the little Priests in *The Reivers*, in 1905, which knows mother love. In no other families with more than one child does the mother survive and adequately fulfill her maternal role. (Addie Bundren did not belong to a leading family and her maternal love was devoted chiefly to Jewel.) There is no family which shows evidence of deep love between the parents; Margaret Mallison comes closest to being an admirable wife and mother, but the narrative deals with situations involving Gavin and Charles rather than Charles and his parents. Despite the Southern tradition, there are few families with kinfolk or with a keen sense of the duties of families and the purpose of family life. The Priests, in 1905, are the only example of a complete and harmonious family, including grandparents, parents, and four little boys, with Uncle Ike McCaslin and Zachary Edmonds as part of the family group. By implication the Priest family is continuing the tradition of a close grandfather–grandson relationship such as existed in the Falkner family.

What is the basic reason for the dying out of families in Yoknapatawpha? Perhaps lack of love between parents and between parents and children which would make marriage and family life attractive to the children and enable them to grow up seeking and making friendships leading to courtship and marriage. What Jung called "The omnipresent and ageless image which corresponds to the deepest reality in man," the image of Woman, is singularly lacking as a motivating force in Faulkner's young men in making them seek marriage. In a region noted in fact and in legend for feminine beauty and charm, Yoknapatawpha is an anomaly.

VI • HEROINES AND HEROES

The myth of the South illustrates that, in the development of a hero, myth is the last stage, as Mircea Eliade said in *Cosmos and History*. Colonel John Sartoris was a hero in *The Unvanquished* and becoming a myth in *Sartoris*. This concentrating on heroic figures may seem to be going back from myth. But Eliade was speaking of cultures in which the memory of a person or an event survives "for two or three centuries at the utmost." The telling and retelling of tales about characters, the very ground on which Yoknapatawpha was built, is one criterion for assigning heroic status to individuals. Enrico Garzilli justifies consideration of heroes in literature, in terms especially applicable to Yoknapatawpha: "The kind of hero that is revered is often an excellent barometer in defining the type of mythology and value system of a particular culture." In the absence of present belief in Greek mythology and the fragmentation of Christian mythology, "Contemporary man," Garzilli continues, "sees himself at his best only in vestiges of these former myths, and at his worst in the more recent parodies or cults of these myths." Garzilli's definition of heroism embraces both submission to God's will and rebellion against it: "Fidelity to his individuality is what constitutes the fabric of heroism."

The image of woman in the Yoknapatawpha chronicles helps to explain why some of the heroes fail to marry and why others when they do marry make poor choices. There may be a relation between the recurrence of the goddess-heroine figures which are most obviously cast in the mythic mold of Southern gyneolatry: the adoration of women as inhumanly pure and chaste or as superhumanly mammalian is characteristic of some of Faulkner's male characters who elevate women to goddess stature, reflecting one of the values "harmful to the post–Civil War South" which, Elizabeth Downey said, made "the creation and persistence of the magnolia myth" a tragedy. The myth of "spotless Southern womanhood," according to Dolores Brien, "shaped Southern culture by hardening into social codes and conventions."

The psychic limitations of the Southern myth are apparent in comparison with M.-L. von Franz's account of Jung's four stages in the development of the anima, as revealed in men's dreams. The first stage is "symbolized by the figure of Eve," representing "purely instinctual and biological relations." The second is "Faust's Helen," personifying "a romantic and aesthetic level . . . still characterized by sexual elements." The third is the Virgin Mary, "a figure who raises love to the heights of spiritual devotion." Sapientia symbolizes "wisdom transcending even the most holy and the most pure." Wisdom was scarcely associated in the myth of the South with women. Von Franz explained the knightly cult of the lady, a chief source of the Southern myth, as "a personification of the anima, fused with the Virgin Mary."

Jung explained that "an inner figure" which appears in dreams represents the unconscious self, "a female personification" if the dreamer is a man, a male personification if the dreamer is a woman; the male form Jung called "animus" and the female "anima." Both have their good and bad aspects. The anima, the woman within the man, has such positive aspects as helping a man to find the right woman to marry, to discern hidden facts, and to be in tune with the right inner values. The animus, the man within the woman, may lure a woman away from real men; it may encourage passivity or a destructive attitude. But it may encourage creativity. If she faces the realities of her animus, he "can turn into an invaluable inner companion who endows her with the masculine qualities of initiative, courage, objectivity, and spiritual wisdom." In Yoknapatawpha, a young woman so endowed is unlikely to be appreciated, but as an elderly widow she may enjoy esteem and independence.

The myth of Yoknapatawpha shows more clearly in the women because women are presented for the most part either objectively by the author or through the point of view of male characters, whose Southern susceptibility contributes to their deification. None of the men through whose eyes we see the chief heroines have had normal experience of love as lovers and husbands; if they married, they did so late and had no children. Partly in the concepts of these interpreters and partly in the author's, women are endowed with intuitive powers and instinctive wisdom and a pragmatic realism which distinguish them from men and which render unnecessary or irrelevant the experiences through which boys and men achieve maturity and identity. Just as the mother myths and rites and the order of Mother Night preceded the reign of the patriarchal gods and the heroic age, so the Earth-goddess and her sisters in Yoknapatawpha can here take precedence over the heroes and their quite different patterns of experience.

The most fully developed goddess-heroine is Eula Varner, heroine of *The Hamlet* and *The Town*. The magnification to mythic stature begins when she is introduced in *The Hamlet* by the omniscient author: it is carried to such an extreme that she seems subhuman rather than superhuman in her size, mammalian charms, and immobility. Any toys which involved physical activity had no more appeal to her than "the pot of cold tea to the old drunkard" (*H* 96). Through the obsession of Labove, the schoolmaster, Eula is seen as Venus and the goddess of fertility; he imagined her as married to a "crippled Vulcan," like "the fine land rich and fecund and foul and eternal and impervious to him who claimed title to it . . . producing a thousandfold the harvest he could ever hope to gather and save" (*H* 119). The wooing of Eula by all the teen-age boys in the area is like the wooing of Helen by her suitors, and the procession of vehicles suggests a ceremonial procession. In "Faulkner's Women: 'Demon–Nun and Angel–Witch,'" Naomi Jackson cited Eula in *The Hamlet* as the apotheosis of the Eternal Feminine among Faulkner's women, who "become reflections, or distortions, of the White Goddess, as life-giver and destroyer."

When Hoake McCarron, alone among the band of rivals, possessed Eula, he was so envied that five of the others also fled to Texas right after Eula was married to Flem (*H* 145). Eula was married to Flem by her parents to give her child a name. When Ratliff saw her crossing the Square to be married in the courthouse, "the calm beautiful mask beneath the Sunday hat" (*H* 147), she was still like a goddess but no longer grotesque. In a passage added in the revision of "Spotted Horses" for *The Hamlet*, it was also Ratliff who saw Eula in the moonlight, standing in a window of her father's house after returning with her husband and infant.

> She did not lean out, she merely stood there full in the moon, apparently blank-eyed . . . the heavy gold hair, the mask not tragic and perhaps not even doomed: just damned, the strong faint lift of breasts beneath marble-like fall of the garment; to those below what Brunhilde, what Rhinemaiden on what spurious river-rock of papier-mâché, what Helen returned to what topless and shoddy Argos, waiting for no one (*H* 306).

In *The Town* this note is continued, more by Gavin Stevens than by Ratliff.

Having described Eula in *The Hamlet* as an incredible "absurd, grotesque caricature," Dolores Brien recognized her as a tragic figure in *The Town* but consistently archetypal in either role. In "Primitivism in the Fiction of William Faulkner," G. W. Sutton explained the change in Eula by her experience of motherhood. He considered her intuitive, not stupid, with wisdom beyond rational intelligence, a Venus or Lilith.

In *The Town* Gavin Stevens regarded Eula and Manfred de Spain as exemplifying "the divinity of simple unadulterated immortal lust" (*T* 15). It was Gavin also, newly returned from eight years in Europe, who reacted to his first sight of Linda, a teen-ager, much as he had to Eula before 1914, and who used "Motion" to epitomize the cause of the anguish caused by "that incandescent shape." He spoke of Eula in terms encompassing the whole range of myth and history: "that Frenchman's Bend Helen, Semiramis—no: not Helen nor Semiramis: Lilith: the one before Eve herself whom earth's Creator had perforce in desperate and amazed alarm in person to efface, remove, obliterate, that Adam might create a progeny to populate it . . ." (*T* 133, 44).

In a study of themes and characterization in *Snopes*, Donald Petesch covers the whole range of women with whom Eula is compared, from Eve and Lilith through ancient myths of the Earth Mother, classical mythology, Near East legends, and Roman history. In addition to explicit allusions are the implicit ones in Faulkner's themes and suggested parallels, from *Golden Bough* figures to the Waste Land. The story of Eula is only an ironic parallel to those of "the Helens and Juliets and Isoldes and Guineveres," with Manfred de Spain as the lover and the impotent Flem as the husband and Gavin as "next-best to Paris." But, as Ratliff concluded, "Not ever body had Helen, but then not ever body lost her neither" (*T* 101). Ratliff's parallels from myth and legend and literature suggest Gavin's role: the knight serving his lady according to the most idealistic code of courtly love.

Maureen Waters regarded Eula as the archetypal mother, representing the creative forces of life but exploited by men incapable of love. In *The Town* Waters recognized Eula's compassion and understanding but regarded her as still mythic and inscrutable, not tragic. Manfred de Spain's passion for her was physical, Gavin's spiritual. The retelling of her story in *The Mansion*, by the three narrators of *The Town*, retains her mythic sexuality, according to Waters, but otherwise shows deterioration. Such retelling is a fundamental device in the creation and growth of Yoknapatawpha; in this instance there is no shift to a subjective view of Eula or to the omniscient author.

As a mother, Eula became less a goddess and more human, with a new self-awareness noted by Sutton. She was most human when her love for her daughter, Linda, made her kill herself to spare Linda the scandal that would result from exposure of the fact that Manfred de Spain was Eula's lover. Apparently Jefferson was like upper-middle-class Victorian England, as described by Peter T. Cominos: "an unmarried or married woman's known sexual behavior classified her either as a respectable member of the social system of the family or one who had fallen below the line of respectability into the subsocial system of prostitution, the negation of the family." In England, also, "Women were classified into polar extremes . . . sexless ministering angels or sensuously oversexed temptresses of the devil . . . these polarities shared an attitude of disguised masculine hostility toward women." Although "the world of respectability . . . placed women on a pedestal," it "admitted and lamented the latent depravity of women, but exalted them in their angelic innocence." "Known sexual behavior" explains the reason why Eula could commit suicide and leave Linda an unblemished heritage: the whole town had known about Eula and Manfred for eighteen years and, as Charles Mallison realized, feared the revelation of its "own baseness in helping to keep it hidden all this long time" (*T* 308). After Eula's suicide, Charles realized some years later, the "wreath on the bank door" was "not the myrtle of grief, it was the laurel of victory . . . the eternal and deathless public triumph of virtue itself proved once more supreme and invincible" (*T*

337). And Flem understood and responded appropriately: Eula's tombstone bore the inscription: "A Virtuous Wife Is a Crown to Her Husband," Anybody in Jefferson who did not know the following line
could find it as soon as he could lay hands on a Bible and turn to the
obvious source. Proverbs: "A good wife is the crown of her husband,
but she who brings shame is like rottenness in his bones." One can
scarcely believe that Eula would not get a divorce and marry Manfred
and give Linda a suitable stepfather, rather than risk the discovery of a
much more reprehensible offense against respectability than a bastard
and a divorce.

Just before her death, when Gavin last saw Eula, her eyes were not
blank but were "the blue of spring blooms, all one inextricable mixture
of wistaria cornflower bluebells weeds and all, all the lost girls'
weather and boys' luck and too late the grief, too late" (*T* 332).
Faulkner's recurrent detail of blank eyes, used also for Caddy and
Temple, may imply what Joseph Campbell said was signified by the
blank eyes in classical sculpture: "there had been no gazing forth of an
interior spirit into space." As a mother, Eula had gained a spirit.

As Helen, Eula is the goddess of love and beauty; as earth goddess,
she is the symbol of fertility, like the land in having her fruitfulness
wasted. In both roles she is violated and victimized and is ruled by
instinct. As a woman she loved and must have exercised qualities other
than instinct to avoid scandal for eighteen years. As a mother she made
a choice that is the chief act of maternal devotion in the annals of
Yoknapatawpha. She is never represented as the ideal upper-class
woman; she is too vital and natural. Gavin idealized her, but never in
the way in which Horace Benbow idealized Narcissa's purity. Gavin's
comment on the tragic waste of Eula's life may explain not only Gavin,
who did meet her too late, but all the other men in Faulkner's cosmos
who permitted womanhood to be wasted or sacrificed to their concept
of virtue as synonymous with chastity and coldness and who put
respectability above vitality: "She loved, had a capacity to love, for
love, to give and accept love. Only she tried twice and failed twice to
find somebody not just strong enough to deserve, earn it, match it, but
even brave enough to accept it" (*T* 359; *M* 150).

Gavin proved the truth of his statement in regard to Linda, Eula's
daughter, whose love he was not brave enough to accept. Linda, a
goddess also, is presented entirely through the eyes of Charles Mallison, Ratliff, and Gavin Stevens. In *The Mansion*, Ratliff related events
from *The Town* in terms of Eula as Helen and Linda as Helen's daughter. Eula as Helen had "inexhaustible capacity for passion" and power
(*M* 139). Linda, deaf, was "immured, inviolate in silence, invulnerable,

serene," "the inviolate bride of silence" (*M* 203): Charles used terms
that recall those of Horace concerning Narcissa. Charles also spoke of
Eula in terms of Venus, with a Swinburnian echo: "the god she represented . . . was a stronger one than the pale and desperate Galilean
who was all they [the preachers] had to challenge with" (*M* 212). Linda
sought love and security, but Gavin never would cease being self-sacrificing and noble long enough to marry her. At the end of *The Mansion*
Linda is a solitary and deaf widow and Gavin is married to the woman
he should have married in his youth and whose children he, not
Harriss, the rich gangster, should have fathered. Putting women on
pedestals does a disservice to the women, to the men who idolize them,
and to the future of society.

Some of the inconsistencies and anomalies in *The Town* and *The
Mansion* are the result of the lapse of time between the writing of *The
Hamlet* and *The Town* during which events in Faulkner's life greatly
changed his earlier plans. The synopsis of the trilogy which Faulkner
sent Robert Haas in 1938, hoping to get an advance which would make
it possible for him to work on the trilogy instead of writing potboilers,
bears remarkably little resemblance to *The Town* and *The Mansion*.
The publication of the synopsis in Blotner's *Faulkner: A Biography*
(pp. 1006–1008) and in Blotner's *Selected Letters* (pp. 107–109) has
made it easily accessible. Faulkner's Hollywood romance with Meta
Carpenter Wilde, told by her in *A Loving Gentleman*, and his less
intense and briefer love affair with Joan Williams, revealed in his letters to Joan published by Blotner, throw light on the characterization
of Eula and Linda, as has already been noted. The change in Flem, his
desire for respectability, symbolized by his mansion, is not suggested
in the synopsis, in which the Snopeses "eat up Jefferson," and the one
Snopes who seemed potentially a Snopes of another color, Sarty, is the
father of a son who marries the counterpart of Linda and who has "all
the vices of all Snopeses," including those from which he contracted
syphilis. Neither heroes nor heroines seemed to be in Faulkner's mind
when he wrote the synopsis. Neither Eula nor Linda can be imagined
from it, although the slots in which they were fitted into the plots are
recognizable. There is no slot for a Gavin Stevens nor one big enough
for Ratliff, although he was a character in short stories revised for
Snopes. Nothing in the synopsis prepares for a study of society which
emphasizes the role of women as shaped by the concepts and influence
of men.

Sally Page's statements that "Eula is a mock-heroic goddess of
love" and that "Eula and Lena Grove are "aliens in the fictional
worlds they inhabit" sound plausible until one considers that French-

man's Bend is Eula's world, however incongruous she is in it, and that she was victimized by the world and married to Flem Snopes to preserve the respectability of the Varner name and to give her child a father such as he was and a name, whereas Lena was free at beginning and end to ''light out for the territory ahead.''

Criticism of Lena as lacking in intelligence does less justice to her rare qualities than G. W. Sutton's explanation of Lena as a primitive who does not distinguish between life and concepts of life, an explanation that is consonant with Otto Schlumpf's statement that Lena's standard of morality is provided by nature. This accounts for her major role as alienated from the standards of conformity imposed by the town, as are the other major characters who, as outcasts, are responsive to her redemptive powers. For Lena is not merely a primitive but has mythic qualities, most notably those identified by Beach Langston as those of Diana of Nemi which involve a constellation of mythic parallels to be found in Frazer's *Golden Bough*. Lena is also identified by attributes and images with the Virgin Mary: the relationship of ''the old goddesses of fertility'' to ''the cult of the virgin'' is explained, in the context of initiation, by Joseph Henderson. Maureen Waters ascribed some of Lena's moral force to her lack of a sense of guilt. The significance of this quality is amusingly but cogently stated by Sally Page:

> Lena Grove is not a virgin. It is significant that Faulkner should endow Lena with the qualities of serenity, tranquility, and purity, which his romantic idealists dreamed were possessed by beautiful and virgin young women, despite that fact that she is unvirgin, unmarried, and very pregnant. . . . He is able to present her very real human limitations without diminishing the significance of her character or the value of what she represents.

Crediting Lena with a more complex character than most critics do, Michael Routh grants her a major place in Faulkner's cosmology. In ''A Body Does Get Around: The Life-Force in Lena,'' Routh deals with Lena's relationship with ''what are called most precisely . . . essential things'': time, motion, nature, home. (Home was simply where Burch lived.) Routh recognized in Lena ''a sustained intuitive perception of the perpetual present,'' of cyclical time, but ''she also knew linear time,'' because, for Faulkner, ''Life involves a simultaneous dual perspective: it repeats itself (cyclical time) while it moves forward (linear time).'' Characters who perceive only one kind of time are out of touch with reality. Lena also has the right pattern of motion: in peaceful, quiet motion she proceeds on a progressive journey, displaying the right kind of motion. (Routh's use of "goal" is misleading, as suggesting a specific place: "quest" is preferable, in both denotation and connotation.) She also has a right relationship with nature, one criterion in Faulkner's moral testing of characters. Those who can "accept and embrace outer nature are likewise able to accept and embrace their own inner natures." A passage from Bergson's *The Two Sources of Morality and Religion* "provides a remarkably apt portrayal of Lena's habit of life." Her simplicity, her intuitive decisions, her "effort, endeavor, and perseverance," "develop . . . in a soul . . . whose liberty coincides with the divine activity," with energy which "flows from a spring which is the very source of life." Lena as a lady and Byron as a courtly lover have not been tainted with the myth of the South but belong to the mythic cosmology of Yoknapatawpha.

Eula and Lena most fully represent mythic powers of women but for that very reason do not reflect that the "symbolic center" of the myth of the South is virginity and that Faulkner's men, as Dolores Brien said, were obsessed with the idea. She cited Gavin Stevens' description of Linda when he first saw her, in her early teens, as "the virgin bitch, immune now in virginity" (*T* 132). What happened to women who did not enjoy being put on a pedestal or who enjoyed it too much is illustrated by those who illustrate Maureen Waters' label, "Women as Nemesis." Temple Drake in *Sanctuary* bears a name that suggests worship, and her story recalls such ancient customs as temple prostitution and ritual defloration described by Malinowski, with the season suggesting ironic inversion of fertility rites. Temple rebelled against the Southern ideal and openly broke all the family and university rules that were designed, no doubt, to protect her virginity. But she posed as an injured innocent to escape the consequences of her folly and allowed Lee Goodwin, innocent of the rape, to be lynched. In *Requiem for a Nun* she admitted her natural affinity for sin and hired Nancy as a servant who spoke her language. As a mother, Temple was no nearer to the ideal of motherhood than to that of virginity. To save Temple's baby girl from a life corrupted by her mother's flagrant immorality, Nancy killed the infant. Nemesis was visited, however, not on the society and the family which Temple rebelled against but on Nancy, who sought to aid in the redemption of Temple at the cost of her own execution for murder. It would seem impossible in *Sanctuary* to encounter another even more reprehensible result of the Southern myth of woman, Narcissa, who cherished the myth by molding herself in its image, thanks to her brother Horace's idealization of her. At least as Nemesis she aimed in the right direction: in betraying Horace's defense of Lee Goodwin by tipping off the district attorney concerning Horace's activities, she was as involved in the lynching of Goodwin as was Temple. Horace may not have known that she betrayed him, as Cleanth Brooks noted in *The Yoknapatawpha Country* just before his condemnation of Narcissa: "Next to Popeye, Narcissa is the most frightening person in this novel, as she pitilessly moves on to her own ends with no regard for justice and no concern for the claims of truth." Ruby, the unmarried mother of Lee's child, was persecuted by Narcissa and the community for being a wife and mother without being legally married.

Horace put Narcissa on a pedestal but Caddy Compson was put there by her mother and Benjy and Quentin, when she sought love outside the loveless Compson household dominated by Mrs. Compson's fanatically Calvinistic concepts concerning sexuality, with which she indoctrinated Quentin, instead of loving him. To Compsons as to Varners, a marriage license was a magic stain remover for the blot on the scutcheon, and any marriage was better than no marriage. As Dolores Brien said, "Caddy is, perhaps, Faulkner's most sympathetic example of the tragic effect of the myth on the women." The myth rose from the necessity of men, Brien explained: "The myth that woman is wise, chaste, and virtuous serves as a psychological foil with which men hope to protect themselves against the woman, whom he [sic] secretly believes to be allied with the powers of darkness." Caddy's child, Miss Quentin, inevitably met the same fate as Caddy, with both Mrs. Compson and Jason preaching the same text. Caddy was Nemesis to Quentin, rather than to Mrs. Compson, whose plaints revealed self-pity, not love.

The real Galatea on a pedestal was ironically the Nemesis with the best aim—she struck at the Pygmalion who would not take her off her pedestal. Eula's daughter Linda remains enigmatic because only three male Southerners tell her story. They will be dealt with later. But Gavin never gives any reason to doubt Linda's repeated expressions of love for him and willingness to marry him, before and after her mother's suicide and after her return from the exile Gavin imposed on her by sending her away from Jefferson. When Gavin visited her before her marriage to Barton Kohl one can read between the lines that this was Gavin's last chance—and he did not take it. Ratliff shared his speculations with the reader (*M* 163–64). But Ratliff went to the wedding of Linda and Barton in 1936, before they went to Spain to fight. By that time Linda certainly knew Gavin was no young Lochinvar. Gavin himself narrates his visit to Linda in Pascagoula and his refusing her direct proposal of marriage. But when she urged him to get married, he did it (*M* 252). (The reader of "Knight's Gambit" knows the time is near when he will marry Melisandre.) So Linda finagled Gavin into helping her get Mink released from prison, and, after Mink murdered Flem, she rode off in the red Jaguar that, Gavin learned, she had ordered in July (*M* 423). Linda is a true nemesis, but Gavin already had taken Melisandre off her pedestal and was no doubt suffering more from wounded pride than from repentance at having been obsessed by the myth of the South.

The solitary woman, widow or spinster, not seeking or sought by a man, adds to the roster of Yoknapatawpha women. It has been generally recognized that several of Faulkner's most admirable characters belong to that category, of which the Sartoris family furnishes a cluster. In *The Unvanquished*, Granny Millard and Aunt Jenny are impressive. Granny Millard was forced into being the man of the family during Colonel John Sartoris' service in the army. With the highest moral principles, Granny used the respect for ladies, of whatever age, to swindle the Union army, beginning with Colonel Dick who had gallantly let Granny get away with hiding Bayard and Ringo under her skirts (*U* 36). One lieutenant who was aware of the forged orders appealed to Granny's benevolence because, he said, "I have a family; I am a poor man; I have no grandmother" (*U* 166), and he would have to pay any outrageous warrant to Mrs. Rosa Millard which the auditor might find. Having so worked her feminine wiles on enemy army officers, Granny gambled one last and fatal time that *any* Southern man would not hurt a woman (*U* 173). She lost. Aunt Jenny Sartoris, who took Granny's place after the war, was widowed early in the war and had the family of Colonel John Sartoris to provide a home for her and a useful and welcome role. Sharp-tongued and tender-hearted, she is one of Faulkner's most delightful women characters. But Narcissa's hypocrisy was literally more than she could endure: her death was caused by learning that Narcissa bought back Byron Snopes's obscene letters by sleeping with an FBI agent ("There Was a Queen"). Since Narcissa had what she really wanted, status, she was not interested in marriage: her son Benbow she could dominate as she had Horace.

Drusilla Hawk and her mother represent extremes: Drusilla was glad to serve in the army after her fiancé was killed and wished to live with the Sartorises and work like a man rebuilding the house; her mother forced Drusilla to marry Colonel John—and was surprised, and probably disappointed, that Drusilla was not pregnant. Mrs. Hawk and Mrs. Compson are similar parodies of Southern ladies. As the wife of Colonel John, Drusilla tried to seduce Bayard, Phaedra to his Hippolytus, and as Colonel John's widow, tried to force upon Bayard the weapons of the revenge demanded by the male code. Drusilla was more an anomaly in her time than was Linda, serving in the Spanish Civil War, but Linda was also a victim of the myth of the South.

Notable as are Rosa Coldfield and Judith Sutpen, their lives were lived in such exceptional circumstances that they are not useful as examples. But two spinsters in Jefferson deserve mention. In *Intruder in the Dust*, Miss Habersham (the counterpart of Miss Worsham in "Go Down, Moses") lived a self-sustaining life after the Civil War by dealing in chickens and vegetables, with the aid of two Negro servants, herself peddling her wares. She was respected, but one doubts that she had any social life. The other spinster was a sadder and more horrifying case. Miss Minnie Cooper in "Dry September" was "thirty-eight or thirty-nine," living with an invalid mother and an aunt. The only unmarried woman of her contemporaries, she was "relegated into adultery by public opinion" (*CS* 175) and took to drinking. Her only pleasure was going to movies with women neighbors: "her idle and empty days had a quality of furious unreality" (*CS* 175). What Miss Minnie Cooper said did not matter: she was a white woman and Will Mayes was a Negro. Mere rumor was enough for McLendon and his fellow defenders of the purity of women who cared nothing for the truth. The barber who knew and defended Will Mayes said to them: "I dont believe anything happened. I leave it to you fellows if them ladies that get old without getting married dont have notions that a man cant—" (*CS* 170). Referring to Miss Minnie's Victorian British counterparts, Peter Cominos said that "the repressed daughter" "became subject to motives and desires of which she was not aware. She acted upon motives unconscious of their origins, and was spared the knowledge of what she was doing." But there were no black scapegoats in England. Miss Minnie went to the movies with her friends after the lynching and laughed herself into hysterics, and her friends took her home and called a doctor. "Then to one another: 'Do you suppose anything really happened?' their eyes darkly aglitter, secret and passionate" (*CS* 182). McLendon, at home, assaulted his wife.

By the 1950s, however, Faulkner made a quantum leap from Miss Minnie Cooper to women who, though wives, were real helpmates to their husbands, with competence and energy to be independent if need arose. And these new women are typical of their society from the 1930s to 1946, not exceptions like Drusilla in her generation, Miss Habersham in hers, and Linda before and after widowhood.

Chronologically Mrs. Wall Snopes came first. (Like his father, Eck, Wall was not a real Snopes.) His wife's "implacable enmity . . . toward the very word Snopes" (*T* 282) was manifest in her cooperation with Wall in his establishment of a wholesale grocery supply house that expanded into a chain scattered through "half of Mississippi" and eventually into Tennessee and Arkansas (*M* 420). They were run "by the outrageous un-Snopes method of jest selling ever body exactly what they thought they was buying, for exactly what they thought they was going to pay for it" (*M* 153). Ratliff, approving Wall's principles, invested in the business. "A not quite plain-faced girl with an ambition equal" to Wall's and a will even greater than his to escape from the swamp of Snopeses, Wall's wife clerked in the store and did chores and delivered groceries (*T* 146).

Essie Meadowfill achieved success by her solitary efforts before she married. She was the only child of "a old broke-down wheel-chair gentleman," with a "gray wife," whose feud with Orestes Snopes over ownership of a piece of land provides the complex conflict between Snopes and non-Snopes in *The Mansion*. Essie graduated from high-school in 1942 "with the highest grades ever made in it." She declined a scholarship offered by the president of the non-Snopes bank, who persuaded her to take a job for life in the bank and paid for the bathroom which Essie had planned (*M* 328–29). Old Meadowfill's "heights of outrageousness" are relevant here as making life hell for his wife and daughter after he "retired permanently" into a wheelchair which served as a kind of mobile throne (*M* 330).

Essie's engagement and marriage to a Marine corporal, McKinley Smith, astonished the town: where and how she met him was a mystery, unless it was through "a lovelorn correspondence agency." Love turned Essie from a mousy girl to a blooming one, determined rather than quiet (*M* 328).

McKinley Smith put up with his in-laws and built a house for himself and Essie within sight of her parents' house. The happy ending finds Essie and her husband on the farm they established on land they bought through Gavin Stevens' deft management of the land deal between Orestes and Meadowfill. The cotton is up and Effie is pregnant. But her combination of loyalty, determination, intelligence, and common sense proved effective because she could get and succeed in a job in a bank. The quantum leap was from the myth of the South to ERA.

Considering what Essie's father was like, one wonders if the gray woman was coerced into marriage and if Essie is like Miss Quentin and Linda. A more destructive animus than old Meadowfill is difficult to imagine; Essie was loyal to her mother, but her sterling qualities seem unlikely to have been generated by her undeserving parents.

As we proceed from "William Faulkner's Myth of Women," to use Dolores Brien's title, to his Myth of Men, it is interesting to note her grouping of the male characters by their attitudes toward women. First are the psychically impotent males, "emasculated, quixotic, and ever perverse," ruled by a code of chivalry to try to save women who do not wish to be saved. The physically impotent men have direct, uncomplicated dealings with women: Gavin and Flem nicely illustrate the two types. There are the bachelors, with V. K. Ratliff the "eunuch priest of the cult," those who dogmatize on women. The unwilling victims of women include men as different as Jack Houston and Joe Christmas. One may well question Brien's classification of "submissive victim" for Byron Bunch. The men who shaped women in the image of the myth of the South were themselves shaped by that myth, which had a boomerang power. Narcissa, woman as nemesis, Brien described as displaying a "moral righteousness" which is "nothing more than a whited sepulchre of hypocritical respectability." But Horace shaped her in his ideal image which she fell in love with, as her name suggests. (The "Narcissus" Faulkner knew was the black nurse of his daughter Jill.) The ways in which the myth of the South shaped the lives of the men who ruled it are even more interesting than the ways in which the men dominated the women.

The thought of the Southern family romance conjures up thoughts of handsome young men wooing beautiful women, marrying them, and founding generations whose lives follow the same pattern. Paradoxically, however, the most popular plot, how a man wins a wife, is notably absent in the main action in Yoknapatawpha; this includes a wide range of life patterns, from the archetypal to the distinctly American, which reflect concepts and dilemmas extending from the classical age to the twentieth century. Most of the patterns can be summed up under two basic classifications: man's quest for spiritual self-realization and man's quest for material success. The first quest most frequently follows the pattern of initiation, with its obvious relation to the Edenic fall from innocence, and its rebirth analogous to spiritual salvation. The second follows the pattern of the American success story: the self-made man.

Wholly satisfactory attainment of either goal requires the achievement of integration of personality through self-acceptance and self-realization. In a society in which fidelity to tradition is an ideal, the dominance of the instinctive and the irrational is a danger to be avoided. But to break away from tradition is an equally great danger: observing that "the progressive ideal is always more abstract, more unnatural, and less 'moral' in that it demands disloyalty to tradition," Jung warns not only of the "Promethean debt" that may pile up from our progressiveness but also of the dangers of the "retarding ideal" of traditionalism. "Viable progress comes only from the co-operation of both": the unconscious and the conscious in the psyche, instinct and will, tradition and progress. "The irrational cannot and must not be wiped out" because "the rational attitude of culture necessarily goes over into its opposite, the irrational devastation of culture."

This Heraclitean principle of enantiodromia, the fluctuating tendency of everything to go over into its opposite, may be implied in Faulkner's polarities and antitheses. If the ego identifies with one basic instinct, Jung says, "there develops a craze, a monomania, or possession, a most exaggerated one-sidedness which endangers the psychical equilibrium most seriously." One thinks immediately of Flem Snopes and Thomas Sutpen and is gratified by Jung's comment that one-sidedness is fostered as a secret of success. And as Faulkner's fiction creates a tension between opposites which may suggest *his* concept of "viable progress" for society, so Jung suggests how the individual may achieve equilibrium: "through tension between the opposites, the collective unconscious brings forth images, which as symbols make possible an irrational union of the opposites." Such symbols are one of the means which Faulkner used to achieve his ends.

To Faulkner, the salvation of man "is in his individuality" (*FN* 195). The text on which he would preach would be "against belonging to anything": "now I don't belong to anything except the human race" (*FU* 269). Man must work out his salvation from within, rather than from without through such social institutions as organized religions (*FU* 73). The artist in particular, he said, must be an individuality, bound to no group or ideology (*FU* 101).

Initiation as a means of developing individuality has been rediscovered in the twentieth century. In *Thresholds of Initiation* Joseph L. Henderson cites such works of literature as T. S. Eliot's *The Waste Land* and Thomas Mann's *The Magic Mountain* as notably exemplifying the works of literature which revealed the experience of initiation into death and rebirth in reaching manhood. The response of readers showed "our nostalgia for the simplicity and unity of primitive ways of life." As an analytical psychologist and psychiatrist, Dr. Henderson's purpose was "to discover . . . specific thresholds of initiation, the rites of passage which make possible the transition from childhood to adolescence, from adolescence to early maturity, and from maturity to the experience of individuation." Study of the problem of arrested development has revealed that such arrest of the developing ego is caused "not only by what has previously happened, but also by its fear of taking the next step in its development" and suffering a recoil. This "renegade tendency tends to isolate the individual from his normal relationship with others."

Defining "individuation" as Jung did, "an internal subjective process of integration . . . and an equally indispensable objective process of relationship," Henderson specified the three conditions necessary for the individuation to become an "actuality": "separation from the original family or clan; commitment to a meaningful group over a long period of time; liberation from too close an identity with the group." Particularly interesting, in view of the gulf between men and women, even in family life, in Yoknapatawpha, is Henderson's insistence that "the bisexual motif occurs on all levels of initiation in certain tribal rites as a psychic, not a physical ordeal," and that "the symbol of bisexual union presents the attitude of wholeness or integration necessary to maturity . . . a desirable, permanent acquisition, not just a phase of development to be outgrown." In *The Wisdom of the Serpent*, Henderson commented on the "balance of the male and female principles" honored in the Grail legend, an important source of the chivalric tradition, as well as in ceremonies at stages of initiation.

Discussing the promince of the Grail quest in medieval romances, Mircea Eliade pointed out that "the majority of the scenarios" of the Arthurian cycle "have an initiatory structure" with "a long and dramatic 'Quest'." Shifting his attention in *The Quest* to "Initiation in the Modern World," Eliade defines three types of initiation which have long survived in many societies; two have their equivalents in the modern world. Puberty rites introduce the novice into the spiritual and cultural values of a particular society and make him a "responsible member of the society." Such rites often "imply the revelation of sexuality." The second category is that of secret societies. "The rites of entrance into a secret society correspond in every respect to those of tribal initiations." Fraternity initiations are the most familiar example in our society; in the recent past deaths have resulted from such initiations and been publicized. Secrecy and cruelty have been characteristic of such societies; only the most extreme cruelty would cause the secrecy to be violated.

Eliade summarized the function of secret society initiation: "it reveals to every new generation a world open to the transhuman, a world . . . that is 'transcendental.'" Referring specifically to "Levels of Maturity" in Faulkner's novels, G. L. Friend defines "three basic steps on the ladder of maturity": "From the family to the community to the world." Thus the family should prepare its youth for a universal brotherhood without boundaries of "class, caste, religion, country." But all who would and should achieve individuality and integration do not climb the ladder to the top or realize their potential.

Individuality and integration are achieved, according to Otto Rank, in three stages, the third of which few in any society attain. In Faulkner's works, few in the twentieth century represent the first, but a number reach and remain in the second stage, the neurotics who have artistic tendencies without artistic capacities. In the first stage, conventional or traditional, the individual depends on external reality, follows the will of the majority, is duty-conscious, and strives for universal norms. The majority remain in this stage. In the second stage, the individual seeks new goals and satisfactions, leading either to the third stage, creativity, or to neurotic inhibition succeeding the initial rebellion. This type rejects external reality, is guilt-conscious, and follows impulse, ecstatic and even orgiastic, in opposition to society and ethics. Following this principle may lead to madness. The third stage is reached especially by the creative artist who creates and projects his own world and follows his own inner reality, adjusting environment to himself. Self-motivated, he accepts himself as his ideal and achieves true self-knowledge and self-creation.

As a creative artist Faulkner should and does represent the third stage, having in his early years passed through the second, unlike his neurotic characters who remain in the second stage. Faulkner's principle of individualism is in harmony with Rank's analysis of the process of self-realization. Faulkner believed that man could better his condition by his own efforts and that art is the force through which man is able to "record the history of his invincible durability and courage beneath disaster, and to postulate the validity of his hope" (*FN* 158, 186). The better world to which man aspires and which he may in part attain, perhaps with aid from outside or "from a greater power," lies inside himself (*FU* 86). The fatalism and pessimism in Faulkner's fiction do not reflect his own attitudes and beliefs but those of his characters, especially those who cannot escape from their neurotic inhibitions to achieve the third stage of creative effort. But this stage, Jung shows, has its own perils: the "divine hero" or the "inspired soul" may be "torn asunder between the pairs of opposites, which, being attributes of deity, also belong to the divine man, who owes his godlikeness to the overcoming of his gods." The artist may pay this penalty for his creative achievements; it is possible that Faulkner did so. But he did not present in fiction the conflict between artist and society, so prominent in the works of Thomas Mann, and a chief subject of James Joyce and of Thomas Wolfe.

The quest for self-realization is usually characteristic of the American myth and its modern treatment in literature, involving the concept of innocence, as in the new Adam in the New World Eden, and the fall from innocence into guilt. Loren Baritz might be speaking of the

Yoknapatawpha chronicles and their basic themes: "the fall of the People, the rape of the Land, the liquidation of the Indian—these were the formative sins of God's Country, the consciousness of which contributed to the birth of culture. Concretely, the fall contributed to secularism, the rape to materialism, and genocide to imperialism." Eliade in *The Quest* noted both "the Protestant Reformation seeking an earthly Paradise" and "the arrival of Catholics which seemed to reduce everything into a conflict between Good and Evil" with "an almost Manichean eschatology." The fervor of Southern Calvinism, as Wilbur Cash explained, was a heritage from New England.

Ike McCaslin had a vision of the Lost Paradise as the Lord looked at it:

> . . . this land, this South for which he had done so much with woods for game and streams for fish and deep rich soil for seed and lush springs to sprout it and long summers to mature it and serene falls to harvest it and short mild winters for men and animals and saw no hope anywhere and looked beyond it where hope should have been, where to East North and West lay illimitable that whole hopeful continent dedicated as a refuge and sanctuary of liberty and freedom from what you called the old world's worthless evening . . . [*GDM* 283].

What the Lord saw was the sin and guilt, especially that of regarding the Negro as "another specimen, another example like the Brazilian macaw brought home in a cage" (*GDM* 284). This new world had become "the same worthless tideless rock cooling in the last crimson evening" except for the lone voice of "just one simple enough to believe that horror and outrage were first and last simply horror and outrage," a man named Brown who was "*against the weak because they are niggers being held in bondage by the strong just because they are white*" (*GDM* 284–85).

Ike had taken what R. W. B. Lewis describes as the "journey from innocence to conscience," traveled by Donatello in *The Marble Faun*: "the soul's realization of itself under the impact of and by engagement with evil—the tragic rise born of the fortunate fall. It is a New World action—my supposition is that it is *the* New World action, the tragic remainder of what Lawrence called the myth of America. It is what has to happen to "golden youth" if it is to mature . . . ."

The facts about the South which Ike perceived exploded "the powerful and persuasive myth of the Southern plantation" which, Henry Nash Smith said of the 1830s, "could not compete with the myth of the garden of the world as a projection of the American experience in the West." The "external war between the dream of nobility and order and the fact of disorder and failure and sorrow," fought across the landscape of Yoknapatawpha, does indeed have "meanings immediately translatable for anyone anywhere," but Leslie Fiedler, in opposing dream to history in meanings and in denying that Faulkner's images have historical meanings, is ignoring the central historical fact with which Faulkner was concerned and obsessed: the weak being held in bondage by the strong because of difference in color of skin. Myth begins "with the recognition of realistic significance in a story": in contrast with the wishful thinking of the fairy tale and such utopian dreams as those of the New Eden or the garden of the world, the "typical theme" of myth, as Susanne Langer observed, is tragic.

Ihab Hassan's concept of the new hero and his "radical innocence" is relevant to the themes of innocence and guilt in the American Edenic myth. The new hero's innocence is radical because it is inherent and "goes to the root or foundation" of his character but also because "it is extreme, impulsive, anarchic, troubled with vision." This new hero brings "American conscience and imagination to bear" on present culture: "His innocence . . . is a property of the mythic American Self, perhaps of every anarchic Self. It is the innocence of a Self that refuses to accept the immitigable rule of reality, including death, an aboriginal Self the radical imperatives of whose freedom cannot be stifled." Faulkner's heroes both exemplify innocence and illustrate Hassan's point that "heroes do not only incarnate our history but recreate it with artifice. The hero is one mirror fiction uses to surprise reality—and identify its forms." Hassan sees in this innocence both Jung's consciousness close to the animal and the Dionysian creative innocence "which D. H. Lawrence hoped to find in the American Adam." That the new hero experiences "two critical moments in his encounter with experience, the moments of initiation or defeat" from which "the form of fiction takes its shape" is particularly true of Faulkner's heroes and his fiction.

Hassan's types of heroes also are pertinent to Faulkner's myth. The situation of the hero may show "the disparity between the innocence of the hero and the destructive character of his experience." But the way in which he meets the situation identifies the kind of hero: in response to the dialectic "between the essential Yes and the radical No" the anti-hero or the rebel-victim may "affirm the human" by the rebel's denying "without saying No to life" or the victim's succumbing "without saying Yes to oppression." But the "other major response to experience" is that of the initiate, "the second major incarnation of the dialectic between affirmation and denial," who accepts the invitation of the world to become part of it. Initiation leads to "a *viable* mode of life *in the world*," to *confirmation*; Victimization leads to "*estrangement from the world*," to *renunciation*.

The response made by the hero may be determined by his society and the stage he has reached in the process of self-realization; Rank's analysis throws further light upon Hassan's. The neurosis of youth prevents participation: the cult of youth, with its defense of self by "resistance, rebellion, and denial," as in Rank's second stage, is an impediment to initiation. The emblem of this spirit of contradiction, Hassan says, is "the antithesis between Eden and Utopia based on an unresolved view of man's place in the world." The context of the encounter may determine the election of initiation or victimization: a Rousseauistic context, like that of Ike McCaslin, leads to choice of initiation; a Calvinistic context, like that of Joe Christmas, leads to choice of victimization. Belief in the American Dream and the New Adam or belief in Original Sin and the Old Adam conditions the responses of the individual.

The two major incarnations of the anti-hero, the rebel and the victim, Prometheus and Sisyphus, may converge: Hassan cites the paradox of Jaspers: "Although I am an anvil, as a hammer I can consummate what I must suffer." The initiate, instead of denying the world, withdraws and contemplates it, then arrives at an understanding of necessity in human terms and accepts the "instinctual renunciation" which necessity requires in building civilization.

Initiation is the pattern which Faulkner repeats more often than any other in fully developed, directly presented narrative. The pattern may be carried through the ritual death and rebirth which signifies integration or individuation, or it may lead to rejection of life or rejection of an adult role.

The purpose and pattern of initiation in primitive cultures are preserved in myth and in literature with mythic qualities, but frequently curtailment of the pattern may render it obscure. The functions and elements of initiation as defined by anthropologists and psychologists provide a basis for understanding the significance and recognizing the pattern of initiation in literature. It is an experience often of more emotional than intellectual significance to the initiate, and gives rise to new attitudes analogous to religious conversion. Malinowski sums up the general purpose and method:

> The rites of tribal initiation . . . entail a dramatic break with the old life and the creation of new bonds. The novice is made to forget his associations with the family, especially his female relatives, above all with the mother. In the course of the moral and mythological training which he receives, he is taught in a systematic way what kinship means, . . . the duties and responsibilities towards his kindred and relatives.

Themes and patterns involved in literary use of initiation patterns include, Hassan notes, "the classic pattern of withdrawal and return; its context is the conflict between social and instinctive behavior, ideal choice and biological necessity"; it is the alternative to victimization. Although initiation is the means of achieving self-realization, the experience does not ensure lasting integration.

The characteristics and stages of the initiation ritual can be applied to fiction as a test of the pattern. The masculine world to which the initiation removes a boy generally is one of nature and animal life, often involving hunting, for the Hunter, as Daniel Hoffman said, is often a "seeker after truth." The wilderness and the hunt and the plantation and agriculture represent the same contrast in activities and values as noted by Joseph Campbell between the paleolithic and neolithic ages: the contrast between individual judgment and excellence and "the virtues of group living and submission to authority." Daniel Hoffman identifies the American version of "the traditional myth of the Huntsman as culture-hero" as the fable of the hunt "in which the quarry . . . personifies nature and the hunter demonstrates his prowess and strength." The combination of the hunt and the initiation is both a primitive and a literary pattern; *Moby Dick* combines these two patterns with the quest.

The initiate in the group of men confronted with nature must undergo an ordeal and suffer privation. In primitive and religious initiation, Jung says, the ordeal may involve "all kinds of tortures, circumcisions and similar rites being not uncommon." The initiate's elders introduce him into the mysteries and esoteric lore, much as students are initiated into a fraternity. The initiate undergoes a ritual representing achievement of maturity or rebirth. Mythic battles between a hero and a monster and night journeys under the sea symbolize a rebirth into a new attitude, as the hero asserts individuality. Joseph Campbell explains the rebirth theme and the imagery of the rites of passage: "every threshold passage—not only . . . from the darkness of the womb to the light of the sun but also those from childhood to adult life and from the light of the world to whatever mystery of darkness may lie beyond the portal of death—is comparable to a birth and has been ritually represented, practically everywhere, through an imagery of re-entry into the womb."

The analogy with birth may be extended to the life of the initiate after his initiation and rebirth: he is born into the adult world in which he must engage actively in adult life if his rebirth is genuine and effective, if, Maud Bodkin says, "passing perhaps through conflict and disillusion, he has achieved a sincere relation to the values he can assimilate from amongst those which social institutions and traditions offer." In terms of Rank's three stages of integration, initiation should enable the initiate, if he has creative ability, to make the transition from the second to the third stage. But to go through the initiation and return to the old life or to wish to remain in the world in which the initiation took place signifies that the rebirth has not occurred.

Faulkner's repeated use of the initiation pattern indicates the high value he placed on maturity and individual participation in adult life; his dislike of groups represented his own mature attitude, not a rejection of group experience as part of growing up (*FU* 269). But each initiation in Yoknapatawpha has distinctive characteristics.

In *The Unvanquished* Bayard Sartoris endured two ordeals which were in effect a two-stage initiation. In "Vendée," he undertook a task or quest which, as the "man of the family" in the abnormal circumstances of wartime, he had to accept: when Granny had been killed by Grumby, Bayard was bound by the aristocratic male code of honor, which even a boy would know, to avenge Granny's death. The pursuit, in which he was accompanied by Uncle Buck and Ringo, was in the wilderness; thus he was isolated in a male world of nature. The ordeal was severe and extended, entailing great physical hardship and mental anguish: from December to late February, in snow and rain and "iron frost" the two boys and the old man hunted Grumby (p. 187). After Uncle Buck became ill and had to go home, there was added to the ordeal the very lack of adult counsel which normally guides the initiate. Bayard here accepted the non-Christian code and savagely wreaked vengeance on Grumby, not only killing him but pegging him out on the compress door like a coon hide and putting on Granny's grave Grumby's right hand (p. 211). As a boy, thrown upon his own resources and stricken with grief and guilt over Granny's death—although he was only fifteen he "could have held her" and kept her from going to her death (p. 174)—Bayard acted like the conventional person, following a conventional code, and lost his innocence.

His rebirth as a mature, responsible, Christian adult is delayed until he is twenty-four ("An Odor of Verbena"). Again faced with the "duty" of avenging a murder, that of his father, he won a battle during his night journey back to Jefferson. Like the hero's night journey under the sea, Bayard's journey is a symbol of the feat, in Jung's terms, of overcoming "the monster of darkness: it is the long-hoped-for and expected triumph of consciousness over the unconscious," the triumph of Christian enlightenment, into the mysteries of which Granny had initiated him during his childhood, over the dark, primitive, traditional code of a life for a life. When he arrived home, he was "the Sartoris," the sole male authority. Drusilla spoke for the male community in giving him the pistols. Aunt Jenny spoke for his conscience.

Bayard had arrived at Rank's third stage, guided by his own ideals as
he had learned them from Granny and Aunt Jenny and neither "duty
conscious" nor "guilt conscious." His ordeal was both mental and
physical: he required moral courage to oppose the force of all male
opinion in his class in the community; he required physical courage to
face unarmed a guilty, perhaps panicky murderer. An interesting variation in the initiation pattern is that the truths that enabled Bayard to
become a mature individual he had learned not from men but from
Granny and Aunt Jenny. His rejection of Drusilla's male code seems a
triumph of moral progress over tradition. Unarmed he entered
Redmond's office and found Redmond seated at his desk, "holding a
pistol flat on the desk." When Bayard walked toward him, Redmond
fired twice, not aiming at Bayard, and Bayard "heard no bullet" (*U*
285–87). Redmond walked out of the building, through the group of
Colonel Sartoris' followers, and took the train out of Jefferson.

But the indolent old man in *Sartoris*, bemused with relics and memories of a heroic past, gives no evidence of ever having experienced a
successful initiation. Aunt Jenny had encouraged him in following his
conscience in avenging his father's death. In *Sartoris* she scorned his
lackluster existence. The apparent inconsistency between the old and
the young Bayard is explained by William Ramsey in "Coordinated
Structures in Four Faulkner Novels." By a close examination of
Bayard's actions in the stories preceding "An Odor of Verbena,"
especially in comparison with those of Ringo, his Negro companion
who, no older than Bayard, played an active role as Granny's assistant
in swindling the Union Army, Ramsey showed that Bayard avoided
action and responsibility until Granny was dead. In the manhunt,
Ringo was as active as Bayard. Although in his double role as narrator
and character Bayard established heroism, as Ramsey said, as a quality
often valuable and necessary, he showed a psychological incapacity for
heroic action.

In *Sartoris* the indolent old man cherished the memory of Sartoris
heroism in war, but he had not distinguished himself during peace
because, as Ramsey said, he misunderstood "the nature and value of
an active life" and "never prepared himself for one."

Considering *The Unvanquished* as an extended initiation story in
which "the challenge to order represents more than a boy outgrowing
his childhood: it represents a man outgrowing his culture," Henry
Peabody ignored *Sartoris*, in which Bayard is immured in his culture.
Peabody does not consistently focus on the initiation patterns and on
Bayard. His conclusion that Bayard was the unvanquished and that the
power of the dream and the tradition did not cause him to lose dignity

and self-respect is not consistent with "a man outgrowing his culture," a development of which *Sartoris* shows no evidence. G. L. Friend also deals with *The Unvanquished* as an extended initiation, with Bayard's dual role providing a mature perspective that clarifies the process of growth. He concluded that Bayard failed to live up to his early action.

The story of Young Bayard in *Sartoris* is the only example of Faulkner's use of his favorite twin motif which serves to illuminate both the psychology of twins and the process of initiation. Brief through it is, as an identity crisis in twinship, complicated by grief and guilt, it merits consideration. In *Jung, Man and his Symbols*, Dr. Joseph Henderson cites Dr. Radin's study of the Winnebago by which he distinguished "four distinct stages in the evolution of the hero," of which the first is the Trickster and the fourth the Twin. The Twins were said to be the sons of the Sun. "They are essentially human and together constitute a single person. In these two sides of man's nature . . . one of them . . . is acquiescent, mild and without initiative; the other . . . is dynamic and rebellious." In some stories, Henderson said, one is the introvert "whose main strength lies in his powers of reflection, and the other is an extravert, a man of action who can accomplish great deeds."

Young Bayard certainly reacted as if he had lost the better part of himself: unfortunately he had no "main strength" of his own. In his acts of suicidal recklessness he was trying to equal Johnny, whose feats were legends in Jefferson. Perhaps they may be regarded as rituals to appease his sense of guilt, the exact reason for which is not made clear. The most obviously initiatory experience is his stay at the MacCallums, but his earlier night in the police station, where he was in safe keeping, was similarly a foreshadowing of what his life would be: "Hell" (*Sar.* 160). At the MacCallums, where he fled when his grandfather died of a heart attack caused by Bayard's reckless driving, Bayard had a vision of hell, an eternal search for Johnny, "never the two to meet" (p. 322). He got out of bed and went through the ice-cold house, found a shotgun, remembered where the shells were, and put the gun back. This is one of the few additions Faulkner made to *Sartoris* after Ben Wasson shortened *Flags in the Dust*. The rejection of suicide is made overt. His final flight in a plane no one else would fly is almost as obviously suicidal choice; he was no Icarus, ego-exalted and overconfident.

What Henderson has to say about twins, trickster, and war heroes in *Thresholds of Initiation* sounds like a psychiatrist's analysis of the Sartoris twins. Johnny is the *puer aeternus*, "an essentially irresponsible power-driven, pleasure-loving" figure. The trickster, however, though similar is capable of being converted into the Hero cycle. "The experience of initiation has to bridge" an "overlapping between the trickster cycle and the hero cycle" so that elements of the two cycles may be transformed either into a psycho-social modality or into a quest for individual identity." Bayard, it seems, reverted to the trickster cycle after John achieved the hero cycle and met his death.

Henderson's account of an actual case history of an Army Air Corps pilot of the Second World War explains part of Bayard's problem, in addition to his grief and guilt: "He looked upon civilian life as a humiliating descent into mediocrity from the high, even heroic, position sustained by adulation, which he had learned to enjoy." Being a Sartoris, Bayard no doubt felt he was born to enjoy such status. "In the Navaho myth, when the masculine powers become too strong, the Twins find female helpers and perform duties toward the feminine, and so it is in the dream material of modern people." As a female helper, Narcissa was a disaster!

Susan Parr discerned some positive aspects in Quentin's suicide: he was unable to negate reality, to stifle his thoughts, to act effectively. By the act of suicide he could achieve those goals and win silence and nothingness. But to Faulkner Quentin was not a hero. Otto Schlumpf believed that those Faulkner viewed as successful heroes were those who escaped from "the tyranny of the past" because "the sense of the past" should not be allowed "to stifle human potential and creativity in the present." Michael Routh extends his perspective to the cosmology of Yoknapatawpha and views Quentin's "shadow deed of a shadow mind" as "microcosmic of a far larger doom Faulkner sees looming over a world unable to align its rational intellect with its emotional faculties: Quentin's disease is really that of modern man." It would be premature to decide whether Routh's view is valid.

Two facts about *Intruder in the Dust* have gradually surfaced after the initial misinterpretations which prevented a proper appraisal of it after it was published in 1948. The first fact, the significance of this novel in the Yoknapatawpha chronicles, could be revealed only in the course of time: Garvin Davenport, in *The Myth of Southern History*, recognized it as Faulkner's closest approach "toward explicit participation in the final and more directly political aspect of the myth of Southern history," that of the Mission of the South in the nation. The second is that *Intruder in the Dust* is not only Faulkner's story of the most successful initiation in Yoknapatawpha but it conforms most completely with initiation patterns. To begin with, Faulkner changed the age of Charles Mallison to make him sixteen at the time of the action, after 1945 (*ID* 149), a suitable age for initiation into his culture. (In "Knight's Gambit" he turned eighteen in December 1941.)

The game of one-upmanship between Charles and Lucas Beauchamp had gone on for four years when the story begins with the arrest of Lucas for murder. Lucas had fished Charles out of an icy stream, taken him into his house, and given him dinner while his clothes dried. Not understanding that the laws of hospitality know no color lines, Charles had tried to pay Lucas. Lucas told his son and Aleck Sander to pick up the coins Charles dropped when Lucas would not take them. To regain his self-respect as a superior white man and erase his shame, Charles plied Lucas with gifts, which Lucas always acknowledged by gifts in return. Charles now finds himself with a unique opportunity "for re-equalization, reaffirmation of his masculinity and his white blood" (*ID* 26).

The situation of Charles resembles that found in the teaching of the Hebrew prophets, as described by John Macquarrie: "a quest for a genuinely human existence" requires "acknowledgment of guilt, acceptance of responsibility, a quest for individual integrity and for social justice." Charles is at the stage on the threshold of initiation specified by Dr. Henderson in "Ancient Myths and Modern Man": "when one is still attached to the original family group," one may experience "that moment of initiation at which one must learn to take the decisive steps into life alone." Dream symbols at this stage suggest a "lonely journey or pilgrimage, . . . on which the initiate becomes acquainted with . . . death . . . it is a journey of release, renunciation, and atonement, presided over and fostered by some spirit of compassion . . . more often represented by a 'mistress' rather than a 'master' of initiation." Enter Miss Habersham.

When Charles responded to the request of Lucas, who was being taken to jail, to bring Gavin Stevens, his uncle, to the jail, he learned the futility of seeking aid from Gavin, who simply assumed that a black man accused of murder must be guilty. Therefore the responsibility rested upon Charles to find the evidence which would exonerate Lucas: the kind of gun Vinson Gowrie was shot with. The traditional initiation rites here take on variations: Charles took himself from Gavin, the man who had been his guide and companion, and left home with only his Negro companion Aleck Sander and Miss Habersham, foster sister of Lucas' wife Molly. Only the next day did Charles move into a world of men. This "mistress of initiation" had the invaluable asset of a pickup truck (*ID* 74, 82).

Charles's moment of choice was extremely difficult and demanded his assuming adult responsibility and facing very real danger. The alternative was attractive and no one would blame him for not taking it or even realize that there had been a choice: he could get on his horse Highboy and ride away and not return until late enough on Monday for the sacred-time of Sunday to have passed and the Gowries and their allies to have accomplished their profane-time sport of lynching Lucas. No one would suspect that a white boy would have thought of interfering with such normal events. The narrative method, third-person but the point of view of Charles, adds enormously to the effectiveness, because all Charles's imaginative anticipation of what may lie ahead proves his courage and the realization proves that his imagination was correct. Unfortunately, only the bare bones of the initiation pattern can be considered here.

The crucial part of Charles's experience is the night journey to the graveyard to dig up the body, the familiar testing by conquest of the dark. The state of tension of the inhabitants of the locality is a real threat of danger. This archetypal journey, "alone or . . . accompanied by a friend," Dr. Henderson described as following the mythic "ritual sequence of separation, transition, and incorporation." In psychiatric cases, "those who undertake the initiation journey . . . have exhausted the absolutism of their group identity." To an amazing degree the narrative method combines the physical experience and the inner quest: seemingly endless sentences combine numerous layers of consciousness which, of course, are often experienced simultaneously. The separation ritual is entirely secret: Charles knew better than to say: "*Let me have the keys to the car, Pop, I want to run out to the country and dig up a grave*" (*ID* 82). The mythic separation from the Mother is followed in the initiation of Charles by a return to Mother and Father after re-entering ordinary life by breakfast at the sheriff's, the end of the transition. Gavin Stevens, not the Father, then takes over as master of initiation, with a daytime return to the graveyard; incorporation with the community includes the presence of the sheriff on his journey.

The ordeals include not only the night journeys but the ritual death of digging up a body—the wrong one, not Vinson Gowrie but Montgomery—and reburying it. It was trial of strength as well as of courage, and an endurance test which included sleeplessness and hunger, as did ancient tribal initiation rites. Dr. Henderson added one feature of these rites not found in Yoknapatawpha: novices did not leave "the maternal universe . . . of the profane world" for the sacred world. But what was only a dream in Henderson's account, in which the patient "perceives the actual madness of the purely collective mass man," was a walking nightmare for Charles: the mob that gathered in the Square to lynch Lucas and that fled, repudiating the actual murderer, the fratricide, Crawford Gowrie, "—not faces but a face, not a mass or even a mosaic of them but a Face: not even ravening nor uninsatiate but just in motion, insensate, vacant of thought or even passion" (*ID* 182).

The rites of incorporation which began at the sheriff's extended through the return to the graveyard, with Charles observing with new sensitivity his native land. A suggestion of ritual occurred when Charles was having breakfast at home and his mother poured him a cup of coffee although he had promised not to ask for or accept coffee before he was eighteen years old (*ID* 127): his mother recognized that he had grown up overnight. Dr. Henderson described the myth cycle of rupture with the community at one end and union with the community at the other, with appropriate rites. In *The Wisdom of the Serpent*, Henderson recognized Christian communion and the prototype, the Last Supper, as symbols of incorporation. The first two pages of Chapter Ten are given to the thoughts of Charles on the symbolic meaning of food: maybe only by the act of eating did "he get himself into the world . . . into that vast teeming anonymous solidarity of the world." In Yoknapatawpha there was no group who could share with Charles a meal symbolizing communal beliefs. In his thoughts he had withdrawn from his people in repudiation, but after his private incorporation rite he made a private declaration of reconciliation: "he wanted no more than to stand with them unalterable and impregnable: one shame if shame must be, one expiation since expiation must surely be, but above all one unalterable durable impregnable one: one people one heart one land" (*ID* 209–10).

Garvin Davenport's concluding comment on *Intruder in the Dust* I can fervently endorse, having been present at "the tragedies of Oxford." "Chick is the first white character in Faulkner's Southern saga to make a positive act, not only of atonement for his region's past, but also toward racial justice for the nation's future. The response to history which is suggested in his action, had it actually materialized among white Americans, might have prevented the tragedies of Oxford . . . ."

Charles Mallison in *The Mansion* shows maturity and self-integration in his responsible participation in the affairs of the community, particularly in his realization that God must be able to trust in man (*M* 321). Because the private life of Charles is peripheral to the story he helps to narrate and is interrupted by his service in the Air Force, the degree to which his initiation is effective is not developed.

The only character who undergoes an initiation and for whom the essential facts of later life are given is Isaac McCaslin. The story of his initiation, in "The Old People" and "The Bear," is the best example of the traditional initiation myth and combines a number of main themes of the Yoknapatawpha chronicles. The initiation myth pattern includes the themes of innocence of childhood and the burden of inherited guilt, and the contrast of nature with civilization and of instinct with reason.

The McCaslin family history ("The Bear" 4) adds the themes of the exploitation of the land and of human beings as represented in the plantation and in racial relations; of the decay of the family, and of Ike's renunciation of the family tradition and heritage for moral progress. Faulkner confirmed the interpretation of "The Bear" as an initiation, "his discovery of the world, of life" and of the bear "as symbolic of nature in an age when nature in a way is being destroyed" (FN 93).

Unlike the heroes of initiation myths already discussed, Ike is a kind of culture-hero. Except that Ike is not "aggressive, competitive, shrewd," and that he does not seek mastery over nature in the usual American sense of subduing nature to the purposes of man, Ike fits Daniel Hoffman's description of the American folk-hero, who undergoes a ritualistic metamorphosis comparable to the rebirth of initiatory rites: "The self-determinative hero turns out to have as his goals a set of concepts more characteristic of the culture of the early American republic than of human history at large. . . . With respect to society, he seeks to demonstrate superiority over other individuals but not ordinarily does he recognize society as an organic structure, in which power can be exercised for extra-personal ends." R. W. B. Lewis places Ike in the mainstream of the tradition of the American Adam but specifies the contrasts in development of themes related to the "hopeful or Adamic tradition":

> He knows . . . that the legend is false and that the New World began with its portion of historic, sinful inheritance. The knowledge protects him from the danger of innocence; but the memory of a lost hope sends him on a lifelong errand of private atonement for everything that had betrayed it. The notion of original innocence tantalizes Isaac's sensibility not less than the accepted fact of original sin. In The Bear, perhaps Faulkner's finest story, the hero's achievement of conscience and the author's achievement of drama both result from the application of imagination to old and familiar materials. Isaac is a Natty Bumppo re-created by the dark energies of a Hawthorne.

Various untypical aspects of Ike's background and life both before and after his initiation are in direct variance with initiation as a cultural rite but somewhat less at variance with the American myth. Ike never is presented in a social context in which women are significant and seldom in one in which they even exist; the male world in which he seems generally to live thus is not merely part of the initiation phase but suggests the world of the frontiersmen before settlers with families arrived. Ike's mother, who was most vivid in her husband-hunting phase ("Was"), died before Ike's experiences in hunting began. Ike's father died even earlier. In his study of parent–child relationships in Faulkner's works, Albert Devlin commented on the lack of white male–female relationships in *Go Down, Moses*. Nothing is known of the marriages of Cass and Zack Edmonds. Lucas Beauchamp commented on Zack's lack of grief at his wife's death (*GDM* 46). Roth was still a bachelor and Devlin doubted that he would have married the mother of his child if she had been white. Tomey's Turl, the slave, and Uncle Buck, his owner, show a significant contrast: "Turl actively pursues the female; the white Buck McCaslin desperately fears women." Of Buck and his twin Buddy, Devlin said, quoting Ike, "Buddy should have been a woman in the first place" (*GDM* 272): "Buddy clearly plays a feminine role in the womanless world of the white McCaslins. Buck, as his name suggests, plays a more masculine role." (Buddy served in Colonel Sartoris' regiment only because he won the poker game with Buck.)

After his father's death, Ike had several foster fathers: his cousin, Cass; the old Indian, Sam Fathers; the other hunters—Major de Spain, General Compson, Boon Hogganbeck, Walter Ewell. General Compson in particular assumed parental authority on occasion and bequeathed his hunting horn to Ike (*GDM* 362). As G. L. Friend remarked, Ike had more spiritual guides than any other Faulkner character. The group of hunters thus represents a feature of primitive society recognized by Malinowski: "The 'father' or 'brothers' act as a group on certain occasions and they are therefore a well-defined social class and not merely a name." Of these fathers, old Sam was Ike's spiritual father, who initiated him into the wilderness and taught him his own moral values. Both Sam and Ike were childless. In the short story "Lion" Ike has a grandson, Theophilus: *Go Down, Moses* thus represents a deliberate and very significant change in Faulkner's concept of Ike's adult role in society.

The relationship between Sam and Ike has another significance: Sam, having both Indian and Negro blood, represents the victims of white exploitation; the relationship between Sam and Ike therefore symbolizes the reconciliation between races. In dealing with the theme of love in American fiction between male whites and Negroes, especially between a white boy and a Negro, Leslie Fiedler refers to "the ennobling love of a white man and a colored one" which contrasts with "the ignoble passion of man for woman," and with the "dark desire which leads to miscegenation." Fiedler points out that "Nature undefiled" is "the inevitable setting for the Sacred Marriage of males," and interprets the relation between Charles Mallison and Lucas as homosexual. Between Charles and Lucas and between Ike and Sam, the relationship according to the text is filial, as befits their ages, their characters, and their circumstances. Fiedler is obsessed with the idea of interracial homosexuality. The bonds of love between Ike and Sam embody the spiritual contribution of the subject races to the master races, with Sam in the quasi-paternal role of initiation mentor. The setting of "Nature undefiled" is represented in the wilderness in "The Bear." In the cosmology of Yoknapatawpha, the Yoknapatawpha wilderness represents "the primitive element within [man] that must be confronted, defined, and accepted." Michael Routh continues with an explication of the "yearly pageant rite" of the hunters as a ritual designed to accomplish that confrontation, Old Ben himself "as a Cosmic Creature identifiably . . . with mankind." In a "dimension free of both time and space" (*GDM* 354) "ten-year-old Ike can witness 'his own birth' psychologically" (*GDM* 195). The world of nature, the animal life, and the hunters form a mythological complex in which Ike's initiation takes place, and from which are derived the values of his adult life. The wilderness provides the setting for the "archetypal motifs of the Hunt, the Quest, the Initiation," in which, Daniel Hoffman says, "ancient myths of the hunt are born again in actual deeds" on "every American frontier where the larger mammals are found," and "the quarry, endowed by superstition with magical powers, personifies Nature, against which the American hunter sees himself in a combative relationship."

The buck, in "The Old People," is Ike's first quarry; the first stage of his initiation as a hunter is symbolized by "the blood with which Sam had marked him forever one with the wilderness which had accepted him" (p. 178). The buck is also a symbol of Nature and the wilderness and even of the most ancient origins of human life; Sam's "Oleh, Chief, Grandfather" may signify not only Freud's explanation of the totem animal as "their common ancestor and primal father" but Jung's theory of the survival in the collective unconscious of "the residue of the animal ancestry of mankind." The bear being the animal most like man, Old Ben is named and personified. Like the animals "revered as spiritual fathers" in Campbell's account of "mythologies of the Great Hunt" Old Ben seems a model for the hunters, like the father for the son. Ike seeks to establish a relationship with him, to be approved by him; Old Ben is the animal parallel to Sam as a spiritual father, a representative of nature. For Ike, animals are not totems so much as part of the nature with which he feels an affinity and seeks to establish a close relationship, a manifestation "of the powers and mysteries of nature" and of a covenant between man and beasts. The serpent, which Ike greets as Sam had greeted the buck, is "the old one, the ancient and accursed about the earth" (*GDM* 329). It is the serpent from the Garden of Eden as well as the serpent of the New World wilderness. As representing old Carothers, it is the serpent which brought sin into the wilderness. Like the archetypal symbol of the labyrinth, Dr. Henderson explained, the serpent is a significant symbol for the life of the unconscious. Lion, the dog, is as wild as the creatures of the wilderness. Sam, the priest, and Boon, the acolyte, prepared Lion for his function as the instrument of destruction of Old Ben. Ike "should have hated Lion" but did not; Lion is part of the inevitable fatality, the last act, of which Ike the novice is a humble participant or just an observer (*GDM* 226).

The bear is so ancient a figure in mythology that G. W. Sutton's explanation of the bear as a totem animal in American Indian initiation rituals sounds up-to-date. The Indians credited the bear with human understanding and beheld the bear with the spirit of love and companionship. Dr. Henderson takes us farther back. The bear-woman, he says, is "perhaps the oldest known example of . . . what we may call the animal master of initiation, forming an archetypal image which can be traced . . . to paleolithic man." Both the bear and the snake are symbols of rebirth because they emerge in the spring. In prehistoric rituals the bear was a numinous figure. The bear mother is "more attentive and self-sacrificing with her cub than the human mother." But when it is "time for him to be on his own, she leaves him in the tree never to return." The bear Ike saw, which had "climbed as high as it could and clung" to the ash sapling, "its head ducked between its arms as a man (a woman perhaps) might have done" (*GDM* 319), was frightened by the logging train but perhaps remembered when its mother left it up a tree. The appendix, "The Bear as Archetypal Image," ends impressively by extending the meaning of the bear rituals to all mankind and all initiations as representing the "right kind of awareness of mankind's paradoxical identity with and separation from the animal world."

Ike's initiation extends over a six-year period, from his first hunt in 1877 to the killing of Old Ben in 1883. The hunting trips and his ordeals and privations follow a ritualistic pattern, although each part of the ritual is not given for each trip. There are two seasons when the hunters go to the wilderness, in June to celebrate the birthdays of Major de Spain and General Compson (*GDM* 204) and in November. The journey out in the surrey, the setting up of the camp, the ritual drinking by the men—"not of the blood they spilled but some condensation of the wild immortal spirit, drinking it moderately, humbly even"—in salute to the wilderness and its inhabitants (p. 192), the ever-present pot of Brunswick stew—all are part of the life of the hunter which Ike shared with his elders.

The individual initiatory experiences of Ike follow a pattern. After being marked with the blood of his first buck, Ike must learn to know the wilderness which has accepted him. First with the compass he teaches himself to be a fair woodsman (p. 205), before he sets out alone in the individual adventure and ritual of hunting, to track down Old Ben and be accepted by the hunted as a hunter, in that violation of nature which was permissible because man and beast followed a code. Campbell explains that the hunt is a sacred rite of sacrifice, the proper sacrifice being the animal itself; "a mutual understanding, supposed to exist between the two worlds," is represented "in rites, upon the proper performance of which depended the well-being of both the animals and their companions and co-players, men." The "proper performance," to be rewarded by sight of the quarry, is the climax, for Ike, to a sequence of incidents. Ike "entered his novitiate to the true wilderness," witnessed "his own birth" at the age of ten when he began his apprenticeship (p. 195). He heard the dogs when Old Ben was near (p. 197), and saw the bitch raked by Ben's claws. He saw the log scored and gutted by Ben, and "the print of the enormous warped two-toed foot" (p. 200). He knew the bear was looking at him but did not see it (p. 203). And then, he relinquished all the trappings symbolic of civilization which gives man an advantage over the beasts—gun, compass, and finally watch—and was rewarded by seeing the bear. Dr. Henderson compares this experience with one typical of dreams, and quotes Eliade on the initiation version: "The novice's solitude in the wilderness is equivalent to a *personal* discovery of the sacredness of the cosmos and of animal life. All nature is revealed as a hierophany."

Thereafter he could find Ben's print whenever he wished (p. 210). One more episode preceded the climax: when the fyce attacked Ben, Ike rescued the dog but did not shoot, but knew that sometime, "when even he dont want it to last any longer," he would have some part in the slaying of Ben (p. 212). That time, which did not come until Ike was sixteen, was the end of another sequence of incidents, on three successive hunting trips, in which Ike did not play a lone part. But just before the death of Ben, Ike was "baptized" in the river; as spectator at the death of Ben he was like a participant in a sacrifice performed by a priest, as Boon killed the bear with a knife. The death of Old Ben is less the climax of Ike's initiation than is the collapse of Sam, with whom Ike insisted on staying until Sam died.

From the hunt Ike had learned to abide by the rules, to be both proud and humble, and to have courage and endurance. From Sam, who taught Ike what he knew of the wilderness, Ike learned that the worth and wisdom of a human being are not determined by the color of his skin. Sam chose his way of life, lived it with integrity, pride, and humility, and willed his own death when the rest of the "old people" and the wilderness were gone. Wisdom, as represented by Sam, is achieved by intuition and discipline in the wilderness, rather than by reason on the plantation. But that was not the end of wisdom for Ike, for the other source of wisdom upon which Ike based his conduct after his initiation and baptism was the Bible; the integration he achieved is not that of a return to nature and primitivism but a harmonizing of the values of nature with Christian principles, seeing in primitive man's relationship between men and between men and nature the image of human brotherhood.

In other terms, Ike reconciles his conscious and rational principles with the instincts brought into play in the wilderness and represented by Sam's wisdom, thus achieving one purpose of initiation, the individuation process represented in Jung's "archetypal forms of the hero-myth." This is the purpose of the rebirth rituals: to bring about "a new and deeper awareness" which "distinguishes the mature personality from the infantile one," "a new attitude on the part of the experiencing subject towards himself and towards his life." The symbol of the wholeness which is the goal of this rebirth is the mandala, "all those symbolic representations of the circle motif, more specifically in its manifold combinations with the square." Carvel Collins called attention to the mandala image at the end of "The Bear," where the platform on which the body of Sam had rested is in proximity to the circle formed by the tree in the clearing. Whether or not Faulkner so intended it, the symbol can be taken as a mandala, one of the archetypal motifs produced by the psyche; the fact that circle and square are only proximate, not combined, may signify Ike's failure to achieve full integration.

Ike's encounter with the serpent is an explicit reminder of the Garden of Eden. His repudiation of old Carothers is a repudiation of the sin represented by the serpent. Thus Ike seems to represent the theme of the New Adam, as dealt with by R. W. B. Lewis, the idea that the New Adam might re-enact the drama of innocence and avoid the errors of the first Adam. But the new Eden did not cancel out the story of man's fall, of original sin and the plan for man's redemption by which Christ, as the second Adam, atoned for the sin of man. Jung explains the story of the fall as psychologically related to the myth of initiation: "the legend of the Fall . . . is the expression of a deep presentiment that the emancipation of ego consciousness was a Luciferian deed." To Henry James, R. W. B. Lewis notes, that emanicipation was the goal of initiation: "In the Book of Genesis he found an allegory of every individual's spiritual adventure, of everyone, that is, who had the energy to grow up. Growing up required the individuating crisis which in Genesis is dramatized as the fall of Adam: the fatal, necessary quickening within the unconscious chunk of innocence of the awareness of self." The inference that Ike by his repudiation demonstrated his lack of "the energy to grow up" is confirmed not only by Faulkner's explicit classification of Ike as the type who avoids evil instead of acting to remedy it (*FU* 246) but also by his statement that we must not go back to "an idyllic condition" in which we thought we were "free of trouble and sin," but "we must take the trouble and sin along with us, and we must cure that trouble and sin as we go" (*FU* 79).

The correct interpretation of Ike's repudiation is vital in the mythology of Yoknapatawpha. Ihab Hassan regards Ike's action as "one of the most radical attempts of the American conscience to resolve the contradictions of the American past," which it certainly is. But he considers Ike to represent youth which "takes upon itself the cumulative sins of God's country, and in the guise of a sacrificial victim redeems that act of Original Innocence which was the discovery of America."

But Ike was not a sacrificial victim, having explicitly declined the altar that his name suggests (*GDM* 283); he had no desire to possess the property which should be his, with the burden of responsibility it would entail, and being fatherless, he could the more easily refuse it. His participation in adult life and in the community was limited. He worked in a hardware store and did carpenter work, whereby he earned his living in part by the destruction of the wilderness by lumbering companies. He married a woman who was more interested in the property she hoped to make him repossess than she was in Ike; he paid the penalty of his error and hers by being childless. The Eve in his Eden was "born lost," meaning, according to Faulkner, that she thought sex was evil, "to be justified by acquiring property. She was ethically a prostitute. Sexually she was frigid" (*FU* 275).

In his repudiation Ike repudiated Sam, who, Otto Schlumpf said, would not have "taught Ike to avoid his responsibility in a futile attempt to forestall the inevitable." He chose narcissism instead of responsibility and "made himself impotent in effect and sterile in fact" by "trapping himself in the past." Furthermore, as Schlumpf indicated, Ike repudiated also "the amelioration of the injustice and the restitution for it" that Buck and Buddy had started before the war. In "Delta Autumn," he had become "a martyr to his own ideals, a victim of the terror of history."

In terms of initiation, Dr. Henderson explained the effects which Schlumpf observed. The purpose of initiation is to form "an ego which has the capacity for individual response and the power of individual choice." Henderson quotes Erik Erikson on the desire of the late adolescent to be "a disciple, a follower," and if this fails, he suffers from "a painfully heightened sense of isolation." The death of Sam Fathers made it impossible for Ike to consult him when the time came for the efficacy of Ike's initiation to be tested. Henderson commented on the danger of the adolescent ego being "pressed upon, molded, or even dissolved by the family or social group surrounding him." Of the other hunters, General Compson was the one most interested in Ike and most paternal toward him, bequeathing him the hunting horn. The account of General Compson's "three avatars" in the appendix to *The Sound and the Fury* indicates his deficiencies. Cass, by all means the most competent of Ike's closest companions, is Ike's adversary in the colloquy. Henderson described "two basic archetypal images, Moira and Themis": Moira signifies "social order as a Way of Nature" and Themis as "the Way of Civilized Man." If Sam had lived, he could not have initiated Ike into the Way of Nature because it had ceased to exist.

The long colloquy between Ike and Cass in the plantation commissary, which covers the history of man since Eden, the history of the South, the story of the McCaslins, and Ike's personal memories, constitutes Ike's defense of his decision to relinquish the inheritance and Cass's protests against it. Few critics have attempted to sort out the component parts and extract any logical reasoning process to justify Ike's decision. But some critical comments are pertinent to this context. G. L. Friend considered the colloquy as evidence of Ike's immaturity, exhibiting his resistance to change, his romanticism and passivity, and his lack of moral commitment. He relinquished his bond with his Negro relatives. Gloria Dussinger's analysis of the rhetoric and the underlying psychology and her translation of Ike's impassioned prose bear out her theory that the self-contradictory elements emerge when Ike, a natural man accustomed to following his instincts, attempted to find persuasive logical motives for his actions. His rationalization reveals his "dual nature and . . . his conscious denial of the existential circumstances." In her study of "Eschatological Thought in Faulkner's Yoknapatawpha Novels," Mary Culley deals with Ike under "Judgment." In a highly mythologized judgment derived from the Old Testament Ike tried to justify his concept of himself as a kind of Moses, a mediator between God and man in the New World. The colloquy is in part an elaborate "Biblical mythology of the South." But in "Delta Autumn" the girl pronounced "the central and authentic judgment," the "stinging judgment upon Ike in the present."

The limitations of Ike's initiation and the vision it provided are confirmed by a contrasting story of initiation in which Ike, as an old man, is one of a company of hunters. "Race at Morning" (1955) was told by the foster son of "Mister Ernest," a hard-working farmer who adopted the boy, deserted by his parents. As M. E. Bradford demonstrated in "The Winding Horn: Hunting and the Making of Men in Faulkner's 'Race at Morning,'" "the completion of the boy's induction into the fellowship of hunters is the direct cause of the development of his foster father's ethic into a self-conscious world-view." As Mister Ernest puts it, when he tells the boy he must go to school and not be just a farmer and hunter like Mister Ernest (*Big Woods*):

> Time was when all a man had to do was just farm eleven and a half months, and hunt the other half. But not now. Now just to belong to the farming business and the hunting business ain't enough. You got to belong to the business of mankind. . . . So you're going to school. Because you got to know why. You can belong to the farming and hunting business and you can learn the difference between what's right and what's wrong, and do right. And that used to be enough—just to do right. But not now. You got to know why it's right and why it's wrong, and be able to tell the folks that never had no chance to learn it . . . [p. 196].

And the boy himself learned that he must earn the right to hunt: farming was not just something to do to fill the time between hunts but "it was something we had to do, and do honest and good during the three hundred and fifty-one days, to have the right to come back into the big woods and hunt for the other fourteen"; hunting and farming were "jest the other side of each other" (p. 195).

But Ike, when he was an old man, still regarded hunting with his "fathers" as the image of eternal bliss. And the comments of the girl in "Delta Autumn" confirm one's conclusion that Ike's wisdom was not deep enough to make him a really redemptive figure, that his initiation did not mark the beginning of the constant growth and maturity which should be the goal of his new knowledge. In his failure to be reborn, Ike is typical of the American folk hero described by Daniel Hoffman: "the transformations are metamorphoses without being rebirths," and reflect a "psychological plane comparable to that of adolescent or pre-adolescent fantasy." Thus the American folk hero falls short of the goal of initiatory rites: "To be worthy of this knowledge the child in him had to die; his soul had to seek its sources in the power that created the world; and he had then to be reborn into his responsibilities and his grace." The hero myth, Henderson also observed, "did not ensure that the hero could relate himself to his adult environment and

maintain the developing consciousness that an individual needs to live a
useful life and . . . achieve the necessary sense of self-distinction in
society." To live in society requires making the commitments that
society, according to Malinowski, demands and needs and that were
made by Phil Stone whose initiation was the model for Ike's: "no
individual initiative is ever culturally relevant unless incorporated into an
institution." Ike might be said to have lived his life in the second stage,
that of transition. As Emily Stone related, Phil Stone stopped hunting and
became a lawyer in Oxford. Compared with Mr. Ernest or Phil Stone,
Ike's role as "uncle" was ineffective, as "Delta Autumn" clearly
shows.

This survey of Jefferson and its leading families shows that what
Ike's society needed was vigorous families, united by love and cooperative parenthood, producing individuals who could vitalize a
decaying civilization by throwing off the shackles of tradition. In this
Ike failed, and he failed even in Christian love for his own kinswoman,
the mother of Roth's baby, because of her Negro blood. That Faulkner
did not regard Ike as an ideal should be remembered: "McCaslin says,
This is bad, and I will withdraw from it. What we need is people who
will say, This is bad and I'm going to do something about it, I'm going to
change it" (*FU* 246). Much of the meaning of the mythology of
Yoknapatawpha County depends on a correct interpretation of "The
Bear"; to regard Ike as an ideal and a saint distorts the meaning. And
no better authority on the subject could be found than Thomas Merton,
himself a monk: in "Baptism in the Forest," Merton remarked that in
"Delta Autumn" Ike revealed "the almost total loss of any prophetic
charisma" he might have had. "Ike McCaslin remains a failed saint
and only half a monk."

Paradoxically Ike showed evidence of both initiation and victimization, the opposed choices in Hassan's categories of heroes. Initiation
should lead to "a *viable* mode of life *in the world.*" But Ike's mode of
life was neither viable, in the sense of allowing complete self-realization and normal experience, nor really in the world; he remained
wedded in spirit to the wilderness: "but still the woods would be his
mistress and his wife" (*GDM* 326). Victimization leads to renunciation,
according to Ihab Hassan: "its characteristic mode is *estrangement
from* the world, and its values are chiefly inward and transcendental."
Despite his initiation, Ike is, in Hassan's terms, a sacrificial victim; he
renounced and he was estranged. But ironically he renounced what he
did not desire, because he preferred loafing in a hardware store when
not hunting or fishing (*M* 323) to earning his right to hunt by commitment, like that of Mr. Ernest, to productive labor for three hundred and
fifty-one days a year.

He did not take upon himself the "cumulative sins of God's country" nor even the sins of his own family; he failed Roth and he failed the last of the descendants of his grandfather's Negro children. Conscious as he was of his succession to Buck and Buddy, he did not "go the McCaslins one better," as M. E. Bradford suggests Mr. Ernest will urge the boy to do, and become "hunter *and* leader, private man *and* patriarch" and also "help his people not only in their physical distress but also in their moral and intellectual development." Ike's convictions were sound; his error lay in withdrawing from the battle for right, in refusing the inheritance which would have permitted him to practice his beliefs. Although his failure might have been prevented if he had married the kind of wife who would have loved him and understood his feelings and who would have showed him how to help the Negroes instead of abandoning them (*FU* 276), Mr. Ernest shows how even a solitary widower may effectively transmit wisdom to a younger generation. As Bradford observed: "a man or a culture is in one sense incomplete without a son, a 'tomorrow' to continue its work; and a son who has not been made a man is no son at all."

The initiation of the boy in "Race at Morning" is an exception to a generalization derived from Faulkner's other initiation stories: initiation which is not supplemented by the wisdom of women, as it is with Bayard Sartoris and Charles Mallison, seems to be incomplete as a foundation for adult life in society. The devaluation of the female in patriarchal mythologies, as noted by Joseph Campbell, may be compared with the devaluation and paradoxical elevation of woman in the myth of the South. Especially in "An Odor of Verbena" Faulkner restored the accent on "initiations received by the male from the female side" which, Campbell explained, was displaced by patriarchal society "to support the patriarchal notion of virtue."

The Reivers, the last initiation story in the Yoknapatawpha chronicles, is also the conclusion of the chronicles. It was published only a few months before Faulkner's death, and he may have written it intending it to be the last. Both his remark to his friend Mr. Reed when the manuscript was ready to mail, "I been aiming to quit all this," and the internal evidence indicate that the Yoknapatawpha cosmos had been completed. The significance of *The Reivers* as marking the completion of the cosmos and of Faulkner's writing will be considered in the next chapter. Here *The Reivers* will be regarded as the third in a complexly related series of initiation stories: the Ike McCaslin trilogy in *Go Down, Moses*, the story of Charles Mallison in *Intruder in the Dust*, and the initiation of Lucius Priest in *The Reivers*. The absence of Ike McCaslin in the short story "Go Down, Moses," which ends the story-novel about the white and the black McCaslins, the latter called Beauchamp, signifies, when viewed retrospectively, that Ike had no place in the world of Miss Worsham, whose family love and loyalty knew no color line. In *Intruder in the Dust* Miss Worsham becomes Miss Habersham, but the change is in name only. Together she and Charles Mallison saved Lucas Beauchamp. Lucas is the link between the three initiation stories: he is referred to in *The Reivers* (p. 229) as the cousin of Bobo Beauchamp, whose problems set off the chain reaction of Uncle Ned's manipulations and provided Lucius with horse races as initiation ordeals. But Uncle Ned is Uncle Ned McCaslin, not Beauchamp, because he was "an actual grandson to old Carothers," as Ike McCaslin was, and the mother of Lucius insisted that the relationship be recognized by her family's calling him Uncle Ned McCaslin, though she herself had no McCaslin blood (*R* 30).

Thus there is an intimation early in *The Reivers* of a change in the theme of race relationship from that in *Go Down, Moses* but closely linked with that in *Intruder in the Dust*: the crucial issue in the initiation of Charles Mallison was the acceptance by white people of racial equality. The same theme of race relationships is basic in *The Reivers* but is not part of what Lucius learned: he already knew and observed the principle his grandfather taught him: "no gentleman ever referred to anyone by his race or religion" (*R* 143). This was in 1905! This specific theme is part of the general one of the Priests as a family of sound values and principles which instill in Lucius the security, as Albert Devlin put it, "of being positively directed by adults who are committed to his welfare." What he already had learned prepared Lucius for what his initiation held in store.

Like the theme of human relationships, the theme of good and evil is derived from the code of a gentleman but achieves a breadth and depth that the maxim of the child Lucius could not convey and that is possible only for a wise old man. The theme is repeated from the preceding initiation stories but is articulated in a fashion not suitable for the memories of Ike or the many-layered consciousness of Charles.

The new theme which is the very foundation of *The Reivers* had been gradually built up in the earlier works: the dawn of the motor age. From the buggies of Eula's suitors in *The Hamlet* to the racing cars of Manfred de Spain and Matt Levitt in *The Town* to Linda's Jaguar in *The Mansion*, all symbols of love, and from Colonel John Sartoris' railroad to Bayard Sartoris' airplane, Faulkner finally brings us to the means of transportation which really joined Yoknapatawpha with the outside world as neither train nor plane did, and which necessitated the network of roads which facilitated travel by any vehicle with wheels.

Boon Hogganbeck is the hero of the future: in Boss Priest's automobile he recognized "his soul's lily maid, the virgin's love of his rough and innocent heart" (R 28), and eloped with it on a honeymoon, oddly chaperoned, to Memphis.

This last theme introduces into the initiation pattern a new time pattern. Ike's initiations followed the mythic cyclical time, as did initiations from time immemorial. Charles Mallison's initiation covered too little time to extend beyond clock time, daylight and darkness. Vernon Hornback commented on the fact that Lucius renounced cyclical time for linear time, progress in space and in "Christian existential time."

The narrative method of *The Reivers* is unique in the Yoknapatawpha chronicles and is indicated in the first two words: "GRAND-FATHER SAID:" There is one narrator but there may be more than one grandchild listening. The book is dedicated to Faulkner's three grandsons, of whom the oldest was only six when Faulkner died. But the idea of telling stories to a cluster of grandchildren no doubt was attractive to Faulkner: for good measure he added in the dedication the son of his stepson and the daughter of his stepdaughter, of an older generation than his own daughter's children. Surely no other author got so much out of two words and a colon as Faulkner did to set the stage, as it were, and prepare the reader for Grandfather's digressions and his leaps from 1905 to 1961. The great advantage of this variation on the narrator device is that it allows references to what the listeners know and to the time of the telling. The age of the narrator provides the greater maturity and broader perspective that "An Odor of Verbena" lacked. The close parallels between "Grandfather" and Faulkner himself and the fact that he had this tale on the back burner for twenty years justify the reader in assuming that "Grandfather" speaks for Faulkner in the perspective with which he views life.

The initiation pattern in *The Reivers* is interwoven with other patterns of action and types of characters and social background which enhance the richness and complexity and the mythic reverberations beyond what one could expect in the initiation experiences of an eleven-year-old fugitive from authority and seeker of adventure. The prevailing and visible parallel is that between the initiation pattern and that of chivalric romance, which often included a quest involving a marvelous journey. Many details in Northrop Frye's analysis in *Anatomy of Criticism* can be identified in *The Reivers*: for example, "A threefold structure is repeated in many features of romance." Although Lucius did not set out, or was not taken out, with any idea of rescuing maidens in distress and engaging in combat with their enemies or matching his skill with that of others in a public performance, his initiation adventures did include these which are more typical of romance. In considering the characters and actions and the significance of the experiences, I shall indicate those which are more typical of romance than of initiation and which are associated with the courtly lover as a hero.

In addition to the companions of Lucius on his journey, who are initiation mentors like the hunting party which accompanied Ike McCaslin, there are older parental, spiritual guides at the beginning and the end. Boss Priest is not only the patriarch of the Priest family but "a far-sighted man, a man capable of vision" (R 38). He bought the Winton Flyer, learned to drive and taught Boon to drive and take care of the car, and took the family and the servants for rides, in rotation. The "separation" in this initiation was the departure of Lucius' parents and grandparents to go to a funeral in Bay St. Louis. The separation of Lucius from the custodians appointed by his parents is difficult strategically, not emotionally: he and Boon had to get away in the car undetected. Lucius chose Non-virtue to gain their ends, especially the lies which were the first cause of his sense of guilt.

The three adventures on the road to Memphis are definitely the stuff of romance. Although Boon as the driver is the leader, Lucius is smarter than Boon and therefore more culpable, like Faustus "doomed and irrevocable" (p. 53). The first adventure was negotiating a series of mudholes to reach the wooden bridge across Hurricane Creek (p. 68). Lucius had to take the wheel—having learned to drive that morning—while Boon raised the car out of the mud. Ned McCaslin emerged from his stowaway hiding place and asserted his right to the adventure as the senior member of the McCaslin family. The next day the adventure at Hell Creek bottom brought them into conflict with their first real adversary, the owner of the cultivated mudhole who watched their vain attempts to get out of the mudhole and then made them pay for the use of his mules. Hell Creek bottom resembles a profane version of Van Gennep's transition area, a natural boundary "mediated by frontier divinities" with the traveler wavering "between two worlds" and observing enforced formalities before he can continue. The Iron Bridge was no such problem.

The trio suggest a Knight-Warrior (Boon), his squire (Lucius), and their servant on a quest. The first night they spend at the wayside inn of Miss Ballenbaugh. In Memphis they seek shelter in a castle, as it were, where they are welcomed, not by the lord and his lady, but by Mr. Binford, proprietor of what might be called, in romantic terms, a Bower of Bliss, and by Miss Reba, the chatelaine, Minnie, their gold-toothed servant, and the beautiful Corrie, Boon's ladylove—by instinct a lady, by ill fate a bond-maid, let us say. Corrie learned from Lucius how a gentleman behaves. From his first adversary, her nephew Otis, Lucius learned how to fight for a lady: Otis had run a peep-show, with Corrie as the unwitting attraction. Lucius fought Otis and suffered an initiatory mutilation, a cut on his hand, which was a handicap to him later in acting as a jockey in the horse races. Of Boon's three-point speech to Lucius on the future value of his present initiatory experience, the third point was "not to tell" when he got home. Secret rites, in other words.

By this time Ned's triple role as clown, as trickster, and as astute observer of human nature has been revealed, with a climax in the consultation between Miss Reba and Ned concerning the strategy for the horse races. The second transition stage had been from Memphis to Parsham Junction by train, with the horse on board. Miss Reba, Corrie, Minnie, and Otis joined Lucius and the men in Parsham Junction.

At Parsham Junction a new group of characters appears. The secret society motif is introduced, but not as part of the initiation. Ned and Uncle Parsham are Masons and have their own secret means of communication. Boss Priest is a Mason, too, but does not need to hide the fact. Uncle Parsham is the black counterpart of Boss Priest, and when Lucius is given a choice of where to spend the night he chooses Uncle Parsham's. He also chooses to sleep with Uncle Parsham: "I sleep with Boss a lot of times. . . . He snores too. I don't mind" (p. 250). Lucius riding Lightning and McWillie on Acheron, Lucius won the third heat because Lightning behaved as Ned had said he would. Boss Priest bet on Lightning on a fourth heat and lost, because Ned had no "sour dean" for him. Ned bet on Acheron!

The evil adversaries of Lucius and his mentors at Parsham include Otis, the child wonder in evil deeds, who stole Minnie's gold tooth, and Butch Lovemaiden, a grown-up Otis, who as deputy sheriff from Hardwick could, as Miss Reba said, have taught Pharaoh or Caesar something about "kinging"—until Mr. Poleymus, the constable, snatched Butch's pistol and ripped off his deputy's badge (pp. 210, 256). Boon's defense of Corrie from Butch's persecution of her resulted in the imprisonment of Boon, his fight with Butch, and Corrie's submission to Butch to recover the horse for the benefit of Lucius and his friends. Lucius reacted to the defilement of Corrie with rage until Miss Reba persuaded him that Corrie did "have to," to get Lightning back (p. 280). Corrie proved that she was truly reformed by taking a job as servant to care for the invalid wife of Mr. Poleymus.

The final transition in the initiation of Lucius was from Parsham

Junction to Jefferson, with Boss Priest driving. Lucius was amazed that nothing at home had changed. He summed up his guilt and his gain: "lying and deceiving and tricking," things "seen and heard and learned" that his parents would have forbidden. But if nothing had changed "then something would have been thrown away, spent for nothing; either it was wrong and false to begin with and should never have existed or I was wrong or false or weak or anyway not worthy of it" (pp. 299–300). In Henderson's terms, this is a cyclic transition, a return, not an evolutionary one.

"Incorporation" follows. Lucius' father gave up the customary punishment of whipping with the razor strop as debasing to both of them. Then Boss Priest took over and put in simple terms of universal validity what Lucius had learned: a gentleman has to live with the memory of his misdeeds and he has to accept responsibility for his actions (p. 302). This scene explicitly restores Lucius to his family, his proper incorporation at this stage, with recognition of his new maturity.

The fact that Boss Priest and Ned and Uncle Parsham are all Masons gives serendipitous relevance to Dr. Henderson's two images of initiation. The first is the "stepladder evolutionary view" of the stages "as moving from a lower to a higher sphere of enlightenment, on the assumption that the novice must learn to overcome, by transcending, his animal nature." The "principle of masculine friendship" "as a form of group solidarity," such as Freemasonry, was the model for Mozart's *The Magic Flute*, one of the stories of this evolutionary initiation. The old pattern is cyclic, return to old patterns instead of progression to new ones. It is perfectly illustrated in Ike McCaslin, in "Delta Autumn," having to follow new roads in a motor vehicle to reach a scene where the old rites can be enacted.

Lucius had undergone an identity crisis usually associated with late adolescence, as described by Erik Erikson and cited by Dr. Henderson: it "shows parallels, first to the hero myth and then to the later developmental stages arrived at by means of the initiatory 'ordeal' or 'trial of strength' associated with certain father-figures, masters of initiation, and the corporate life of the group." At "its peak of intensity" the crisis reaches the stages of "'sexual identity vs. bisexual diffusion,' 'leadership polarization vs. authority diffusion,' and 'ideological polarization vs. diffusion of ideals' as comprising the full range of inner and outer conflicts to be experienced and, if possible, resolved." The combination of the romance pattern with the initiation pattern is justified in light of Erikson's analysis: the unique "father-figures and masters of initiation" and the components of "the group" and the settings in which it shares its experiences may well increase the reader's appreciation of the serious meaning if he can stop laughing and soberly reconsider this happy ending of the Yoknapatawpha chronicles which began more than thirty years earlier with the uninitiated young Bayard Sartoris and Quentin Compson who threw their lives away.

Through his ordeals of physical and mental strain and a guilty conscience, of conflict and mutilation, of loss of innocence and of confusion in an adult world, of childish desire to quit and go home, Lucius had learned a great deal. He had learned to drive a car and to ride a race horse. From observing Butch, he had learned about the injustices of the law and about man's lust for power and authority. But he had also learned that human dignity and decency and intelligence know no color lines, that law officers can act with courage and justice. He learned about the evils of gambling but also about one's responsibility for kinfolk. He learned how women can be degraded but also how they can be redeemed. He learned how to live like a gentleman. But by himself he learned that childhood innocence can never be regained, and that one cannot travel back into the past. He learned that man has a natural inclination toward Non-virtue. He learned not to shirk or dodge but to finish what he and others had started, but not to do it for money.

But unlike Faust, Lucius gained knowledge but was not damned; because of his gentlemanly ideals and conduct, he redeemed Corrie and restored to her the name Everbe Corinthia. She had never met a gentleman before but had an instinctive desire for virtue and self-respect. She married Boon and they named their son Lucius Priest Hogganbeck. (The Lucius Hogganbeck who drove an automobile jitney in *The Town* and *The Mansion* before 1914 was not born after 1905.)

All the characters who accept initiation represent, in their youth and inexperience, a version of Jung's child archetype, "equipped with all the powers of nature and instinct," and impelled "by the urge to realize itself." Because Faulkner was adapting myth to realistic fiction, his initiates may not achieve full self-realization or their stories are left incomplete and unresolved. But they do gain insight into themselves and their world, and all of them either demonstrate freedom from race prejudice or achieve that freedom during their initiation and renounce the traditional attitude. Thus these initiation stories are relevant to the basic theme of the exploitation of men as well as to the individual themes and contribute significantly to the mythology of Yoknapatawpha and the archetypal patterns it embraces.

Complementary to the theme of primal innocence is the utopian dream of ultimate perfection: both were cherished, as Ihab Hassan shows, in the New World.

> At first glance, the utopian motive seems an affirmative projection of the self into active life, and the Edenic a nostalgic withdrawal from it. A more sober view, however, will discover in both motives, carried far enough, a mode of escape from that realm of uncertainty and compromise which *is* the world. Both, in a sense, are a form of radical innocence. Looking too far ahead or too far back amounts to the same thing: escape from the present, escape from time and death. . . . Childhood and youth satisfy at once the demands of our past and the hopes of our future. This is our national neurosis, the form of *our recoil from an actual world* that brings Failure, Age, and Death.

Thus we should expect to find, among characters who do not undergo initiation, examples of utopianism to parallel Quentin Compson's rejection of the present to cling to the past or to reject life itself. Utopianism may, however, lead people forward with anticipation and get them past the period of adolescent despair; when disillusionment strikes, the utopian may be able to go on living.

The utopian dream of perfection is most relevant to Yoknapatawpha in relation to the myth of the South. The perfection with which the myth endowed ladies and the quixotic dreams of the gentlemen were derived in part from the chivalric romances and the novels of Sir Walter Scott. The Courtly Lover has been identified as a distinct character type in Yoknapatawpha. In "The Fatal Illusions: Self, Sex, Race, and Religion in William Faulkner's World," Jewel H. Gresham divides her study into five chapters which indicate her approach and its scope: I Yoknapatawpha and the Chivalric Myth: The South as Invention; II The Cavalier Myth: *Sartoris*; III The Cult of Virginity: *The Sound and the Fury*; IV The Black Scapegoat: *Light in August*; V Blood Guilt and Cultural Casualties: *Absalom, Absalom!*. The writer's purpose is to show that the prototype for the culture of the Old South is the system of medieval chivalry and that Faulkner's fictional world is "overlaid . . . by two layers of the past: the Old South past and . . . the feudal past." She demonstrates the society's "concern with the inherited Chivalric myth" but concludes "that it is a false Camelot which betrays the Chivalric dream of honor and valor even as its members structure a cultural façade paying homage to that dream." Since Gresham is dealing with entire novels and not with single characters exemplifying her theme, there will be no occasion to deal further with her useful study.

"Courtly Love in the Writings of William Faulkner," by Anderson Clark, is precisely on my present topic but in isolation from the broader context. The omission of *The Reivers*, in a 1975 dissertation, is regret-

table: Lucius as the Courtly Lover and Everbe Corinthia as the redeemed Lady are original, charming, and significant. Clark identifies
three characteristics of courtly love: worship of woman, doctrinaire
free love, and sublimation of love into chivalric activity. In addition to
the three advocates of courtly love with whom he deals—Quentin
Compson, Gavin Stevens, and Byron Bunch—Joe Christmas and Gail
Hightower were initially susceptible to the chivalric impulse. The
development of the tradition of courtly love is traced. Courtly attitudes, ritual, and rhetoric in Faulkner's work are examined.

The Courtly Love tradition was derived in part from the "Pure or
Cathars," also known as the Heresy or the Albigensian heresy. Their
dualistic belief was based on the concept that "Good and
Evil . . . exist in absolute heterogeneity," God and Satan. Denis de
Rougement's account of the Cathars includes their vow "*to abstain, if
married, from all contact with a wife*." The Manichaeans had "the
same sacraments as the Cathars." The polarity in Faulkner's works is
reminiscent of Manichaeanism; to find that the Courtly Love doctrine
is related to the Cathars and to Manichaeanism, which condemned the
flesh, casts a new light on the emphasis on chastity in the myth of the
South.

Cleanth Brooks cited Rougemont, referring to Quentin Compson as
"a classical instance of the courtly lover," and to Faulkner's statement
that Quentin "loved not his sister's body but some concept of
Compson honor" as sounding like Rougemont's *Love in the Western
World*. The pattern of activity of Quentin's last day on earth closely
resembles that of initiation stories, as has been indicated, but the impulse which drove him to death was the ideal of courtly love, as Clark
shows, including both *The Sound and the Fury* and *Absalom,
Absalom!*. Although Clark views Quentin leniently, he concludes that
"the tale of this unstable and ineffective lover ends pathetically, not
tragically," and regards Henry, Bon, and Judith as a tragic triangle of
courtly romance. But of course it is Quentin's vision that Clark interprets.

The Courtly Lover figure appeared early in the Yoknapatawpha
chronicles, in Horace Benbow. He was poetic and idealistic and very
susceptible to feminine charms. The only woman, however, whom he
idealized in courtly lover fashion was his sister Narcissa. Horace was
never the seducer, but always the seduced. This is much more apparent in *Flags in the Dust* than in *Sartoris*. In fact, in *Flags in the Dust*
and the revisions of the unpublished galleys of *Sanctuary*, every
woman in Horace's life, from his mother to his stepdaughter, Little
Belle, plus his wife, Belle's, sister who was deleted from *Sartoris*, and

Ruby and Temple in *Sanctuary*, evokes an emotional response of which Horace was more aware than in the shortened versions. Horace's idealistic concept of man and his appalled realization of the evil represented by Popeye impelled Horace to act as Lee Goodwin's lawyer; having had no experience in a criminal case, he was like a knight without armor engaging in a tournament. Horace left a vacancy for a lawyer in Yoknapatawpha when he returned to his wife. Because Faulkner ultimately filled that vacancy with Gavin Stevens, Horace cannot be ignored.

Horace had served an apprenticeship until he was forty-three (*San.* 272), and Gavin in some ways was incorrigibly adolescent, but what Dr. Henderson said about middle-aged men applies to the experience of both of them: "between the first and second halves of life, not only the introvert but all men experience a sense of failure and a sense of panic that they may be unequal to the task of becoming truly mature." He illustrates by the examples of T. S. Eliot's Prufrock, "with his outworn infantilism and mistrust of feeling" and Gerontion, with his "thoughts of a dry brain in a dry season." Gavin's remarks about himself recall Henderson's *puer aeternus*, referring to his Courtly Lover rivalry with Manfred de Spain as "playing the fool" using "my own delayed vicious juvenility," "my own clowning belated adolescence" (*T* 89, 133).

Recognizing Gavin Stevens as more than the Quixotic hero or the preacher or a mouthpiece for Faulkner, Mary M. Dunlap in a dissertation, "The Achievement of Gavin Stevens," accomplished a most useful, complete account of Gavin Stevens from his first appearance in "Hair" (1931) to the last in *The Mansion* (1959). She noted Gavin's resemblance to Horace Benbow as an intellectual and to Quentin Compson as obsessed by myth and stated his unique distinction in the Yoknapatawpha fiction: for the last eleven of twenty-eight years he was the major character in the mythical world Faulkner created. Tracing the development of Gavin from his first appearance, she specified the role he played in each short story and the relation of those roles and the themes involved in his later major roles in works published after 1946. In *Light in August* the ΦBK key was added to the identifying details in his appearance and his family was added to the oldest families in Yoknapatawpha. In that novel, "Stevens is as rigid in thought as Grimm is in action," but his rationalism was needed in creating a credible world. In *Intruder in the Dust* he became a family man living with his father and the three Mallisons. The close reading and perceptive interpretation extend to all aspects of Gavin's character and his roles.

Gavin's first major role in the story of Charles Mallison's initiation reveals him as a man born out of time, whose "rhetoric becomes a metaphor defining his historical place and attitudes," and whose values were fixed by history. With these attributes and his propensity to talk rather than to act, Gavin is a potential Courtly Lover, but his appearance in that role at the end of the detective short stories in *Knight's Gambit* is surprising in that context, with the chess game as the "organizing metaphor," as Dunlap observed. The relationship between chess and courtly love is clearly a clue to Gavin's involvement in the legend of Melisandre. The names of the chess pieces are explicit: King, Queen, Castle, Bishop, Knight. But the fact that "a radical change in the game of chess" took place as a result of the Cult of the Virgin should be mentioned: instead of the four kings of the original Indian game, "a Lady (or Queen) was made to take precedence over all other pieces, save the King, and the latter was actually reduced to the smallest possibility of real action, even though he remained the final stake and the consecrated figure." This little nugget from Denis de Rougemont's *Love in the Western World* has ironic implications concerning the myth of the South which inhibited the action of women and Gavin as a Courtly Lover who acts like a Knight as a detective and like a King with women until middle age. His marriage to Melisandre in "Knight's Gambit" Faulkner accepted as a fact with which he had to deal in *The Mansion*.

"Knight's Gambit" is a story of detection and crime prevention rather than one of the Courtly Lover, but he at least casts his shadow when the events of twenty years previously emerge. Melisandre got the wrong letter and thought Gavin did not want her, that she was not smart enough (*KG* 345). So she married Mr. Harriss to save her father's plantation. Some of Dunlap's observations about Gavin are very pertinent to his role in *The Town* and *The Mansion*. Commenting on Gavin's need to balance the masculine and feminine principles to function positively, she remarked that Gavin had to overcome his feminine, passive sensitivity and attain masculinity by proving he could cope with her children before he could claim Melisandre. Her comment on brother–sister relationship or twinship as aiding masculine–feminine balance is a reminder that Melisandre and Margaret Mallison were Academy friends and that Gavin was "going on thirty years old" when Melisandre was sixteen (*KG* 234). In *The Town* Margaret and Gavin are twins.

Anderson Clark isolated the romantic dimensions of Gavin in *Snopes* and summed up his attitude toward Eula and Linda: Gavin's "expression of courtly love rejected the proffer of physical-sexual involvement

. . . for an overwhelming, transcendent spiritual worship." In the eyes of men Eula retains a mythic dimension in *The Town* even when it is known that Manfred de Spain is her lover and Flem Snopes her husband. De Spain was a successful foil to "the romantically unsuccessful antagonist," Gavin. When Manfred was elected mayor, Chick saw him as "the Godfrey de Bouillon, the Tancred, the Jefferson Richard Lionheart of the twentieth century" (*T* 13). Gavin is "a second-string courtly lover," a Don Quixote with Ratliff as his Sancho Panza. Richard Milum described his marriage to Melisandre as happy but not passionate, his attitude toward courtly love having been demythologized.

In the series of one-upmanship encounters between Manfred, the proved champion, and his "second-string" opponent, both act like retarded adolescents. Dunlap refers to their "ritual preening" before each other (*T* 57). Now that she is Gavin's twin, Maggie is his accomplice; even though Jefferson women cannot forgive Eula the way Jefferson men look at her, Maggie facilitates Eula's entry into Jefferson society as the beginning of Gavin's crusade to save Eula from being unchaste with Manfred de Spain (*T* 48, 49). Maggie's reference to Melisandre, four years younger than she, as the girl Gavin should have married and her prediction that he will marry a widow with grown children (*T* 50) prove that Melisandre's appearance in *The Mansion* was not a belated afterthought. The Christmas Ball of the Cotillion Club was Gavin's first chance to show his colors, which he did by sending Eula a corsage and then having to send each member of the club one, and Manfred, being alerted by the florist, did the same. In the meantime they played sophomore tricks on each other.

The sight of Eula and Manfred dancing together precipitated the first encounter, with Gavin, not Flem, "the protector in the formal ritual" (*T* 75). He was "simply defending forever with his blood the principle that chastity and virtue in women should be defended whether they exist or not" (*T* 76). In the repetition of this episode in another generation, Gavin fought Matt Levitt, the challenger, over a copy of John Donne's poems (*T* 189–90). Clark said, of the two chivalric actions, that "Eula and Linda have Gavin for life" (or at least until Linda left Jefferson in her Jaguar).

Similarly repeated are two confrontations between Eula and Gavin, with parallel episodes between Gavin and Linda in *The Mansion*. As acting city attorney, Gavin sued Manfred de Spain's bonding company for malfeasance after Flem stole the brass from the power plant. Eula came to Gavin in his office in the evening. He thought she came to intercede for both Manfred and Flem or for Manfred and that if he had not been a dreamer, it might have been him instead of Manfred. But that would have been against his nature: "I wouldn't have been me then" (*T* 94). When she drew the shade, a sign that it was Flem, not Manfred, she wanted Gavin to "buy," Gavin opened the door and told her he would value Flem as highly as her coming indicated that she did (*T* 94–96). (Horace Benbow reacted the same way when Ruby offered to "pay" him for helping her [*San.* 267–68].) In the next confrontation, also in Gavin's office, on the last night of Eula's life, she asked Gavin to marry Linda—he supposed, so she and Manfred could leave together. (Gavin's "complete belief in the fidelity of adultery," as Dunlap said, had defended Eula and Manfred to Mr. Garraway: "Nothing for constancy, nothing for fidelity, nothing for devotion, unpoliced devotion, eighteen years of devotion?" [*T* 314].) Gavin promised: "At any time, anywhere. No matter what happens" (*T* 333). Dunlap refers to Gavin's unsmoked pipes in this last scene and Eula's crushing out her cigarette (*T* 320, 333).

Gavin then lied to Linda, after Eula's suicide, and assured her that Flem was her father. As Dunlap said, after Linda leaves, Gavin "retreats to escape the passion of grief and the knowledge of the enormity of his own failure and the evil inherent in human actions, his own included. It is in confronting evil that Stevens fails as a human being."

Linda proved like Eula in failing to find a worthy recipient for her potential love. Gavin would not have accepted love from Eula if he had met her before her marriage. But Linda he tried to form in his favorite image: "Forever will he love and she be fair." Unlike Eula, Linda had a wider field in which to choose someone worthy of her love, both before and after her marriage to Kohl. From beginning to end, she repeated that she loved Gavin. But Gavin had selected an ideal of fidelity to implant in, first, Melisandre and then Linda, when they were young and malleable. Melisandre escaped, although Mr. Harriss was no prize. But Gavin practically forced Linda to live up to *his* prophetic image of her—as if Maggie had maneuvered the marriage of Gavin to Melisandre to prove *her* a good prophet—he's "doomed to marry a widow with grown children" (*T* 50). Ratliff quoted the rest of Gavin's earlier remarks: "Doomed to fidelity and grief . . . To love quick and lose him quick and for the rest of her life to be faithful and to grieve" (*M* 158). Ratliff refused to go to the "housewarming" of Linda and Barton Kohl, but Gavin was already sure Linda would fulfill his expectations. (It is possible she was giving Gavin a chance to dissuade her before the marriage took place. Gavin never would admit that he might be right and be "it.") Ratliff considered that it was Gavin who was doomed, perhaps from the time Eula first "laid eyes on him": his "was the right and privilege and opportunity to dedicate forever his capacity for responsibility to something that wouldn't have no end to its appetite and that wouldn't never threaten to give him even a bone back in recompense" (*M* 163). And when Linda returned to Jefferson, a deaf widow, Chick continued from what Ratliff had told him: "she was lost; she had even lost that remaining one who should have married her for no other reason than that he had done more than anybody else while she was a child to make her into what she was now. But it wouldn't be him; he had his own prognosis to defend, make his own words good *no matter who anguished and suffered*" (*M* 219, italics added).

The evidence of Linda's love for Gavin is sufficient to warrant Dunlap's interpretation: Gavin's rejection of her, symbolized by the lighter he never used, left Linda with nothing but revenge "to satisfy her destiny as Eula's daughter." The will Linda made out in Flem's favor because, she told Mr. Stone of Oxford, "I love and admire and respect him" (*M* 328) was reinforced by the lie Gavin told her, that Flem was her father. If Gavin had fulfilled Linda's love, Eula's sacrifice would have been justified. Clark traced the change in Gavin's attitude toward Linda from love to friendship. After his final refusal of physical intimacy at Pascagoula, Linda told Gavin to marry (*M* 252). (Her reactions when he did can only be surmised.) The irony of the juxtaposition of his concept of her fidelity and of his Courtly Lover ideal of love without intercourse, following one of his refusals of marriage, in black and white, helps one to understand her revenge motives: Gavin saw in Linda's eyes "the immeasurable loss, the appeaseless grief, the fidelity and the enduring . . . while I wrote *because we are the 2 in all the world who can love each other without having to . . .*" (*M* 239).

The collaboration of Linda and Mink in their revenge murder of Flem and Linda's involvement of Gavin as an accessory before the fact led to Gavin's very ultimate disillusionment. Clark considered that Gavin and Linda were more than "technically implicated" in the murder of Flem. Gavin resisted admitting the truth to himself about the red Jaguar. His one crumb of comfort was her statement: "At least I didn't lie to you" (*M* 423). That was more than he could say to her. When she said: "You have had nothing," he knew what she meant: "he had offered the devotion twice and got back for it nothing but the privilege of being obsessed, bewitched, besotted . . . ." And he realized that Linda knew he would find out that she ordered the car as soon as "she knew for sure he could get Mink the pardon" (*M* 424–25). There is no reason to doubt her final statement concerning Gavin: "I have never loved anybody but you" (*M* 424). The last scene in the drama of Gavin's life, one hopes, provided him with appropriate *Catharsis*.

The acme of total devotion and self-abnegation in the Courtly Lover is reached just once, in the most extravagant and poetic language. At the end of a description of dawn, which alludes to "Troy's Helen and the nymphs and the snoring mitered bishops, the saviors and the victims and the kings," the lover looks into the eyes of his beloved: "Within the mild enormous moist and pupilless globes he sees himself in twin miniature mirrored by the inscrutable abstraction; one with that which Juno might have looked out with he watches himself contemplating what those who looked at Juno saw. . . . He squats beside her and begins to draw her teats" (*H* 184–85). In the extravaganza which descends from the sublime to the ridiculous, Faulkner used the story of Ike Snopes and the cow to ridicule the overblown and fantastic elements in the tradition of courtly love and to pay tribute to the power of unselfish love and devotion, even in a subhuman creature.

The name of the last of the Courtly Lovers is most appropriate for the character: Byron Bunch, the romance hero of *Light in August*, bears one of the favorite aristocratic–romantic given names, "Byron," found even among the Snopeses, and "Bunch," one of the common herd, a name found in the Oxford, Mississippi, area. As described by the furniture dealer who relates the departure of Byron and Lena from Mississippi, no hero, courtly or otherwise, could be less impressive: "he was the kind of fellow you wouldn't see the first glance if he was alone by himself in the bottom of a empty concrete swimming pool" (*LA* 469). The myth of the South has vanished, as it did at the beginning with the very pregnant Lena hitching rides. But Faulkner might have created Byron Bunch to exemplify the statement by C. S. Lewis in discussing courtly love: "Love advances the most lowly born to true nobility, and humbles the proud." Of "the four marks" of courtly love listed by Lewis, the first two are superlatively represented by Byron, Humility and Courtesy, despite his lack of elegant rhetoric. The third precisely explains Gavin Stevens' idealization of Manfred and Eula but only in terms of medieval society. "Adultery," the third mark, is explained by Lewis: "any idealization of sexual love, in a society where marriage is purely utilitarian, must begin by being an idealization of adultery." Inasmuch as Eula's marriage was utilitarian, Gavin's view was not unreasonable. (The fourth mark applies only to medieval culture.) The very name of Byron Bunch and his image suggest that *Light in August* is reduced to lowly human dimensions, but demythologizing is only partial: Lena's mythic qualities are apparent in the total context of *Light in August* more than in her role as Byron's Lady.

In "Courtly Love in the Writings of William Faulkner," Anderson Clark stated Byron's qualifications as a courtly lover: both ritual and courtly behavior and "an inward passion for the well-being of his be-

loved, his mistress, to whom and for whom he will sacrifice any principle or possession." To Byron Lena's welfare took precedence over his
own sexual desires or the return of her love. But, as Clark said,
Byron's story is a parody of courtly love in simple rural terms. Because
Byron's "courtly love enables him to worship" Lena "with strength
and endurance beyond his awareness" and because his love and fidelity are unqualified, there is no element of ironic inversion as there often
is in Faulkner.

   Byron worked in a planing mill, working on Saturday afternoon and
keeping record of the time himself. On Sunday he rode a mule to a
church thirty miles away to lead the choir in an all-day service (*LA* 43).
"Then Byron fell in love . . . contrary to all the tradition of his austere
and jealous country raising which demands in the object physical in-
violability" (p. 44). He dedicated to her his instant devotion and assumed responsibility for her protection, of both body and mind. When
he appeared at Gail Hightower's on Sunday night, when he should
have been riding back to Jefferson on a mule, Gail realized that the
rigid pattern of his life had changed. Apparently his conversion to
natural instead of clock time was effected by Lena's query, when
Byron was going to keep track of how much time he spent listening to
her, "A few minutes wouldn't make no difference, would it?" (p. 47).
The few minutes transformed his life, so it was Lena's question that
was unrealistic. When Byron realized that the Lucas Burch Lena was
seeking was the man he knew as Joe Brown and when the discovery of
Joanna Burden's multilated body put the town in a frenzy, he sheltered
Lena by taking her to Mrs. Beard's where he roomed and where he
secured an accomplice in Mrs. Beard in shielding Lena from the dis-
turbance. He kept Brown in ignorance of Lena's presence until after
her baby was born. In his account to Gail Hightower on Tuesday night
of what had gone on, he explained Lena better than he could understand himself: one part of Lena knew Lucas was a scoundrel, and the
other part thought of him as her husband and father of her child. Byron
was determined that "never the twain should meet" (p. 285). At her
request Byron was going to establish her in the cabin where Brown and
Joe Christmas had lived, against the strong objections of Hightower to
his "interfering" between Brown and Lena.

   The next night, when for the first time Byron did not stumble on
Hightower's steps, Hightower, as Byron realized, was not pleased:
Byron had gained self-confidence and assurance and, as G. L. Friend
suggested, pride (*LA* 294). Byron had made the cabin ready for Lena,
put a bolt on her door, and slept in a tent where he could hear if she called.
Hightower told him to go away and marry a virgin (p. 298). But when

Byron sought Hightower's aid when Lena's baby was being born and he himself went for the doctor, Hightower consented. The experience had a redemptive effect, short-lived though it was (p. 385). He never ceased to try to separate Byron and Lena, but he did realize all that Byron gave and restored to him (p. 392).

The birth of Lena's baby brought the two parts of Byron's mind together: he had believed that she was a virgin and that a doctor would not be needed (pp. 297–99). Convinced of the reality of Lucas Burch, he was ready to tell Burch about Lena. Lena made no effort to hold Byron, and when he asked her to marry him, she refused. So he had the sheriff send a deputy with Brown–Burch to Lena to let them make their own choice, and he rode off on a mule. As Clark said, Byron gave Burch a chance to assume responsibility and give the child a name.

After patent lies to Lena, until with her eyes "she released him by her own will deliberately," Brown escaped through a window, the deputy being outside the door (p. 409). In the meantime, Byron on his mule has what Routh termed an "apocalyptic vision" on the crest of a hill and in an "epiphany" sees himself as an "avatar" (pp. 401–402). Then he sees Brown fleeing from the cabin and decides there is one more thing he can do for Brown: "I took care of his woman for him and I borned his child. . . . I may not can catch him. . . . And I may not can whip him if I do. . . . But I can try it. I can try to do it" (p. 403).

At last, the Courtly Lover hero confronts the cowardly villain, who is bigger than the hero and a fighter if the odds are with him. "Finally, in the best of the courtly tradition," Clark said, Byron "sublimates his love into chivalric battle designed to champion his love's cause, to bring honor to her humiliation and abandonment." Byron, a "knight in bedraggled armor but undiminished virtue," Clark concluded, had achieved a moral victory in physical defeat.

The final account of Lena and Byron is related by a furniture dealer to his wife on his return from a trip in his new truck with "a housed-in body with a door at the rear" (LA 468). He had picked up a "young, pleasant faced girl," carrying a baby, and an unremarkable man. The man gave the impression that he had "tried everything else until he was desperate" (p. 471). Most of the story reveals how meticulous Byron was to do what Lena wanted and to take the best possible care of her: the narrator even alludes to Alphonse and Gaston, not named, and their insistence that the other go first. When Byron climbed into the back of the truck where Lena and the baby were, the furniture dealer heard Lena say, "Why, Mr. Bunch. Aint you ashamed. You might have woke the baby too," and saw the man emerge through the back door of the truck, apparently picked up and set on the ground. The furniture man imagined how ashamed Mr. Bunch must be. In the morning he was gone and the girl rode in the back of the truck. But around a curve the man was waiting, *"hang dog and determined and calm . . . desperated . . . to take the last chance. . . ."* When the driver stopped the truck, the man stood at the back of the truck where she was sitting at the door and said "I be dog if I'm going to quit now." "'Aint nobody never said for you to quit,' she says." Courtesy he had demonstrated in the consideration he had shown for her wishes, Humility he had, as it were, proudly endured. But not Adultery, even with an unwed mother carrying a bastard. The furniture dealer figured she was going to enjoy as much travel as possible before she settled "for the rest of her life" (p. 480). The particularly Faulknerian touch is that, in relation to the depiction of Lena at the beginning, she was obviously both a Diana and a Virgin Mary figure and the ending re-establishes her as a mythic figure: Mary and Joseph and the Child on the flight into Egypt. The closeness of Lena and now of Byron to the natural world and their instinctive goodness prevent any suggestion of sacrilege. Michael Routh sums up the cosmological significance of Lena and Byron: Byron has changed from anti-life traits to positive attitudes. Both Lena and Byron now represent positive forces in the universe which can transcend the ambiguities of the world.

The Mary and Joseph analogy at the end of *Light in August* is a reminder that Mrs. Hines confused Lena's child with Joe Christmas, her grandson. The use of the story of Lena and Byron as a framing device for the story of Joe Christmas is more suitable than it may seem: Regina Fadiman's study of Faulkner's revisions of *Light in August* shows that Faulkner worked out the structure very carefully, with parallels between the stories of Lena and Joe as well as the beginning and ending frame. Although Joe is an obvious Christ figure, Lena is the redemptive figure, having faith in mankind and in life and communicating that faith to Byron Bunch and then through him to Hightower, at least briefly. Christ figures in Faulkner are more frequent than redemptive figures or than characters with positive Christ-like qualities.

The Christian myth as exemplifying suffering and sacrifice and hope is represented in archetypal figures, in the Jungian sense, in Faulkner, even in suffering victims who are villains, like Popeye, or idiots, like Benjy Compson, a point made by both Mary Culley and Stanley Elkin. Elkin deals comprehensively with Christ figures, including Goodyhay, whom Mink encountered on his way to Memphis in *The Mansion*. The most self-conscious Christ figure in Yoknapatawpha, Ike McCaslin, Elkin regarded as a denier of life, whose religion was renunciation: "He remains, at the last, a kind of unleavened, unrisen

Christ." Elkin noted the clues which identify Benjy Compson as a Christ figure: his age, the emphasis on Christmas and Easter—with the empty room on Easter morning—his castration as symbolic crucifixion. The inarticulate suffering of an idiot thus recalls Christ's passion. But Benjy as the judge of the Compsons unwittingly conveys deep meaning: as Culley said, all but Caddy, who had loved him, remained in "self-chosen darkness" and in truth, as Jason said, "had never resurrected Christ" (*SF* 348). The transformation of R. W. B. Lewis' type of the "mere helpless innocent into a figure of redemption" is illustrated in both Lucius Priest, who accepted the burden of sin and redeemed Everbe, and in the more experienced but uncorrupted Lena, who brought Byron into life.

The crucifixion symbol in Faulkner is associated less often in Yoknapatawpha than with the rebel-victim or scapegoat. Joe Christmas, the best example of this type of anti-hero, is also the best example of Lewis' "isolated hero 'alone in a hostile, or at best, a neutral universe,' who begins to replace the Adamic personality in the New World Eden." But Joe was a tormented distortion of this prototype until his dying moments. That the successor to the Adamic personality should become a Christ figure has a certain inevitability.

The rebel-victim also is the successor or the alternate to the initiate as the hero in modern fiction. Ihab Hassan said: "The Hero, who once figured as Initiate, ends as Rebel or Victim." His problem is "essentially one of identity. His search is for existential fulfillment, that is, for freedom and self-definition." Joe Christmas' Negro blood intensifies his problem: "The case of Joe Christmas is [a] . . . reminder of our unacknowledged passion for the violence of repudiation." In "Identity Diffusion: Joe Christmas and Quentin Compson," Glenn Sandstrom used Erik Erikson's theory of identity crisis and came to the conclusion that Faulkner had "a profound perception into the darkest and deepest wells of the human personality, . . . a brilliant, raw psychological intuition which could cut like a laser to the center of human thought and emotion."

Joe did not refuse initiation; being rootless he was offered no initiation, for McEachern was himself not a part of the society in which he lived and could not initiate Joe into that male world but only into the world of his Calvinism. Joe listened to the other boys telling what they knew about female sexuality and went out alone the next Saturday, shot a sheep, and dipped his hands "in the yet warm blood of the dying beast" (*LA* 174), thus in his own way being washed in the blood of the lamb. In this instance, Lawrence Dembo remarked, the "blood of the lamb" was sacrificial, not redemptive. Malinowski would accept this ritual as significant: "Even when a magical act is performed in solitude and secrecy, it invariably has social consequences." Though for a time Joe seemed to have "bought immunity" from his horror of sex, he was unable to accept or reject sex. Otto Rank's explanation of "*sexuality* as a kind of racial will forced upon the individual, the final acceptance of which is made possible through the individual love choice" throws light on Joe's problem: he was resisting both races but he desperately needed the only human relationship available. Hassan cited the homosexual as "the hopeless victim of love, who neither indulges nor abdicates the sexual will but perverts it." If Faulkner had intended Joe's problems to include homosexuality, as some critics have supposed, there is no reason why that aspect of his character should not be as explicit as his violent and strained relationships with women.

Judging by Hassan's generalizations, however, Joe's private initiation had consequences that were typical:

> Sacrifice, regression, defeat—these summed up the recurrent expense of initiation. The face of the initiate in modern America began early to shade into the face of the victim, less spiteful than vulnerable and elegiac perhaps, but still rebellious and still outraged. Initiation did not end with communion; it led to estrangement. Its stages were not broadly ritualized into viable modes of knowledge or action; each stage, rather, was attended by an acute sense of personal anxiety, a feeling of rage, loss, or despair.

The first decisive social consequence of Joe's initiation was the conflict with McEachern which resulted in the fight. Joe became the guilty wanderer, representing the archetypal figure that goes back to the story of Cain, and that, in this instance, involves also the crime of son against father. (There was nothing Oedipal, of course, in Joe's feeling for his foster father, especially in view of his dislike of his foster mother.)

In the last stage of his life, after fleeing Joanna Burden in rebellion against her and society, Joe changed from flight to return, from rebel-fugitive to victim. Having escaped capture repeatedly, by people who recognized him, Joe reflected that "there is a rule to catch me by" and, "*tired of running, of having to carry my life like it was a basket of eggs*," he went to Mottstown, in the Negro shoes, to be captured according to the rule. As he was betrayed by Lucas Burch, so Joe accepted capture in the way that suggests a parallel with the story of Christ.

But Joe is an ironic Christ figure, because he suffers for his own sin, in the literal sense. The last part of Joe's story, from his capture to his

actual death, is "distanced" by presenting it only after it is over; by
this means Faulkner shifts the emphasis to those aspects of the story
which make Joe a scapegoat and a genuine Christ figure. The death of
Joe reflects both the universal human obsession with suffering and
blood-lust, as it is satisfied by a scapegoat or a sacrificial victim, and the
Southern characteristics of obsession with race in crimes against white
women and "hypnosis by evil" which Amos Wilder said "a bankrupt
Calvinism had visited upon the nostalgic."

Mircea Eliade's explanation of the scapegoat ceremony, observed as
a ritual preceding and following the New Year, enhances the meaning
and significance of the fate of Joe far beyond the awareness of the
people of Jefferson. The expulsion of the scapegoat or of a person was
symbolically "the expulsion of demons, diseases, and sins." After
purification was effected through the expulsion, the cosmogonic act
would be repeated by Jahweh, with twelve intermediate days, prefiguring the twelve months. Michael Routh's comment does not refer to Joe
as a scapegoat but is illuminating: Joe had come "to emblemize, ironically, the violence of the Southern Community": "in a sense it has
helped create his own violence, then hunts him down and kills him for
it." Joe Christmas and Lucas Beauchamp both exemplify the scapegoat
ritual as a means by which a man can commit a crime, as Lucas Burch
and Crawford Gowrie did, and depend on ordinary men to participate in
a rite from the forgotten past to avoid personal responsibility for crimes
of violence in their society. Dembo commented on the Calvinist tradition that created the "sin-dynamics" that destroyed Joe, Joanna, and
Hightower, and produced Doc Hines. The castration of Joe was "an
explicit completion of this ritual action." The ritual quality of the pursuit of Joe by Percy Grimm was noted by Vernon Hornback, a quality
which was heightened by the image of Percy Grimm: "Above the
blunt, cold rake of the automatic his face had that serene, unearthly
luminousness of angels in church windows" (*LA* 437).

In addition to the initial parallel between Christ as the crucified
scapegoat and Joe Christmas, numerous less obvious parallels have
been detected by critics. Mary Culley's reference to the last week of
Joe's life as his Passion Week is general, but François Pitavy identified
specific details which are less obvious. Christmas gave himself up on
Friday (that was changed to Saturday by Faulkner). He did not deny
that he was called Christmas. Grimm's guards played poker. Grimm
slashed Joe's garments. To the crucifixion images is added the ascen-
sion image at the moment of Joe's death. Even more parallels were
detected by Stanley Elkin: the fourteen Stations of the Cross, from
Joe's flight to his giving himself up in Mottstown, the fourteenth.

Like the scapegoat, animal or human, Joe was sacrificed by the community. The blacks of Yoknapatawpha, as Culley said, were the archetypal suffering victims: Joe's belief that he had Negro blood made him one of them, even though the townspeople had only the word of Joe Brown that Joe Christmas had killed Joanna and that he had said he had Negro blood. The Calvinistic fanaticism of Percy Grimm and Doc Hines, however, activates the others: without Percy Grimm there is no certitude that Joe's fate would have been the same. There were only three men with Grimm, in whose memories "the man seemed to rise soaring . . . forever and ever" (*LA* 440). He was not a part of the myth of Yoknapatawpha so far as the community was concerned.

The very name "Joe Christmas" symbolizes the Calvinistic union of Old and New Testaments, "Joseph" being of primary importance in both Testaments as "Christ" is in the New Testament. In "The Calvinist Burden of *Light in August*," Ilse Lind noted the irony in the fate of Christmas: "martyred by the austerity of a faith rooted in the Old Testament [he] becomes a symbol of the suffering endured by Christ in the New."

In view of Joe Christmas' name and the emphasis on Calvinism and crucifixion, Robert Slabey's contention that Joe Christmas is not a Christ figure but a *Golden Bough* figure is unsound in its either–or premiss but is useful in extending the significance of Joe beyond the Christian connotations. Joe is both a Christ figure and a *Golden Bough* figure, precisely as Lena is both Diana of the Wood and the Virgin Mary. Slabey's account of Joe as a *Golden Bough* figure is a supplement to, not an alternative to, Joe as a Christ image. The "eternal framework" Joseph Campbell used in *The Hero with a Thousand Faces* Slabey also recognized in *Light in August*:

> The events of his life story and the imagery with which they are told are related to an archetypical experience. *Light in August* is part of an "eternal" framework: the journey of the classical hero in his mythological descent into the abyss and meeting with the Shadow (the Shadow which is his own "dark" side); the similar pattern in the modern existential encounter with Nothingness; the timeless sequence of withdrawal; and return, death and rebirth, analogous to the principle of organic growth, a rhythmic experience close to the heart of Man, recorded in art and literature from prehistoric time to "atomic" time. Myths present fundamental attitudes about fundamental matters.

Joe Christmas is a superb example of the degree to which Faulkner used in his myth not only archetypal patterns and Christian symbolism but also heroes and dilemmas particularly characteristic of the South and of modern American fiction.

Joe Christmas also illustrates in some respects the birth of the arche-typal hero, distinguished by unusual circumstances, concealment of his origin, and hazardous infancy. The hero also eventually discovered his true parentage. Joe, however, found his grandparents, not his parents, and was killed, not honored and rewarded.

A better example of the birth of the hero and his adventures, follow-ing the archetypal motif of the Quest, is Jewel Bundren in *As I Lay Dying*. Concealed beneath the inner monologue or stream-of-con-sciousness passages through which the story is narrated is an ironic inversion of the quest romance form of the hero myth, as outlined by Northrop Frye in *Anatomy of Criticism*, "The Mythos of Summer: Romance." The "standard saga" of the hero, as summarized by Rank, will serve as a brief statement of this pattern, with which to compare the story of Jewel:

> The hero is the child of distinguished parents . . . . His origin is preceded by difficulties, . . . such as prolonged barrenness. During or before the pregnancy there is a prophecy in the form of a dream, . . . usually threat-ening danger to the father . . . . As a rule, he is surrendered to the water, in a box. He is then saved by animals or lowly people.

At the end the hero finds his parents and achieves honor. The birth of Jewel is unusual: Addie was resolved to have no more children and looked upon Anse as dead (p. 166). Jewel, the son of Whitfield, thus has "an origin preceded by difficulties." The parallel with the story of Hester Prynne and Dimmesdale in *The Scarlet Letter* is underlined by the names of the children: Hester's "Pearl" and Addie's "Jewel."

Darl's statement "Jewel's mother is a horse" (p. 95) introduces the idea of the animal foster mother, the horse being for Jewel a surrogate for Addie but not in the period of infancy. The prophecy is displaced by Addie's prophecy after Jewel is born, a prophecy that he will save his mother rather than threaten his father (p. 160). In the quest romance, succeeding the archetypal story of the hero's birth, the hero engages in a life-giving quest, usually to rescue a lady. In Jewel's quest death is substituted for life: the box on the waters associated with the hero's birth is the coffin on the flood after the mother's death; Jewel performs Herculean labors to save the body of his mother from flood and fire. Rank explains flood myths as a universal expression of exposure myths. Jewel shows Oedipal hostility toward his father and is hostile toward his brothers, especially Darl; with the archetypal hero, Rank saw "a certain tension between father and son, or still more distinctly a competition between brothers, competition for the tender devotion and love of the mother." Jewel, like the hero of the quest romance, faithfully serves his lady, but thus serves death, not life. He is aided by lowly people along the way and by animals in getting his mother's body to Jefferson for burial, but he is the only one of the family, except Darl who was sent to the asylum, who received no reward and had no desire gratified except burial of the mother. The archtypal patterns in *As I Lay Dying* are the clue to the ironic inversion, which I have dealt with in an article, "*As I Lay Dying* as Ironic Quest."

The story as a myth of Yoknapatawpha is one of a family more devoted to death than to life: none of the sons are married or show any inclination to be, and Dewey Dell, unmarried but pregnant, is devoting her energies to having an abortion. The "villain" in the story, according to Faulkner, is "the convention in which people have to live, which in that case insisted that because this woman had said, I want to be buried twenty miles away, . . . people would go to any trouble and anguish to get her there . . . in order to follow the dying wish, which by that time to her meant nothing" (*FU* 112). Conventional piety and the desire to go to Jefferson, for various ulterior motives, united this family in the service of death. They are not an exception to the generally discouraging accounts of family life in the Yoknapatawpha myth. Since the Bundrens appear only in *As I Lay Dying*, except for one brief and obscure mention, they were not considered previously among the leading families of Yoknapatawpha.

Not the least of the ironies in *As I Lay Dying* is the objective presentation of the hero, which leaves us unaware of what the journey means to Jewel, despite the fact that, as Daniel Hoffman observed, the quest, like the initiation, is one version of the "journey of self-discovery" of the hero of American legend or romance. As a "journey of self-discovery," the hero of *As I Lay Dying* is Cash, as G. L. Friend and Calvin Bedient have demonstrated.

The heroes in the other main pattern, the quest for material success, are not typically concerned with self-discovery and are therefore generally presented in maturity, either in years or in seeming never to have been young. Since myth has to do with content, rather than with literary form, characters may be considered in relation to their dominant motives, not in relation to their literary roles, and all the information about them, no matter how it is presented, is pertinent. Whereas a hero in a story of initiation is presented largely from inside, the hero of a success story may be presented wholly from the outside. The success may lead to tragic reversal and downfall or may be comic, but the hero is actively engaged in the community, shares community values, and first becomes a public figure and then a public legend.

The most eminent of such heroes is Colonel John Sartoris. Not a hero of tragedy in the literary sense, Colonel John most fully represents the hero of myth who meets a tragic fate. But he is a hero of Faulkner's myth, not of the myth of the South. He was a forward-looking man of business who could accomplish the change from the old plantation system, in which change was chiefly seasonal, to the new society typified by the railroad. Like the archetypal hero, fashioned to represent men's ideals, his was an image fashioned by men to represent pioneer America, as the legendary figure of Colonel Falkner was fashioned. Like both the epic hero and the tragic hero, described by Honig, he is an aristocrat and a leader of men, "carrying his men along by force of his own ideas, purposes, and character," whether in war or as a railroad builder. He is "a repository for all the virtues the group needs to believe in to survive. Other men live vicariously in his deeds, his courage, and self-sacrifice," as old Falls does in recalling old times and the Colonel's deeds in *Sartoris*. His life describes the tragic pattern of the fall from greatness to death, which is due to his own errors, his hubris, revealed in his arrogance and disregard of others. He illustrates the principle expressed by Maud Bodkin that "the death or fall of the tragic hero has in some sense the character of a purifying or atoning sacrifice." His renunciation of violence exposed him to the violence of Redmond, but in his death he atoned for his own previous violence and for that of the times in which he lived. But Faulkner in using this universal pattern "distances" the hero by having his post-war achievements and death presented only in the memories of Bayard; thus Colonel John as a character does not achieve the tragic and mythic stature that the pattern would warrant had Faulkner wished to glorify him as an ideal. The point of view of Bayard in *The Unvanquished* and of old Falls in *Sartoris*, plus the many references to the Sartoris legend and to its visible symbol, Colonel John's effigy monument, lend a patent mythic magnification as easily recognized as the cothurnus and mask of the hero of tragedy.

The strategy which Faulkner used to raise his heroes or anti-heroes to mythic stature is not abandonment of realism but utilization of psychological realism; by the process of projection of dominants in the collective unconscious through fictitious narrators as in *Absalom, Absalom!* or through the point of view of various characters both Sutpen, the demon, and Flem, the trickster, are created. Jung cites as dominants "almost always met with in the analysis of projections from the collective unconscious" the "magical demon" which is the "archetype of Faust himself." Thus Sutpen as demon is part of his characterization by Rosa, but out of this projection the mythic hero takes shape.

Thomas Sutpen is presented only through such projections. He combines the classic, the Renaissance, the romantic, and the American aspects of the tragic hero. He is a figure of doom and fatality, guilty of hubris and, by his innocence, blinded to his sin and guilt. A self-made man in the American pattern, he took over the vices of the South when he copied the Tidewater plantation and added his own insensitivity, seeking to be admired for what he *had*, rather than for what he *was*. Like Colonel Sartoris, he was a leader of men. The demonic quality projected by the narrators makes him a Faustian figure, with the term specifically applied, thus linking the archetypal demon with the Renaissance individualist. Sutpen also fits Edwin Honig's characterization of the Romantic egoist: "the Romantics, disdaining mere success stories and pat views of salvation, revered the outcast, despot, madman, dandy and intellectual superman . . . a rebellious strong-man prophet who remade the world in his own image and then brought the whole fabrication down with him in a last delirium of destruction."

In fact, as Patricia Tobin said, Sutpen appeared godlike, with no past, and re-enacted "all creation myths." His narrators elevated him to "the man of myth, the founding father," whose origin they relegated to "a mythical time that is absolutely discontinuous with the historical time in which they draw beneath." In "Ancient Myths and the Moral Framework of *Absalom, Absalom!*," Lennart Bjork perceived in Sutpen, Faulkner's "foremost tragic character," the fusion of Greek, Hebrew, and Christian cultures, similarities to Agamemnon as well as to David.

Sutpen remade the world in the image he chose, knowing nothing in his innocence of the ethical and religious basis of the culture he imitated. He forgot that he belonged to the human family and sacrificed his two wives and his children to his dream of a dynasty. As Faulkner said, "people like that are destroyed sooner or later" (*FU* 81). His innocence, according to Philip Wheelwright, is really the ignorance which prevents union with the godhead: "The deadly ignorance consists in the illusion of individuation, the belief that one can decide one's purposes and way of life entirely by and for himself, and that the greatest felicity is attained by so doing." This is quite different from the self-realization of the truly creative individual.

Because the story is that of Sutpen's children as well as Sutpen, the tragic pattern in his life must be extracted from the chronology Faulkner provided. The pattern is the familiar one of rise from low estate to wealth and power, followed by a reversal, with loss of wealth and prestige and often of life. When time ran out on Sutpen and he had no sons to leave his estate to, he was destroyed by the nemesis he had created. Wash Jones, another "boy at the door," was satisfied to retain the status Sutpen rejected. Applying Bergsonian concepts to Sutpen, Susan Parr saw a deeper meaning in the scythe with which Wash killed Sutpen. Time indeed had run out on him, but the episode also reflects Bergson's concept of the impossibility of manipulating natural events and of escaping the passage of time. Like Agamemnon, Sutpen experienced no enlightenment before his death. In "Apotheosis and Apocalypse in Faulkner's 'Wash,'" Jack Stewart interprets Sutpen's death and its agent in Judaic-Christian terms, "Apocalypse" connoting Time, Death, and Judgment. Stewart explained Wash, in the short story version, as being guilty of "vicarious hubris," reflected glory of Sutpen's status. His "epiphany brings with it the ironic reversal of all his cherished ideals," and in his "true apotheosis of courage" he seems almost "an allegorical figure of revenge." Ironically Sutpen was the only character vitally concerned in the continuation of his family, but because he desired it to gratify his ego, both ego and dynasty were destroyed.

Sutpen responded to humiliation by conceiving his grand design which destroyed his family and finally himself, at the hands of Wash. Mink Snopes responded to the affront to his dignity of Flem's refusal to acknowledge the obligations of kinship by himself destroying the offender. As the hero of a tragedy of revenge Mink is unique: a "durn little half-starved wildcat" (*M* 374); his passion for justice and his inflexible will are his heroic qualities. A statement by Clement Eaton, quoted from a Scottish traveler in the South before the Civil War, applies to both Wash Jones and Mink: common people in the South "considered themselves men of honor, resenting any indignity shown to them, 'even at the expense of their life or that of those who insult them.'" Wash's instant revenge and Mink's incredibly delayed revenge had similar motivation.

Mink's first murder, however, followed the affront without undue delay. Mink accepted the judgment that he owed Houston for having pastured his cow at Houston's and claiming to have sold it. To work out what he owed, Mink would work all day on his own land and then walk two miles to Houston's for thirty-seven days to dig postholes. But the imposition of an additional dollar pound fee before he could get his cow was the last straw. Mink's code of ethics obliged him to work out the last stint, discharging his obligation to Houston before shooting him. Then he had to wait for days before Houston rode into his ambush. (The version of the story in *The Hamlet* is focused on events after the murder, with night journeys to dispose of the body, rather than daytime ones to plow and dig. Mink experienced tragic enlightenment: "I thought that when you killed a man, that finished it . . . . But it dont. It just starts then" [*H* 243]).

This first murder was revenge for denial of recognition as a man. But when Flem, the prosperous Snopes, completely ignored Mink during his imprisonment and trial, Mink's motive was denial of recognition of him as a Snopes. Mink's physical and psychological endurance and his inflexible purpose are amazing. During Mink's thirty-eight years in the penitentiary at Parchman, Flem provided another motive, although the first was "enough. 'Twill serve," like Mercutio's wound. Flem tricked Mink, with the aid of Montgomery Ward Snopes, into trying to escape and consequently having his sentence extended twenty years. Montgomery Ward's description would seem to make this the stronger motive: "the damn little thing looking like a little girl playing mama in the calico dress and sun bonnet . . . as forlorn and lonely and fragile and alien in that empty penitentiary compound as a paper doll blowing across a rolling mill" (M 85).

As soon as he was released from prison Mink demonstrated his honesty again, at great hazard to his quest for revenge: he did not take the money Linda sent him to pay him not to return to Jefferson but only pretended to: he did not even think about it when he left the prison with $13.85 of his own. Mink's consistent honesty and integrity according to his own code of ethics is a vindication, as Otto Schlumpf decided, of the murder which to Mink was an act of justice. Stanley Elkin interpreted Mink as an un-Christian hero, living by an archaic philosophy and therefore to be judged by his beliefs, in which a passion for justice prevailed. Mink's quest–journey for revenge combines a romantic quality with a Rip Van Winkle quality of utter strangeness: he went into prison in 1908; he came out in 1946. From Parchman to Memphis he not only had various adventures or rather misadventures but he also saw motor vehicles and neon lights and all the other transformations in Memphis; at least the railroad depot had not changed (M 288). And the railroad tracks still ran from Memphis to Jefferson "and that but eighty miles" (M 293), and he had a pistol and three bullets.

Mink had spent his life waiting for revenge, and Flem had spent his waiting for nemesis. Mink's life had been divided between walking in circles before and after he killed Houston and being immobilized in jail and the penitentiary. His last journey on foot was straight toward his goal. He found Flem seated in his mansion: with only one bullet left, after testing it en route, Mink aimed at Flem, the gun misfired; Mink rolled the cylinder back and fired again. Flem's complete immobility is tantamount to the admission that he had it coming.

The myth of innocence of the Bible, the mythos of love of the Middle Ages, the tragedy of ambition of the Greek drama and Shakespeare, and the Elizabethan tragedy of revenge are joined in the Yoknapatawpha chronicles by another myth which seems to be pure Yankee, the success story. But it is really as old as the others. The Helen of Yoknapatawpha County was linked not only with Paris–Manfred but, to carry out the parallel, with Menelaus–Flem. However, Flem's prototype is the trickster, a role played at times by the wily Odysseus, according to Joseph Henderson. As Daniel Hoffman observed, "the Yankee villager is one expression of the myth of innocence, the Yankee peddler of the myth of competence." But America developed one myth pattern in which innocence and competence are combined, and shrewdness is compatible with honesty and the rest of the Christian virtues: the success story, formalized but not invented by Horatio Alger. In its innocent form, this story is one of virtue rewarded. But there is an obvious possibility of turning it inside out and upside down and making the innocence merely an illusion and the virtue a disguise for calculation. The typical Alger hero is born of poor but honest parents and achieves success by unflagging cultivation of the middle-class virtues of honesty, sobriety, thrift, and industry—the ideal of Benjamin Franklin. By taking the tide of the affairs of men at the flood, which usually involves marrying the boss's daughter, the hero wins success with never an action which he need conceal from the closest scrutiny of his most godly friends. Hogarth's series of "The Industrious Apprentice" is the pictorial version of the story.

A summary of the story of Flem which merely listed the events in his life and ignored the means by which he gained his ends would sound just like the success myth. But his career, Hyatt Waggoner shows, is actually one of paradoxes and ironic inversions:

> He parodies the American dream, caricatures the American success myth. He has ambition, go-ahead, gumption, a head for figures: everything deemed necessary for success in the Ben Franklin–Dale Carnegie popular philosophy. He is cautious, discreet, self-controlled, soft-spoken. He never loses his temper, is never driven to self-forgetful rashness or violence by any lust, passion, need. He keeps his eye on the main chance and looks out for number one. He is rewarded by riches. . . .

With these qualifications for the role, Flem proceeds through the usual stages in the rise from rags to riches. But behind each stage is an ironic reversal of the usual motives or circumstances. He gets his first job, from Jody Varner, not because Jody is impressed by Flem's sterling virtue but as a bribe to keep the Snopeses from burning Varner's barn. He is strictly honest in money matters but completely ruthless: he will not make a mistake in giving change, but he will collect every cent due him even if children must suffer, as in the five dollars he got from the Armstids in a perfectly "legal" fashion. He married the boss's daughter, not as a reward of virtue or for love but because he was paid to do so to give her child a father. Here the themes of love and money join and Flem, in contrast with Eula, seems even more shabby. Married to the goddess of love and fertility, Flem is impotent. Not religious, he makes religion a rung in the ladder of getting ahead and being respectable (*M* 420). He conforms to his Algerian prototype chiefly in giving jobs to his relatives, but he shows no interest in his parents. Having reached the top in Jefferson, as president of the bank and owner of the finest mansion in town, he should, according to the myth, die full of years and honor and be mourned by the entire community. Instead he is shot like a sitting duck by puny little Mink Snopes with a gun that "looked like a old old mudcrusted cooter" (*M* 429).

In the 1938 synopsis of the trilogy, published in Blotner's *Faulkner*, Flem left "all his property to the worthless boy" (Sarty's son) because "this boy will get rid of it in the way that will make his kinfolk the maddest" (p. 1007). All the kin but that boy came to the funeral. In *The Mansion*, Wallstreet Panic Snopes came to the funeral, and a summary of Wall's profitable and admirable career is given (*M* 420). Faulkner had a remarkable change of intentions when he finally wrote *The Town* and *The Mansion*. Flem and the Snopeses are less despicable. The chief resemblance between the two versions of the funeral is that they were both well attended.

For Flem was a legend, the tales of his rapacity and shrewdness having a lively currency in a region in which horse trading was a favorite sport. The parallel between Sutpen and Flem is heightened by the fact that both are killed for the same reason, the affronts they offer to human dignity. Wash Jones is a kind of instant nemesis and Mink Snopes a delayed-action one, with an incredibly long-burning fuse of revenge. Wash and Mink have their place in the myth as representing the limits of tolerance among the socially downtrodden whites.

Flem has his prototype in folk heroes. Both his career and his marriage with Eula might well be added to Hoffman's examples of "the literary enlargement of the native folk heroes . . . often drawn against a contrasting set of heroic values, those of the world-mythical heroes whose fates and powers are so different from their own." Eula as the world-mythical heroine and Gavin as the romantic idealist provide that contrast. Eula at the beginning is raised to the stature of a goddess, and Flem's deeds make him a local legend. To elevate him as the trickster to a height comparable with Eula's, thus sharpening the ironic contrast, we have Ratliff's fable of Flem in hell, claiming hell from the Prince, a fable that apotheosizes Flem as more soulless and implacable than the Devil himself in insisting on keeping to the terms of a bargain. Donald Petesch devoted a chapter to "Flem as a Devil Figure."

The Alger success story is represented by another character whose success is moderate and admirable and who not only narrates much of the Yoknapatawpha legend but also helps to create it, in his own inimitable and unabashed colloquial style: V. K. Ratliff. The contrast between V. K. and Flem Snopes is explicit in *The Hamlet*, in which Ratliff engaged in competitive deals with Flem. But Ratliff is also the character most clearly based on mythic heroes and on more recent but more primitive folk heroes. And he is the only character who plays a part in both the first and the last of the Yoknapatawpha novels in which the action takes place chiefly in Yoknapatawpha County.

In *Sartoris* he is named V. K. Suratt but thereafter in the novels he is V. K. Ratliff. Not only do families of both names live in the Oxford area, but according to the *Military History of Mississippi* W. T. Ratliff was a lieutenant in the First Regiment, Mississippi Artillery, and M. Suratt was Quartermaster in the Second Regiment, of which William C. Falkner was Colonel. The shift from *Suratt* to *Ratliff* may have been more than coincidental. The reasons Faulkner gave for the change are unconvincing and are irrelevant here. Identical in attributes and occupation with Ratliff, V. K. was still Suratt in "Spotted Horses," published in *Scribner's* in June 1931, and in "Lizards in Jamshyd's Courtyard" (*Scribner's*, February 1932); as narrator in "Spotted Horses," his name is less prominent than in "Lizards," in which II begins with a detailed account of Suratt and his accouterments which leaves the reader of *Uncollected Stories of William Faulkner* (*US* 38) puzzled if he is familiar with Ratliff in *Snopes* but not Suratt in *Sartoris*.

In *Sartoris*, V. K. Suratt is unmistakable and unforgettable. When Bayard Sartoris was thrown by the stallion, V. K.'s auto was commandeered to take Bayard to Doc Peabody, and Suratt then offered to take Bayard home in "the impressed automobile": "It was a Ford body with, in place of a tonneau, a miniature one-room cabin of sheet iron, no larger than a dog kennel . . .; in it an actual sewing machine neatly fitted, borne thus about the countryside by the agent . . . V. K. Suratt and he now sat, with his shrewd, plausible face, behind the wheel" (*Sar.* 135). The episode which follows is a realistic pastoral, enacted on a run-down farm, in which Suratt provided Bayard and Hub with whisky from a jug. Suratt's account of his bare-footed, cotton-chopping childhood can be accepted as Ratliff's (*Sar.* 141–42).

In *The Hamlet* the initial passage on Ratliff is, unfortunately, too long to quote, but the essentials can be summarized. He lived in Jefferson and covered four counties in his buckboard with a mismatched team and the "dog-kennel" for the sewing machine. (Ford cars did not yet exist.) V. K. talked not only to men at country stores but to women, amid their clotheslines and wash pots or "decorous on a splint chair on cabin galleries, pleasant, affable, courteous, anecdotal, and impenetrable" (*H* 13). He seems to have been the only man in Yoknapatawpha who treated women as people, not as sex-objects or serfs, to be dominated by men. He listened more than anyone believed. "He sold perhaps three machines a year, the rest of the time trading in land and livestock and second-hand farming tools and musical instruments . . . ." He served as a newspaper, a bearer of personal messages "about weddings and funerals . . . with the reliability of a postal service. He never forgot a name and he knew everyone, man mule and dog, within fifty miles" (*H* 13). In *The Hamlet* he is a re-creator of tales that had been published as short stories, such as "Fool about a Horse" and "Barn Burning."

In Yoknapatawpha, in addition to his trading and his intuitive wisdom, conveyed in colloquial but eloquent language, Ratliff's functions suggest the attributes of Hermes as given in *The New Century Classical Handbook*: "he was the messenger of the gods, the bringer of dreams, the god of the flocks and herds, and of the market place; he was the god of commerce and trade, of inventions, science, and the arts, and of craft in oratory." (A notable characteristic of Ratliff's was his readiness to change his mode of transportation and his stock-in-trade, ranging from "a used music box" (*H* 25) through Victrolas, radios, and TV sets.) "Altogether, Hermes was a most helpful god; a deity of great ingenuity and craft, and, on the whole, good will." His staff, the caduceus, bore two wings, diligence and activity, and two serpents, symbols of wisdom; the staff itself was a symbol of peace, prosperity, and commerce. (Unlike the gods, and especially Hermes, who loved many women and had many children, Ratliff was asexual.) The caduceus also symbolizes the integration of the four elements, according to Cirlot, and expresses "the idea of active equilibrium" and "balanced duality."

Ratliff's uniqueness in Yoknapatawpha consists in his close relationship with both men and women, with intuitive understanding of both sexes without becoming too much involved emotionally with either. Norman O. Brown stressed the association in Greek mythology of Hermes and Aphrodite as deities of love: "A lover might invoke Aphrodite 'weaver of tricks' or Hermes the Trickster. In fact, Hermes and Aphrodite were frequently associated in ritual, and even combined in the figure of Hermaphroditus."

Although Ratliff bridged the gulf between the sexes, even in marriage, he did so as a storyteller rather than as a seducer. His initial choice of sewing machines as his chief stock-in-trade brought him closer to women than any other article would. When Ratliff was telling the "fool about a horse" story of Ab Snopes and Pat Stamper, the omniscient author described what the listeners could see with their mind's eye although they were sitting on the veranda in the dark: Ratliff "easy and relaxed in his chair, with his lean brown pleasant shrewd face, in his faded blue shirt, with that . . . air of perpetual bachelor-hood . . . that hearty celibacy as of a lay brother in a twelfth-century monastery—a gardener, a pruner of vines . . ." (*H* 42).

Again the mythical figure suggested differs from Ratliff in sexual experience: Tiresias, recalled to literary readers of Faulkner's generation by T. S. Eliot's *The Waste Land* (1922), had lived for some years as a woman before being restored to manhood. In the dispute between Zeus and Hera over which sex enjoyed sex more, Tiresias being at the time the unique voice of experience, sided with Zeus: if the pleasures of love are counted as ten, women get nine parts and men one. In one version of the story Hera in her rage blinded Tiresias but Zeus gave him long life and power as a soothsayer. One assumes that Ovid's *Metamorphoses* was not required reading in the South, but Gavin, with his Harvard education, might be expected to know such myths and not accept so readily the myth of the South which denied that women—or at least ladies—had sexual urges.

In line with his concentration on Hermes, Norman Brown denied that Hermes was originally regarded as a thief; "tricky" might mean "technical skill" or magic. "Hermes the Trickster," Brown said, "is identical with Hermes the 'giver of good things,' the culture hero." "This combination of trickster and culture hero is a recurrent phenomenon in primitive mythology." Furthermore, and more pertinent perhaps to Ratliff as a hero, Brown observed that "in the mythology of the North American Indians there is a recurrent figure that appears in the mixed role of altruistic culture hero, shaman, and trickster." A comment by Karl Kerényi in Paul Radin's *The Trickster* both confirms Brown and warns against exaggeration of the similarities: the Trickster of Indian mythology "has nothing like the universality and plasticity of the Greek divinities" or even of the hero Heracles. But Winnebago trickster stories remind one of Heracles rather than of "the divine trickster of Greek mythology, Hermes." But Hermes "like every other trickster . . . operates outside the fixed bounds of custom and law." With his interest in and understanding of people and his satisfaction in a contest of wits with a competitor, Ratliff as a trickster is remarkable for the rarity with which he operates outside "the bounds of custom and law" and his motives for doing so.

The title of an article by Joseph Trimmer indicates the unique function of Ratliff in *Snopes*: "V. K. Ratliff: A Portrait of the Artist in Motion." As co-narrator with the omniscient author in *The Hamlet* and as one of three character-narrators in *The Town* and *The Mansion*, with the omniscient author narrating the story of Mink in *The Mansion*, V. K. Ratliff not only has a creative role in all three novels in *Snopes* but he is the most reliable narrator. Charles Mallison was too young in *The Town* to rely wholly on his own observations and was absent too much of the time in *The Mansion* to do so. As Trimmer neatly puts it, in *The Mansion* Ratliff's "ironic realism" is needed to counteract Gavin's "quixotic idealism." Because of Ratliff's "desire to know," his addiction to people-watching, "his love of aesthetic strategy and narrative manipulation," and because of his ability to cope with "the furious motion of experience," Ratliff symbolizes Faulkner's conception of the artist. He maintains contact with life without being overwhelmed by it, perhaps because he is asexual. He battles with Flem but observes and interprets throughout *Snopes* and also, being aware of "alternative interpretations," retells tales from the previous volumes. Having experimented with "tentative engagement" with Flem in *The Hamlet* and with "tentative detachment" in *The Town*, Ratliff gives us in *The Mansion* his "tentative creation, his own Snopes trilogy" (Chapter 6). Like the shaman, as described by Stephen Larsen, Ratliff served as "a mediator between the bright world of myth and ordinary reality": "the shaman is man's basic creative response to the presence of the mythic dimension."

Roger Davis traced the appearance of Ratliff in short stories and the changes in his role when some of the stories were incorporated in *The Hamlet*. The publication of *Uncollected Stories of William Faulkner*, edited by Joseph Blotner (1979), makes it possible for the reader to refer to the first published version of each story. Unfortunately, Davis did not deal with *The Town* and *The Mansion*, in which Ratliff's role is both narrator and creator of Yoknapatawpha legends. A most significant part of Davis' treatment of Ratliff in *The Hamlet* is his careful comparison of Flem and Ratliff as opponents: except for Flem's impotence and Ratliff's asexuality, the two are opposites in characteristics and attitudes, although they are occasionally competitors in trade. The image of Ratliff as a guardian in a monastery (*H* 42) is a clue to the fact that although both Flem and Ratliff are excluded from sexuality, Ratliff is in harmony with the world of fertility, of nature and of women, and Flem is interested only in money and in the gratification of pride made possible by money.

Roger Davis and other critics have recognized the contrast between Ratliff and Gavin Stevens as narrators, Ratliff as being the more reliable and therefore, as Davis said, "speaking with authorial presence" and revealing admirable personal qualities and values. Davis' recognition of Ratliff as a Tiresias figure enhances his awareness of Ratliff's empathy with both sexes and his powers of perception and prediction, most striking in his anticipation of what Mink was likely to do when he was released from the penitentiary. In *The Hamlet* Davis observed that Faulkner used Ratliff's colloquial language and "tall tale" humor to deflate and counterpoint his own extravagant rhetoric as uttered by Gavin.

In *The Hamlet* Ratliff is sometimes the protagonist, initiating action to involve Flem; at other times he is the antagonist. Flem's only moral opponent, as Davis remarked. Again Ratliff resembles the shaman, the champion of the community: shamanism in general, according to Mircea Eliade, "defends life, health, fertility, the world of 'light,' against death, diseases, sterility, disaster, and the world of 'darkness.'" In his youth, in *The Hamlet*, Ratliff was part of a community in which the chief male activity was barter, a term which connotes much more than buying and selling. It is a game which, like poker or chess or checkers or craps, can be won honestly or dishonestly and which involves both skill and luck. Faulkner used all four games in crucial situations. The formal games with their codified rules and standardized equipment are less a challenge to ingenuity and what might be called creative activity than barter is.

The term "the trickster tricked" has been used of the Snopeses and their competitors but with little attention to the antiquity and mythic aspects of such male contests. But as Ratliff initiates or observes or is taken in by "tricks," his mythic dimensions are verified, Dr. Joseph Henderson stated that "the fundamental goal of initiation" lies in taming the original "Trickster-like wildness of the juvenile nature"—notably demonstrated by that pair of retarded adolescents, Manfred de Spain and Gavin Stevens, in *The Town.* Henderson returns to the Trickster theme which appears "at the most archaic level" of the symbolism of transcendence: The Trickster "has become the shaman— . . . —whose magical practices and flights of intuition stamp him as a primitive master of initiation." Roger Davis credits Ratliff with Bergsonian intuition.

Most amazing and amusing, however, are the references to Hermes as a Trickster. Henderson so describes him in his role "as a messenger, a god of the cross-roads, and finally the leader of souls to and from the underworld." Michael Grant, in discussing *Prometheus Bound*, refers to Hermes as bringing the message of Zeus to Prometheus and remarks that as "the agent of Zeus" Hermes shows "the two faces of Zeus." Grant continues: "Hermes is generally the clever, non-moral, *dieu tzigane* [gipsy god]—another aspect of the Trickster"—who rules animals and is patron of "trickery in the common man."

What seems an inexplicable and unnecessary interruption of Ratliff's activities lends itself to shamanistic interpretation and to none other that I can discover. Ratliff played a major role in the invasion of Frenchman's Bend by the Snopeses. The reader is suddenly informed (*H* 67) that Ratliff has been sick and is on his way to Frenchman's Bend after an absence of a year. Except that Bookwright and Tull have a chance to bring Ratliff up-to-date on news of the village, his absence and return seem to have no purpose. But in the context of shamanism, a long illness has great significance. An initiatory sickness is a distinctive feature of shamanism as a vocation. Stephen Larsen quoted Eliade's statement that "the shaman is not only a sick man; he is, above all, a sick man who has been cured, who has succeeded in curing himself." If his vocation has been revealed during his sickness, "the initiation . . . is equivalent to a cure." Joseph Campbell described the effect of the shamanistic crisis in terms applicable to non-shamanistic societies and to individual crises which may not be a "vocational summons": "the shamanistic crisis, when properly fostered, yields an adult not only of superior intelligence and refinement, but also of greater physical stamina and vitality of spirit than is normal to members of his group." Larsen quoted this passage from Campbell but added his own summary of Campbell's explanation of the universal validity of shamanism: "The shaman is . . . a cosmically instructed man." In Faulkner's cosmos, Ratliff may well be regarded as having shamanistic qualities.

When Ratliff returned to Yoknapatawpha from Memphis, where a doctor put him to sleep and cut out his pocketbook (*H* 68), Ratliff had a subcontract to sell goats which he expected to buy in the Frenchman's Bend area, hoping, as Olga Vickery said, to enjoy three satisfactions: "Barter is for him at once a source of profit, an exciting game, and a way of extending and cementing personal relationships." In this activity Ratliff is engaged in a "Trickster tricked" contest with Flem, rather than operating on the shaman level. Whoever wishes to know all the facts about goats, sewing machine, and a legacy of ten dollars each to Mink, Ike, and Flem Snopes from their grandmother will find them obligingly presented by Cleanth Brooks in *William Faulkner: The Yoknapatawpha Country*. The episode is significant as a revelation of Ratliff's character. When he learned that Ike was an idiot and that Flem could make a profit on the note which was Ike's part of the inheritance, Ratliff gave up the profit which he had anticipated but which was of less importance than the satisfaction of outsmarting Flem. Ratliff burned the note and gave its value, with interest, to Mrs. Littlejohn to use for Ike's benefit. She used it to buy for Ike his lady-love, the cow. Ratliff had the satisfaction of the moral victory over

Flem, in addition to what Joseph Trimmer called the fun of "designing the complicated economic trap."

But when Ratliff found that another Snopes, Lump, was demoralizing the community and making money by running a sodomic peepshow of Ike with the cow, he felt that both Lump and the peepers must be stopped, even if Ike suffered the loss of the cow. He held a family conference, thinking that Ike's relatives should buy back the cow for the $16.80 which Ratliff had given Mrs. Littlejohn and butcher it to provide the only known cure for Ike's obsession, the flesh of the cow being analogous, it seems, to the "hair of the dog," the drink to cure a hangover. Whitfield, the minister, had seen it tried once, with success. Ratliff was inspired, when I. O. Snopes protested against giving money, by remembering that "it's got to be done by the fellow's own blood kin, or it won't work" (*H* 203). Perhaps Ratliff was inspired by shamanistic intuition rather than memory! The fact that Eck Snopes was persuaded by I. O. Snopes to bear the chief burden of paying for the cow because he had fathered so many Snopeses may be further evidence that Eck was a bastard: no Snopes would pay fifteen dollars for moral value and Snopes honor. I. O. said, "the Snopes name has done held its head up too long in this country to have no such reproaches against it like stock-diddling," but he paid one dollar and eighty cents (*H* 201, 204). Ratliff gave up the whole sum rather than have the community corrupted by the greedy Lump and their own prurient desires.

The episode of the horse auction diverted the attention of the villagers from Flem to the Texan with whom he returned from Texas: the performance of the horses and the showmanship of the Texan held the men spellbound until the horses were penned in for the night and brought them back in the morning, their desire to own at least one of the wild creatures being undiminished by Ratliff's warning that Flem was behind the whole deal and that, so far as he was concerned, he would "just as soon buy a tiger or a rattlesnake" (*H* 279). Such warnings were as far as one could go in interfering in another man's business ventures. The next day Ratliff was conspicuously absent during the horse auction, and Mrs. Littlejohn was conspicuously going about her usual chores. When the men tried to take possession of the horses they had paid for, including Henry Armstid who had given a five-dollar bill earned by his wife, the horses broke out of the lot and escaped, leaving the buyers with neither money nor steeds. But Henry Armstid was left with a broken leg. Ratliff had gotten back to Mrs. Littlejohn's just in time to be chased out of his own room by a horse.

In the episode which follows, however, Ratliff, the only one who escaped Flem's horse trick, becomes the Trickster tricked. We never know what goes on in Flem's mind, but it is safe to assume that he knew Ratliff had been too smart to be taken in by the bargains in horses and that Flem set up his trick with Ratliff as the victim. The dramatic irony at the end of "Flem," with Flem instead of Will Varner sitting in the flour-barrel chair beside the ruined mansion, becomes apparent. Even more ironic is Ratliff's vision, at the end of "Eula," of "the calm beautiful mask seen once more beyond a moving pane of glass." The fable of Flem in hell follows, in which Flem, having no soul to be redeemed "into eternal torment" (*H* 150), confronts the Prince of Hell and demands hell—but might take Paradise if it is the Prince's to offer. The figure of the shaman, rather than of Hermes, seems appropriate in this vision of Ratliff's. Mircea Eliade explained that the shaman as a healer may have to "descend to the nether world" if the soul of a sick man has been "stolen by demons." Another "complicated and danger-ous enterprise" is "the voyage of the shaman to the other world to escort the soul of the deceased to its new abode." The shaman's access to the nether world is the essential element which, in combination with Ratliff's power of mythic creation, accounts for the effectiveness of this vision in a realistic context of cotton-picking in September. From the vision of Eula's "calm beautiful mask" to the image which opened the gates of hell—"the straw bag, the minute tie, the constant jaw"— the diction is Ratliff's; the debate between Flem and the Prince of Hell is couched in the legalistic terms which are all that Flem would under-stand. Flem is immune to the sinful pleasures hell has to offer: "for a man that only chews, any spittoon will do" (*H* 151). (Flem had not yet arrived at the ultimate austerity of chewing on air.)

Flem on the flour-barrel chair and Flem in hell should have made Ratliff immune to Flem's buried-treasure trick. (The tales of buried treasure which Faulkner used also as a basis for incidents in *Go Down, Moses* and "My Grandmother Millard" had their source in historical reality.) In this episode Ratliff reveals characteristics of all three an-cient heroic figures—what Stephen Larsen called "the ubiquitous Hermes-trickster figures" and the less ubiquitous shaman. But in dis-cussing "the shaman's vision," Larsen said: "The hero's quest of treasure or boon often takes him to the bottom of the sea or deep within the earth." The suggestion of hell, the underworld, is provided by the madness of Henry Armstid, digging frantically from the sheer despair of poverty. A quite fascinating detail is found in the short-story ver-sion, "Lizards in Jamshyd's Countryard" (a quotation from Fitzger-ald's translation of *The Rubáiyát*). No doubt it is merely an interesting coincidence that the car or chariot of Hermes was drawn by lizards, according to Eva Hangen in *Symbols*. If this episode were less loaded with details which fit Hermes in his trickster role but do not fit tricksters in general, the aptness of the original title of the story would not be apparent.

The action in Chapter Two of Book Four, "The Peasants," begins on a moonless August night and the action continues to be largely in darkness and as much as possible in silence. Armstid has found it easy to persuade Ratliff to join him and Bookwright in digging for treasure at the Old Frenchman place because he had suspected there must be something of value in the ruined house and the ten acres when Varner bought it and had his suspicions confirmed when Flem took over the place. Ratliff drove Bookwright out there and found that they had to proceed through a deep ravine, a "black abyss," despite Henry's lame leg, to reach the place where Bookwright and Henry had heard the sound of digging, Henry for ten nights. Bookwright and Henry were sure it was Flem, seeking buried treasure, as people had done for thirty years. The next night they went back at midnight with Uncle Dick Bolivar, who searched for metal with "a forked peach branch" with a tobacco sack, with a gold-filled tooth in it, hanging from the branch. The peach fork works—it arched down, "the string taut as wire" and Uncle Dick's arms "jerking faintly and steadily." Armstid digs and finds a sack with coins in it. Uncle Dick feels "four bloods lust-running . . . four sets of blood here lusting for trash." The invisible fourth they heard gallop off on a horse (*H* 346–47). There were three bags with twenty-five silver dollars in each. This proof that the buried treasure existed and could be found if they could dig long enough and deep enough made all three eager to own the property.

Norman Brown's account of Hermes includes the distinctive details in this episode. Hermes has been called Hermes the Thief, but Brown explained that the epithet meant "stealthy" and was not derogatory. Similarly, the word usually translated "trickster" in reference to Hermes meant "secret action," and "trickery" meant something mysterious, magical. Uncle Dick, with his "magic wand," has the Hermes qualities in this part of the action, but he acts at Ratliff's request. Hermes shared one epithet with Aphrodite and Eros: "the whisperer." Of course this applies to all three: "Ratliff whispered," "Bookwright whispered," and "Armstid's dry whisper" are repeated during their secret action which is mysterious and magical.

Believing that Eustace Grimm is a prospective buyer, Ratliff speeded up the deal: they met with Flem in the store in Frenchman's Bend and bought the Old Frenchman place, ostensibly "to start a goat-ranch": Ratliff paid with a quitclaim deed on his half-interest in a lunchroom in Jefferson; Armstid, with a mortgage on most of what little he possessed; Bookwright, with cash. Ironically, Ratliff was the goat, responsible for the misfortune of those who trusted him.

All three moved into the ruined house, prepared to sleep and eat there until they found the rest of the treasure. They dug all that night and the next day and night. Before dawn the second morning Ratliff belatedly remembered that Eustace Grimm was related to Flem, and Bookwright dug out the details from his memory bank: Eustace was the son of the youngest sister of Ab Snopes, Flem's father (*H* 360). When Ratliff and Bookwright looked at the coins in the bags Uncle Dick had unearthed, none were minted before 1861—one dollar had been minted the previous year. But Armstid went on digging. Ratliff played his Hermes role by leading Armstid to the underworld from which he never returned to freedom: "Armstid dug himself back into the earth which had produced him to be its born and fated thrall forever until he died" (*H* 366).

Only Ratliff's pride was injured; when he recovered his normal self-respect and confidence, it was apparent that his defeat by Flem was "a fortunate fall." Roger Davis summed up the effect: "Ratliff's humanistic values, sense of honor and individual responsibility, his concept of community and comradeship, his business ethics, his relationship with nature and the land, and his sense of humor have each been severely tested and traumatically bruised, but he and they are all the stronger for it."

The Town is much more the story of Gavin Stevens as the courtly lover, first of Eula and then of Linda, than of Ratliff, whose role is diminished but necessary as a contrast to Gavin's. In *The Mansion*, in addition to his re-creation of the Snopes story, Ratliff performed one action of great value to the men of good will in Jefferson, in Mississippi, and in the United States: he prevented Clarence Snopes, the unscrupulous racist politician, from running for Congress or continuing his career in state politics. Here barter was not involved, but Ratliff's method was that of the Trickster, aided by twin boys. Thus in Ratliff's last and best trick, the Winnebago Trickster and the Twin hero cycles, cited from Paul Radin's schema by Joseph Henderson, are linked in Ratliff's last trick. As Charles Mallison, the narrator, said, Ratliff was working as "an instrument of God," no matter how ludicrous a method he chose (*M* 321). As Norman Brown said of Hermes, "the tricky": "his function is to promote human welfare."

At the end of Mink's story, the accomplishment of his long-delayed revenge, Ratliff showed much greater understanding of Mink through intuition than Gavin did through reason or wishful thinking. He eased his conscience by assuming that Mink must have died from the shock of freedom before he got far from Parchman (*M* 392–93). Ratliff, however, went to Parchman and verified his theory that Mink had accepted the money Linda sent on condition that he would not return to Jefferson; Mink had to accept the money to get out of prison, and he had to get out of prison to achieve his revenge. As Ratliff realized, Mink was, as Faulkner might have said, "incorrigibly" honest: he left the money with a trusty to return to the warden. Thus when Mink left he undoubtedly headed for Jefferson. Ratliff understood that Mink was scrupulously honest as a man and indomitable as a murderer, with no awareness of moral inconsistency. After Mink shot Flem and fled, Ratliff resumed the Hermes role he played at the end of *The Hamlet* when he led Armstid into what was a pit of madness, a hell on earth. When Gavin and Ratliff sought Mink to give him money from Linda, Ratliff drove Gavin's car. When they got out Ratliff led the way to "the cave, the den" underground, where they found Mink. But in this resting place Mink was no longer enslaved by the earth, its "thrall" as Armstid was; Mink would soon be free, "equal to any, good as any, brave as any" (*M* 435).

From the arrival of the Snopes tribe in the early 1900s to 1946, when *The Mansion* ends, the presence of V. K. Ratliff in the chronicles of Yoknapatawpha provides a positive, eloquent character whose humanistic attitudes and sound ethical and moral values are essentially the same as Faulkner's. Ratliff achieves Otto Rank's third stage of development: he accepts himself and exercises his creative impulses to create himself as an individual, guided by his own tastes and values instead of superficially adopting community values without discrimination, and to create the legend of Yoknapatawpha in recounting the episodes in its history which he had witnessed or had heard about from the principals. Roger Davis described Ratliff as "the only major character in Faulkner's fiction" who combines intellect and intuition and can grasp temporal reality and permanent truths. Ratliff's varied functions as the narrator or narrator-participant are combined with the point of view of the omniscient author in *The Hamlet* and of two narrators in *The Town* and *The Mansion*. The characterization of Ratliff by other narrators and the checks they provide on his credibility contribute to both subjective and objective realization of Ratliff as a character in a real world. But the mythic qualities and patterns suggested by his resemblance to gods and heroes and by his own creation of the myths of Yoknapatawpha give breadth and depth to Ratliff as a character and also to other characters and events which are included in his penetrating vision of Faulkner's cosmos. Returning to *The Waste*

Land, Roger Davis decided that Ratliff not only possessed attributes of T. S. Eliot's Tiresias but spoke with the voice of the Thunder: "Give, sympathize, control."

In the conception of *Flags in the Dust* and the publication of the shortened version, *Sartoris*, the mythology of Yoknapatawpha began, with neurotic paralysis or death in the leading families. It ends with man in motion and, in *The Reivers*, with implied perpetuation of a vigorous family. The meaning of the mythology of Yoknapatawpha, the norms and ideals implied by the abnormalities and imperfections, will be dealt with in the next chapter. Although, as Daniel Hoffman said, Faulkner "has based his work more firmly on the documentation of social reality than any other major novelist of our time," he has also created the most timeless and universal world in American fiction: "mythic patterns as antique as time . . . are bulwarks still of his vision of the tensions between individual experience and the heritage of his culture."

But this "mythical primitiveness" is "psychological, yes psycho-analytical modernity." Not only does this remark by Thomas Mann about Wagner precisely fit Faulkner, but other statements in the same essay apply equally well to the myth of Yoknapatawpha and to the process by which it was created: "Such a unique reanimation of antiq-uity, with such freedom of form, such masterly humor, so full of genius in its lively perceptions, in a style of the finest artistry." Thomas Mann, the best possible authority on these matters of myth and composition, conjecturally presents what went through Wagner's mind in creating his trilogy, which was written in reverse order as an epic poem before the music was composed: "What if he spread out his method, his theme-fabric, not only over one scene but over the whole drama; what if he vastly broadened it, applied it not to one drama alone but to a whole epic sequence of them, in which everything was brought in, from the very beginning on? That would be a very feast of associa-tion, a whole world of profound and brilliant allusion."

As Mann regards myth as the bridge between Wagner and Goethe, so myth reveals an analogy between Wagner and Faulkner and be-tween Goethe and Faulkner. What Mann said of Goethe applies to Faulkner: "He does not celebrate the myth, he jests with it, treats it with affectionate, teasing familiarity; he controls it down to the small-est and remotest detail and makes it visible in blithe and witty words, with a niceness which has in it more of the comic, yes of gentle parody, than of the sublime."

The conclusion Virginia Hlavsa reached in "St John and Frazer in *Light in August*: Biblical Form and Mythic Function" is pertinent to a comprehensive view of the mythology of Yoknapatawpha. She showed that the themes in the twenty-one chapters of *Light in August* parallel "the 21 chapters of the St John Gospel" "to reach for the mythic or primitive tradition" which might lie behind the stories in John. She concluded that Faulkner chose John rather than "the Synoptics, who primarily addressed the Jews," because he chose a universal view, like John's or Frazer's. "So too we might see that Faulkner was addressing not merely the Southern bigots or the Northern busybodies; rather he was showing that the universal forms of belief can restore to us our sense of terror and compassion over the human condition." In creating his Cosmos, Faulkner used resources beyond the Biblical and the mythical.

By tapping the resources of antiquity and of the collective unconscious, by reading intensively and widely and creatively, by keeping attuned to the currents of thought of his own time and to its literature, and by remaining rooted in his own native soil, William Faulkner was able to transmute into the mythology of Yoknapatawpha themes, symbols, literary patterns and figures which are at once native and universal, timely and timeless, reaching back into the past and looking into the future.

3

The Quest for Freedom

TO ARRIVE AT THE TOTAL MEANING of the myth of Yoknapatawpha County, to answer the basic questions, is not easy. What is Faulkner's fundamental concept of man and society? Can one derive from the myth any positive concept of man and the life worth living? Is there any redemptive vision of how man may overcome the evil in life and his own errors and weakness and bring himself closer to the authentic life? The difficulties encountered in trying to answer these and other such questions are caused by the complexity of style and structure, the impersonal techniques, and the prevalence of irony but also by the facts of publication of the Yoknapatawpha chronicles. But Faulkner was a serious and responsible author; he might choose to communicate his vision in ways which render interpretation difficult, but he did not abdicate the author's moral responsibility, insisted upon by Wayne Booth, to make the meaning available to those who choose to learn how to read his books.

> When human actions are formed to make an art work, the form that is made can never be divorced from the human meanings, including the moral judgments, that are implicit whenever human beings act. And nothing the writer does can be finally understood in isolation from his effort to make it all accessible to someone else—his peers, himself as imagined reader, his audience. . . .

The author makes his readers. . . . if he makes them well—that is, makes them see what they have never seen before, moves them into a new order of perception and experience altogether—he finds his reward in the peers he has created.

The moral judgments are inherent in the fiction; the structures and techniques are means of giving inflection, as it were, to the moral judgments. "In the greatest fiction the writer's moral sense coincides with his dramatic sense, and I see no way for it to do this unless his moral judgment is part of the very act of seeing, and he is free to use it." Flannery O'Connor, in thus commenting on her own writing and other Southern fiction, explained the frequency with which grotesque and violent aspects are chosen: "writers who see by the light of their Christian faith will have, in these times, the sharpest eyes for the grotesque, for the perverse, and for the unacceptable." The violence, she explained, serves as shock technique: "The novelist with Christian concerns will find in modern life distortions which are repugnant to him, and his problem will be to make these appear as distortions to an audience which is used to seeing them as natural; and he may well be forced to take ever more violent means to get his vision across to this hostile audience."

This aspect of Faulkner's work caused readers of his earlier books, readers who had not yet been "well made," as Wayne Booth would say, to accuse Faulkner of lack of moral meaning or of immoral meaning, and to see in his fiction either the fantastic Gothic horror of the sensationalist or the gutter-scraping of the naturalistic novelist. And of course Faulkner was neither; he was a highly observant, imaginative, and impassioned writer, with a unique gift and a penetrating vision, fulfilling his role as a writer as described by Maud Bodkin: "The poet—. . . and . . . in our own day, the more imaginative writer of fiction—performs for the community . . . the function of objectifying in imaginative form experience potentially common to all, but exceptionally deep and vivid, and revealing a certain tension and ideal reconcilement of opposite forces present in actual life."

The "ideal reconcilement" is extended throughout the Yoknapatawpha chronicles and is in part implied. Each of the component parts contributes its separate order, but the reader is left to exercise his own imagination on the whole. Saul Bellow explained that "a novelist begins with disorder and disharmony, and he goes toward order by an unknown process of the imagination." When Faulkner wrote *The Reivers*, he may well have intended it to be his last novel. Although the action covers less than a week, mostly outside of Yoknapatawpha, the list of characters in *The Reivers* given in Robert Kirk's *Faulkner's People* requires more pages than does that for *The Mansion*, which covers thirty-eight years. Faulkner packed into what was, in fact, his last novel as many allusions to familiar characters, as much retelling of incidents, and as many new characters with familiar surnames as possible before the main action began, requiring unfamiliar characters and names in a new setting. The Yoknapatawpha chronicles constitute a whole that cannot be sliced up without destroying the continuity of existence in the world Faulkner created. And much of the meaning of that world is revealed only when it is viewed as an aggregate extended in both space and time, like the world in which we live.

In his introduction to the Riverside Edition of *Bleak House*, Morton Zabel specified what it means to create a world as Dickens did on a larger scale than did most writers of single novels, which may range from the microcosmic to the panoramic. A writer's "world," Zabel said, "must communicate its human wholeness, its moral unity and relevance to us, and convince us that they are real, authentic, inclusive." He continued with an explanation of what is required to achieve the necessary wholeness: "It requires both extension of scene and continuity of value; both the scope of drama and unity of idea; both multiplicity of means and singleness of vision. Comprehensiveness of sympathy must join with coherence of judgment. The complex must come to terms with the simple. The creator of such a world is at once inclusive and radical—compendious in the material he undertakes to master; radical in the root-values to which he refers the truth or significance of the life he portrays." Zabel regarded Dickens as attempting "to mediate between . . . the dead past and the violent future," as being "radical in the justice he demanded for humanity, but conservative in the moral authority he saw as a necessary cognate of such justice." Faulkner's world, Zabel said, required "a more realistic necessity in social and psychological analysis" than did the world of Dickens. Among his favorite books, Faulkner listed "most of Dickens" instead of naming a few titles (*FU* 150).

In creating a world that bears obvious similarities to Lafayette County, Mississippi, Faulkner used a geographic and social reality as the basis of his "cosmos" in which he could "move these people around like God, not only in space but in time too." The last paragraph in the interview with Jean Stein reminds the reader that geographic dimensions and sociological facts are inadequate tools in Yoknapatawpha, as Ike McCaslin learned that man-made tools must be discarded if he was to see Old Ben. In seeking the total meaning of Faulkner's cosmos one discovers, as has been apparent, cosmological and eschatological dimensions in the "little postage stamp of native soil" from which Faulkner created Yoknapatawpha. He explained to Loïc Bouvard that the South is "the only really authentic region in the United States, because a deep indestructible bond still exists between man and his environment. In the South . . . there is still a common acceptance of the world, a common view of life, and a common morality" (*LG* 72). He had previously said to Bouvard: "God . . . is the most complete expression of mankind, a God who rests both in eternity and now." And although "neither God nor morality can be destroyed," man may cause God to fade away for himself "by the very act of . . . doubting Him" (*LG* 70). Faulkner used his total creation, Yoknapatawpha, in all its aspects to convey his total meaning.

Failure of critics to recognize this achievement of Faulkner's as rendering illogical a comparison of one novel by Faulkner with one novel by another writer as representing similar worlds is illustrated by David Jarrett's "Eustacia Vye and Eula Varner, Olympians: The Worlds of Thomas Hardy and William Faulkner." Hardy's fictional world comes so close to offering the kind of opportunity which Faulkner recognized as a challenge to his creative powers that it seems inconceivable that such a comparison as Jarrett's could be made with no reference, even, to the striking contrast between Hardy's world and Faulkner's. Jarrett's reference to "an environment which is generally confining and restricting" in both novels is in a paragraph dealing with Diggory Venn and V. K. Ratliff, precisely the context in which the contrast is most notable and significant. But even Jarrett's mention of Gavin Stevens does not indicate that Gavin is not a character in *The Hamlet* or that the roles of both Gavin and Ratliff in *The Town* and *The Mansion* are essential to the creation of the myth of Yoknapatawpha. In fact, Jarrett's comment on Ratliff's "lack of any deep human relationship" occurs in a sentence following a reference to Gavin but it suggests that Jarrett had not read *The Town* and *The Mansion*, in which Ratliff's relationship to Gavin, especially in *The Mansion*, is certainly deep and personal. Jarrett's purpose in his essay was to show that Hardy and Faulkner had "a similar vision of the working of time on those localities" and that Faulkner was influenced by Hardy in characters, imagery, narrative methods, and names. Comments on Linda Snopes in *The Mansion* give no hint that *The Town* preceded *The Mansion* or that *The Hamlet* was the first volume of the trilogy *Snopes* or that Ratliff is the only character with a major role in all three volumes. Similarities between Hardy and *The Hamlet* do not prove that Faulkner drew extensively upon Hardy.

Hardy is not listed in the index of *Faulkner in the University*. The few references in the index of Blotner's *Faulkner: A Biography* are to comments by Blotner, chiefly to some similarities between Hardy's poetry and Faulkner's. In writing about *The Hamlet*, in *The Triumph of the Novel*, Albert J. Guerard said that Ratliff "was perhaps suggested by Hardy's itinerant reddleman," but in *Thomas Hardy: The Novels and Stories* Guerard did not ascribe similarities between Hardy and Faulkner to the influence of Hardy. It is ironic, therefore, to find Hardy credited with precisely what he did not create: Robert Carpenter said, "Hardy's Wessex is a symbolic microcosm like Faulkner's Yoknapatawpha." Novels are written not about the land but about people, and the characters in Hardy seem to live cut off from their communities without even coincidental encounters, in an area much more thickly populated than Yoknapatawpha, with road maps on a scale of an inch to four miles. A comparable map of Mississippi is on a scale of one inch to about seventeen miles. A Geological Survey map of Mississippi is on a scale of about one inch to fifteen miles. My regret that Hardy did not create a microcosm similar to Yoknapatawpha was greatly increased by my travels in the Hardy country, with its inexhaustible wealth of villages and hamlets near to Dorchester and the varied beauty of the countryside and the coast.

The influence of the *Comédie humaine* of Balzac, however, is unquestionable. Faulkner generally included Balzac among his favorite novelists. Malcolm Cowley suggested that Faulkner might divide his work into cycles as Balzac divided his into "Scenes," and followed a somewhat analogous scheme in his division of the selections in *The Portable Faulkner*. Cowley's introduction to that collection, the source of his reference to Balzac, was the first and is still one of the best accounts of Faulkner's Yoknapatawpha fiction. To find an account of Balzac's work that applies perfectly to Faulkner's Yoknapatawpha in Mircea Eliade's *The Quest*, in a chapter entitled "The New Humanism," was pure serendipity. The *Comédie humaine*, Eliade said, is "the work of an exceptional individual. . . . But the working-out of this gigantic *oeuvre* must be studied in itself, as the artist's struggle with his raw material, as the creative spirit's victory over the immediate data of experience . . . here lies the role of the literary critic. It is he who deals with the work as an autonomous universe with its own laws and structure."

In *The Age of the American Novel*, first published in 1948, Claude-Edmonde Magny, in a section of the chapter on Faulkner entitled "Rivalry with God the Father—Faulkner and Balzac," said that not enough attention had been given to reappearance of characters and interweaving of stories in Faulkner, a statement which is still generally true. Magny cited Cowley's statement about Balzac in *The Portable Faulkner* and referred to the map in that volume as materializing the whole "in a Faulknerian geography as objective as the map of France in *La Comédie humaine*." The Yoknapatawpha novels and stories "are part of one living reality . . . that constitutes Faulkner's true literary work," with "its extraordinary power of suggestion and sense of reality." Confronting "the totality of his vision" is for Faulkner like being "face to face with the God he has been in all but actuality." Magny considered Faulkner's work to be a "manifestation of the widespread malady of the modern spirit": "to live in the time before the birth of Christ and thus to find oneself in the same situation as that of the entire Jewish people." This, Magny explained, was "responsible for Faulkner's almost unconsciously adopting, with regard to his creations, the position that is traditionally that of God the Father."

Thus from Balzac we have arrived at Faulkner's twentieth-century competitor as creator of a world, James Joyce. But Joyce's world differs from Faulkner's in significant respects and need not be examined further than to specify those respects. Joyce's Dublin, presented in *Dubliners*, *A Portrait of the Artist as a Young Man*, and *Ulysses*, is a closed universe presented with photographic realism: it is the Dublin Joyce lived in until he went into voluntary exile on the Continent, in the year after the action in *Ulysses* took place, June 16, 1904. The routes of the characters can be followed, street by street, even today, with remarkably few changes; a good map of Dublin is all one needs. The characters in general are identifiable as of the time of Joyce's youth. But after that no one could get out and no one could get in: all must remain as Joyce knew it. The reappearance of characters and the development of Stephen Dedalus from early childhood to young manhood and the vicissitudes of the Dedalus family create a sense of living reality, but it is fixed in place and limited in time. Faulkner's world is one of time and change, in which the necessity for man to accept these realities is paramount.

Unlike James Joyce's Dublin, Yoknapatawpha County does not retain the geographic dimensions and configurations of Lafayette County, as the combination of Faulkner's map from *Absalom, Absalom!* with the actual map of the county makes clear. In the fictitious map Faulkner seemed to follow the injunctions in Isaiah 40:3 for those who are to make "a highway for our God": "Every valley shall be exalted, and every mountain and hill shall be made low: and the crooked shall be made straight, and the rough places plain." The actual map by its absence of straight roads suggests the hilliness of the area.

Faulkner's map gave credence to the error made by many readers of locating Yoknapatawpha in the Delta region, where roads really are straight. In "Darkness to Appall," Charles Gregory describes Yoknapatawpha as Faulkner might have seen it in his mind's eye, in a kind of cosmic vision, "as an ever-expanding collection of concentric circles with Jefferson at the center and Mississippi, the South, and the world symbolized by the outer circles; or as a wheel with Jefferson the center and the roads that lead from Jefferson the spokes connecting the themes of Yoknapatawpha to all men's actions." Two descriptions from the point of view of characters suggest the cosmic dimensions, that of Gavin Stevens in *The Town*, from the vantage point of Seminary Hill (pp. 315–17), and Charles Mallison's vision on a spring morning of his "whole native land" and beyond it the river and the two oceans and finally "the uttermost rim of earth itself, the North" (*ID* 151–52). Gregory describes the "rigid, stratified society" of Yoknapatawpha as consumed by external codes of honor, 'designs' for living based on possessions, and a religion whose external piety hides an internal corruption." In this society, obsessed characters, "driven by the rightness of their obsessions, . . . repeat the same actions without any signs of having learned from their failures." Gregory interpreted Faulkner's attitude as that of recognizing the "old verities" as manifest in tradition and the social structure but wishing to change and improve society.

As the dimensions of Yoknapatawpha in space are decidedly limited, so the dimensions in time are virtually limited to the life of Faulkner himself from the end of World War I to the end of World War II: to be precise, from the return of young Bayard Sartoris to Jefferson in the spring of 1919 to the return of Mink Snopes to Jefferson in the fall of 1946. *The Unvanquished*, narrated by young Bayard's grandfather some time after 1874, gives accounts of his experiences as a youth, 1862–1865, and his becoming a man, "the Sartoris," after the death of his father, Colonel John Sartoris, in 1874. The Civil War and Reconstruction do not play a large part in the chronicles of Yoknapatawpha. The publication of *The Reivers* only months before Faulkner's death in July 1962 brings fiction and reality closer together than does any other Yoknapatawpha narrative. "Grandfather" is telling the story in 1961 to one or more grandsons. Because Faulkner had three grandsons at the time and the Priest family are almost mirror images of three generations of the Falkners in 1905, the time of action in *The Reivers*, "you" as addressed to the listeners may easily be imagined as including three little boys. The Yoknapatawpha fiction covers Faulkner's whole writing career, from *Sartoris* in 1929 to *The Reivers*.

A listing of the Yoknapatawpha novels, with dates of publication and time of action, shows that repeatedly Faulkner dated the action as occurring about the time of the writing. This listing also indicates relationships between novels, in addition to the formal trilogy, *Snopes*, and between short stories and novels. For example, "Wash" remained a separate story, although *Absalom, Absalom!* dealt with the same incident, Wash's murder of Sutpen. "Spotted Horses" as a short story related by Ratliff and the account of the horse auction in *The Hamlet* differ significantly. Like Ratliff, Faulkner was disinclined to tell the same story the same way when retelling. Their imaginations did not stop working when one creative process had been completed, as is illustrated when short stories were incorporated in novels, with significant changes. Or an episode might acquire significance apparently unanticipated by the author, as when Melisandre Backus emerged in "Knight's Gambit" (1949), after her ancestry had been established in "My Grandmother Millard" (1943), before Gavin Stevens was a fully realized major character in a novel. The reader has to put together "Knight's Gambit" and *The Town* to make sense of Gavin's marriage to Melisandre Backus Harriss in *The Mansion*. The fact that most of the tales in novels and short stories become part of the myth of Yoknapatawpha and are common property, to be told and retold, makes more remarkable the omission of a few major incidents and characters from the myth, especially the Bundrens and Joe Christmas. Robert W. Kirk's *Faulkner's People* is most enlightening in making apparent such examples, as well as showing the frequency with which other characters reappear.

The vicissitudes of Yoknapatawpha through a hundred years provide scope enough to reach conclusions about the viability of that society. The questions James Gustafson asked himself in *Christian Ethics and the Community* are suitable to ask about the Yoknapatawpha community, as represented by two races, by leading families in both, and by many individuals of varied economic and social status whose lives and narrative roles are less fully developed but who provide the milieu in which the major characters live out their lives. Gustafson asked three questions: " 'Can a human community exist without faith, both as trust and as faithfulness or loyalty?' 'Can a human community exist without hope, both as expectation or anticipation and as the affirmation of new possibilities?' 'Can a human community exist without love?' " Those questions seem to be implicit in the Yoknapatawpha chronicles, with the emphasis on "that measure of devotion and respect that is necessary for men to live together." As a Protestant theologian belonging to a tradition with an affinity "with the work of Calvin and [Jonathan] Edwards," Gustafson's perspective has an affinity with the Yoknapatawpha fiction.

Amos Wilder is one of several theologian–critics of Faulkner whose views are of particular significance even when not referring directly to Faulkner. Discussing the potential value of theologians to contemporary literary criticism, Wilder cited Fr. Martin Jarrett-Kerr as believing that form and style are conditioned by the world view of an author and that the faith of a novelist is "in his work as a whole, in his style, its imagery, its preoccupations, and his technique of novel-writing." In dealing with Faulkner's world view as revealed in the world he created, religion and philosophy, morals and ethics, as professed or implicit in action in Yoknapatawpha, will be our concern.

The most eminent of the theologian–critics of Faulkner, Nathan A. Scott, Jr., states specifically the relation between the beliefs of an artist and his creations, in terms that are particularly applicable to Faulkner: the artist

> can transmute the viscous stuff of existential reality into the order of significant form only in accordance with what are his most fundamental beliefs about what is radically significant in life, and these beliefs he will have arrived at as a result of all the dealings that he has had with the religious, philosophical, moral, and social issues that the adventure of living has brought his way. The imaginative writer's beliefs . . . do not generally involve a highly schematized set of ideas or a fully integrated philosophic system. He customarily has something less abstract, namely, a number of sharp and deeply felt insights into the meaning of the human story that control all his reactions with the world that lies before him.

From the world that in reality lay before him Faulkner created the world of Yoknapatawpha, past and present. Because the past cast so dark a shadow over some of Faulkner's characters, it is often a factor which must be taken into account in interpreting action in the present. Or the failure to act in the present. The exceptional use of time in the entire content of the Yoknapatawpha chronicles has an unusual if not unique effect upon what is called the "situation ethic" in existentialism, in which the situation is of more significance than laws and rules. John Macquarrie explains that "in such an ethic the course of action is determined by the unique situation in which the agent finds himself." But the agent in Faulkner may respond to influences from the past which the reader is aware of from reading other works in the chronicles: he shares the memories of the characters. Furthermore, the consequences of actions can be covered in another work. Thus long-range consequences, as in Mink Snopes's revenge murder of Flem, can be accommodated, although that murder was accomplished in *The Mansion* in 1946, thirty-eight years after Flem provided the motive, in *The Hamlet*. There was a lapse of seventeen years between the publication of *The Hamlet* and *The Mansion*, with *The Town* appearing two years before *The Mansion*. For those who read the Yoknapatawpha fiction as it appeared, a unique opportunity was provided to test their own judgment of actions and predictions of consequences.

Macquarrie commented on the difference between the legal ethic based on the past and the situation ethic, oriented toward the future, and on the constructive influence "the existential stress on the situation and the future" can have on the contemporary world.

"The task of criticism" is defined by Nathan Scott in *Negative Capability* as "that of deciphering given work at hand in such a way as to reveal the ultimate concerns which it implies." When the "work at hand" is the Yoknapatawpha chronicles, the task is formidable, not only in scope but also in complexity, which obliges the reader to discern the truth in varied versions of events. For readers and critics Faulkner offers an invitation and a challenge. Stanley Elkin remarked that "the novels may have ultimately to be read together in order to obtain a true perspective on them," because "Faulkner seems to see his commitment to Yoknapatawpha County in terms of a continuum." Louis Rubin also regarded "a time continuum" as Faulkner's aim, but he went on to discuss variations in point of view from that of a single character to that of a single consciousness, "a fixed, centered viewpoint, a perceiving eye and mind, which takes in the actions and conjectures the thoughts of men and women in time." Rubin's explanation of what Faulkner requires of the reader well expresses the unique experience of being a participant which is ample reward for "the exhausting performance."

> . . . in *The Sound and the Fury*, none of the participants themselves can be credited with the role of being the single, encompassing percipient; rather it is we as readers who are made . . . to furnish the focus of consciousness in which what has happened can be resolved and given order and meaning. . . . Faulkner forces the reader to become an actual participant in the consciousness of the drama; the reader plays his role, just as the characters do, is made to learn and to speculate and actually to take part. . . . By witholding information, revealing it at certain times and in certain ways, conjecturing and hinting, suggesting and teasing, he introduces the reader into the actual story, makes the stream of consciousness that of our own consciousness.

Thus the reader becomes involved in the whole Yoknapatawpha chronicle, described by Louis Rubin in its totality: "Seen as one tremendous action in time, the whole drama is a chronicle of human history in which the forces of continuity and change contend with one another. The numerous problems of definition, values, morality, and community that beset men in a time of transition are dramatized and explored." Thus what Nathan Scott identified as "the task of criti-

cism'' takes on unique breadth and depth in dealing with the Yoknapatawpha chronicle: the task ''of deciphering the given work at hand in
such a way as to reveal the ultimate concern which it implies.'' Of the
major writers of this century listed by Scott two pages later—Pound
and Gide, Joyce and Lawrence, Kafka and Faulkner—only Faulkner
and Joyce demand the study of a society revealed in interrelated works
produced during the whole creative lifetime of the author.

II • FAULKNER'S INDIVIDUALISTIC CHRISTIAN HUMANISM

Faulkner was an imaginative, impassioned, and highly skilled writer of
fiction and must be judged on his merits as such; he was not a philosopher or a great thinker. He did, however, have some relatively simple, consistent, and deeply sincere convictions about man and his
condition that constitute a moral philosophy. In *Faulkner at Nagano*
and *Faulkner in the University*, in answer to questions he expressed
these convictions adequately to provide a coherent account of his beliefs. These beliefs, Judeo-Christian in orientation but not limited by
any specific theology, are definitely humanistic, using the term as defined by Robert Olson: ''a doctrine according to which individual persons are the source of value and intelligibility.'' He said himself, in
Faulkner at Nagano: ''the only school I belong to, that I want to
belong to, is the humanist school'' (p. 95).

''Humanism'' is a broad term with a wide range of meanings.
Faulkner's connotation for it was no doubt that of the ''New Humanism'' which flourished in academic centers of culture in the East from
1900 until the late 1920s. Faulkner's Oxford friend Phil Stone was a
student at Yale, where Faulkner visited him in 1918. Another friend
from Oxford, Stark Young, was a professor at Amherst. The leading
critics and editors among the New Humanists—Stewart Sherman, Paul
Elmer More, and Irving Babbitt—were nationally known. The account
of their basic religious, philosophical, and ethical principles given by
Gorham Munson, in *The Dilemma of the Liberated: An Interpretation
of Twentieth Century Humanism*, closely resembles Faulkner's explicit and implicit beliefs about man and the principles that should guide
human life. A few quotations from Munson will serve to introduce an
account of later varieties of humanism. The ''foundation idea for all
modern Humanism,'' Munson said, is the dignity of man, which ''consists in the fact that whereas other creatures must obey their destiny,
he can have an active part in forming his.'' ''American humanism'' is
free of theological or political alliances. ''The New Humanist maintains the seat of authority in himself: he studies with zeal the wisdom

stored in tradition, but he insists on his internal corroboration of that wisdom.'' For the humanist ''the true liberty'' lies in ''responsibility for his natural self.'' To achieve and exercise this liberty man must develop the will, for on the will ''everything in American Humanism depends.''

Gorham Munson's book was first published in 1930, when his variety of New Humanism was waning. In 1933 *The New Humanist* published ''A Humanist Manifesto'' by Roy Wood Sellars. In *The Humanist Alternative: Some Definitions of Humanism,* edited by Paul Kurtz (1973), Sellars in ''The Humanist Outlook'' redefined humanism forty years after the ''Manifesto.'' He emphasized the new orientation provided by the support of humanism by science, technology, and philosophy and stated that ''the human spirit must concentrate on its table of values and define the spiritual in this context.'' In the same volume edited by Kurtz, Edwin Wilson referred to the ''Humanist Manifesto'' as a valid religious quest for the good life, reported on the international growth of humanist societies, including as members both conservative and reform rabbis, and described humanism as ''essentially affirmative,'' centered in the faith in man's potentialities to live a good life. Paul Kurtz in ''Humanism and Moral Revolution'' stressed the moral aspects of humanism as based on man's needs, the potential contribution of scientific intelligence and critical reason in reconstructing moral values, and the good life and social justice as moral ideals. Humanism has no party line and regards mankind as a whole. Kurtz expressed the humanist ideal as rejecting creeds and dogmas and commandments which repress needs and vital inclinations and restrict autonomy, causing man to ''lose his sense of responsibility and urge for creativity.'' In discussing ''Religious Humanism,'' Herbert Schneider desired a religion that would free faith and devotion from dogmas and from religious institutions but would affirm religious faith and authentic devotion. Faulkner's adverse criticism of the Christian religion as he had experienced it was directed at the churches, not at Christian faith.

Specifically Christian humanism is dealt with by David Eggenschwiler, in *The Christian Humanism of Flannery O'Connor.* ''The Christian humanist,'' he said, ''believes that even man's attempts to deny or defy God cannot destroy the infinite within him.'' As a spiritual creature man is free, and ''in his freedom he is both more divine and more capable of separation from God.'' In *Negative Capability,* Nathan Scott, himself a theologian and an authority on Faulkner, stated his ideal of Christian humanism, following comments on Paul Tillich's *The Protestant Era*: ''The genius of authentically Christian humanism is most truly expressed when, in its dealings with the 'secular culture,' it so takes this body of witness up into itself that the distinction between the sacred and the secular ceases to exist."

Like Faulkner, Nathan Scott is an Episcopalian. Pierre Teilhard de Chardin was a Catholic priest and a distinguished paleontologist. In Christian humanism he perceived "two trends of collective unconsciousness," toward God and toward mankind, which reveal the divine purpose. His three principles of the rights of man, also in *The Future of Man*, he wished to be affirmed "in any new Charter of Humanity": "The absolute duty of the individual to develop his own personality. The relative right of the individual to be placed in circumstances as favourable as possible to his personal development. The absolute right of the individual, within the social organism, not to be deformed by external coercion but inwardly super-organized by persuasion . . . in conformity with his personal endowments and aspirations." Emile Rideau, in *The Thought of Teilhard de Chardin*, saw in his Christian humanism the hope man has been seeking: "The complete solution to happiness is . . . a Christian humanism, . . . which enables us not only to serve the world of man but to cherish it and transform it."

In shifting from religious and philosophical views of humanism to humanism in a literary context, our first leap is to Peter Faulkner's *Humanism in the English Novel*—another example of serendipity: Peter is unrelated to the Mississippi Faulkners. Peter Faulkner defined humanism in the English novel as either founded on religion as in Dickens or as replacing the loss of faith in the old religion, as in George Eliot. "Humanism is a philosophical position, not a matter of casual good will, and its basis is the belief in human responsibility and human potentiality." The humanist is "committed to free will, the possibility of ethical choice."

Now we come to critics of Faulkner who define his attitude as that of Christian humanism. My conclusions were reached before theirs were published. In "Faulkner's Vestigial Christianity," Richard O'Dea said he called Faulkner "Christian" because he emphasized the Christian virtues: "He demands of his characters that they accept themselves, that they realize they are men and not angels, and that they humbly recognize the consequences of that fact." (One is reminded of Henry in "The Fire and the Hearth": he replied to Roth, who had just asserted his racial superiority to his foster brother. "I aint shamed of nobody. . . . Not even me" [p. 114].)

Comparing "The Nature of Man in the Writings of Reinhold Niebuhr and William Faulkner," R. J. Trobaugh said that both Faulkner and Niebuhr were opposed to forces in Western culture which threatened man's integrity and struggled "towards a rich affirmation about man."

What Trobaugh said about Niebuhr is equally true of Faulkner as a layman and novelist rather than a theologian: he speaks "in behalf of the freedom and responsibility of man as he is apprehended through the insights of the Hebraic-Christian faith." Stanley Elkin's study of Faulkner's religion recognizes the Hebraic-Christian ideas and habits of action as "the basic framework of his creative efforts" but goes beyond and perceives Faulkner's theology as "an ultimately irreconcilable blend of the two systems, the Christian stoic and the existential."

The stoic element in Faulkner is postulated by John W. Hunt in *William Faulkner: Art in Theological Tension.* Both the aristocratic tradition and the Calvinism prevailing among the other social classes fostered a most un-Stoical tendency to violence—political, social, and personal. Faulkner's own statements about his beliefs show no basis for assuming that he held as highly exceptional views as, in his society, Stoicism would be. An element of Christian Stoicism is apparent in the patient endurance of some of Faulkner's characters, such as Dilsey, but Hunt's thesis is that "the Stoic and Christian assessments . . . have formed the poles of a theological tension" in Faulkner. He recognizes the contrast between the Stoic "refusal to recognize guilt" and the consequent Stoic renunciation and the Christian existentialist attitude; he quotes Paul Tillich: "the courage to face one's own guilt leads to the question of salvation instead of renunciation." Un-Christian Stoicism as in tension with Christianity in Faulkner's work appears to be an invalid explanation, in face of the strongly existential patterns which other critics and I have found to pervade Faulkner's work, as this chapter will show.

The basis of Faulkner's Christian humanism is his belief in man and human dignity, a belief nowhere more convincingly, though implicitly revealed than in his characterization of Mink Snopes in *The Hamlet* and *The Mansion.* His concern for the individual is sufficiently apparent throughout his work, so that what he said about man does not suggest the escape from individuality "through some sort of identification with the race of mankind or a large social unit such as the nation" which Robert Olson specifies as characteristic of one kind of humanism. In his writing, Faulkner sought to convey the message of "man's hope and aspiration which has enabled him to prevail above his condition and fate and his own self-created disasters" (*FN* 177).

> . . . I think that the purpose of writing, of art, is a record. The reason that the books last longer than the bridges and the skyscrapers is that that is the best thing man has discovered yet to record the fact that he does

endure, that he is capable of hope, even in darkness, that he does move, he doesn't give up, and that is not only a record of his past, where he has shown that he endures and hopes in spite of darkness, but it is a promise of the validity of that hope. That that is one thing in which he can show tomorrow that yesterday he endured. He knows that since his own yesterday showed him today that he endured, was capable of hope, was capable of believing that man's condition can be bettered, is his assurance that after he is gone someone will read what he has done and can see what man yesterday was capable of believing and of hope that man's condition can be changed; and man's condition does change. There are evils of yesterday that don't exist any more, the evils of today will be gone tomorrow by the advancement, woman [sic] will have more freedom in this country than they had once. There will be a time when the older people that get the world into wars won't be able to get the world into wars any more for the young people to get killed in. That will come, it will take time, it will take patience, and it will take a capacity of people to believe that man's condition can be improved, not as a gift to him, but by his own efforts [*FN* 157–58].

The only problems which Faulkner had no hope that man would solve are "the problems which he is doomed forever to, simply because he is flesh and blood" (*FN* 27). Faulkner's demonstrated awareness of the extent and ineradicability of those problems keeps his statements of his beliefs from implying utopian optimism. His optimism was based on a Christian concept of man.

Faulkner's denunciation of organized religion was occasioned by his conviction that the churches had too often failed to practice Christianity. Faulkner himself believed in God and Christianity in his own way, but without espousing any specific theology and probably without any systematic knowledge of doctrine. Asked at Nagano whether he believed in God, he replied, "Well, I believe in God. Sometimes Christianity gets pretty debased, but I do believe in God, yes. I believe that man has a soul that aspires towards what we call God, what we mean by God" (pp. 23–24). He added that Christianity had never really been tried. At the University of Virginia, Faulkner explained his "relationship to the Christian religion"; "the Christian religion has never harmed me. I hope I never have harmed it. I have the sort of provincial Christian background which one takes for granted without thinking too much about it, probably. . . . Within my own rights I feel that I'm a good Christian—whether it would please anybody else's standard or not I don't know" (*FU* 203).

Basic to Christianity is belief in the soul and immortality. Faulkner believed in immortality, both of the race and of the individual. Immortality of the race is implied in his belief that man will endure. Faulkner more specifically stated this belief in terms which deny any overly

optimistic concept. When asked at Nagano, "Do you consider human
life basically a tragedy?" he replied: "Actually, yes. But man's immortality is that he is faced with a tragedy which he can't beat and he still
tries to do something with it" (p. 4). Proof of man's immortality, he
believed, lay in man's ability to change his ways of living to avoid
perishing (*FN* 41) and in the fact that "he has lasted this long in spite of
all the anguishes and griefs which he himself has invented and seems to
continue to invent. He still lasts, and still there is always some voice,
some essay, saying, 'This is wrong, you must do better than this'" (*FN*
28). That Faulkner did not conceive of immortality only as that of "man
in the abstract, not the concrete individual person," to be achieved
through "identification with the species," as Olson said, is indicated in
his response at Nagano to a statement that he was "one of the very rare
writers of the world who have most strong belief in immortality of
mankind, immortality of man's soul." Recognizing that he might seem
old-fashioned to young people in America, Faulkner continued: "To
think of immortality is not only old-fashioned but it implies a certain
amount of ignorance. But maybe in my own case it's ignorance in the
sense that I am not a trained thinker, not a school man, but I don't feel
the shame about believing in immortality that I might feel expressing a
belief in it if I were an educated man and could refer to philosophy"
(pp. 82–83). Both personal immortality and the immortality of the artist
are involved in another statement at Nagano:

> To me, a proof of God is in the firmament, the stars. To me, a proof of
> man's immortality, that his conception that there could be a God, that the
> idea of God is valuable, is in the fact that he writes the books and
> composes the music and paints the pictures. They are the firmament of
> mankind. They are the proof that if there is a God and he wants us to see
> something that proves to him that mankind exists, that would be proof.
> And if we want to stay on good terms with God, then we better keep in
> mind that we are, and I don't know of a better way to do it, than with the
> music, the books, the sculpture, the pictures, poems [p. 29].

The ethical ideals which Faulkner held as personal values and imperatives were in the tradition of Judeo-Christian and classical humanism. He did not, however, credit classical influence with inspiring the
Latin virtues of *pietas, gloria, virtus*:

> . . . I doubt very much if the Latins invented glory and pity and integ-
> rity. I think that the Latins, like all the people, inherited a knowledge of
> glory and pity and integrity. . . . I don't think that one has to have stud-
> ied any literature to believe that glory and pity and integrity are important
> and valuable. I've seen ignorant people that didn't know the words, that
> acted on the belief that they were valuable and important [*FN* 83].

This statement suggests that Faulkner believed in a kind of Original Virtue as well as in Original Sin; his humble and uneducated characters such as Mink Snopes often display an integrity which can be explained in no other way than as a kind of innate, instinctive virtue.

An innate, instinctive wisdom or insight is intuition. Teilhard de Chardin credited the intuition of Galileo with not only the collapse of geocentrism but with the consequent psychic upheaval. Émile Rideau in turn said that Teilhard "arrived, through his known intuition of world-wide currents, at a vision of mankind that gradually embraced its differences and divisions in a universal humanism." In a chapter on Radhakrishnan, V. S. Naravane explained that "at the highest reaches of knowledge intuition offers advantages which neither perception nor reason can offer." But he quoted Radhakrishnan's warning that the intuitive method is effective only if there has been adequate moral preparation and that intuition requires "continuous creative effort" and long and arduous study. R. J. Trobaugh observed that both Niebuhr and Faulkner gave an important place to the intuitions of the heart as well as to the wisdom of the mind. Dreams show man's intuitive capacity to project images of perfection.

But intuition and imagination are not enough: the essential virtue for a writer, Faulkner believed, is "an integrity to hold always to what he believes to be the facts and truths of human behavior, not moral standards at all. But that man in his books does what man will do, not what man should do but what he will do, maybe what he can't help but do" (*FU* 267).

A comment by Charles Anderson on the ethical principles of Faulkner supplements the statements quoted above. He identifies Faulkner's principles of conduct as Senecan and Ciceronian, derived perhaps from Southern tradition and personal and literary influences rather than directly by study of the Latin classics. He defines *virtus* as including bravery and fortitude, the heroic qualities of manhood; *gloria* as the honor and fame won by glorious deeds, immortalized by aristocratic pride in ancestry; *pietas* as respect for tradition, for duty to family, religion, and country, and as compassion. Alfred Kazin comments on the significance of integrity to Faulkner: it is not a "luxury," as Stuart Chase calls it in "The Luxury of Integrity," but for Faulkner "*integrity* represents not that hoped-for state of 'integration' which enables us to 'function,' but that which alone enables us to grasp our existence." Faulkner's criticism of the modern world may well have been founded upon the fact that in it integrity is too often a luxury.

But what keeps integrity alive and functioning is conscience. In *Man's Search for Himself*, Rollo May defined "conscience" as "*one's capacity to tap one's own deeper levels of insight, ethical sensitivity and awareness, in which tradition and immediate experience are not opposed to each other but interrelated.* . . . For there is a level on which the individual participates in the tradition, and on that level tradition aids man in finding his own most meaningful experience."

The eternal verities of Faulkner's Nobel Prize speech were at the heart of his attitude toward man; failure of readers to see this before Faulkner made his explicit statement may have been the result of failure to see Faulkner's deep distress and sense of outrage behind his revelation of man's inhumanity to man, a failure less excusable in view of his creation of such characters as Dilsey. Personification of "love and honor and pity and pride and compassion and sacrifice" in a humble but admirable Negro woman should have been sufficient evidence that Faulkner cherished such qualities and believed man capable of possessing them. After the Nobel Prize speech, Faulkner continued to affirm his consecration to those verities in his writing; the Stockholm address meant what it said to young writers, "to remind them that the things to work toward, to write about, were the verities which later he would never be ashamed of," the verities which every man must try to live up to (*FN* 66). These verities are "to be practiced not because they are virtues but because that's the best way to live in peace with yourself and your fellows" (*FU* 134).

The truth which Faulkner sought was the truth of heart and conscience: "Truth to me means what you know to be right and just, truth is that thing, the violation of which makes you writhe at night when you try to go to sleep, in shame for something you've done that you know you shouldn't have done" (*FN* 101).

And it is the heart, not necessarily the reason, which recognizes this truth. As Isaac McCaslin said to McCaslin Edmonds, about the truths in the Bible: "The heart already knows. He didn't have His Book written to be read by what must elect and choose, but by the heart . . . there is only one truth and it covers all things that touch the heart" ("The Bear," p. 260).

How far removed Faulkner's moral philosophy was from cynicism or pessimism or even stoicism is now apparent. Patrick Hogan refuted the interpretation that Faulkner's was a "Myth of Cosmic Pessimism": "Indeed, Faulkner's basic preoccupation with the necessity of faith in eternal verities, such as love and fidelity, with commitment to a spiritual life, with self-respect, honesty, and compassion, demonstrates a view essentially optimistic. But it is not an easy optimism."

Faulkner's moral vision has, implicitly or explicitly, been consistently in harmony with Christian humanism. His recognition of evil and his depiction of it are closer to Dante than to modern theories which explain vice chiefly in terms of environment. The original misinterpretations of Faulkner might be compared to what readers may think about Dante if they read only the *Inferno* and have no concept of its place in the larger whole. One can work out Faulkner's plan for salvation from his works, as well as from his concept of man. Faulkner's consistent Christian humanism is recognized by Neal Woodruff, referring in particular to "The Bear":

> Faulkner's moral vision . . . clearly invites formulation in humanistic, not religious terms. His fiction, it must be granted, is often ambiguous in the values it expresses; no perversity is required to decide that they are Christian values, for it is at least plain that they are consistent with Christian values. The Christian motifs and Biblical analogies . . . seem to me to parallel a humanistic vision, to illuminate and reinforce it, but not to transform it into a Christian account of man. They are part of the structure of individual works, but they do not determine the essential burden of the work as a whole. Similarly, I view the shift in Faulkner's work neither as a changing expression of Christian values, at first tentative or submerged and later brought into the open, nor as a revision of moral outlook from a notion that most men must be damned to a notion that most may be saved. The values expressed in his work seem quite consistent from first to last. The shift reflects less a change of emphasis from negative values to positive than a change in the manner of representing those values, a change from the dramatic and implicit to the rhetorical and explicit.

Faulkner's concept of man, based upon his general humanistic philosophy, is even more essential to interpretations of his fiction than are his personal beliefs. Central to both is the premiss of free will and, as a corollary, the belief in man's capacity to change. Faulkner's essentially Christian principles and belief underlie his fiction: his interest in man, in individual human beings and in the race as composed of individuals, is the passion which animates it. Cleanth Brooks, agreeing with Randall Stewart's view of Christian elements in Faulkner's writings, qualifies the phrase "profoundly Christian":

> Perhaps it would be safer to say that Faulkner is a profoundly religious writer; that his characters come out of a Christian environment, and represent, whatever their shortcomings and whatever their theological heresies, Christian concerns; and that they are finally to be understood only by reference to Christian premises.

Faulkner repeatedly expressed his faith in man's ability to endure and in the virtual immortality of the human race. The famous Nobel Prize speech is but one of a number of statements of this idea: "I believe that man will not merely endure; he will prevail. He is immortal, not because he alone among creatures has an inexhaustible voice, but because he has a soul, a spirit capable of compassion and sacrifice and endurance" (*ESPL* 120). As he told Jean Stein, his central thesis, which he was "always hammering at," was "that man is indestructible because of his simple will to freedom" (*LG* 241). Faulkner specified the conditions under which man's will to freedom can cause him to prevail; man must have hope and believe in man; he must believe "in justice, in truth, in freedom, in liberty" and be willing "to work at it" and "to sacrifice his life that justice will prevail" (*FN* 186, 196).

Faulkner's basic concept of life as motion is fused with his belief that man must make choices which are dictated by his moral conscience; both passivity and deterministic involuntary action are ruled out:

> Life is motion, and motion is concerned with what makes people move—which are ambition, power, pleasure. What time man can devote to morality, he must take by force from the motion of which he is a part. He is compelled to make choices between good and evil sooner or later. Because that moral conscience demands that from him in order that he can live with himself tomorrow. His moral conscience is the curse he had to accept from the Gods in order to gain from them the right to dream [*LG* 253].

It is always the individual man in whom lies the hope for the race. As he told his daughter's high school class at commencement:

> It is not men in the mass who can and will save Man. It is Man himself, created in the image of God so that he shall have the power and the will to choose right from wrong, and so be able to save himself because he is worth saving; . . . who will refuse always to be tricked or frightened or bribed into surrendering, not just the right but the duty . . . to choose between justice and injustice, courage and cowardice, sacrifice and greed, pity and self;—who will believe always not only in the right of man to be free of injustice and rapacity and deception, but the duty and responsibility of man to see that justice and truth and pity and compassion are done [*ESPL* 123].

Faulkner's belief in man's free will has as its corollary his belief that liberty and freedom are man's most precious possessions, and that to deserve and win or retain them man must exercise his free will as befits a responsible individual. A favorite quotation of Faulkner's is taken from John Curran, the Irish statesman: "God hath vouchsafed man liberty only on condition of eternal vigilance; which condition, if he break it, servitude is the consequence of his crime and the punishment of his guilt" (*ESPL* 132). Faulkner's application of this principle is of significance to the South and to the United States in general as well as relevant to themes in Yoknapatawpha:

. . . man's hope is in man's freedom. The basis of the universal truth
which the writer speaks is freedom in which to hope and believe, since
only in liberty can hope exist—liberty and freedom not given man as a
free gift but as a right and a responsibility to be earned if he deserves it, is
worthy of it, is willing to work for it by means of courage and sacrifice,
and then to defend it always.

And that Freedom must be complete freedom for all men; we must
choose now not between color and color nor between kind and kind nor
between ideology and ideology. We must choose simply between being
slave and being free. Because the day is past when we can choose a little
of each [*FN* 187–88].

Man must be a responsible individual in his personal life, but his
personal life involves his responsibility as a member of the community.
Intensely individual as were Faulkner's beliefs and principles of conduct, he never lost sight of man as a social being nor presented with
approval a character who did not function as a responsible individual in
his social context. As Charles Anderson said: "Morality to him is a
method of behavior for the individual aimed at a full realization of his
potential character, always of course in his relation to society." In
developing his individual potential, man must both accept the present
as it grew out of the past and make his choices in the present with a
view to a better future. Walton Litz defined "Faulkner's Moral
Vision":

Man's freedom is an inner, moral one. It is his responsibility to endure
and attempt to expiate the evils which he inherits from the past. Then,
secure in the knowledge that this free choice will improve the lives of
succeeding generations, he will be able to reconcile himself to his fate and
prevail over it.

The responsibility of the individual as artist Faulkner believed lay in
maintaining independence of groups except to exchange ideas, not to
protect artists against the rest of the community (*FN* 195).

There is no paradox involved in Faulkner's insistence on both man's
individualism and his social responsibility. Olga Vickery well distinguished between the social and the moral definitions of man:

Out of Faulkner's sharply realized portraits of individual men and
women, there gradually emerges a view of man which involves making a
crucial distinction between the social and the moral definitions of his
nature. The former simply places the individual in certain exclusive categories, the latter restores to him his identity with all humanity. The one
provides a formula for morality and enforces it with law, the other leaves
moral action undefined and therefore unfettered. In short, the social
definition of man predetermines the individual's response to experience
by creating an expectation of conformity to certain codes which govern

the behavior of each social unit. The moral definition forces man to assume responsibility for recognizing and enacting his own moral nature.

The perfect example of the individual faced with the choices between the social and the moral definitions of his nature is Bayard Sartoris, after the murder of his father: he made the moral choice to refrain from a murder of vengeance which social tradition demanded of him.

The great violence done to Faulkner's actual concepts and his intentions in his fiction by the notion that he accepted the "formula for morality" of the Southern tradition should now be apparent. As Vickery says:

> Far from idealizing the Old South, Faulkner sees in it, as in the army, an instance of the paralyzing influence that a rigid caste system and a closed society can exert on the individual. Born into such a society, men are automatically labelled and cross-filed in terms of color, class, clan, and possibly religious and political affiliations. Each of these categories defines a separate world and a distinct code of behavior; all of them together constitute the Southern way of life.

As Gavin Stevens says in *Intruder in the Dust*: "No man can cause more grief than that one clinging blindly to the vices of his ancestors" (p. 49).

To Faulkner, the "rigid caste system" and "closed society" of the South were among the major vices of his ancestors; he might nostalgically recall the *virtus*, *gloria*, *pietas*, and *integritas* of some people of the past, just as he appreciatively immortalized those qualities in some of his most humble characters of the present century, but "the Southern way of life" was alien to his deepest convictions. The recognition of that fact must have dawned upon him gradually and occasioned the anguish of an inner conflict between loyalty to the traditional concepts and values of his region and class and loyalty to the dictates of his own moral conscience. He perfectly illustrates Vickery's distinction between the moral and the social definitions of man. As an artist, to whom unconventionality is indulgently allowed, Faulkner could make his moral choice without violating his obligations to his family and his community and without violating his conscience by adherence to the code.

One of man's primary responsibilities in the community is to raise his voice against injustice:

> It's the single voice that's the important thing. When you get two people, you still got two human beings; when you get three you got the beginning of a mob. And if you get a hundred all focused on one single idea, that

idea is never too good. Man has got to be, if he's got to be a collection, or
a gang, or a party or something, he's got to be a party of individual men
[*FU* 29].

Because man has free will and should exercise both his social and
moral responsibilities, the best government is that in which the individual has the greatest responsibility and the greatest freedom. Faulkner
admitted that democracy "is a very clumsy, inefficient way for people
to govern themselves, but so far I don't know a better one" (*FN* 131).
He denied that the world is now divided between two ideologies: he
considered the United States to be based on "simply a human belief
that no government shall exist immune to the check of the consent of
the governed" and to be "simply a mutual state of man mutually believing in mutual liberty." Democracy, with its creaks and rattles, will
do until we find a better form of government, "since man is stronger
and tougher and more enduring than even his mistakes and blunder-
ing" (*FN* 188).

In *Children of Light, Children of Darkness*, Reinhold Niebuhr supported democracy for the same reasons that Faulkner did: "Ideally
democracy is a permanently valid form of social and political organization which does justice to two dimensions of human existence: to
man's spiritual nature and his social character; to the uniqueness and
variety of life, as well as to the common necessities of all
men. . . . An ideal democratic order seeks unity within the conditions
of freedom; and maintains freedom within the framework of order."

Faulkner was, logically, opposed to governmental bureaucracy, and
expressed his protest in "The Tall Men," with its example of the
McCallum family objecting to government subsidy but not to army
service. Faulkner believed that a certain amount of hardship does one
no harm and feared that lack of struggle weakened man's integrity and
moral strength. To retain his superiority over the state, which is the
servant of the individual, "the individual must be independent of the
state, he mustn't accept gratuity from the state. He mustn't let the state
buy him by pensions or relief or dole or grant of any sort" (*FU* 100–
101).

The same principle of individualism explains Faulkner's unfavorable
view of organized religion, particularly Southern sects which are
strongly Calvinistic: he believed that man must work out his own religion and that religious groups, such as the groups of women who hounded Ruby Lamar in *Sanctuary* and reformed to death the old druggist in
"Uncle Willy," were motivated by other than Christian sentiments.
Even more than organized religion did Faulkner distrust and denounce

those persons like McEachern and Hines in *Light in August* who suffered from religious megalomania and, as agents of the Lord, exercised domination over other individuals in a spirit of Old Testament wrath and vengeance instead of treating others with Christian charity and love. He would have agreed with Nietzsche: "And whatever harm the wicked may do, the harm of the 'good' is the harmfulest harm."

Stanley Elkin's account of the various Protestant denominations in Oxford in Faulkner's youth puts the Southern Baptists at the top, with the Methodists second and the Presbyterians third. All three denominations were Calvinistic, for reasons explained by Douglas and Daniel in "Faulkner's Southern Puritanism"; in the North only the Presbyterians were Calvinistic. Elkin indicated that Faulkner had had experience with all the denominations: his mother was Baptist and his father Methodist; the Faulkner boys went to the Methodist Sunday School. After his marriage Faulkner and his family were Episcopalians; the Episcopalian church had the fewest members but had prestige socially and had the only ante-bellum church building in Oxford. Elkin said of Faulkner: "He has been called a Christian humanist and such a label is . . . ultimately just, but one interested in Faulkner must not overlook the fact that he was Christian first and humanist second." In that environment a man of Faulkner's generation was most unlikely to be a humanist in the modern sense. He did not stop being a Christian when he became a humanist or stop being a humanist when his convictions encompassed existentialist ideas.

Before we leave the Christian-humanism phase of Faulkner's writing, the Calvinistic aspect needs further consideration. It was part of the culture in which Faulkner grew up and was particularly oriented to emphasis on the Old Testament concepts of man and God. Critical interpretation of Faulkner's works involves study both of his use of Old Testament stories and images and of his characters who represent Calvinistic beliefs. In the collection of essays *Religious Perspectives in Faulkner's Fiction,* edited by J. Robert Barth, S.J., Calvinism is a major aspect: Barth's own essay is entitled "Faulkner and the Calvinist Tradition." Having stated that "the term 'Puritanism' has been equated with Calvinism pure and simple," Barth conceded that "there was indeed a stern foundation of Calvinist thought in much of American Puritanism," and its theologians, such as Jonathan Edwards. ("Faulkner and the Concept of Excellence," a dissertation by Alma Ilacqua, deals with Jonathan Edwards and the Puritan influence to be discerned in four novels and several short stories in the Yoknapatawpha cycle.) Barth identified two elements in Puritan theology, and said that Faulkner "stands quite unmistakably within the orthodox strain.'' In *The Reivers*, however, ''Faulkner's final vision is one of hope: man sinful, but striving for the good; man shackled by bonds within and without him, but struggling to be free.'' Barth fails to recognize the most significant fact about *The Reivers*: it is the only one of Faulkner's novels in which the narrator-hero and his family closely resemble Faulkner and his parents and grandparents, with Faulkner as the grandfather speaking to his grandsons. Richard O'Dea's criticism of Barth applies to other critics: the theology of the characters is not necessarily shared by Faulkner: ''their tragedy consists in their very Calvinism,'' and Faulkner ''implicitly rejects their deterministic theology.''

In ''Faulkner's Southern Puritanism,'' also in Barth's collection, Harold Douglas and Robert Daniel explain why Calvinism became so widespread in America that it is ''apt to turn up almost anywhere that religious belief impinges upon Southern life.'' Therefore it is bound to be evident in novels dealing broadly with Southern life. ''The influence of Calvin is to be detected,'' they say, ''not so much in a literal application of the doctrine of the elect and the damned, as in a serious and often gloomy view of man's fate, in an insistence upon the strictness of behavior, particularly on the Sabbath, and in the belief . . . that sexuality is the chief sign of man's fallen nature.'' (In *Intruder in the Dust* the Gowries piously refrained from lynching Lucas on Sunday; fortunately Charles Mallison made good use of his time on Sunday, but not by going to church.) The many parallels between Hawthorne's novels and Faulkner's show that Faulkner was continuing the Calvinism, whether or not he was influenced by Hawthorne in all the parallels.

In ''William Faulkner: The Calvinistic Sensibility,'' a dissertation by Mary D. Fletcher, Puritanism was compared with Manichaeism as stressing the dualistic nature of man and the separation of flesh and spirit. The symbolism of light and darkness is significant especially in Quentin's shadow, the dark side of his nature. The title correctly suggests a psychological rather than a theological influence of Calvinism on Faulkner. Faulkner's mature choice of the denomination least influenced by Calvinism, the Episcopal church, would seem to indicate that his sensibility was not unalterably Calvinistic.

III • EXISTENTIAL ASPECTS OF FAULKNER'S CHRISTIAN HUMANISM

In calling into question the ''goodness'' of traditional society and showing the isolation and alienation of those who seek the guidance of their own conscience or who are excluded from communion with their fellows by barriers of class or caste, Faulkner reveals the human condition in a small rural area to be startlingly similar to that which is typical of modern urban life. In his humanist concept of man as endowed with freedom and in his appeal to man to exercise his freedom as an individual, Faulkner was in essential agreement with the most pervasive literary philosophy of the century, existentialism. In *Radical Innocence,* Ihab Hassan described "our awareness of the modern experience" as "supremely existential," and found the "dramatic center of the modern novel in Europe and America" to lie in "the encounter between the new ego and the destructive element of experience." The consequence of this encounter is such "alienation of the self, its response in martyrdom or rebellion or both to the modern experience." In the preceding chapter Hassan had observed that Faulkner, in his isolated heroes or scapegoats, had used American themes and that his creation of a myth of the South, using those themes, places him in the American literary tradition. His use of existentialist themes and characters places his major works in the mainstream of both Western humanistic literature and current American fiction. A brief statement in Paul Kurtz's *The Humanist Alternative: Some Definitions of Humanism* links the two philosophic developments: "Humanism . . . is what it is through its existential value."

Faulkner's existentialism seems not to have been based on existentialist philosophy; he belonged to no school of writers and did not follow systematically any school of thought. William Barrett, both a philosopher and a critic of Faulkner's works, said: "Faulkner certainly never read Heidegger; he may never even have heard of him. So much the better; for the testimony of the artist, the poet, is all the more valid when it is not contaminated by any intellectual preconceptions." A remark Barrett made about T. S. Eliot applies even more generally, perhaps, to Faulkner: he had "an almost radar-like sensitivity to contemporary life." Rather than with the concepts of any existentialist philosopher or school, therefore, we are concerned here with the philosophical attitudes covered by the more broad and general definitions of *existentialism* in a society with a strong Protestant tradition.

It is interesting to note, however, that there was a source of radio waves, as it were, of Mississippi origin and existentialist import within the range of Faulkner's personal knowledge and sympathetic interest. The eminent Percy family, of liberal views and literary talents, included William Alexander Percy, who not only was one of the Delta aristocrat families most actively opposed to Vardaman and Bilbo, whom Faulkner detested, but who was the author of *Lanterns on the Levee,* an account of life on a Mississippi Delta plantation. His home, Robert

Coles remarked, "was a mecca for writers, artists, and scholars. Faulkner came to play tennis." A few years later, in the early 1930s, he had adopted his cousin's son, Walker. Robert Coles wrote *Walker Percy: An American Search* because he and Percy belong to the "tradition of Christian existentialism." Percy *did* read Heidegger and wrote philosophical and theological essays before expressing his ideas in novels, beginning with *The Moviegoer*, published in 1961, the year before Faulkner's last novel, *The Reivers*. But Faulkner's personal and professional associations brought him closer to existentialism than one might suppose, and as sharers of the same tradition, Faulkner and Walker Percy shared the values of Christian existentialism.

Implications as to "how existentialism can issue in a living Christian philosophy" had appeared in Faulkner's fiction before Marjorie Grene raised that question in *Introduction to Existentialism* or Paul Tillich provided an answer. Grene described existentialism as "a courageous and an honest attempt at a new morality" which prizes "integrity of character and action rather than of vision alone," "an ethic of integrity, in which running away from one's self is evil, facing one's self is good." Faulkner expressed and dramatized similar concepts, positively or negatively. He shared the "central and significant insight of existentialist philosophy": the perception of "the dichotomy between fact and value, between what merely and irrationally but undeniably is, and what we aspire to, yet what as undeniably is not." The humanistic orientation of existentialism is suggested by both the individualism and the faith in man's potentialities which are reflected in the above general definitions.

In *Existentialism* (1972) John Macquarrie makes an authoritative statement about the themes common to all existentialist philosophers: "Such themes as freedom, decision, and responsibility are prominent in all. . . . These matters constitute the core of personal being. It is the exercise of freedom and the ability to shape the future that distinguishes man from all the other beings that we know on earth. It is through free and responsible decisions that man becomes authentically himself." Despite the agreement on themes, Macquarrie stated that existentialists could "not be counted as forming a 'school' in the usual sense." The division into Christian and atheist existentialists is oversimplified, partly, Macquarrie explained, by the paradoxical relation an existentialist may have "to his Christianity or his atheism." Macquarrie devoted one chapter to "Existentialist Influence in the Arts and Sciences," and listed the important areas: "psychology (including psychiatry); education; literature; the visual arts; ethics; theology. . . . psychology, literature, and theology have been especially infiltrated by existentialist ideas." In his early Yoknapatawpha novels Faulkner was not, as he seemed to be, taking off into the wild blue yonder from the solid ground of the novel, but was blazing trails through a wilderness.

Although Jean-Paul Sartre defined existentialism in humanistic terms, in "Existentialism Is a Humanism," Christian humanists disagreed with his concept. Sartre's "first principle of existentialism," that "man is nothing else but that which he makes of himself," places upon the individual "the entire responsibility for his existence" and makes him also "responsible for all men." Thus man is the measure of man and the creator of man: "I am thus responsible for myself and for all men, and I am creating a certain image of man as I would have him be. In fashioning myself I fashion man." John Macquarrie expressed the Christian humanist disagreement with Sartre, based on Sartre's view that "man starts from nothing and invents his values and images for himself." "It seems to me" Macquarrie continues, "that already with existence there is given an image or goal of existence . . . a basic awareness of the direction of human fulfillment. This is conscience. . . ."

Sartre's concept of *existential humanism* is explicitly stated in "Existentialism Is a Humanism":

> Man is all the time outside of himself: it is in projecting and losing himself beyond himself that he makes man to exist; and, on the other hand, it is by pursuing transcendent aims that he himself is able to exist. Since man is thus self-surpassing, and can grasp objects only in relation to his self-surpassing, he is himself the heart and center of his transcendence. There is no other universe except the human universe, the universe of human subjectivity. This relation of transcendence as constitutive of man (not in the sense that God is transcendent, but in the sense of self-surpassing) with subjectivity (in such a sense that man is not shut up in himself but forever present in a human universe)—it is this that we call existential humanism.

Faulkner disagreed with Sartre because Sartre "denied God" (*FU* 161). Unfortunately Sartre was the best-known of the existentialist writers in the twentieth century; consequently readers who were unfamiliar with contemporary philosophical and theological thinkers assumed that other existentialists were usually atheists, like Sartre. In Faulkner's less philosophical but more Christian terms he did believe in man as self-surpassing: "Man tries to be better than he thinks he will be. I think that that is his immortality, that he wants to be better, he wants to be braver, he wants to be more honest than he thinks he will be and sometimes he's not, but then suddenly to his own astonishment he is" (*FU* 85).

The genealogy of existentialism confirms its religious humanistic concern with the individual and suggests various channels through which Faulkner's radar sensitivity may have implanted existentialist ideas before the existentialist school of literature developed. Arthur Fallico gives the "existential motif" a long and general tradition:

> Existentialism represents a strand of thought present in every age and among all peoples; the persistent sensitivity, the fundamental mood, the disturbing awareness which it represents, is stamped on every product of the human spirit that attests man's radical ontological insecurity, born out of the deepest self-consciousness.
>
> This is the tradition of existing man's concern with his individual self—with his own soul. He has forever reflected upon the irremediable contingency of his being, his mortality, his forlornness, his solitariness, his uncertain fate. Under the sway of this mood, existing man has time and again become aware of his unessentiality of being, his essence-lessness, as if awakening naked and homeless in a Parmenidean universe of immobile Essence. This, surely, is the state of awareness which has ever instilled in man the feeling of being a stranger, a wanderer without abode or destination, or a prisoner awaiting release or execution for some original, forgotten crime.

In *The Broken Center*, Nathan Scott traces existentialism only to writers and artists "who belonged to that nineteenth century vanguard of revolutionaries . . . distinguished for the clarity and courage with which they acknowledged the bitter facts of alienation and estrangement as the central facts of modern existence," and recognizes 1914 as the point at which "the existentialist experience ceased to be the experience of a sensitive minority and became the dominant experience of the age."

In *Existentialism and the Modern Predicament*, F. H. Heinemann explained how he coined *Existenzphilosophie* and used it in *Neue Wege der Philosophie* (1929), thus giving rise to *existentialism* as a philosophical term. He started with "man as being-within-the-world," standing "in a threefold relationship with man, the Universe, and God." Heinemann traced the course of existentialism from 1929 to 1957: "from religion, through agnosticism and atheism back to religion." (The dates chance to be those of the publication of *Sartoris* and *The Mansion*.)

In the introduction to *The Worlds of Existentialism*, Maurice Friedman defined *existentialism* as "a movement from the abstract and general to the particular and the concrete," but not "at the expense of all generality and abstractions." "Forerunners of modern existentialism" are innumerable, including "the whole range of literature, which has always had a strong tendency toward the particular and the personal."

The "particular and the personal" aspect of life Heinemann perceived to be in conflict with "the progressive mechanization of life," resulting in what he termed "technological alienation": "Words, tools, and machines have the natural tendency to become independent of their creator and to appear as foreign to him." Heinemann interpreted existentialism "as a reaction to the all-embracing powerful influence of technology," and quoted Paul Tillich to support his view:

> What all philosophers of Existence oppose is the *irrational* system of thought and life developed by Western industrial life and its philosophic representatives. During the last hundred years the implications of this system have become increasingly clear: a logical or naturalistic mechanism which seemed to destroy individual freedom, personal decision and organic community; an analytical rationalism which spans the vital forces of life and transforms everything, including man himself, into an object of calculation and control; a secularized humanism which cuts man off from the creative source and the ultimate mystery of existence.

The solution to the problem of technological alienation, Heinemann said, begins with a "return to facts, to concrete experience, to reality"—back to the "particular and the personal."

Although Faulkner did not refer specifically to existentialism, his remarks about Sartre and Camus are evidence that he was familiar with their philosophic views. In aligning himself with Camus rather than with Sartre, he took the position of Christian existentialists:

> I think that no writing will be too successful without some conception of God, you can call Him by whatever name you want. . . . That to me is the difference between Camus and Sartre, the difference between Sartre and Proust, the difference between Sartre and Stendhal. That Sartre has denied God. . . . I think that Camus will get better, but I think that Sartre will never be better [*FU* 161].

Faulkner believed that Camus was "the best of the living Frenchmen" because "Camus has stuck to his principles, which was [sic] always to search the soul, which I think is the writer's first job. To search his own soul, and to give a proper, moving picture of man in the human dilemma" (*FU* 282–83). Faulkner's reasons for preferring Camus are more significant in this context than is his interpretation of Camus.

In "Albert Camus: Sainthood Without God," John Cruickshank recognized that Camus stood "quite distinctly in a relationship of tension to Christianity" and "experienced a religious need in its widest sense yet was unable to accept religious belief. . . . He attempted to teach his contemporaries that it is both possible and vital to arrive at a rigorous personal and social ethic starting from the premises of doubt

and despair and independently of dogmatic *a priori* foundations."
There was no such tension between Sartre and his dead God. Faulkner
made the statements quoted above while Camus was still living and
there was a possibility that Camus might have found satisfaction for
what Cruickshank described as "a hint of a possible nostalgia for God"
in *L'Homme revolté*: "Nothing can discourage the appetite for divinity
present in the human heart."

An interesting similarity between Camus and Faulkner may be more
than merely coincidental. If my reading of Faulkner is correct, Ratliff
comes closer to being Faulkner's ideal humanist than does any other
character. A prototype of the Yankee peddler, the type of which Ratliff
is an idealized version, is Odysseus. William Barrett said of Camus,
whose message is "very much in the main stream of existentialist
thought":

> What Camus wishes to affirm against the dehumanizing tendencies of
> ideologies is a renewed sense of the human, which means a renewal of the
> classic sense of moderation and limits that is to be found in the Greek
> poets, if not in Plato. His final hero from the Greek mythology is Ulysses,
> prudent, reasonable, tenacious, and above all the most *human* of all the
> warriors who went to Troy.

The most obvious use of Ulysses as a prototype is, of course, James
Joyce's. The fact that William Barrett devoted to Camus the Postscript
to the Introduction to Part Four, "Phenomenology and Existentialism," in *Philosophy in the Twentieth Century*, lends a unique distinction to Camus as "a writer singularly equipped by temperament and
experience to address himself" to our century. Faulkner's radar tuned
him in on Camus, and Barrett confirmed Faulkner's preference for
Camus rather than Sartre.

As a kind of postscript of mine to Barrett's, his comments on the rise
and decline of French Existentialism help to explain American reactions. Camus, Sartre, and Simone de Beauvoir gave rise to a cult of
devotees which had died out by 1958; when Barrett was writing *Irrational Man*, Camus had split off from the group and continued his
own explorations of existential themes, Sartre and De Beauvoir were
still producing, and existentialism was still influential in the non-
academic world, but philosophers had rejected it. But by 1962, when
Philosophy in the Twentieth Century was published, Barrett wrote:
"As a popular cult, existentialism no longer generates any news or
excitement, while as a subject for serious study it has already entered
the academy" as a subject for courses and dissertations.

Barrett's statement about the academic status of existentialism can be checked as represented in scholarly criticism of Faulkner's works: John Bassett, *William Faulkner: An Annotated Checklist of Criticism*, (1972); Thomas McHaney, *William Faulkner: A Reference Guide* (1976). McHaney used "Existentialism" as a subject index, with fewer than fifteen entries from 1958 to 1973. Bassett included dissertations, in a separate section: only three can be identified by title as dealing with existentialism.

That existentialist elements have been recognized in Faulkner's fiction is evident from the modest number of entries listed under "Existentialism" in McHaney. Brief statements identifying Faulkner as an existentialist writer or citing existentialist aspects in his work occur in discussions of existentialism as well as in critical treatment of Faulkner's works. In discussing existentialism in "The Broken Center," Nathan Scott listed Faulkner with Conrad, Kafka, and Malraux as among the "great charismatic seers of modern literature," along with Baudelaire and Pirandello. In *The Philosophy of the Twentieth Century*, William Barrett ascribed the "new and more serious interest" in existentialism to "the continuing and mounting influence of modern art and literature," and referred to "the strange and powerful art of the first fifty years of this century— . . . the disturbing world of a Kafka or Joyce or the early Faulkner."

Another group of critics deals with Faulkner rather than with existentialism. Theodore Greene recognized Faulkner's "existential convictions" revealed "in specific human motives, decisions, and acts": "they constitute . . . not only Faulkner's own philosophy of life; they comprise that aggregate of interrelated basic attitudes and ultimate beliefs which, on Faulkner's diagnosis of human nature, are the chief source and fruit of man's spiritual strength, as their opposites are the demonic forces within him which drive him to self-destruction." In "Faulkner's Waste Land Vision in *Absalom, Absalom!*" Robert Slabey described "Faulkner's vision" as "existential and mythic, and at the same time, powerful in its expression, scope, and originality."

Concluding "A Passion Week of the Heart," his interpretation of Christian symbolism in Faulkner's works, Hyatt Waggoner said:

> Faulkner's fiction is existentialist, and to say this is not really to change the subject. It is existentialist as much of modern painting is existentialist, and the fiction of Kafka, and the earlier poetry of Eliot, and the theology of Paul Tillich. And as Tillich himself . . . said, existentialist art rediscovers in a manner appropriate to our time "the basic questions to which the Christian symbols are the answers." Faulkner's fiction breaks up and reconstitutes the conventional and expected elements and patterns and feelings of experience, imposing on us the burden of painful-

ly fresh perception. From its sometimes violent dislocations of the familiar, the old questions of man's nature and destiny emerge with fresh relevance and unexpected urgency.

The most thorough published treatment of existentialism in Faulkner, Ralph Ciancio's "Faulkner's Existentialist Affinities," states that "Yoknapatawpha County . . . is existentially oriented" and reviews existentialist themes. In his many examples Ciancio breaks up his accounts of characters; he proves his point that existentialist themes abound in Faulkner's fiction, but he does not deal with characters as existentially conceived and developed or with the consequences to society of the inhabitants' choices of authentic or unauthentic lives.

Despite the similiarities in basic principles between Faulkner's beliefs and existentialist philosophy, differences in values between Faulkner and various prominent modern existentialists are due in large measure to Faulkner's acceptance of some traditional values and to his Christian orientation. Ralph Ciancio recognized that Faulkner's world, unlike that of atheist existentialists, had a moral center. The individual, according to Faulkner's concept, chooses his values, rather than creating them: *virtus*, *gloria*, *integritas*, *pietas*—the truths of the heart are to be sought in the heritage of man. Camus, like Faulkner, believed that values precede action, that existence does not precede essence. In theory Sartre believed that existence precedes essence: "There is no human nature, because there is no God to have a conception of it. Man simply is. . . . Man is nothing else but that which he makes of himself." The ideals Sartre postulates, however, are ideals in the tradition of Western humanism; he did not conceive of man, acting existentially, as following the animal pattern of survival. In theory, it seems, he thought of each man as inventing his game of life and setting up the rules for it. Faulkner used the game analogy significantly in crucial situations as a bond between men, made possible because they accepted the same rules. Faulkner frankly recognized tradition as the source of his ideals and evidence of their validity. His use of Latin terms for his most cherished values is a reminder of his cultural tradition.

The high place Faulkner gave to compassion, explicitly illustrated in the Nobel Prize speech, is a deviation from the values of some existentialists, among whom, Robert Olson remarked, compassion is not typically a value. They reason that the achievement of the goal of elimination of suffering would ultimately make compassion unnecessary. Like Dostoevsky and Gabriel Marcel, Faulkner did not regard "compassion as an insult to human dignity" and was no doubt too realistic to conceive of the elimination of suffering as humanly possible, in a world in which emotion is stronger than reason, death is inevitable, and disasters resulting from natural causes and human folly and fallibility are almost equally inevitable and ineradicable. Euthanasia as a way of ending suffering due to disaster would seem unlikely as an existential choice by the individual and unthinkable as a remedy imposed by others. Although Faulkner specifically stated that "disaster seems to be good for people," he also expressed his belief that many causes of suffering, "the misery which we create for ourselves," can and should and will be removed (*FU* 37, 40). Compassion would seem to be man's consolation and spiritual recompense for the suffering which is irremediable.

John Macquarrie's explanation of the themes "prominent in all the existentialist philosophers," freedom, decision, and responsibility, is brief and lucid: "These matters constitute the core of personal being. It is the exercise of freedom and the ability to shape the future that distinguishes man from all the other beings we know on earth. It is through free and responsible decision that man becomes authentically himself." But "every decision is a decision against as well as for" and limits "the range of possibilities" for "future decisions." He cites Kierkegaard's emphasis on the decisions familiar to most people: "marriage, friendship, and vocation." All three of these are likely to have "lasting consequences for the whole life of the individual who makes the choices." And by these choices he chooses the possibilities of his own future. He makes promises, he supports policies, he marries, he makes friends. . . ." Macquarrie, presenting Gabriel Marcel's concept of "engagement," adds: "Marcel sees fidelity as a basic human virtue, making genuine community possible." This simple and realistic framework for a human life can be used in studying a living person or a fictional character, and is most appropriate when applied to the creations of an author with existentialist affinities.

Freedom is essential before one can make choices. "The Quest for Freedom" as the title of this chapter signifies the first goal that an individual, a society, a nation, or the human race must reach before the human potential can be realized, individually or collectively.

In his interpretation of existentialism written in the 1960s, Frederick Olafson reminded his readers of how recently changes in life circumstances had allowed people to "conceive their powers and responsibilities as moral agents," to think of controlling significant aspects of their roles rather than having "the claims of custom and authority . . . set the course of an individual life." Although Faulkner's Yoknapatawpha is vastly different from the Paris and France of Sartre and Simone de Beauvoir, it is significantly different from much of the

United States in the twentieth century. The world of Yoknapatawpha is closer to nature and less highly organized, mechanized, and industrialized than urban settings. Even after the passing of the wilderness, people had access to nature and to the simple and natural life. (In Faulkner's Oxford, the residential area is spreading into uncultivated wooded land where people whose occupations are in Oxford can literally live in the woods.)

The community of Jefferson is relatively homogeneous and has a meaningful tradition if its sound values are preserved. Except for poor whites, especially tenant farmers, and Negroes, alienation in Yoknapatawpha is more likely to be due to individual circumstances, to deviations from the norm, than to society in general. The security of accepted status in the community and a sense of individual relationship to a continuing tradition is a natural condition for many people in this society. This situation is to the advantage of those whose families enjoy some prestige, even if prosperity has vanished. It is to the disadvantage of the "risers," like the Snopeses whose lowly beginnings were known to everyone. The three choices—marriage, friendship, career—would be limited by family status. V. K. Ratliff is unique in establishing friendship with his social superiors, Gavin Stevens and Chick Mallison. But the most serious limitations of freedom are taken for granted: this is not merely a "closed society" which shuts out the Negroes, but a closed society which shuts in the women. It is male-dominated, and women even of good social status do not have freedom to choose a husband, friends, or a career. There are two victims of the closed society in "Dry September": Miss Minnie Cooper and Will Mayes.

Mississippi: The Closed Society was written by Faulkner's friend James Silver, who stated in "A Note from the Author" that Faulkner was one of the "six men," all natives of Mississippi, who "beyond all others, have influenced my thought and action." Faulkner died in July 1962. On September 30, 1962, the riot occurred at the University of Mississippi which, Silver wrote, "released me from whatever obligation I might theretofore have assumed of maintaining silence for fear of possibly hurting the institution to which I had devoted most of my adult life." Existential choice! Silver had succeeded in having Faulkner address the Southern Historical Association in Memphis in 1955. Faulkner's remarks on freedom and choice were thoroughly and daringly existential:

Soon now all of us—not just Southerners nor even just Americans but all people who are still free and want to remain so—are going to have to make a choice. We will have to choose not between color nor race nor religion nor between East and West either, but simply between being slaves and being free. And we will have to choose completely and for good . . . [*ESPL* 150].

In the context of existentialism, denying freedom and opportunity to others and treating them as things, not people, is the depth of inauthenticity. Sartre's analysis of anti-Semitism in "Portrait of the Anti-semite" needs only painting the Jew black to represent the white racist—except that instant recognition of the enemy simplifies the initial stage. Gabriel Marcel, an anti-Sartrean religious existentialist, in *Man Against Mass Society* has a chapter, "Techniques of Degradation," which deals most directly with Nazi methods in Germany against the Jews but which applies also to the Jim Crow laws in the South after the Civil War. Marcel explained the chapter title:

> a whole body of methods deliberately put into operation in order to attack and destroy in human persons belonging to some definite class or other their self-respect . . . in order to transform them little by little into mere human waste products, conscious of themselves as such . . . in the very depths of their souls . . . .

Marcel ends with a warning: "in the long run all that is not done through Love and for Love must invariably end in being done against Love . . . ." Those who use such techniques have lost "awareness of these transcendental laws which allow him to guide his behavior and direct his intentions. . . ."

In light of some of the realities which Faulkner was painfully aware of but which he could not focus on in his fictional world, one can assume that he would agree with the existentialist view of human life as stated by Robert Olson:

> Frustration, insecurity, and painful striving are the inescapable lot of humankind, and the only life worth living is one in which this fact is squarely faced; for, if the existentialists are right, a life of frustration, insecurity, and painful striving itself generates values, and the values so generated are the only ones actually realizable and genuinely worthy of human pursuit.

The values derived from such a life are based primarily on "freedom of choice and individual dignity" and embrace "personal love and creative effort." With these values and the following three points in respect to them Faulkner and "all existentialists without exception" are in agreement: the values can be experienced only under condition of "a resolute acceptance of anguish and suffering"; existentialist values "liberate man from . . . degenerate and unwholesome forms of anguish," such as "tedium or petty anxiety, apathy or craven fear"; and finally, "existentialist values intensify consciousness, arouse the passions, and commit the individual to a course of action which will engage his total energies."

Although Faulkner's direct statements of his beliefs are useful in interpretation of his fiction, his fiction constitutes his contribution to existentialist literature. Characters which can be interpreted in existentialist terms must be viewed *in toto*, not fragmented by examination of separate aspects of their situations and actions.

A substantial number of Faulkner's major characters falls into two basic groups, in existentialist terms, according to their choices and actions or their failures to choose and to act; *authentic* and *inauthentic*. The life worth living is described by Olson. It is "an authentic life, based upon an accurate appraisal of the human condition." This human condition, to both Sartre and Heidegger, is that of "the radical duality between the human and the nonhuman," of the necessity of man's living in the world without "being-in-the-midst-of-the-world" like a mere material object. Despite his rejection of Sartre's atheism, Faulkner would agree with Sartre that the authentic man "is the person who undergoes a radical conversion through anguish and who assumes his freedom." Olson sums up:

> To be free is to be under the necessity of transcending one's past. On the other hand, authenticity, or, if you prefer, moral responsibility, consists in an unwavering recognition of the necessity one is under to be free. Only the morally responsible or authentic man recognizes his past for what it is, recognizes that it is *his* past and assumes responsibility for it, while at the same time recognizing that his future is free and that at every moment he is called upon to transcend his past and to make himself anew, for the future, too, is his.

Rollo May, regarded by John Macquarrie as a leading psychiatrist using the existentialist approach, warned against mere rebellion against conventions: "Rebellion acts as a substitute for the more difficult process of struggling through to one's own autonomy, to new beliefs, to the state where one can lay new foundations on which to build. The negative forms of freedom confused freedom with license, and overlooked the fact that freedom is never the opposite to responsibility."

The concept of Camus differs from that of Sartre chiefly, in this context, in affirming, Fallico said, that "authentic existence is possible only as we squarely face and accept the total *absurdity of life* and the world, determining to make our humanity count in spite of and against it" (italics added).

Olson's pragmatic view, similar to Sartre's, although not based on the same definition of man, preserves us "against those opposite extremes of bourgeois conformism and romantic idealism":

> In concrete and commonsensical terms the requirement of authenticity is that man assume responsibility for his past while simultaneously recognizing his responsibility to surpass it toward a future. It forbids us to be ourselves only in so far as being oneself means a slavish and supine acceptance of one's past history and the world as presently constituted. It forbids us to refuse to be ourselves only in so far as refusing to be one's self means a quixotic rejection of one's past history and the world as one finds it.

In short, one must neither cling to the past nor reject it but accept and use it.

Authentic human relationships not only must be based on "mutual respect for one another's freedom" but necessarily involve conflict in personal relations, as the natural consequence of individual integrity. (Faulkner would no doubt have been less insistent than Sartre on "conflict as the very foundation of human relations.") Thus the authentic man strives for his own self-creation and transcendence while recognizing that others have a right and a duty to the same striving; conflict, if it arises, is not due to the attempt of one *authentic* person to subdue another to his will, but it may arise through an authentic person's resistance to being so subdued by an inauthentic person.

The achievement of authenticity, Fallico explains, is likely to involve not only conflict but also guilt: "Our moments of authenticity and spontaneity of being, when and if we ever achieve them, contaminate us with guilt. Life is a grave business: innocence and spontaneity are reserved only for very small children or for the outcast." Guilt is caused by "conscience" if it is used to mean "a person's awareness of the moral code accepted in his society" and his consequent discomfort at breaking the rules. Macquarrie contributes another meaning of conscience: "the kind of moral conviction that will sometimes lead a person to reject the accepted standards of his society in response to what he believes to be a more deeply founded imperative." Existentialists hold only the second kind of conscience important. Insight which carries with it moral conviction would seem to be a kind of intuitive conscience, not a code imposed from without; Radhakrishnan's statement that "Reason must work in cooperation with Intuition" suggests a corollary: "Reason must work in cooperation with Conscience."

In a dissertation, "Religious Themes and Symbols in the Novels of William Faulkner," Stanley Elkin deals with what existentialists would call values characteristic of authenticity, but he seldom refers to existentialism and his subject is not focused on characters and their actions. He does present relevant observations about Faulkner's moral and religious ideas. The basic terms for existentialist values are too common to be interpreted as aligning Elkin with the existentialists. His dissertation, from 1961, is listed by Bassett as 53 in the 173 from 1941 to 1971. (Marjorie McCorquodale's "William Faulkner and Existentialism" [1956] preceded Elkin's dissertation and Ralph Ciancio's "The Grotesque in Modern American Fiction: An Existential Theory" [1964] followed it.)

In citing the values specified by Elkin as significant in Faulkner's novels, only those not in the existentialist vocabulary of values will receive special mention. "Rendered truth" being "the test of art," the artist must deal with "concepts which make a difference and result in a habit of action for the people who hold them." Such ideas provide a "frame of reference" for a system, criteria which "create a kind of heritage of intent" and give meaning to action. These ideas are derived from the Hebraic-Christian myth. Action requires will and self-control and responsibility. The lack of congruity between action and self-control Elkin regards as causing "an ultimately irreconcilable blend of two systems: the Christian Stoic and the existential." (John Hunt's dissertation, "William Faulkner's Rendering of Modern Experience: A Theological Analysis," also 1961, is 55 in Bassett. The only item on Stoicism in McHaney is Hunt's book *William Faulkner: Art in Theological Tension* [1965].) Robert Olson is one of the few existentialists who recognize a relationship between Stoicism and existentialism: Elkin's interpretation is more in line with existentialist thinking.

Other values in Faulkner's novels which are cited by Elkin include: courage, action, duty, honor, pride; faith, commitment; free will, choice, action: "executed choice." Values not typical of existentialism are *courage, honor*, and *pride*. To these might be added *loyalty* or *fidelity*, although specified by Elkin in this context. These qualities are likely to be misdirected, as honor and pride would have perpetuated the revenge code, and seldom would defiance of that code have required the courage Bayard demonstrated in facing Redmond unarmed. No doubt Faulkner was well aware of the aristocratic tradition that honor demanded that one pay gambling debts but not that one pay his tailor. But in Yoknapatawpha loyalty to some traditional values might deter freedom of choice and action in life-promoting ways. And of course the Christian values of faith, hope, and love would be esteemed in either the fictional or the actual society.

Freedom is essential if the individual is to act as an autonomous being, able to make choices, to act in accordance with the choices made, and to assume responsibility for the consequences. Frederick Olafson deals in particular with the relation between values and actions: value concepts involve the rightness of a specific action in a specific situation and therefore must be capable of serving as a guide to conduct. Action is free in the sense that "the direction and goals of human action must be self-generated." Despite the passivity of many of Faulkner's characters or even their self-destructiveness, Stanley Elkin recognized that Faulkner's characters might "seek suffering because it fixes identity" and might use memory as "vicarious existence," but he described Faulkner's religion as one of life, not death. Therefore, Elkin said, Faulkner "eschews the suicide, the hermit, the seeker after safety."

What might be called a constellation of values is found in the Nobel Prize address: "the old universal truths": "love and honor and pity and pride and compassion and sacrifice"; "the courage and honor and hope and pride and compassion and pity and sacrifice which have been the glory of his [the poet's] past."

The values and patterns of action specified are those that identify what existentialists call the authentic life. John Macquarrie defines *authentic* and *inauthentic* in terms of the ideal: "True community allows for true diversity." "Authentic being-with-others . . . promotes existence in the full sense; . . . it lets the human stand out as human, in freedom and responsibility." "Inauthentic being-with-others suppresses the genuinely human and personal." It "depersonalizes and dehumanizes," it "imposes uniformity" and suppresses "any kind of excellence." It cannot "tolerate . . . the different."

Arturo Fallico's definition of the unauthentic man explains basic attitudes and motives. He tries to evade the moral responsibility of freedom "by denying the essential ambiguity of human existence. Objectivist and subjectivist alike fail to realize that man both is and exists. The one denies that he must choose his future; the other, that the past is his. . . . They cannot bear to envision the possibility of genuine freedom. . . . A past that is irremediably gone or a future which is of their own making is as frightening to them as the infinite spaces were to Pascal."

The unauthentic man may be most easily recognized in his attitudes and relationships to others; he may merely, Grene says, seek a "fraudulent togetherness," for the "sense of belonging with nothing genuine to belong to," but he may become part of a mob; Fallico's description particularly fits Faulkner's lynching mobs:

> . . . he is a noisy crowd rather than a single personality. Hence, too, he is in perennial conflict—a conflict which forces upon him the most stringent

self-surveyance, if he would hold the pieces together. He must talk fast and continuously, in that inner dialogue with oneself that we call thought, so that he can silence whatever original utterance may still burgeon in him. If he hangs together at all in his conflicting parts, it is due to no self-renovating inward spontaneity of purpose, but precisely to a studied and systematized practice of escaping renewal. This stultifying feat he is usually best able to accomplish in association with other men, where the others' noises are added to his own to produce a din which makes his waning ability to speak sincerely to himself altogether ineffectual. This divided and self-oblivious state fuses him with what Heidegger calls *das Man*, the epitome of depersonification, where he reaps all the benefits of individual irresponsibility, others' approval, and of course, material security. He is then the "one-hundred-percenter" of whatever you like.

This kind of unauthentic person tries to avoid direct confrontation with another person who could look him in the eye and size him up. Sartre gave special attention to the look of another that transforms him into an object: "such an annihilation I am bound to try by every means in my power to overcome. Therefore, between myself as subject and the other who sees me as object, between my freedom and its destruction by another's possession of me, there arises a circle of conflicts." Sartre believed that conflict was the whole pattern of interpersonal relationships, a fact of life. In presenting Sartre's theory of the Other and the look which is a threat, a source of humiliation to him as the object in encounters or confrontations, Marjorie Grene suggested that "to see eye to eye" with another has a different meaning and "that the original relation of myself to another lies in the recognition of another *like* myself, who enriches and completes my freedom rather than threatens to annihilate it." Because confrontations between characters present realistic and meaningful images in fiction, especially when "look" or a synonym is used, the reader should be alert to the existential significance, without assuming a Sartrean interpretation.

The term "situation comedy" is sufficiently common that to refer to existentialism as situation ethics not only implies that ethical judgments are based upon a specific situation, not on rules, but, by analogy, suggests that fiction or drama would be suitable means of presenting existentialist ideas. John Macquarrie deals only with avowedly existentialist writers in "Existentialism and Literature," or with forerunners of existentialism such as Dostoevsky and Kafka. But "Existentialism and Ethics" provides the useful term "situation ethic" for Faulkner's fiction which is grounded in realities of time, place, and people. Faulkner's technique of "freezing" motion enables him to stress details that would otherwise be too fleeting—a facial expression, a look, a gesture.

Arturo Fallico's classification of "existing men" provides a useful differentiation among three kinds of unauthentic individuals:

> There are those who secretly or overtly are running away in panic from what they have been and done, without direction and knowledge of what they want to be or do. There are those who, by devious ways, have convinced themselves that they can find their meaning in the repetition of their former or present roles, resisting to the death any change. There are those who somehow succeed in entering a state of self-oblivion or insensitivity, remaining immobilized in indifference and passivity, suffering external changes not of their own initiation.

Fallico's fourth type is the authentic man who "having come to the realization that there is no fulfillment in the past or the present cautiously opens" himself "to the envisionment of new possibilities." Fallico is viewing men as potential modern artists. In Faulkner's fiction, however, there are other types which are closer to the authentic than to the unauthentic but which do not belong under Fallico's category. Because Faulkner presents a traditional, homogeneous society, with some sound values, he created characters of integrity who deliberately choose acceptable ends in a meaningful world. Their values are authentic in relation to their circumstances and way of life, though the world may have changed around them so that what were once the values of society have become the values of the individual, retained through the integrity of free choice. A character may have integrity and may make choices in crises and accept responsibility for his actions, suffering the penalty for errors but without experiencing conversion or achieving transcendence. And finally, characters of deep faith or of strongly instinctive and intuitive natures may lack the self-consciousness and intellectual quality of the typical existential character but may still be fully authentic in the sense of accepting themselves, exercising choice, and bearing responsibility.

In considering the existential situation of specific characters in Yoknapatawpha there are two basic aspects to take into account: what we are told about that individual and his family and his social environment and what we are not told, even in the broad span of the chronicles. If some aspects of ordinary life are never experienced by a character in direct narrative or are not remembered, when Faulkner gives so much space to memory, the reader might assume that these aspects were not important or did not exist in Yoknapatawpha. But if certain normal and universal kinds of events rarely or never are presented in narrative or thought of or remembered, then the question is: What was Faulkner, consciously or unconsciously, conveying about the viability of life in Yoknapatawpha and in what ways did the choices and actions of the characters affect that viability?

Cleanth Brooks has been particularly concerned with the sense of community in Yoknapatawpha, both in *William Faulkner: The Yoknapatawpha Country* and in "The Sense of Community in Yokna-patawpha." The latter, being much the more recent and the less well known, is the source of my quotations. Brooks uses a set of categories formulated by W. H. Auden—*crowd, society, community*—to differentiate between social groups: "a *community*—a group of people united by common likes and dislikes, aversions and enthusiasms, tastes, lifestyle, and moral beliefs." He regards such communities as having "an important place in the world that he [Faulkner] created in the fiction," and views as "a genuine loss" the "loss of cultural cohesion." But Brooks uses "A Rose for Emily" to illustrate his point. The narrator speaks for the town, as in "Our whole town went to her funeral." "His story," Brooks says, "is about what Miss Emily's life and death meant to the community." But she is never mentioned again, not even by Charles Mallison, quoted by Brooks as saying: "So when I say 'we' and 'we thought' what I mean is Jefferson and what Jefferson thought." Other examples Brooks gives of community consensus are the congregation of Gail Hightower and the community opinion of Hightower and Joe Christmas in *Light in August*. Those two unforgettable characters, however, do not enter the minds of anyone in Yoknapatawpha thereafter, not even Charles Mallison. He did remember a less terrible example of community violence: in *The Mansion*, Charles was telling the story of Tug Nightingale and Captain McLendon (including a reference to Miss Joanna Burden's mailbox) and mentioned McLendon as a leader "in something here in Jefferson that I anyway am glad I don't have to lie down with in the dark every time I try to go to sleep" (p. 185). The answer to that riddle is the lynching of Will Mayes in "Dry September."

Charles and Gavin Stevens and, even more so, V. K. Ratliff are characters who identify themselves with the community and are familiar with its varied aspects. But with the exception of the Sartorises and the Mallisons, the chief characters belong to families that live in isolation, neither joining in events outside the household nor entertaining guests. Shared experiences such as weddings and funerals, church services, and special celebrations such as Easter and Christmas, county fairs, Halloween, Confederate Memorial Day (Fourth of July may be dispensable in that community), athletic events—such normal activities which bring people together are strangely lacking not only in the Compson family but also in the McCaslin and the Edmonds families, the Sutpens, and even the Mallisons; the family takes little part in community life.

When there are exceptions, there may be something bizarre about the occasion or the way it is presented. Caddy's wedding appears as flashes of memory, but that of Sutpen and Ellen, as related by Mr. Compson, is seen as a travesty in which a mob gathered outside the church and only a few of the one hundred invited guests were in the church. The funerals are equally lacking in grief and solemnity: the burial of Addie Bundren is told by Darl, the most sane and sensitive of the Bundrens: "we got it filled and covered" (*AILD* 227). Not the least remarkable of the funeral scenes is that of Mr. Compson as Jason describes it: the outward decorum, Uncle Maury's retreats behind a tombstone to take "another one from the bottle," Mrs. Compson's predictable tears "when they begun to get it filled up," and Jason, unpredictably, "began to feel sort of funny" when they were "throwing dirt into it." He quickly recovered his normal lack of feeling when Caddy showed up and wanted to see her baby (*SF* 249–51). Only Flem's funeral was a real community event—without mourners!

In the existential situations in which the characters must choose and act, it is necessary to consider whether the person had had the requisite relationship with others in the community to be able to make a choice and to act responsibly. The reader who is familiar with the major Yoknapatawpha fiction is better able to judge the situation than is the reader of a single novel. We know that Miss Emily did not "come close to being a legend, a fable, even a parable." Faulkner could have provided the evidence if he had wished.

IV • EXISTENTIAL ELEMENTS IN FAULKNER'S YOKNAPATAWPHA CHRONICLES

Existential elements in the Yoknapatawpha chronicles are apparent in the choices and actions of characters and their values, stated or implied, and in related themes. Such elements provide some of the philosophical groundwork for aspects of form and content, as Donald Kartiganer demonstrated. In *The Fragile Thread: The Meaning of Form in Faulkner's Novels,* he was concerned with what a Faulkner novel implies "about consciousness, reality, and moral value." He discovered that "the design . . . never denies its dubious status, its origins in contingency," and concluded that "for Faulkner the imagination of form is a moral act, an exploration of the possibilities and the value of human conduct." As the terms Kartiganer used in stating his purpose suggest, his interpretations and mine at times are complementary, but with a different focus. Analysis based on existential criteria is independent of but not inapplicable to literary form; it may, however, be applied to living agents or to personages in histories or biographies. We shall here be concerned, therefore, with characters and their attitudes, their choices and actions, rather than with such aspects as literary scenes and patterns as such or with style, other than with existentialist terms in the vocabulary, or with motifs, such as the "look," which have existential significance. For maximum clarity and continuity, works will generally be considered in chronological order according to events, except where several works deal with the same group of characters and should be taken in sequence or where there is a double time scheme such as the time of the narration and the time of the action. Attention will be focused on the configuration of major characters in a work or in related works as the essential basis of the interpretation; classification of existentialist attitudes, authentic or unauthentic, as outlined previously, will deal with groups of related characters within a work or a sequence of works. Recurrent characters will be considered in relation to their different roles, even though the works may not be constructed as a sequence. Regarding the Yoknapatawpha chronicles as a whole, I followed Amos Wilder's principle before I discovered it: "Any social or religious meaning that a novel or poem may have is finally to be defined in terms of the work as a whole."

Existentialism as a philosophy or literature emerging from crisis which forces the individual to confront reality and to meet the exigencies of times of stress lends itself particularly to examination of conduct during conditions of social upheaval such as war. *The Unvanquished,* Faulkner's only work dealing chiefly with the Civil War, presents a series of crises as viewed by Bayard Sartoris, the narrator, as he recalled events which occurred during his adolescence, the last when he was twenty-four years old. The time of telling is not specified; there is no evidence that he was much older than he was when the last event took place. The last and longest story, "An Odor of Verbena," was published for the first time in *The Unvanquished.* Except "Skirmish at Sartoris," the other stories were written for and published by *The Saturday Evening Post.* Changes for publication as a story-novel were comparatively few but, with the mature point of view in the last story, greatly increased the significance, existential or general. The major characters, Granny Millard and Bayard Sartoris, son of Colonel John Sartoris, are involved in a succession of wartime crises requiring Granny to make choices and assume responsibility for the family, Colonel John being away fighting the Yankees at the time.

In the earlier stories, when Bayard was still a boy, Granny tried to retain her integrity and to instill in Bayard and his black companion, Ringo, her own principles and behavior. She was responsible for protecting the property of Colonel John, her son-in-law, and the safety of the inhabitants of the plantation. When the situation became dangerous and she had to deal with the enemy troops, she tried to secure means to restore Sartoris after the war and to alleviate the suffering of the poor people in the region. To achieve her goals, she had to make choices which violated her principles. She was so ardent a believer in truth that she prayed to be forgiven for the lie which saved the lives of Bayard and Marengo, both twelve years old. The boys saw Yankee soldiers approaching and shot at one on a horse. Ringo announced to Granny, "We shot the bastud" (p. 31). The arrival of a Yankee sergeant looking for the boys he had seen run into the house made Granny forget the language Ringo had used. Granny had just time to sit down and get the boys under her skirts before the sergeant got into the house. He was followed by a colonel who said the shot had killed one horse. The colonel was a gentleman and accepted Granny's lie as truth. After Granny prayed to be forgiven for lying, she made the boys wash out their mouths with soap (p. 39).

So Granny and other Southern ladies, supposed to be paragons of virtue who needed the direction and control of a man, found themselves responsible for running the plantation and supervising the slaves. Anne F. Scott's subtitle for *The Southern Lady* is *From Pedestal to Politics*. The lady did not make it in one leap. Nor did Granny. She saw the "hand of God" in the misunderstanding whereby a Union officer restored to her far more than the Union troops had taken. She did not really lie—she just did not speak up and tell the truth. Frederick Olafson raised the moral question of whether it may not be better to tell a lie than cause suffering by telling the truth. Having persuaded herself that she could help the poor people if she did deliberately what she had done inadvertently, Granny carried on a highly successful trade with forged orders, getting livestock from the enemy to help the poor in her area. Courage to stand on one's own convictions is an affirmative choice, according to Rollo May. But except for the Union officers, Granny fooled no one, not even herself. She publicly confessed in church and asked the congregation to pray for her, before she distributed to the needy another issue of welfare funds, courtesy of the enemy, and conscientiously tore up the old receipt before she issued a new one (pp. 156, 157). Then in the empty church, with her two young partners in crime, she addressed God, justified her actions by the need, and took upon her own conscience the sins of the two boys (p. 167).

Granny learned to leap too well and leaped once too often. She did not realize that once she was off the pedestal of the Southern lady she would meet men who were not gentlemen. With Ab Snopes doing the traveling and Ringo as her office assistant, she was doing well until the Yankees began to evacuate and cut off her supply of stolen livestock. She set off to see Grumby, against the advice of Ringo and Bayard: "They won't hurt a woman" (p. 173). The boys could have stopped her but were too used to obeying her. And Granny was still dreaming of having fifteen hundred dollars for Colonel John when he returned "to his ruined plantation" (p. 172).

When Bayard and Ringo found her body in an old cotton compress, Bayard's responsibility and Ringo's loyalty were tested. Granny's funeral was attended by Fortinbride, the minister, and the entire community in that rural area and most of the Jefferson people (p. 178). It is the most impressive funeral we see in Yoknapatawpha, and Fortinbride's last words at her grave reflected her spirit. For Bayard, there was no choice: a fourteen-year-old boy, son of a Colonel, whose helpless little grandmother was shot in cold blood, all he could even think of doing was to get a pistol and start after Grumby. He was "mixed up" (p. 183), but Uncle Buck led Bayard and Ringo as long as his rheumatism and a shot in the arm let him. It was not only a test of courage but one of endurance, in foul weather, for two months. Granny had shown one kind of courage described by Rollo May: "Courage is the basic virtue for everyone so long as he continues to grow, to move ahead; the only lasting virtue." As if he had been reading Faulkner, May defines in the next paragraph Bayard's courage: "Courage is the capacity to meet the anxiety which arises as one achieves freedom. It is the willingness . . . to move from the protecting realms of parental dependence to new levels of freedom and integration."

After a series of narrow escapes the boys find Grumby, Ringo jumps on his back, Grumby gets loose and turns and runs and Bayard shoots him in the back. Only when the boys had pegged out Grumby's body on the compress door and brought Grumby's severed hand and put it on Granny's grave could Bayard get relief from the nightmare of guilt; as Ringo said beside Granny's grave (p. 211): "It wasn't him [Grumby] or Ab Snopes either that kilt her . . . It was them mules. That first batch of mules we got for nothing." But if Bayard had been killed instead of his killing Grumby, Granny's responsibility, after choosing repeatedly to do what she knew was wrong because it would serve her ends, would have been more terrible than her own death for having too much faith in the sanctity of women in the South.

Colonel John Sartoris in *The Unvanquished* resembled the authentic man who envisions new possibilities and makes responsible choices: his "will to endure" and his "declining of self-delusion" (p. 11), his dream of the railroad which he made come true, his realization that violence must be renounced and peace must be gained through law and order, his going unarmed to death rather than continue to yield to the necessity of killing—in all these choices and attitudes he was authentic. Like Granny, Colonel John's deviations from authenticity caused his death: in Bayard's own words, his "violent and ruthless dictatorialness and will to dominate" and his offenses against the pride of Redmond— as George Wyatt put it, "there ain't any use making a brave man that made one mistake eat crow all the time"—impelled Redmond to shoot him (pp. 258, 260). But this is Bayard's story.

When Bayard received news that Redmond had shot his father, he had time to consider what he should do. He knew his father's friends would assume that he would shoot Redmond, as the old tradition called for. He also remembered what he had learned from Granny, not to kill. He is no longer a boy. He proves Rollo May's point that "the creative use of tradition makes possible a new attitude toward conscience, as telling one what *to* do, rather than what not to do." May said one should ask: "What does the tradition have to teach me about human life, in my particular time and my problems?" It was a time of peace after war, at the beginning of his adult life; he wished to prove his courage and save his honor but not to kill, as he knew his father had made the same decision. Although he had faced a similar decision after Granny's death, he realized that a new moral choice might be called for. (Olafson stated the principle that no individual action can commit one "to a moral principle once and for all.")

When he got to Sartoris, his young stepmother, Drusilla, met him with a pair of duelling pistols, holding them out to him. He took them but she realized, infuriated, that he would not use them. Aunt Jenny said she would think well of him whatever he chose to do. He went unarmed into Redmond's office and stood while Redmond shot twice, missing both times. Then Redmond fled Jefferson and was not seen again.

After Drusilla's fiancé had been killed, Drusilla joined Colonel Sartoris' troop as a soldier. After the war she went to Sartoris with him and helped to rebuild the house which had been burned by the Yankees. Society provided no respectable role but marriage for a young woman. Her daring unconventionality wilted under the blast of letters from her mother, shriveled under the gaze of her mother's lady friends in Jefferson, and was gone with the wind when her mother arrived with trunks full of Drusilla's ante-bellum wardrobe. The wedding was interrupted by an election in which she helped her not-yet husband to prevent Negroes from voting. In her torn wedding dress, she acted as voting commissioner (p. 240), enacting Anne Scott's subtitle, *From Pedestal to Politics*, by making the leap in the brief interval between bride-to-be and wife. Her amorous overtures to Bayard, as his step-mother, gave her the hope, one assumes, when she handed him the pistols with which to avenge her dead husband, of marrying Bayard and then controlling him. Melvin Bradford recognized the hope, but saw Drusilla only as a displaced person, not as a woman with some masculine qualities which would make her always displaced. Her anger when she realized that Bayard would not shoot Redmond was that of a foiled Phaedra. Drusilla is unique among Faulkner's young women in her desire for a dominating male role.

After Drusilla kissed Bayard's hand, which held the pistol she hoped would kill Redmond, she stared at him "with intolerable and amazed incredulity" (p. 275) and went into hysterics. (She recognized his courage by leaving a sprig of verbena on his pillow before she disappeared from Yoknapatawpha.) Drusilla's stare is one example of the Sartrean "look" with which one confronts the Other, each regarding the other as an object, usually one attempting to dominate the other, as Drusilla had assumed she could dominate Bayard. A succession of looks are exchanged in "An Odor of Verbena." Bayard's eye-level look at his father, when he tried to confess his amorous interlude with Drusilla, was not met by the Colonel's "intolerant eyes" with the "transparent film" of "the eyes of carnivorous animals"; Colonel John was too lost in dreams of the future to hear his son in the present (pp. 265–66). This is a perfect example of what Camus said in *The Rebel* : "The climax of every tragedy lies in the deafness of its heroes." Bayard's look was his only weapon against Redmond, but it sufficed to make Redmond flee in shame after shooting wide of the mark at Bayard (p. 287). The rare look of equality, between "two centers of liberty which can be free together," as Grene said, "not endangering each other but united through understanding" of similar aims, is exchanged between two authentic persons, Aunt Jenny and Bayard. Aunt Jenny's eyes "were not intolerant but just intent and grave and . . . without pity" when she told him that she would think well of him no matter what he did (p. 280). At the end of the story, her eyes were full of tears as she said, "Oh, damn you Sartorises!" (p. 292). The contrast between Aunt Jenny and Drusilla is that between the authentic person who lives by her own code and the person who can be forced by convention to conform outwardly to a code and way of life she does not believe in, as in her marriage.

Bayard's action apparently had no effect on the community: George

Wyatt, his father's friend, admired Bayard's courage but would not follow his example. Panthea Broughton compared Bayard and Colonel John: they "resist the traditional code of violence." In rejecting one code of honor, Bayard "rejected a meaningless abstraction for a meaningful one." Bradford decided that both Granny and Colonel John had a positive influence on Bayard. But both made choices that left Bayard with a potentially deadly responsibility to fulfill in his youth.

But Bayard was not guiltless. As Ringo said, what killed Granny was not Grumby or Ab Snopes: "It was them mules. That first batch of mules we got for nothing." Bayard remained silent and inactive and Ringo ably assisted Granny, and both of them let Granny go alone to her death when they could easily have held her.

In *Sartoris*, Bayard is Old Bayard, at seventy dull and listless. An explanation of the apparent inconsistency between the young and the old Bayard is provided by William Ramsey, who traced a pattern of behavior of Bayard, in *The Unvanquished*: he chose inaction, leaving the initiative to an older person. Ringo, a slave the same age as Bayard, played as courageous and responsible a role as Bayard did in their quest for vengeance in "Vendée" but had been much more helpful to Granny in her illicit trading. In the way in which Bayard chose to prove his courage and defend his honor, he left the initiative to Redmond. He tells the story, so we do not know all his thoughts: he might well have believed that Redmond would not shoot a "standing duck" and risk the vengeance of the friends of the Colonel for a double murder. Bayard was brave still but not in the wholly courageous and active way he chose in avenging Granny's murder. Ramsey also explained Old Bayard in *Sartoris*: Bayard "misunderstands the nature and value of an active life, and he consequently never prepares himself for such a life, either practically or psychologically." He went to Law School because his father sent him there, but he left after his father's death and did not become a lawyer. His role at his bank was largely that of a figurehead. He seems to have transcended his natural capacity for choice and action in "Vendée." In *Sartoris* his was the unauthenticity that clings to the dull routine of a sedentary life. In *Sartoris*, Doc Peabody told him bluntly that nobody got less fun out of living than he did (p. 100), and Aunt Jenny told him he could spend the rest of the day "being a Sartoris and feeling sorry for himself" (p. 104).

Aunt Jenny figures more prominently in *Sartoris* than in *The Unvanquished*. Her "piercing old eyes that saw so much and so truly" (p. 369) supply the only authentic vision in the Sartoris family: she saw through the fustian and the bombast but loved and cherished the Sartoris men even while she damned them. Having lost her young husband in the

Civil War, she chose responsibility, going to Mississippi and giving the Sartoris men her unsentimental devotion without self-pity. Honesty, rectitude, and moral sensitivity governed her relationships with others and herself. Being honest herself, she was taken in by Narcissa's performance as the Southern lady and did not suspect that Narcissa was engaged to Bayard when she kept coming to Sartoris to see Aunt Jenny. Aunt Jenny could live through anything, even knowing that Narcissa had lied to her about the engagement, but she could not live with the knowledge of Narcissa's utter lack of principles: she died in her wheelchair when she learned how Narcissa bought back the letters Byron Snopes wrote to her before her marriage ("There Was a Queen"). Aunt Jenny provided the one example of sustained authenticity in the Sartoris family; without her backbone, the Sartorises would have collapsed long ago. Unfortunately, young Bayard was too young and blinded by the Sartoris legend to realize that a Sartoris old woman could be a source of understanding and wisdom as well as of love.

Young Bayard, the central character in *Sartoris*, is an amazingly existential hero for a novel published in 1929, when F. H. Heinemann had just coined the term, in German. Bayard is a perfect example of the unauthentic type who runs away from his problems, endures the anguish of grief and despair occasioned by death, and chooses death. As Panthea Broughton said, "Faulkner ironically implies that both the Sartoris twins and Horace [Benbow] are in reality making similar evasions" but with different endings. Actually, Byron Snopes belongs to the same type except that he is a Snopes; all three were about the same age, from the same community, and with war experience. The cutting of passages dealing with Byron and Horace in the shortened *Sartoris* version made Bayard definitely the hero, an improvement in the novel over *Flags in the Dust* but a loss of psychological studies of two very unauthentic characters.

Bayard's problem was basically that he loved no one but his twin brother. Cold and unfeeling and soulless, with a cold mask of a face and bleak and haunted eyes, Bayard found in marriage only "the temporary abeyance of his despair and the isolation of that doom he could not escape" (p. 289). (The moment of choice is not presented but whenever it occurred, Narcissa no doubt took the initiative.) Tormented by self-accusation after the death of his brother John, Bayard could not go on living but neither could he commit suicide. The whole pattern of seeking danger and violence—by means of stallion, racing car, and airplane—in his flight from his problem involves risk which is bound eventually to cause his death, releasing him from "a bleak and barren

world" (p. 160). The climax of Bayard's misery and lack of moral
courage came after the death of his grandfather, old Bayard, in the
wrecked car. After Bayard fled to the MacCallums, he could confront
himself:

> he saw the recent months of his life coldly in all their headlong and
> heedless wastefulness; saw its entirety like the swift unrolling of a film,
> culminating in that which he had been warned against and that any fool
> might have foreseen. . . . *You were afraid to go home.* . . . *You, who*
> *deliberately do things your judgment tells you may not be successful,*
> *even possible, are afraid to face the consequences of your own acts.*
> Then again something bitter and deep and sleepless in him blazed out in
> vindication and justification and accusation; blazing out at what, Whom,
> he did not know: *You did it! You caused it all; you killed Johnny* [p. 311].

Self-deception is stripped away and *you* involves self-accusation for his
inability to keep Johnny from going to his death (p. 45). So fully did he
identify himself with Johnny and so complete was his despair in the
"black chaos" of his isolation (p. 323) that he even wondered if he too
was dead and "this was hell, through which he moved for ever and
ever with an illusion of quickness, seeking his brother who in turn was
somewhere seeking him, never the two to meet" (pp. 321–22). Self-
acceptance, self-creation, a vision of new potentialities were impossible for Bayard, feeling and reason being frozen by grief, and death
seeming less appalling than the "long, long span of man's natural life"
(p. 160). The look with which he regarded others signified the isolation
of his private hell; the nightmare from which he woke to gaze at
Narcissa "with wide intent eyes in which terror lurked, and mad, cold
fury, and despair" (p. 250) was little worse than the reality in which he
relived the experience of Johnny's death as he told it to Narcissa,
inwardly struggling with his "false and stubborn pride" (p. 251). The
mask which hid his cold despair was as bleak and cold as his eyes. The
contrast with the warm and gay and loving Johnny suggests that
Johnny had been Bayard's means of communication with life and
people, the human and loving part of the twinship without which
Bayard could not live. Like the Twins in Paul Radin's account of the
Winnebago Twin cycle, "together they constitute a single person,"
"the two sides of man's nature." Joseph Henderson, in *Jung's Man*
and His Symbols, goes on to cite a refined story of Twin Heroes in
which "one figure represents the introvert, whose main strength lies in
his powers of reflection, and the other is an extravert, a man of action
who can accomplish great deeds." The particular division of the
Sartoris twins may be unique, but the principle of division which
makes one twin only half a person helps one to understand Bayard's
problem. One might say that he was born unauthentic.

The episode at the MacCallums' introduces, by way of contrast, what seems to be a simple, authentic way of life, except for the all-male family: father and sons who live according to their own values and who are united by love. Albert Devlin, however, said that they reveal "much of the same frustration and perversion usually associated with the wasteland" and supported his view by an analysis of the father and his sons. A passage added in *Sartoris* to the *Flags in the Dust* version confirms the significance of Bayard's choice of risking his life rather than committing suicide: on his night prowl at the MacCallums', a pause in his quest for death, he found a shotgun and remembered where the shells were, but he put the gun back in the corner (p. 322). He was also showing consideration for his hosts, but undoubtedly Faulkner intended that brief incident to confirm what was implied before: that the Sartoris legend demanded that his death must be a gamble, an act of spectacular violence, not as cold-blooded an affair as shooting himself.

Bayard's wife, Narcissa Benbow, and her brother Horace Benbow provide a bridge between *Sartoris* and *Sanctuary* and in the two novels furnish an interesting contrast, existentially speaking. Both Horace and Bayard had returned from the war, in which Bayard was in the Air Corps and Horace was in the Y.M.C.A. Despite the contrasts between them, Broughton considered them as the first example in Faulkner, in *Flags in the Dust*, of Faulkner's "revealing similarity beneath apparent dissimilarity": both are in flight from reality, a romantic flight from the "entanglements and caprices of the human community." It would be difficult to say which was the more unfortunate in being chosen as a husband. Belle and Narcissa are both utterly repulsive.

Horace in *Sartoris* tried to return to the past, to take up the life of a lawyer which he adopted as a duty to the family tradition and left to serve with the Y.M.C.A. overseas. Horace's unauthentic, passive acceptance of the family tradition is emphasized in a passage in *Flags in the Dust*, describing his inherited law practice as consisting of "polite interminable litigation" (p. 165). By creating fragile glass vases with the "crucibles and retorts" he brought back from Europe, he escaped from creating himself and facing the reality of his situation and his excessive attachment to Narcissa: an almost perfect vase he apostrophized and called by his sister's name as "Thou still unravished bride of quietness" (p. 182). Horace released himself from Narcissa only by yielding to seduction by Belle Mitchell and accepting the role in which she cast him (p. 194). Knowing "the sad fecundity of the world and time's hopeful unillusion that fools itself" when Belle said she wanted to have his child (p. 195), he chose to be entrapped, to break up the marriage of the Mitchells and marry the mercenary Belle who could drown him "in a motionless and cloying sea" (p. 257). At least he and Belle had no child, but unfortunately Horace's feeling for his stepdaughter, Little Belle, as she grew older was not purely paternal, although his remarks in a letter to Narcissa soon after his marriage sound proper (p. 353).

Panthea Broughton cited Horace and Belle, Ellen and Sutpen, and Joanna Burden as using "role playing to escape themselves; they feel that, by playing a role, they may lapse out of their own personal identities." Horace as the one with secure status and at least reasonably normal family background is the least excusable for this Sartrean "bad faith," as Broughton defined role playing. In *Sartoris* Horace was an unauthentic, dependent, irresponsible person combining bourgeois conformism and romantic idealism in behavior that even when rejecting conventional standards, as in his affair and marriage with Belle, lacks honest feeling and deliberate, responsible choice. Devlin discussed the failure of Belle as wife and mother in *Sartoris* and the consequent problems of Little Belle.

A far more detailed account of Horace and Narcissa in *Flags in the Dust* eliminates any ambiguities concerning their inner life and their attitudes toward others. Horace's affair with Belle's sister Joan, "a lady tiger in a tea gown," is not even mentioned in *Sartoris*. Horace's relations with all women, including his mother, Narcissa, and Little Belle, are explicitly presented in his thoughts and dreams. Faulkner's concern over these moral and psychological problems is particularly apparent in his dwelling on them in *Flags in the Dust* beyond the limits of artistic effectiveness.

In *Flags in the Dust*, Narcissa's reactions to John and Bayard Sartoris are developed more fully, with an addition of three pages after the break on page 75 in *Sartoris* (*FD* 65-67). The fact that she is both attracted to and repelled by violence is evident in incidents she remembered. The repeated use of inanimate objects to symbolize Narcissa, such as the vase Horace made, is to "attempt exclusion from human ravishment," as Broughton said, "and to accomplish instead exclusion from human bliss." Horace's admiration of Narcissa's serenity and his idealization of her as the pure virgin clad in white created for her a role she delighted to play to conceal her true self and her motives, not only her gratification with the mash notes Byron Snopes, the voyeur, sent her, unsigned, which made her keep them instead of destroying them as Aunt Jenny advised, but also her pursuit of Bayard as the substitute for the dead Johnny, using Aunt Jenny as a means of access to Sartoris. When she found that she had lost her ascendancy over Horace, there was antagonism and desperation and hopelessness in her look (pp. 255–

56). The image Horace created which provided her role was the traditional one of the Southern Lady as described by Anne Scott, based on the accepted belief "that only men and depraved women were sexual creatures and that pure women were incapable of erotic feeling." She readily accepted the idealization because women expected to be formed by men's hands before being put on a pedestal. The fact that these were the ideals of the nineteenth century made no difference to Horace and Narcissa in the twentieth.

The presence of both Narcissa Sartoris and Temple Drake in *Sanctuary* is another instance of the similarity–dissimilarity Broughton noted. They were sisters under the skin, like a white widow spider and a Venus' flytrap. Horace had to pay for choosing another female to dominate him. After leaving his wife in Kinston, not because of what she was but because she ate shrimp, he came face to face with evil, in Popeye. The opening scene, so placed in the revision of the galleys shown in Gerald Langford's collation, is one of the most existential confrontations in Faulkner. Each man is acutely aware of the Other as they face each other across the spring. Popeye with his death-like mask and eyes like rubber knobs viewing Horace with hostility.

After the weak, capricious choice which brought him back to Jefferson, Horace made an authentic and crucial choice, to defend the innocent Lee Goodwin against the charge of murder: thus he sought to defend himself after the forty-three-year apprenticeship of his soul (p. 272). But Horace's experience as a lawyer in *Flags in the Dust* makes it perfectly clear that he was totally unqualified to defend anyone in a criminal case. As Goodwin's lawyer, Horace attempted to counteract the forces of convention and respectability which he realized were not promoting justice. His appalled recognition of the logical pattern of evil and of the self-deception in his feeling for Little Belle contributed to his failure. The danger of his choice to defend Goodwin and thus to oppose the legal system, represented by the district attorney with political ambitions and Judge Drake, is dramatized in a completely new episode in the published version. In the galleys, Horace went back to Kinston and wrote to Narcissa, saying he was putting the case in the hands of "the best criminal lawyer" he could find—what he should have done in the first place. In the book, Goodwin was found guilty of killing Tommy but was lynched by burning for raping Temple. He was innocent of both crimes. Horace was a witness of the lynching until he lost consciousness. He later returned to Kinston.

A previous scene was strangely prophetic of Sartre. When he returned from seeing Temple in Memphis at Miss Reba's and hearing her story of what happened to her at the Old Frenchman place, he looked at a photograph of Little Belle: her image merged with that of Temple and his realization of the evil and injustice in the world built up to a climax in his sudden awareness of the self-deception in his feeling for Little Belle: he was violently nauseated and envisioned a girl bound to a flatcar going through a tunnel. Sartre's *La Nausée*, which was based on his own experience in the 'thirties, was published in 1938. No doubt it was what Hazel Barnes had in mind when she wrote, "according to the existentialists, man discovers his Being in anguish and nausea."

The other cause for Horace's failure was the actions of Narcissa: sacrificing people to conventionality, the living present to the dead past, Narcissa revealed the true nature behind the serene mask. With cold selfishness and irresponsibility she encouraged the attentions of the callow Gowan and then insultingly rejected him. She hounded the suffering Ruby, devoted to Lee and to her baby, from every decent haven. She caused Horace to lose his case and return to his loveless marriage. But Horace was partly to blame for Narcissa's faults: he created the image she adopted and was too bemused with a shallow idealism to perceive the reality. The visit Narcissa made to the district attorney provides a perfect example of the "look" at the "Other" as a "Thing": "again she put that cold, still, unfathomable gaze upon him as though he were a dog or a cow and she waited for it to get out of her path" (p. 257). His expression "when he found himself facing Narcissa across the desk in his dingy office . . . was like that when he had put the forty-two dollars into the pot" in a legendary poker game (p. 256). Since he used the information she provided to further his career, not to further justice, he was guilty of the same sin she was, but was not betraying trust and love. Broughton commented on the lack of relationship between legality and justice. Faulknerian characters, she said, "confuse law with justice, propriety with morality, or the literal terms of an agreement with the intent. They grant full reality status to procedure alone."

Gowan Stevens in *Sanctuary* is fully unauthentic. Vain, irresponsible, he ran away in rage and shame and left Temple at the Old Frenchman place: though the world appeared "as a black cul-de-sac," "the prospect of facing Temple again was more than he could bear" (p. 83). In the blindness of self-deception he wrote to Narcissa: "I have injured no one save myself by my folly" (p. 126). Gowan's reform and his "magnanimous" action in marrying Temple, for which he demanded unlimited gratitude, were followed by a life so conventional by country-club–set standards, as it is described in *Requiem for a Nun*, that he seems more sober, rather than more authentic. Gavin Stevens postulates the greater integrity of Red's blackmailing, wife-stealing brother (p. 170).

Popeye appears to be the inhuman extreme of unauthenticity: voyeur, sadist, fearful of all that is natural, enemy of all who did not yield to his domination, he accepted death unperturbed because he had never really lived. The story of Popeye's life which Faulkner added to the galleys makes clear that he was born with abnormalities which caused his psychopathic personality. From insensitivity he passed into oblivion when he was executed for a crime he did not commit. But the next most terrifying character in *Sanctuary*, according to Cleanth Brooks, was Narcissa, "with her quiet and efficient ruthlessness."

Yoknapatawpha reflects social history: the time of action in *Sanctuary*, 1929 or 1930, was a period which James Gustafson described as a turning point in Protestant Christian ethics as a response to social crisis on the part of both Catholics and Protestants who were "fundamentally interested in morals" and made an issue of prohibition. Popeye and Lee Goodwin were brought to Yoknapatawpha by the profits available to bootleggers. The choice of many leading citizens to defy national law may have been an expression of free will but it fostered crime. In Mississippi, prohibition lasted until after Faulkner's death, supported paradoxically by the clergy to promote sobriety and by the law officials, paid off by bootleggers. The existence of Lee Goodwin's group at the Old Frenchman place and the presence there of Gowan and Temple would not be realistic at other times.

Temple Drake is of course the central figure in *Sanctuary*, but she must be considered as she appears in both *Sanctuary* and *Requiem for a Nun*. Not only does the latter shed light, through Temple's own words, on her motives and actions in *Sanctuary* but the two works, viewed existentially, lead from the extreme of unauthenticity to the threshold, it seems, of authentic choice. The central pattern of Temple's actions in *Sanctuary* is her deliberate choice of evil and her irresponsible flight from the consequences afterward. She deliberately chose wrong when she got off the train, but she repeated, until it became a mocking refrain on the lips of the town boys, "My father's a judge" (p. 30). As Panthea Broughton observed, Gowan's parallel formula was being a Virginia gentleman (which meant being able to hold his liquor). And both had to face "the inefficacy of their codes." Aware of being the object of masculine stares, she accepted that role by her "taut-toothed coquetry" (p. 47). Otherwise her eyes are usually described as blank. As she left for Memphis, Temple looked at Ruby, her face "like a small, dead-colored mask," with no sign of recognition: Ruby was not even a thing (p. 100). Temple's constant use of her mirror is the obverse of her blank gaze at the world and at others to whom she was not an object of desire. The fantasies which she told Horace were other attempts to escape the consequences of her provocative rashness. She not only used others as a means to her ends—her father and brothers, the whole conventional society of Jefferson—and allowed Lee and Ruby to be sacrificed on the altar of her "innocence" but also allowed herself to be used by Popeye, both to gratify his perverse tastes and to protect him from the consequences of his guilt. Dr. Kubie suggested that the death of the only potent men, Lee Goodwin and Red, might be explained as a revenge "on those who had not harmed her, but who are essentially normal in their masculinity," and that she hated her father and "her four stalwart brothers" enough to take revenge on "all . . . men who are really men."

The degree to which Temple was a free agent and therefore responsible for her choices and the consequences is apparent only in *Requiem for a Nun*: what the reader could only guess at in *Sanctuary* is confirmed. Because *Requiem for a Nun* is in dramatic form with prologues which cover Yoknapatawpha from the creation, which it must have shared with Jackson with its "gilded pustule" (p. 99), it cannot be dealt with in the same way as the novels. Stanley Elkin dealt with the rituals of false witness and confession in *Sanctuary* and *Requiem*. The false witness of Temple's perjury dooms her to damnation, but the confession Gavin seeks to obtain from her could lead to salvation.

In "Eschatological Thought in Faulkner's Yoknapatawpha Novels," Mary Culley deals with *Requiem for a Nun* under "Judgment" and "Heaven." The judgment to be rendered is that of Temple; Nancy has confessed and has faith in her salvation.

The courtroom setting, Culley said, is the "metaphor for the judgment": "*Requiem* dramatizes the working out of the consequences of the choices Temple made in *Sanctuary*." The uncle of Temple's husband, Gowan, Gavin Stevens by his questioning succeeds in eliciting significant truths from Temple: she admits that she was responsible for Nancy's execution from the time she "got on the train at the University" (*RN* 209); that she could have saved herself; that she chose Popeye, the murderer, instead of saving Goodwin by telling the truth (pp. 139–42); that she liked evil (p. 135). She admits also that she committed perjury to escape the consequences of her actions (p. 128).

As father-confessor, Gavin Stevens provides the existential crisis: by seeking the truth, he is determined to force Temple to face her past and to see herself without deception. Not only Gavin and Nancy use traditional Christian concepts and terminology but also Temple, with self-irony: "So good can come out of evil!" (p. 208); "for the good of my soul!" (p. 90). Gavin asserts the power of truth and love; Nancy affirms the power of suffering and faith. Faulkner leaves the salvation of Temple problematic; she lacks Nancy's faith, and even if she could "believe" by willpower, one doubts her capacity for attaining belief. Albert Devlin found something compulsive about Temple's recurring rebellions and was not convinced that she had reformed and was redeemed. Mary Culley stressed the significance of Faulkner's insight that "we become our choices": when Temple chose the murderer, she became the murderer of her own child.

In *Absalom, Absalom!* the boy Thomas Sutpen showed marked characteristics of authenticity when he encountered a look that reduced him to an object: "he stood there before that white door with the monkey nigger barring it and looking down on him in his patched made-over jeans and no shoes" (p. 232). Morris Beja cites this experience of Sutpen's as the "single epiphany" which "brings about all the subsequent events of his life and thus forms the basis of the entire novel." Nowhere in even the most existentialist of fiction could a "look" have more far-reaching consequences.

Sutpen's logical premiss, that if he wanted to be equal to the plantation owner he must have comparable possessions, revealed his complete lack of cultural traditions acquired, like the aristocrat's treasure, through generations. The "truths of the heart" to which conscience responds have no cash value and cannot be subdued by logical reasoning. Sutpen's weakness was not "innocence" but ignorance: he had no way of knowing the depths of his ignorance. As Donald Foran put it, "Sutpen had embraced a form, believing that he had acquired its substance." And conversely, the community was horrified by him because of his "naked version of its own deepest principles." General Compson could listen to Sutpen but could not convey to him the best aspects of a tradition within which Sutpen had never lived and which money could not buy. Nor did Sutpen envision the other pattern which unwittingly he was fashioning in the American tradition: Stanley Elkin described Sutpen as the classic example of the "Self Made Man." But he destroyed himself by imitating the evil of the society he aspired to: the evil of the closed society, the closed door, the "wonderfully functional symbol," as Elkin said, "of the inelasticity of Southern society."

Amazingly, Sutpen created a new self, a self with force and dignity, and created Sutpen's Hundred in the wilderness as the foundation for his future and for his dynasty. By his marriage to Ellen Coldfield he bought the necessary respectability. Anne Scott's *The Southern Lady* might have served him as a text: "The weakness and dependence of women was thrown into bold relief" by her husband's "virility and mastery of his environment."

Sutpen well exemplified Broughton's comment that "man wants to believe . . . that other human beings will react within the roles assigned them according to established rules" and no doubt considered Ellen a proof of the principle. If we discount Miss Rosa's obviously prejudiced account and rely chiefly on Mr. Compson's version of the town tradition and on his father's personal knowledge of Sutpen, we see Sutpen as he arrived in Jefferson, ready to begin to realize his design: "his pale eyes had a quality at once visionary and alert, ruthless and reposed" (p. 33). Acting in the existential pattern of "self-generated action" toward freely chosen goals, in Olafson's terms, the willpower required would encourage ruthlessness and the design itself was a vision to be created into reality.

Sutpen's basic unauthenticity is that of using people as means, not as ends, of denying human beings their human dignity, precisely the sin that forced Sutpen to go to earth and emerge reborn (pp. 233–34). They all had to pay for his humiliation: the Negroes he brought to Jefferson and used to build Sutpen's Hundred, the females being subjected to his lust; the French architect, kept a prisoner and hunted like an animal when he escaped; Coldfield, whom he contrived to use "to further whatever secret ends he still had" (p. 43); Ellen, the mother of his children, essential to his design and his respectability but never treated as a person; Rosa, outraged, and Milly, scorned—all were merely instruments in his grand design. And before and above all, the first wife, provided for and put aside as not "adjunctive or incremental to the design," and her son Charles, turned away from the door more cruelly by his father than ever young Sutpen was turned away by a strange servant, are the discarded instruments.

Sutpen made a series of choices, based upon the authentic concept of "freedom's bright aura" which was his poor-white heritage. He chose to build a career for himself; he chose to marry and to put aside that wife and begin his design anew; he presumably chose to reject Charles Bon, not knowing that by doing so he would lose his legitimate son and heir; presumably he chose to tell Henry the truth that would cause Henry to kill Charles, thus losing one son by death and the other a second time in flight as a fugitive from justice; he chose to try a third time, without marriage, to produce a male heir. Except the first choice which, at Supen's then tender age, could not clearly entail specific means, each choice involved the same violation of human dignity which precipitated an existential crisis in the boy and drove him to define and create himself.

Sutpen's innocence was not innocence in existential terms; it is rather, in Sartre's terms, the Fall: "The problem of freedom is placed on the level of Adam's choice of himself." Sutpen's innocence was an attempt, through spiritual blindness, to be as a god without seeing that he was naked, without recognizing good and evil and seeing his guilt before all the Others:

> I am guilty first when beneath the Other's look I experience my alienation and nakedness as a fall from grace which I must assume. This is the meaning of the famous line from Scripture: "They knew they were naked." Again I am guilty when in turn I look at the Other, because of the very fact of my own self-assertion I constitute him as an object which he must assume. Thus original sin is my upsurge in a world where there are others; and whatever may be my further relations with others, these relations will only be variations on the original theme of guilt.

The guilt is compounded by the denial of it.

The other members of Sutpen's family fall into different patterns of authenticity or inauthenticity, but none of them follows a code of cold logic like Sutpen's, excluding the irrational and the emotional. Through courage and fortitude and responsibility Judith acquired a calm, impenetrable mask which was a symbol of her acceptance and endurance; her sense of duty made her reject the idea of suicide (p. 128). Lawrence Dembo regarded her survival after Bon's death as manifesting her will to endure. Her death manifested her will to save others: she nursed Charles Etienne when he had yellow fever, caught it from him and died before he did, when she was still in her mid-forties. Freedom was an illusion to Judith, who was always bound by duty. She pictured human beings as puppets trying to weave their own patterns into the rug and getting their strings entangled: "it can't matter, you know that, or the Ones that set up the loom would have arranged things better, and yet it must matter because you keep on trying or having to keep on trying . . ." (p. 127).

Henry rejected truth in repudiating his heritage and choosing Bon instead. His choice to give himself and Judith to Bon, of his own free will (p. 328), is conjectural. His final choice, to kill Bon, is presumably based upon the taboo against miscegenation, a tradition which violates human dignity, although he had apparently waived the more universal taboo against incest. The last look with which Henry regarded Bon was one in which the Other was the victim. Henry was unauthentic both in trying uncritically to preserve one tradition, racism, after critically rejecting the more universal taboo against incest, and in sacrificing others as well as himself by murder and by subsequent flight, and by his ultimate return to be a secret prisoner.

Knowledge of Charles Bon's motives is too conjectural to permit more than speculation. He may have sought self-definition in seeking a father. He may have loved Judith enough to risk and give his life for her. We do know enough about his son to recognize a strongly existential pattern: there is a definite similarity between Charles Etienne Bon and Joe Christmas. Charles Etienne's reaction to the doom of his black blood was to deny his white blood. Lonely, sullen, inscrutable, implacable, he married a very black, animalistic woman after episodes of violence, of "furious protest" and "indomitable desperation" which were "an indictment of heaven's ordering" (p. 202). He decreed and created his own Gethsemane and crucified himself in protest against the alienation forced upon him (p. 209). In so doing he acted significantly: as the mirror of the Southern image of the Negro, he reflected authentically the unauthentic status to which he was doomed. Rejected by society, he rejected himself; denied a future, he fathered an idiot for whom there could be no future. He met hate with hate. The transformation from Bon, the good, to Bond, the enslaved, was the ultimate consequence of Sutpen's grand design and the tradition upon which it was founded. The course followed by Charles Etienne resembles the "heroic negativity" by which "existentialism displays the limits of rebellion, defiance, and perversity," to quote Kingsley Widmer in "The Existential Darkness: Richard Wright's *The Outsider*." Charles Etienne was like Wright's hero in taking "the path of demonic purgation" required by the quest for the authentic.

The three Coldfields present interesting contrasts. Ellen, wife of Sutpen, patterned her life after the conventions of her social status and retreated into a world of pure illusion, "a shadowy miasmic region" in which Judith was a daughter to arrange a marriage for and Charles Bon was "one inanimate object for which she and her family would find three concordant uses: a garment which Judith might wear as she would a riding habit or a ball gown, a piece of furniture which would complement and complete the furnishing of her house and position, and a mentor and example to correct Henry's provincial manners and clothing" (p. 75). Coldfield was a man of inflexible moral strength, deviating from his principles only in whatever deal he entered into with Sutpen. He freed his Negroes, refused to sell to secessionists, and finally nailed himself into his own attic and died there. He illustrated the existential crisis described by Arturo Fallico: "when the world collapses around the existing man" and, freedom of choice being impossible without flight, "in the desperate need to be himself against all the pretense and the lying, he utters to himself the honest though frenzied and mad word, rejecting existence itself as unbearable hell."

Rosa Coldfield is the most fully presented character, largely as self-revealed. Her life of loneliness and uselessness was sustained by her outrage for forty years. She need not have been either lonely or idle had she been willing to learn skills and to help others when every able-bodied woman was needed. She was not only nursing her wrath to keep it warm but she was clinging to the ante-bellum image of the white lady when there was money for neither food nor hired help. No doubt her image of herself as an instrument of retribution sustained her: one of the most unauthentic patterns, in which the individual renounces freedom and regards himself as a thing. In her impassioned self-defense to Quentin and her disingenuous account of her acceptance of Sutpen's proposal, she conceals her choice: to be used by the "demon" in return for status and security. Lawrence Dembo commented on Rosa's transferal of her antipathy toward her father to Sutpen. Although Dembo was correct in saying that Ellen's plea that Rosa protect Judith and Henry was the only recognition she ever received, the plea was absurd, Rosa being younger than they and having chosen to be useless. Dembo credited Rosa's denial of Sutpen as the cause of his death. But she probably would not have had a son.

Mr. Compson suggests that Rosa, the outraged and the unforgiving, may have "*gained that place or bourne where the objects of the outrage and the commiseration also are no longer ghosts but actual people to be actual recipients of the hatred and the pity*" (p. 377). Quentin's vision of Sutpen and Wash Jones in that same bourne, under the scuppernong vine, a companion piece for Mr. Compson's, adds one final character who ended a life of indolent acceptance of tradition by one authentic act of assertion of human rights: Wash Jones avenged all the victims of Sutpen's violation of human dignity. He voiced the protest for all who were silent: "*Better if his kind and mine too had never drawn the breath of life on this earth. Better that all who remain of us be blasted from the face of it than that another Wash Jones should see his whole life shredded from him and shrivel away like a dried shuck thrown into the fire*" (pp. 290–91).

As Wash's thoughts ended, he heard the dogs and horses and saw the lanterns. De Spain heard Wash say, "Hit wont need no light, honey. Hit wont need no light." And then "he was running toward them all"; "he ran with the scythe above his head, straight into the lanterns and the gun barrels" (p. 292). In "the most magnificent gesture in the novel," as Robert Slabey said, Wash repeated the gesture which preceded his murder of Sutpen, like old Father Time. Slabey continued with comments on the "violent, destructive, disastrous, and suicidal" acts in the novel and defined Faulkner as a realist: "Faulkner implicitly affirms man's existential integrity as being free to choose good or evil." Sutpen's choice was "to perpetuate not love, which could transcend self and death, but ruthless and egotistical pride."

To that pride, from his earliest choices, Sutpen sacrificed two wives, two sons, two daughters, and Rosa and Milly. The irony of the title is that Sutpen uttered no words of grief for either son, not even when Judith told him Henry had shot Bon, and shed no tears (p. 159). Mary Culley observed that Sutpen sowed seeds of death from the beginning. Wash Jones, from roots like Sutpen's, executed judgment upon him, and the final destruction of his design was an apocalypse of fire and smoke.

In *Absalom, Absalom!* Sutpen was a father figure to Quentin. There is no hint in the events of September 1909, when Quentin heard the Sutpen story from Miss Rosa and his father, or of January 1910, when Quentin and Shreve reconstructed it to give love a place in it, that Quentin would drown himself in the Charles River in June. Quentin's love–hate feeling toward the South, revealed in his last words to Shreve, is inadequate as a motive for his suicide. Why Faulkner did not follow his usual method of reminding the reader that Yoknapatawpha was a cosmos and encouraging him to remember one book when reading another, as he did in *Sartoris* and *Sanctuary*, remains a mystery. Had the narrator device been used exclusively, one could understand why there is no hint in *Absalom, Absalom!* that Quentin had a sister, much less that he was obsessed by her. But the narrative was broken both by passages given to Quentin's thoughts and by the author's unobtrusive comments and explanations, in either of which information about the rest of the Compson family could have been given. Most puzzling is the fact that in revision, as Gerald Langford's collation of the manuscript and the published book and his comments indicate, Faulkner eliminated most of Shreve's recital, substituting a presentation of the events through several shifts to Quentin's reverie. But Caddy did not enter Quentin's thoughts even when his father's interpretation of Henry and Judith applied to Quentin and Caddy. There was no upsurge of suppressed memories as in *The Sound and the Fury*. In *Doublings and Incest | Repetition and Revenge,* John Irwin ignored the lack of textual evidence for his statement that "there can be no question that Quentin reconstructs the story of Bon, Henry and Judith in light of his own experience." To treat the two books about Quentin as "a structural whole" makes such good sense that Irwin is justified in pretending that Faulkner built a two-way bridge between them, but not in assuming that Faulkner expected readers of one book to be familiar with the other. Since our concern here is with choices and actions for which there is external evidence, Irwin's psychological analysis we must forgo. Obviously Quentin in *The Sound and the Fury* cannot be influenced by the Sutpen story, and equally obviously Faulkner did not expect the reader to graft onto the Sutpen story all that is learned about the Compsons.

In *Absalom, Absalom!* Quentin is already so bound by the past that he has no probable future: he is a ghost, who has heard too much too often, to whom the past is more vivid than the present. Unlike those characters who try to escape from and deny the past, he is so entangled in the past that he thinks *"Maybe nothing ever happens and is finished. Maybe happen is never once but like ripples . . ."* (p. 261). The two children of Sutpen are relevant to Quentin's sense of involvement; he and Shreve, in their reconstruction of the story, stress the incestuous love of Henry for Judith and his homosexual love for Charles Bon. A "look" between Quentin and Shreve confirms the implications of their identification with Henry and Charles: ". . . they looked at one another . . . not at all as two young men might look at each other but almost as a youth and a very young girl might out of virginity itself—a sort of hushed and naked searching . . ." (p. 299). A similar suggestion occurs later (p. 324). The thoughts attributed, presumably in Quentin's mind, to Henry because of the incest anticipate Quentin's image of himself and Caddy in Hell (*SF* 135), a parallel "acceptance of eternal damnation" because of "the irrevocable repudiation of the old heredity and training" (*AA* 347).

Quentin's sense of being a ghost and his identification with young men of the past suggest his obsession with time in *The Sound and the Fury*. His attempt to forget time is symbolized by his twisting the hands off his watch after remembering his father's remark about forgetting time now and then and not spending all his breath "trying to conquer it" (pp. 102, 93).

Patricia Tobin explains "the structure of a genealogical novel" as committing the novelist "to a definition of individual identity through its familial connections, and to an elaboration of time as the continuity between an inheritance and a legacy." She regarded Quentin's suicide in *The Sound and the Fury* as "a swerve away from genealogical destiny," explained *post factum* by the Sutpen story. But in his last day on earth Quentin was only too aware of the passing of time, marked by clocks and watches and by natural phenomena.

Quentin's unauthenticity is apparent as soon as we realize that, in living toward death and using the present to remember the past and prepare for death, Quentin is rejecting the other half of the "story of the contingency and transiency of our being" as stated by Fallico: "We live also in expectation, waiting for something which is not death, but the fulfillment of life itself: We live enduring every *now* for the sake of a future which, like a mirage, is ever receding from view." Quentin denies the basic principle of authenticity as stated by Robert Olson: "To be free is to be under the necessity of transcending one's past." The passing of time and the changes it brings, the changes in which man has an opportunity to transcend his past, are precisely what Quentin rejects: the wound of his love for Caddy and her loss of virtue must not be healed. Before he goes to the river, his last memory is of his father's remarks about suicide: a man "does it only when he has realized that even the despair or remorse or bereavement is not particularly important to the dark diceman" (p. 221). The word "temporary" is a sad refrain through this remembered conversation: the unendurable thought, to Quentin, is that "someday it will no longer hurt . . . like this." The conversation in Quentin's thoughts ends thus: "i temporary it will be better for me for all of us and he every man is the arbiter of his own virtues but let no man prescribe for another mans wellbeing and i temporary and he was the saddest word of all there is nothing else in the world its not despair until time its not even time until it was" (pp. 221–22).

"Every man is the arbiter of his own virtues" has an existential ring, but in the context it means merely that Mr. Compson is evading responsibility for what his young son does, who has been brought up on Mr. Compson's nihilistic philosophy. Life is a gamble with the dark diceman, in which "no battle is ever won. . . . The field only reveals to man his own folly and despair, and victory is an illusion of philosophers and fools" (p. 93). Quentin summarized the concepts he learned from his father: "Father was teaching us that all men are just accumulations dolls stuffed with sawdust swept up from the trash heaps where all previous dolls have been thrown away the sawdust flowing from what wound in what side that not for me died not" (p. 218). The nihilistic concepts of Quentin and his father are in harmony with the title, voiced but meaningless in Benjy's screams when Luster turned the horse to the left at the monument (p. 400). But Faulkner was no idiot: he would have agreed with a character in Vercors' *You Shall Know Them*, as quoted by Hazel Barnes: "Humanity is not a state we suffer. It's a dignity we must strive to win. A dignity full of pain and sorrow. Won, no doubt, at the price of tears. . . . But now I know, I know that all this isn't 'a tale told by an idiot, signifying nothing.' "

Into his father's nihilism Quentin introduced the fire-and-brimstone idea of a family curse: He said to Caddy, "There's a curse on us its not our fault is it our fault?" (p. 196). Either concept allows him to avoid a sense of responsibility, and not without justification in the deficiencies of his parents and his upbringing by the Compsons. Dilsey did her best but Quentin was not responsive: he realized "that a nigger is not a person so much as a form of behavior; a sort of obverse reflection of the white people he lives among" (p. 106). In his vision of the captives in the dungeon, his father and mother are in a weak light and the children are "lost somewhere below even them without even a ray of light" (p. 215). Amos Wilder saw in the Compson son Quentin "the prenatal history, as it were, of later giant traumas and obsessions; the inculcation of social and racial distortions; the inbreeding of desiccated feudal-Christian survivals."

Quentin's vision of himself and Caddy in hell "*amid the pointing and the horror beyond the clean flame*" (p. 144) and his plunge into the river represent hell and death: Culley interpreted his suicide as the archetypal image of the sex act and its form of death. After the apocalyptic Easter service, the weekly journey to the cemetery is ironic, Benjy being the uncomprehending participant, with an addiction to graveyards because death is an ever-present reality to the Compsons who have wasted their lives and lack Dilsey's faith.

Quentin's choice of death involves two alternative concepts, hell and the clean flame with Caddy forever or peace and escape from evil. It is a moot point whether his suicide is an act of courage, as he believed and his father conceded as a possibility, or a piece of self-deception like his idea that if the world believed he had committed incest "it would have been so" (p. 220). Lawrence Dembo pointed out that Benjy and Quentin had similar dominant images and conflicts, Quentin being intellectual and moral and Benjy emotional and moral. They both tried to keep Caddy from growing up. Having failed in that endeavor, Quentin stopped his own clock because he could not stop time. Although Michael Routh limited his study of Yoknapatawpha cosmology chiefly to *Light in August*, he used the term "Quentin's disease." "The test consists of whether a particular character can remain true to, and hence follow, the call of the natural, intrinsic life-conducing powers within. . . . If he can, his Life-Force will achieve fulfillment." If not, he will become afflicted with "Quentin's disease," "in which the life-drives are inverted and the sick soul quests not for life but for death." The quest for death is the depth of unauthenticity.

Quentin's awareness of others and theirs of him is emphasized by the repeated "looks," most frequent in the sequence in the present with the little girl who is a substitute sister (pp. 155–65), and in the memory sequence into which the present reality "fades," recalling Caddy at the branch and Quentin's conflict with Dalton Ames (pp. 185–202), and ending with Dalton metamorphosed into Gerald Bland. The little girl's gaze, variously *black, friendly, still,* and *inscrutable,* showed more perception of Quentin that did his memory images of Caddy. With Quentin's knife at her throat, Caddy had "her eyes wide open looking past my head at the sky" (p. 189). When Quentin asked Caddy if she loved Dalton Ames, "she looked at me and then everything emptied out of her eyes and they looked like the eyes in the statues blank and unseeing and serene" (p. 202). Julio's "Italian face and his eyes" impressed Quentin as Julio sprang upon him; Dalton Ames's "look" is unqualified, as with forbearance tinged with contempt he first tried to avoid fighting and then demonstrated his superiority to Quentin. The fact that this memory was so long suppressed and then blocked out reality suggests that part of Quentin's self-deception is his failure to admit to himself the significance of this memory, which shows that he was not the kind of man who could attract Caddy and that he was utterly incapable of playing a protective role as her older brother. His suicide may thus have been not only a protest against the healing power of time but an indication of his inability to transcend his limitations, an inability confirmed by his fight with Gerald which re-enacted his fight with Dalton (p. 204).

In a meaningless world, obsessed by the past and lacking desire and will to face the future which would be a losing gamble with the dark diceman, Quentin ended his shadowy life in the river. His suicide was the final unauthentic choice—an abdication of responsibility, a denial of freedom, an act of bad faith. (But he waited until the end of the college year to get the full value of his paid-in-advance tuition" [Appendix, p. 411].) As Hazel Barnes said, in reference to Simone de Beauvoir, "We are equally wrong if we give up the struggle for innocence or if we seek to evade that guilt which is inseparable from the human condition." In *The Tragic Vision in Twentieth-Century Literature*, Charles Glicksberg cites Quentin as a nihilist hero who often has nothing to live for and takes his own life; he quotes some of Mr. Compson's disillusioning views which gave Quentin "a vision. . . of a life that is without meaning and beyond redemption." In the chapter "Existentialism and the Tragic Vision," dealing with Sartre, Glicksberg emphasized that "Existentialism calls man to take up a life of authentic striving," but "the freedom he cherishes is freedom in the face of death."

The cause of Quentin's suicide and of Caddy's promiscuity is the lack of agreement of their parents on how to rear children. Mr. and Mrs. Compson led unauthentic lives. Mr. Compson's nihilism and his idea that "no live or dead man is very much better than any other live or dead man" (p. 125) made him abandon his responsibilities and drink himself to death. Mrs. Compson lacked sensitivity and understanding and really cared for none of her children but Jason. Her unfeeling refusal to let Caddy's name be spoken was partly responsible for Mr. Compson's lapsing into dipsomania, as her rigid conventionality had been responsible for Caddy's disastrous marriage and for the harsh and loveless upbringing of Miss Quentin that ruined her as Caddy had been. Incompetent to care for her own family, a self-indulgent hypochondriac, a hypocrite whose morality was limited to concealing sin and refusing to know about wickedness, Mrs. Compson represents the callous emptiness of those who pay lip service to the old values but are weak, cold, selfish, and irresponsible. Mr. Compson's decanter and Mrs. Compson's camphor-soaked cloth and hot-water bottle symbolize, existentially speaking, escape from responsibility.

The faults of the parents of the Compson children Robert Caserio diagnosed as Mr. Compson's distrust of authority and refusal to exercise his own and Mrs. Compson's determination to control her children by rigid rules. They represent a kind of perversion and parody of Southern ideals. Mr. Compson showed the proper respect for a lady, even to sending Quentin to Harvard to gratify Mrs. Compson's pride. By denying Quentin the affirmative advice and even punishment Quentin sought and needed, Mr. Compson turned the Harvard venture into a disaster. Mrs. Compson and Jason, as Broughton observed, regarded only the code of propriety as real: dinner with Jason at the head of the table represents what Mrs. Compson wanted. The fact that Caddy and Miss Quentin are ruined by Mrs. Compson's and Jason's treatment is evidence of the unauthenticity of their principles, a kind of "save the surface and you save all" policy. Herbert Head was hoodwinked into marrying Caddy to give her child a name, and Jason stole the money Caddy sent for Miss Quentin, but took pride in the public image he created of paternal responsibility. Mrs. Compson "raised the children" and "set the standards for behavior" as Anne Scott's "Southern Lady" was expected to, and Mr. Compson, having granted her "the custody of conscience and morality," had discovered that she applied it "to inordinate addiction to alcohol" which, along with his nihilism, completed his abdication of paternal authority. Caserio decided that Faulkner was "philoprogenitive" in the concern he showed, in plot and story, for "the formation of children, for their growth and development."

Jason as a parody of the *paterfamilias* is both comic and distressing. He is an ironic reversal of the authentic type which responsibly chooses acceptable ends in a meaningful world. Ostentatiously he supports the family, preserves family unity, observes the conventions, and outwardly is a good son and solid citizen. But he reveals himself, and quotes others to the same effect, as having a cold heart and no conscience. His detestation of hypocrisy is the height of his own hypocrisy: "If there's one thing gets under my skin, it's a damn hypocrite" (p. 285). He shows scorn and contempt for everyone, including his mother, except his mistress, Lorraine, and for her he lays down rigid rules. He is motivated by vengeance against Caddy and the family for his not getting the position in the bank promised him by Caddy's husband and for being given no opportunity like Quentin's. He takes sadistic delight in torturing others, from making the family go through the motions of a happy family meal to burning the passes to the show in front of Luster. His anti-Semitism and contempt for Negroes is predictable unauthenticity.

Judging by Benjy's replays of incidents in their childhood, one can say of Jason "the child is father of the man," and with even more assurance can say "like mother, like son." In *The Faraway Country*, Louis Rubin's statement about Jason concludes his account of *The Sound and the Fury* as "a story of moral and spiritual collapse": "only Jason survives in Yoknapatawpha County, and the price he pays for survival in the modern world is to lose all attributes of honor, virtue, and kindness, and to become a vicious, materialistic scoundrel." I would change two words: "lose" and "become." He imbibed the necessary qualities for survival with his mother's milk, figuratively speaking; both he and his mother could not or would not express their pattern of behavior: to "look like the innocent flower but be the serpent under't."

The "look" repeatedly conveys his hostility and suspicion. Between Jason and Miss Quentin and between Jason and Caddy, the "look" is eloquent. Pleading with Jason to use the money she sends to see that little Quentin "has things like other girls," she looks so beseechingly that even Jason felt "her eyes almost like they were touching my face" (p. 261). After Jason's veiled accusations of her and the man with the red tie, Miss Quentin looked at him with eyes "that looked like they were cornered or something"; after a second such look, she said: "If I'm bad, it's because I had to be. You made me. I wish I was dead. I wish we were all dead" (pp. 323, 324).

Jason met no one on equal terms. He deceived everyone, stealing from Miss Quentin the money Caddy sent her, buying a car with the money his mother gave him to invest in the hardware business, telling Earl lies about his absence from the store. He even deceived himself: his tone of self-satisfaction and self-congratulation for his own cleverness suggests confidence that he made a good case for himself that would favorably impress others. His one acceptable motive, a sense of responsibility for the family, is negated by the ways in which he exercised his responsibility and the hate and suspicion engendered by his sense of injustice. Responsibility for the souls of others was violated while he made a show of concern for their bodies. And even that concern will last only until he can make a killing: "And once I've done that they can bring all Beale Street and all bedlam in here and two of them can sleep in my bed and one can have my place at the table too'' (p. 309).

Benjy, of course, is not a moral character. Panthea Broughton's account of Benjy as subhuman, "immune to the agony of consciousness," stresses his inability to "abstract details." The series of images from the past and from his present serve, however, "as a kind of moral mirror," quoting Lawrance Thompson, of the Compson family. Broughton convincingly rejects the various sentimental interpretations of Benjy and supports her interpretation by quoting what Faulkner said about Benjy in the interview with Jean Stein. In the story of the Compsons, whose collapse resulted largely from living by abstract codes and impossible ideals, rejecting and destroying their own lives and the lives of Caddy and her daughter, Benjy's photographic memory and perception of the present allow the reader to arrive at moral judgments without distortion of point of view: Benjy could not even select and control images as a photographer can. Benjy's insistence on order is not a virtue: his "howling outrage indicates just how subhuman is preabstracting rigidity." Broughton arrived at a sound and useful generalization: "Faulkner's fiction offers no justification either for idealizing Benjy's incapacity for abstraction or for approving Addie Bundren's rejection of abstraction."

The only authentic character in the Compson household is Dilsey, to whom everyone, even Benjy, is a child of the Lord, and whose courage, fortitude, and patience enable her to bear the whole responsibility of the household and to provide what tenderness and love will be tolerated by the sadism of Jason and the selfishness of Mrs. Compson and the tortured misery of Miss Quentin. Dilsey is a superb example of the authentic character whose self-acceptance and responsibility are largely instinctive and non-intellectual but who is sustained by Christian faith and who faces death as a release and salvation: "En I be His'n too, fo long, praise Jesus" (p. 396). Because of her capacity for love, Dilsey accepts as a free soul a life that others might have considered bondage. "They endure" because they can accept and transcend suffering. Faulkner seemed to be in agreement with the attitude of Gabriel Marcel toward suffering, as stated by Temple Kingston: "It is through suffering and the trials of life that one can reach the heights, because through suffering one may be led into a far deeper insight into the nature of reality and to an appreciation of the suffering of others. However, to abandon oneself to suffering is to abandon oneself to absurdity."

The accolade bestowed upon Quentin's section in particular but *The*

Sound and the Fury as a whole by William Barrett is most appropriate in this context: "a masterpiece, perhaps as great as anything yet written by an American; . . . to be recommended to anyone who wants to know the concrete feel of that world with which in his thinking the existentialist philosopher has to deal."

Although William Barrett referred to the world of Quentin Compson as existential, another kind of existential world, that of the Outsiders, is depicted in *Light in August*. Martin Buber's images of two kinds of epochs in the "history of the human spirit" serve admirably to symbolize these two worlds: "epochs of habitation and epochs of homelessness. In the former, man lives in the world as in a house, as in a home. In the latter, man lives in the world as in an open field and at times does not even have four pegs to set up a tent." A purely fortuitous parallel image appears in Byron's account to Hightower of how he had provided for Lena: he had established her in the cabin where Joe and Lucas Burch had lived. He had arranged to protect her without harming her reputation: "I aint in the house with her. I got a tent. It aint close, neither. Just where I can hear her at need" (p. 297). Lena and Byron and Joe Christmas are the homeless. Jefferson represents the world as habitation. Gail Hightower and Joanna Burden are self-imprisoned in their own homes but excluded from the homes of Jefferson citizens and therefore are Outsiders like Joe and Lena and Byron.

David Eggenschwiler commented on the frequency of "displaced persons" and their significance in the fiction of Flannery O'Connor: "These displacements are important socially as manifestations of destroyed or decaying human community . . . ." Olga Vickery's comment on Joe, Joanna, and Hightower and Jefferson may be relevant also to Southern society depicted by Flannery O'Connor: these three are "the key figures"—"the Negro, the Yankee, the Apostate—. . . in a society which defines itself by exclusion." That exclusion is at the root of "The Failure of Community," the chapter on *Light in August* in Walter Sullivan's *William Faulkner and the Community*. In *The Individual and the Community Values in the Novels of William Faulkner*, Donald Kartiganer interpreted Faulkner's view of the traditional community as bound up with the "tyranny of conventionality," supported by an institutionalized religion which bred "self-righteousness and intolerance" and which tried to keep original sin in check and maintain order by suppression of individuals. It is the Outsiders whose existential predicaments and crises dominate *Light in August*.

The few characters in *Light in August* who appear in other Yoknapatawpha fiction play minor roles. The strongest tie with the rest of the chronicles is Joanna Burden's account of the murder of her grandfather and her brother by Colonel John Sartoris, related by his son Bayard in "Skirmish at Sartoris." Although Panthea Broughton's comment is true, it applies chiefly to characters who are Outsiders: "In *Light in August* a mythic mode of thought is used to divide man against man and to transfer to some power outside the human sphere the responsibility for man's own acts."

Joe Christmas is consistently portrayed in existential terms as the individual alienated from the world, lacking knowledge of his family and racial identity. In the terms Hazel Barnes used to describe Genêt, Joe chose "himself as myth rather than as freely self-creating history." *Light in August* answers Barnes's question: "Can an author write at once myth, case history, and contemporary social document?" One answer to her question was provided a few years later by William Sowder in "Christmas as Existentialist Hero" (1964). He recognized that Joe "endured the most painful suffering of all existential anguish" and that *Light in August* was Faulkner's first important contribution to existential literature and possibly a work that influenced Sartre.

Subjected as a child to the insane hostility of Doc Hines, to the scheming of the dietician at the orphanage, and to the domination of his fanatically Calvinistic foster father, McEachern, Joe grew up rootless, proud, lonely, and ruthless. François Pitavy indicated that in Joe's hopeless quest for identity and an impossible perfection he tried to maintain his own integrity and dignity. But each experience took him further from knowledge and acceptance of himself and consequently increased his alienation. By the time he arrived in Jefferson he had to cope with the sense of community in a Calvinistic racist society. Stanley Pinsley described Joe as "a dislocated particle swimming volitionless in an immense void." Had Joanna Burden not been a kind of female version of McEachern, with New England Calvinism in her heritage as well as the Southern version in her environment, Joe might not have been driven to murderous action. Paul Tillich traced the opposition between Existentialist and anti-Existentialist theology and philosophy, with particular attention to Calvinism which transformed man "into an abstract moral object": "The rational subject, moral and scientific, replaced the existential subject, his conflicts and despairs." When one considers whose grandson Joe was, his responses to environmental influences and concepts seem amazingly moderate and sane.

By the time Joe arrived in Jefferson, his attitude toward others was one of cold suspicion. After "ignoring Byron as if he were another post," Joe contemptuously refused the food Byron offered, too proud to admit that he was penniless and to be grateful (p. 31). The "look" appears as a motif most frequently in *Light in August*: there are over thirty passages in which Joe is the "looker." His look was so contemptuous that a millworker remarked, ". . . that's a pretty risky look for a man to wear on his face in public" (p. 28). Joe's look is not a means of communication—it is a barrier to communication. Because he had been used by others and had met hostility and violence, he rejected others as he rejected himself.

Joe's flight from his problems and the consequences of his action began when he fled after knocking McEachern down, leaving him unconscious and never seeking to know whether he lived or died. His second flight was parallel to the first. Joanna Burden, like McEachern, sought to make Joe fit into a pattern not of his choice, even repeating the compulsory praying that triggered Joe's homicidal violence, like a conditioned reflex, by recalling his previous rebellion against McEachern's attempt to make him deny his own nature. Before the final encounter with Joanna, Joe paced the streets of Jefferson, an alien in the white sections and in Freedmantown alike. Thus for fifteen years he had paced "a thousand streets" that "ran as one street," alienating himself if he found acceptance. When he got far enough north to find a woman who did not care when he told her he had Negro blood, he almost killed her. He thought he was fleeing from loneliness, not from himself (pp. 210–13).

In this choice of action, however, Joe seemed to succumb to a contagion of belief in God's will as determining human action: When he "rose and moved toward the house," he "didn't think even then *Something is going to happen. Something is going to happen to me*" (p. 110). And before he went to the house he had a mental preview of what he would do and what he would see and hear after he entered the house. When he sat waiting for the courthouse clock to strike, "he believed with calm paradox that he was the volitionless servant of the fatality in which he believed that he did not believe. He was saying to himself *I had to do it* already in the past tense; *I had to do it. She said so herself!*" (p. 264). After the confrontation with Joanna and her attempt to make him choose between life determined by her choices or death, he fled when her pistol did not go off and discovered it in his right hand after he had flagged a car and got out after riding a short distance. Both Joe and the sheriff found two loaded chambers; upon one the hammer had fallen without a shot and the other was still intact: " 'For her and for me' " he said (pp. 270, 281). The report of the boy and girl who gave him a ride gave no evidence of a bloody throat-cutting with a razor.

After Joe fled, streets and roads became a closed circle, the "no

exit'' of the unauthentic individual who refuses the choice of self-acceptance and self-creation. Because Joe could not transcend his past and
build toward a future, his choice was negative. At the end of the narrative which presents Joe directly, there are signs of authenticity after
the first act of desperate humility, his donning of the Negro shoes
(p. 321). Joe experienced the peace and quiet which were all he had
wanted; he escaped from the picket fence of time. When he saw fear in
the eyes of others, he responded politely and quietly; he was appalled
by the terror and distress which Negroes showed toward him: ''of their
brother afraid'' (p. 317). Then a need for purposeful action, rather than
a conscious choice, urged him to return to the human community, to
recognize that he could not escape his past and his identity but must
accept himself and the consequences of his actions: ''I have never
broken out of the ring of what I have already done and cannot ever
undo.'' On his feet were ''the black shoes smelling of Negro; . . . the
black tide creeping up his legs, moving from his feet upward as death
moves'' (pp. 320, 321). His re-entry into the world of time and nature
was followed by his resolute, unhurried progress to Mottstown. Here
he allowed himself to be arrested without protest, after visiting the
barber shop and buying some new clothes: he accepted the consequences of his past life with pride and dignity.

The measure of Joe's change is to be read in his last look, at his
killers. He had escaped when being taken from the jail to the courthouse, fled to Hightower's where Percy Grimm and his three followers
cornered him. Joe had a pistol and knocked Hightower on the head
with it but did not shoot. Percy Grimm emasculated Joe before he
killed him. Joe ''just lay there, with his eyes open and empty of everything save consciousness, and with something, a shadow, about his
mouth. For a long moment he looked up a them with peaceful and
unfathomable and unbearable eyes'' (p. 439). The murder of Joanna
Burden and the racist killing of Joe may have lingered in the memories
of the men who were in at the kill, but no one else in Yoknapatawpha
thought or spoke of the events.

Joe's death, like that of Meursault in Camus' *The Stranger*, is
authentic. Panthea Broughton explained Joe's death in thoroughly
existential terms. ''In choosing to stand before Percy Grimm and not to
shoot, Joe has chosen in one sure act of free will to be himself. . . .
Though the shadow lingers, Joe himself is no longer a shadow. Though
he has found respite in one shadow identity after another, at the time of
his death he ceases to be a shadow and beomes himself. Only then does
he at last discover, not what he is, but who he is.'' G. L. Friend
suggests the alternative: ''he chooses rather to relinquish his life than

to resort to a savage method of retaliation. . . . It is a heroic act of mature decision and courage."

Joanna Burden was as much an alien in Jefferson as Joe was, but she was not rootless. She was one of the third generation of Burdens in Jefferson; her father and grandfather, she told Joe, came to Jefferson with a government commission "to help with the freed negroes" (p. 238). Colonel John Sartoris' murderous reaction provided an example for the community of how to deal with alien invaders. After her grandfather and brother were killed, she and her father remained on their land. He left to Joanna the legacy of bearing the curse of the white race, the black shadow (p. 239). She tried to get away but failed and lived in ostracism, carrying on her mission to help the Negroes in Yoknapatawpha and elsewhere. She represents both the permanent Outsider and the character, significant in Faulkner's fiction, who is obliged to play a role imposed by another person's decisions. Because she owned the land and the house she could remain, but she tried to preserve simultaneously two opposed traditions, that of her abolitionist family and that of the racist community. Shunning Joanna while she lived, the townspeople rallied to her defense when she was murdered, supposedly by a black man. The only evidence of Joe's black blood was the word of Brown, who might have been the murderer himself (p. 369). The most plausible explanation of Joe's final flight is that Mrs. Hines told him, when she visited him in jail, who he was (p. 423).

Ironically, Joanna shared with the white community their Calvinism. Her frenzied love affair with Joe was the consequence of the sexless life forced upon her by her heritage. Her Calvinistic sense of guilt, when the sexuality was ended, caused her to repeat the sins of the white community by regarding Joe as a Negro and trying to force him into a Negro pattern. And her Calvinistic fanaticism made her regard herself as an agent of the Lord when she demanded that Joe kneel and pray with her. Her last look at Joe as she pointed the pistol at him, "like the arched head of a snake," showed the confidence of fanaticism: "And her eyes did not waver at all. They were as still as the round black ring of the pistol muzzle. But there was no heat in them, no fury. They were calm and still as all pity and all despair and all conviction. But he was not watching them. He was watching the shadowed pistol on the wall; he was watching when the cocked shadow of the hammer flicked away" (p. 267). Apparently he blacked out until he was standing in the road with his right hand lifted—holding the gun that he did not know he had.

When Joe envisioned the three stages of Joanna's sexual life, he showed an existentialist imagination: "During the first phase it had

been as though he were outside a house where snow was on the
ground, trying to get into the house; during the second phase he was at
the bottom of a pit in the hot wild darkness; now he was in the middle
of a plain where there was no house, not even snow, not even wind"
(p. 254, 255). "Not even four pegs to set up a tent," as Martin Buber
would say. Describing the "existentialist revolutionaries" of the end of
the nineteenth century among artists, poets, novelists, and dramatists,
Paul Tillich said they were "full of discoveries in the deserts and
jungles of the human soul."

Both Joe and Faulkner use "house" as a symbolic image. Joanna's
was a prison which she inherited and in which she had no guests until
Joe's arrival. Referring to Hightower's house, Michael Routh noted
that "house" may be used as a symbol of the self, and observed that
Faulkner's working title for *Light in August* was "Dark House." (He
later used the same working title for the story of Sutpen, in which the
house was the creation of the central character.) Hightower's house is
comparable with Joanna's in that both allow the owner to live in
privacy in or near a community which ostracizes them. Since Edgar
Guest's *A Heap o' Livin'* was published in 1916, Faulkner and his
readers would be likely to add "in a house to make it home," a perfectly suitable association for both Hightower's and Joanna's lifeless
houses. Unlike Joanna, however, Hightower's unauthentic, useless life
was the result of a series of wrong choices, beginning with his choice of
a career, whereas Joanna had a role imposed upon her as a duty to her
family and a moral and religious obligation.

During the time of events in *Light in August*, Hightower led a life of
inaction and indifference, a renunciation of life and a refusal to play
any role. His one redeeming quality is his compassionate sensitivity,
but he deliberately avoided experiences that would evoke the pain of
compassion. He spent his days sitting at the window waiting for night
to bring the vision, a kind of self-induced hallucination, in which was
concentrated a moment from the past, all that yet remained to him "of
honor and pride, of life" (p. 55). Not only did Hightower try to preserve the past and refuse the present: he tried to arrest the past in one
moment of "glorious action" by his grandfather. In giving himself up
to this ideal vision of the past, he made a series of unauthentic choices:
he chose his cavalier grandfather, dead in a dead past, in preference to
his puritanic father who came home from war, "looked forward and
made what use he could of defeat by making practical use of that which
he had learned in it. He turned doctor" (p. 415). Gail Hightower entered the ministry in the belief that God would call him to Jefferson
because that was where his grandfather was shot on a galloping horse

during the Van Dorn raid. The seminary meant "quiet and safe walls within which the hampered and garmentworried spirit could learn anew serenity to contemplate without horror or alarm its own nakedness," "where the spirit could be born anew sheltered from the harsh gale of living" (p. 453). He accepted a position in Jefferson not to fulfill his duties but to indulge in his vision of galloping horses. He married and used his wife for his own selfish ends and then forgot her and let her seek, first in a love affair and then in suicide, escape from an intolerable marriage. As he finally realized, he "became her seducer and her murderer, author and instrument of her shame and death" (p. 462). He had been equally irresponsible as a clergyman: "I came here where faces full of bafflement and hunger and eagerness waited for me, waiting to believe; I did not see them" (p. 461). Having lost his wife and his church, Hightower found oblivion not by flight but through reading, through withdrawal, in indifference, from the life of the community, through a life of sloth which recalls both the sin of accidie and the sin of the damned in the Vestibule of Dante's *Inferno*.

Byron Bunch's visits to Hightower at night, several times a week, are Hightower's one link with the community. His habitual reaction to Byron's information about events in Jefferson is one of shrinking and denial. He is determined to remain uninvolved, to preserve his immunity from life, to escape the despair of love and the prices of goodness. When Byron looks at Hightower sleeping in his chair, "it seems to Byron as though the whole man were fleeing away from the nose which holds invincibly to something yet of pride and courage above the sluttishness of vanquishment like a forgotten flag above a ruined fortress" (p. 343). Hightower had tried to keep Byron as uncommitted as he was. The authenticity of existential communication, as defined by Karl Jaspers, is violated by Hightower's attitude: "Neither the submission nor the domination of the other permits me to become myself. Only in mutual recognition do both of us become ourselves. . . . I also must commit myself, for I become myself only in communication."

To an extreme degree the statement Jaspers made about himself would apply to both Hightower and Byron, since each had only the one Other: "True communication excludes other possibilities. I cannot reach all human beings," and communication with too many will "destroy communication." But "in communication I am revealed to myself together with the other." Two crucial confrontations present Byron in the process of self-revelation and decision and Hightower resisting any change in the convictions which have ruined his life. In the first, Byron sits with "his face lowered" because what he has to say will be unpleasing and will not be believed. "Downlooking" and "does not look up" are repeated. Hightower throughout "watches" Byron, most graphically when he "looks across the desk at the other's still, stubborn, ascetic face: the face of a hermit who has lived for a long time in an empty place where sand blows" (p. 285). Byron is explaining what Lena needs to live safely in the midst of the turmoil in Jefferson, with Lucas Burch as the informer who was murderously accompanying the police with bloodhounds, hunting down Joe Christmas. Lena wants to go out and stay in the cabin, Lucas being in jail when not "out running with dogs the man that took him up and befriended him," a fact Byron had kept from Lena (p. 288). And still "the stubborn, dogged, sober face . . . has not yet looked" at Hightower (p. 289). A "wave of exultation, of triumph" seems to go through Byron and he looks "for the first time at the minister, with a face confident and bold and suffused. The other meets his gaze steadily" (p. 290). Hightower accuses Byron of trying to come between man and wife and is totally unconcerned for the welfare of Lena and her unborn child even if Lucas Burch would marry her and assume the responsibility from which he had fled. Finally Hightower accuses Byron of being helped "by the devil" (p. 291). Byron has clearly made a decision but feels the need to confess his intent.

The second confrontation takes place after Byron has installed Lena in the cabin. For the first time he does not stumble on the bottom step. "He enters immediately, with that new air born somewhere between assurance and defiance. 'And I reckon you are going to find that you hate it worse when I don't stumble than when I do,' Byron says" (p. 295). He is quite right. Hightower is still determined to preserve his immunity from life, and to prevent Byron Bunch from making any moral commitment and assuming any responsibility for Lena. This time Byron looks at Hightower and then looks away (p. 295). Knowing that Hightower will disapprove, he nevertheless speaks "in that new voice: that voice brief, terse, each word definite of meaning, not fumbling" (p. 296). He gives an account of how he has established Lena in the cabin and is staying in a tent, to be close enough to protect her physically and visibly separated to protect her good name. Hightower is still adamant as they look at each other: Lena made a choice and Byron is under no obligation to sacrifice himself for her; men have suffered more from good women than good women ever suffered from men. The two men are "already impregnable each in his own conviction." But only Byron has become his authentic self. As Elkin noted, Byron and Hightower have exchanged roles.

After Hightower's brief experience with life, when Byron sent him on the mule to help Lena at her child's birth while Byron ran for the doctor, he envisioned the wasteland restored to fertility as he returned in the afternoon to see Lena. One wonders if his advice to Lena would have been different if she had named the child for him. As it was, he told her to send Byron away. But when he found that she had refused to marry Byron and learned that Byron had left without saying good-bye to him, he regretted not being able to tell Byron what Byron had restored to him (p. 392).

Hightower did achieve some measure of authenticity by choices which made him act purposefully in the present: he allowed Byron to bring Doc and Mrs. Hines to see him but refused to give Joe an alibi, not yet being willing to re-enter life. He helped Lena at the birth of her baby and regained "a glow of purpose and pride" (p. 383). One of the most explicit statements about Hightower's refusal to bear the respon-sibility for his actions is made by Byron. While trying to persuade Hightower to provide Joe with an alibi for the time when Joanna was killed, Byron appealed to Hightower as "a man of God." Hightower replied: "Not of my own choice that I am no longer a man of God," and accused the members of his church of "insult and violence" in defrocking him. Byron replied: "You made your choice before that. . . . You were given your choice before I was born" (p. 345). Members of Hightower's congregation had told Byron of his obsession with the Civil War and of his misuse of the pulpit, "using religion as though it were a dream" (p. 96). Hightower's final, sudden choice, his attempt to save Joe, when he took refuge at Hightower's, by a feeble and false alibi, failed of its purpose but resulted in Hightower's brief experience as an authentic man, seeing the truth of himself and his whole life, fifty years of being "a single instant of darkness in which a horse galloped and a gun crashed" (p. 465).

The meditation of Hightower after he was wounded by Joe and Joe was killed by Percy Grimm is of particular significance in existential terms as revealing not only Hightower's unauthentic life and his wrong choices but also aspects of the society which conditioned his desires and ideals. He saw the Church as being destroyed "by the profes-sionals who control it and who have removed the bells from its steep-les" (p. 461). But as a minister he was "a charlatan preaching worse than heresy, in utter disregard of that whose very stage he preempted, offering instead of the crucified shape of pity and love, a swaggering and unchastened bravo killed with a shotgun in a peaceful henhouse, in a temporary hiatus of his own avocation of killing" (p. 462). And when he tries to defend himself on the grounds that he tried to achieve more than was in his power, he sees the Face and hears: "It was not to accomplish that that you accepted her. You took her as a means toward your own selfishness. As an instrument to be called to Jefferson; not for My ends, but for your own'' (p. 463). When the wheel of thinking whirls fast and smooth, he sees a halo ''full of faces,'' including his own. Then one face which is confused and another interchanging with it: Christmas and ''the boy with the black pistol,'' Percy Grimm.

At the end of his meditation Hightower has an existential, Pascalian glimpse of nothingness: ''With all air, all heaven, filled with the lost and unheeded crying of all the living who ever lived, wailing still like lost children among the cold and terrible stars.'' Then as if ''to be reaffirmed in triumph and desire with, with this last left of honor and pride and life'' (p. 466) he sees his obsessive vision of the galloping horses and seems to hear ''the wild bugles and the clashing sabres and the dying thunder of hooves'' (p. 467). Presumably he is at the point of death. But this is no tragic enlightenment. The significance of Hightower's last vision is clear in an existential context. Morris Beja regarded Hightower's ''pathetic self-delusion and persistence in his vision'' as ''revealing more than anything else the full depths of degradation and futility to which that vision has brought him.''

''The debilitating effect of the Calvinistic tradition upon the individual himself or upon his descendants'' Robert Burrows regarded as ''one of the most tragic results of religious fixation in Yoknapatawpha County.'' His study covered attitudes toward institutional Christianity in Faulkner's works.

In a comparatively early article, later published in *The Tangled Fire of William Faulkner*, William Van O'Connor described *Light in August* as being at center ''a probing into the terrible excesses of the Calvinist spirit,'' the force that with its ''rigidity of principle and harshness of spirit menaces Joe Christmas . . . and that persecutes Hightower.'' Until the latter part of the novel, when Doc Hines and Percy Grimm are pernicious additions to the cast of characters, the truth and significance of O'Connor's statement are not apparent. Both as an aspect of Southern culture and as the basis of religious concepts antithetical to existentialism, Calvinism merits special consideration in the context of *Light in August*. An error of Faulkner's, ignored or reinforced by some critics, must be corrected. The Burden family, strongly Calvinistic, were Unitarians from New England who brought their religion into the South. Calvinism, usually associated with Presbyterianism, in the South infiltrated other Protestant denominations as well. (See W. J. Cash and Clement Eaton.)

John Macquarrie's quotations from Calvinist doctrine and comments upon the concepts make the conflict obvious. Calvinism held that the

Fall of man stripped him of "sound intelligence." Consequently "the Calvinist believes that he himself, as one of the elect, has been rescued from this sea of error and that his mind has been enlightened by the Holy Spirit. However much he may insist that this is God's doing and not his own, his claim is nevertheless one of the most arrogant that has ever been made." Calvinists believed that the "secret directions" of God bring to pass all that happens. As Macquarrie said and as any existentialist would agree, "If this were indeed the case, it would make utter nonsense of any belief in human responsibility." Understood as a system "in which all happenings are rigidly determined in advance," Calvin's doctrine of Providence debases the relation between man and God "to the subpersonal level where man is little more than a puppet and God too has been degraded to the one who pulls the strings." The doctrine of election means that God chooses or rejects every person, "the elect who have been marked out for salvation or the reprobate whose destiny is damnation." The Compson family provide a good example: Mrs. Compson and Jason think they are among the elect and Quentin and Caddy think they are damned and Mr. Compson is a nihilist. The doctrine of election also deprives "man of any responsibility or . . . of any genuine humanity."

Although Panthea Broughton recognized characters in *Light in August* who believe, as Joe Christmas did, paradoxically, that he was "the volitionless servant of . . . fatality" (p. 264), McEachern, Joanna Burden, and Doc Hines believed this doctrine consistently, Doc Hines even madly. Broughton does not identify Calvinism nor recognize it as significant in Southern society in the past. She does, however, realize that this particular abstraction "projects upon a man the role . . . of an object which has no free will and thus is not responsible."

Ilse Lind emphasized the parallels between Joe and Joanna which can be explained by similar religious training when they were young: the similarity of Joanna to McEachern caused Joanna's death, whether Joe knocked her out with the pistol and Lucas Burch found her unconscious and cut her throat or Joe killed her in some mysterious fashion that would leave a bullet in the pistol and no trace of blood on Joe. Of *Light in August*, Lind remarked on its excellence as "a psychological study . . . of an alienated personality who is not articulate or intellectual" and commented on "the cunning with which Faulkner has personified in two neurotic personalities forces at work in the culture of the South." Joanna, Lind said, has a will that "has become absolute under the delusion of having surrendered itself to the Almighty," a respect in which she resembles McEachern.

McEachern and Doc Hines have similar ideas of how to treat wives: train them to be submissive. Of Mrs. McEachern, Lind said: "McEachern's sovereignty over her is moral, impersonal, and absolute." McEachern, Hines, Joe at times, and Percy Grimm have one power that is remarkable: they can act instinctively and with certainty and confidence, as when McEachern rode in pursuit of Joe and Percy Grimm pursued Joe. "Clairvoyance" indicates "seeing" what is out of sight, as Darl Bundren did when he was away from home. "Intuition" or, in colloquial language, "hunch" would be adequate in this context.

Ilse Lind differentiates between the other Calvinists and McEachern who is a Scotch-Presbyterian, one of a special group known in the South for "its extreme literalism of Calvinistic doctrine." He is not cruel, but his principles "outlaw the affections." Joanna's "fanaticism in her mature life is rabid." Doc Hines seems never to have been sane. More than the others he is convinced that he is the instrument of God to whom all deeds are permitted. His obsession with Negroes and female sexuality made him murder his daughter and Joe's father and let the infant live only because he believed God had a plan and had left Doc to watch it (p. 362). Like McEachern pursuing Joe, Doc knew intuitively which road his daughter and the man from the circus had taken: "It was like he knew" (p. 355).

These characters, brought up as Calvinists and without association with people outside their family, did not begin with a choice, because it would not have occurred to them that they had a choice. The lives they led would not lead others to choose them as models. Joe believed that he was free but found he had been inside the circle for thirty years (p. 321). Death may have been his choice.

Percy Grimm grew up in Jefferson and certainly there were still Calvinistic ideas and attitudes in the community. He is a Nazi type before the Western world knew about Nazis, but the KKK would provide a reasonable facsimile, with the right kind of prejudices. In *William Faulkner: The Yoknapatawpha Country*, Cleanth Brooks said that "the most fascinating instance of the alienated person" in *Light in August* is Percy Grimm, and that Faulkner was "almost as careful in working up the background of Percy Grimm's spiritual starvation and alienation" as he was for Hightower. Percy needed so badly to be part of the community that he attempted "to seize the community values by violence." His unconscious motives took over when he confronted Joe and his face lost "that serene, unearthly luminousness of angels in church windows" it had had when he was moving "with that lean, swift, blind obedience to whatever Player moved him on the Board" (p. 437). Percy Grimm is the personification of "the apotheosis of his own history" which Hightower heard in church music: "Pleasure, ecstasy, they cannot seem to bear; their escape from it is in violence, in drinking and fighting and praying: catastrophe too, the violence identical and apparently inescapable. *And why should not their religion drive them to crucifixion of themselves and one another?*" (p. 347).

"Sitting beside the road, watching the wagon mount the hill toward her, Lena thinks, 'I have come from Alabama: a fur piece.'" Between this first sentence and the last—"Here we aint been coming from Alabama but two months, and now it's already Tennessee"—Joanna Burden has been murdered, Joe Christmas has been crucified, and Hightower has probably died. But Lena and her baby and Byron Bunch, like Mary and Joseph and the infant Jesus, are on their way, to Memphis most likely, if not to Egypt. The framing of the story of Joe Christmas in that of Lena and Byron was achieved by careful revision of the manuscript, including skillfully worked-out parallel actions of Joe and Lena, as Regina Fadiman showed. This structure not only produces a contrapuntal effect between tragedy and low-keyed comedy but provides a contrast between unauthentic and authentic characters, the latter "framing" the tragedy.

As Heinrich Straumann observed, Lena is a unique character in Faulkner, and her story at beginning and end provides a measure for the rest: courage, helpfulness, unselfishness, and good humor enable Lena to face an open but uncertain future with Byron, whom she has won by leaving him free to choose. Mary Culley interprets Lena as a Madonna figure and contrasts her journeys toward life and the future with Joe's journeys toward death. She notes the parallel between Byron and Lena and Mary and Joseph.

In "Faulkner's Psychology of Individualism," Stephen Ballew used the tradition of self-reliance of Emerson and Whitman, rather than existentialism. Noting the shift from "divinely sanctioned to individually created values and actions," Ballew remarked that Faulkner's novels "reflect a radical subjectivity in which self-definition, self-validation, and self-judgment are totally contingent upon personal values."

Richard Chase suggests the mythic quality in Lena: "The surviving, enduring character, Lena Grove, lives in a timeless realm which seems at once to be eternity and the present moment." In endowing Lena with "an unvarying inner harmony" which reconciles or renders meaningless "all opposites or disparates," Faulkner praises "the quiet enduring stoicism and wisdom of the heart which he finds among . . . marginal types." Her "self-hood is whole; it is congruous with experience, with nature and with time." Michael Routh identifies Lena as both life-promoting, in giving birth, and life-conducing. Homes figure in all the story lines, he observes, but only Lena and Byron can establish one. Lena feels at home wherever she goes, and she will make a home wherever she stays.

Lena accepted herself and her responsibility—one doubts that she had much choice—on an instinctive level. Her behavior was innocent and spontaneous, but her self-respect and self-image, "like a lady travelling" (p. 23) because "a family ought to be all together when a chap comes" (p. 18), impressed those she met. She graciously and gratefully allowed others to help without becoming too dependent. She looked at Lucas Burch with "her grave, unwinking, unbearable gaze" and "released him by her own will, deliberately" (pp. 406, 409). She made no attempt to hold Byron (p. 389). Free, confident, responsible only to herself and her child, she left others free to take her or leave her. Fortunately Byron refused to leave.

Lena's faith and her wholesome acceptance of human nature were the qualities Byron needed to rid himself of his fear of responsibility and sin and change: "a fellow is more afraid of the trouble he might have than he ever is of the trouble he's already got. He'll cling to trouble he's used to before he'll risk a change. Yes. A man will talk about how he'd like to escape from living folks. But it's the dead folks do him the damage. It's the dead ones that lay quiet in one place and dont try to hold him, that he cant escape from" (p. 69).

Stephen Ballew noted that the circle and the line which were repeated motifs change significantly in Byron's vision from a hill outside Jefferson; he thinks of "the terrific and tedious distance which, being moved by blood, he must compass forever and ever between two inescapable horizons of the implacable earth" (p. 401). The circle and line join in the circularity of the compass: "the joining of motion with order to create direction." This suggests that "a man can be fully free and responsible and maintain those qualities as he changes and learns in response to events and people." Lena and Byron, female and male, become more fully human by combining "complementary aspects of human personality."

Byron's new life began, as François Pitavy observed, when Lena's baby cried (p. 379). He had not really believed until then that Lena was not a virgin. Panthea Broughton commented on the change in Byron when "he had got himself desperated up to risking all" (p. 475): "His development hinges upon awareness, acceptance, and affirmation and further exemplifies that, to lead an authentic existence in Faulkner's scheme of things, it is necessary to go beyond the empty precept but not to discard the vital abstraction." Lives like Byron Bunch's are not "so unrestricted that relevant abstractions such as justice, loyalty, and responsibility do not pertain."

Faulkner deliberately created Byron Bunch as so unimpressive a character that the furniture dealer in the final chapter utters the last word: "He was the kind of fellow you wouldn't see the first glance if he was alone by himself in the bottom of an empty concrete swimming pool" (p. 469). If we take a second, careful look, we discover that he has admirable qualities, including modesty, sincerity, and courage. In his study of individualism in Faulkner, Stephen Ballew comments on distinctive aspects of Faulkner's characters which apply notably to Byron. Faulkner's fiction "dramatizes the insistent, significant presence of a man's instinctual and emotional desires" and confronts "the sexual dimensions of self-actualization": "a Faulknerian character is not caught between innocence and experience or between Being and Becoming but between desires—for happiness and freedom—and fears—of failure and retribution." Byron unselfishly considers Lena's welfare first and subdues his own "instinctual and emotional desires" until Lena can make her own decisions without pressure. His desires were so instinctual and so new in his experience that he was in love before he knew it. Instead of the self-assertive male of "the frontier tradition" Faulkner creates "a new self-reliant man, both adventurous and responsible" who can "act freely in the face of personal doubts and fears as well as social and religious pressures."

Not only does Byron exemplify this self-reliant man but he is the true chivalric lover, governed by lofty ideals and unselfish devotion to his lady's welfare. If Lena really wanted to marry the father of her child, she had a chance to do so: Byron sent Lucas Burch to her, accompanied by a deputy, and gave Lena a chance to confront Lucas in private (the deputy stayed outside the cabin). The "looks" which were exchanged revealed their reactions: Lena "watching him with her sober eyes in which there was nothing at all—joy, surprise, reproach, love—while over his face passed shock, astonishment, outrage, and then downright terror . . . while ceaselessly here and there about the empty room went his harried and desperate eyes" (p. 406). Lucas escaped the deputy by leaving through the window.

Cleanth Brooks, in "Gavin Stevens and the Chivalric Tradition," cited Byron Bunch: "the gallant little unhorsed knight who selflessly comes to Lena Grove's rescue" is "at once comic and admirable. . . ." But Brooks missed the point. Byron had the courage to challenge Lucas, to defend Lena's honor as her champion, when Lucas was running away and no one but Byron would know of his chivalric action. Byron knew he would be defeated. Byron thought: "You've done throwed away twice inside of nine months what I aint had in thirtyfive years. And now I'm going to get the hell beat out of me and I dont care about that, neither." When Byron let Lucas, the large man, get to his feet instead of springing on him from behind, Lucas took that as an insult and fought like "a starved and desperate rat." In two minutes Byron lay "bleeding and quiet," before he re-entered "the world and time" (p. 416). No better examples of the authentic Christian humanist and the Demonic Misfit, as described by David Eggenschwiler, can be found than Byron and Lucas. Man "can accept himself, his limitations, his freedom, his responsibility, and his proper relation to God; he can accept peace and have faith." Or he can live in "a sustained flight from dread and freedom, a sustained and compulsive denial of reality." The Misfit "has complete freedom of choice" because alternatives are "equally meaningless."

Panthea Broughton recognized Byron's development to the point where "he is mature and independent enough to act . . . according to his own understanding of right." Byron's "own understanding" is his conscience, which is definitely existentialistic. John Maquarrie, in *Existentialism*, defines "conscience" in two ways: awareness of the moral code of his society and discomfort or satisfaction with his own conduct in relation to the code. Only the second way is regarded by existentialists as important: a person's moral convictions impel rejection of accepted standards if necessary to act according to his own "more deeply founded imperative." Byron's conscience obliged him to respond in both ways: when he established Lena in the cabin alone, he took great care to make clear that he was in a tent by himself, maintaining both the inner and the outer concepts of propriety. When peace was restored to Jefferson, Byron's conduct would have made it possible for them to stay in Jefferson. The furniture dealer makes it clear that Byron continued to act with propriety until Lena welcomed him back into the truck the second day (p. 479).

The "open-ended quality of the conclusion," Stephen Ballew commented, "enhances the possibility of Lena and Byron joining together in mutual freedom." This ending emphasizes Faulkner's belief that man can "structure his life with the desire for happiness, personal responsibility for action, freedom for others."

The story of Byron and Lena is given in detail because it has received less than its due. The myopia of the furniture dealer seems to have been shared by some critics. Byron is an excellent example of the Faulknerian hero as defined by Broughton: He "entertains no illusion that he may escape the world's troubles either by seeking a better place to live or by retreating inward. His affirmation of spirit and humanity in fact is contingent upon his remaining in the 'sorry shabby world.' Such affirmations may be rare in the fiction, yet they are there. And they are not vaguely implied but rather portrayed and actualized." The context of the quotation abounds in "authenticity" and "inauthenticity," indicating that Panthea Broughton used existentialist standards of critical judgment without so identifying them.

Dealing with novels according to time of action rather than date of publication brings us to a gap between *Light in August*, in which time of present action and date of publication are the same, 1932, and *Go Down, Moses*, in which time of action in the stories stretches from 1859 to 1941 and therefore leaves only the publication date, 1942, to be considered. (*Snopes* will be treated as a whole.)

In the first story in *Go Down, Moses*, "Was," the destiny of both slaves and free men rests upon the outcome of poker games. Actual games, activities analogous to games, sports, and the life of man as a game are significant in Faulkner, particularly in the remaining novels, and assume philosophic dimensions. He began by using metaphors for God, as at the end of *Sartoris*: ". . . the Player, and the game He plays. . . . He must have a name for his pawns, though. But perhaps Sartoris is the game—a game outmoded and played with pawns shaped too late and to an old dead pattern, and of which the Player Himself is a little wearied." Mr. Compson described life as a game to Quentin, a game man never won, "with dice already loaded against him." But still "he risks everything on a single blind turn of a card" and will give up the game "only when he has realized that even the despair or remorse or bereavement is not particularly important to the old diceman" (pp. 220–21). Games and sports, as action or as metaphor, are prominent enough in Faulkner to provide subjects for dissertations, one on "Game-Consciousness and Game-Metaphor in the Works of William Faulkner" by N. M. Rinaldi, and another on sports in the works of Ring Lardner, James Farrell, Ernest Hemingway, and Faulkner, by Stewart Rodnon.

The existentialist significance of games is most obvious in Sartre, and Faulkner no doubt would have agreed with Hazel Barnes that Sartre's concept of life as a game constitutes "bad faith." Sartre contrasted the idea of a serious world "with the lighter attitude of one playing a game. No matter how serious the stakes, the player knows that the rules have been *invented*. If they are to apply to him, it is because he has consented to regard them as binding: there is always the possibility of initiating a change in the regulations or of playing an entirely different game." Fortunately the Player handed me just the card I need to win against Sartre for the existentialists and Faulkner. Radhakrishnan used the game metaphor to explain Free Will:

> Life is like a game of bridge. The cards in the game are given to us; we do not select them. . . . we are free to make any call we like and to lead any suit. Only, we are limited by the rules of the game. We are more free

when we start the game than later on, when the game has developed and our choice becomes restricted. But till the very end there is always a choice. A good player sees possibilities which a bad player does not. The more skilled a player, the more alternatives does he perceive. A good hand may be cut to pieces by unskillful play; and bad play need not be attributed to the frowns of fortune. Even though we may not like the way the cards are shuffled, we like the game and we want to play.

Obviously, in these terms, one of the problems of some of Faulkner's characters is that they do not want to play the game.

But sometimes the game is literal and too high a value is set on winning or losing. Uncle Buddy's skill at poker won Tennie as a bride for Tomey's Turl—who dealt the cards—and saved Uncle Buck from marrying Sophonsiba in 1859. (His immunity ran out after the war.) The McCaslin–Beauchamp story in *Go Down, Moses* depended on that final poker game in "Was." Buddy won another poker game, with Uncle Buck, and Buddy went to war and Buck had to stay at home (*U* 57).

But *Go Down, Moses* is more about hunting than white man's games. And old Sam Fathers is a notable example of simple and natural authenticity, inherent in the wilderness and its creatures. Retaining in his eyes the look of the cage, "the knowledge that for a while that part of his blood had been the blood of slaves," Sam was "himself his own battleground, the scene of his own vanquishment and the mausoleum of his own defeat" (p. 168). He won his freedom by resisting the demands of white men and finally going out to the Big Bottom to live as his Indian ancestors had done. His own people having been dispossessed, Sam had to choose between identifying himself with Negroes, whose ways and work were alien to him, or to be independent of society. His choice, freely made, allowed him to retain his independence and dignity. His fellow creatures were the animals and the hunters; he was the human patriarch of the wilderness as Old Ben was the animal one: the "look" with which Sam gazed at Old Ben was "darkly and fiercely lambent, passionate and proud" (p. 198); the "look" that accompanied his salute to the phantom buck was from one free and equal creature to another. The anguish of death was conquered by Sam's willing his own death so that he and his animal counterpart, Old Ben, might end their lives together. The precise manner of Sam's death is less significant than the doctor's statement that "he just quit" (p. 248). This death is unlike suicide which rejects life, often by choosing a painful, frightening death. Robert Olson explained that existentialists recognize "the values which consciousness of death brings with it." He quoted Nietzsche: "My death, I praise to you, the free death, which comes to be because I want it. . . ." Nietzsche specified what his free death should be like: "free, conscious, without hazard, without ambush."

Although McCaslin Edmonds is not developed in great detail and is seen only through the memories of Ike, as Ike's guardian and his opponent in the colloquy in "The Bear" his ideas and attitudes merit consideration. The fact that he maintained the plantation after the Civil War and made it prosper and that he continued to do so when Ike refused to accept his heritage manifests a strong sense of responsibility exercised within the tradition and for acceptable ends. Other evidence of authenticity lies in his belief in life and in man's ability to choose life or death: "after all you dont have to continue to bear what you believe is suffering; you can always stop that, put an end to that. And even suffering and grieving is better than nothing; there is only one thing worse than not being alive, and that's shame" (p. 186). And from Cass Ike learned about the truth of the heart: "*Courage and honor and pride, and pity and love of liberty. They all touch the heart, and what the heart holds to becomes truth, so far as we know truth*" (p. 297).

In contrast with McCaslin Edmonds is Roth, the youngest of the family, who appears in "The Fire and the Hearth" and "Delta Autumn." He began his unauthentic choices when, as a child of seven, he asserted his white superiority: "Then one day the old curse of his fathers, the old haughty ancestral pride based not on any value but on an accident of geography, stemmed not from courage and honor but from wrong and shame, descended on him" (p. 111). Thereafter he and his foster brother Henry were never equals. Molly, Henry's mother, taught him that he should be "gentle with his inferiors, honorable with his equals, generous to the weak and considerate of the aged, courteous, truthful and brave to all" (p. 117). But her teaching proved in vain. As a man, in "Delta Autumn," Roth had a cynical philosophy which denied man human dignity; he asked Isaac, who had expressed faith in man, where he had been all the time he was dead, if that was what he had "learned about the other animals" he lived among (p. 345). Roth's bitterness and cynicism, his opinion that only the law makes a man behave, reflect his own guilt and self-condemnation. As Panthea Broughton observed, Ike "seems to have been unable to pass on any of his code of honor even to his kinsman Roth Edmonds." Roth had seduced a girl whom his code would forbid him to marry; although she shared the McCaslin blood of which Roth was so proud, the black blood with which it was mingled was all that Roth was aware of. Like old Carothers McCaslin, Roth rejected his own son and thought that money was a substitute for recognition of paternity. Roth's uncritical repetition of the tradition when he was a child and his evasion of the consequences of his actions as a man show that he lacked a sense of honor and that he denied human beings, even his own son, human dignity.

Although Isaac McCaslin in his role as the hero of an initiation into the wilderness life has already been reviewed, as a character he gains a new dimension through the existential interpretation of his ideas and actions. He is an excellent example of the authentic choice of freedom, inspired by the vision of new possibilities and the cycle of rebirth and transcendence. In "Pietism and the American Character," William McLoughlin identified pietism as the basis of the American moralistic view of life in Faulkner and others, defining "pietism" in terms which apply particularly to Isaac McCaslin. Pietism held the individual to be the "single most competent judge of moral truth." Pietists' belief in the continual revelation of God in new ways and their consequent belief in an open society are relevant to the convictions on which Isaac based his choice. But he failed to strive for the ideal of American perfectionism which "lies in movement, in action and in the future," an ideal much like Faulkner's of "man in motion." Thus Isaac lapsed into unauthenticity for the rest of his long life. In *The Reivers* "Grandfather" refers to Ike as still living in 1961, the time he is telling the story: he says to his grandson, "the same camp which you will probably continue to call McCaslin's camp for a few years after your Cousin Ike is gone . . ." (pp. 19–20). In 1905, the time of action in *The Reivers*, Ike, still in his thirties, "lived alone in a single room over his hardware store" (p. 54).

Isaac McCaslin's beliefs were thoroughly existential. His realization of man's solitariness and his voluntary testing of himself in solitude are part of the initiation which preceded his rebirth. Thomas Merton identified the "shift in consciousness" which occurred in "The Old People": "in order to find himself truly he has to make an existential leap into this mysterious other order, into the dimension of a primitive wilderness experience." His passion for truth—"there is only one truth and it covers all things that touch the heart" (p. 260)—his assertion of freedom and of choice, as well as his belief that he has been chosen, his ideal of the earth being held "in the communal anonymity of brotherhood," and his passionate rejection of the tradition which used human beings like any other property—all are fully in accord with Christian existentialism. His repudiation of his grandfather and his relinquishment of his material heritage was a rebellion against a slave society. Rollo May, in *Man's Search for Himself*, deals with rebellion in a section entitled *What Freedom Is Not*: ". . . rebellion is often confused with freedom itself. . . . it gives the rebel a delusive sense of being really independent. The rebel forgets that rebellion always pre-supposes an outside structure—of rules, laws, expectations—against which one is rebelling; and one's security, sense of freedom and strength are dependent actually on this external structure." The struc-ture Ike repudiated was Southern slave society, which no longer exist-ed. What Ike did not rebel against was the establishment of Jim Crow laws which began in Mississippi before the federal troops were with-drawn in 1877: Mississippi in 1865 passed a law forbidding "any freed-man, negro, or mulatto" to ride in "first-class passenger cars, set apart, or used by . . . white persons." C. Vann Woodward in *The Strange Career of Jim Crow* states the purpose of the Jim Crow laws: to make sure "that the Negro would be effectively disfranchised throughout the South, that he would be firmly relegated to the lower rungs of the economic ladder, and that neither equality nor aspirations for equality in any department of life were for him." Laws were being passed and codes of etiquette being enforced in Mississippi from 1865 to 1890—two years after Ike's twenty-first birthday—which are re-corded in Vernon Wharton's *The Negro in Mississippi, 1865–1890*. The story of Ike McCaslin gives no hint that he was even aware of what was happening in his own state to assure white supremacy. He rebelled against what no longer existed but accepted, it seems, the external structure which was replacing slavery.

Ike's concept of God and view of himself seem, in light of the reality, to be ironic. He conceived of God as having to "accept responsibility for what he Himself had done in order to live with Himself in His lonely and paramount heaven" (p. 282), even as man has to be responsible and win peace of conscience: "I have got myself to have to live with the rest of my life and all I want is peace to do it in" (p. 288). Even in 1888 when Ike said that to Cass, he was, as "Grandfather" said, "abdicating" his responsibility and opportunity to assume his author-ity over the McCaslin plantation. Even more ironic, one realizes, is his belief that "most men are a little better than their circumstances give them a chance to be," transcending their limitations (p. 288). Ike's little room over his hardware store in 1905 is a symbol of his limiting his limitations. When one considers that Ike regarded himself as chosen, a new Moses, but never acted to improve life for the Negroes, and creat-ed himself as a Christ figure by becoming a carpenter, but never gave up his trade for a spiritual mission, the paucity of his accomplishments is even greater in comparison with his grandiose ambitions. The in-flated rhetoric of Ike in the colloquy with Cass is regarded by Gloria Dussinger as an attempt "to reason logically, seeking motives for his

actions," although he aspired to be a natural man, "who acts instinctively, and his deed contains its own justification." Ike's rationalization proves his "dual nature . . . his conscious denial of the existential circumstance."

That Ike was a natural man and not even a Christian in his eschatological ideas is proved in "Delta Autumn," in which he conceived of
his life span and that of the wilderness running out together "not toward oblivion, nothingness, but into a dimension free of both time and
space," inhabited by the spirits "of the old men he had known and
loved," where "the wild strong immortal game ran forever" (p. 354).
Eternal bliss was for Ike the happy hunting grounds of the Indians,
even as in his youth he had realized that, although he might marry,
"still the woods would be his mistress and his wife" (*GDM* 326).

Not only in the absence of anguish at the thought of death and
nothingness but also in his attitude toward nature and in the implications of his choice Ike deviated from the seemingly authentic pattern of
his life. A statement by Karl Jaspers precisely fits Ike, in that Ike
retained throughout his life a preference for nature, rather than human
society:

> Solitary devotion to nature—this deep experience of the universe in the
> landscape and in the physical nearness to its shapes and elements, this
> source of strength to the soul—could seem like a wrong done to human
> beings, if it becomes a means of avoiding them, and like a wrong done to
> myself, if it tempted me to a secluded self-sufficiency in nature. Solitude
> in nature can indeed be a wonderful source of *self-being*; but whoever
> remains solitary in nature is liable to impoverish his self-being and to lose
> it in the end. To be near to nature in the wonderful world around me
> therefore became questionable when it did not lead back to community
> with humanity and serve this community as background and as language.

Considering the aversion of Uncle Buck and Uncle Buddy to marriage
and women and the choice of Edmonds men to remain widowers if
happily a wife died after a son was born, one may well question both
the will and the wisdom involved in Ike's choice of a wife. Like Ike's
mother, his wife may have taken the initiative: Faulkner said that she
expected when she married Ike to be the "chatelaine of a plantation and
they would have children" (*FU* 275). Then she discovered that he
was wedded to the woods! The girl's accusation of Ike in "Delta
Autumn" as having failed, in giving up his inheritance, to fulfill his
responsibility as the head of the family justifies the application to Ike of
Jasper's warning against setting nature above community.

Mary Culley interpreted the girl's denunciation as undercutting his
mythologizing in the colloquy in "The Bear," envisioning himself as a

Moses. "An authentic judgment has been spoken to Ike," whose "attractive, simple vision" of a future judgment diverted his attention from the present and left him a "foolish, fond old man." The girl's "stinging judgment upon Ike in the present" was that "he set no one free, not even himself." Culley said that Ike did not "accept, confess, and integrate guilt and thereby reach an authentic integrity": "His journey led not to Sinai or the Cross but back behind the flaming gates of Eden."

Ike had a duty to family and society precisely because of the spiritual strength he had won in the wilderness. He continued to go hunting. Faulkner's "Race at Morning" implies what Faulkner said about Ike. Of the three stages of coping with problems, "The first says, This is rotten, I'll have no part of it. I will take death first. . . . McCaslin is the second, He says, This is bad, and I will withdraw from it" (*FU* 246). In "Race at Morning," Ike is an old hunter. The foster father of the little boy told him that he must earn the right to go hunting for two weeks by working the other fifty weeks in the year, and that "the farming business and the hunting business ain't enough. You got to belong to the business of mankind" and be able to teach people what's right and wrong and why (*BW* 196). The existentialist interpretation of Ike's adult life as a decline from youthful authenticity confirms the mythic interpretation of Ike's initiation as ineffective. When hunting ceases to be a game but becomes the game of life, man lives by the rules he made, once he has progressed beyond totemism and primitive weapons. The close group of hunters fails to have equally close family and community relationships. The hunters in Ike's group do not even assume responsibility for the preservation of the wilderness where they hunt: De Spain's sale of the land to a lumber company aroused no protest, not even from Ike.

As Isaac McCaslin is the chief white character in *Go Down, Moses*, Lucas Beauchamp, also a grandson of Carothers McCaslin, is the leading Negro character. In "The Fire and the Hearth" and *Intruder in the Dust*, Lucas is remarkable for his stubborn refusal to fit into the stereotype of the Negro or, with one exception, to adopt the materialist values of the white man. He is authentic but without fitting into any category. He rejected everything but his own dignity as an individual. Because of his Negro blood and his secure status on the McCaslin plantation, he was outside the patterns of social advancement. His self-acceptance is one aspect of his uniqueness: ". . . it was not that Lucas made capital of his white or even his McCaslin blood, but the contrary. It was as if he were not only impervious to that blood, he was indifferent to it. . . . He resisted it simply by being the composite of the two races which made him, simply by possessing it. Instead of being at once the ground and victim of the two strains, he was a vessel, durable, ancestryless, nonconductive, in which the toxin and its anti stalemated one another . . ." (p. 104). Thus ancestryless, he was self-created; *"who fathered himself, intact and complete, contemptuous . . . of all blood, black, white, yellow or red, including his own"* (p. 118). Panthea Broughton dwells on the way in which "the overweening concern for an immobile abstraction like 'name' is intolerant because it is absolute." The concept is dissociated "from the human sphere and therefore from the context of meaning and value." She cites Olga Vickery's explanation of "the communal mind and thought of the South": "a complex of concepts, such as 'Calvinism, racial purity and white supremacy'" has been established and accepted so that "its reference to experiential realities has been utterly obscured." "Blood" is "another specious concept," as in the pride Lucas took in his McCaslin blood: "He acquired arrogance and intolerance through deference to the abstract concept of blood." But Broughton does not stress that Lucas derived enough confidence from his feeling of superiority, which as a person he did possess over many whites, to live his life more freely than he could have otherwise, and he did not make others suffer. It is true that Ike and Lucas "both are guilty of the intolerant use of abstractions" such as blood. When Lucas collected from Ike his inheritance from old Carothers on his twenty-first birthday, he wanted to be able to do what he wanted. And Ike knew that Lucas considered that Ike had betrayed his blood *"for what he too calls not peace but obliteration, and a little food"* (*GDM* 108, 109). (Zack was paying Ike an allowance.)

Because Lucas took pride in his McCaslin blood, he followed his own standards, risking his life in his defiance of racial etiquette, when, in self-assertion, he transcended self-acceptance. He challenged Zack Edmonds as man to man, face-to-face, willing to risk the coal oil and the rope in defense of his rights as a husband (*GDM* 53–58). For a Negro to face a white man and look him in the eye, as Lucas did Zack, lends the "look" new intensity: the Negro was used to being an object. But Lucas faced reality: it was old Carothers' blood that gave him the courage, but "How to God," he said, "can a black man ask a white man to please not lay down with his black wife? And even if he could ask it, how to God can the white man promise he won't?" (*GDM* 58, 59).

Lucas' mask is one of inscrutability, intractability, and imperturbability. In *Intruder in the Dust*, his mask and his self-possession drove a white man to fury in a crossroads store. In response to the man's curses, "Lucas looked at the white man with a calm speculative detachment" and went on eating gingersnaps (*ID* 16). While other white men forcibly restrained the man from killing Lucas, Lucas did not even quicken his pace or stop his chewing.

Only in the episodes of the still and the buried treasure in "The Fire and the Hearth" did Lucas adopt the conventional Negro mask of deception and "stupid impassivity." Only in those episodes did he sink to an unauthentic level, making use of other people for his own unworthy purposes and practicing deceit. He was recalled to his senses by his wife, Molly, who herself insisted on her freedom to escape God's curse and to save her daughter from it if Lucas persisted in his violation of God's land and God's laws. Lucas' choice to give up treasure hunting in order to save his marriage is consistent with his ideal of marital fidelity, symbolized by the fire on the hearth, and with his grief-stricken abstraction later, when Molly died, which revealed to Charles Mallison that "*You don't have to not be a nigger in order to grieve*" (*ID* 19).

In "Pantaloon in Black," Rider had derived his ideal for his own marriage from the fire on Lucas' hearth. The account of his inconsolable anguish over the death of his wife is Faulkner's most powerful and sympathetic study of a man's "rejecting existence itself as unbearable," to use Fallico's terms. The fact that Rider killed the white night watchman for cheating at a dice game with a second pair of dice, as he had been doing for fifteen years when playing craps with the niggers at the mill, made Rider himself his "old diceman" (*GDM* 153, 156).

As Lyall Powers stated, "To read *Intruder in the Dust* against the background of *Go Down, Moses* is to achieve a much richer experience than to read it alone as a discrete novel." But in suggesting a comparison between Sam Fathers and Ike McCaslin and Lucas Beauchamp and Charles Mallison, Powers did not recognize the most important truth revealed by that comparison: Ike's training as an initiate with Sam as his mentor trained him only to be a hunter, not to live in his own society. Lucas had a much greater influence on Charles as a host with a guest, and in a few encounters transformed Charles from such typical attitudes as Roth's toward his own part-Negro relatives to complete rejection of racist codes. Ike McCaslin is the most significant example of unauthenticity in Yoknapatawpha because he had the greatest potential and the longest life in which to be a power for good but rejected his responsibility at twenty-one. Charles Mallison is the most significant example of authenticity because his mentor, Gavin Stevens, failed him, and on the strength of his own intuition and conscience Charles at sixteen had courage to defy the whole structure of Southern society and to risk his life in so doing.

In *Intruder in the Dust* the "look" dominates the episodes in which
Lucas and Charles appear together, exemplifying Paul Tillich's definition of existential knowledge: "In all existential knowledge both subject and object are transformed by the very act of knowing. Existential
knowledge is based on an encounter in which a new meaning is created
and recognized." In the first episode, Lucas watched Charles, flound-
ering in the icy creek, "without pity commiseration or anything else,
not even surprise" (p. 6). Lucas did not even look at Charles as he
ordered the Negro boys to pick up the money with which Charles had
tried to pay for hospitality (p. 16). Facing the mob when he was
brought to jail charged with murdering a white man, Lucas "was not
even looking at them but just toward them, arrogant and calm and with
no more defiance . . . than fear: detached, impersonal, almost musing,
intractable and composed, the eyes blinking a little in the sunlight"
(p. 44). In jail, Lucas watched Gavin with "a look shrewd secret and
intent" (p. 60). The "mute patient urgency" of Lucas' gaze made
Charles return alone to the jail: "the mute unhoping urgency of the
eyes" then had the power to send Charles on his terrible mission (pp.
66, 69). By "using" Charles to do what he himself could not do and
Gavin would never consider doing, Lucas provided Charles with an
opportunity to act with courage, dignity, and authenticity beyond his
years. Rollo May explicitly specified Lucas' "look" at white people in
Intruder in the Dust: "such contempt for the conquerors keeps the
person still an identity in his own right even though outward conditions
deny him the essential rights of a human being." Lucas' "look" at
Charles exemplifies that in Tillich's "encounter."

The power of Lucas' gaze toward Charles is that of human appeal.
The anguish Charles had undergone when Lucas refused the money is
that of betrayal of self and of race. The fifty cents haunted him: "to
hang fixed at last forever in the black vault of his anguish like the last
dead and waneless moon and himself, his own puny shadow gesticulate
and tiny against it in frantic and vain eclipse: frantic and vain and yet
indefatigable too because he would never stop, he could never give up
now who had debased not merely his manhood but his whole race too"
(p. 21). His sense of responsibility to himself and his race involved also
the need "simply for re-equalization, reaffirmation of his masculinity
and his white blood" (p. 26). Charles's definition of life is amazingly
mature and existential: "that agony of naked inanesthetisable nerve-
ends which for lack of a better word men call being alive" (p. 26).

As an initiation hero, Charles established his identity as an authentic, responsible, mature member of the community, an individual with
courage to assert his freedom, "in direct defiance of wise and cautious
and practical adults," and to transcend the limits of his youth to serve

truth and justice. Panthea Broughton continued with an account of the few characters in Faulkner who make it possible for God to depend on men sometimes: "They are dependable and courageous precisely because they do not depend upon anything foreign to themselves; they may trust, that is, but they do not depend; thus they manage not just to endure but also to prevail."

Charles's first assertions of freedom were specious. He was trying to be free of his conscience, of the necessity to make a choice consonant with his humanity. His plan to ride away on Highboy clearly identified his choice as that between irresponsibly running away from the problem, safe from all but his own conscience, and acting responsibly, with compassion, in defiance of family and society, in whose eyes he had no obligation whatever to act in behalf of Lucas. In terms of Frederick Olafson's existentialist criteria, Charles is an excellent example of "moral judgment" as "a decisional act," a choice of alternatives which the person has envisaged. Charles "envisaged" during a good part of the night, in interludes of his furious reviewing of all the reasons why shooting a Gowrie was the most stupid thing Lucas could have done. In the morning he was still planning on saddling Highboy, tying a sack of feed behind the saddle and riding for twelve hours "in the opposite direction from Fraser's store" (p. 41), and riding back the next day when it would be all over. Instead he waited across the street from the jail the next morning until Lucas was brought in and "looking straight at him" said, " 'Tell your uncle I wants to see him' " (p. 45).

Charles had incredible luck in the co-conspirator he found when Uncle Gavin proved incapable of even being an adviser. R. J. Trobaugh described Miss Habersham as authentic, one of the best representatives of tradition. Like Miss Worsham in "Go Down, Moses": she and Mollie Beauchamp grew up as sisters and Mollie and Lucas were her family (*GDM* 375). Aleck Sander, companion to Charles, was angry with Lucas for being the kind of nigger that made life difficult for the rest of his race; he explained to the sheriff why he went to help dig up a dead man. "Aleck Sander said, 'I didn't even know I was going. I had done already told Chick I didn't aim to. Only when we got to the truck everybody seemed to just take it for granted I wasn't going to do nothing else but go and before I knowed it I wasn't' " (p. 113). As Olafson observed, a choice made unconsciously does not manifest "bad faith." Thus in what was practically a contagion of authenticity, Charles and Miss Habersham and Aleck Sander carried out their mission. Charles achieved "his own one anonymous chance too to perform something passionate and brave and austere not just in but into man's enduring chronicle worthy of a place in it . . . in gratitude for the gift of his time in it . . ." (p. 193). He learned also that "it's all *now*" and that "you escape nothing, you flee nothing; the pursuer is what is doing the running and tomorrow night is nothing but one long sleepless wrestle with yesterday's omissions and regrets" (pp. 194-95).

Although Gavin Stevens voiced the last thought and was able to express the significance of Charles's experience, Charles surpassed Gavin in achieving the fullest and rarest kind of authenticity: that which involves rebirth and transcendence and reintegration into the community and which not only envisions new possibilities but courageously acts to help bring them about. In Chapter Ten Charles meditated on his experience, realized that "by the act of eating and maybe only by that did he actually enter the world" (p. 207), "expiated his aberration from it," became "once more worthy to be received into it" (p. 209). His identification with the community, sharing its shame and its expiation, is the confirmation of his authenticity.

Having analyzed "the different courses open to Man on the threshold of the socialization of his species," Pierre Teilhard de Chardin had observed four possibilities: "to cease to act, by some form of suicide; to withdraw through a mystique of separation; to fulfill ourselves individually by egotistically segregating ourselves from the mass; or to plunge resolutely into the stream of the whole in order to become part of it." Charles's declaration of his reintegration into his community may be the equivalent of Faulkner's third way of coping with evil: "What we need are people who will say, This is bad and I'm going to do something about it, I'm going to change it" (*FU* 246). Teilhard was thinking in truly cosmic terms, Faulkner in terms of the foreseeable future of his cosmos, but their views seem complementary.

In *Intruder in the Dust*, as later in *The Town* and *The Mansion*, Gavin is the advocate of the values of existentialism. In his defense of the tradition of the South, he emphasized the humanistic values of that tradition, especially "that minimum of government and police which is the meaning of freedom and liberty" (p. 154). He recognized the evils wrought by uncritical conformity to traditional vices. He defended the privilege of the South to set free the Negro, in accordance with "the postulate that Sambo is a human being living in a free country and hence must be free" (p. 154). His use of "Sambo," however, is a sign that Gavin is not free of the taint of Southern prejudices, confirmed by Gavin's inability to treat Lucas as he would a white man of the same age in a commercial transaction: "'My receipt,' Lucas said" is not really a comic ending. Gavin is doing what Charles did in trying to pay for his dinner: being patronizing instead of acting as a guest or as a professional man being paid for his services. Aaron Steinberg stressed Gavin's refusal to regard Lucas as an adult and his paternalistic attitude toward an older man. Gavin referred to Lucas as "old Luke Beauchamp" in *Go Down, Moses* (p. 377). Gavin is more credible in his humanistic, existentialistic pronouncements than in his views on race. Man's transcendence, Gavin said, is seen in human history: "the whole chronicle of man's immortality is in the suffering he has endured in his struggle toward the stars in the stepping stones of his expiations" (pp. 154–55). Man tries to be right "if they who use him for their own power and aggrandisement let him alone. Pity and justice and conscience too—that belief in more than the divinity of individual man . . . but in the divinity of his continuity as Man" (p. 202). Gavin admitted his own initial error in not aiding Charles and confirmed the rightness of what Charles did and of the principle on which he acted: "Some things you must never stop refusing to bear. Injustice and outrage and dishonor and shame" (p. 206). As Lyall Powers said, "More important . . . than Gavin's resignation and withdrawal is young Chick Mallison's active and affirmative triumph; and in a very real sense it is a triumph over his Uncle Gavin and those whom he represents" (p. 203).

As *Intruder in the Dust* represents most fully the authentic individual in social action and the expression of the philosophical concepts of freedom and responsibility, it also most horrifyingly reveals the extreme of unauthenticity: the mob is the antithesis of individuality and freedom and responsibility. Charles's view of the mob as a Face is the ultimate of volitionless in-Humanity; ". . . not faces but a face, not a mass or even a mosaic of them but a Face; not even ravening nor uninsatiate but just in motion, insensate, vacant of thought or even passion: an Expression significantless and without past . . . without dignity and not even evocative of horror: just neckless slack-muscled and asleep, hanging suspended face to face with him just beyond the glass of the back window" (p. 182). "The mob," as Panthea Broughton said, "is ready to follow a code according to which Negroes are automatically lynched for killing white men." But when Lucas is found to be innocent, "the mob turns and runs. . . . Their actual physical flight is intended as an escape from self-recognition." The power of the "look" is indicated in the sheriff's explanation that lynchings do not begin by daylight "because then they would have to see one another's faces" (p. 114).

Equally impressive as a symbol of the volitionless unanimity of a mob is the flight of the mob when Crawford Gowrie was found guilty of fratricide: again the individual was absorbed in the mass and the action magnified, as the Face was magnified, but the flight was an expression of "one indivisible public opinion": "They didn't want to destroy Crawford Gowrie. They repudiated him. . . . they deprived him to the full extent of their capacity of his citizenship in man'' (p. 202).

Charles Mallison in *Intruder in the Dust* is the best example of the Faulknerian hero as described by Panthea Broughton, in terms of what existence entails rather than in terms of situations but not incompatible with existentialism. "What the Faulknerian hero should do is to cut himself loose from whatever would desensitize or insulate or assure, from whatever would hold him outside of flux. To do so he must dismiss all the rigid abstractions by which he has distanced himself from reality. . . . For existence demands that man must be aware of all it offers: that man acknowledge the impossibility . . . of exhausting experience and that he accept grief, suffering, and injustice and nevertheless struggle to do whatever he can to cure them."

To proceed from this point with an account of Gavin Stevens and Charles Mallison in *The Town* would be simple and would seem logical. But *Snopes* was planned as a whole before *Sartoris* was published, and a summary of the story of Flem from his arrival in Jefferson until he became vice president of the Sartoris bank was given in *Sartoris* (pp. 172–73). Byron and Eck Snopes are recognizable but not named. At that time Gavin Stevens was not even a gleam in his creator's eye. Moreover, when Faulkner sent a full synopsis of the Snopes trilogy to Robert Haas in December 1938 (Blotner, II, 1006–1008), the only characters recognizable in the published novels were Flem, his wife, and her daughter. Flem as the Alger-type hero provided the only plot line which survived the long interval between inspiration and composition. The creation of Gavin Stevens and Charles Mallison as leading characters in the novella, "Knight's Gambit," and *Intruder in the Dust* provided him with ready-made characters for *The Town* and *The Mansion* and for "facts of life" which would have to be coordinated with the role of Gavin. (Charles was "born again" in *The Town*; the dates of his birth differ. See the Stevens Genealogy in Cleanth Brooks, *William Faulkner: The Yoknapatawpha Country*.) To consider the whole life in Yoknapatawpha of Flem Snopes, Mink Snopes, V. K. Ratliff, and Eula Varner Snopes, it is necessary to go back to *The Hamlet* (1940) and to keep in mind that Faulkner was "re-creating" the last two novels to accommodate what his imagination and his life had provided since he created the Sartorises and Snopeses in the 1920s.

In Frenchman's Bend, the game of life is economic: in a poor farming community most of the interaction between villagers is trading with each other, by barter which becomes a contest for both profit and the satisfaction of winning. A good example of the literal horsetrading game is V. K. Ratliff's tale in which Ab Snopes was bested by Pat

Stamper who resorted to such skulduggery as coloring a bay horse black and inflating it with a bicycle pump so that Ab did not recognize it as the one he had left home with that morning (*H* 43). V. K. himself originated the goat deal which he hoped would bring him both profit from and victory over Flem. As Cleanth Brooks said, "The whole transaction is typical of Ratliff. He likes a devious game." Ratliff, however, was devious but honest and gave up his profit on the deal rather than take advantage of Flem's idiot nephew, Ike. Cleanth Brooks not only gives a detailed account of the transaction but includes bookkeeping entries worked out by Hervey C. Lewis. Mary Culley credits Ratliff as being the source of the sense of community by bringing people together to listen to his tales. With Ratliff, as she said, human and economic motives do not conflict, but with Flem Snopes in particular and all Snopeses in general, only their own advantage matters. The inhabitants of Frenchman's Bend are defending their own vested interests, as R. J. Trobaugh observed, against the Snopeses, the out-group, the aggressors. The same situation occurs when Flem rises on the economic ladder and goes to Jefferson, followed by his relatives. The horse auction engineered by Flem but conducted by a Texan, a stranger, expresses "the theme of the perversion of the natural" identified by Lyall Powers. Significantly, Ratliff was absent or merely an observer; he knew that the buyers of the horses would be victimized, as they were when the horses proved wild and escaped. But a man would not interfere in the business transactions of another. In the final perversion of nature, Flem triumphed over Ratliff, tricking him into thinking there was buried treasure at the Old Frenchman place. It was the one time Ratliff yielded to greed; he recovered his authentic ways and values, but Armstid, having lost money on the horse at the auction and broken his leg, was driven into complete madness by hopeless poverty. Not the least notable characteristic of Flem is that he rarely looks at anyone, eye to eye.

Mink is the third major character who appears throughout *Snopes*. He is a curious, unparalleled example of the unauthentic character whose very limitations evoke sympathy. Physically, psychologically, and economically "underprivileged," Mink's only way to transcend his limitations and assert himself as an individual, according to his code of honor, was to murder: thirty-eight years of his life were spent literally as "time served" between his murder of Houston and his murder of Flem. His unauthentic choice was rigidly adhered to. But his admirable qualities are most evident in *The Mansion*.

The other major theme in *The Hamlet*, represented by Eula Varner, is corollary to the all-male economic competition. The "ideal of masculinity," as Panthea Broughton said, "is defined in such narrow terms that it excludes the possibility of a relationship between a man and a woman based upon mutual respect and love. Marriage, to most of the characters in *The Hamlet*, is simply a contest for dominance." Strangely enough, Mink Snopes did marry for love but felt "an overriding compulsion to mask love as conquest." Broughton goes on to explain that in *The Hamlet* "the male identifies masculinity and honor with absolute self-sufficiency." Lyall Powers remarks on the intensity of Mink's and Yettie's love and on their loving "with honor and respect and a willingness to sacrifice." But "we are made to feel that Mink's peculiarity as a lover—not so much his almost obsessive concern with honor, perhaps, but especially his hot waspish sexuality—results from his social and economic condition. . . . But he is fiercely monogamous, fiercely moral, fiercely proud." Flem, however, "is mean and deadly, and evidently willfully so" and "represents simply the absence of love—its negation, in fact." By the time we find out that Flem is impotent we are ready to believe that he is "willfully so" in that respect also. Powers sums up the themes in *The Hamlet*: "love, exploitive barter and abuse, and nature."

By the end of *The Hamlet*, Eula, the Helen of Troy of Yoknapatawpha, has been pursued by youths in their chariots, has yielded to only one, Hoake McCarron, and Flem Snopes has been paid to marry her to give her unborn child a name. At the end, somewhat like Lena and Byron and the baby, Flem and Eula and baby Linda are headed for Jefferson. Different as the Varners are from the Compsons, they solve their similar problems the same way: between Herbert Head and Flem Snopes as a son-in-law a choice would be difficult.

In *The Town* the Snopes tribe are even more "outsiders" than they were in *The Hamlet*. Gavin Stevens assumed responsibility for defending Jefferson from the "herd of tigers" named Snopes, with V. K. Ratliff as his second-in-command: "it's for us to cope, to resist" he told Ratliff before leaving for Europe. "You'll have to hold the fort now. You'll have to tote the load" (p. 102). Unlike Mr. Compson who left the old diceman to play the game of life, Gavin and V. K., and Chick Mallison when he had been born and was old enough, shared the awareness James Gustafson spoke of as having impact on theological thinking: "we are the players, as well as the cards and the stakes."

Unfortunately Snopeses and their kind do not see themselves as "*participants in creativity*" as Gustafson saw mankind, "the shapers rather than conformers to static established shapes." Flem tried to make himself into the shape of the respected town leaders. When Manfred de Spain succeeded old Bayard Sartoris as bank president, Flem became vice president, thanks to Will Varner's bank stock. Flem's efforts to gain wealth and power constituted a series of "games" of his own invention to enhance his own status and to remove any threat to it. When he brought Eula to Jefferson he had made her sin pay for his advancement. He was not only a "voluntary cuckold," as Lyall Powers said, using Manfred's "interest in Eula to further his own welfare," but he was a typical Snopes "pander to perversity." He played Tom Tom and Turl, his helpers at the power plant, against each other to conceal his theft of the brass and was "the basic evil in the illicit union of Eula and Manfred." But when Montgomery Ward Snopes set up his "Atelier Monty" which was discovered to be a cover-up for pornography and thus a threat to Flem's status, Flem put moonshine whiskey into bottles which had had Kodak developer in them and thus got Monty sent to the state penitentiary for a federal offense. When he seems to be on the same side as Gavin, saying "I'm interested in Jefferson. We got to live here," and when Ratliff explained that Flem really wanted respectability, we may be taken in. We learn in *The Mansion* that Monty was sent to Parchman so that he could persuade Mink to try to escape so that his sentence and Flem's life would be lengthened. Having got rid of Monty, Flem got rid of I. O. whose habit of letting his livestock be killed by trains and collecting damages was becoming embarrassing. "Mule in the Yard" is very amusing before Flem enters the scene and engages Gavin as witness to the deal he makes with I. O. to get him out of Jefferson. That is the point at which Ratliff explains that to gain respectability Flem will stop at nothing: "aint nobody or nothing within his scope and reach that may not anguish and grieve and suffer" (p. 259). And that is evidence of Flem's unauthenticity: that to attain his perfectly acceptable ends he will sacrifice others ruthlessly. "Beneath that cloak of respectability," Lyall Powers said, "Flem will continue to manipulate human beings, to capitalize on man's potential for evil, to be . . . as fiendish as ever— but much less visibly so." And Linda was being manipulated, to the extent of making out a will in his favor so that no matter what happened to Eula, Flem would inherit the Varner money.

The cloak of respectability was ready-made for Flem. What Flem said to Gavin about living in Jefferson was sincere up to a point, for only a person who has not been respected can crave to achieve respectability as Flem did. Town life was a new game: he watched others playing it and imitated as best he could the way those people lived whose status he envied. They went to church: so did he and became a Baptist deacon. Reinhold Niebuhr perfectly expressed the social aspects of Calvinism, which was particularly strong in the South: "In

Calvinist thought prosperity as a mark of divine favor is closely related to the idea that it must be sought as part of a godly disciplined life." He quoted Max Weber's thesis: "Calvinism was responsible for creating the standards of diligence, honesty and thrift which would lie at the foundation of our capitalist culture." What Faulkner showed through Flem is, as G. W. Sutton said, how respectability may be a way of pursuing bestial goals while professing idealistic motives.

The games that Flem invented to gain the prosperity and power he desired were complicated, and the narrators, Gavin Stevens and V. K. Ratliff chiefly, were usually trying to figure out what Flem was up to rather than presenting solid facts. Therefore when Flem engaged in the final game, for the highest stakes, to get rid of De Spain by taking the bank from under him, "snatch it intact," as Gavin put it (p. 278), Flem's weapon is the fact that he had known and concealed for eighteen years, that Eula was De Spain's mistress. Flem rarely said anything. The only person who knew what the situation really was between Eula and Flem and Linda was Eula. Before considering her account to Gavin, one of the few occasions when the two of them had a long conversation, her previous choices, actions, and fulfilling of responsibility must be examined.

Neither the young men who were attracted to Eula nor her parents seemed much interested in Eula's marriage. When she finally yielded to Hoake McCarron and he and the other youths fled to Texas, Eula's parents paid Flem to marry Eula. The omniscient author tells us how Eula despised Flem, who had lived at Varners since she was fourteen, and how suddenly her parents dressed her up, took her to town, and married her to Flem. She was offered no choice, but apparently she registered no protest. After Linda was born, in Texas, Flem and Eula returned to Frenchman's Bend and then went to Jefferson. There is no omniscient author in *The Town*. But everyone in Jefferson, it seems, had known and kept the secret until, as Charles Mallison put it, "the saw of retribution" was about "to touch that secret . . . buried in the moral tree of our community" (*T* 307). Eula not only chose infidelity and deception for eighteen years but chose to bring up her daughter in such a situation. There is no evidence that Eula considered getting a divorce from Flem and marrying Manfred or separating from both Manfred and Flem and living on what her parents could well afford to provide for her.

In Gavin's office, when the saw of retribution was at work, Eula told Gavin that by being generous with Linda and finally letting her go away to the university, Flem had made Linda believe he really loved her. In gratitude she willed to Flem whatever she might inherit from Eula's share of the Varners' wealth. Flem took Linda's will to Varner, who knew nothing about Eula and Manfred. Eula said that Manfred was to give Flem the bank and she and Manfred were to leave town, which, she said, "was what we should have done eighteen years ago" (p. 329). Now her responsibility as a mother Eula considered seriously: she asked Gavin to marry Linda. She begged him repeatedly to promise to marry Linda and he promised; she said "swear" and he said "I swear" (T 332, 333).

Eula went home and committed suicide. As Charles Mallison said, Manfred had outraged the town and "flouted the morality of marriage" and "outraged the economy of marriage which is the production of children" (p. 338). And Eula committed suicide because she had "been an abomination before God for eighteen years" and reached "the point where she would have to choose death in order to leave her child a mere suicide for a mother instead of a whore" (p. 340). The unauthenticity of Flem throve on the unauthenticity of Eula and Manfred.

As Lyall Powers points out, Flem was "dog in the manger, willing cuckold, eager pander," but Manfred was at fault. Powers suggested that Manfred and Eula might have gone away and redeemed "the adultery by finally legalizing their union," but he wondered "just how willing Manfred was to take on full responsibility for Eula." And Linda!

Flem again secured the cooperation of Gavin as in the cases of Montgomery Ward and of I. O. Snopes. This time Gavin helped him get a marble likeness of Eula carved in Italy and put on a monument, on which the inscription read: "A Virtuous Wife Is a Crown to Her Husband / Her Children Rise and Call Her Blessed." The monument closely resembles that of Faulkner's grandmother in the cemetery in Oxford, and the second line also is on her monument. The first line people usually interpret as another example of the cloak of respectability. In the Bible Belt anyone who did not know what the next line is could find out as fast as I did: Proverbs 12:4, "but she that maketh him ashamed is as a rottenness in his bones." V. K. Ratliff explained that Flem's "game of solitaire was against Jefferson" and that the monument was the last thing needed to make it all "right and proper and decorous and respectable" (p. 348). Flem made Linda wait until the monument was erected and then let her go to Greenwich Village. She had been given by Will Varner "a good-size chunk of what would be Eula's inheritance under that will . . ." (p. 351).

Lyall Powers felt that Gavin not only failed Eula "through basic cowardice" but also aided "Flem's progress, thus helping to call down upon Jefferson and Yoknapatawpha County the general plague of Snopesism." Powers used the "Second Chance" as a term for the repeated situations in which Gavin failed to redeem a previous negative choice or failed in action: first as Eula's champion and then as Linda's Gavin was beaten, by Manfred de Spain and by Matt Levitt. The same pattern recurs in *The Mansion*, with significant effects. Gavin's un-authenticity includes repeated lies and broken promises. He asked Linda if he had ever lied to her and she replied: "You are the one person in the world I know will never lie to me." He answered: "I swear to you then, Flem Snopes is your father" (*T* 346).

The successive stages in Flem Snopes's socio-political views were neatly listed by Charles Mallison after Flem had restored the De Spain mansion to somewhat more than its pristine glory and had ensconced himself therein: Flem "had begun life as a nihilist and then softened into a mere anarchist and now was not only a conservative but a tory too: a pillar, rock-fixed, of things as they are" (*M* 222). The revelation of what really happened in the story of Montgomery Ward Snopes in *The Town* prepares the reader for less crude economic games on Flem's part, "Flem being a banker now," Ratliff said, "and having to deal not jest in simple usury but in respectability too" (*M* 53). When Montgomery Ward Snopes tells his own story, the only Snopes to be so privileged, he reveals that Flem's real reason for getting M. W. sent to Parchman was to trick Mink into attempting to escape; an unsuccessful attempt would add twenty-five years to Mink's sentence and thus that many years to Flem's life. With Lawyer Stevens and Hub Hampton as witnesses that bottles of moonshine whiskey were found in Monty's studio, Monty's guilt was indubitable and he was sentenced to two years at Parchman. Monty has real merits as a raconteur, with ironic humor and even a trace of compassion at times, as when he described Mink walking slowly across "that empty penitentiary compound" in a calico dress and sunbonnet (p. 85). It took five men to knock him out. Mink only mildly resented the woman's dress. Monty confirmed, at the end of his narrative, the suspicion Ratliff had that Eck Snopes was a bastard: "the one technically true pristine immaculate unchallengeable son of a bitch we ever produced wasn't even a Snopes" (p. 87).

The other economic game was initiated by Jason Compson, who should have known better than to assume that Flem was stupid. Jason wanted to sell what was left of the old Compson property and spread the word that it was likely to be the site of an airfield, a hilariously funny idea to anyone familiar with the Oxford topography Faulkner had in mind. Gavin thought that "Jason was simply waving that imaginary airfield around the Square, to spook Mr. Snopes into making the first move" (p. 324). And by January 1943 Flem owned the Compson place.

Flem was not deluded: he knew that as soon as the war was over, there would be great demand for new houses. He opened up a new subdivision, named it Eula Acres, and built modest little houses on it. Oxford has its equivalent. And Oxford even has Zillah Avent Drive, wittingly or unwittingly linking real-life Snopeses with Lot and his wife Zillah. The competition between Jason and Flem ended with the tricker tricked. Part of the Compson land was occupied by Orestes Snopes, who became involved in a feud with old Meadowfill, over a disputed title and a wandering hog, which almost led to murder and which required the professional services of Gavin Stevens.

But Flem was remote from such uncouth disturbances of the peace. He had no friends and no relatives with whom he was on friendly terms, but lived alone in the Mansion except for a few years before World War II and part of a year after 1945 when Linda lived with him. When he was at home he sat "with his feet propped on that little unpainted ledge nailed to his Adam fireplace and chewing steadily at what Ratliff called his little chunk of Frenchman's Bend air" (p. 222). Thus, as R. J. Trobaugh said, "Life and Flem conspire together to confine him within a tiny lonely universe." Mary Culley described him as a most "utterly diminished Faust." His trips to take Linda to the bootlegger's must have been a welcome diversion. Between Linda's deafness and Flem's taciturnity, her presence would not enliven the household, if one could call it that.

Neither Flem nor Mink can speak for himself. But in *The Mansion* Faulkner modified his technique and used the omniscient author as the teller of Mink's story, thus making the murderer more human than his victim. The real triumph in *The Mansion* is Mink, the personification of the humanist principle as stated by Paul Kurtz: "All men, as free persons, should be accorded some measure of respect, some dignity and value, as individuals." The dignity and integrity of Mink are inseparable from his determination to kill Flem to avenge his honor and that of the Snopes family.

The additions to and the alterations in the story of Mink as given previously contribute to the effect of authenticity of Mink's two choices, both of murder, and his undiminished determination to commit the second as soon as he has served his sentence for the first. A choice is added in *The Mansion*: Mink was offered the choice of going to the penitentiary or of spending the rest of his life in the insane asylum in Jackson, where he would have nothing to do but rest. He refused the second trial to which his lawyer thought his obvious madness entitled him. All that he insisted on was a written statement of what he must do to be released in twenty to twenty-five years. What he must not do was to try to escape; if he did, twenty-five years would be added to his sentence. And through Flem's villainy Mink served thirty-eight years in the penitentiary.

The other alteration, in the story of Mink and Houston, consists in the detailed account of the cow deal, when Mink tried to get his cow pastured free for the winter at Houston's. When Varner judged the case and fixed $18.75 as what Mink should pay, Houston offered him a chance to earn it digging post holes. Both Houston and Varner offered him money. But after his initial deception and lie about selling the cow, Mink insisted on paying the full amount, working literally night and day. And then because Mink did not take his cow out of the pound before dark, Houston charged him the regular one-dollar pound fee. Varner would have paid it but Mink refused. He worked the two more days to earn the dollar, and took his cow home. And after he had got a ride to Jefferson, had to spend the night there, and returned without the shotgun shells because Ike McCaslin would not sell them to him, he had to take a chance on his old shells firing and wait in ambush until Houston came along several days later. To the dead Houston he told his reason: "I killed you because of that-ere extry one-dollar pound fee." Mink proved as indomitable as he had been indefatigable. Mink possessed nothing but pride and honor as proof of his manhood and nothing but kinship as a bond with mankind. He literally gave his life to be able to live with himself.

Mink's journey from Parchman to Jefferson, via Memphis to buy the murder weapon and ammunition, is a large-scale version of the trip to Jefferson before he shot Houston. But this time he had been imprisoned for thirty-eight years, was leaping from 1908 into the motor age with little warning, and had $13.85 left from the $40 Monty (not Flem) had sent him, to get to Jefferson. Rip Van Winkle's problems were nothing to Mink's. He left with a trusty the fortune—two hundred and fifty dollars—the price paid to keep him out of Mississippi; since he was going to Mississippi, he could not honorably keep the money. Mink's conscience was selective but strict and enduring.

When Mink got to Flem's house, only his faith that "Old Moster dont play jokes: He jest punishes" gave him courage to face Flem with only one cartridge in his pistol. But "there must be that moment, even if it lasted only a second, for him to say, 'Look at me, Flem' " (p. 412). He had waited in the jail and in the courtroom for Flem to come and look at him. Surely no "look" was longer sought, first in hope and then in unrelenting, deadly anger. But "He didn't need to say, 'Look at me, Flem.' His cousin was already doing that, his head turned over his shoulder. Otherwise he hadn't moved, only the jaws had ceased chewing in midmotion" (p. 415). The pistol clicked and Mink had to roll the cylinder back so that the one shell would come under the hammer. But with faith in Old Moster he cocked the pistol again, "his cousin not moving at all now though he was chewing faintly again, as though he too were watching the dull point of light on the cock of the hammer when it flicked away" (p. 416).

The words of Ratliff as he and Gavin approached Mink's den in the old cellar anticipated Mink's thoughts: "He's free now. He wont never have to kill nobody else in all his life" (p. 432). No longer feeling threatened by the pull of the earth, he thought: "*I'm free now, I can walk any way I want to*" (p. 434). With the money from Linda, he could walk west. In harmony with the earth and with mankind, "equal to any, good as any, brave as any," he envisioned, perhaps at the point of death, "Helen and the bishops, the kings and the unhomed angels, the scornful and graceless seraphim."

The elegiac ending was derived, as Richard Adams discovered, from *The Playboy of the Western World* by J. M. Synge, and was echoed twice in *The Hamlet* in the Ike Snopes idyll, once at the coming of dawn and the second time when Ike and the cow lay down together (pp. 184, 189). The context in *The Mansion*, Mink's concept of having transcended earthly limitations, justifies the heightened style which surpasses his powers of expression.

Mink's choices and deeds must be judged in relation to his culture and his life of deprivation which failed to destroy his virtues and convictions. G. W. Sutton in "Primitivism in the Fiction of William Faulkner" explained the violence of Mink as characteristic of primitivism in the South; in Mink it was combined with pride in himself and his family, with determination, and with tenacious endurance. Mink's primitive code included his sense of "a sacred obligation to atone for the affronts to his human dignity." Mink's insistence on the "look" as a sign of recognition from Flem is related to his insistence on man-to-man dealings with others. Sutton commented on Mink as a "loner," with social concepts limited to his family who have rejected him. R. J. Trobaugh regarded Mink as lacking nobility but without a tragic flaw within his universe of meaning. His belief in some kind of divine justice was the source of his courage when all the odds were against him. Although Mink's faith in Old Moster was not shared by Lucifer, Cleanth Brooks suggested that Mink could have understood "the greatest of the scornful and graceless seraphim":

> All is not lost, the unconquerable Will,
> And study of revenge, immortal hate,
> And courage never to submit or yield. . . .

It is not quite fair to Gavin Stevens, with his many opportunities and his pleasant, easy life, to place him in juxtaposition with Mink, whose courage and willpower were notable. Even readers who have read "Knight's Gambit" and expect Melisandre to surface by 1942 can scarcely regard Gavin as an authentic married man. As Panthea Broughton noted, in commenting on the numerous bachelors in Yoknapatawpha, "Faulkner presents marriage as an ethical responsibility." "Bachelorhood, therefore, may be an attempt to hold the self outside ethical and emotional complexity. But bachelorhood is just one paradigmatic instance of the retreat from human commitment. Married and unmarried men and women throughout the fiction mistakenly conceive of a life disentangled from human ties as an ideal existence." In the context of what constitutes an authentic life, this comment is of primary significance.

The change which Faulkner made in the "facts" about Gavin and Margaret Stevens made Gavin's bachelorhood more convincing: with Margaret his twin sister instead of his younger sister, and Gavin and his father living with the Mallisons, Gavin had not only companionship with a congenial woman his own age but he enjoyed the closeness of twinship that Margaret described in reference to John and Bayard Sartoris: "they don't even know that they loved themselves first" (*M* 190). There is no indication that Gavin and Margaret were like Horace and Narcissa Benbow, but there was a rapport between the Stevens twins which made Margaret aware of Gavin's feelings and needs in relation first to Eula and then to Linda. Gavin avoided permanently the responsibility of fatherhood but was an excellent uncle to Charles: "Father just talked to me while Uncle Gavin listened to me" and would say "*'Let's try it.'* Not *YOU* try it but *US* try it" (*M* 321).

Stephen Ballew, dealing with "Faulkner's Psychology of Individualism," said that Faulkner believed "in man's inevitable relationships in communities. Adult figures who embody communal values and authority make an indelible imprint on the psyches of his self-reliant men." Both Gavin and V. K. Ratliff are such adults. Still with Emerson's "Self-Reliance" in mind but primarily in relation to *Light in August*, Ballew made a statement which applies particularly to Charles Mallison: a man who has been deeply influenced by his society can gain independence "by achieving a measure of control over past impressions so that he can form his own system of values and freely make decisions."

Gavin's attitude toward Linda repeats his response to Eula, when Eula was a married woman with a lover. But with Linda it remains the same when she is a schoolgirl, when she is a grown woman celebrating a housewarming without marriage, and when she marries Barton Kohl. We have only Gavin's account, of course, of episodes involving only

himself and Linda. When she married, Gavin prognosticated that
Linda's doom would be to love once and lose him and then to mourn.
And when she did lose him, as Charles said, Gavin "had his own
prognosis to defend" (*M* 219). And he went on defending it and rejecting her, even in Pascagoula where, as a middle-aged, deaf widow,
Linda no doubt figured that no one would pay much attention to her
and her elderly gentleman friend. But Gavin treated her just as he had
her mother. Finally she gave up and told Gavin to marry someone else.
That was in the summer of 1941. When she returned in the fall of 1945,
she found he had done so: he married Melisandre Backus Harriss in
1942—of whom, apparently, she had never heard, although he had
formed Melisandre's mind not many years before he formed Linda's.
Linda had been telling Gavin back in the late twenties that she loved
him. It never occurred to him that *he* was the one she was doomed to
love and lose, eventually by his marriage to a millionairess, with a
country estate.

This was the situation when Linda ran out of injustices, as Ratliff
said, and whatever cause she took up would prove dangerous for
Gavin. Melisandre proved that Gavin was not impervious to love: his
vulnerability lay in the one choice he had made and assumed responsibility for: his profession. And he refused to believe the evidence
which proved that he had been manipulated into being an accessory
before the fact of murder. Only a clue as garish as the new British
Jaguar could not be ignored. Gavin's one consolation was that Linda
did not lie to him. That was a consolation Linda did not have. She no
doubt told the truth when she said she had never loved anybody but
Gavin (p. 425). After giving Gavin the money to take to Mink, Linda
looked at him for the last time: "no faint smile, no nothing: just the
eyes which even at this distance were not quite black" (p. 426).

Linda, like Eula, is seen only through the eyes of men. But since she
is only a temporary resident of Yoknapatawpha, her beliefs and actions
do not reflect the influence of the society she belonged to by birth.
Cleanth Brooks commented on Gavin's failure to understand Linda
"as a woman or as a committed human being," "a person who believes
sufficiently in direct action to liquidate an enemy." Although Brooks is
right in saying that with few of Faulkner's characters are we "taken
into the decision chambers of their souls to watch the process by which
they come to act," Faulkner did precisely that, magnificently, with
Mink, but the only woman whose decision chamber he entered was
Addie Bundren, after she was dead. Linda may be "a sort of Medea,
an implacable avenging spirit," as Brooks said. But there is no evidence that she returned to kill Flem, rather than to be near Gavin.

Flem is, as Brooks said, "the perfect incarnation of all she has been taught to hate in the system of finance capitalism." But she lived with Flem from 1938 to January 1941, when she went to Pascagoula, and again on her return in the fall of 1945. Mink was released in October 1946 and killed Flem as soon as he could get to Jefferson. A Medea would not wait like that for an agent whose time was not his own and the date of whose release was not fixed. The only time that Linda and Melisandre appear together is a scene in Charles's account of one of the monthly dinners at Rose Hill which apparently began in the spring of 1946, when Gavin began "acting the squire." The next chapter covers from the beginning of negotiations to get Mink released until after Flem was killed.

Linda may well have returned to Jefferson in 1938 in the hope that Gavin would marry her. After he repeated his refusals to have Linda on any terms, Gavin married a woman from his past, with grown children, perhaps a grandmother. It was not marriage, then, that Gavin refused: it was Linda. Just before she drove away in the new Jaguar, she said to Gavin: "I love you. . . . I have never loved anybody but you" (*M* 425). There is no reason to doubt her word. Gavin was the one who could say "I swear" and then tell a lie. If killing Flem had not been Mink's sole purpose in life, her using Mink as a tool could be held against Linda. But with the childhood Linda had endured and the new world of Greenwich Village that Gavin thrust her into, where would Linda learn about authenticity after Gavin had lied to her and she had met her father?

V. K. Ratliff's role as companion to Gavin, witness, and narrator of events allows new revelations of his character and his capacity for effective action. The trip to New York with Gavin to attend Linda's wedding to Barton Kohl took him into a totally unfamiliar world where his self-respect and respect for others and his intuitive understanding stood him in good stead. He was as much at ease with Allanovna, the designer of ties, and Barton Kohl, the sculptor, as he was with Linda's father, Hoake McCarron, whom he had known in Frenchman's Bend, and he was more appreciative of the creations of artists than were sophisticated intellectuals.

This episode, however, is less significant than his unaccustomed political action, with its potential national and international effects. Will Varner had long exercised paternalist control of political candidates in his district. Memorable in *Sanctuary* as the voyeur at Miss Reba's as well as the source of Horace's information about Temple, Clarence Snopes had risen in politics to the state legislature, needing "no other platform than Uncle Billy Varner's name" (p. 301). "Having been designated by old Varner custodian of the public peace," he advanced in politics through his capacity to employ men "like mules or oxen, with one eye constant for the next furrow" (p. 301). His procedure was to join any organization "which he might compel or control or coerce through the emotions of religion or patriotism or just simple greed" (pp. 303–304). Uncle Will Varner as the paternalistic political "boss" and Clarence as his tool illustrate the point made by Frederick Olafson that "moral paternalism" which professes to know what is good for the individual moral agent is "alien to the general ethos of existentialism."

The dismay which overwhelmed Gavin and V. K. and the rest of the small group of "unreconstructed purists" in 1946 when Clarence Snopes decided to run for Congress is understandable. His opponent was Colonel Devries, who had volunteered to command Negro troops and had won a Medal of Honor and lost a leg while so engaged. All Clarence had to do to defeat Devries was to stress his military record. Ratliff was telling Charles what had happened before he got home in September and explaining to Gavin why it happened. As Gavin said, the Medal of Honor awarded Devries "for risking death to defend the principles" on which our nation was founded "had destroyed forever his chance to serve in the Congress which accoladed him" (p. 312).

When Ratliff explained why Clarence suddenly retired from politics after Uncle Will Varner's annual picnic for his political constituents, we learn of his last and best trick. (He concealed his own role until the end of the tale.) V. K. knew of a thicket he described as a "dog postoffice," and directed to it the twin nephews of Devries. They armed themselves with well-irrigated switches with which they gently stroked the back of Clarence's trouser legs. The horde of dogs quickly got the message and lined up behind Clarence before he knew what was happening. When he did and got into a car, the dogs circled around it until the owner came and drove Clarence home, with the dogs trailing for two miles. That finished Clarence with Varner, who refused to have his state and county represented by a man dogs could not tell from a fence post. V. K. saw to it that Varner hushed up the incident. This is the most admirable of V. K.'s devious tricks: Clarence was a trickster himself who deserved to be tricked, and V. K. did so in a way that did no more than temporarily embarrass Clarence but enormously benefited the voters who were really dedicated to the principles on which the nation was founded. V. K. tried to give Devries credit for "a little political strategy" but said that a man should "keep his eyes open" and use what he has as best he can (p. 320).

It remained for Charles to point out to Gavin the moral. He repeated what Gavin had said in 1937 about political activity: "We are too old, too tired, have lost the capacity to believe in ourselves"; and "America: the greatest country in the world if we can just keep on affording it." God saved them this time, Charles said, "using V. K. Ratliff as His instrument." But Ratliff might not be there the next time. "So what you need is to learn how to trust in God without depending on Him. In fact, we need to learn to fix things so He can depend on us for a while" (p. 321).

After Linda had driven off in her new car and before Gavin and Ratliff delivered the money she had given them for Mink, in his hole in the ground, a "den like an animal," Gavin remembered Flem's funeral. Not just the town but the county came too, although Flem "had no auspices . . .; fraternal, civic, nor military: only finance, not an economy. . . . He had been a member of a Jefferson church true enough, as the outward and augmented physical aspect of the edifice showed, but even that had been . . . simply an armistice temporary between two irreconcilable tongues" (p. 419). Except Wall Snopes and his family, who were not really Snopeses and whose success and respectabililty were both genuine, Gavin identified other Snopeses, like "*wolves come to look at the trap where another bigger wolf, the boss wolf . . . died: if maybe there was not a shred or scrap of hide still snared in it*" (p. 421).

In their last dialogue, as they are driving out to Mink's den, Gavin and V. K. discuss Gavin's ordeal. V. K. will not let Gavin deceive himself: "So you think she really didn't know what he was going to do when he got out?" By giving Gavin information he had collected by examining the pistol Mink threw away when he fled, V. K. brought up the question of why Flem sat there while Mink snapped "them two shells at him until one of them went off and killed him" (p. 430). Then V. K. explained in terms of a game, "Give-me-lief," in which one boy would hit another with a stick or switch or throw something at him, and then the "target" would do to the other boy, who had to stand and take it, what had been done to him. So, as V. K. said, "Flem had had his lief fair and square like the rule said, so there wasn't nothing for him to do but jest sit there . . ." (pp. 430–31). V. K. was sure that both Linda and Flem knew what Mink would do as soon as he was freed. "So she had a decision to make too that once she made it, it would be for good and all and too late to change it." She could have waited for two years when Mink would have been released and "saved herself not jest the bother and worry but the moral responsibility too, even if you do say there aint no morals" (p. 431). V. K. believed in moral responsibility, but he compassionately saved Gavin from assuming more responsibility than was his. Mink's success showed him that Old Moster favored him. What, then, could mortals like V. K. and Gavin do to prevent divine justice from operating? V. K., of course, did not know all that went on between Gavin and Linda and would not ponder what would have happened if Gavin had married Linda before Melisandre turned up. In the short last chapter in "Linda," Charles told the story of Gavin's marriage to Melisandre much as it is given in "Knight's Gambit," but without the earlier story of Gavin and Melisandre as given in *The Town*. Conjectural though Linda's motives may be, Gavin was unquestionably unfair to her to insist that she play the role he doomed her to and then to prove that he was not immune to marriage and to choose a widow.

James G. Watson's interpretation of the signs of the zodiac (*M* 417, 433) is useful: Libra, the scales of justice, symbolic of Gavin; Scorpio, scorpion, symbolic of Mink (*M* 287); Virgo, symbolic of Linda. But his statement that throughout *The Mansion* Linda is "imagined as a virgin, 'the inviolable bride of silence, inviolable in maidenhead' [*M* 203], who frees love from its ritual enactment" ignores the facts that Charles is the narrator, referring particularly to Linda's deafness, and that on the next page Charles says: "She's going to marry him." Furthermore, freedom from ritual enactment of marriage does not mean preservation of virginity. Linda married Barton after living with him unmarried. Watson interpreted Libra as "signifying not only Mink's and Linda's commitment to justice but also the justness of their commitment." If Gavin was persuaded of the justness of Mink's commitment, why did he try so hard to prevent Mink from fulfilling his only remaining purpose in life? If Gavin believed in the justness of Linda's commitment, why was he so shocked when he discovered her collusion in the murder of Flem? Flem was not the cause of Eula's suicide. When he had Manfred de Spain's bank, Manfred could have his wife and welcome. Eula's suicide was caused by her choice to live a life of adultery, for eighteen years, with Linda bound to find out the truth as she grew up, the truth being less excusable as long as Linda thought Flem was her father. "Gavin's reaffirmation of their love" does not, as Watson asserts it does, exonerate either of them "of cruelty or inhumanity" to the other, although it might signify forgiveness. Gavin denied Linda physical love and an opportunity for a life of shared love with a family and then married Melisandre, another widow. Linda deliberately chose to deceive Gavin and to let Mink bear the literal guilt of murder while she, who made the murder possible, rode off scot-free. Gavin was left with the guilt of his complicity. The evidence of Linda's love for Gavin is adequate to explain her intervention in Mink's release as motivated by revenge and conceived after Linda's second return to Jefferson and discovery of Gavin's marriage. Gavin is the only one with enough knowledge of all that transpired in his relationship with Linda to realize that her motive might be revenge. His compassion is undeniable, but equally undeniable is his self-deception. V. K. Ratliff made Gavin face evidence that Linda made him an accessory to murder. V. K. is compassionate too, but when he says "The pore sons of bitches" (*M* 429), he is soothing Gavin, not denying personal responsibility as an existential element of human life.

V. K. Ratliff's last trick was the most significant: it involved national and international issues with which Faulkner was deeply concerned, as his speeches during the 1950s indicate. The authenticity of Ratliff's motives and actions is not lessened by the ridiculousness of his methods, just as Faulkner in his fiction might choose to convey serious ideas through comic action. If Flem Snopes represented the "unpalliated amorality of an aggressor whose successes are excruciatingly injurious," in Watson's words, why was an intelligent, well-educated lawyer like Gavin Stevens unable to defeat Flem by legal means during over twenty-five years? Flem was incredibly solitary (*M* 419). He had low animal cunning but no great intelligence and no creativity; all he could do was imitate what he could observe in his very restricted environment. Gavin failed in another area of justice, equality before the law. He did not act to aid Negroes, not even Lucas Beauchamp. Butch Lovemaiden in *The Reivers* resembles Clarence Snopes when he was a constable (*M* 198–301). Butch is described by Ned and Miss Reba as a familiar type of law officer (*R* 210–11, 185–86).

No doubt few readers now dealing with Faulkner read *The Reivers* when it was Faulkner's latest novel, not his last. I had just read *The Reivers* when his death was announced; I found some consolation in the thought that he had obviously much enjoyed writing what proved to be his last novel. It had a special quality which reminded me of his remark to Jean Stein: "My last book will be the Doomsday Book, the Golden Book of Yoknapatawpha County. Then I shall break the pencil and I'll have to stop" (*LG* 255). When I wrote an article on *The Reivers*, I borrowed "golden" to convey my sense of the quality of the book and used as my title "*The Reivers*: The Golden Book of Yoknapatawpha County." On going back to Cleanth Brooks's chapter on *The Reivers*, I was pleased to rediscover that his reactions had been similar to mine even in the concluding imagery: "Some of his basic convictions about human nature receive their happiest and most skillful dramatic treatment here. Moreover, Faulkner has been extremely successful in his handling of the tone of his novel, casting over Yoknapatawpha County and its inhabitants a kind of golden retrospective atmosphere.'' Knowing more now about Faulkner's struggles and problems than even Joseph Blotner knew in 1962, I feel that this "reminiscent" and "valedictory novel,'' as Brooks called it, might be regarded as "a valediction forbidding mourning.'' William Faulkner had completed his cosmos and in doing so had expressed a final affirmation; he had enjoyed modest success financially; he had succeeded beyond his wildest dreams in his literary fame and beyond his wildest nightmares in the attention he received. And he had three grandchildren. It is pleasant to know that Faulkner did enjoy writing *The Reivers* so much that as he handed Joseph Blotner a newly completed section to read, he said: "This book gets funnier and funnier all the time" (II, 1795).

Olga Vickery felicitously described the combination of romance and reality: "In *The Reivers* Faulkner has created his enchanted land; it is Prospero's island compounded of the innocence of youth and the wisdom of old age, of dream, imagination, and fantasy, which are, nevertheless, firmly anchored in the reality of Jefferson and Yoknapatawpha County. It encompasses elemental good and elemental evil, but above all it is a world of infinite freedom and therefore of infinite possibility.'' Faulkner's references to his creation as a cosmos reminds one of Dante's "construction of a complete universe,'' the *Commedia*. In discussing Dante, John Gardner suggested that "an unspoken premise in his way of thinking,'' "his test of authenticity in himself,'' was that he was capable of "at least sensitivity to goodness in others.'' That premiss in Faulkner's creation seems more likely in *The Reivers* than in some other Yoknapatawpha novels. But, as Cleanth Brooks said, the experience of Lucius "may verge on the improbable . . . but it never becomes, in the telling, soft-headed or irresponsibly soft-hearted.'' Its unique quality is that the authenticity is that of both the boy living the events and the grandfather telling of them.

In *The Reivers* there is a suggestion of Dante's Hell, Purgatory, and Heaven: the worst ordeal of their journey is at Hell Creek bottom; the expedition thereafter causes physical suffering and pangs of conscience for Lucius that may well be redemptive punishment, and the return to his loving family and the wisdom and understanding of his grandfather is as close to bliss as Lucius can hope for. But *The Reivers* itself is the *Paradiso* in Faulkner's cosmos. I was anticipating with pleasure, even though it might steal some of my thunder, the chapter on *The Reivers* in *The Yoknapatawpha Comedy* by Lyall Powers, until I discovered that, although the thesis is that "The Yoknapatawpha Saga is our modern American divine comedy,'' it appears at the end of the book and neither "Dante'' nor "The Divine Comedy'' is listed in the index. The only mention of *The Reivers* is in the introduction: it is omitted "as falling outside the Saga proper: it is, rather, an engaging and altogether charming 'Afterword.'" Powers apparently thinks that *The Reivers* was planned after *Snopes* was concluded. But in *Faulkner* Joseph Blotner included a letter to Robert Haas giving a 1940 synopsis of "a sort of Huck Finn" novel which is much closer to *The Reivers* than the 1938 synopsis of *Snopes* was to the finished work. Leaving out *The Reivers* is a bit like omitting an account of a church steeple because it was put on last.

Critics writing before Joseph Blotner's biography of Faulkner was published might fail to realize the special significance of *The Reivers*, but Cleanth Brooks, Olga Vickery, and Michael Millgate did not. Millgate concludes his chapter on *The Reivers* with a comment which would be even more valid if it specified the Yoknapatawpha fiction: "it seems, in retrospect, an entirely appropriate final volume in that long row of novels and short story collections which demonstrates . . . the security of Faulkner's claim to major status." Cleanth Brooks does so specify: "It is appropriate that Faulkner's last novel should exhibit . . . the full range of the classes and kinds of people who live in his famous county." The unique feature of *The Reivers*, however, is that it depicts the only family in Yoknapatawpha which extends to three generations living in harmony and showing serious concern for the spiritual, intellectual, and emotional well-being of the children in the family. The other side of that uniqueness is that it is closer to reality than any of the other families in Yoknapatawpha: the Priests are much like the Falkners, and Grandfather Priest and Grandfather William Faulkner are at times as difficult to tell apart as are identical twins. John Faulkner's *My Brother Bill* and Murry C. Falkner's *The Falkners of Mississippi* are both valuable as sources of information which increase one's understanding of the family and the society in which William Faulkner grew up and about which he wrote in *The Reivers*. In a foreword to Murry Falkner's book, Lewis Simpson said that it is free from "what may be termed . . . the tyranny of Yoknapatawpha . . . the power of the fictional world of Yoknapatawpha, one of the most convincingly illusory worlds ever developed, to impose itself upon anything written about Oxford and Lafayette County, Mississippi." In Murry Falkner's book, "we seem to be seeing the Falkners and their world in . . . pre-Yoknapatawpha times."

Because so little of the action in *The Reivers* takes place in Jefferson, the Priest family life plays little part, but the basic make-up and living quarters of the Priest grandparents and Lucius' family are parallel to those of the Falkners. The description of "what was Grandfather's house" (*R* 66) precisely fits the reality as it existed when I first went to Oxford. Other allusions are in general equally realistic. Murry Falkner adds to details of family life accounts of their grandfather's first auto and of a trip to Memphis in 1910: the passengers in the Buick included Chess, the driver, the Colonel (Grandfather Falkner), Bill and Murry, and their aunt and her daughter. The trip took two long days and created an incredible number of mechanical and tire problems. They did not stay at Miss Reba's.

The Reivers is an initiation story, both similar to and different from previous ones. Lucius is the intiate and frequently emphasizes the fact of his introduction to unfamiliar people, places, and situations not usually available to a boy of eleven. Boon, his mentor, is not as smart as Lucius. The familiar patterns of the heroic journey with its many hazards and complicated tests of skill suggest knights and tournaments. Cleanth Brooks provides a useful term for this initiation story in which the standard of behavior that Lucius is trying to maintain, as he has been taught, is that of a gentleman: "a latter-day 'courtesy book.'" Miss Reba and her "girls" were amazed when Lucius "drug" his foot, "made" his "manners." (The male equivalent of a female curtsy.) Olga Vickery differentiated the three heroes, Boon, Ned, and Lucius, by knightly terms: Boon, the warrior, who performs feats of strength; Ned, the leader, the doer of glorious deeds who achieves a personal triumph; Lucius, "the knight as moral exemplar . . . who is pure of heart, noble of thought, courageous in deed." Instead of the tournament, there are horse races, the same two horses in several heats, with much betting. Lucius is the jockey, on the horse Ned has custody over. Of all the complicated bartering and dickering and "life is a game" elements in Yoknapatawpha fiction, the horse races and the preliminary and what might be called postliminary bargaining are the most complicated and amusing, but with genuine concern for the welfare of all involved. In *Faulkner's Vitalistic Vision*, Peter Crow entitled the chapter on *The Reivers* "Motion Glorified by Regeneration and Growth" because, he said, the actions and characters in the novel imply "a summing up of the spectrum of Faulkner's vitalistic vision which reaches symbolic proportions in the Parsham horse race."

The horse race, with Lucius as the jockey, is the crucial event upon which the return to Jefferson in the Buick depends and which converts the initiation situation into one which places such a burden of responsibility upon Lucius that the existentialist values are singularly appropriate. Free will, choice, action, responsibility for the action chosen provide the framework for the thoughts and actions of Lucius and

frequently for his expression of his inner experience. The keen awareness of Lucius of his choice of evil began with his repeated lying to
make possible the four-day trip to Memphis with Boon in his grandfather's Buick while his parents and grandparents were in Bay St.
Louis. Although early in the game Lucius had "told more lies" than he
had thought he could invent and had had them believed with spellbind-
ing consistency (p. 62), he was "*sick and tired of lying, of having to
lie*" (p. 64), and his confession to Boss Priest began "I lied" (p. 301).
Ernst Breisach devoted a third of his last chapter in *Introduction to
Modern Existentialism* to "Existentialists on Truth and God." He said:
"the existentialists have never abandoned their emphasis on truth as
an individual concern." Murry Falkner testified to truth as basic in
Faulkner's system of values: "He felt that the ultimate in weak and
worthless character was the man who would lie to advance his own
cause or to save his own skin." The lies of Lucius and those of Gavin
to Eula and Linda were not those which are unavoidable, "to ease a
mental or physical burden on one more feeble and unfortunate than
himself."

From the beginning Lucius knew Boon would respect his views, but
knew that Lucius was corruptible (p. 45). Boon could go by himself if
Lucius "had been incorruptible." But what lends this initiation an
unusual twist is that Lucius knew that he was more culpable than Boon
because he was smarter and therefore "of we two doomed and irrevocable, I was the leader, I was the boss, the master" (p. 53). Therefore
the choices are his and also the responsibility, although the action is
shared by Boon and Ned. In his meditations on good and evil or Virtue
and Non-virtue, Lucius repeatedly compared himself with Faustus and
used game imagery: "already a lost liar, already damned by deceit;
why didn't I go the whole hog and be a coward too; be irrevocable and
irremediable like Faustus became? glory in baseness, compel my new
Master to respect me for my completeness?" (pp. 60–61). When he had
told all the lies needed and had them believed, "if Non-virtue still
wanted either of us, it was now her move" (p. 62). When they were on
their journey and had gone through Hell (Creek bottom), Lucius
thought that maybe "Virtue . . . had given us up, relinquished us to
Non-Virtue to cherish and nurture and coddle in the style whose right
we had won with the now irrevocable barter of our souls" (pp. 93–94).
Here we have barter added to the game pattern of man's life.

Even before he had left Jefferson, Lucius felt the burden of the
"dreadful freedom" of some existentialists and reverted to his childish
self: "I wanted . . . no more of free will; I wanted to return, relinquish,
be secure, safe from the sort of decisions and deciding. . . . But it was

too late now; I had already chosen . . .; if I had sold my soul to Satan for a mess of pottage, at least I would damn well collect the pottage and eat it too . . ." (p. 66). R. J. Trobaugh said that Faulkner "believes man has an essential freedom and responsibility." "Exercising this freedom . . . implies all the sordid and magnificent possibilities of moral and responsible existence. It implies that man is capable of shame and grandeur, corruption and compassion, responsible guilt and responsible goodness." He cited Lucius Priest as learning that freedom and guilt are inseparable, and said that "authentic human freedom" involves sin and suffering.

The journey from Jefferson to Memphis provided Faulkner with an opportunity to have Grandfather Lucius tell his grandson about the people and history of the region they were traversing. John Gardner's explanation of "the good creative artist" is "a man who has learned . . . to drop at will almost anywhere he wishes in his experience, recapturing an infinite variety of impressions from the past." That past for Faulkner was both the cosmos he had created and the world of actuality; those worlds are most prominently and significantly represented in *The Reivers* because Faulkner the creator is imagining an experience in his own familiar world. Parsham Junction is not in Yoknapatawpha but it is well known to residents of Oxford. It is Grand Junction, Tennessee, where indeed the Grand National Trials take place for bird-hunting dogs, and the men named are real, except Colonel Linscomb and Colonel Sartoris. The town is still much as it is described, and the actual plantation is the Ames plantation. Faulkner was doing what Thomas Mann did in *Death in Venice*, according to John Gardner, giving accurate descriptions that can be verified: "the truth of place . . . gives increased weight, increased authority." To treat the racing portion of the story as purely romantic is a misrepresentation and misinterpretation: the force of romantic concepts as motives for action is much more convincing if the locale is ordinary. And Grandfather Priest is presumably telling his story to a child who is familiar with the places and local history and legends.

The initiation at Miss Reba's goes far beyond what Boon had intended: he was unaware of Corrie's dormant affinity for good and of even the existence of Otis, with his rampant affinity for evil. Boon specified three points. The first is that a boy can learn things he may have use for later if he remembers them, like what Lucius learned about driving a car to Memphis. The second is that Lucius is about to learn some more things he had not thought about that "a lot of folks" would try to claim he was not old enough to bother with knowing. And the third, Lucius put into more simple and direct terms: "What you mean is, whatever I see on this trip up here, not to tell Boss or Father or Mother or Grandmother when we get back home'' (p. 105).

When Lucius made his manners again for Corrie, Miss Reba said to Corrie, ''You brought that nephew of yours over here hunting refinement. Here it is, waiting for him. . . . Maybe Lucius could learn him to at least ape it'' (p. 102). Corrie's instinctive desire for refinement made her an eager novice in the world of gentlemen and ladies. Lucius learned a good deal about houses and house rules from Mr. Binford and Miss Reba, in language which he had not heard at home, and described Mr. Binford, the landlord, as ''the prince and paragon, a man of style and presence and manner and ideals; incorruptible in principles and impeccable in morals''—that is, among landlords of whorehouses (p. 114).

But before Lucius could learn more about this subculture, he had to help load a horse onto a boxcar. When he returned, he shared a room with Otis, Corrie's nephew, who was impervious to refinement but even more corrupt and greedy for money than Lump Snopes was. Having made his choice and accompanied Boon, Lucius had to listen to Otis. ''There are things, circumstances, conditions in the world which should not be there but are, and you cant escape them and indeed, you would not escape them if you had the choice, since they too are part of Motion, of participating in life, being alive. But they should arrive with grace, dignity'' (p. 155). When Lucius learned about Otis' peephole and his exploitation of Corrie, beyond that by Aunt Fittie—''the demon child who debased her privacy and the witch who debauched her innocence'' (p. 157)—he fought Otis and cut his hand on Otis' knife. His real victory came when Corrie learned what had happened, that she had been the lady defended by a gallant knight. She told Lucius: ''it won't be my fault any more. . . . You can choose. You can decide. You can say no. You can find a job and work.'' And that is what she promised Lucius she would do and made him say out loud ''I'll take it'' (p. 160). The action of Lucius, the gentleman defending a lady, was the beginning of the authentic life of Corrie.

Having swapped the Buick for a race horse with which he expects to win money to pay off his kinsman Bobo's debt and repossess the car, Ned emerges as the leader. He exemplifies Peter Crow's ''true comic character,'' who ''chooses his or her role on the basis of inclination and natural attributes.'' ''The main value of the comic mode,'' Crow said, ''is nothing less than the preservation and perpetuation of life and motion.'' Crow describes Ned as ''a pattern-free character'' whose ''value to his community depends largely upon the motives of his actions.'' Ned's motives and value are ultimately made clear. At

Parsham Junction, where the race track is, Ned is the first male Negro—as Minnie was at Miss Reba's—to play a role parallel to that of a white person, with no diminution of dignity except when he is deliberately playing a comic, stereotyped role. When he first told Miss Reba about the race, Lucius said: "Now Ned looked at her, for a full quarter of a minute; the spoiled immune privileged-retainer impudence of his relations with Boon and the avuncular bossiness of those with me, were completely gone" (pp. 127–28). And again, when Ned was training Lucius to ride the horse, Lightning, Lucius commented: "He spoke, quiet and succinct. He was not Uncle Remus now. But then, he never was when it was just me and members of his own race around" (p. 182). That statement, as succinct as Ned could be, indicates the unique value of the portrayal of the numerous Negro characters in *The Reivers*: the point of view of Lucius is more that of a Negro than that of a white person, especially a white adult. The same code of a gentleman is observed by Negroes in terms of respect such as "Mr." whether the man is black or white: when Lycurgus called Ned "Mr. McCaslin," Lucius refrained from asking "What?" and admitting his progress "in weary unillusion" (p. 228). Ned said to Lucius: "Make your manners to Uncle Possum Hood" and Lucius did so (p. 168). (Hodding Carter was one of the first Southern journalists to put "Mr." or "Mrs." with the name of a Negro.) Because of the point of view of young Lucius and the fascinating adventures, the reader is left to note with due care the innumerable details revealing race discrimination except when they are embodied in Butch Lovemaiden and the situation is too exciting and humorous or too threatening for the reader to pause and meditate. Because Butch is outside Yoknapatawpha he is not treated here as a major character.

Lucius accepted his role as jockey in the race because of his responsibility for the consequences of his choice, although his wildest dreams or nightmares could not have envisioned a horse race as the result of borrowing an auto. As Lucius "had gone too far to quit," Everbe's promise to Lucius made her resist Boon and tell him she had quit. Boon's protest to Lucius made clear that between women and slaves there was little difference: both could be bought (pp. 196, 197). Miss Reba's "cat-house problems" now included Otis, who stole Minnie's gold tooth, and Lucius, who was driving her "damned girls into poverty and respectability" (p. 209).

By the time Ned had got the male members of his retinue to the Linscomb plantation where the race track was, Lucius realized how he and Lightning carried the fate of the rest of them, "certainly Boon's and Ned's, since on us depended under what conditions they could go back home, or indeed if they could go back home'' (p. 224). If he and Lightning ''were not the last desperate barrier between Boon and Ned and grandfather's anger, even if not his police,'' they were all ''engaged in a make-believe not too different from a boys' game of cops and robbers'' (p. 230).

Butch's machinations having deprived Lucius of his companions' company overnight after the first day of racing, Lucius chose to spend the night with Uncle Parsham. In this episode one becomes almost as color-blind as the mules at Hell Creek bottom, unless one remembers to color Uncle Parsham black. He and Boss Priest are so similar, even in both being Masons, that Lucius could not have made a better choice. Uncle Parsham's courtesy and dignity, his compassion, and his profound understanding of just what Lucius needs to overcome traumatic experiences make this episode one of the most memorable. The lesson in how to drive a mule restored to Lucius a sense of the ''power, . . . intelligence, sagacity; . . . the willingness to choose when necessary between two alternatives and to make the right decision without hesitation'' (p. 246). In relief Lucius dissolved in tears ''against Uncle Parsham's shirt.'' That night, when Lucius was given a choice of a bed to himself or sharing Uncle Parsham's bed, Lucius chose the latter, giving the only possible reason why he might take Lycurgus' bed: ''I sleep with Boss a lot of times. . . . He snores too. I dont mind'' (p. 250).

When Lucius learned from Ned that Corrie ''bought Lightning loose'' to race again, and how, and that Boon had ''whupped that gal'' and then tried to tear Butch's head off, until little old Mr. Poleymus took Butch's pistol and ripped off his badge, Lucius said, ''I dont believe it. She quit'' (pp. 256, 257). Like David without a slingshot attacking Goliath, Lucius jumped on Boon. But Lucius still refused to go home when Mr. Poleymus, now aware of the whole situation, offered to send him. Mr. Poleymus gave Boon some money to bet for him.

When Lightning finally won, Lucius refused to take any of the winnings. Money was the last thing he would have done it for. When everyone except him and Ned had quit, ''it was as though only by making Lightning run and run fast could we justify . . . any of it. Not to hope to make the beginning any less wrong—I mean, what Boon and I had deliberately, of our own free will, to do back there in Jefferson . . .; but at least not to shirk, dodge—at least to finish—what we ourselves had started'' (279). Lucius' conscience is a reliable source of his moral judgments.

When Ned and Lucius confronted Boss Priest and Mr. van Tosch at Colonel Linscomb's plantation house, Lucius *had* quit: he was not "making choices and decisions any more" (p. 284). When Ned had told the whole story of his attempt to help a foolish young black relative who could get no help from Mr. van Tosch—" 'You're a white man,' Ned said gently. 'Bobo was a nigger boy' "—his confession was accepted and he was forgiven to the extent of the white men betting on a race between Lightning and Coppermine the next day. (In that race Boss Priest proved "he aint got enough sense to bet on horses" [p. 304].)

Lucius, Ned, and Corrie exercised their capacity to use their free will to choose, to act upon their choice, and to accept the responsibility of their actions. As Panthea Broughton said, "The scarcity of such examples evidences . . . Faulkner's awareness of how much easier it is to believe in the efficacy of formulas and the suitability of the codified response than it is to confront face-to-face, without the defense of code or precept, a living and fluid irrational world." Ned also confirmed his choice to be a comic leader and his capability as "a pattern-free character" like Ratliff, as Peter Crow said, to perform "unassuming deeds of benevolence in the community sufficiently far-reaching to make a lack of comic dependable regularity or of tragic intensity seem insignificant."

The true artist, Faulkner the novelist or Lucius Priest the storyteller, is, as John Gardner said, "a passionate, easily tempted explorer who fully intends to get home again, like Odysseus." The meaning of Lucius' initiation was expressed twice after the return to Jefferson. Lucius was amazed and distressed to find that nothing in Jefferson had changed in his absence: "if those four days—the lying and deceiving and tricking and decisions and undecisions, and the things I had done and seen and heard and learned . . .; if all that had changed nothing . . . then something had been wasted, thrown away, spent for nothing; either it was wrong and false to begin with and should never have existed, or I was wrong or false or weak or anyway not worthy of it" (p. 300). When Lucius' father gave up the usual razor-strop whipping as debasing to both of them, Boss Priest took over. Boss Priest's "courtesy book" ends with the admonition that Lucius cannot forget: "Nothing is ever forgotten. Nothing is ever lost. It's too valuable." He must live with it. To Lucius' protest that he can't, Boss Priest replied: "A gentleman can live through anything. He faces anything. A gentleman accepts the responsibility of his actions and bears the burden of their consequences, even when he did not himself instigate them but only acquiesced to them, didn't say No though he knew he should" (p. 302).

The Reivers does not end on this entirely practical and realistic version of existentialistic principles, intelligible to an eleven-year-old boy. It is quite fitting that Ned is not going to return to Boss Priest the money he lost by betting on Lightning in the last race. Because Ned had no "sour dean" to offer Lightning, Lightning lost the race and Boss Priest his bet: therefore he should accept the consequences of his action. Ned was too prudent to offer to return the money Boss bet, because the consequences of that action might be that Boss would take it. The last line, however, spoken by Everbe to Lucius, is an affirmative ending, testifying to the regenerative power of goodness and love: "His name is Lucius Priest Hogganbeck." *The Reivers* is the only Yoknapatawpha novel in which a new life is beginning as the consequence of the choice of goodness and love, inspired by a young gentleman.

To dismiss *The Reivers* in a critical study of the Yoknapatawpha fiction as an amusing but negligible coda would be an injustice to Faulkner as a creative artist. *The Reivers* is a rare combination of a significant initiation story with what Nathan Scott called "the bias of comedy": "In its deeply affirmative attitude toward the created orders of existence, in the profound materialism of its outlook, the comic imagination . . . summarizes an important part of the Christian testimony about the meaning of human life." An appreciation of "this profoundly affirmative quality of the comic vision" requires "a strenuous effort of the moral imagination." Comedy is defined by Northrop Frye as moving in its action toward "the incorporation of the hero into the society that he naturally fits." The hero is "socially attractive" but "seldom very interesting," and "virtue is rewarded" in the heroine as it is in *Pamela*. It is clear that Lucius is an initiation hero and Boon and Everbe Corinthia are ironic comedy hero and heroine.

And what Lucius learned and where he learned it involves other irony. Olga Vickery interpreted Grandfather's account of "the bright rewards of sin and pleasure" (*R* 52–53): "Non-virtue offers freedom, unlimited possibilities of action and experience, and . . . life grasped in its immediacy rather than through those rules and codes designed to encompass and control it." But the untraditional initiation of Lucius prepared him for adult life in which he retained "the truths of the heart" and presumably made wise choices and assumed his responsibilities. Isaac McCaslin was instructed in the old rituals and consequently let the McCaslin family die out. Lucius Priest experienced time, motion, and change, and promoted family life through three generations.

The broad spectrum and the inclusion of many Negro characters, some of whom have white counterparts, imply that Christian existentialist principles are applicable to all the inhabitants of this oddly assorted little social world. We have come full circle to the principles of Granny Millard and Bayard of *The Unvanquished*, with whom we began, and to the basic Christian humanism which underlies William Faulkner's existential focus on the human condition.

V • TIME, MOTION, CHANGE

In his interview with Jean Stein, Faulkner revealed his intention to use his "own little postage stamp of native soil" as a "kind of keystone in the universe," the "cosmos" he created. In the introduction to the Compass Books Edition of *Writers at Work*, Malcolm Cowley quoted that passage. In another paragraph from the same interview, Faulkner stated his concept of life and morality which provided a basis for his existentialist values and which is particularly relevant to Grandfather Priest in *The Reivers* and the truths he learned as a child from *his* grandfather: "Life is motion, and motion is concerned with what makes man move—which is ambition, power, pleasure. What time a man can devote to morality, he must take by force from the motion of which he is a part. He is compelled to make choices between good and evil sooner or later, because moral conscience demands that from him in order that he can live with himself tomorrow" (*LG* 253).

In "Mythology: A New Frontier in Southern History," George Brown Tindall dealt with "the standard image of the Old South, the plantation myth," and with "the Southern Renaissance in literature," in which "at the center—in Ellen Glasgow, in Faulkner, Wolfe, Caldwell—there is the consciousness of change, of suspension between two worlds, a double focus looking both backward and forward," evidence that "southerners still feel a persistent pull toward identification with their native region as a ground for belief and loyalty" in their "quest" for "a viable myth of the South." Tindall concluded, in "The Benighted South," that "the twentieth-century South has not produced a positive and viable myth of its own identity powerful enough to challenge the image of the benighted South," despite "the Oxford riot" (in September 1962, after Faulkner's death in July).

The symbols and images which Faulkner used in his myth of Yoknapatawpha and the myth itself take on universal dimensions when considered in relation to such existential values as motion. In *Faulkner: Myth and Motion* Richard Adams said that Faulkner's technique involves "imagery in which the dynamic quality of life is immediately and sharply opposed to artificial stasis," and some of Faulkner's "most useful characters . . . provide the most dramatic contrasts between the motion of life and the static obstacles": "But they are not morally admirable."

Motion and change are inseparable. What Boss Priest told young

Lucius, that "nothing is ever forgotten" but that one must "live with it" (*R* 302), Faulkner told the Japanese at Nagano. He rejected the idea of Rousseau's that we can return to "an idyllic condition, in which the dream [made us think] we were happy, we were free of trouble and sin. We must take the trouble and sin along with us, and we must cure that trouble and sin as we go." He suggested that "time is a [forward] and continuous thing which is a part of motion" (*FN* 78). Maybe it was true in Kipling's time that "East is East and West is West, and never the twain shall meet," but the most succinct statement of Faulkner's idea, in terms eminently suitable to the Western world, is a statement by Jawaharlal Nehru: "There is only one-way traffic in Time."

Time, Motion, and Change are the existential conditions of the cosmos Faulkner created, which was based upon his values. Like Nehru's statement, Faulkner's statement about time implied his rejection of the contrasting mythic concept of time as cyclic or circular, which has been replaced in the Judeo-Christian areas of the Western world by the concept of linear, historic time. Thus in creating Yoknapatawpha as not only an open society, unlike James Joyce's Dublin, but as an open cosmos, Faulkner left himself free to portray his "keystone in the universe" as a cosmos in which time was conceived by its inhabitants in either cyclic or linear dimensions. Faulkner's own concept of time is both implicit and explicit in his creation. As Otto Schlumpf observed: "Faulkner's mythology and morality" are linked in the sense of time and are "integral and complementary."

In his cosmological approach to Yoknapatawpha, Michael Routh stressed that Faulkner as a writer had a goal "bound inextricably to an impulse toward universalization." In the macrocosm of the universe, man is a microcosm. The story Faulkner was telling "over and over," he wrote to Malcolm Cowley, was "myself and the world." In cosmology Routh observed an inherent "vitalistic current of creative energy—a Life Force—streaming through the universe at large and also through the microcosm, man." This Life Force a cosmological writer perceives as engaged in a struggle with death.

But, as Mircea Eliade explained, there is a religious connection between the cosmos or world and time: "They are both sacred realities, divine creations." " . . . cosmic life was imagined in the form of a circular course; it was identified with the year. The year was a closed circle; it had a beginning and an end, but it also had the peculiarity that it could be reborn in the form of a *new* year." Liturgical Time in Christianity preserves the pattern of the life of Christ and thus "is a circular Time. Christianity, as faithful heir to Judaism, accepts the linear Time of History: the World was created only once and will have only one end; the Incarnation took place only once, in historical Time, and there will be only one Judgment." For the religious man, Eliade explained, there is the reversible, recoverable sacred time celebrated by traditional rites, and the profane time of ordinary temporal duration. For the non-religious man, Eliade said, "time constitutes man's deepest existential dimension": it begins with his birth and ends with his death.

In Mississippi, as Eugene Genovese noted, the prevailing Judeo-Christian concept of historical time was contrary to the West African tradition of time as "cyclical and eternal." For the slaves time was flexible, "subordinated to the natural order of work and leisure," ruled by seasons rather than by timeclocks. In his account of Evangelicalism in the South, Donald Mathews stressed the lack in African tradition of a concept of history "as a linear progression toward a valued, sublime goal in which true believers would be vindicated for all the persecution that they had suffered in God's name." In taking "Christianity from the whites," Mathews explained that the slaves "had discovered that it passed cosmic judgment upon whites and promised something far better for black people than the world which the slaveholders had made."

Yoknapatawpha, however, shared the Judeo-Christian tradition, including the concept of "time as a forward motion," J. T. Fraser's parallel to Nehru's traffic image. Christianity, Fraser said, added "to the one-way progress of Hebrew history . . . the idea of a unique event or, philosophically, the idea of contingency." To "lawfulness or being, in form of the divine design" is added "contingency or becoming in form of the idea of the unique. Time now could be regarded as progressive and nonrepetitive, and a philosophy of history, including the idea of progress, became thinkable." The Neoplatonist philosophers attempted "to reconcile the lawful and the eternal with the free will of man."

But Fraser recognized the variations in individual perception of time, which might be directed toward the past or toward the future, which might regard time as destructive or creative, which might prefer the non-motion of being to the risks and uncertainties of becoming.

In "William Faulkner and the Terror of History," Vernon T. Hornback, Jr., interpreted Faulkner's perspective as "strongly existential," depicting "the traditional time scheme of Western, Judeo-Christian man," as contrasted with cyclical time which fosters mere repetition and denies freedom and responsibility. His characters have to accept lack of freedom in the repetition of cultural patterns or accept "the terrible freedom of linear time" and responsibility for their actions. J. T. Fraser's statement, superbly exemplified by the Yoknapatawpha novels, justifies Faulkner's use of both cyclical and linear concepts of time: " . . . the traditional novel, a Western piece of art, insists on accommodating free will, fate, and causality as understood in the modern West. Consequently, the novel as a literary device displays the orientation of its characters to time and to the hierarchy of conflicts in temporality."

John Macquarrie's theological definition of existence would apply also to fictional characters who live in Judeo-Christian linear time: " . . . what constitutes existence is temporality, the stretch of existence through the dimensions of past, present, and future; and moreover, what constitutes selfhood is the bringing into a unity of these three dimensions of temporality, as the existent draws them into one through acceptance of the remembered past, commitment to an overarching possibility of the future, and openness in the present to both of these."

In explaining man's unique characteristic, invaluable to the novelist, of being able to "stand outside his present time and imagine himself ahead in the future or back in the past," Rollo May quoted Alfred Korzybski on man's "*time-binding* capacity": " . . . the capacity to use the fruits of past labors and experiences as intellectual or spiritual capital for developments in the present . . . the capacity of human beings to conduct their lives in the ever increasing light of inherited wisdom; . . . the capacity in virtue of which man is at once the heritor of the by-gone ages and the trustee of posterity." The moral implications of the concept of linear, historical time derived from Judeo-Christianity are an essential aspect of Faulkner's cosmos and its inhabitants. Faulkner transcended time by creating his cosmos, to show the world of the future that "Kilroy was here" (*FU* 61).

Robert Penn Warren identified the distinctive quality in Faulkner's literary creation:

> Time fluid versus time fixed. In Faulkner's work that's the drama behind the drama. . . . Time spreads and is the important thing, the terrible thing. A tremendous flux is there, things flowing away in all directions. Moments not quite ready to be shaped are already there, waiting, and we feel their presence. . . . You have the sense of the small becoming large in time, the large becoming small, the sweep of time over things—that, and the balance of the frozen, abstracted moment against violent, significant action. These frozen moments are Faulkner's game.

Time is of vital significance in Panthea Broughton's *William Faulkner: The Abstract and the Actual*. Having quoted Faulkner's statement at Nagano (p. 78) about man's having to take the past with him, Broughton examines Faulkner's attitude toward the past, burden though it may be. "Faulkner's fiction . . . establishes that man escapes history only by coming to terms with it, by living with it and accepting all its implications. . . . To refuse to accept the past is to grant it power and to doom oneself to repeating it. Only by accepting the past, living with it, does one gain control over experience." Time is a key factor in linking "the abstraction which is Faulkner's fiction" with the actuality of life.

Approaching the study of time in a broader context, Patricia Tobin chose "to study time in the novel as it had been construed thematically and structurally in those family novels that follow a dynastic family through its generations," with a time line, a family line, and a story line. Obviously Tobin is concerned with linear time, but in dealing with eighteenth- and nineteenth-century novels she dealt with conflicts between generations, such as the breaking away of children from linearity. Tobin observed in Quentin and Shreve (*AA*) a move from subjective mythologizing to the historical past. Her discussion of *Absalom, Absalom!* emphasized Quentin's concept of "life as doomed repetition, past as prophecy, and time as a circle," and Quentin's identification of himself "with the single genealogical family that contains the whole mythic significance of the South." Tobin's concern with dynasty as a pattern shaping time in novels is pertinent to the Yoknapatawpha novels but peripheral to Faulkner's concepts of time in creating his cosmos.

Directly relevant to those concepts is the philosophy of Bergson which has been observed by various critics as a significant influence on Faulkner or at least as in harmony with Faulkner's ideas on time and the nature of reality. In his interview with Loïc Bouvard in 1952, Faulkner made a number of statements concerning his concepts of time and art, of God and man. His expression of belief in "a God who rests both in eternity and in the now" reminded Bouvard of the God of Bergson. Thereupon Faulkner explained his conception of time to Bouvard in Bergsonian terms: "In fact I agree pretty much with Bergson's theory of the fluidity of time. There is only the present moment, in which I include both the past and the future, and that is eternity. In my opinion time can be shaped quite a bit by the artist; after all, man is never time's slave." Faulkner's statement that he knew "nothing about oriental civilization" indicates that he had no knowledge of cyclical time comparable with that of Judeo-Christian linear, historical time (*LG* 70, 71).

Several dissertations emphasize the similarities between Bergson's and Faulkner's ideas about time. In "Bergsonian Dynamism in the Writings of William Faulkner" (1962), Shirley Callen began with

Faulkner's concept of life as change and motion and his technique of time in dealing with the dichotomy of characters who destroy themselves and those who survive and prevail. Faulkner's technique of contrasting motion with stasis Callen relates to Bergson's *Creative Evolution* concept of *élan vital* or life force. Her summing up of a basic concept in Bergson applies implicitly to Faulkner: "Because it is contrary to the nature of reality and life, resistance to change is disintegrative to the individual, destructive to the social order, and offensive to the moral order of the universe." Callen quoted the Bouvard interview and stated that Faulkner fused "subject matter, structure, and style to present a consistent attitude toward the process of living."

The complete title of Vernon T. Hornback's dissertation is self-explanatory: "William Faulkner and the Terror of History: Myth, History, and Moral Freedom in the Yoknapatawpha Cycle" (1964). Hornback explained southern entrapment in the past in cyclical time as a means of retaining identity, in contrast to alienation from the past which is a denial of guilt and responsibility. The third way of coping with time requires acceptance of "the terrible freedom of linear time": it involves moral freedom, an understanding of the lessons of the past, and responsibility for one's actions. Like Bergsonian time it depends on free will shaping the future and retaining connections with the past.

Despite the title, "And by Bergson, Obviously" (1972), Susan Parr wrote "From a Bergsonian Perspective" and dealt less with philosophical concepts than with techniques and analogues. In "Uses of Time in Four Novels of William Faulkner" (1973), Daniel Ford dealt with duration and with voluntary, sequential clock-time memory and involuntary, psychic, intuitive memory, citing both Bergson and Proust. He described Faulkner's "creative memory" in *Absalom, Absalom!* as combining the clock time of reality with the psychic time of memory.

Ralph Ellison's general comments in "Society, Morality, and the Novel" are particularly applicable to Faulkner, one of the American novelists Ellison discussed. "As an art form," he said, "the novel is obsessed by the relationship between illusion and reality as revealed in duration, in process." Ellison believed that "the primary social function of the novel . . . is that of seizing from the flux and flow of our daily lives those abiding patterns of experience which . . . help to form our sense of reality and from which emerge our sense of humanity and our conception of human value." Equally applicable to Faulkner's Yoknapatawpha novels is Ellison's statement of "one of the enduring functions of the American novel": "defining the national type as it evolves in the turbulence of change, and . . . giving the American experience, as it unfolds in its diverse parts and regions, imaginative integration and moral continuity.'' Ellison's comment on Isaac McCaslin as an example of how one can achieve moral identity was published in 1957, before Faulkner demonstrated ''imaginative integration and moral continuity'' by his responses to questions at the University of Virginia and Nagano and West Point about Isaac, published ''Race at Morning,'' and in *The Reivers* concluded the story of Isaac when he was still living in 1961, the narrative ''now.'' Isaac's moral identity as a youth was inadequate to serve him for a life of almost a hundred years of motion and change. But Ralph Ellison was correct in describing Faulkner as ''involved both as a Southerner and as an artist with those issues which most white Americans have evaded since the Civil War.'' Faulkner's Yoknapatawpha fiction exemplifies Ellison's reference to fiction in which ''the difficulty is the mark of the writer's deepest commitment to life and to his art.''

John Macquarrie's explanation of how images and myths can be translated into contemporary language of existence suggests how Faulkner achieved the contrast between cyclical and linear time without, as he said to Bouvard, a knowledge of oriental civilization. Macquarrie, a Protestant theologian, observed ''sufficient affinity between the Biblical understanding of man and the philosophy of existence to ensure that existential interpretation does not force the Biblical material into an alien mold.'' This affinity may help to explain how Faulkner's existentialistic ideas could evolve from his understanding of the Bible, part of his personal culture, and from his ''radar'' sensitivity to contemporary cultural currents in the United States and France.

Absalom, Absalom! is probably the richest, most comprehensive example of Faulkner's fusion of Biblical tales and the Southern past. In ''A Flash, A Glare: Faulkner and Time,'' Morris Beja dealt with epiphanies in Faulkner, experiences defined by Hugh Holman in the sense used by James Joyce: ''an event in which the essential nature of something—a person, a situation, an object—was suddenly perceived . . . an intuitive grasp of reality achieved in a quick flash of recognition.'' Beja stressed such insights in Faulkner's novels in which the past exists in the present. The confrontation between Sutpen as a boy and the Negro at the door is the ''single epiphany'' that ''brings about all the subsequent events of his life and thus forms the basis of the entire novel.'' More than that, however, it is the ironic obverse of Sutpen's rejection, as a white man, of his part-Negro son, Charles Bon. The destruction of the Sutpen dynasty by this rejection of his son symbolized the potential destructiveness of the rejection by white Southerners of their part-black children.

In "Faulkner's Defeat of Time in *Absalom, Absalom!*" Ruth Vande Kieft perceived Sutpen's obsessive desire to found a dynasty as analogous to Faulkner's desire as an artist to work out his destiny in time—one might add, to create a cosmos. Both Sutpen and Faulkner were possessed by "demonic fury." Faulkner was also like Rosa telling her story to Quentin; the novel to Faulkner was what Rosa hoped that her story would become: "the written word that endures." The narrators also resemble Faulkner in seeking "to arrest motion." By seeing in all the different attitudes of characters and narrators parts of Faulkner's vision, Vande Kieft justifies her title as it applies to Faulkner as an artist; the initial parallel between Sutpen and Faulkner is less satisfactory because it ignores the vast differences between them as fathers: Sutpen wanted a dynasty, but Faulkner was philoprogenitive, like the two grandfathers in *The Reivers*.

Olga Vickery's "Faulkner and the Contours of Time" is a third felicitous title. Vickery categorized the effect of concepts of time on the lives of characters and reached some general conclusions. "Deliberate reduction to the purely physical, vegetative life is stultifying, for it is out of conflict and struggle that understanding of himself [man] grows." Man's doom may be determined by action or events, but it is "fused with doom as time or process," the inevitable death which all must experience. Those who evade doom as time, seek doom as death, as Quentin Compson did. Patriarchs try to evade doom by control of the future through a dynasty. "Man's dignity consists of submitting to time and change while preserving his identity and his sense of continuity."

In his *History of the Idea of Progress* Robert Nisbet explained that idea as "inseparable from a sense of time flowing in unilinear fashion" which prevails in the Western world and traced it from Hesiod through the classical world and from St. Augustine, especially his *The City of God*, through Christianity to Pierre Teilhard de Chardin. Near the end of the last chapter on the past, Nisbet quoted a prophetic statement from Teilhard's *The Future of Man*: "*I am convinced that finally it is upon the idea of progress and faith in progress that Mankind, today so divided, must rely and reshape itself.*"

Inseparable from time is motion, and, as Faulkner said, the writer is "interested in all men's behavior. . . . it's motion, it's life, the only alternative is nothingness, death" (*FU* 267). Shirley Callen perceived in Henri Bergson's concept of "*élan vital*," in *Creative Evolution*, a source of Faulkner's dynamic concept of man which rejected stasis and rigidity. For Bergson, Callen said, "morality lies in a spirit of living characterized by flexibility" and good must be dynamic. "Resistance to change is a blindness to the nature of reality which can mean the crippling or the destruction of an individual or a society."

J. T. Fraser's description of the Hebraic concept of time after it was changed by the theology of St. Paul recalls Nehru's statement: "There is only one-way traffic in time." The Yahwists, Fraser said, "came to regard time as a forward motion with an identifiable beginning in the divine act of creation and leading to the fulfillment of the divine purpose." Through "the perception of motion and change" man recognized "the instinctual separation of the world into . . . the necessary and the contingent" and discovered that the "chronic conditions of existence" resulted from the tensions between "what is expected and what is encountered."

The emphasis on time and motion in Faulkner's fiction may have had its origin in what Willie Morris, in *Sense of Place: Mississippi*, described as "a profound feeling for communal origins." The cult of ancestor worship which is one manifestation of that feeling and which is revealed in ceremonial display of Confederate flags and homage to the legendary founding fathers pays little heed in Faulkner's region to the mobility—and often the economic necessity—which brought those specific pioneers to the unsettled West.

Peirce Lewis, also in *Sense of Place,* discussed American mobility as giving freedom and becoming the symbol of freedom; he compared movement west in America with movement forward in time. Lewis deplored the "horrendous" consequences of "the lack of a sense of place" which in these post-frontier days encourages flight from a community instead of preservation and rehabilitation of a place "that can be directly experienced, intimately known, and passionately loved by its inhabitants." His closing scornful remarks about the "new Snopeses" are undeserved by Flem, the successful Snopes: he restored the De Spain house, after he ousted Manfred de Spain from the bank, and restored it to greater glory, even though his life there was bleak and lonely. (If my guess is right about which mansion was *the* Mansion, it was saved by being moved from the center to the edge of town, largely through the efforts of Oxford women to prevent its demolition. Handsomely restored, it is the headquarters for the spring pilgrimage to Oxford stately homes.)

The mobility represented by the ancestors who crossed the Appalachian Mountains and settled in Mississippi is not, however, what Faulkner had in mind in "motion." Stanley L. Elkin, dealing with "Religious Themes and Symbols in the Novels of William Faulkner," interpreted "motion" as the life struggle in which there are no final victories. The motion is "toward but not to a goal"; the goal may retreat, like the horizon, as one moves toward it.

Although Faulkner was probably unfamiliar with Teilhard de Chardin's concept of the evolution of man as "the finest proof of the transcendence of Christianity," specifically Catholicism, and probably would not have accepted it, Teilhard's view of human possibility might have attracted Faulkner: "Happily for us, not only is mankind, considered experientially, in its organic wholeness, still constantly in motion . . . unlike all the zoological species . . . it is converging upon itself. And this irresistible biological folding-back . . . suggests to our minds the wild idea and the wild hope that perhaps there really does exist an ultimate centre of reflection (and hence of beatifying consummation) ahead of us, at the upper end of evolution" (*Activation of Energy*).

Another affirmation that man must live in a world of motion comes from India. Radhakrishnan might have addressed the same message to any ancestor-worshipping society: "The scriptures of an earlier age cannot answer the problems of our time. The great representatives of Indian culture were men of mobility and ceaseless adventure. We are not loyal to their spirit if we mark time in a world of perpetual motion by sitting still and chanting ancient hymns. We cannot command the sun to stand still in the plains of Hindustan."

Even India could not produce a more extreme example of the attempt to halt the flow of time and to withdraw from a world of motion than Gail Hightower in *Light in August*. In his study of cosmology based on *Light in August*, Michael Routh observed that Hightower tried to live in the moments at the beginning and end of Sunday and Wednesday church services twenty-five years previously. Even his fleeting recognition of the reality behind his self-induced hallucination of his grandfather on a galloping horse—"a swaggering and unchastened bravo killed with a shotgun in a peaceful henhouse, in a temporary hiatus of his own avocation of killing" (*LA* 462)—he was unable to sustain: at the moment of his death, apparently, the image of motion returned for which he had given up a life of motion for himself in the service of others in the profession he had chosen.

In Hightower Faulkner created a character representing stasis. In "Flux and the Frozen Moment: The Imagery of Stasis in Faulkner's Prose," Karl Zink dealt with the technical method Faulkner used most frequently, what Daniel Ford called "images of stasis from which the readers intuit reality" and explained as arising from "an impulse to images of stasis" originating in "the need to retain the past."

Faulkner explicitly rejected stasis. At West Point he repeated his basic idea that "any . . . human living situation will have to change because life is motion and the only alternative to motion is stasis—death" (*FWP* 98). Daniel Ford regarded Faulkner's "imagery of stasis" as sometimes an experimental representation of "Faulkner's concept of a perpetual present which contains past, present, and future."

In *Faulkner: Myth and Motion*, Richard Adams explained the purpose served by devices which presented stories and characters from "sharply separate views, which become simultaneous in the reader's mind": thus Faulkner could "arrange his static impressions of moving life in clusters and patterns that heighten both the motion and the stasis." In the introduction Adams quoted from the interview with Jean Stein: "The aim of every artist is to arrest motion, which is life, by artificial means and hold it fixed so that a hundred years later, when a stranger looks at it, it moves again since it is life."

Focusing on Bergsonian dynamism in relation to Faulkner's fiction, Shirley Callen considered that Faulkner embodied Bergsonian concepts by fusing "subject matter, structure, and style to present a consistent attitude toward the process of living." He used "imagery and symbolism" to "guide the intuition to the point at which reality can be grasped," having realized "the appeal and value of imagery as a medium of relating the world of appearances to a cosmic background." The reality of flux and change was conveyed by images of "terrific stasis," of "force-filled rigidity," as in the confrontation between Rosa and Clytie (*AA* 139–40). This image well exemplifies what Richard Adams described as "concentrations of force" confined in "the most tightly blocked possible situations."

Recognizing that the dimension of time is the most important in motion in the actual world, Richard Adams analyzed Faulkner's technique as sometimes a "scrambling of the time dimension" which "short-circuits our intuition so as to concentrate the energy of a large amount of motion on a single, artificially fixed and isolated moment." Thus "time is held still for esthetic contemplation." "The arrest of motion is accomplished most often," Adams said, "by imagery in which the dynamic quality of life is immediately and sharply opposed to artificial stasis"—the "frozen moment." Faulkner's world of motion had "moral implications" specified by Adams. The characters who are "fundamentally opposed to life," like Quentin Compson, "are desperate because a living world keeps forcing them into action in spite of their desire for security, peace, stasis. They are crushed because they are trying not to move and . . . the only way to be motionless is to be dead."

In her study of three Faulkner novels "from a Bergsonian Perspective," Susan Parr dealt with use of stasis as providing aesthetic insights. In *Absalom, Absalom!* in particular she cited images which stress works of art, not life—references to painting, photography, film, and drama—and dwelt on the dreamlike quality and often *déjà vu* effect conveyed by the narrative method which makes the reader identify with the characters and become in effect the sixth narrator.

In "Faulkner's Vitalistic Vision" Peter Crow brings out several points concerning time and motion which are of special significance as reflecting not only the fictitious narrator and his adventures but also Faulkner himself in 1961, the last year of his life. In 1904 Boss Priest said, "People will pay any price for motion." In 1961 the narrator, a grandfather, had seen that prediction come true, transforming life in Yoknapatawpha. In *Sartoris,* before the "now" of *The Reivers,* young Bayard's obsessive actions dramatized the change from horses to automobiles to airplanes which was taking place even in rural areas. As Peter Crow remarked, *"The Reivers* is centered around the excitement and fulfillment of motion," in the innovation of the automobile and the ancient sport of horseracing juxtaposed. The automobile operates in linear time on roads that lead from Jefferson to Memphis and from Parsham Junction to Jefferson. The race was on a circular track. Crow described the three heats as respectively cyclical, suspended, and linear; the return in the fourth race to cyclical motion Crow considered as appropriate to the comic world. The three-heat race he regarded as the epitome of "vitality and motion" in Faulkner's work.

Precisely to the point of change as related to motion is Shirley Callen's comment on Faulkner's literary creation: "The man who based his writing on the principle of life as change and motion has surely achieved his own artistic goal of arresting the motion of life so as to attain his desired immortality by creating a living body, something that will always move since it is life." But motion without change, the eternal return of everyday going around in circles, is analogous to cyclical time: such motion may be repetitive and resistant to change, not linear and progressive.

Believing that change is a principle of reality, Faulkner aimed to represent in his style, according to Callen, "the elusive reality of change and flux, a reality difficult to articulate." Faulkner considered change a necessary "continual, inexorable process" providing "a continual flexibility toward the present and future." In the life of the individual, integration and a sense of identity are achieved by change, thematically represented, Callen observed, in *As I Lay Dying.*

Writing about the South of Faulkner's time and later, George Brown Tindall saw the change manifest in the 1960s and 1970s as arousing "a

heightened awareness of something that is passing away." but he recognized that "to change is not necessarily to disappear": "to change is
not necessarily to lose one's identity; to change, sometimes, is to find
it." Despite the contrast between Faulkner's young initiates and their
companions—Ike McCaslin, who never outgrew his ideal of the happy
hunting ground, and Sam Fathers; Charles Mallison, who grew up
overnight and accepted his social and moral responsibility, and Aleck
Sander; Lucius Priest, who learned to accept himself and live with his
past, and Boon Hogganbeck and Uncle Ned McCaslin—they all illustrate Tindall's observation that "southerners white and black share the
bonds of a common heritage."

The significance of the contrast between Ike and the two other initiates is that Ike spent the rest of his life "living" so far as possible only
in "sacred time," defined by Mircea Eliade as "circular time, reversible and recoverable, a sort of eternal mythical present that is periodi-
cally reintegrated by means of rites." Eliade explained that thus primitive man strove "to thrust himself out of time (and change) into eternity." Not only does Ike in "Delta Autumn" exemplify this attitude as
an old man, even with a vision of eternity, but he shows that in human
understanding and moral responsibility he has advanced no further
than his grandfather did: he refused to acknowledge kinship with even
a distant relative with black blood. To reinforce the implications in *Go
Down, Moses* Faulkner showed again in "Race at Morning" that Ike
never grew up and assumed responsibility or successfully played an
adult, paternal role or outgrew the hunting stage.

Chick Mallison and Lucius Priest, living in our modern "profane
culture," show what Eliade calls "the nostalgia for initiatory trials and
scenarios," featured in many literary works, which "reveals modern
man's longing for a total and definitive renewal . . . capable of radically changing his existence." Chick and Lucius each chose motion and
change in activities outside of family and community.

As Immanuel Kant concluded, " . . . the possibility of changes is
thinkable only in time; time is not thinkable through changes, but only
vice versa." Kant's "idea of time" J. T. Fraser described as "pure
intuition," constituting "direct experience of sensory content." In a
chapter section with a heading fortuitously pertinent to this context,
"Being, Becoming, and Existential Tension," Fraser deals with the
"contradictory views of the nature of time": that "there is an ultimate
reality of permanence" and that "the ultimate reality" is "pure
change." The latter concept involves past, present, and future, a world
of *becoming* rather than of *being*. In the world of becoming "process
and function [are] more fundamental than matter and space"; it is a

world of free will and indeterminism," not a being-like world of "determinism and strict causation." The two concepts reflect "two aspects of temporality": the "lawlike, stationary, or permanent" and the generative or creative aspects of time. "Our experiential world," Fraser said, "is the world of passing and change."

The two aspects of time suggest also the polarity of being and becoming and of stasis and motion as related to characters and events in Yoknapatawpha. Fraser refers to "cultural filtering as one element that conditions our habits of separating permanence and change," which are rooted in human biology and "modulated by social values." The Myth of the South and the Myth of Yoknapatawpha provide contrasting examples of "cultural filtering" and "social values" which Fraser might enjoy. And Faulkner might have approved of Fraser's statement that supports the Myth of Yoknapatawpha in its implications: "Christian ethics is the source of the idea of progress as the summum bonum of the good, and the idea of progress has come to command the attention and guide the aspirations of most peoples on the earth."

Fraser's reference to "cultural filtering" and "social values" applies to the process which took place in the South before Faulkner's time. Eugene Genovese traced the use of "religion as a method of social control" in the South after 1831. Although the success of this "political strategy" occurred only because the masters had "a considerable degree of genuine Christian concern" for their slaves, the resistance to social change was encouraged by political strategy and thus strengthened "the South's commitment to slavery as a permanent social order."

The paternalism of the slave system survived variously after emancipation, again demonstrating the resistance to change as a cultural characteristic in both races. Genovese stated that "the legacy of paternalism" kept former slaves and successive generations of blacks "from a full appreciation of . . . individual strength." Furthermore, "paternalism with racism" catastrophically "transformed elements of personal dependency into a sense of collective weakness." The break between white and black children came when they ceased to be playmates and "the white children began to go to school" and both races became aware that their lives henceforth would be forever separate—and not equal. The points made by Genovese are exemplified by Bayard and Ringo in *The Unvanquished*. Ringo disappeared from the Sartoris story thereafter. In *Sartoris* Bayard was a static, backward-looking old man.

The Unvanquished is the only novel in the Yoknapatawpha chronicles which deals with the Civil War and Reconstruction, from the limited point of view of Bayard recalling events of his boyhood and youth. Events in Mississippi from the end of the Civil War through the Radical Reconstruction in 1871 to the achievement of white supremacy by the establishment of the Jim Crow laws, from 1875 to 1896, are scarcely hinted at by Faulkner. Disfranchisement is dramatized in "Skirmish at Sartoris." As John Hope Franklin said, "Once the Negro was disfranchised, everything else necessary to white supremacy could be done." And he traced the necessary steps, beginning with the convention in Mississippi in 1890, "for the primary purpose of disfranchising the Negro." Segregation was established by the Jim Crow laws. The Ku Klux Klan was only one of many secret societies established to promote white supremacy. In Yoknapatawpha, Colonel John Sartoris was the only leading character involved in such activities; he prevented Negroes from voting and was an organizer of night riders "to keep the carpet baggers from organizing the Negroes into an insurrection" (U 256). (Bayard's sympathies were with Sutpen, who refused to join the night riders.) The contrast between the Myth of the South, as represented in Thomas Dixon's novels and especially the movie The Birth of a Nation, and the Myth of Yoknapatawpha is most impressive when one is aware of what Faulkner left out in his myth, the darker side of Mississippi history which produced the closed society.

Resistance to change is only one side of the South. In the preface to The Ethnic Southerners (1976), George Brown Tindall remarked that "the South has repeatedly displayed a striking knack for accepting change without losing the sense of its separate identity," and to support his statement gave evidence from the 1920s through the 1960s. His essays in this volume had been published from 1958 to 1975, beginning when Faulkner's work and his life were near their end.

In "Mythology: A New Frontier in Southern History," Tindall assigned "the ideas of the South" to "the order of social myth," in which "mental pictures . . . portray the pattern of what a people think they are," thus, in Henry Nash Smith's words, fusing "concept and emotion into an image." "The standard image of the Old South," Tindall agreed, was "the plantation myth." But he cited enough examples to confirm the "infinite variety of southern mythology" and "the proliferation of paradoxical myths." C. Vann Woodward is cited as noting "several crucial factors" which give rise to paradoxes: "the experience of poverty in a land of plenty; failure and defeat in a land that glorifies success; sin and guilt amid the legend of American innocence; and a sense of place and belonging among a people given to abstraction." Woodward might have been referring to Yoknapatawpha.

In the Southern Renaissance in literature, which of course included Faulkner, Tindall perceived "the consciousness of change, of suspension between two worlds, a double focus looking both backward and forward." He linked this consciousness of change with southerners' "pull toward identification" with the South "as a ground for belief and loyalty." The "quest for myth" having been powerful in contemporary southern literature, Tindall asks: is there "a viable myth of the South?" Tindall listed non-fictional "trails" that have been "blazed," such as William Taylor's *Cavalier and Yankee* and Paul Gaston's *The New South Creed*, and decided that the "key to the enigma" lies in "the mythology that has had so much to do with shaping character, unifying society, developing a sense of community, of common ideals and shared goals, making the region conscious of its distinctiveness."

In "The Benighted South," Tindall confirms observations reflected in the works of Faulkner. "The defensive temper of the 1920s" is dramatized in "Dry September." Mencken's "vilification" of the South Tindall referred to as anticipating "William Faulkner's saga of the Snopes family." Faulkner's replies to questions about Southern Baptists explain the phenomenon as the result of spiritual starvation, not limited to the South: "no books, no theatre, no music" (*FU* 190) could be a mini-version of Mencken's "The Sahara of the Bozart," the "drying-up of civilization," a key phrase quoted by Tindall. After World War I the "consciousness of change" and the consequent "intolerance and repression" observed by Tindall were manifest in McLendon in "Dry September" and in self-destructive ways in *Sartoris* in young Bayard and Byron Snopes and in dangerous assertion of equality in the black Caspey, until Colonel Bayard knocked the nonsense out of him with "a stick of stove wood" (*Sar.* 83).

Referring to "the Oxford riot," which occurred in September 1962, after Faulkner's death in July, Tindall observed that "the image of the benighted South had not yet been replaced by "a positive and viable myth of its own identity." In 1964, when "The Benighted South" was published, having been delivered in 1963, Tindall could not predict what would occur by the 1980s. But having been on the University of Mississippi campus during the riots and returned to Oxford almost every year since then until 1980, I can testify that unpredictable changes *have* taken place; visible to the casual observer are scenes which could not have been imagined in 1962. An image that lingers in my memory from 1975 is of two young blacks in the cocktail lounge of a nice restaurant, in what used to be the warehouse of the Oxford cotton gin (a fact which added spice to the scene for me). There they sat, with their caps on, and nobody but me paid them any mind! With a companion image of a black woman police officer directing traffic in front of the Confederate monument and the courthouse on the Square, the two youths seem to be images for a viable myth in which blacks *and* women have freedom to make choices.

At the end of her dissertation, "Faulkner's Sense of History: Criticism of the Magnolia Myth in the Novels of William Faulkner," Elizabeth Downey cited Faulkner's use of that monument as a symbol: "those who look toward the past alone are looking like the statue of the Confederate soldier in Jefferson, for reinforcements that can never come." A full-page photograph of that statue is given in *Harper's: The South Today* (p. 134).

In an earlier essay than "The Benighted South," "The Central Theme Revisited," George Tindall said, "The churches have never been the spearhead of social change in the South." In 1962, Oxford clergymen, led by Duncan Gray, pastor of the Episcopal church which Faulkner attended, tried to prevent the riots; they were verbally abused in the Oxford *Eagle* and were personally in danger. Typical of the paradoxes of the myth was the "Memory Selection" in the same issue of the *Eagle*: "Truly I perceive that God shows no partiality" (Acts 10:34). I was more suprised to read that verse in that issue than to learn from Donald Mathews that the verse "was one of the most popular passages in black Christianity."

That segregation existed in churches before the Civil War is evident near Oxford in the traces remaining of a slave gallery in the College Hill Church, built in 1844. It now attracts sightseers as the church where William Faulkner and Estelle Oldham were married. Eugene Genovese commented on the acceleration, during the thirty years before the Civil War, of the trend "toward racial separation within the churches."

Tindall recognized the activities of groups seeking "fair-play" for Negroes, "while assuming the inevitability of white supremacy." John Hope Franklin traced the Supreme Court decisions which ended segregation practices initiated by the *Plessy* v. *Ferguson* "separate but equal doctrine" in 1896. After the May 17, 1954, decision "outlawing segregated public schools," the governor of Mississippi was one of several governors who "threatened to abolish public schools rather than permit any black children to attend the same schools." Faulkner accepted the Supreme Court decision: in answer to a question at Nagano he said: "It's right, it's just." But the problem of enforcement would take time—"maybe in three hundred years" in which "the Negro himself has got to be patient and sensible" (*FN* 6). For someone who viewed reality as "time, motion, and change," this pronouncement seems an unwarranted deep-freezing of all three!

But Faulkner saw clearly enough what the White Citizens Councils were up to and the KKK and how they were built up by people in other states. But this is "something that is going to change whether we like it or not": "to live in this country, anywhere in the world today, and to be against giving a man what equality, cultural, educational, economic that he's capable of and responsible for, is like living in Alaska and being against snow . . ."(*FU* 222–23). In answering the next question, Faulkner said that Klan members were usually "poor unsuccessful white" men who envied Negroes for "beating him at his own poor game" and clung to their own single claim, literally only skin-deep, to superiority (*FU* 223).

In *The Mansion* the career of Clarence Snopes and the political victory of Colonel Devries show Faulkner's political sympathies and his realization that Gavin Stevens is a man of talk, not of action, and that Clarence is dangerous. Perhaps Faulkner's admiration for Adlai Stevenson and regret that he lost because he "had three strikes against him: wit, urbanity, and erudition" motivated this one venture into Yoknapatawpha politics, in which the seriousness of the issues involved is absurdly contrasted with the means by which Ratliff ended the political career of Clarence Snopes.

In September 1962 I ceased to regret the death of Faulkner in July. Less fortunate than Boswell, who only "*began* to think that the hope which I had long indulged of obtaining his acquaintance was blasted," *my* hope was forever blasted before my stay in Oxford that year began. But Faulkner was spared the traumatic experience of dissension with friends and relatives and of seeing the University of Mississippi under the control of National Guard troops—black and white, an aspect particularly shocking to some citizens. Now, twenty years later, the desegregated university, achieved faster and with less violence than Faulkner might have expected, would raise in Faulkner's mind only the capacity of both blacks and whites for a university education.

In "On Fear: Deep South in Labor: Mississippi" (*Harper's,* June 1956), Faulkner dealt with the whole problem of freedom and education and justice, and said what he was not alive to say in 1962. On equality he said: "There is no such thing as equality *per se,* but only equality *to:* equal right and opportunity to make the best one can of one's life within one's capacity and capability, without fear of injustice or oppression or violence. If we had given him [the Negro] this equality ninety or fifty or even ten years ago, there would have been no Supreme Court ruling about segregation in 1954." The choice that remains is "simply between being slaves and being free": "the time is already past when we can choose a little of each." And we must make "inimical forces" fear us "because we practice freedom" (*ESPL* 105, 106).

Faulkner's belief in equal rights was equally firm in relation to education and to justice. Joseph Blotner's account of Faulkner's reaction to the Willie McGee case in 1951, in which he considered that the death penalty for rape was based on racism, not on legal evidence of force and violence, can now be reviewed with amplification of the facts Blotner gives. Faulkner was correct in associating with leftist politics the women from the Civil Rights Congress, none of them identified, who interviewed him on the McGee case: they were indeed "being used." In the chapter "Mississippi" in *A Fine Old Conflict,* Jessica Mitford's account of the interview with Faulkner was written after she had herself discovered the "fairly obvious thralldom to the Soviet Union" of the American Communist Party and had resigned from it. Her version of the interview suggests the intensity of Faulkner's commitment to the humanistic values involved in the case: "Faulkner himself came to the door, and when we explained the reason for our visit, greeted us most cordially, invited us in, and held forth on the McGee case for a good two hours." Such loquacity, especially with a group of strange women, was not typical of Faulkner. After telephoning the brief press release she wrote to the CRC national office, she took the copy to Faulkner and had him initial it. When he had done so, he murmured, "I think McGee and the woman should *both* be destroyed." Equality in guilt, as well as equality in race and sex: the woman had long been McGee's mistress.

Jessica Mitford interpreted Faulkner's final remark as expressing "the deepseated schizophrenia then endemic among white liberals and racial moderates of the region." Observations of "white liberals and racial moderates" of changes in Mississippi since the time of Willie McGee and of James Meredith provide a context in which Faulkner's convictions and expectations can be viewed. In *Harper's: The South Today* (1965), C. Vann Woodward described the reaction of the South to the Supreme Court decision of 1954 and to the subsequent Civil Rights Acts. Southern whites imagined their nightmares materialized: "Negroes at the ballot boxes, federal bayonets in the streets, a rebirth of scalawags, a new invasion of carpetbaggers, and battalions of abolitionists and Yankee schoolmarms in the form of Freedom Riders and sit-ins . . . ." By 1954 "the old regional syndrome of minority psychology and rejection anxiety" had stifled "debate and dissent." Many Southerners felt suspicious of outsiders and feared "all outside ideas, movements, and opinions." In the extreme instance these paranoid impulses resulted in what James W. Silver has described as " 'the closed society' of Mississippi." (Professor Silver was Faulkner's chief personal friend on the faculty of the University of Mississippi.)

But in this "Second Reconstruction," Woodward said, "The Negro himself was a decisive participant, not an instrument of white purpose." But although "dark Faulknerian themes" of "defeat and failure, . . . guilt and tragedy . . . will continue to play a part in defining a Southerner," in the new era both races are looking to the future. "In this new search for identity the Negro is fully engaged. In fact, he has taken the initiative and the white man reacts to him. Their discovery of each other will define a distinctively new period of Southern history and a new Southern identity."

In the same special supplement of *Harper's: The South Today,* Walker Percy, of an old and distinguished Mississippi family, contributed "Mississippi: The Fallen Paradise." He noted that in 1965 Mississippi had "refused to change," although in 1882 George W. Cable had been welcomed at the University of Mississippi and his address was "warmly accepted" even when he accused the South of "conservatism to the point of absolute rigidity." Percy doubted that in 1965 Cable would even be allowed to speak at Ole Miss. In 1965 he may have been right, but in 1971 I heard Charles Evers, brother of the assassinated black leader Medgar Evers, speak there in Fulton chapel to a large audience of blacks and whites of all ages. And he was honored at a reception given by Ole Miss faculty. Walker Percy regarded Medgar Evers and James Meredith as "the bravest Mississippians in recent years."

Percy's view of Gavin Stevens as an "influential white moderate" is disproved in *The Mansion,* in which Gavin as usual talked to those who agreed with him and refrained from political action. Percy may have been right about Ole Miss students in 1965 being "good-looking and ferocious young bigots, indoctrinated by White Citizens Councils." But I remember an Ole Miss student in 1962 who reminded me of Chick Mallison and who predicted that the trouble-making rioters would prove to be chiefly the younger students, as yet uninfluenced by university education.

Walker Percy recognized the prominent role of religion in Mississippi and correctly described it as "a religion . . . which tends to canonize the existing social and political structure and to brand as atheistic any threat of change." Churches such as the Episcopalian, much a minority in Oxford, are less subject to control by majority sentiment than those in which the congregation has free choice in hiring and firing ministers. As Percy noted, Faulkner "at last changed his mind about" federal intervention and "came to prefer even enforced change to a state run by Citizens Councils and the Klan." In recognizing that "in the light of recent history in Mississippi, the depersonalized American neighborhood looks more and more tolerable," and "people generally leave each other alone," Walker Percy did anticipate changes that have come to pass in Oxford.

Willie Morris, editor of *The South Today,* a native of Mississippi and at times a resident in Oxford, perceived a transformation in Mississippi directly related to the violent change imposed in 1962. In "A Sense of Place: The Americanization of Mississippi" (1978), Morris observed that "Mississippi . . . is catching up to the older social ideals and values of the more pristine America." In addition to integration of public schools there are "manifestations of this vast social change" which would not have been predicted when Meredith was admitted to Ole Miss, "emerging biracialism"—"in the newspapers, television, parent–teachers meetings, in a courtesy and politeness between the races in public places." Although the "catalyst to the process" was "the federal presence," Mississippi responded "to its own genuine heritage: whites and blacks living together" (as they had done before the Jim Crow laws).

In light of my familiarity with Confederate symbolism that marks football games, especially homecoming games overwhelmingly attended by alumni at Ole Miss, Morris' most impressive image of change is that of "black and white Ole Miss players" embracing each other to the strains of "Dixie," with confederate flags "waving in the stands." And a "black boy from Yazoo County" was "elected Colonel Rebel."

Willie Morris recalled nostalgically the memories of childhood, when "Time seemed to stand still for us when we wished it to." Although he recognized the gains that accompanied the losses during change and progress, one may question his view that our "communal heritage" is threatened by "that relentless urge to mobility and homogeneity which . . . is the hallmark of the greater society." As in most areas in the United States, the original founding fathers displayed precisely that "relentless urge" in establishing their settlements. In the 1980s in Milwaukee, the current culture is concerned with preserving the ethnicity of non–English-speaking residents whose mobility brought them here: ethnicity versus homogeneity is still an issue. One agrees with Willie Morris, however, that "It is no accident . . . that Mississippi produced Faulkner, the greatest of all the American novelists. . . ."

Another native of Mississippi, a journalist of an earlier generation than Willie Morris and one who pursued his career in Mississippi, Hodding Carter assessed the healthy provincialism of Mississippi at the end of *Southern Legacy* (1950), after a critical examination of its unhealthy provincialism: "when loyalty makes the regional patriot blind to imperfection and resentful of inspection . . . it becomes a deteriorative force; the obligation to examine, to protest and to propose change must accompany affection, else devotion can destroy." Dissatisfaction and discontent he accepted: "for the soul is nurtured on inquietude . . . . Out of inquietude the South, so long bemused in the twilight of its self-satisfaction, stirs now before the dawn.'' In the foreword of the paperback edition of *Southern Legacy* Ralph McGill, another distinguished Southern journalist, spoke from the perspective of November 1965: ''Many Southern white men and many Southern Negroes have accepted the responsibility necessary to cope with change and with opportunity. There are still those who betray their legacy by interpreting change as something which enabled them to have and to hold a special privileged status. There are still those who persist in thinking that their Southernism enables them to be outside the laws and obligations of their national citizenship.'' Change requires of citizens responsibility and obligation.

Writing after Hodding Carter and not long before Ralph McGill, as quoted above, Louis Rubin in ''The Literature of a Changing South'' dealt with social change:

> what can happen if a society which has one kind of identity and one kind of texture of values, attitudes, beliefs, customs, and assumptions that constitute its social and moral fabric is suddenly confronted with great changes in its way of doing things? . . . it is a change in the basic premises under which a society functions . . . that involves religious ideals, moral values, social structure, historical memories, blood ties of kith and kin, political loyalties, aesthetic inclinations. Any society is predicated upon such values and attitudes, which together define its image of the good life, its worthy ideals and standards.

Writers, Rubin said, ''in creating an image of human life . . . are attempting to reconcile . . . the apparent contradiction in ideals and values . . . and the nature of actual existence . . . .'' But what the South must retain, however much it changes, Rubin said, is what ''Faulkner called . . . 'love and honor and pity and pride and compassion and sacrifice' '' and what Robert Penn Warren called '' 'the awful responsibility of Time.' Whatever it is called, it is the old human impulse to look deeply and honestly at what we are, never to deny what we must be, never to settle for less than what we might become, and always to seek to understand and cherish our experience. Another name for this, in our own time, has been William Faulkner.''

Change and ''the awful responsibility of Time'' bring us from Faulkner's concept of life as time, motion, and change to the values, such as those listed by Louis Rubin, which represent what Faulkner considered admirable exercise of man's free will in the conduct of his life. Michael Millgate's comments in ''A Cosmos of My Own'' serve to recall the unique aspects of Yoknapatawpha which make it possible and essential to view it as a whole in examining the values which are reflected in the lives and fates of its inhabitants, ''the embodiment of Faulknerian ideas about human existence.'' Millgate quoted Faulkner's statement about them: "I can move these people around like God, not only in space but in time too." As Millgate said, "Faulkner's whole world seems to have remained perpetually alive and active in his imagination, as something quite apart from his capacity, as a time-bound human being, to realize that world on paper." "Yoknapa-tawpha," Millgate continued, "is . . . to an extraordinary degree an organically unified world, a cosmos, ordered and harmonious, growing progressively and ever more richly out of a single original conception. But it is also . . . an infinitely fluid world, in which the maturing creative imagination of the author is under no obligation to observe a rigid consistency in such matters as geography, chronology, or characterization." But Millgate commented on the "unmistakable coherence" of the "Faulknerian world. The novels and stories illuminate, modify, and support each other to a degree with which we have scarcely as yet begun to come to terms." Yoknapatawpha retained in Faulkner's "imagination an absolute integrity and reality." As Faulkner said: "I like the idea of the world I created being a kind of keystone in the universe." Faulkner's "keystone image," Millgate remarked, "was absolutely to the point, so integral has his work become to the whole texture of our civilization."

In considering this world in relation to the values motivating the motion and action of the characters, which depend in part on their initiative and volition, the other two principles of reality, time and change, might seem unrelated to values. As Quentin Compson demonstrated, only in death can one escape from time and change. But the principles by which one makes effective use of time and contributes to desirable change lie within the individual's own powers of choice and action.

The moral principles which Faulkner regarded as the foundation of an authentic life are those of Christian existentialism, which is based on Judeo-Christian time. Existential time should be considered, therefore, before dealing with concepts and values less inherent in religion and culture.

"William Faulkner and the Terror of History: Myth, History, and Moral Freedom in the Yoknapatawpha Cycle" suggests the "existentialist perspective" which Vernon Hornback observed in Faulkner's cosmos. The absence in cyclic time of freedom and responsibility Hornback constrasted with the Bergsonian concept of time in which free will retains connection with the past and shapes the future. Faulkner cast the actions of his characters, Hornback explained, against mythic archetypes and cyclical time because the Southern dilemma involved being entrapped by the past and repeating cultural rites and patterns or accepting "the terrible freedom" of linear time in which "what is done . . . is uniquely the responsibility of the agent alone."

Faulkner's life-long commitment as a creative artist to his own cosmos is obvious in the chronological list of his major publications: from *Sartoris* in 1929 to *The Reivers* in 1962, only *A Fable* indicates a long departure from the creation of his cosmos. Faulkner's return to *Snopes* (*The Town*, 1957, *The Mansion*, 1959) and his final creation, *The Reivers*, brought the end of his life as a creative artist very close to the end of his life—"a consummation devoutly to be wished" in the existentialist concept of time.

But even concentration on the cosmos Faulkner created does not ensure comprehensive treatment of that subject. *The Heart of Yokna-patawpha* by John Pilkington, a longtime resident of Oxford, was published too recently for me to deal adequately with it, and his anatomical approach had little in common with my cosmic one. I regretted, however, that Dr. Pilkington, as a cardiologist, did not consider *The Town*, *The Mansion*, and *The Reivers* as belonging to what Graham Greene would call *The Heart of the Matter*.

Unfortunately *Yoknapatawpha* in the title of a critical volume on Faulkner's fiction suggests a comprehensive treatment of the cosmos he created; if such a work does not make it clear that Faulkner went on creating until his death shortly after the publication of *The Reivers*, the reader may receive the impression that the creator outlived his creation and no longer dwelt in that universe. One might wonder if he lost the key! Or if, like James Joyce's artist, "the God of the creation," the creator of Yoknapatawpha remained "invisible, refined out of existence; indifferent, paring his fingernails."

Faulkner, however, used his last years creatively. The long-contemplated "Huck Finn" story was narrated in *The Reivers* by "Grandfather" in 1961. Faulkner lived long enough to enjoy his last creation: he had so enjoyed writing it that he wished he "could do it again" (*FWP* 68). And there he is in his own creation, visible at last. "The mark of his genius," according to Ben Vorpahl, "is finally his recognition of his own double involvement as creator–participant in the novel and his ability to implicitly express it."

In Rollo May's terms, Faulkner's use of time was qualitative: "The more a person is able to direct his life consciously, the more he can use time for constructive benefits." For himself and his readers, Faulkner must have considered writing *The Reivers* a "constructive benefit," the use of time for creation and self-creation until his death.

For the servant of the time clock, Rollo May said, "The more conformist and unfree he is, the more time is the master." He "serves time," as if he were in jail. Writing as a psychologist, not as a philos-

opher, May's statement that "one's goal is to live each moment with
freedom, honesty, and responsibility" approximates the existentialist
meaning of "authenticity" as man's goal. May cited Otto Rank as
pointing out "that the past and the future live in the psychological
present." "The most effective way to ensure the value of the future,"
May said, "is to confront the present courageously and constructively.
For the future is born out of and made by the present."

John Macquarrie's comments on the future serve to complement
May's: the will that dwells on the future may become mere wishing or
"irresponsible idealism or utopianism" and may "result only in an
unrealistic and impractical mode of existence in which action has been
. . . stifled and overcome by fantasy." And preoccupation with the
past and resistance to change result in "no act of will that breaks into
the future, but rather an attempt to find security in the routines and
rituals of the past."

In *Time in Literature* (1955) Hans Meyerhoff and the authors he dealt
with were "thinking of time as directly and immediately experienced."
He recognized "man's temporal existence" as constituting "a crucial
concept" in existentialist philosophy and literature: Bergson's "notion
of time . . . as experienced and lived . . . enters into all varieties of
existentialism." Furthermore, Meyerhoff considered that "existentialism in our age is practically indistinguishable from literary trends and
the arts" and named Dostoevsky, Tolstoi, Kafka, and Faulkner as
examples.

The title of the last chapter in Mircea Eliade's *Cosmos and History*,
"The Terror of History," is intelligible in light of his account of
cyclical time and "the myth of the eternal return." In comparison with
the mythic world, the anxieties of those living in history in the modern
world and the consequent rise of existentialism can well be explained
as "the terror of history." Eliade cited the work of T. S. Eliot and
James Joyce as "saturated with nostalgia for the myth of eternal repetition and . . . for the abolition of time." To explain how modern man
endures the "terror," Eliade discussed "Freedom and History."
Modern man, he said, "can be creative only insofar as he is historical;
. . . all creation is forbidden him except that which has its source in his
own freedom; . . . everything is denied him except the freedom to
make history by making himself." Thus the life of the authentic man
becomes a "quest for freedom." "The test of progress," according to
Robert Nisbet, "was the degree of freedom a people or nation possessed."

Not only is Christianity the religion of modern historical man, "who
simultaneously discovered personal freedom and continuous time,"

but according to Eliade, "the existence of God forced itself far more urgently on modern man . . . than upon the man of the archaic and traditional cultures. . . ." That William Faulkner did exercise his freedom in creating himself as well as Yoknapatawpha and that his belief in time, motion, and change was inseparable from his belief in God suggest that he also may have escaped from the terror of history by his Christian existentialism.

Because the statements quoted in *Faulkner at West Point* were made in April 1962, shortly before Faulkner's death in July, they have been less frequently quoted than those in *Faulkner in the University* and *Faulkner at Nagano*; they express the beliefs he held at the end of his life.

In response to a question about why he presented characters who displayed "perversion and corruption" rather than "courage and honor," Faulkner replied that the artist must show man "in his base attitudes, his base conditions," despite which "he has outlived the dinosaur" and "in time . . . will even outlive the wheel." Man's "aberrations are part of his history." His inner nature "makes him want to endure, . . . makes him believe that war should be eradicated, that injustice should not exist, that little children shouldn't suffer." Man should "never be afraid of dirt or filth, of baseness or cowardice" but should try "to be braver, to be compassionate" but should not fear or try to avoid the evils of life; "the worst perversion of all is to retire to the ivory tower. Get down in the market place and stay there" (*FWP* 54, 55).

Although Faulkner disavowed following any right or duty to improve his readers and said that he wanted to tell about "the magic and passion of breathing" rather than be limited to right and duty and truth, he concluded that inverview with an affirmation of his belief in telling "a true and moving and familiar old, old story of the human heart in conflict with itself for the old, old human verities and truth, which are love, hope, fear, compassion, greed, lust" (*FWP* 56, 57, 59).

Faulkner believed that "man in his essence in the long view doesn't change" but slowly improves and eventually "will get rid of war and disease and ignorance and poverty." He dealt with "men and women who are moving, who are involved in the universal dilemmas of the human heart." A writer must love all mankind "even when he hates individual ones," and he should not judge them (*FWP* 80, 81, 82, 83).

Only a few months before the problem of equality of opportunity for Negroes erupted in the riot at the University of Mississippi, Faulkner responded at West Point to questions on the problem; he said it was a moral problem with only one answer: education for the Negro. He affirmed his belief in democratic government and in the capacity for democracy of any ethnological group if "educated to it" (*FWP* 90, 91, 92). At Nagano he had expressed his belief in democracy as the best form of government because it is based on belief in "mutual liberty." "Only in liberty," he said, "can hope exist—liberty and freedom not given man as a free gift but as a right and a responsibility . . . ." "And that Freedom," he said, "must be complete freedom for all men; we must choose now not between color and color . . . nor between ideology and ideology. We must choose simply between being slave and being free" (*FN* 187, 188).

Freedom is the foundation upon which the authentic life must be built. In addressing scholars, in *The Stubborn Structure*, Northrop Frye used "concern," a term from existentialists, to include "the sense of the importance of preserving the integrity of the total human community." Morality, "in the sense of obligation that enables man to preserve his relation to society, is the central expression of concern." John Macquarrie summed up his definition of "concern": "To be in the world is to be concerned with the world, to be engaged in ceaseless interaction with the things we find within the world." This means that "the world of everyday existing is an instrumental world," "viewed from the perspective of practical concern" of man for his environment and for "the beings around him."

Morality as defined by Frye is exemplified in the relationship of a foster parent to a child in Faulkner's "Race at Morning." "Mr. Ernest" explained to his twelve-year-old foster son that farming and hunting are not enough: "You got to belong to the business of mankind." It is no longer enough to know "what's right and what's wrong. . . . You got to know why it's right and why it's wrong, and be able to tell the folks that never had no chance to learn it; teach them how to do what's right. . . ." Uncle Ike McCaslin was the oldest member of the hunting group; the boy "reckoned" Uncle Ike "had been hunting deer in these woods for about a hundred years." The contrast between Mr. Ernest's concern for the boy and their world and the lack of such concern on the part of the parents who had deserted him and of the other hunters—Uncle Ike, Roth Edmonds, Willy Legate, and Walter Ewell—has implications in relation to Yoknapatawpha society.

In *The Reivers* Ike McCaslin, born in 1867, is still living in 1961. Roth Edmonds presumably has a son, whereabouts unknown. Only the Priests, of the whole McCaslin–Edmonds–Beauchamp tribe, have a third generation, to whom the grandfather is telling the story in *The Reivers*. He gives no evidence of grandchildren in any of the other leading families in 1961. If Yoknapatawpha families are examined according to existentialist values, it is apparent that the dying out of families was implicit in their motives and actions, derived from the society which suppressed such dissenting views as those of Uncle Buck and Uncle Buddy on slavery and which limited individual responsibility by the rigid social structure. Donald Mathews recognized in Old South evangelicalism such values as intuition and commitment. But the prevalence of Calvinism in Protestant denominations even in the New South gave predestination an appeal for those who regarded themselves as among the elect and could escape personal responsibility even for murder, as Doc Hines and Percy Grimm did (*LA*) by acting as agents of God. *Light in August* gives examples of devastating family religion, but of rigid Calvinism rather than the ante-bellum evangelical Christianity which made "the family the cadre of their movement." The McEachern, Burden, and Hines families, which were not natives of Yoknapatawpha, illustrate the point made by James Gustafson that "the legacy of a left- and right-handed God," of law and justice and of love, has been unfortunate: "Justice and order can become depersonalized, untempered by love and mercy, restricted to the preservation of the old and not opened to the creation of the new."

Such valuing as characterizes existentialism implies, Rollo May said, an open system. In the concluding paragraph of *Psychology and the Human Dilemma* he continued to stress "valuing as an *act*," involving "a commitment" which "implies some conscious choice and responsibility" on the part of the individual. In *Man's Search for Himself* May stressed that "ethical judgment and decision must be rooted in the individual's own power to evaluate." He must choose and affirm the value and the acting "as part of the way he sees reality," "with responsibility for his action." In *Psychology and the Human Dilemma* May explained the origin of existentialism as the individual's need "to look deeply within himself to discover a new basis for orientation and integration" which society no longer can provide. What Faulkner found deep within himself was Yoknapatawpha, in which he depicted a society that, in May's terms, "no longer provides the individual with adequate psychological and ethical orientation."

Man "becomes authentically himself," John Macquarrie said, "through free and responsible decisions." Freedom, however, is found only in "the good society," defined by Rollo May as "the one which gives to its people the greatest freedom," "the opportunity to realize ever greater human values." May specified that any "collectivism, as in fascism and communism," denies these values and must be opposed. J. T. Fraser interpreted Heidegger and his followers as seeing "the source of man's freedom in his potential to act and choose and thereby change his dread into courage" and put "mortal terror into the service of life." V. S. Naravane expressed very simply and briefly Radhakrishnan's concept of the good and moral life: "the good life is a life of freedom. There can be no question of good and evil where the agent has no command over his own actions."

The positive, volitional existential values are based on freedom in society and free will in man. Man exercises his free will in making a choice of action, often requiring courage, and thereafter bears the responsibility consequent to his choice. Although willpower cannot cause conscience or intuition to function, it can aid the individual in being receptive to such "truths of the heart." Radhakrishnan's metaphor for Free Will, of life as a bridge game, is particularly suitable in relation to Faulkner's concept, considering his various uses of game episodes or analogies in his fiction. In determining why the leading families in Yoknapatawpha have been defeated in the game of life, Radhakrishnan's metaphor is useful in identifying the types of player: those who break the rules, those who do not want to play, those who lack skill, those who never get a fair deal. And in Yoknapatawpha the game would be poker, not bridge: cards were not even dealt to the women.

The families upon whom the viability of the society rested and about whom we have sufficient information are white, middle-class or upper-class, play prominent roles in at least one book, and appear or are referred to in other narratives. The genealogies and character indexes provided by Cleanth Brooks in *William Faulkner: The Yoknapatawpha Country* and Robert W. Kirk in *Faulkner's People: A Complete Guide and Index to Characters in the Fiction of William Faulkner* are useful sources of vital statistics but not of "truths of the heart."

Like Faulkner we can begin with *Sartoris*, *Flags in the Dust*, and fill in earlier facts from *The Unvanquished*. Colonel John Sartoris, the founding father and an early settler in Yoknapatawpha, was married twice. Bayard, his only son, survived until 1919. After the Civil War, Colonel John married Drusilla only to placate her mother and preserve Drusilla's respectability. Colonel John was too busy building railroads and saving white supremacy to pay attention to Drusilla's Phaedra-like attachment to his son Bayard. He seemed little interested in women or fatherhood. His son Bayard seemed interested only in being a father and did not remarry when his wife died. *His* son was the father of twins and thus served a purpose. Old Bayard did not arouse the admiration of his grandson as Colonel John had aroused the hero worship of old Bayard when he was young. When young Bayard returned after World War I, his first wife and their infant son having died during his absence, he married Narcissa Benbow; probably it was Narcissa's choice more than his, carefully prepared for by her intimacy with Aunt Jenny. One male Sartoris survived in Yoknapatawpha, Benbow, son of Bayard and Narcissa, born the day of his father's suicidal plane crash. Dominated by Narcissa, with her superficial ideal of purity, Benbow continued the unauthenticity of the Benbow men. Aunt Jenny Du Pre, sister of Colonel John Sartoris, could not preserve the family, beyond providing a wise and loving woman to run the household for four generations of Sartoris men.

Horace Benbow, Narcissa's brother, let himself be victimized, first by Narcissa because he idealized her as a Southern virgin, a "still unravished bride of quietness" (*Sar.* 182), and second, by Belle Mitchell, whose wiles and ruthlessness he perceived but yielded to. Horace's choice of the family law business was motivated by a sense of duty and a desire for peace. He regarded the law as the "final resort of the lame, the halt, the imbecile, and the blind" (p. 184). Horace's susceptibility to the charms of women included all ages and even blood relatives, as *Flags in the Dust* reveals more clearly than does *Sartoris*, the shortened version. In *Sanctuary*, having deserted his wife, Belle, Horace made a decision of some moral significance but with disastrous results. Lacking experience as a criminal lawyer, he undertook to defend Lee Goodwin. Narcissa betrayed Horace to the unscrupulous district attorney in order to keep the Benbow name unsullied, although Horace is the only Benbow left, Narcissa being Mrs. Sartoris. The lynching of Lee Goodwin and the suffering of Ruby and her baby resulted from Horace's irrational decision and his inability to bear the responsibility. Fortunately the Benbow family as well as the Sartoris ends in Benbow Sartoris. Horace was replaced in Jefferson by Gavin Stevens who survived to the end of *The Mansion* but left no offspring.

The MacCallum family continued in the chronicles of Yoknapatawpha from *Sartoris* to *The Town* and *The Mansion*, appearing from the end of World War I, in *Sartoris*, to World War II in "The Tall Men." They are an all-male family consisting at first of a Civil War veteran father and six sons, one of whom, Buddy, fought in World War I after running away and enlisting. The family represents patriarchal domination and the preservation of an old way of life close to nature. Except for the Negro servant, Mandy, it is an all-male household, with a tacit understanding "that some day Buddy would marry and perpetuate the name." In "The Tall Men" Buddy had done so and had twin sons now of draft age. Faulkner used the MacCallums to represent a way of life which men might find attractive, but which Albert Devlin showed was not a viable way of life offering normal freedom of choice to grown

sons. In "The Tall Men" Buddy and his brother refused to quit growing cotton in order to receive a government subsidy in return. Like
Faulkner they "still believed in the freedom or liberty to make or break
according to a man's fitness and will to work" (*CS* 56). Because
"honor and pride and discipline . . . make a man worth preserving,
make him of any value" (p. 60). Buddy, unlike his father, was eager to
have his twin sons go to Memphis and enlist, too eager to let them wait
until his leg had been amputated. But the twin sons acted like automa-
tons, not as if they had made a significant choice, when they kissed
their father and left.

The Compson family are more fully represented in dialogue, interior
monologue, and stream-of-consciousness than other families. At the end
of *The Sound and the Fury*, Quentin had committed suicide, Caddy had
been disowned and her name never spoken in the Compson family, Mr.
Compson had died, of grief and alcoholism, Benjy had been castrated
and had reached his thirtieth year of idiocy, Caddy's daughter, Miss
Quentin, had run away with a carnival man taking with her the money
Caddy had sent for her and Jason's legitimately acquired money. Mrs.
Compson and Jason had chosen to imitate Southern gentility: Mrs.
Compson refused to know about sin, and Jason, like his mother a
Bascomb at heart, went through the motions of being a *paterfamilias*
but had no intention of marrying his mistress. Mrs. Compson forced
Caddy to marry Herbert Head to give her bastard—father unknown—a
name and to preserve Compson respectability. Jason made life so intolerable for Miss Quentin that she fled, no doubt to ruin. Mr.
Compson in his youth might have been a victim of Caroline Bascomb's
flirtatious wiles, which she dredged up as bait to catch Herbert Head as
a son-in-law. The inactivity of Mr. and Mrs. Compson, the frenzied
activity of Jason, divided between profit-seeking and spying on Miss
Quentin, are contrasted with Benjy's timeless and mindless wander-
ings and Quentin's meticulously planned and successfully carried out
choice of death to escape time and change. Even Dilsey can scarcely
be regarded as existentially authentic: she had no freedom of choice
because in her society subservience was inescapable, and her first
duties were to the Compsons, not to her own family. In her religion and
in her capacity for loving care she transcended the responsibility she
had to assume without free choice. Mr. Compson's nihilism was at
least an individual view of life, not cultural role playing, but his love for
Caddy and for Quentin was not deep enough to move him to action in
their behalf. His concern for Mrs. Compson as a lady caused him to sell
the pasture to send Quentin to Harvard, and Quentin showed his concern by finishing the academic year before he committed suicide; both
father and son had warped values.

When Quentin was resurrected in *Absalom, Absalom!* as the medium to whom and through whom the Sutpen story is narrated, one may conjecture that the Sutpen ability to reach decisions and carry them out and to resist being defeated by time constituted the fascination the Sutpen story held for Quentin. Time, motion, change were challenges to Sutpen. What destroyed Sutpen was his original choice of the slave society which had so humiliated him that he had to spend the rest of his life making the world respect him. He had had no opportunity to learn the values that were part of the society he chose to imitate; *noblesse oblige* was beyond his comprehension. He fulfilled his responsibility financially to his first wife, which was more than most slaveholders would have done under similar circumstances. But he lacked the conscience that education as a Southern gentleman might have cultivated in him. Mr. Compson's interpretation of the Charles Bon–Henry Sutpen–Judith Sutpen relationship confirms the impression in *The Sound and the Fury* that Quentin's interpretation of his father is somewhat warped. Mr. Compson and Quentin are the only Compsons in *Absalom, Absalom!*. The fact that the only Sutpen descendant living in Quentin's time is the idiot Jim Bond might incline one to accept Shreve's theory—until one remembers that the Compsons produced an all-white idiot and that the choice of a wife by Mr. Compson would thus parallel that of Charles Etienne Bon of a "coal-black and ape-like woman," mentally subnormal (*AA* 205).

The dynasty pattern which Sutpen chose and strove to achieve was destroyed by time, literally by the scythe in the hands of Wash Jones. Sutpen's choices, the last one being Milly Jones, were never based on love. But the presumed choice of Charles Bon to marry Judith because he did love her was equally fatal: Henry shot him, not because of his Sutpen blood and incest but because of his mother's part-Negro blood and thus miscegenation.

The white McCaslin family is still extant in Yoknapatawpha in 1961, in *The Reivers*. But Isaac, the only legitimate McCaslin left, is ninety-four. The son of Roth Edmonds and the unnamed grandaughter of Tennie's Jim Beauchamp, in "Delta Autumn," is presumably still living. Lucas and Mollie Beauchamp have no living grandchildren. In *The Reivers*, as previously noted, the collateral Priest branch of the descendants of Mary McCaslin, sister to Uncle Buck and Uncle Buddy, and Isaac Edmonds, had three boys younger than Lucius, the narrator. The parallels between the Priests and the Faulkners warrant a comparison between fact and fiction. William Faulkner and two of his three brothers (the other one had no children) were grandparents to twelve children, according to Joseph Blotner's genealogy in *Faulkner: A Biography*, II.

The McCaslins differ from the other leading white families in Yoknapatawpha in acknowledging many part-Negro descendants of L. Q. C. McCaslin, called Beauchamp after Tennie Beauchamp ("Was"), until Lucius Priest's mother insisted that Uncle Ned be called Uncle Ned McCaslin (*R* 30). It seems reasonable to assume that this departure from the previous custom indicates what Faulkner considered preferable. Enough information is given about the McCaslins to explain the decline of the family: after the Civil War Uncle Buck was finally captured by Sophonsiba Beauchamp and married her; Isaac was born in 1867 when Uncle Buck was sixty-eight years old. Mary McCaslin Edmonds and Isaac Edmonds were the ancestors of several generations with only one child. Too little is told about some of the marriages to explain the low productivity. Zack, father of Roth Edmonds, did not remarry when his wife died; Lucas Beauchamp's wife Mollie was wet nurse and mammy to Roth, who was the same age as Henry, son of Lucas and Mollie. This example, as well as that of L. Q. C. McCaslin himself, may account for the failure of white men to remarry if they could gain the benefits without the responsibility. But the long married life of Lucas and Mollie had no parallel among the McCaslin and Edmonds families. When Mollie died and Lucas grieved so deeply that he did not even recognize Chick Mallison, Chick discovered that "*you dont have to not be a nigger in order to grieve*" (*ID* 25).

The reluctance of Buck and Buddy to marry and the marriage of Buck's son Ike to a woman who refused to give him a second chance to father a son suggests that she caught him as Sophonsiba apparently caught Buck, and that assumption is supported by Faulkner's statement that "she assumed when they got married that she was going to be chatelaine of a plantation and they would have children" and took her revenge by denying him children when he denied her the plantation (*FU* 275–76). Thus Ike made one choice, to give up his inheritance, but it was a choice by which he escaped responsibility and hard work; the plantation was run by Cass Edmonds and his descendants. Ike had no regular, continuing occupation; after being a carpenter (*GDM*), he owned a hardware store (*T*), taken over eventually by Jason Compson (*M*). "Race at Morning" confirms the impression that Ike resisted change and "lived" only during the hunting season. The measure of Ike's failure as a mentor to younger men is exposed in "Delta Autumn," in Roth's lack of authentic values, as well as in the contrast between Ike and Mr. Ernest. Ike lived in cyclical time, and for him the "eternal return" was the hunting season, and eternal bliss would be hunting with the older men of his youth. This was a concept natural to

Sam Fathers, who had been Ike's mentor, but not natural to a member of a Christian culture who saw himself as a Christ figure when he became a carpenter (*GDM* 309).

The Stevens–Mallison family, with the exception of Gowan, possessed qualities which might have produced a healthy, growing family. (The young choices of Gowan and Temple caused the murder of one of their children and the execution of Nancy. Temple's redemption at the end of *Requiem for a Nun* is merely a possibility. Temple and Gowan seem unlikely to reverse the trend in Yoknapatawpha from declining to burgeoning families.) Gavin and Maggie Stevens are unique. They were at first older brother and younger sister, with difference in age inconsistent. But in *The Town* and *The Mansion* Gavin and Maggie are twins and Gavin and Judge Stevens live with the Mallisons after Maggie marries Charles Sr. In "Knight's Gambit" Gavin married Melisandre Backus Harris, a widow with two grown children, in 1942. Gavin's comfortable life with Maggie, enhanced by the close bonds of twinship, and with her husband and son, who was more like a son to Gavin, would explain his prolonged bachelorhood without absolving him from full participation in and responsibility to the community, both as a citizen and as a lawyer. His semiliberal principles were not demonstrated in his legal activities, not even to the extent that his forerunner, Horace Benbow, risked his career in defending Lee Goodwin. Gavin took it for granted that Lucas Beauchamp was guilty of murder, in *Intruder in the Dust*, and wanted him to plead guilty and spend the rest of his life in prison (*ID* 64–65). Gavin's failure to act politically is emphasized in *The Mansion*, when it is Ratliff who prevents the defeat of Devries in the campaign for senator and destroys the vicious career of Clarence Snopes. Charles Mallison pointed the moral of that tale: Gavin had failed to act according to his moral convictions when he should have let God depend on man (*M* 321).

The story of Charles Mallison's initiation in *Intruder in the Dust* perfectly illustrates "time, motion, and change" as accepted and used to good purpose, to save the life of Lucas Beauchamp, innocent of the murder of Vinson Gowrie. At the end of *The Mansion*, in 1946, Charles is at home again, after serving in the Air Corps since 1942 (*KG* 239); he returned in 1945 (*M* 350). Faulkner changed the age of Charles between *Intruder in the Dust* and *Knight's Gambit* and the Snopes trilogy. Since Charles makes his last appearance in *The Mansion*, in which Cleanth Brooks estimated his birth year as 1914, instead of 1923 or 1924 as in *Intruder in the Dust* and *Knight's Gambit*, the earlier date should be used. Charles would then be thirty-two in *The Mansion*, an age suggesting that he was neither uxorious nor philoprogenitive in his inclina-

tions. The Mallisons may well be a family without a future, despite the
sound values and motivations Charles demonstrated in *Intruder in
the Dust*. After all, he had really been brought up by his Uncle Gavin,
who idealized women but did not marry one who might have children.

Yoknapatawpha so far is a moribund society. In 1944 J. Donald
Adams diagnosed the problem: "the lack of a normal and mature relationship between a man and a woman. Every such relationship remains
on an infantile, depraved, or . . . an adolescent level." There is not "a
single family in which the relationships are not twisted either by perversion or insanity. The vital currents of life are stepped up in his pages
to an unparalleled intensity, so that sexual intercourse is conducted
always on the level either of rape or of nymphomania. It is a nightmare
world, wearing a mask of reality." Whether viewed as insane and
perverse or merely unhealthy, Yoknapatawpha had not changed radically by 1961.

Thus Faulkner seems to have created *The Reivers* to exemplify the
qualities needed for the survival of families and a healthy society.
Young Lucius made a choice that required only silent acquiescence to
Boon's scheme to "borrow" Boss Priest's car for the fabulous journey
to Memphis, symbolizing motion and change that would transform the
world and create new concepts of time. Lucius learned about sin,
gleefully chosen by Otis and helplessly accepted by Everbe Corinthia,
an innocent victim. But Lucius learned from Everbe that one may
choose virtue, as she did when she realized that she had freedom and
exercised her free will. Having chosen Non-Virtue himself, Lucius
bore his responsibility as jockey, to recover Boss Priest's car, until the
very end, taking no profit. He already knew how to behave like a
gentleman, without racial or religious prejudice and showing gallantry
to and respect for women. And he learned that one must live with the
memory of his wrongdoing. Thus Lucius learned truths to live by and
chose to play the game of life.

The most fundamental and significant explanation for the dying out of
Yoknapatawpha families seems to be the attitude of men toward
women in this male-dominated society. Men could live without white
wives if they did not care about fatherhood and preservation of the
family. Living without women was not necessary. Ratliff and Gavin
Stevens until he was past middle age seemed to find companionship
with congenial women, Ratliff with customers and Gavin with Maggie,
adequate for their needs. Marriages in Yoknapatawpha were not based
on love but on necessity: a name for a child, as with Eula Varner and
Caddy Compson; a bride's dowry, as with Flem Snopes; conformity to
social custom to gain or to preserve status, as with Sutpen and Ellen
Coldfield, Caroline Bascomb and Mr. Compson, Drusilla Hawk and

Colonel John Sartoris, Narcissa Benbow and Bayard Sartoris. (The woman may conceal her motives, for an open choice was not a woman's privilege.) Other Sartoris wives were barely mentioned, with no details about the marriage situation. The MacCallums and the McCaslin–Edmonds men married only to preserve the family and did not remarry if a wife died. Isaac McCaslin chose to let the McCaslins die out rather than to assume responsibility as head of the family and heir to the land in order to have children of his own. The Mallisons represent a potentially good marriage and family, but the belated change in Faulkner's concept to twinship for Gavin and Maggie provided Maggie with Gavin as a companion and member of the family until they were in their fifties. Her husband did not seem indispensable to Maggie or Gavin or young Charles. The lack of love between husband and wife in Yoknapatawpha is in ironic contrast to the incestuous love between brothers and sisters in *The Sound and the Fury* and *Absalom, Absalom!* and hinted at in *The Town* and *The Mansion* and between father and daughter in "Was." The only enduring love among major characters in Yoknapatawpha was the adulterous love between Manfred de Spain and Eula Varner, a life-denying and life-destroying love. Presumably Eula chose to live a lie and impose it on Linda rather than getting a divorce and marrying Manfred and providing Linda with a desirable father. Between respectability and morality, she chose respectability.

Yoknapatawpha seems too fragile as the keystone in the universe unless we consider *The Reivers* as a final positive, though comic, comment on what Yoknapatawpha needs in order to survive. The existentialist values demanded by time, motion, and change are needed to overcome the life-defeating impulses which destroyed Yoknapatawpha families by maintaining a closed society excluding even kinfolk with black blood, and which denied freedom of choice to women in the male-dominated society. Radhakrishnan's analogy between life and a bridge game reminds one that the card game that figures in Yoknapatawpha is not bridge but poker, played by men. Chick Mallison remembered an elderly spinster who taught all the young women to play Five Hundred, which to Chick was a "stakeless," "childhood game," not a man's game like poker (*ID* 60, 61). Southern women had their lives determined, figuratively speaking, by games played by men, according to rules formulated by men, and even enforced by Southern ladies like Mrs. Hawk, Mrs. Varner, and Mrs. Compson. Only women of superior social class and independent means were free to remain single without loss of status, like Aunt Jenny Du Pre—but she had been married and was born a Sartoris.

The Reivers not only provided a vision of a viable myth in Yoknapatawpha, that of a free society based on Christian existential values, but completed the cosmos which had been in the process of creation from the writing of *Flags in the Dust*. In concluding her examination of Faulkner's novels, Olga Vickery commented on the significance of the three heroes—Boon, the comic hero; Ned, the successful leader; Lucius, the young initiate—and their "triumphant reentry into an established society which serves to unite the world of romance and reality." "The dominant tone of *The Reivers* . . . is a blending of innocence and experience and of acceptance and wonder. . . . It offers a heightened, poetic awareness of the beauty of normal humanity, . . . always worthy of man's faith." It is, indeed, as Vickery declared, "a tribute to Faulkner" that in his last book he "created his 'brave new world' by describing man not tragically, satirically, or comically but simply lovingly."

Olga Vickery's specific statement confirms and complements John Gardner's general statement about "true art's divine madness": it "is shot through with love: love of the good, a love proved . . . by active celebration of whatever good or trace of good can be found by a quick and compassionate eye in this always corrupt and corruptible but god-freighted world." Together the concepts of Vickery and Gardner can be firmly applied to Faulkner's cosmos only as *The Reivers* confirms and concludes the implications of the Yoknapatawpha fiction.

The last word of Vickery on *The Reivers* expressed her intuitive understanding of a quality in Faulkner with which he was not usually credited. But in 1976, the title of Meta Carpenter Wilde's story of her personal experience with Faulkner was *A Loving Gentleman*.

Almost twenty years after William Faulkner's death, his "brave new world" was called to my mind by "Liberal Catholic" expression of ideas on sexuality and marriage and God's design which were both catholic and existential. A "positive theology of human sexuality" was called for by Archbishop Joseph Bernardin as "an expression of the dignity entrusted to the man and woman who were to function with the twofold purpose of dispelling each other's existential loneliness and cooperating with the Creator in the injunction to 'increase and multiply.'" The Most Reverend Vincent de Couesnongle echoed I Corinthians 13: "God's design is a design of love. . . . This is the fundamental law of the gospel. We must return to it without fail in all things. For it is on love that we will be judged." The "loving gentleman" narrator in *The Reivers* is the creator of Yoknapatawpha, looking on his creation and suggesting what goodness it needs to survive and take delight in God's design.

Afterword

THE OMISSION of the third twentieth anniversary in 1982 which would be of concern to readers of Faulkner, the riots at the University of Mississippi, seems inexplicable in 1983. The publication of this book had been originally planned for 1982, with no thought of events late in the year being included. But publication was carried over into 1983; the manuscript had been completed before the announcement was made that in the fall semester of 1982 commemorative ceremonies would be held at the University of Mississippi in recognition of the admission of James Meredith in 1962, the first Negro enrolled. Although the riots of 1962 have been dealt with and some observations made of the effect of desegregation, chiefly by critics of Faulkner and of Southern literature, a twentieth-anniversary report provides a more significant conclusion concerning a crucial event than an interim report, such as *The South Today* (1965). Those events are very pertinent to William Faulkner and the cosmos he created.

When Faulkner's political views and his religious and philosophical beliefs are considered in relation to local, regional, and national issues and events, the consistency between his Christian-humanist existentialism as an author and his belief in democracy and the Constitution of the United States and the responsibility of citizens as individuals is apparent and impressive. The gulf between his beliefs and those of a majority of his fellow Mississippians becomes strikingly clear: his sudden death in July 1962 seems providential, sparing him a painful experience.

The same gulf is revealed in the lives of two other natives of Mississippi whose experiences parallel those of Faulkner in significant respects and who have been connected with the University of Mississippi. Will Campbell told the story of his life and that of his brother in *Brother to a Dragonfly*. Son of a farmer in the Deep South, near McComb, Mississippi, Will grew up during the Depression. When he was "a sixteen-year-old fundamentalist" Baptist, he was "a full-fledged preacher." When the Supreme Court decision on segregation was three months old, in 1954, he was "Director of Religious Life" at the University of Mississippi. Neither blacks nor whites took desegregation seriously. The organization of White Citizens' Councils to preserve White Supremacy was a major factor in Campbell's changing his social and religious views. He became active in opposition against the bigotry he observed and left the South. In the National Council of Churches he spent much time combating KKK violence. He was active in interracial activities, knowing the chief Negro leaders of the 1960s. He visited Meredith at Ole Miss six weeks after Meredith was admitted. He quoted what Faulkner said in a letter to the Memphis *Commercial Appeal* while Campbell was still at Ole Miss: "I hate to see the South destroyed twice in a hundred years over the same issue."

Personal experiences of Ole Miss faculty members during the 1962 riots were related in a long article in the Memphis *Commercial Appeal* before the commemorative ceremonies in 1982. Evans Harrington, of the English Department, and the son of a minister in Mississippi, said that until the night of the riots he was "a kind of James Joyce type, a nonparticipant in political life. But that sure shook me out of my ivory tower." Harrington became engaged in professionally and personally hazardous interracial activity. Now as Chairman of the English Department at Ole Miss he is responsible for the annual summer conferences, "Faulkner and Yoknapatawpha."

After the Supreme Court decision that "separate but equal" was no longer acceptable and that segregation must end, Faulkner wrote a number of letters to the Memphis *Commercial Appeal* stressing the folly of those who sought to retain the "two identical systems" when there was not enough money for "one school system good enough for anybody." With such a system, "the best that schools can be . . . the schools themselves will take care of the candidates, white and Negro both, who had no business there in the first place." The implication that White Supremacy might be based not on belief in Negro inferiority but on fear of Negro superiority, not merely equality, is confirmed by explanations William Faulkner and Will Campbell gave for the existence of the White Citizens' Councils: they were being used by "respectable organizations and institutions of which they were a part and party, all of which," Campbell belatedly learned, were "more truly racist" than Klans in Klan country in Mississippi. The White

Citizens' Councils of "Mississippi and the South" were originated by "a small group of Delta aristocrats" who could not be called "ignorant rednecks." In *Integration at Ole Miss*, Russell Barrett said that the Citizens' Council in 1962 was "the dominant factor in Mississippi," controlling "the leaders of the state—business, newspaper, political, religious, educational, . . . This conquest by the Citizens' Council . . . was the most important single cause of Mississippi's legal resistance and physical insurrection."

In the South during Reconstruction the aristocratic status of night riders like Colonel Sartoris endangered them: the Ku Klux Klan were—and are—disguised by masks and robes. Although the Klan was not involved in the riots at Ole Miss, the explanation in "Learning to Hate," in *Special Report: The Ku Klux Klan*, casts light on the reactions of students at Ole Miss. Gordon Allport's study, *The Nature of Prejudice*, "discovered that bigoted people go through life feeling threatened," and that the young person "begins to harden into the pattern of adult bigotry that is shared by his or her parents": "it takes the entire period of childhood and adolescence to master prejudice."

Faulkner provided both an example of that general rule and an exception. Roth Edmonds, bound by the traditions of his family and society, cast aside Henry and Lucas and Molly as "family." Charles Mallison risked his life to follow the dictates of his conscience and save Lucas. The students at Ole Miss behaved like the boy who did not sign the letter he wrote in favor of racial equality. Faulkner wrote to the paper, praising the letter but commenting: "in Mississippi communal adult opinion" can reach such a pitch that their children "dare not, from probably a very justified physical fear, sign their names to an opinion adverse to it."

One of the best-known and most significant expositions of Faulkner's stand on equality and desegregation is the speech he made to the Southern Historical Society at the Peabody Hotel in Memphis, November 10, 1955. He gave the speech at the request of James Silver, Professor of History at the University of Mississippi. That historic occasion, as well as the admission of James Meredith to the University, has been repeated, even more recently. *The Faulkner Newsletter & Yoknapatawpha Review*, published in Oxford by Dean Faulkner Wells, Faulkner's niece, and her husband, devoted a column and a half of the January/March 1983 issue to "Silver Recalls Role in Faulkner Speech." The occasion for Silver's recollection was the twenty-seventh anniversary celebration, on November 3, 1982, in the same place, of the 1955 meeting to discuss "The Segregation Decisions." "It took months of negotiations," Silver said, to arrange with the Peabody "for blacks to socialize at organizational meals, but renting rooms for them remained taboo." Only reluctantly was Benjamin Mays, then and now a distinguished historian, allowed to sit at the head table, where he delivered "an impassioned sermon on the immorality of segregation."

Faulkner based his address on that occasion on the American Constitution, "the idea of individual human freedom and liberty on which our nation was founded . . . individual liberty and equality and freedom," which is our only defense against communism. To preserve our freedom, we must practice it: "our freedom must be buttressed by a homogeny equally and unchallengeably free, no matter what color they are, so that all the other inimical forces everywhere—systems political or religious or racial or national—will not just respect us because we practice freedom, they will fear us because we do." "The question," he said, "is no longer of white against black. It is no longer whether or not white blood shall remain pure, it is whether or not white people shall remain free."

Faulkner's belief in racial equality did not vary, but he advised the Negroes to be patient and moderate in their methods to achieve equality. To a challenge from Dr. W. E. B. Du Bois to "debate desegregation in Mississippi," Faulkner replied with a telegram saying that they were in perfect agreement that desegregation "IS RIGHT MORALLY LEGALLY AND ETHICALLY" and that only their views on practicality of methods might differ. In "A Letter to the Leaders in the Negro Race, 1956," he advised moderation, and added: "This was Gandhi's way." They should be unflagging and flexible, patient, without violence.

In the last few days of Faulkner's life, before his sudden death caused by a coronary occlusion, he was concerned with political issues and with James Meredith. In the election in which Ross Barnett was elected Governor, thereby ensuring a battle between Mississippi and the federal law at Ole Miss, Faulkner had voted for a Democrat, Frank E. Smith. Faulkner retained his admiration for Adlai Stevenson, whom he had known personally in the 1950's. (When Stevenson lost in the presidential election in 1956, Faulkner said: "Adlai Stevenson . . . had three strikes against him: wit, urbanity, and erudition.") If Stevenson's *Papers* had been published before 1962, Faulkner would have been pleased with what Stevenson said about him, to illustrate the "new vitality and creative energy of the 'New South'": "so it was that the Nobel Prize for Literature came to the Mississippian, William Faulkner, a prize that he accepted in an exalted address, extolling the unconquerable spirit of man." And he would have endorsed Stevenson's pledge to "continue our efforts to eradicate discrimination based on race, religion, or national origin."

On July 2, 1962, Aubrey Seay remarked to Faulkner: "Meredith is supposed to come on the thirteenth. Do you suppose we'll have trouble?" Faulkner replied, "If we do . . . it will be because of the people out in Beat Two who never went to the University or never intended to send their children to the University." These back-country White Supremacists Faulkner foresaw as an influence in the opposition to Meredith if he came to the University as the first Negro student. Ross Barnett was elected, Faulkner said, by "eighty-Beat Twos." (His readers will remember that the Gowries were identified by their "Beat.")

The vulgarity of the language of students, male and female, at Ole Miss which shocked James Meredith may reflect family origins. The student chants in Chad Walsh's "Ode on the University of Mississippi" (September 30–31, 1962) are authentic, not his creation.

Hotty, toddy, God A'mighty,
Who in the hell are we?
Flim flam, bim bam,
Ole Miss, by damn.

Never, Never, Never, Never, No-o-o Never Never Never.
We will not yield an inch of any field.
Fix us another toddy, ain't yieldin' to nobody.
Ross's standin' like Gibraltar, he shall never falter.
Ask us what we say, it's to hell with Bobby K.
Never shall our emblem go from Colonel Reb to Old Black Joe.

James Meredith considered that his "most remarkable achievement" in fighting the White Supremacy system was his survival. His physical survival was ensured by the constant protection of U.S. marshals, of whom he said: "They had been as good an example of the American ideal as probably could be found. They were men dedicated to the idea of human equality and freedom for all." But Meredith's own character was the other essential factor in his psychological survival. He kept his sense of humor and silently had the last word: on the last day of classes he wore on his lapel one of the "NEVER, NEVER buttons that Barnett had made so popular"—but Meredith wore it upside down.

William Faulkner would have been essentially in agreement with the basic beliefs of James Meredith as well as those of Will Campbell and Evans Harrington, although each chose his own way of expressing and furthering his beliefs. In *Three Years in Mississippi* James Meredith repeatedly stated his purpose in submitting himself to a situation so dangerous that, without his body guard of marshals, he might well have met the fate Medgar Evans did, June 12, 1963. That death, Meredith said, "had a most profound effect on me both publicly and privately. Since I had been considered the most likely victim, it took time to absorb the reality of his death."

Meredith's analysis of the problems of desegregation sounds familiar to readers of Faulkner. "The basic problem is that none of us knows how to make the transition from one way of life and status to another. People are afraid of change." That fear of change, of the loss of "White Supremacy," explains why "raw, demonstrative violence has become a religion to the whites; its ceremonial and ritualistic aspects are a vital part of the Mississippi way of life." And why the long out-moded symbols of the Confederacy are cherished by the whites as if they represent a reality. The White Citizens' Councils, a reaction to the Supreme Court decision in 1954, and the revival of the Ku Klux Klan provide the violence to bind white society together and preserve White Supremacy. The Councils create "an image of respectability," and the Klansmen continue to wear the masks and robes which conceal identity and create mystery and fear.

Meredith felt that he had a "Divine Responsibility" to liberate his people from the restrictions imposed by White Supremacy: he wanted his people to be able to take pride in themselves. By so doing, he believed that he could aid "the cause of directing civilization toward a destiny of humaneness." "Freedom of opportunity" is necessary before a person can exercise "the greatest of all human freedoms . . . the freedom of choice." But choice involves responsibility: Meredith was alarmed because he received letters from Negro students who were leaving it to God and Meredith "to prove to the world that Negroes are somebody," instead of each making a contribution of his own "to the accomplishment of his freedom." After the murder of Medgar Evers, Meredith felt that it was his responsibility to advise the Negroes and offer "an alternative to violence": his suggestion of "a massive nation-wide 'passive resistence movement'" is similar to Faulkner's recommendation to Negro leaders of "Gandhi's way."

The invitation to James Meredith to attend the commemoration in 1982 of his admission to Ole Miss in 1962 elicited varied replies, but after months of indecision he agreed to come and to speak at one of the sessions. The events at Ole Miss again received nation-wide publicity, which revealed both desirable changes and continued or even increased resistance to national policies and ideals. One of the requests of Meredith was the abandonment of "the Confederate flag, Colonel Rebel, and the song 'Dixie' as symbols of Ole Miss," one of the issues disputed in 1962. But in 1982 the Ku Klux Klan marched around the

Square in Oxford to protest the refusal of an Ole Miss cheerleader to carry the Confederate flag. There was not a large crowd of spectators, and their booing of the marchers was their chief response. I was told by a friend in Oxford that visible indication of a change for the better was the presence of black police on duty keeping order in the Square.

The reappearance of the Klan is of ominous significance: *The Poverty Law Report* (Nov.–Dec. 1982) reported both anti-Klan political and legal activity and nation-wide Klan and Nazi incidents, including the march in Oxford: "University students and faculty on both sides of the issue said they resented the Ku Klux Klan injecting itself into the controversy." The *Report* announced a new Confederation of Klans, "a coalition of White-Supremacist organizations." Although "the Klan has long been both anti-Semitic and anti-black," "the new Klan Confederation basically consists of those groups which make no attempt to disguise their Nazi orientation." H. Brandt Ayers provided the perfect metaphor for the Ole Miss symbols, whether cherished by students or the Klan: "A viral weed of mythology has been allowed to grow up like kudzu over the South." Kudzu flourishes incredibly in the Oxford area.

Although the concept of such an observance as that of 1982 at Ole Miss, with blacks and whites freely mingling, would have been unthinkable in 1962, progress toward equality of opportunity among both black students and black faculty members has been slower than Meredith wished. In this context, the most encouraging news item is that the Milwaukee *Journal*, January 2, 1983, published an article on James Meredith, with a photo, and the headline: "Meredith wants to work at Ole Miss." No longer "the staunch individualist and loner," he has decided that he can have greater effectiveness in an organization or institution. He also has an idea for a "Black African Volunteer Corps," similar to the Peace Corps. James Silver's description of Meredith suggests that such a change would be contrary to his nature: "Mr. Meredith is a very complicated human being, above all an individualist."

William Faulkner once tried to change his life in a somewhat similar way. He consented to President Eisenhower's request that he head a section of writers, American and foreign, in a "people-to-people program," to "help bridge international gaps widened by the Cold War." When the plan failed, he said that it had been doomed by "the mystical belief, almost a religion," in our culture "that the individual man can no longer exist," to speak to other individuals of such simple things as honesty with oneself and responsibility toward others and protection for the weak and compassion and pity for all." If James Meredith should read this, he might have second thoughts about relinquishing his freedom to choose and to be personally responsible for the consequences of his choice.

And if William Faulkner could have read *Three Years in Mississippi*, might he have recognized in James Meredith what Yoknapatawpha lacked before 1962, a black existential hero?

Faulkner and Meredith seem to speak in unison:

> Home again, his native land; he was born of it
> and his bones will sleep in it;
> loving it even while hating some of it.
> But most of all he hated the intolerance and injustice:
> the lynching of Negroes not for the crimes they committed
> but because their skins were black;
> the inequality: the poor schools they had then when they had any,
> the hovels they had to live in;
> who could worship the white man's God
> but not in the white man's church.

> Loving all of it even while he had to hate some of it
> because he knows now that you dont love because:
> you love despite; not for the virtues, but despite the faults.

The conclusion I arrived at before there was any need for an Afterword was confirmed when I reread "Mississippi" which embraces both that reality and the mythic land called Yoknapatawpha. The last lines of "Mississippi" confirm also Louis Rubin's decision on what Faulkner's solution would be to the problem of the South and of any society: "He wanted a world to be a place where love is stronger than fear, compassion is stronger than hate."

BIBLIOGRAPHY/INDEX

A READER'S GUIDE

This section provides the essential information about critical sources which is usually given by a system of obtrusive or elusive superscript numbers in the text, with their accompanying notes at the foot of the page or at the end of the chapter, if not at the end of the book. In lieu of this system, each author cited is named in the text, with the title if more than one work by that author has been used; and in this Bibliography/ Index a complete entry for each author and each work cited is given in a single alphabetical listing. Those readers who make use of notes will find the requisite information here, in a single listing without duplication of data. Those who find notes an interruption or irritation can ignore the Bibliography/Index.

Each bibliographical entry is followed by numbers in brackets. The numbers in **boldface** indicate pages of *this* book on which reference(s) to cited work(s) will be found. The numbers after the colon are set in lightface, and indicate the page(s) in the source for the passage(s) cited on that page in our text. For example:

Vickery, Olga W. *The Novels of William Faulkner: A Critical Interpretation.* Rev. ed. Baton Rouge: Louisiana State University Press, 1964. [**38**: 20; **79**: 133; **142**: 261; **231**: 175; **259–60**: 253; **310**: 75; **356**: 228; **358**: 237; **365**: 229; **373**: 258, 259, 260, 258; **401**: 239, 239].

Entries under an editor's name have no index or source numbers unless the editor is quoted. See, for examples, the various entries under Rollo May as author and editor.

The same index and source page-number system used for non-fiction works cited in the text applies to the non-fiction works of Faulkner and to Joseph Blotner's *Faulkner: A Biography* and *Selected Letters of William Faulkner*, listed in the first section of this Bibliography/Index. Quotations from Faulkner's novels in the text are followed in parentheses by page numbers in the edition specified in the list of novels.

For a few authors of several works cited, like Mircea Eliade, a title has to be given in the text, but short titles or key words are adequate to identify the specific work in question.

The Ph.D. dissertations listed, with most of the other dissertations and theses on Faulkner, are available for use in the Faulkner collection in the University of Mississippi Library. Most of them are in book form, enlarged and reproduced from microfilm. As far back as October 1975, a print-out by the Comprehensive Dissertation Query Service already listed more than 270 dissertations on William Faulkner's works. I have referred to only those dissertations which proved germane to my subject.

By authors' names in the text and the data in the Bibliography/Index, I have given due credit to all writers who have contributed to my understanding and interpretation of Faulkner's Yoknapatawpha novels.

The following editions of the fiction and non-fiction work of William Faulkner have been used. They and the two works by Joseph Blotner are published in New York by Random House. Consult the Abbreviations on p. vi to see how they are cited throughout this book.

Yoknapatawpha novels and stories:
Flags in the Dust. Douglas Day, Ed. 1973.
Sartoris. 1929, 1956.
The Sound and the Fury. Modern Library College ed. (facsimile of first printing, 7 October 1929).
Sanctuary. 1931, 1958.
Light in August. Vintage ed. (facsimile of first printing, 6 October 1932).
Absalom, Absalom! Modern Library ed. (facsimile of first edition, 1936).
The Unvanquished (facsimile of first printing, 15 October 1938).
Go Down, Moses. Modern Library ed. 1942.

Intruder in the Dust. Twelfth printing, 1948.
Knight's Gambit. Fourth printing, 1949.
Collected Stories of William Faulkner. N.d.
Requiem for a Nun. 1950, 1951.
Snopes: A Trilogy. 3 vols. 1964.
  1 *The Hamlet.* Third ed., 1964.
  2 *The Town.* Fourth printing, 1957.
  3 *The Mansion.* Third printing, 1959.
The Reivers. 1962.
Big Woods.

The index of Faulkner's fiction begins on p. 438.

Collections of non-fiction:
Faulkner at West Point. Joseph L. Fant, III and Robert Ashley, Eds.
  1964.

63: 55	**391**: 54, 55, 56	**392**: 90, 91, 92
376: 98	**391**: 57, 59	

William Faulkner: Essays, Speeches, and Public Letters. James B.
  Meriwether, Ed. 1965.

258: 120	**383**: 105	**406**: 147, 151
258: 132	**383**: 106	**406**: 109, 111
274: 150	**404**: 216, 219	**410**: 36, 37, 42, 43
	405: 222	

Lion in the Garden: Interviews with William Faulkner, 1926–1962.
  James B. Meriwether and Michael Millgate, Eds. 1968.

9: 245	**242**: 72	**366**: 253
12: 255	**258**: 241	**370**: 70, 71
240: 255	**258**: 253	**376**: 253
	355: 255	

Published versions of recorded conferences and speeches:
Faulkner at Nagano. Robert A. Jelliffe, Ed. Tokyo: Kenkyushà, 1956.

3: 68	**174:** 158	**256:** 66
10: 78	**174:** 186	**256:** 101
16: 50	**186:** 93	**258:** 196
20: 91–92	**252:** 177	**258:** 186–87
44: 103	**253:** 23–24	**260–61:** 29
51: 143	**253:** 157–58	**261:** 131
78:86–87	**254:** 4	**261:** 188
79: 50–51	**254:** 41	**367:** 78
110: 77–78	**254:** 28	**392:** 187
172: 195	**254:** 29	**392:** 188
	254: 83	

Faulkner in the University: Class Conferences at the University of Virginia, 1957–1958. Frederick L. Gwynn and Joseph L. Blotner, Eds. Charlottesville: University of Virginia Press, 1959.

2: 65	**106–107:** 197	**174:** 86
2: 121	**108:** 190	**179:** 269
2: 147	**108:** 267	**192:** 246
10: 206	**108:** 67	**192:** 79
14: 110	**109:** 277	**195:** 246
15: 39	**109:** 5	**219:** 112
32: 249	**109:** 68	**221:** 81
32: 254	**109:** 98	**241:** 150
35: 42	**112:** 43–44	**253:** 203
38: 119	**113:** 79	**255:** 267
38: 76	**113:** 98	**256:** 134
42: 87	**113:** 94	**261:** 100–101
44: 64	**124:** 254, 119	**266:** 85
52: 74	**125:** 81, 282	**286:** 161
60: 199	**147:** 275–76	**268:** 281–82
61: 74	**149:** 256	**331:** 275
62: 103	**172:** 269	**337:** 246
81: 8	**172:** 73	**369:** 61
95: 168	**172:** 101	**398:** 275–76

Blotner, Joseph L. *Faulkner: A Biography*. 2 vols. 1975.
——, Ed. *Selected Letters of William Faulkner*. 1977.

Adams, J. Donald, Ed. William Faulkner, "It Is a Nightmare World, Wearing a Mask of Reality." *The Shape of Books to Come*. New York: Viking, 1944. Rptd in *The Idea of an American Novel*, Louis D. Rubin and John Rees Moore, Eds. New York: Crowell, c. 1961. [**400**: 352]

Adams, Richard P. "The Apprenticeship of William Faulkner." *Tulane Studies in English* 12 (1962), 113–56. [**47**: 152; **54**: 130–31]

———. "Faulkner and the Myth of the South." *Mississippi Quarterly* 14 (Summer 1961), 131–37. [**9**: title; **348**: 164, 189]

———. *Faulkner: Myth and Motion*. Princeton: Princeton University Press, 1968. [**91**: titles; **108**: title; **115**: title; **345**: 29; **366**: 12, 13; **376**: 3–4, 5, 7, 12, 12, 12, 13]

Anderson, Charles. "Faulkner's Moral Center." *Etudes Anglaises* 7 (January 1954), 48–58. [**255**: 49; **259**: 50]

Ayers, H. Brandt, Ed. *You Can't Eat Magnolias*. L. Q. C. Lamar Society Publication. New York: McGraw-Hill, 1972. "You Can't Eat Magnolias," 3–24. [**409**: 5]

Ballew, Stephen. "Faulkner's Psychology of Individualism: A Fictional Principle and *Light in August*." Ph.D. Dissertation, Indiana University, 1974. [**322**: 165, 163, 162; **323**: 164, 167; **324**: 164, 163; **325**: 168; **349**: 177, 177]

Barnes, Hazel. *Humanistic Existentialism: The Literature of Possibility*. Lincoln: University of Nebraska Press, 1959. [**294**: 41; **304**: 46; **306**: 41; **311**: 29–30; **326**: 48–49]

Barrett, Russell H. *Integration at Ole Miss*. Chicago: Quadrangle Books, 1965. [**405**: 11, 12]

Barrett, William. *Irrational Man: A Study in Existential Philosophy*. Garden City: Doubleday Anchor, 1962. [**264**: 53; **310**: 52]

———, and Henry D. Aiken, Eds. *Philosophy in the Twentieth Century*. 4 Vols. New York: Random House, 1962. [**264**: Vol. 4, 619; **269**: Vol. 3, 169, 169, 142, 142; **270**: Vol. 4, 142; **310**: 695; **311**: 657; **335**: 650]

Barth, J. Robert, s.j., Ed. *Religious Perspectives in Faulkner's Fiction: Yoknapatawpha and Beyond*. Notre Dame: University of Notre Dame Press, 1972. [**262**: 11, 13, 31]

Bassett, John. *William Faulkner: An Annotated Checklist of Criticism*. New York: Lewis, 1972.

Beach, Joseph Warren. *Obsessive Images: Symbolism in Poetry of the 1930's and 1940's*. William Van O'Connor, Ed. Minneapolis:

University of Minnesota Press, 1960. [**3**: 22; **45**: 3–12; **94**: 273; **114**: 307]

Beauchamp, Fay E. "William Faulkner's Use of the Tragic Mulatto Myth." Ph.D. Dissertation, University of Pennsylvania, 1974.

Beck, Warren. *Man in Motion: Faulkner's Trilogy.* Madison: University of Wisconsin Press, 1961. [**108**: title]

Bedient, Calvin. "Pride and Nakedness: *As I Lay Dying.*" *Modern Language Quarterly* 29 (March 1968), 61–76. [**219**]

Beja, Morris. *Epiphany in the Modern Novel.* Seattle: University of Washington Press, 1971. "6. William Faulkner: A Flash, A Glare," 182–210. [**319**: 208; **372**: 208]

Bellow, Saul. "Distractions of a Fiction Writer." *The Living Novel.* Granville Hicks, Ed. New York: Macmillan, 1957. [**240**: 6]

Beringause, A. F. "Faulkner's Yoknapatawpha Register." *Bucknell Review* 11 (May 1963). [**10**: 71; **11**: 81, 82]

Billingslea, Oliver L. "The Monument and the Plain: The Art of Mythical Consciousness in William Faulkner's *Absalom, Absalom!*" Ph.D. Dissertation, University of Wisconsin, 1971. [**115**: vii]

Bjork, Lennart. "Ancient Myths and the Moral Framework of Faulkner's *Absalom, Absalom!*" *American Literature* 35 (May 1963), 196–204. [**221**]

Bodkin, Maud. *Archetypal Patterns in Poetry.* New York: Vintage Books, 1959. [**4**: 81; **20**: 84–85; **90**: 4, 7–8; **96**: 18, 19; **178**: 272; **220**: 15; **240**: 317]

Booth, Wayne C. *The Rhetoric of Fiction.* Chicago: University of Chicago Press, 1961. [**239–40**: 397–98]

Bowling, Lawrence. "Faulkner and the Theme of Isolation." *Georgia Review* 18 (Spring 1964), 50–66. [**49**: 52–53]

Bradford, Melvin E. "Faulkner's Doctrine of Nature: A Study of the Endurance Theme in the Yoknapatawpha Fiction." Ph.D. Dissertation, Vanderbilt University, 1969.

——. "The Winding Horn: Hunting and the Making of Men in Faulkner's 'Race at Morning'." *Papers on English Language and Literature* 1 (Summer 1965), 272–78. [**194**: 273; **196**: 277, 278]

Breisach, Ernst. *Introduction to Modern Existentialism.* New York: Grove, 1962. [**359**: 205]

Brien, Dolores. "William Faulkner and the Myth of Women." *Research Studies* (Washington State University) 35 (June 1962), 132–40. [**159**: 132; **161**: 135; **171**: 133, 136]

Brooks, Cleanth. *William Faulkner: The Yoknapatawpha Country.* New Haven: Yale University Press, 1963. [**32**: 383; **293**: 128; **204**:

332, 196–97; **321**: 60, 61; **340**: 403; **348**: 243; **350**: 228, 236; **355**: 351; **356**: 350, 351; **356**: 360, 351; **357**: 366; **358**: 351]

——. *The Hidden God*. New Haven: Yale University Press, 1963. [**259**: 22–23; **295**: 26]

——. "Gavin Stevens and the Chivalric Tradition." *Studies in English* (University of Mississippi) 15 (1978), 19–32. [**324**: 31]

——. "The Sense of Community in Yoknapatawpha Fiction." *Studies in English* (University of Mississippi) 15 (1978), 3–18. [**281**: 3, 4, 5]

Broughton, Panthea Reid. *William Faulkner: The Abstract and the Actual*. Baton Rouge: Louisiana State University Press, 1974.

26: 51	**309**: 190, 191, 189, 130	**333**: 120, 121, 122
288: 194, 195	**311**: 156	**335**: 181
289: 141	**313**: 137	**338**: 100
291: 141, 142	**320**: 156	**339**: 182
292: 102	**323**: 197–98	**340**: 118–19
292: 51	**325**: 196	**349**: 47
294: 89	**325**: 164	**364**: 106, 107
295: 81	**328**: 140	**369**: 45–46

Brown, Norman O. *Hermes the Thief: The Evolution of a Myth*. Madison: University of Wisconsin Press, 1947. [**228**: 23, 24; **234**: 4, 10, 7, 14; **235**: 22]

Brylowski, Walter. *Faulkner's Olympian Laugh: Myth in the Novels*. Detroit: Wayne State University Press, 1968. [**23**: 52, 53; **115**: cited]

Buber, Martin. *Philosophy in the Twentieth Century*, William Barrett and Henry D. Aiken, Eds. Vol. 4. Part 6, *Neo-Orthodoxy*. [**310**: 695]

Burroes, Robert N. "Institutional Christianity Reflected in the Works of William Faulkner." *Mississippi Quarterly* 14 (Summer 1961), 138–47. [**319**: 145]

Callen, Shirley P. "Bergsonian Dynamism in the Writings of William Faulkner." Ph.D. Dissertation, Tulane University, 1962. [**371**: 19, 26; **373**: 19; **376**: 44, 44; **377**: 141–42, 30, 34, 73]

Campbell, Harry Modean, and Ruel E. Foster, *William Faulkner: A Critical Appraisal*. Norman: University of Oklahoma Press, c. 1951. [**70**: 36]

Campbell, Joseph. *The Hero with a Thousand Faces*. New York: Meridian, 1956. [**217**: title and "framework"]

——. *The Masks of God: Primitive Mythology*. New York: Viking, 1959. [**188**: 129; **190**: 293]

——. *The Masks of God: Occidental Mythology*. New York: Viking, 1964. [**113**: 105, 78; **114**: 227; **163**: 397; **178**: 34, 61–62; **188**: 505; **196**: 158]

Campbell, Will D. *Brother to a Dragonfly*. New York: Seabury, 1979. [**404**: 239, 241, 201, 246, 111]

Carpenter, Robert A. "Faulkner Discovered." *Delta Review* 2 (July–August 1965), 27–29. [**242**: interview with Cowley]

Carter, Hodding. *Southern Legacy*. Baton Rouge: Louisiana State University Press, 1966. [**386**: 186]

Caserio, Robert L. *Plot, Story, and the Novel: From Dickens and Poe to the Modern Period*. Princeton: Princeton University Press, 1979. [**307**: 276]

Cash, W. J. *The Mind of the South*. New York: Vintage, 1960. [**95**: 138–39; **97**: ix, ix, x, x; **98**: 127, 127, 69, 131; **100**: 189, 117; **103**: 320, 28, 29; **104**: 5, 124; **105**: 135; **105**: 158]

Cassirer, Ernst. *The Philosophy of Symbolic Forms*. Vol. 2: *Mythical Thought*. Trans. Ralph Manheim. New Haven: Yale University Press, 1960. [**11**: 40; **21**: 135–36; **88–89**: 69, 69; **95**: 230, 157, 5, 24; **110**: 125, 126]

Chase, Richard. "The Stone and the Crucifixion: Faulkner's *Light in August*," 205–17. *William Faulkner: Two Decades of Criticism*. Frederick J. Hoffman and Olga W. Vickery, Eds. East Lansing: Michigan State College Press, 1951. [**64**: 210; **65**: 205, 206]

Chesnut, Mary Boykin. *A Diary from Dixie*. Ben Ames Williams, Ed. Boston: Houghton, Mifflin, 1961. [**129**: 122]

Ciancio, Ralph A. "Faulkner's Existentialist Affinities." *Studies in Faulkner*. Neal Woodruff, Jr., Ed. Carnegie Studies in English, Vol. 6. Pittsburgh: Carnegie Institute of Technology, 1966. [**271**: 89]

Cirlot, J. E. *A Dictionary of Symbols*. Trans. Jack Sage. Foreword by Herbert Read. New York: Philosophical Library, 1962. [**6**: xxix, 1; **28**: 247, 310; **149**: 273; **226**: 35, 36]

Clark, Anderson A. "Courtly Love in the Writings of William Faulkner." Ph.D. Dissertation, Vanderbilt University, 1975. [**203**: 2, 108; **204**: 184, 185, 114; **206**: 129, 126; **207**: 157; **209**: 171; **211**: 100]

Clough, Wilson O. *The Necessary Earth: Nature and Solitude in American Literature*. Austin: University of Texas Press, 1964. [**110**: 121; **112**: 123]

Coffee, Jessie A. "Empty Steeples: Theme, Symbol, and Irony in Faulkner's Novels." *Arizona Quarterly* 23 (Autumn 1967), 197–206. [**26**: title]

Coles, Robert. *Walker Percy: An American Search.* Boston: Little, Brown, 1978. [**265**: 58]

Collins, Carvel. "A Note on *Sanctuary*." *Harvard Advocate* 135 (1951). [**57**: 16]

——. "A Note on the Conclusion of 'The Bear'." *Faulkner Studies* 2 (Winter 1954) 58–60. [**191**: 58–60]

——, Ed. *William Faulkner: New Orleans Sketches.* New York: Random House, 1958. [**3**: Introduction, xvi]

Cominos, Peter T. "Innocent Femina Sensualis in Unconscious Conflict," 155–72. *Suffer and Be Still.* Martha Vicinus, Ed. **102**: 157, 157, 157, 157, 159; **102**: 163, 164, 165; **103**: 165, 167, 167, 167, 168, 169, 168, 172; **162**: 167, 168]

Corridori, Edward L. "The Quest for Sacred Space: Setting in the Novels of William Faulkner." Ph.D. Dissertation, Kent State University, 1971. [**131**: 107, 111, 114, 115, 125, 121–22]

Cowan, James C. "Dream-Work in the Quentin Section of *The Sound and the Fury*." *Literature and Psychology* 24, No. 3 (1974), 91–98. [**7**: 91]

Cowley, Malcolm. *The Portable Faulkner.* Rev. ed. New York: Viking, 1967. [**243**: xiii]

Crow, Peter G. "Faulkner's Vitalistic Visions: A Close Study of Eight Novels." Ph.D. Dissertation, Duke University, 1973. [**358**: 271, 287; **361**: 304, 305; **364**: 13; **377**: 281, 299, 297]

Cruickshank, John. "Albert Camus: Sainthood Without God," 314–24. *Mansions of the Spirit.* George Panichas, Ed. New York: Hawthorne, 1967. [**268–69**: 324, 317]

Cullen, John. *Old Times in the Faulkner Country.* In collaboration with Floyd C. Watkins. Chapel Hill: University of North Carolina Press, 1961. [**62**: 81, 93–97]

Culley, Mary M. Mulvehill. "Eschatological Thought in Faulkner's Yoknapatawpha Novels." Ph.D. Dissertation, University of Michigan, 1972. [**116**: 119; **193**: 66; **213**: 84, 85; **216**: 87, 86; **296**: "Judgment" in *Requiem for a Nun*; **302**: 62, 43, 65; **305**: 33; **332**: 66, 71, 70, 71; **340**: 122, 123; **346**: 134]

Daiches, David. *Critical Approaches to Literature.* Englewood Cliffs: Prentice-Hall, 1956. [**3**: 348]

Dauner, Louise. "Quentin and the Walking Shadow: The Dilemma of Nature and Culture." *Arizona Quarterly* 21 (Summer 1965), 159–71. [**46**: title]

Davenport, F. Garvin Jr. *The Myth of Southern History: Historical Consciousness in Twentieth-Century Southern Literature.* Nashville: Vanderbilt University Press, 1967. [**95–96**: 43, 24, 24; **105**: 34; **131**: 149, 100–101, 105; **182**: 127; **185**: 130]

Davis, Roger L. "William Faulkner, V. K. Ratliff, and the Snopes Saga (1925–1940)." Ph.D. Dissertation, UCLA, 1971. [**229**: 221, 222; **230**: 277, 277, 264; **235**: 302; **236**: 305]

De Laszlo, Violet, Ed. C. G. Jung, *Psyche and Symbol: A Selection from the Writings of C. G. Jung.* Garden City: Doubleday Anchor, 1958. [**6–7**: xxi, xxi; **108**: xxii]

Dembo, Lawrence S. "William Faulkner: The Symbolic Action of Sin and Redemption." M.A. Thesis, Columbia University, 1952. [**214**: 161; **215–16**: 166, 173; **299**: 142; **300**: 130; **305**: 105, 107]

Devlin, Albert J. "Parent–Child Relationships in the Works of William Faulkner." Ph.D. Dissertation, University of Kansas, 1970. [**197**: 152; **291**: cited; **292**: cited; **297**: cited]

——. "Sartoris: Rereading the MacCallum Episode." *Twentieth Century Literature* 17 (April 1971), 83–90. [**139**: title, titles]

Douds, Edith Brown. *William Faulkner of Oxford.* James W. Webb and A. Wigfall Green, Eds. [**34**: "Recollections of William Faulkner and the Bunch," 51]

Douglas, Harold J., and Robert Daniel. "Faulkner's Southern Puritanism," 37–51. *Religious Perspectives in Faulkner's Fiction: Yoknapatawpha and Beyond.* J. Robert Barth, Ed. Notre Dame: Notre Dame University Press, 1972. [**263**: 39]

Downey, Elizabeth. "Faulkner's Sense of History: Criticism of the Magnolia Myth in the Novels of William Faulkner." Ph.D. Dissertation, University of Denver, 1972. [**159**: 70; **382**: 190]

Duclos, Donald P. "Son of Sorrow: The Life, Works, and Influence of Colonel William C. Falkner, 1825–1889." Ph.D. Dissertation, University of Michigan, 1962. [**33**: 182; **99**: 5, 5]

Dunlap, Mary Montgomery. "The Achievement of Gavin Stevens." Ph.D. Dissertation, University of South Carolina, 1970. [**205**: 2, 15, 40; **206**: 69, 107; **207**: 172; **208**: 198, 203, 207; **209**: 219]

Dussinger, Gloria R. "Faulkner's Isaac McCaslin as a Romantic Hero Manqué." *South Atlantic Quarterly* 68 (Summer 1969), 377–85. [**193**: cited; **330–31**: 381–82]

Eaton, Clement. *The Waning of the Old South Civilization, 1860–1880's.* Athens: University of Georgia Press, 1968. [**120**: 159]

——. *The Growth of Southern Civilization: 1790–1860.* New York: Harper, c. 1961. [**18**: 25]

Eggenschwiler, David. *The Christian Humanism of Flannery*

O'Connor. Detroit: Wayne State University Press, 1972. [**250**: 19; **310**: 30; **325**: 32, 50]

Eliade, Mircea. *The Sacred and the Profane: The Nature of Religion.* Trans. Willard R. Trask. New York: Harcourt, Brace & World, 1959. [**24**: 46; **25**: 47; **118**: 68, 72; **378**: 70]

——. *Cosmos and History: The Myth of the Eternal Return.* Trans. Willard R. Trask. New York: Harper Torch, 1959. [**116**: 144; **117**: 10, 11, 12, 14, 137; **118**: 86, 156, 161; **119**: 6, 12, 21, 25; **120**: 27–28, 29, 30; **158**: 43, 43; **391**: 153, 156, 161]

——. *The Quest: History and Meaning in Religion.* Chicago: University of Chicago Press, 1969. [**106**: 170, 172, 172; **173**: 121, 112–13, 115; **174**: 93, 95; **243**: 5; **378**: 126]

——. *Myths, Rites, Symbols: A Mircea Eliade Reader.* Wendell C. Beane and William G. Doty, Eds. New York: Harper & Row, 1976. [**230**: 280; **233**: 264]

Elkin, Stanley L. "Religious Themes and Symbolism in the Novels of William Faulkner." Ph.D. Dissertation, University of Illinois, 1961. [**214–15**: 271, 273, 285, 235, 237, 230; **216**: 245–47; **223**: 175; **248**: 22; **252**: 12; **277**: 12; **278**: 22, 22–23; **296**: cited; **297**: 34, 36; **374**: 24]

Ellison, Ralph. "Society, Morality, and the Novel," 58–91. *The Living Novel: A Symposium.* Granville Hicks, Ed. New York: Macmillan, 1957. [**371**: title, 62, 65, 69, 86; **372**: 86, 88–89]

Fadiman, Regina K. *Faulkner's Light in August: A Description and Interpretation of the Revisions.* Charlottesville: University Press of Virginia, 1975. [**213**: title and subject stated; **322**: author named]

Falkner, Murry C. *The Falkners of Mississippi: A Memoir.* Baton Rouge: Louisiana State University Press, 1967. Foreword by Lewis Simpson. [**358**: 190–91]

Fallico, Arturo. *Art and Existentialism.* Englewood Cliffs: Prentice-Hall, 1962. [**267**: 5; **275**: 15; **276**: 80; **278**: 147; **278–79**: 111–12; **280**: 131, 131; **300**: 115; **303**: 78.

Faulkner, John. *My Brother Bill.* New York: Trident Press, 1963. [**23**: 104]

Faulkner, Peter. *Humanism in the English Novel.* London: Elek/ Pemberton, 1975. [**251**: 6, 1, 1, 2]

Feidelson, Charles. *Symbolism and American Literature.* Chicago: University of Chicago Press, 1952. [**6**: 64–65]

Fiedler, Leslie A. *An End to Innocence: Essays on Culture and Politics.* Boston: Beacon Press, 1955. [**112**: 128; **175**: 198; **187**: 147, 148]

Fletcher, Mary Dell. "William Faulkner: The Calvinistic Sensibility."

Ph.D. Dissertation, Louisiana State University and A. and M. College, 1974. [**44**: 46–47; **46**: cited; **136**: 72, 57; **263**: title and subject]

Foran, Donald J., s.J. "William Faulkner's *Absalom, Absalom!*: An Exercise in Affirmation." Ph.D. Dissertation, University of Southern California, 1973. [**297**: 28, 32]

Ford, Daniel G. "Uses of Time in Four Novels by William Faulkner." Ph.D. Dissertation, Auburn University, 1973. [**371**: subject; **375**: 30; **376**: 33]

Foster, Ruel. "Dream as Symbolic Act in Faulkner." *Perspective* 2 (Summer 1949), 179–94. [**3**: 179; **47**: 194]

——. "Further Notes on the Conclusion of 'The Bear'." *Faulkner Studies* 3 (Spring 1954), 4–5. [**81**: 5]

Franklin, John Hope. *From Slavery to Freedom: A History of Negro Americans*. 5th ed. New York: Knopf, 1980. [**380**: 266, 263, 253–54; **382**: 410, 410]

von Franz, Marie-Louise. "The Process of Individuation." Carl G. Jung, *Man and His Symbols*. [**144**: 163–64; **106–107**: 216; **116**: quoted by Michael Routh; **159**: 185, 187, 177; **160**: 180, 194]

Fraser, J. T. *Of Time, Passion, and Knowledge*. New York: Braziller, 1975. [**368**: 22, 23, 23; **369**: 421, 421; **374**: 23, 22, 92, 93; **378**: 35, 44; **379**: 44, 88, 368; **393**: 203]

Frazer, Sir James G. *The Golden Bough: A Study in Magic and Religion*. 1 Vol. abridged ed. Rpt of 1922 ed. New York: Macmillan, 1944. [**61**: 3, 3; **93**: 613–14]

——. *The New Golden Bough*. Theodor H. Gaster, Ed. New York: Criterion Books, 1959. [**56**: 89]

Frazier, David L. "Lucas Burch and the Polarity of *Light in August*." *Modern Language Notes* 73 (June 1958), 417–19. [**64**: 418]

Freud, Sigmund. *Totem and Taboo*. Trans. James Strachey. New York: Norton, 1962. [**151**: 122–24; **188**: 131]

Friedman, Maurice. *The Worlds of Existentialism: A Critical Reader*. Maurice Friedman, Ed. New York: Random House, 1964. [**267**: 4–5, 5; **316**: Karl Jaspers, "Communication," 203, 204]

Friend, George L. "Levels of Maturity: The Theme of Striving in the Novels of William Faulkner." Ph.D. Dissertation, University of Illinois, 1964. [**173**: 77; **187**: 201; **193**: 203, 206, 208; **211**: 259; **313–14**: 170, 171, 172]

Frye, Northrop. *Anatomy of Criticism*. Princeton: Princeton University Press, 1957. [**8**: 99, 102, 118; **10**: 89; **88**: 136; **90**: 136, 139–40; **92**: 147–50; **116**: the Apocalyptic World; **198**: 187; **218**: Mythos of Summer; **365**: 44]

——. *The Stubborn Structure: Essays on Criticism and Society.* Ithaca: Cornell University Press, 1970. [**392**: 26, 27, 36]

Gardner, John. *On Moral Fiction: Premises on Art and Morality.* New York: Basic Books, 1978. [**356**: 34, 34; **360**: 201, 141; **364**: 204; **401**: 204–205]

Garzilli, Enrico. *Circles Without Center: Paths to the Discovery and Creation of Self in Modern Literature.* Cambridge: Harvard University Press, 1972. [**14**: 61; **159**: 2, 3, 4]

Genovese, Eugene V. *Roll, Jordan, Roll: The World the Slaves Made.* New York: Vintage, 1976. [**368**: 290; **379**: 190; **382**: 235]

Gerster, Patrick, and Nicholas Cords, Eds. *Myth and Southern History.* Single Vol. ed. Chicago: Rand McNally, 1974. [**105**: title]

Gibbons, Kathryn G. "Quentin's Shadow." *Literature and Psychology* 12 (Winter 1962), 16–24. [**50**: 23]

Glicksberg, Charles I. *The Tragic Vision in Twentieth Century Literature.* Cross Currents: Modern Criticism. Carbondale: Southern Illinois University Press, 1963. [**306**: 3, 4, 101]

Grant, Michael. *Myths of the Greeks and the Romans.* Cleveland and New York: World, 1962. [**230**: 208]

Greene, Theodore M. "The Philosophy of Life Implicit in Faulkner's *The Mansion.*" *Texas Studies in Literature and Language* 2 (Winter 1961), 401–18. [**270**: 402]

Gregory, Charles T. "Darkness to Appall: Destructive Design and Patterns in Some Characters of William Faulkner." Ph.D. Dissertation, Columbia University, 1968. [**245**: 19, 10, 17]

Grene, Marjorie. *Introduction to Existentialism.* Chicago: Phoenix Books, 1959. [**265**: 149, 144, 10; **278**: 72; **279**: 93; **287**: 93]

Gresham, Jewel H. "The Fatal Illusions: Self, Sex, Race, and Religion in William Faulkner's World." Ed.D. Dissertation, Teachers College, Columbia University, 1970. [**122**: chapter titles; **203**: chapter titles]

Guerard, Albert J. *The Triumph of the Novel: Dickens, Dostoevsky, Faulkner.* New York: Oxford University Press, 1976. [**243**: 214]

Gustafson, James M. *Christian Ethics and the Community.* New York: Pilgrim Press, 1979. [**246**: 154, 15, 47; **295**: 26, 29; **341**: 187; **392**: 174, 175]

Guttmann, Allen. "Collisions and Confrontations." *Arizona Quarterly* 16 (Spring 1960), 46–52. [**38**: title and images]

Hardy, John E. *Man in the Modern Novel.* Seattle: University of Washington Press, 1964. [**44**: 149, 153, 151, 151]

Hassan, Ihab. *Radical Innocence: Studies in the Contemporary American Novel.* Princeton: Princeton University Press, 1961.

[173: 36, quoting Baritz; 175: 6–8; 176: 7, 31, 32, 35, 40, 39, 35, 32, 17; 177: 43; 191: 58; 195: 35; 202: 38–39; 214: 9, 31, 81; 214: 76; 215: 59; 264: 19, 22, 20]

Hawkins, E. O. "Jane Cook and Cecilia Farner." *Mississippi Quarterly* 18 (Autumn 1965), 248–51. [24: 249–50]

Heinemann, F. H. *Existentialism and the Modern Predicament.* New York: Harper Torchbook, 1958. [267: 1; 268: 15, 17, 26, 27]

Henderson, Joseph L. *Thresholds of Initiation.* Middletown: Wesleyan University Press, 1967. [172: 14–15, 15, 19, 21–22; 173: 197, 97; 181: 33, 37; 182: 58, 65; 184: 134, 176, 135; 189: 54–55, 225, 225; 190: 155; 193: 182, 183, 182, 205; 201: 176, 176, 185; 205: 127, 22; 224: 177; 235: 35]

——. "Ancient Myths and Modern Man." Carl G. Jung, *Man and His Symbols.* [181: 112, 113, 114; 183: 152, 151–52; 189: 39; 195: 129; 230: 149; 290: 113]

——, and Maud Oakes. *The Wisdom of the Serpent: The Myths of Death, Rebirth, and Resurrection.* New York: Braziller, 1963. [173: 58; 185: 84, 86]

Hirshleifer, Phyllis. "As Whirlwinds in the South." *Perspective* 2 (Summer 1949), 233–38. [62: 233]

Hlavsa, Virginia. "St. John and Frazer in *Light in August*: Biblical Form, Mythical Function." *Bulletin of Research in the Humanities,* Spring 1980. [237–38: 11, 25, 26]

Hoffman, Daniel. *Form and Fab. in American Fiction.* New York: Oxford University Press, 1961. [112: xi; 178: 235, 232, 228; 186: 81, 82; 188: 228, 232; 194: 80, 79, 80; 219: xiv; 224: 51; 225: 82; 237: 359]

Hoffman, Frederick J. *Freudianism and the Literary Mind.* Baton Rouge: Lousiana State University Press, 1945. [2: title]

——, and Olga W. Vickery, Eds. *William Faulkner: Three Decades of Criticism.* East Lansing: Michigan State University Press, 1960.

Hogan, Patrick G. "Critical Misconceptions of Southern Thought: Faulkner's Optimism." *Mississippi Quarterly* 10 (January 1957), 19–28. [256: 28]

Holman, C. Hugh. *A Handbook to Literature.* Based on the original by W. F. Thrall and A. Hibbard. Indianapolis and New York: Bobbs-Merrill, 1972.

Honig, Edwin. *The Dark Conceit: The Making of Allegory.* Evanston: Northwestern University Press, 1959. [93: 130, 134; 94: 154–55; 220: 155, 157; 221: 39, 40]

Hornback, Vernon T. Jr. "William Faulkner and the Terror of History: Myth, History, and Moral Freedom in the Yoknapatawpha Cycle." Ph.D. Dissertation, St. Louis University, 1964. [**118**: title; **198**: cited; **216**: cited; **388**: 265; **371**: 7–10, 267; **388**: title, 66, 13]

Howe, Irving. "The Southern Myth and William Faulkner." *American Quarterly* 3 (Winter 1951), 357–62. [**99–100**]

Hunt, John H. *William Faulkner: Art in Theological Tension.* Syracuse: Syracuse University Press, 1965. [**252**: 33, 30–31]

Ilacqua, Alma A. "Faulkner and the Concept of Excellence." Ph.D. Dissertation, Syracuse University, 1974. [**262**: title]

Irwin, John T. *Doubling and Incest / Repetition and Revenge: A Speculative Reading of Faulkner,* Baltimore: Johns Hopkins University Press, 1975. [**42**: 7, 6; **303**: 7, 74]

Jackson, Naomi. "Faulkner's Woman: Demon–Nun and Angel–Witch." *Ball State University Forum* 8 (Winter 1967), 12–20. [**107**: title; **160**: 19]

Jaffé, Aniela. "Symbolism in the Visual Arts," 230–71. Carl G. Jung, *Man and his Symbols.* [**66**: 240]

Jarrett, David. "Eustacia Vye and Eula Varner, Olympians: The Worlds of Thomas Hardy and William Faulkner." *Novel: A Forum on Fiction* 6 (Winter 1973), 163–74. [**242**: 170, 171, 173]

Joyce, James. *A Portrait of the Artist as a Young Man.* New York: Viking, 1968. [**389**: 215]

Jung, Carl G. *Psyche and Symbol: A Selection from the Writings of C. G. Jung.* Violet S. De Laszlo, Ed. Garden City: Doubleday Anchor, 1958. [**5**: 293–94, 145, 254; **7**: 292–93; **46**: 6–9; **94**: xv; **153**: 10, 11; **172**: 126, 127; **179**: 130; **191**: xxxi, xxvi, xxxiii, 35, 39, 87; **202**: 136]

———. *Memories, Dreams, Reflections.* New York: Pantheon Books, c. 1961, 1962, 1963. [**94**: 340]

———, et al. *Man and his Symbols.* Garden City: Doubleday, c. 1964. [7: 55; **15**: 29; **108**: 168, 169; **111**: 94–95]

———. "The Personal Unconsciousness and the Super-Personal or Collective Unconscious." *Classics of Psychology.* Thorne Shipley, Ed. New York: Philosophical Library, 1961. [**107**: 729; **172**: 724, 724, 754; **174**: 726; **178**: 749, 743; **188**: 742]

Kahler, Erich. "The Nature of the Symbol," 50–73. *Symbolism in Religion and Literature,* Rollo May, Ed. [**6**: 53; **8**: 63; **9**: 70]

Kartiganer, Donald M. *The Fragile Thread: The Meaning of Form in*

Faulkner's Novels. Amherst: University of Massachusetts Press, 1979. [**282**: 36]

——. "The Individual and the Community: Values in the Novels of William Faulkner." Ph.D. Dissertation, Brown University, 1964. [**310**: 3]

——. "The Role of Myth in *Absalom, Absalom!*" *Modern Fiction Studies* 9 (Winter 1963–1964), 357–69. [**129**: cited]

Kaufman, Walter. *Existentialism from Dostoevsky to Sartre.* Selected and introduced by Walter Kaufmann. New York: Meridian, 1957. [**316**: 147, Jaspers]

Kazin, Alfred. "Faulkner's Vision of Human Integrity," *Harvard Advocate* 135 (1951), 8–9, 28–33. [**255**: 30]

——. "The Stillness of *Light in August*," 247–65. *William Faulkner: Three Decades of Criticism*, Frederick Hoffman and Olga Vickery, Eds. [**73**: 254]

Kerr, Elizabeth M. *Yoknapatawpha: Faulkner's "Little Postage Stamp of Native Soil."* New York: Fordham University Press, 1969, 1976. [**12**: title and purpose]

——. *William Faulkner's Gothic Domain.* National University Publications. Port Washington: Kennikat Press, 1979. [**17**: title; **91**: title]

——. "William Faulkner and the Southern Concept of Women." *Mississippi Quarterly* 15 (Winter 1962), 1–16. [**37**]

——. "The Creative Evolution of *Sanctuary*," 14–28. *Faulkner Studies* I, Barnett Guttenberg, Ed. Coral Gables: University of Miami Press, 1980. [**53**]

——. "*As I Lay Dying* as Ironic Quest Romance." *Wisconsin Studies in Contemporary Literature* 3 (Winter 1962), 5–19. [**90**, **94**, **218**] Rptd in *William Faulkner: Four Decades of Criticism*, 230–43. Linda W. Wagner, Ed. East Lansing; Michigan State University Press, 1973.

——. "*The Reivers*: The Golden Book of Yoknapatawpha County." *Modern Fiction Studies* 13 (Spring 1967) 95–113. [**355–56**]

King, Richard H. *A Southern Renaissance: The Cultural Awakening of the American South, 1930–1955.* New York: Oxford University Press, 1980. [**97**: 153; **107**: 161; **128**: 8, 20, 21, 24; **128**: 34, 35, 77, 79, 82; **128–29**: 128; **142**: 166]

Kingston, F. Temple. *French Existentialism: A Christian Critique.* Toronto: University of Toronto Press, 1961. [**309**: 42, 81]

Kreyling, Michael. "Myth and History: The Foes of *Losing Battles*." *Mississippi Quarterly* 26 (Fall 1973), 639–40. [**118**: cited]

Kubie, Lawrence. "William Faulkner's *Sanctuary*: An Analysis,"

137–46. *Faulkner: A Collection of Critical Essays*, Robert Penn Warren, Ed. [**296**: 142]

Kurtz, Paul, Ed. *The Humanist Alternative: Some Definitions of Humanism.* Buffalo: Prometheus, 1973. Preface, 5–7. "Humanism and the Moral Revolution," 49–55. Epilogue: "Is Everyone a Humanist?" 173–86. [**250**: title; **264**: 43, quoting Van Praag, "What Is Humanism?"; **346**: 179]

Langer, Susanne. *Philosophy in a New Key.* New York: Penguin Books, 1948. [**88**: 143; **175**: 144, 142]

Langford, Gerald. *Faulkner's Revision of Sanctuary: A Collation of the Unrevised Galleys and the Published Book.* Austin: University of Texas Press, c. 1972.

——. *Faulkner's Revision of "Absalom, Absalom!": A Collation of the Manuscript and Published Book.* Austin: University of Texas Press, 1971. [**302**: cited]

Langston, Beach. "The Meaning of Lena Grove and Gail Hightower in *Light in August.*" *Boston University Studies in English* 5 (Spring 1961), 46–63. [**61**: 47; **165**: cited]

Larsen, Stephen. *The Shaman's Doorway: Opening the Mythic Imagination to Contemporary Consciousness.* New York: Harper & Row, 1976. [**229**: 9; **231**: 60, 80–81; **233**: 85]

Lewis, C. S. *The Allegory of Love: A Study in Medieval Tradition.* New York: Oxford University Press, 1958. [**210**: 12, 13]

Lewis, Peirce. "Defining a Sense of Place." *Sense of Place: Mississippi*, Peggy Prenshaw and Jesse O. McGee, Eds. [**374**: 34]

Lewis, R. W. B. *The American Adam: Innocence, Tragedy, and Tradition in the Nineteenth Century.* Chicago: University of Chicago Press, 1955. [**93**: 8; **175**: 122; **186**: 197; **191**: title; **191–92**: 58; **214**: 152, 111]

Lind, Ilse Dusoir. "The Calvinistic Burden of *Light in August*," 79–95. *"Light in August" and the Critical Spectrum*, John B. Vickery and Olga W. Vickery, Eds. [**59**: 79–80; **217**: 93; **320**: 81, 82, 90, 85, 86; **321**: 84]

Linscott, Robert. "Faulkner Without Fanfare." *Esquire* 60 (July 1963), 36–38. [**137**: 38]

Litz, Walton. "William Faulkner's Moral Vision." *Southwest Review* 37 (Summer 1952), 200–209. [**259**: 201]

Loughrey, Thomas F. "Values and Love in the Fiction of William Faulkner." Ph.D. Dissertation, University of Notre Dame, 1962.

MacLure, Millar. "Snopes—A Faulkner Myth." *Canadian Forum* 39 (February 1960), 245–50. [**111**: 249; **125**: 248]

McCorquodale, Marjorie K. "William Faulkner and Existentialism."
Ph.D. Dissertation, University of Texas, Austin, 1956. [277: title]

McGill, Ralph. Foreword to Hodding Carter, *Southern Legacy*. [386–
87: iv]

McHaney, Thomas L. "*Sanctuary* and Frazer's Slain Kings." *Mississippi Quarterly* 244 (Summer 1971), 223–45. [52–53: cited]

———. *William Faulkner: A Reference Guide*. Boston: Hall, c. 1976.
[115: title]

McLoughlin, William. "Pietism and the American Character." *American Quarterly* 17 (Summer 1965), 163–86. [329: 174, 184]

Macquarrie, John. *Existentialism*. Philadelphia: Westminster; London:
Hutchinson, c. 1972. [85: 18, 19; 183: 23; 247: 6, 213–14; 248: 215;
265–66: 4, 5–6, 6, 204; 266: 164; 272: 4, 142, 142, 145, 145; 276: 164;
278: 91, 91; 279: 209–11, 213; 325: 164, 167; 372: 217; 390: 157, 158;
392: 60; 393: 4]

———. *Principles of Christian Theology*. 2nd ed. New York: Scribners,
1977. [107: 255; 319–20: 49–60, 245, 245, 340, 341; 369: 358]

Magnan, Jean-Marie. "Incest et mélange des sangs dans l'oeuvre de
William Faulkner." *Sud: Revue trimestrielle* 14/15 (1975). [152:
title]

Magny, Claude-Edmonde. *The Age of the American Novel: The Film
Aesthetic of Fiction Between the Two Wars*. New York: Ungar, c.
1972. [4: 211n26; 224: 211, 214, 214, 215, 222–23]

Malin, Irving. *William Faulkner: An Interpretation*. Stanford: Stanford
University Press, 1960. [147: title]

Malinowski, Bronislaw. *Sex, Culture, and Myth*. New York: Harcourt,
Brace & World, 1962. [67: 66, 103; 88: 247, 312, 312; 94: 214; 105:
230; 110: 88; 112: 185, 95, 96; 127: 39, 63; 129: 22, 25; 130: 141; 137:
18; 149: 77; 150: 77, 115; 177: 144; 187: 135; 195: 218; 214–15: 240;
215: 257]

Mann, Thomas. "Freud and the Future." *Essays by Thomas Mann*.
New York: Vintage, 1950. [89: 317–18]

Marcel, Gabriel. *Man Against Mass Society*. Chicago: Regnery, 1962.
[274: 42, 75]

Marcus, Steven. *The Other Victorians: A Study of Sexuality and
Pornography in Nineteenth Century England*. New York: Basic
Books, c. 1964, 1965, 1966. [102: cited]

Mathews, Donald. *Religion in the Old South*. Chicago: University of
Chicago Press, 1977. [368: 195, 197; 382: 219]

May, Rollo. *Man's Search for Himself*. New York: Signet, 1967. [255:
184; 275: 135; 284: 203, 193; 285: 191, 192; 286: 183, 179; 329–30:
133; 335: 129; 369: 219; 389: 221, 235, 227, 229; 293: 186, 137–38]

——. *Psychology and the Human Dilemma*. New York: Norton, 1980. [**393**: 220, 70]

——, Ed. *Symbolism in Religion and Literature*. New York: Braziller, 1960.

Meats, Stephen. "Who Killed Joanna Burden?" *Mississippi Quarterly* 24 (Summer 1971), 271–77. [**71**: title; **72**: 277]

Meredith, James H. *Three Years in Mississippi*. Bloomington: Indiana University Press, c. 1966. [**407**: 230, 323, 328, 322; **408**: 304, 229, 231, 243, 240, 243, 206, 247, 307]

Merton, Thomas. " 'Baptism in the Forest': Wisdom and Initiation in William Faulkner," 17–44. *Mansions of the Spirit: Essays in Literature and Religion*. George Panichas, Ed. New York: Hawthorne, 1967. [**85**: 25, 28–29, 130]

Meyerhoff, Hans. *Time in Literature*. Berkeley and Los Angeles: University of California Press, 1955. [**390**: 138, 138, 140, 141]

Millgate, Michael. *The Achievement of William Faulkner*. New York: Random House, 1966. [**357**: 258]

——. " 'A Cosmos of My Own': The Evolution of Yoknapatawpha," 23–43. *Fifty Years of Yoknapatawpha*. Doreen Fowler and Ann J. Abadie, Eds. Jackson: University Press of Mississippi, 1980. [**387–88**: 38, 38–39, 39, 42, 43]

Milum, Richard A. "The Cavalier Spirit in Faulkner's Fiction." Ph.D. Dissertation, Indiana University, 1972. [**207**: 43]

Mitford, Jessica. *A Fine Old Conflict*. New York: Knopf, 1977. [**384**: 181–82, 182]

Morris, Willie. "A Sense of Place and the Americanization of Mississippi," 3–13. *Sense of Place: Mississippi*. Peggy W. Prenshaw and Jesse O. McKee, Eds. Jackson: University Press of Mississippi, c. 1979. [**374**: 4]

——, Ed. *The South Today: 100 Years After Appomattox*. A *Harper's* Special Supplement, April 1965. [**386**: "A Sense of Place"; **403**: *The South Today*]

Morris, Wright. "The Territory Ahead," 120–56. *The Living Novel: A Symposium*. Granville Hicks, Ed. New York: Macmillan, 1957. [**91**: 130]

Munson, Gorham. *The Dilemma of the Liberated: An Interpretation of Twentieth Century Humanism*. Port Washington: Kennikat Press, 1967, c. 1930. [**249**: 13, 12, 105, 109–10]

Murphy, Francis X., C.Ss.R. "Of Sex and the Catholic Church: Liberal Catholics Confront the Intransigence of the Vatican." *The Atlantic Monthly* 247 (February 1981), 44–57. [**402**: 49, 52]

Murray, Henry A. Introduction to "Myth and Mythmaking" issue,

Daedalus (Journal of the American Academy of Arts and Sciences), Spring 1959, 211–22. [**86**: 213]

——. *Myth and Mythmaking*. Henry A. Murray, Ed. New York: Braziller, 1960. [**87**: 355–57, Appendix, Mark Schorer's definition of Myth, from *William Blake*]

Musil, Robert K. "The Visual Imagination of William Faulkner." Ph.D. Dissertation, Northwestern University, 1971. [**31**: 40; **41**: 157, 169]

Naravane, V. S. *Modern Indian Thought: A Philosophical Survey*. Lucknow and Bombay: Asia Publishing House, 1967. Chapter Eight: Radhakrishnan, 230–69. [**255**: 249–53; **326**: 258–59; **375**: 261; **394**: 258]

Nehru, Jawaharlal. *The Discovery of India*. Robert I. Crane, Ed. Garden City: Doubleday Anchor, 1960. [**367**: 393]

The New Century Classical Handbook. Catherine B. Avery, Ed. New York: Appleton-Century-Crofts, c. 1962. "Hermes," 552–56. [**227**: 552, 555]

Niebuhr, Reinhold. *The Children of Light and the Children of Darkness: A Vindication of Democracy and a Critique of its Traditional Defense*. New York: Scribners, 1960. [**261**: 3; **343**: 51]

Nisbet, Robert. *History of the Idea of Progress*. New York: Basic Books, 1980. [**373**: 5, 316]

O'Connor, Flannery. "The Fiction Writer and His Country," 157–64. *The Living Novel: A Symposium*. Granville Hicks, Ed. New York: Macmillan, 1957. [**240**: 162–63]

O'Connor, William Van. *The Tangled Fire of William Faulkner*. Minneapolis: University of Minnesota Press, c. 1954. [**319**: 72, 73]

——. "The Grotesque in Modern American Fiction." *College English* 20 (April 1959), 342–46. [**114**: 343, 343]

O'Dea, Richard J. "Faulkner's Vestigial Christianity." *Renascence* 21 (1968), 44–54. [**251**: 54; **263**: 47]

O'Donnell, George Marion. "Faulkner's Mythology," 82–93. *William Faulkner: Three Decades of Criticism*. Frederick J. Hoffman and Olga W. Vickery, Eds. East Lansing: Michigan State University Press, 1960.

Olafson, Frederick A. *Principles and Persons: An Ethical Interpretation of Existentialism*. Baltimore: Johns Hopkins University Press, 1967. [**272**: 237, 238; **278**: 115–17; **284**: cited; **298**: 73; **336**: 141, 167, 168; **352**: 221]

Olson, Robert. *An Introduction to Existentialism*. New York: Dover, 1962. [**249**: 47; **252**: 46, 47; **254**: 45, 47; **271**: 164; **274**: 14, 17, 18; **275**: 134, 135, 139, 145; **276**: 159; **303**: 145]

Page, Sally. *Faulkner's Women: Characterization and Meaning.* Deland, Florida: Edwards, 1972. [**164**: 140, 139; **165**: 141]

Panichas, George, Ed. *Mansions of the Spirit: Essays in Literature and Religion.* New York: Hawthorne, 1967.

Parr, Susan Dale Resneck. "'And by Bergson, Obviously'; Faulkner's *The Sound and the Fury, As I Lay Dying,* and *Absalom, Absalom!* from a Bergsonian Perspective." Ph.D. Dissertation, University of Wisconsin, 1972. [**182**: 154; **222**: 191; **371**: title; **377**: 224]

Pate, Frances Willard. "Names of Characters in Faulkner's Mississippi." Ph.D. Dissertation, Emory University, 1969. [**11**: title]

Peabody, Henry W. "Faulkner's Initiation Stories: An Approach to the Major Works." Ph.D. Dissertation, University of Denver, 1972. [**180**: 14, 22]

Percy, Walker. "Mississippi: The Fallen Paradise," 166–72. *The South Today,* Willie Morris, Ed. [**385**: 166, 167, 171, 172]

Petesch, Donald. "Theme and Characterization in Faulkner's Snopes Trilogy." Ph.D. Dissertation, Florida State University, 1969. [**182**: 160; **225**: chapter title]

Pilkington, John. *The Heart of Yoknapatawpha.* Jackson: University Press of Mississippi. [**389**: title]

Pinsley, Stanley. "The Embrace of a Chimera: The Dying World of William Faulkner." M.A. Thesis, Columbia University, 1956. [**311**: 42]

Pitavy, François. *Faulkner's Light in August.* Rev. ed. Trans. Gillian E. Cook. Bloomington: Indiana University Press, c. 1973. [**16–17**: 85, 86, 87, 88, 90–91; **216**: 77; **311**: 60–61]

Poverty Law Report: Klanwatch Intelligence Report 10, No. 6 (November/December 1982). [**409**: 9, 3]

Powers, Lyall H. *Faulkner's Yoknapatawpha Comedy.* Ann Arbor: University of Michigan Press, 1980. [**334**: 192; **340**: 150; **341**: 159, 160; **342**: 219–20; **344–45**: 221, 225; **356**: 6]

Radin, Paul. *The Trickster: A Study in American Indian Mythology.* With commentaries by Karl Kerényi and C. G. Jung. New York: Shocken, 1977.

Radhakrishnan: *see* Naravane, V. S., *Modern Indian Thought.*

Ramsey, William C. "Coordinate Structures in Four Faulkner Novels." Ph.D. Dissertation, University of North Carolina, 1971. [**180**: 163; **288**: 163]

Rank, Otto. *The Birth of the Hero and Other Writings.* Philip Freund, Ed. New York: Vintage Books, 1959. [**88**: 8–9; **147**: 307, 304, 297; **148**: 313; **150**: 311, 311; **173**: 286–95; **180**: 195, 265; **215**: 257; **218**: 65]

Rideau, Émile. *The Thought of Teilhard de Chardin*. Trans. René Hague. New York: Harper & Row; London: Collins, c. 1967. [**251**: 210; **255**: 24]

Rinaldi, Nicholas M. "Game-Consciousness and Game-Metaphor in the Work of William Faulkner." Ph.D. Dissertation, Fordham University, 1963. [**27**: title; **326**: games]

Roberts, Bramlett. *William Faulkner of Oxford*, James W. Webb and A. Wigfall Green, Eds. ["A Soft Touch, A Great Heart," 152]

Rodnon, Stewart. "Sports, Sporting Codes, and Sportsmanship in the Work of Ring Lardner, James T. Farrell, Ernest Hemingway, and William Faulkner." Ph.D. Dissertation, New York University, 1961. [**27**: title; **326**: games]

Rose, Maxine Smith. "From Genesis to Revelation: The Grand Design of Faulkner's *Absalom, Absalom!*" Ph.D. Dissertation, University of Alabama, 1973. [**131**: title, 22; **132**: 74, 9, 161, 161]

de Rougemont, Denis. *Love in the Western World*. Trans. Montgomery Belgion. New York: Pantheon, c. 1956. [**86**: 18; **204**: 79, 80, 81; **206**: 111–12]

Routh, Michael. "The Story of All Things: Faulkner's Yoknapatawpha County Cosmology by Way of *Light in August*." Ph.D. Dissertation, University of Wisconsin, 1973. [**106**: 26; **116**: 192–93, 196, 197, 198; **165**: chapter title; **188**: 201; **212**: 114; **213**: 98, 107, 115; **216**: 146; **305**: 26; **322**: 106–107, 107; **367**: 2, 3, 18, 24; **375**: cited]

Rubin, Louis D. Jr., and John Rees Moore, Eds. *The Idea of an American Novel*. New York: Crowell, c. 1961. Rpts William Faulkner, "It Is a Nightmare World, Wearing a Mask of Reality." *The Shape of Books to Come*. J. Donald Adams, Ed. New York: Viking, 1944, [**400**: 353]

——. *The Faraway Country: Writers of the Modern South*. Seattle: University of Washington Press, 1963. "Chronicles of Yoknapatawpha: The Dynasties," 43–71. [**248**: 47–48, 49; **308**: 55, 56]

——. "The Literature of a Changing South," 147–61. *The Deep South in Transformation: A Symposium*. Robert B. Highsaw, Ed. University: University of Alabama Press, 1964. [**387**: 153, 153, 154, 161]

——. "Notes on a Rear-Guard Action," 27–41. *The Idea of the South: Pursuit of a Central Theme*. Frank E. Vandiver, Jr., Ed. Chicago: University of Chicago Press, c. 1964. [**410**: 40]

——. "Notes on the Literary Scene: Their Own Language," 173–75. *The South Today: 100 Years After Appomattox*, Willie Morris, Ed.

Sandstrom, Glenn. "Identity Diffusion: Joe Christmas and Quentin

Compson." *American Quarterly* 19 (Summer 1967), 207–23. [**214**: 223]

Sartre, Jean-Paul. *Existentialism from Dostoevsky to Sartre*, 222–311. Walter Kaufman, Ed. [**266**: 291, 291, 292, 310; **271**: 290–91]

Schlumpf, Otto. "William Faulkner: Myth-Maker and Morals-Monger: Esthetics and Ethics in Yoknapatawpha County." Ph.D. Dissertation, University of California, Santa Barbara, 1974. [**182**: 20; **192**: 74, 72; **223**: 180; **367**: 7]

Schneider, Herbert W. "Religious Humanism," 65–66. *The Humanist Alternative: Some Definitions of Humanism*, Paul Kurtz, Ed. [**250**: title]

Scott, Anne Firor. *The Southern Lady: From Pedestal to Politics 1830–1930*. Chicago: University of Chicago Press, 1970. [**100**: 20, 21, 61; **284**: title; **287**: title, 6, 18, 90; **293**: 54, 19; **297**: 14]

Scott, Nathan A. Jr., Ed. *The Tragic Vision and the Christian Faith*. New York: Association Press, 1957.

——. *The Broken Center: Studies in the Theological Horizon of Modern Literature*. New Haven: Yale University Press, 1966. [**267**: 18–19; **270**: 21]

——. *Narative Capability: Studies in the New Literature and the Literary Situation*. New Haven: Yale University Press, c. 1961. [**247**: 126–27; **248**: 133; **248–49**: 143]

Sellars, Roy Wood. "The Humanist Outlook," 133–40. *The Humanist Alternative: Some Definitions of Humanism*, Paul Kurtz, Ed. [**250**: 137, 139–40]

Silver, James W. *Mississippi: The Closed Society*. New York: Harcourt, Brace & World, c. 1963, 1964. [**114**: title; **273**: "A Note from the Author," xi]

——. "Silver Recalls Role in Faulkner Speech." *The Faulkner Newsletter & Yoknapatawpha Review* 3 (January–March 1983). [**405–406**: 1, 4]

Simon, John K. "The Scene and Imagery of Metamorphosis in *As I Lay Dying*." *Criticism* 7 (Winter 1965), 1–22. [**31–32**: 3]

Simpson, Lewis. *The Falkners of Mississippi*. Foreword by Murry Falkner. [**357**: ix, x]

Slabey, Robert M. "Myth and Ritual in *Light in August*." *Texas Studies in Literature and Language* 2 (Autumn 1960) 328–49. [**61**: 349; **67**: 341; **217**: 347]

——. "Faulkner's 'Wasteland' Vision in *Absalom, Absalom!*" *Mississippi Quarterly* 14 (Summer 1961), 153–66. [**121**: 160; **270**: 151; **301**: 158, 160]

Slatoff, Walter J. *Quest for Failure.* Ithaca: Cornell University Press, 1960. [**11**: title; **108**: 3–4, 11, 23, 25, 17]

Smith, Henry Nash. *Virgin Land: The American West as Symbol and Myth.* New York: Random House, 1957. [**12**: title; **117**: 138, 172; **175**: 172]

Smith, Lillian. *Killers of the Dream.* Garden City: Doubleday Anchor, 1963. [**127**: 111, 113]

Sowder, William J. "Christmas as Existential Hero." *University Review* 30 (Summer 1964), 279–84. [**311**: 281]

Special Report: Klanwatch. The Ku Klux Klan: A History of Racism and Violence. Montgomery: Southern Poverty Law Center, 1982. [**404**: 33]

Stein, Jean. "7. William Faulkner," 119–41. *Writers at Work: The Paris Review Interviews,* Malcolm Cowley, Ed. Rptd, James B. Meriwether and Michael Millgate, Eds., in *Lion in the Garden.* "Interview with Jean Stein vanden Heuvel," 237–56. [**114**: 255]

Stein, William Bysshe. "The Wake in Faulkner's *Sanctuary.*" *Modern Language Notes* 75 (1960), 28–29. [**58**: cited]

Steinberg, Aaron. "Faulkner and the Negro." Ph.D. Dissertation, New York University, 1963. [**338**: 329, 335–36]

Stevenson, Adlai E. *The Papers of Adlai Stevenson,* Vol. 4: *"Let's Talk Sense to the American People,"* 1952–1955. Walter Johnson, Ed. Boston: Little, Brown, c. 1974. [**406**: 109, 111]

Stewart, Jack. "Apotheosis and Apocalypse in Faulkner's 'Wash'." *Studies in Short Fiction* 6 (Fall 1968), 586–600. [**116**: 589, cited; **221**: 597, 598]

Stone, Emily Whitehurst. "How a Writer Finds His Material." *Harper's Magazine* 230 (November 1965), 157–61. [**80**: 159; **193**: cited]

Stonum, Gary Lee. *Faulkner's Career: An Internal Literary History.* Ithaca and London: Cornell University Press, 1979. [**109**: 33, 17, 16]

Strandberg, Victor. "Faulkner's Poor Parson and the Technique of Inversion." *The Sewanee Review* 63 (Spring 1965) 181–90. [**11**: cited]

Straumann, Heinrich. *William Faulkner.* Frankfurt am Main: Athenäum, 1968. [**107**: 164, cited; **322**: 145, 146]

Sullens, Idelle. "A Study of the Incest Theme in Two Works of William Faulkner: *The Sound and the Fury* and *Absalom, Absalom!*" M.A. Thesis, University of Washington, 1954. [**152**: 1, themes]

Sullivan, William P. "William Faulkner and the Community." Ph.D. Dissertation, Columbia University, 1961. [**310**: chapter title]

Sultan, Stanley. "Call Me Ishmael: The Hagiography of Isaac McCaslin." *Texas Studies in Literature and Language* 3 (Spring 1961), 50–66. [**80**: 61]

Sutton, George W. "Primitivism in the Fiction of William Faulkner." Ph.D. Dissertation, University of Mississippi, 1967. [**12**: cited; **161**: 84; **27**: cited; **162**: 280; **165**: 306; **188**: 169; **343**: 28; **348**: 241, 244, 250, 246]

Teilhard de Chardin, Pierre. *The Future of Man.* Trans. Norman Denny. New York: Harper & Row, 1969. [**251**: 35, 13; **337**: 49]

———. *Activation of Energy.* Trans. René Hague. New York: Harcourt Brace Jovanovich, c. 1970. [**255**: 254; **375**: 381]

Thomas, Frank Howard III. "The Search for Identity in Faulkner's Black Characters." Ph.D. Dissertation, University of Pittsburgh, 1972. [**137**: 103]

Thompson, Lawrence. "Mirror Analogues in *The Sound and the Fury*," 211–25. *William Faulkner: Three Decades of Criticism*, Frederick J. Hoffman and Olga W. Vickery, Ed. [**44**: cited]

Tillich, Paul. "The Religious Symbol," 75–98. *Symbolism in Religion and Literature*. Rollo May, Ed. New York: Braziller, 1960. [**88**: May 88*n*, 83, 84, 87]

———. "Courage and Individualization"; "Existentialist Forms of the Courage to Be as Oneself," 652–68. *Philosophy in the Twentieth Century*, Vol. 4. William Barrett and Henry D. Aiken, Eds. New York: Random House, c. 1962. [**311**: 657; **315**: 659; **335**: "existential knowledge" defined]

Tindall, George B. *The Ethnic Southerners.* Baton Rouge: Louisiana State University Press, c. 1976. [**105**: "Mythology: A New Frontier"; **366**: 25, 38, 39, 58; **378**: *The Ethnic Southerners,* 21, 20; **380–81**: "Mythology: A New Frontier," xi, 22, 23, 25, 35, 37, 38, 39; **381**: "The Benighted South," 44, 45, 47, 54, 58; **382**: "The Central Theme Revisited," 77, 79]

Tindall, William York. *The Literary Symbol.* Bloomington: Indiana University Press, 1955. [**4**: 14, 287; **5**: 12–13; **8**: 105, 137, 104; **39**: 264; **87**: 178]

Tobin, Patricia D. *Time and the Novel: The Genealogical Imperative.* Princeton: Princeton University Press, 1975. [**130**: 6; **221**: 110, 111; **303**: 87; **370**: ix, 117, 121, 122]

Trimmer, Joseph F. "A Portrait of the Artist in Motion: A Study of the Artist–Surrogate in the Novels of William Faulkner." Ph.D.

Dissertation, Purdue University, 1969. [**228**: title; **229**: 461, 453; **232**: cited]

Trobaugh, Robert J. "The Nature of Man in the Writings of Reinhold Niebuhr and William Faulkner." Ph.D. Dissertation in Religion, Vanderbilt University, 1966. [**251–52**: 11, 44; **255**: 371, 370; **336**: 58; **340**: 155; **346**: 200; **348**: 171; **360**: 232, 241]

Vande Kieft, Ruth. "Faulkner's Defeat of Time in *Absalom, Absalom!*" *The Southern Review* N.S. 6 (Autumn 1970), 1100–1109. [**373**: 1100, 1103, 1105]

Vandiver, Frank E., Ed. *The Idea of the South: Pursuit of a Central Theme*. Chicago: University of Chicago Press, c. 1964. Louis D. Rubin, "Notes on a Rear-Guard Action," 27–41. [**410**: 40]

——. "The Confederate Myth." *Myth and Southern History*, Patrick Gerster and Nicholas Cords, Eds. [**98–99**: 148, 148, 149, 149]

Van Gennep, Arnold. *The Rites of Passage*. Trans. Monika B. Vizedom and Gabrielle L. Caffee. Chicago: University of Chicago Press, 1961. [**199**: 15–17, 18]

Van Ghent, Dorothy. *The English Novel: Form and Function*. New York: Harper Torch, 1961. [**89**: 52–53]

Vicinus, Martha, Ed. *Suffer and Be Still: Women in the Victorian Age*. Bloomington: Indiana University Press, 1973. [**100**: xii; **101**: ix, x, x, xi, xiv]

Vickery, Olga W. *The Novels of William Faulkner: A Critical Interpretation*. Rev. ed. Baton Rouge: Louisiana State University Press, 1964. [**38**: 20; **79**: 133; **142**: 261; **231**: 175; **259–60**: 253; **310**: 75; **356**: 228; **358**: 237; **365**: 229; **373**: 258, 259, 260, 258; **401**: 239, 239]

Vorpahl, Ben Merchant. "Moonlight at Ballenbaugh's: Time and Imagination in *The Reivers*." *Southern Literary Journal* 1 (Spring 1969), 3–26. [**356**: 24; **389**: 26]

Waggoner, Hyatt H. "William Faulkner's Passion Week of the Heart," 303–23. *The Tragic Vision and the Christian Faith*, Nathan A. Scott, Jr., Ed. [**91**: 312]

——. "A Passion Week of the Heart," Chapter 11. *William Faulkner: From Jefferson to the World*. Lexington: University of Kentucky Press, c. 1959. [**224**: 185; **270–71**: 251]

Wagner, Linda Welshimer, Ed. *William Faulkner: Four Decades of Criticism*. East Lansing: Michigan State University Press, c. 1973.

Walsh, Chad. *The End of Nature*. Chicago: Swallow Press, c. 1969.

"Ode on the University of Mississippi" September 30–31, 1962. [**407**: 9, 102]

Warren, Robert Penn. "William Faulkner," 109–24. *William Faulkner: Three Decades of Criticism*, Frederick J. Hoffman and Olga W. Vickery, Eds. [**91**: cited as a critique of Cowley's 1964 interpretation of Faulkner's mythology]

———. *Paris Review* (Spring 1956) interview by Ralph Ellison and Eugene Walters, 185–207. [**369**: 201–202]

———, Ed. *Faulkner: A Collection of Critical Essays*. Englewood Cliffs: Prentice-Hall, c. 1966.

Waters, Maureen A. "The Role of Women in Faulkner's Yoknapatawpha." Ed.D. Dissertation, Teachers College, Columbia University, 1974. [**134**: 63; **136**: 16; **162**: 152, 158]

Watson, James Gray. *The Snopes Dilemma: Faulkner's Trilogy*. Coral Gables: University of Miami Press, 1970. [**354**: 220, 221; **355**: 218, 216]

Webb, James W., and A. Wigfall Green, Eds. *William Faulkner of Oxford*. Baton Rouge: Louisiana State University Press, c. 1965.

Weisinger, Herbert. *The Agony and the Triumph*. East Lansing: Michigan State University Press, 1964. [**88**: cited]

Wellek, René, and Austin Warren. *Theory of Literature*. 2nd ed. New York: Harcourt, Brace & World, 1956. [**87**: 180]

Wharton, Vernon Lane. *The Negro in Mississippi, 1865–1890*. New York: Harper Torch, 1965. [**155**: 229]

Wheelwright, Philip. *The Burning Fountain*. Bloomington: Indiana University Press, 1955. [**10**: 60; **11**: title, Chapter 12; **87**: 159; **221**: 201]

Whitehead, Alfred North. "Uses of Symbolism," 233–50. *Symbolism in Religion and Literature*, Rollo May, Ed. [**6**: 247]

Widmer, Kingsley. "The Existential Darkness: Richard Wright's 'The Outsider'." *Wisconsin Studies in Contemporary Literature* 1 (Fall 1960). [**300**: 21, 17]

Wilder, Amos. "The Cross: Social Trauma or Redemption," 99–115. *Religion and Literature*. Rollo May, Ed. New York: Braziller, 1960. [**216**: 109–12]

———. *Theology and Modern Literature*. Cambridge: Harvard University Press, 1967. [**247**: 83, 84; **283**: 24; **305**: 120]

Wilson, Edwin H. "Humanism's Many Dimensions," 15–19. *The*

Humanist Alternative: Some Definitions of Humanism, Paul Kurtz, Ed. [**250**: 15–18]

Woodruff, Neal. " 'The Bear' and Faulkner's Moral Vision." Studies in Faulkner, *Carnegie Studies in Literature* 6 (1961), 43–88. [**257**: 44]

Woodward, C. Vann. *The Strange Career of Jim Crow*. Rev. ed. New York: Oxford University Press, 1957. [**330**: 7]

Wright, Andrew. *Henry Fielding: Mask and Feast*. Berkeley: University of California Press, 1965. [**31**: 122]

Zabel, Morton Dauwen, Ed. Charles Dickens, *Bleak House*, Introduction. Boston: Little, Brown, 1956. [**240**: viii, ix, xix]

Zink, Karl. "Flux and the Frozen Moment: The Imagery of Stasis in Faulkner's Prose." *PMLA* 71 (June 1956), 285–301. [**109**: title; **376**: subject and title]

——. "Faulkner's Garden: Woman and the Immemorial Earth." *Modern Fiction Studies* 2 (Autumn 1956), 139–49. [**109**: title; **111**: 149]

FAULKNER'S FICTION